Sociology

4⁵⁰

PHILOSOPHICAL DIMENSIONS OF PRIVACY

Philosophical Dimensions of Privacy: An Anthology

Edited by

FERDINAND DAVID SCHOEMAN

Department of Philosophy
University of South Carolina, Columbia

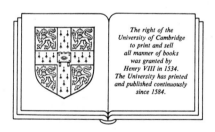

The right of the
University of Cambridge
to print and sell
all manner of books
was granted by
Henry VIII in 1534.
The University has printed
and published continuously
since 1584.

CAMBRIDGE UNIVERSITY PRESS

CAMBRIDGE

LONDON   NEW YORK   NEW ROCHELLE
MELBOURNE   SYDNEY

Published by the Press Syndicate of the University of Cambridge
The Pitt Building, Trumpington Street, Cambridge CB2 1RP
32 East 57th Street, New York, NY 10022, USA
296 Beaconsfield Parade, Middle Park, Melbourne 3206, Australia

© Cambridge University Press 1984

First published 1984

Printed in the United States of America
Library of Congress Cataloging in Publication Data
Main entry under title:

Philosophical dimensions of privacy.

Bibliography: p.

Includes index.

1. Privacy, Right of – Addresses, essays, lectures.
2. Privacy – Addresses, essays, lectures.
I. Schoeman, Ferdinand David.
JC596.P47 1984   323.44′8   84-5898
ISBN 0 521 255555 4 hardcovers
ISBN 0 521 27554 7 paperback

I have looked forward to some occasion like this to express gratitude to my parents for so many years of loving support and devotion. My admiration for their lives and ways will last all of my days. With this in mind, I dedicate this book to Helen and Eugene Schoeman.

. . . .

Contents

Contributors

STANLEY I. BENN   Department of Philosophy, Research School of Social Sciences, Australian National University

EDWARD J. BLOUSTEIN   President, Rutgers University

LOUIS D. BRANDEIS   Former Associate Justice, United States Supreme Court

CHARLES FRIED   Law School, Harvard University

RUTH GAVISON   Law School, Hebrew University of Jerusalem

ROBERT S. GERSTEIN   Political Science Department, University of California at Los Angeles

ROBERT F. MURPHY   Department of Anthropology, Columbia University

RICHARD A. POSNER   Judge, United States Court of Appeals, Seventh Circuit

WILLIAM L. PROSSER   Former Dean, Boalt Hall Law School, University of California at Berkeley

JAMES RACHELS   Philosophy Department, University of Alabama at Birmingham

JEFFREY H. REIMAN   Philosophy Department, American University at Washington, D.C.

FERDINAND SCHOEMAN   Philosophy Department, University of South Carolina at Columbia

JUDITH JARVIS THOMSON   Philosophy Department, Massachusetts Institute of Technology

SAMUEL D. WARREN   Former lawyer

RICHARD A. WASSERSTROM   Kresge College, University of
                          California at Santa Cruz

ALAN WESTIN   Department of Public Law, Law School, Columbia
              University

Preface

The aim of compiling the various essays presented here is to make readily accessible many of the most significant and influential discussions of privacy to be found in the literature. In addition to being representative of the diversity of attitudes toward privacy, this collection has a coherence that results from the authors' focus on the same issues and theories. Although the main issue addressed here is the moral significance of privacy, some social science and legal treatments are included because of their direct bearing on the moral issues that privacy raises. In addition to the classics on privacy, I have included an interpretive essay on the privacy literature; this provides a philosophical guideline as to what the issues are and how various thinkers have contributed to their resolution.

1

Privacy
Philosophical dimensions of the literature

FERDINAND SCHOEMAN

Privacy as a topic is as fascinating as it is important. Though we all acknowledge its value in the abstract, there are numerous grounds for puzzling over its significance, and for being suspicious of its value. The right to privacy is seen as creating the context in which both deceit and hypocrisy may flourish: It provides the cover under which most human wrongdoing takes place, and then it protects the guilty from taking responsibility for their transgressions once committed. The right to privacy often stands in the way of vigorous public debate on issues of moral significance. Without the shade of privacy, many practices that are arguably legitimate though in fact illegal might be thoroughly and rationally debated rather than left unexposed and unexamined. Concern for one's own privacy may be regarded as a sign of moral cowardice, an excuse not to state clearly one's position and accept whatever unpopularity might ensue. Privacy may be seen as a culturally conditioned sensitivity that makes people more vulnerable than they would otherwise be to selective disclosures and to the sense of comparative inferiority and abject shame – a sense engendered by ignorance about the inner lives of others.

The literature and popular lore about privacy is full of surprising claims. Despite the fact that privacy has been identified by contemporary philosophers as a key aspect of human dignity, or alternatively as something even more basic than rights to property or than rights over one's own person, there was no major philosophical discussion of the value of privacy until the late 1960s. Moreover, despite the fact that the right of privacy has been judged as more basic than any of the rights enumerated in the United States Bill of Rights, there was no explicit and sustained legal discussion of the right to privacy until the article by Warren and Brandeis in 1890 [Chapter 4 in this volume]. Although the conviction is widespread that increasingly we are being

Adapted from Ferdinand Schoeman, "Privacy: Philosophical Dimensions," *American Philosophical Quarterly* 21, 1984. © American Philosophical Quarterly, 1984.

deprived of our privacy as a result of technological advances, there is reason to believe that we experience far more privacy than did our ancestors, as Flaherty (1972) has amply documented. Ironically, this increase in privacy is the result of technological changes and the social transformations such changes brought in their wake. One can cite as examples the anonymity of urban life and the marital privacy provided by more elaborate domestic heating systems.

This volume focuses primarily on the philosophical aspects of privacy, including its definition, justification, interconnection with other values, and the estimation of its importance in comparison with other social, moral, and individual goods. It is my hope that by presenting this collection of essays, the primary and representative philosophical views about privacy will be made easily accessible.

In this Introduction I shall aim at two main objectives:

1. To review what seem to be the main philosophical issues relating to privacy.
2. To introduce the particular papers collected here, put them in their philosophical contexts, and make some critical remarks about their contributions.

To a very limited extent, I shall also aim at placing discussions of privacy in their intellectual and historical context. We turn first to the general philosophical issues.

I. The philosophical issues

1. The nature of privacy

a. Proposed definitions of privacy. It is crucial in any discussion to have some measure of agreement about what is meant by the key terms employed. It is especially important to have such agreement secured in a manner that does not beg any of the substantive questions that arise.

Various definitions have been proposed for "privacy." Some have regarded privacy as a *claim, entitlement,* or *right* of an individual to determine what information about himself (or herself) may be communicated to others. Privacy has been identified also as the measure of *control* an individual has over:

1. information about himself;
2. intimacies of personal identity; or
3. who has sensory access to him.

Finally, privacy has been identified as a *state* or *condition* of limited access to a person.

One difficulty with regarding privacy as a claim or entitlement to determine what information about oneself is to be available to others is that it begs the question about the moral status of privacy. It presumes privacy is something to be protected at the discretion of the individual to whom the information relates. Furthermore, although this characterization informs us that privacy is morally significant, we have not been told *what* it is that is so significant. We still need a characterization of what the right to privacy is about.

The second characterization equates privacy with control over access to information about, or to intimate aspects of, oneself; this also presents some difficulties. Although it does not seem to beg any moral questions, it does seem particularly vulnerable to a number of counterexamples. We can easily imagine a person living in a state of complete privacy but lacking control over who has access to information about him. For instance, a man shipwrecked on a deserted island or lost in a dense forest has unfortunately lost control over who has information about him, but we would not want to say that he has no privacy. Indeed, ironically, his problem is that he has too much privacy. To take another example, a person who chose to exercise his discretionary control over information about himself by divulging everything cannot be said to have lost control, although he surely cannot be said to have any privacy.

This brings us to the third proposal, the identification of privacy with a state of limited access to a person. A person has privacy to the extent that others have limited access to information about him, limited access to the intimacies of his life, or limited access to his thoughts or his body. This characterization of privacy leaves open the question of whether privacy is a desirable state, and how valuable it is in relation to other things. By including reference to limited access to the intimacies of life this characterization of privacy leaves open the possibility that issues like autonomy over abortion, birth control, and the gender of one's sexual partner, as well as some issues concerning freedom of conscience, are at least arguably privacy matters. (It should be mentioned that numerous writers take it as obvious that such issues are *not* privacy issues; for them, these issues only raise questions about an individual's rightful sphere of autonomy.)

Furthermore, this third definition enables us to disentangle the question of whether or not one has undergone a loss of *privacy* from the question of whether or not one's *right to privacy* has been infringed or violated. We can imagine situations in which we would want to say that a person has diminished privacy without any infringement of this right having occurred – for example, any time a person reveals something about himself. We can also envision situations in which we would want to say that a person has not in fact suffered loss of privacy but has suffered a violation of his right to privacy. Suppose, for instance, that a national security agency is authorized to monitor, at its discretion, international telephone conversations. We would say about this state of affairs that such authorization obviously affects a person's (legal) right to privacy. Whether such an authorization actually affects one's state of privacy is going to depend in large part on whether one's conversations are among those actually monitored. We should note that we would say that a person's privacy has been violated – not just lessened – only if some relevant norm has been infringed. Thus, if God or Martians monitor all our thoughts and behavior, we have no privacy with respect to them, but we have not been violated either since there is no applicable restricting norm.

Benn and Gaus (1983) have recently argued that the concept of privacy represents something more complex than anything captured in the previous proposals. They suggest that the notion of privacy constitutes a central social concept which infects our way of experiencing the social world, and which affects social life in profound and subtle ways. As a social category, privacy has both normative and descriptive functions which interact with one another. The concept of privacy regulates institutions, practices, activities, and social and individual life generally. It controls what people feel they have legitimate access to and in this way fosters both possibilities and limitations. As Benn (1971) had earlier noted, there are important uses of the term "private" which function to stress the applicability of relevant norms, and not to describe what is.[1]

b. The right to privacy. Much of the privacy literature has focused on the importance of privacy with the aim of arguing for the desirability of recognizing moral and/or legal rights to it. In addition to discussing whether privacy rights and protections should be accorded to individuals formally and explicitly, we should also focus attention on sensitivity to privacy interests when respect for them cannot feasibly become part of any clear and explicit institutional rules. It is possible to act insensitively to the privacy interests of another even though one does not actually violate his privacy rights, and indeed even if he has no privacy rights. A person may be skeptical about recommending a legal right to privacy without having any doubts about the importance of privacy; one may be convinced that no feasible set of explicit limits is defensible.

The question of whether there is a moral right to privacy, even if there is no legal right to it, is difficult to settle. Answering it requires that we distinguish a claim that an interest individuals have in their privacy is very important to their lives and hence is deserving of great moral weight, from a claim that individuals have a moral right to privacy. Individuated interests, when acknowledged to be of considerable significance to our conception of a person, seem to play the role of moral rights, even if not accorded that designation. Whatever stand one takes on the right-to-privacy issue, the literature on privacy is enlightening in exploring the moral importance of privacy as a moral and social virtue.

2. *Is privacy coherent and distinctive?*

Having introduced some of the issues that relate to the nature of privacy, we now turn to some of the substantive moral questions that philosophers have addressed. We shall begin by inquiring whether there is something fundamental, integrated, and distinctive about the concerns traditionally grouped together under the rubric of "privacy issues." In opposing this position, some have argued that the cases labeled "privacy issues" are diverse and disparate, and hence are only nominally or superficially connected. Others have argued that when privacy claims are to be defended morally, the justifications must allude ultimately to principles which can be characterized quite independently of any concern with privacy. Consequently, the argument continues, there is nothing morally distinctive about privacy. For our purposes, I shall refer to the position that there is something common to most of the privacy claims as the "coherence thesis." The position that privacy claims are to be defended morally by principles that are distinctive to privacy I shall label the "distinctiveness thesis."

Theorists who deny both the coherence thesis and the distinctiveness thesis argue that in each category of privacy claims there are diverse values at stake of the sort common to many other social issues and that these values exhaust privacy claims. The thrust of this complex position is that we could do quite well if we eliminated all talk of privacy and simply defended our concerns in terms of standard moral and legal categories. Some argue that what is wrong with privacy invasions always comes down to either the infliction of emotional distress on another, the misappropriation of another's assets, or a trespass onto another's property. According to others, the real basis for privacy concern reduces to a concern for one's property interests or for one's right to one's own person. Still others claim that interest in privacy is exhausted by reference to a person's stake in maintaining or enhancing his or her social or economic leverage. These skeptics agree that there is nothing distinctive, or morally or legally illuminating, about privacy interests.

Motivating the view that there is something fundamental, distinctive, and coherent about the privacy cases is the attitude that something special about human moral or social character is lost in reductive accounts – something that transcends the particular cases being analyzed. Among philosophers who argue that there is something unique to privacy concerns, there is considerable disagreement as to what constitutes this transcending feature of privacy. Some argue that concerns for inviolate personality or human dignity are reflected in the seemingly diverse privacy claims. Others argue that what privacy issues possess in common is their positions as key components in structuring the very possibility of diverse social relationships, and in making possible the deepest kind of love individuals can share. Still others regard privacy issues as sharing a role in protecting "private life" or an individual's intimate self.[2]

3. Is privacy culturally relative?

Two issues relating to the dependence of privacy on cultural variation have been raised. The first of these concerns whether privacy is in fact regarded as important among all peoples. If it is deemed not, this may suggest that privacy is superfluous and hence dispensable as a social value. The second issue that arises focuses on whether there are any aspects of life which are inherently private, and not just conventionally so. This issue is related to the question of whether there is a criterion of the private.

Several writers on privacy have tried to discover whether the esteem with which privacy is held is dependent upon particular cultural conditions in which people are socialized to care about privacy. Not only is an indifference to privacy held by some to be socially feasible, but it is also thought by some to be, in principle at least, desirable. These theorists see privacy as increasing human vulnerability through increased sensitivity to shame and embarrassment. This susceptibility is thought to result from ignorance about the fact that one's own condition is universal and not an idiosyncratic aberration. People who hold this view claim that institutions of privacy are conducive to social hypocrisy, interpersonal exploitation through deception, and even asocial or antisocial loyalties.

This hypothesis about the cultural dispensability of privacy norms is open to diverse kinds of responses. One obvious issue that the thesis raises is the empirical one of whether or not there are cultures in which privacy as such is not recognized and institutionalized. On a somewhat more theoretical plane, we find people arguing that institutions of privacy are in fact psychologically necessary for the development of personality. On a still more Olympian level we find some arguing that the very possibility of important, intimate relationships, and highly significant personal conditions and experiences, are *logically* dependent upon institutions of privacy.

Arguments for the logical dependence of relationships and experiences upon institutions of privacy offer the following considerations: It is claimed that intimacy involves abandoning objectivity – something which cannot occur under the gaze of noninvolved points of view. Second, it is argued that intimacy and trust cannot take place outside the realm of selective self-disclosure. Third, it is claimed that the diversity of social relationships and roles important to social life can survive only in a context of control over which "audiences" have access to the various "faces" we present.

Distinguishable from the question of whether all cultures value privacy is the question of whether there is a realm of life which is inherently private. Some have argued that while privacy is important, what it is that is respected as private by a community is irrelevant; what matters is that some area or other be marked off as private. Others argue that matters related to a person's innermost self are inherently private, though what parts of a person's extended self are private is conceded to be culturally conditioned. Still others argue that each relationship is socially defined in such a way as to demarcate which dimensions of a person's life are accessible and which are inaccessible.

This raises the question of whether there is a criterion of the inherently private. One might propose, for instance, that the only criterion of the private is that it is marked off by those aspects of life that do not, or tend not to, affect the significant interests of others. Such a criterion, plausible at first, is subject to the following difficulty. Whatever one might claim as falling within his or her private realm could be reclassified on the basis of others manipulating the situation so that they have a stake in that state of affairs. For instance, so long as I am in a position to make a large bet on any matter relating to another's life, that matter, on this criterion, thereby ceases to be private. One does not have to be inventive to generate counterexamples. There are institutions with considerable resources and investments devoted to exposing parts of lives we all think of as private. Few would be tempted to think that such practices deprive these domains of life of their private character. While there is concurrence on the view that at least some parts of our lives are regarded as private only because of particular cultural norms, there is considerable disagreement over whether there is any culture-free criterion of the inherently private, and if so, what it is.

II. Critical discussion of the literature

Having enumerated a number of the philosophical issues that are raised in discussions of privacy, we now turn to a more detailed and critical discussion of positions as they developed historically – especially of those represented in this volume.

The privacy literature can be roughly divided into three categories: attempts to define privacy; discussions that emphasize the centrality of privacy to morality; and essays that are morally skeptical about the value of privacy. Defenses of the importance of privacy have generally followed two related strategies:

1. Arguments designed to show that respect for privacy is a key component in the more general regard for human dignity. The appeal here is to such conditions as moral integrity, individuality, consciousness of oneself as a being with moral character and worth, and consciousness of oneself as a being with a point of view, searching for meaning in life.
2. Arguments designed to show that respect for privacy is integral to our understanding of ourselves as social beings with varying kinds of relationships, each in its way important to a meaningful life.

Both of these approaches attempt to demonstrate a connection between respect for privacy and certain individual, social, and political ideals.

Those who are morally skeptical of privacy have generally adopted one of two approaches:

1. Some suggest that the kinds of interests protected by privacy are not really distinctive or morally illuminating, and hence do not constitute an independent moral category.
2. Others argue that protecting privacy and recognition of institutions of privacy may be harmful to the individual in making him psychologically vulnerable, and may be detrimental to the society through the encouragement of asocial or antisocial attitudes.

Although the focus of this volume and its Introduction will be philosophical, contributions to our understanding of the nature and role of privacy have been made from a number of disciplines. Although philosophers have speculated about the extent to which the need for privacy is culture-specific and socially nurtured, there is much anthropological and sociological literature that is also relevant to the issue. I have included two pieces of anthropological argument that deal with the social functions of institutions of privacy. Let me begin with these.

Robert Murphy's essay "Social Distance and the Veil" [Chapter 2 in this volume] is devoted to discussing, theoretically and empirically, the functions of social distance mechanisms like privacy. According to Murphy, not only is privacy recognized and institutionalized in all societies, but it is absolutely essential to the maintenance of both social relationships and the sense of self. It follows from this thesis that privacy is operative in, and highly significant to, not only "individualistic" societies like our own.

Murphy claims that aloofness, removal, and reserve are the means by which a person establishes and maintains social relationships. Self-revelation and self-reserve are necessary components of all social relationships, but they can be found to have pronounced importance in a number of particular settings:

1. In relationships that are most difficult to maintain but are also most important to the parties involved
2. In relationships in which possibilities of role conflict and disappointment of expectations are most likely to emerge

Striking in Murphy's analysis is his claim that privacy is as important in intimate relationships as in more pedestrian relationships, because of the inevitable ambiguity and ambivalence of the parties in intense relationships. Most analyses by philosophers have taken privacy *vis-à-vis the rest of the world* as important to intimacy, but not privacy *vis-à-vis the parties to the intimate relationship itself*. Similarly salient is Murphy's observation that some of a person's public roles may conflict with other public roles of the individual, and that privacy may be necessary to the maintenance of the *public* roles of an individual. Privacy, in other words, may be a precondition of public roles and not always just the simple antithesis of action in the public realm.

Alan Westin's piece, "The Origins of Modern Claims to Privacy" [Chapter 3 in this volume], is a survey of anthropological literature as it relates to the thesis of the cultural relativity of privacy. Westin concludes that privacy appears to be a cultural value in all known human communities, although the forms it takes may vary enormously. Westin indicates that many practices that strike Westerners as performed without concern for privacy are actually structured by privacy norms and are thus protected by psychological shades even if not by physical walls.

It should be observed that not all social theorists elevate the private to the universal and indispensable role attributed to it by Westin and Murphy. Hannah Arendt, for instance, in her book *The Human Condition* (1958), has suggested that what we now take to be the private realm was thought in classical Greek times to be the realm of "privation" or deprivation – a realm in which persons saw to their material dependencies, like sustenance, and not to their creative and rational, or specifically human aspects. This private area was exhausted by activities people shared with lesser beings, and as such was decidedly not the realm in which individuality, meaningful existence, or characteristically human aspirations were expected to flourish. Such qualities could emerge only in political activities performed in the public realm.

Although the first sustained and explicit discussion of privacy appeared in 1890 in Warren and Brandeis's article, their interest in privacy was by no means unprecedented. In order to place the philosophical treatments of privacy in a broader intellectual context, I shall review some efforts at dealing with privacy issues that predate the Warren and Brandeis article, even though these treatments are not represented in this collection.

Many aspects of life connected with privacy have long been recognized under other descriptive headings. Examples include privacy protected through the recognition of private property; privacy protected through the First Amendment to the United States Constitution, which protects freedom of conscience; privacy protected through the Fourth Amendment, which limits the conditions under which legally sanctioned searches of private premises and personal effects may take place; and privacy protected through the Fifth Amendment, which relieves a person of a legal duty to incriminate himself. The American practices closely resemble, in fact derive from, English practices. Seventeen years before the Warren and Brandeis article appeared, James Fitzjames Stephen, the English jurist and philosopher, made the following short but pregnant remarks about privacy in his classic work, *Liberty, Equality and Fraternity:*

Legislation and public opinion ought in all cases whatever scrupulously to respect privacy. To define the province of privacy distinctly is impossible, but it can be described in general terms. All the more intimate and delicate relations of life are of such a nature that to submit them to unsympathetic observation, or to observation which is sympathetic in the wrong way, inflicts great pain, and may inflict lasting moral injury. Privacy may be violated not only by the intrusion of a stranger, but by compelling or persuading a person to direct too much attention to his own feelings and to attach too much importance to their analysis. The common usage of language affords a practical test which is almost perfect upon this subject. Conduct which can be described as indecent is always in one way or another a violation of privacy. (p. 160)

In this passage Stephen emphasizes several points:

1. Privacy relates centrally to the intimate aspects of a person's life.
2. Privacy relates centrally to subtle aspects of relationships between people.
3. Part of what people care about when others know certain things about them is that these things are to be understood in a certain light, or with a particular kind of appreciation for the meaning these have for the subject.
4. Privacy involves allowing a person discretion to decide when, and to what extent, inner feelings and attitudes are to be explored.
5. Certain kinds of affronts to a person's sensibilities can be seen as intrusions into their privacy.

Each of these themes has been developed in subsequent literature and treated as a central insight into privacy.

Several pages later, Stephen comments:

That any one human creature should ever really strip his soul stark naked for the inspection of any other, and be able to hold up his head afterwards, is not, I suppose, impossible, because so many people profess to do it; but to lookers-on from the outside it is inconceivable.

The inference which I draw from this illustration is that there is a sphere, nonetheless real because it is impossible to define its limits, within which the law and public opinion are intruders likely to do more harm than good. To try to regulate the internal affairs of a family, the relations of love or friendship, or many other things of the same sort, by law or by the coercion of public opinion is like trying to pull an eyelash out of a man's eye with a pair of tongs. They may put out the eye, but they will never get hold of the eyelash. (p. 162)

Central to Stephen's idea is that to be a moral being necessitates the existence of certain areas of life that are inherently private, which can be exploited for public purposes only through a willingness to suffer

or inflict personal loss. Stephen acknowledges that there are persons
who appear to give themselves over fully to a cause in which there is
no compromise with anything private, and who nonetheless fare passably well. This recognition of the possibility that what seems like a
moral universal – respect for deeply experienced privacy needs – may
be a cultural peculiarity stemming from a socially conditioned conception of individual and social life is still philosophically pressing.

Many novelists have been concerned with the issues raised by Stephen, and we may take as examples some of Henry James's writing
during this period. In *The Reverberator*, published in 1888, James contrasts two attitudes toward privacy, represented by two families: the
Proberts and the Dossons. In the novel, the Proberts are profoundly
distraught at having become an object of public attention and judgment. Served up to the public in an article that appeared in a scandalous society newspaper, they experience a sense of "excruciation – of pollution." The Dossons, on the other hand, are completely
mystified and bewildered by the Proberts' aversion to, and phobia of,
public exposure. James defines Mr. Dosson's attitude toward public
exposure as follows:

Deep in Mr. Dosson's spirit was a sense that if these people had done bad
things they ought to be ashamed of themselves and he couldn't pity them
(for the publicity) and if they hadn't done them there was no need of making
such a rumpus about other people knowing. (p. 183)

Although presented as uncultured, the Dossons exhibit throughout
endearing personal and familial virtues. Concern for privacy, whether
one's own or another's, is represented in *The Reverberator* as class-
dependent, and not as something indispensable to a life of basic decency.

In "The Private Life," published by James in 1893, the private part
of a distinguished playwright's life is hypostasized into a separate
being, with an existence independent of the person's public self. This
private being is the source of the playwright's creativity and, interestingly, the basis of the ability to relate to others. James's story entitled
"The Death of the Lion," published in 1894, similarly explores the
association between privacy and creativity. To offer just one more
instance of James's preoccupation with dimensions of privacy, his
novel *The Bostonians*, published in 1886, deals with the question of
whether a life can be completely and fully lived if given over entirely
to political and public causes, with no attention paid to one's private
dimension. From a contemporary, feminist perspective, we could also
see raised in this book the issue of whether the sharp distinction drawn
between the private and the public domains of life forces hardships

and closes options on those primarily responsible for maintenance of the private domain. If facets of private life, like child care, were more readily acknowledged in professional contexts, more women could find fulfillment in public endeavors.

As a speculation as to why this interest in the perceived importance in a private life, and hence in privacy, emerged at this time, we might connect it with a social awareness that there may be standards of behavior that do not gain their validity through social approval. Perhaps what emerged at this period, in Europe and North America, was an appreciation of competing sources of evaluation, the traditional standard providing but one, perhaps stifling, source. Theodor Fontane's novel *Effi Briest,* published in 1894, reflects the damage to individuals and the most intimate relationships occasioned by adherence to conventional standards. Once matters are made public, the dynamic aspect of social categories is represented as overwhelming individual attitudes and reservations, requiring a preestablished routine of responses. Moral courage is necessary to suffer the social consequences of acting on the basis of profound sensibilities of the heart. Typically, individuals seeking a way around traditional styles are crushed. Skepticism over the adequacy of conventional standards and the emergence of conflict between sources of value that historically spoke with but one voice sparked the following realization: There is an inner truth that may need some protection if it is to survive the battle with social opinion and ultimately have a role in reforming it. What would differentiate this view – that there is a source of human meaning threatened by the popular standards – from the realizations of the ancient prophets and the sophists, as well as from those of later iconoclasts, is the modern attitude that there may be no unique truth, but possibly diverse, individually defined sources of value, combined with modern pessimism about the ability of social standards to reflect deeply personal needs. Hense the need for privacy rather than merely a replacement for the dominant and dominating conventions.

Alasdair MacIntyre (1981) has recently argued that Kierkegaard and Nietzsche ushered in an era of belief to the effect that beyond choice or will, there is no basis whatsoever for submission to moral rules or principles. Such a conclusion resulted from a realization that reason could not be expected to supply a standard for the resolution of conflicting attitudes or for opposing natural passions. This attitude toward morals coincided with the identification of personality as something essentially divorced from any social or historical roles, hitherto understood to impose an identity replete with obligations and emotional dispositions.

In the treatment of positions that follows, we shall begin with arguments that defend the moral importance of privacy by way of an emphasis on individual values, then consider defenses that are oriented to the preservation of important human relationships, and finally consider various skeptical treatments of privacy. (This structure is only roughly accurate and when it serves philosophically critical, or important historical, purposes, the treatment will be integrated.)

1. Privacy and individual dignity

We turn now to the more technical discussions of privacy, beginning with defenses of privacy that stress the relationship between respect for privacy and respect for individual dignity generally. First under discussion is Warren and Brandeis's paper, "The Right to Privacy" [Chapter 4 in this volume]. Although Warren and Brandeis refer to aspects of privacy such as solitude and control over other's access to one's private thoughts, the real focus of their essay is the violation of privacy occasioned by the publication or public dissemination of information relating to the private domains of a person's life.

The authors cite the advances of civilization as having cultivated new sensibilities and vulnerabilities in us, in effect having created privacy needs. This places the authors among those who argue that the need for privacy is not inherent but only attendant on reaching a certain threshold of cultural sophistication. The authors also believe that the intensity and complexity which increasingly characterize life make crucial a person's ability to retreat from the world. Finally, technological and business developments and the emergence of a certain kind of press – one devoted to reporting the scandalous details of individuals' lives rather than the political and economic issues of the day – resulted in assaults on the "sacred precincts of private and domestic life," and violations of the bounds of propriety and decency.

Although the authors, in defending its importance, never define what privacy is, they connect it with various other values, including an individual's *right to be left alone,* and the respect due an individual's *inviolate personality.* These principles are not explored further except to indicate that they relate to a person's estimate of himself and to others' estimates of that person's feelings.

Warren and Brandeis argue that unless explicit legal recognition is given to privacy, the law will be inadequate to protect privacy. The authors point out that social and legal tolerance for the public exposure of private lives can corrupt a society by encouraging the diversion of attention to such matters away from important economic and political issues. They suggest that although various strategies, including the laws of property, of copyright, of contract, and of breach of confidence, have been employed in the past to protect privacy interests, the law should explicitly entitle persons to determine the extent to which their thoughts, sentiments, emotions, and productions – independent of their commercial or artistic value – become available to the world at large. The point of a shift to explicit legal entitlement is to underscore that the law recognizes the moral and spiritual integrity of individuals, as well as their material interests.

What emerges as most significant about this article is the claim that there is a specific privacy interest, connected in a profound way with the recognition of human moral character, and that for historical reasons this interest is more compelling at the present time than it was in the past. The authors are not merely interested in discovering a legal remedy for a particular, increasingly recurrent problem; they acknowledge that the law has been dealing passably well with such cases as they have arisen. The law's facility in dealing with such problems has been at the expense of remaining oblivious to the fundamental issue at stake: The law should articulate the underlying moral parameters of social interaction.

Diverse reactions greeted the Warren and Brandeis article. One reaction deserves special mention: outright skepticism. Some authors find bewildering the kind of protection Warren and Brandeis sought to make a matter of law. Harry Kalven, for instance, in his 1966 paper "Privacy in Tort Law – Were Warren and Brandeis Wrong?" argues that Warren and Brandeis leave their readers with no sense of what kinds of publications are wrongful, except perhaps the overinclusive criterion that any unauthorized reference to a person is a prima facie violation of that individual's right to privacy. Kalven suggests that had Warren and Brandeis limited themselves to making actionable those public disclosures that outrage the common sense of decency, one would then have had a comprehensible profile of what is wrongful publication. By not limiting themselves to such a threshold, according to Kalven, they show themselves insensitive to issues that people in fact find newsworthy, and to the importance of maintaining a free press.

Summarizing developments in American tort law during the seventy years after the Warren and Brandeis article, William Prosser, in his highly influential paper entitled "Privacy" [Chapter 5 in this volume], argues that there are actually four distinct kinds of invasion and three distinct kinds of interest protected by the law of privacy.

The four categories that distinguish the varieties of intrusions that fall under the privacy tort are as follow:

1. Intrusion upon a person's seclusion, solitude, or private affairs: This intrusion can be physical, visual, or electronic, and it must be into an area which would be offensive or objectionable to a reasonable person. The intrusion must be on a person entitled to be not so treated. The interest protected here, according to Prosser, is avoidance of emotional distress.
2. Public disclosure of private, embarrassing facts: The intrusion here involves three distinct elements:
   a. The disclosure must be public, not private in nature.
   b. The facts disclosed must be of a private nature and not of things that a person has done in public or that are a matter of public record.
   c. The matters made public must be ones that would be offensive and objectionable to a reasonable person of ordinary sensibilities. The interest protected here is primarily that of reputation, but also that of emotional tranquility.
3. Public disclosure of a private person in a false light. This invasion involves publicly attributing falsely to a person some opinion, statement, or behavior that would be regarded as objectionable to a reasonable person. Here again the interests protected are those of reputation and emotional tranquility.
4. Appropriation, for one's own advantage, of another's name, image, or other mark that is an aspect of that person's identity, without that person's consent and where the motivation is pecuniary. The interest protected here is proprietary – a property interest.

   It is interesting to note that Warren and Brandeis began with cases they thought *deserved* to be treated as privacy cases and formulated their defense with just these cases in mind. Prosser, on the other hand, took those situations that any court had regarded as privacy cases and then proceeded with his categorization and analysis. With this contrast in mind, it should not surprise us that Warren and Brandeis found one unified issue that related the cases they discussed, whereas Prosser found no such coherence in the cases he examined. Prosser explicitly remarked that of the diverse intrusions of privacy interests his analysis uncovered, Warren and Brandeis had focused on one: the disclosure of private, embarrassing facts. Insofar as Prosser regarded such disclosures as a single kind of intrusion, he cannot be said to disagree with Warren and Brandeis about the coherence of such cases or about their preferred legal status.

Although Prosser seems to concede Warren and Brandeis their primary legal claim – that there is a unified concern that involves the interest private individuals have in keeping their private lives out of the public light – there is a difference in emphasis regarding what is at stake in violations of this sort. For Brandeis and Warren, at issue is something sacred, connected with inviolate personality. For Prosser, the issue is reputation and protection from emotional distress. Brandeis and Warren thought that privacy represented one coherent and distinctive value; Prosser regards it as a complex of different interests, themselves like values the law seeks to protect generally and thus not particularly distinctive in function.

The terms in Prosser's analysis are straightforward and palpable. Writers like Prosser and Fredrick Davis argue that unless we acknowledge that our interest in privacy really does reduce to interests of reputation, emotional tranquility, and proprietary gain, we condemn ourselves to using confusing and obscure principles for deciding real cases. These reductionists argue that the interests that we seek to protect when we judge something private are not distinctively privacy interests; rather they are the ordinary kinds of interests many laws, having nothing whatever to do with privacy, aim at ensuring.

Others respond by arguing that the price we pay for this kind of reduction of privacy interests is depth of understanding and analysis. They claim that we miss the real injury to personality if we think that we can account for our interest in privacy exclusively in terms of our interest in reputation, emotional tranquility, and proprietary gain.

What emerges in the continuing debate over privacy are two questions about the reducibility of privacy to other interests or rights. First, does an analysis of privacy in terms of a variety of interests rather randomly associated do justice to our conception of privacy? (Earlier I called this question the *coherence* issue.) Second, does an analysis of privacy in terms of other interests point to anything distinctive about privacy, in contrast to other values we find it important to protect? (This question I earlier labeled the *distinctiveness* issue.) As we shall see, authors can and have argued that the interests protected under the rubric of privacy are important but not distinctive; such authors think that privacy represents just one way of pointing to interests or values already recognized as significant under different labels. Much of the philosophical controversy concerning privacy relates to this latter question. One way of arguing that there is something distinctive about the right to privacy is to show that we are unable to justify some of our clear intuitions about legitimate and illegitimate behavior without reference to privacy interests. When discussing Judith Thomson's argument below, I will try to provide just such an example.

Shortly after the publication of Prosser's article, Edward Bloustein took it upon himself to defend Warren and Brandeis's view against Prosser's assault. His defense in "Privacy as an Aspect of Human Dignity: An Answer to Dean Prosser" [Chapter 6 in this volume] deals with both aspects of the "reducibility" issue just mentioned. Bloustein wants to show first of all that the values at stake in privacy incursions are fundamental human values of a sort more exalted and more coherent than those proposed by Prosser. Second, Bloustein argues that there is something distinctive about privacy, in the sense that we cannot eliminate mention of it in discussing certain cases without loss of moral vision.

Bloustein intends to unpack the notion of "inviolate personality" that Warren and Brandeis regarded as central to the role of privacy. "Inviolate personality" is taken to include other notions such as individual dignity and integrity, personal uniqueness, and personal autonomy. Bloustein argues that respect for these values, not merely for things like emotional tranquility, reputation, and proprietary gain, both grounds and unifies our concern for privacy. This is true not only for philosophers but for judges as well. Respect for these aspects of human dignity is the basis for according to individuals the right to determine to whom their thoughts, emotions, sentiments, and tangible products are communicated.

Bloustein's article takes each of the areas that Prosser regarded as discrete and tries to show that something central is missed in the analysis or reduction offered by Prosser. For instance, to take the case of intrusion upon one's seclusion, Bloustein argues that at stake here is not primarily emotional tranquility but rather an affront to human dignity. He observes that when a particularly intimate or private aspect of one's life is intruded upon, one may suffer outrage but not necessarily mental trauma or distress. Even if one does suffer distress, this would be the *consequence* of the realization that one's dignity and freedom had been violated. The distress itself would not be the core of the injury. Additionally, one suffers an injury even if one is unaware of the intrusion – something that cannot be accounted for if the injury is seen as primarily a disturbance of emotional tranquility.

Bloustein also argues that those areas of the law that relate to privacy but do not fall under tort law, such as the Fourth Amendment to the United States Constitution, can also be analyzed by reference to the notion of inviolate personality. The connection between privacy torts and privacy as it arises elsewhere in the law is simply missed in analyses like Prosser's.

Bloustein argues that a person completely subject to public scrutiny will lose his uniqueness, his autonomy, and his sense of himself as an individual – in short, his moral personality. Such an individual will conform to other's expectations and become a purely conventional being – nothing but a part of an undifferentiated mass. The connection between privacy and concerns for individuals is completely lost in the kind of reduction Prosser and others have offered.

Like Bloustein and like Warren and Brandeis before him, Stanley Benn, in his paper "Privacy, Freedom, and Respect for Persons" [Chapter 8 in this volume], argues that something basic to our notion of respect for persons is engaged when we explore the role privacy plays in human interaction. Benn is interested in addressing two issues related to privacy:

1. What is significant about a person's wish to be or act in a way unobserved or unreported by others?
2. Are there realms of life that are inherently, and not just conventionally, private and therefore deserving of more respect than other matters that people might prefer to keep private?

In addressing the first question, about the basis for respecting a person's choice to act in private, Benn characterizes a person as a subject conscious of himself as an agent having projects and his own point of view. Respecting a person, Benn argues, involves appreciating the fact that what others do affects persons as agents with points of view. Others may act in ways that frustrate a person's objectives or violate the conditions under which he chooses to live a part of his life. Characteristically, the presence of another person forces us to take into account the fact that our behavior is being observed, and that we are being judged from another's vantage. This profoundly affects people as social beings. Such a situation forces an individual to acknowledge a different perspective on himself. If a person wishes to behave in a way free from such scrutiny and judgment, respecting that person involves affording a moral presumption to that preference. That is to say, unless we have reasons of a certain sort for observing an individual against his or her will, we ought not to do so. Respecting persons, for Benn, amounts to allowing two principles to govern our interactions:

1. Realize that others have a point of view on the basis of which
   they make choices.
2. Respect the choices of others when morally feasible.

Benn uses these same principles when arguing against surreptitious
observations of persons. Even though surreptitious observation of a
person does not affect the observed person's view of his own behavior,
it nonetheless undermines that person's capacity to make choices and
perform actions on the basis of reasons. Ignorance of circumstances
frustrates efforts at making rational choices. Additionally, one cannot
be said to respect a person if one knowingly and deliberately alters
the conditions for his actions, concealing this fact from him. Benn is
concerned to show that it is not only out of an unwillingness to disappoint persons that we presumptively should accord them privacy,
if they choose it. It is because we are rational agents with individual
and personal points of view, and not because we are mere repositories
of painful or pleasant responses, that our privacy interests should be
respected.

Benn goes on to address the second question of whether there are
inherently private aspects of people's lives. He argues that what is
most intimately connected with qualities of a person that confer respect – having a point of view and the capacity for choice – is inherently private and deserves more respect than matters kept private
simply because people prefer them to remain so. The intimacy of the
connection between a concept of self and one's body qualifies bodies
to be in the category of the inherently private. Accordingly, preferences for privacy regarding one's body are to be treated as deserving
greater deference than do preferences for privacy regarding other
aspects of life. Precisely which parts of a person's environment are
regarded as extensions of the self, and thus as qualifying for the same
level of presumptive privacy as the person himself, varies from society
to society.

Up to this point it may appear as if Benn's account of privacy rests
merely on his presupposition of autonomy as morally basic. As autonomous, an individual is morally entitled to act in ways, or under
conditions, of his choosing so long as there is not a compelling moral
reason to override the choice. Thus stated, the decision to be private
has not been distinguished significantly from a decision such as whether
to go about on roller skates. In the last section of his paper Benn
develops his ideas of what is morally distinctive about a person's ability
to think and act in private.

Benn argues that our privacy ideals are closely intertwined with our ideals about life and character. These include our ideal of personal relationships, our ideal of being free citizens, and our ideal of being morally autonomous. The ideals of moral autonomy and of personal relationships, as these relate to privacy, are explored by other writers represented in this volume, and I will not pursue them now. What Benn has to say about the ideal of being a free citizen is, however, unique. Benn suggests that part of our notion of a person as free is that he is subject to the authority and scrutiny of others only within reasonable and legally safeguarded limits. In other words, people have a right to a *private life*. People can be held *socially accountable* only for respecting the rights of others, and can be thought to have obligations to promote the welfare of society only if these obligations have been voluntarily assumed or if especially pressing reasons are operative.

George Orwell's novel *1984* presents one picture of what life would be like in a society which did not limit itself in the way Benn prescribes. Alternatively, one could suggest that without risking totalitarian political institutions, one may recognize responsibilities to the welfare of others on the basis of need, as well as on the basis of voluntary adoption.

More than any other writer considered in this volume, Jeffrey Reiman, in his essay "Privacy, Intimacy, and Personhood" [Chapter 13], regards it important to defend privacy exclusively in terms of individualistic moral considerations, foregoing any reference to an individual's social needs or dimensions. Reiman's thesis is that privacy represents a social ritual by means of which an individual's moral title to his own existence is conferred. Privacy is taken to be an essential part of a social practice by which a society recognizes and communicates to the individual that his existence is rightfully his own. Reiman speculates that a person's very sense of self as something morally distinctive could neither develop nor survive outside of social institutions instructing and disposing persons to recognize the private spheres of others.

In discussing moral autonomy and personhood, Reiman suggests that having moral title to oneself involves more than simply being able to determine how, and within what limits, one may act. Also included in our understanding of autonomy and personhood is the capacity to determine what about our thoughts and body is experienced by others.

In thinking about Reiman's position, we might ask: What would be lost if people were accorded autonomy over their behavior but not over who has access to their thoughts and bodies (insofar as this loss of control is compatible with behavioral autonomy)? For Reiman, the more one can control who has access to his thoughts, the more sensible it is to say that these thoughts really are *his,* in a normative sense. Without social practices according individuals control over access to their thoughts, people could not take moral title to their own consciousness or regard themselves as persons.

2. *Privacy and interpersonal relationships*

We now turn to examine defenses of privacy that stress the role of privacy in accounting for the ability to maintain important interpersonal relationships and intimate parts of life. In his seminal essay "Privacy" [Chapter 7 in this volume], Charles Fried argues that conventions relating to privacy, while having many practical and instrumental functions, also relate to basic aspects of individual integrity and moral and social personality. With respect to the very definition of oneself, Fried points out that of the various thoughts that appear in one's mind, discretion in selecting which of these to present, and in which contexts, is central to an individual's ability to be a certain kind of person.

Equally fundamental to the development of an individual's moral and social personality is the capacity to form important, intimate relationships involving love, friendship, and trust. These relationships require the spontaneous relinquishment of parts of one's inner self to another, inspired by certain kinds of attitudes. This capacity for sharing presupposes secure possession of those features of self in the first place. Privacy, and the sense of self and the title to the self that it engenders, thus constitute necessary conditions for love, friendship, and the ability to modulate important but less intimate relationships. Without the theoretical prospect of controlling access to one's inner aspects, important personal relationships could not emerge and could not even be envisioned as a mode of human interaction. Independent of the sense of how discretion over sharing certain parts of one's life sets off one class of relationships from others, trust, love, and friendship could not evolve out of other interactions.

Fried's analysis of the importance of privacy in terms of its role in intimacy has come under attack because to some it seems to place too much emphasis on informational sharing and not enough on personal caring. Whether or not this criticism is warranted, Fried's theory has formed the foundation for a number of other defenses of privacy that base their analyses on notions of integrity or the prospects for intimacy.

In his essay "Intimacy and Privacy" [Chapter 10 in this volume],

Robert Gerstein, like Fried, argues that intimacy would be impossible without privacy. Gerstein's analysis contrasts two relationships that a person might have to a situation: the participant role and the observer role. To be a participant is to immerse oneself fully in a situation; to become involved to the extent that one loses the sense of oneself as independent of the situation; to become enflamed and engulfed by the situation. In contrast, to be an observer is to distance oneself from a situation and adopt an objective attitude toward it.

With this distinction in mind, Gerstein argues that intimate communication, and intimate relationships generally, involves the parties as participants and not as observers. However, involvement as a participant can be transformed by becoming aware that one is being observed and judged. The very possibility of the sense of abandon that flourishes within an intimate relationship is undermined by a consciousness of oneself as an object of observation. Intimacy for Gerstein also involves a kind of ecstatic inner focus that is distracted or corrupted by objective judgment. Judgment typically imposes independent and nonpersonal standards for assessing the value of a relationship.

In another treatment of privacy and its connection with intimacy, "California's Constitutional Right to Privacy: The Development of the Protection of Private Life," Gerstein argues that a unified approach to privacy will start not with a definition of privacy, but with an account of the private life. He characterizes the private life as a commonly shared conception of those aspects of life that we most immediately identify with ourselves and that could not exist under the strictures of formal roles. These aspects can be destroyed by either control or surveillance. Accordingly, having a private life depends on having the capacity to make choices or act spontaneously without social constraints.

Gerstein argues that having a private life is central to the development of individuality, for it provides people with the conditions under which they can differentiate from others. Most importantly, a private sphere provides individuals with the resources and the perspective to form independent judgments about the social norms that dominate social life. Without this perspective, the social norms would completely absorb the individual.

In two different articles, "Privacy and Self-Incrimination" [Chapter 9 in this volume] and "Demise of Boyd: Self-Incrimination and Private Papers in the Burger Court," Gerstein argues that privacy is significant in certain contexts because it protects a person's capacity for coming to terms with his own conscience and for developing self-knowledge. The context at issue is that of defending the privilege against self-incrimination. Gerstein's argument begins with the observation that, at least in the case of violations of "core elements" of the criminal code, a confession will typically involve an expression of self-condemnation. Because of this connection, to require a person to admit to violating the law has the effect of causing that person to *condemn himself.* Self-condemnation, involving a profound inner reorganization and commitment, and being so dependent upon the particular motivation inspiring it, is not something with which judicial compulsion should interfere. Such an effort, aimed at affecting a person's innermost self, violates principles of respect for persons. At the same time it may actually impede the moral realization that should result when the guilty contemplate their crimes. (An interesting fictional account of this situation appears in Albert Camus' novel *The Stranger.*)

Again in the tradition of Fried's analysis, James Rachels, in "Why Privacy Is Important" [Chapter 12 in this volume], introduces his discussion of privacy by indicating two conditions that an adequate account of privacy should satisfy. First, an adequate criterion will account for the importance of privacy in normal situations – situations in which an individual is not covering up something deplorable. Second, an adequate account of privacy will help to explain what makes certain information not someone else's business, and will also account for the fact that prying is regarded as offensive.

Explaining why privacy is important to ordinary situations, Rachels observes that associated with different relationships are different patterns of behavior. Each sort of relationship involves a conception of what is appropriate behavior for the parties involved. Furthermore, each role involves a conception of the kind and degree of knowledge concerning one another which it is appropriate for the parties to possess. Thus Rachels's answer to the first question of why privacy is important for ordinary situations is that privacy is central to a person's ability to maintain varying kinds of relationships.

Rachels's treatment of this topic represents a generalization of Fried's position. Whereas Fried pointed to privacy as the means by which we can differentiate intimate from less intimate relationships, Rachels argues that privacy is a means of managing diverse kinds of relationships, many of which will be nonintimate.

Rachels uses his treatment of the first criterion to supply a basis for his treatment of the second, which involves showing what makes certain information about a person not someone else's business. Information about one person is not the business of another if no part of the relationship between the two persons entitles the second to know this information about the first.

One consequence of Rachels's treatment is that information about a person is appropriately sought only by those in relationships that warrant such an exchange of information. But it is also a consequence of this position that no information is inherently more private than any other information. Most of us would feel that although an employer has an understandable interest in whether an employee plans to become pregnant during the first few years of her employment, such a question is nonetheless inappropriate: It violates the employee's privacy. Similarly an employer may have an interest in routinely administering lie detector tests to his employees to deter theft, yet such a practice would strike us as wrong, because it is an invasion of privacy. Interestingly, if a person inquires of an acquaintance what his social security number is, the question is not likely to be regarded as offensive or invasive, even though no part of their relationship warrants interest in such information. Rachels's analysis does not account for our intuition that some information is objectively or presumptively more private than others, independent of the relationship involved.

Ruth Gavison's comprehensive discussion, in "Privacy and the Limits of Law" [Chapter 16 in this volume], is so rich that it defies efforts to abstract its central and important points within the limited space of an introduction such as this. I will confine my remarks to some of the positive functions of privacy which Gavison elaborates: the promotion of liberty, moral and intellectual integrity, important relationships, and the ideals of a free society.

With respect to individual integrity and the maintenance of important relationships, Gavison points out that people at times will not agree and will not be able to effect tolerance for other values or behavior, even though they acknowledge the legitimacy of the other position. In such situations, privacy allows for important interaction without the need to address areas of profound disagreement. Privacy effects practical tolerance for views and behavior which would be difficult to acknowledge directly. Privacy reflects our appreciation of the limits of human nature to deal with situations where there is both disagreement and a need to cooperate.

Besides helping to maintain individuality in the parties to an important relationship, privacy provides people with the emotional and intellectual space to review unpopular ideas and deliberate upon them without the pressure of social sanctions. Privacy makes it possible for individuals holding unpopular views to seek support for their positions and to work toward the expression of their ideas in a way that will be publicly more acceptable.

In a related vein, Gavison observes that privacy alleviates some of the tension between individual standards and social norms by leading to the nonenforcement of some of these standards. This is particularly important for norms that are only controversially applicable to a situation, even though the sentiments for regulation in this area are widespread and profoundly felt. Decisions about homosexual relationships or abortion are examples of areas where an individual's choices are shielded from social norms by privacy.

Discussing the ideals of a free society, Gavison notes that even in a society which prides itself on being open there is always a danger that behavior that deviates from the norm will result in hostile responses. Such a prospect will have an inhibiting effect on behavior that, strictly speaking, the individual should have been free to perform. This applies primarily to areas in which individuals are convinced that there should be few or no norms governing behavior. Privacy provides a context in which such behavior goes unchallenged.

3. Skeptical treatments of privacy

We turn now to skeptical arguments regarding privacy. Typically, critical treatments of privacy have emphasized two positions. The first is that while various privacy interests may be important, the significant moral issues at stake in privacy cases must be analyzed in terms quite independent of privacy or the right to privacy. Because of this, privacy fails to constitute a significant moral category in its own right, and what needs to be said about privacy can be best expressed without reference to privacy at all. The second position is that theorists who defend privacy fail to give sufficient weight to the socially and individually demoralizing aspects of a society in which respect for privacy is institutionalized. Both themes are expressed in the essays we are now to discuss.

Judith Jarvis Thomson's "The Right to Privacy" [Chapter 11 in this volume] represents the first kind of skeptical position. Although Thomson regards privacy interests as important, I regard her position as skeptical because she argues against both the coherence thesis and the distinctiveness thesis. Recall that in denying the coherence thesis one denies that there is any one interest or value that is the primary focus of privacy issues. In denying the distinctiveness thesis, one denies that something morally significant will be lost if we stop talking in terms of privacy and instead confine ourselves to the discussion of other values. Thomson argues that whatever rights to privacy a person has, such rights can be fully expressed using notions such as property rights, and the rights a person has over his own person. Privacy, for Thomson, is entirely derivative in its importance and justification. A person's right to privacy is violated only if another, more basic right has been violated.

To give some instances of this account of privacy, Thomson suggests that what is specifically wrong with reading another person's private papers is that such papers belong to that individual; part of the right of owning such papers is discretion concerning who has access to them. In Thomson's view, the specific problem with a person peering through the draped windows of another's house to get a view of the occupant is that part of what is involved in having rights over one's own person is discretion regarding who has access to views of oneself. In this way, characteristic cases of invasion of privacy can be formulated as dependent on property rights and personal rights.

Of course, any defense of privacy will involve reference to other values or ends. Thomson's claim is that there is nothing morally illuminating about introducing the concept of privacy, provided we are clear about what other rights a person can legitimately claim.

Consideration of an example can be used to show that there *is* something distinctive about the right to privacy that is not captured by reference to property rights or to rights over the person. Suppose that there are two types of sound wave interceptor available. One type records the speech carried by the sound waves. The other type converts the sound waves into usable energy but makes no record of the speech itself. Now compare the uses of these interceptors from a moral perspective. If two neighbors, each possessing one of the two types of receptor, train their receptors at my house to gather the emanating sound waves, would we want to say that each gathering violates equally my rights? If I do not like my neighbor with the sound-wave-to-energy converter, and if I do not want to be instrumental in lowering his energy bills, do I have the right to stop that neighbor from collecting my sound waves? (Of course, I may surround my yard with receptors and in this way make it less likely that any usable energy ever gets as far as my neighbor's yard; but that is not relevant to the issue at hand.) Whatever rights a person has over uses that may be made of him, such rights cannot be thought to preclude numerous potential uses of his sound waves. It is incorrect to think that because a person's voice is his own he can determine all limits on how others use it.

My neighbor with the sound wave interceptor that records conversations does violate my rights, and Thomson agrees with this. The reason such use of my sound waves violates my rights is that it interferes with my right to privacy, and not, as Thomson supposes, because it violates my right to determine what happens to my sound waves. Reference to ownership of sound waves will not suffice, since, as we just observed, that ownership does not preclude certain uses, even without consent. Indeed, in order to acknowledge any ownership rights in such situations, we must establish that a privacy right has been violated. The suggestion here is that without reference to privacy rights specifically we shall not be able to account for the wrongness of certain acts consistent with the innocence of certain others. Without reference to privacy, we will not be able to draw moral distinctions that are important to describe.

In a pair of skeptical essays, "An Economic Theory of Privacy" [Chapter 15 in this volume] and "The Right of Privacy," Richard Posner, like William Prosser before him, argues that the kinds of interests protected under the rubric "privacy interests" are nondistinctive. Posner also argues that the way we generally assign personal privacy rights is socially injurious because it is economically inefficient. Posner is interested in finding an entitlement scheme that will maximize investment in the production and communication of socially useful information. This criterion will then be used to assign privacy rights to such information.

With respect to the communication of information, according to Posner, privacy is to be ensured in just those cases where making it freely accessible to others would either eliminate the communication altogether or reduce its value by the inclusion of other misleading information. For example, making recommendations about a student accessible to the student discourages truthful assessments and consequently diminishes the value of the recommendation to potential employers or graduate schools.

Personal information can fall into one of two categories: discrediting or not discrediting. If the information is discrediting and accurate, then, according to Posner, we have a social incentive to make this information available to others who might have dealings with this person. Accurate information enables others to gear their interactions with this person in a reliable way. For Posner, revealing discrediting information about a person to others with whom he may come in contact is like revealing a fraudulent scheme. Since such revelations will make others better-informed "consumers" of personal interactions, it is socially most efficient to invest rights to discrediting information to the society at large, and not to the individual whom it concerns.

With respect to nondiscrediting or false information, the value to the individual of keeping such information from being widely disseminated is higher than the value of having these kinds of information freely available. Nondiscrediting information typically will not change others' bases for interactions with the person, and thus is not socially useful. False information is disruptive to rational decision making and for that reason is not usefully disseminated. Posner's general account of why people wish to maintain information about themselves as private is instructive. According to Posner, people are most interested in reticence when they want to maintain a social or economic advantage.

Richard Wasserstrom, in "Privacy: Some Arguments and Assumptions" [Chapter 14 in this volume], also suggests that not revealing information about oneself may be morally equivalent to deception and thus presumptively improper. After reviewing numerous rationales for valuing privacy, related mostly to our understanding of personhood and to our appreciation of human vulnerabilities, Wasserstrom develops his own basis for being suspicious of privacy. He places his argument in the context of what he calls "counterculture" considerations.

Wasserstrom suggests that we may make ourselves unnecessarily vulnerable by accepting the notion that there are thoughts and acts about which we ought to feel embarrassed or ashamed. We would be less vulnerable if we were to discover that others are similarly structured and that we are not uniquely defective or unusual. According to Wasserstrom, reserve and reticence constitute the preconditions for maintaining this level of vulnerability.

Wasserstrom observes that many kinds of behavior are regarded as shameful unless performed in private. But anthropological evidence suggests that acts we regard as inherently private are regarded as such because of our particular enculturation. What we feel we must do only in private, people elsewhere are comfortable doing publicly. Presumably, we could change our conventions about these acts and come to feel that such behavior is appropriate in a wider range of contexts.

Wasserstrom suggests, again in the context of the countercultural speculation, that privacy encourages hypocrisy and deceit. If people were more comfortable with who they were as private beings, their personalities would become more integrated and they would come to feel less threatened and less pressured to present themselves as other than they really are.

The picture that both Posner and Wasserstrom, in the latter's counterculture mode, present of human nature is something like this: People are really and fundamentally unitary. We act either authentically or inauthentically as we present ourselves in various contexts. If we do not reveal all of what we are to those who have reason to interact with us we are being partially deceptive. Furthermore, in the case of Wasserstrom's critical treatment of privacy, the suggestion is implicit that were the world made up exclusively of psychologically understanding, morally trustworthy, and anthropologically informed persons, our interest in privacy would diminish radically if not disappear entirely. For both Posner and Wasserstrom, what we are private about relates presumptively to matters we wish to conceal because of the different images of ourselves that would be projected through such a disclosure.

Each of these presuppositions or pictures is open to critical treatment. Perhaps people can behave in different ways in different contexts without exhibiting any inauthenticity in any of these contexts. People really may be complex in the sense that they are not basically one thing. Persons may have different dimensions in their lives, find these important to maintain, and yet not be very clear how they all fit together. The notion of the self as an integrated substratum that explains the consistency of human activities in divers contexts has come under attack from several theoretical quarters. Walter Mischel (1968), the psychologist, has argued that one of the primary reasons we have for positing the self – the supposed consistency in behavior irrespective of context – is not well founded in practice. This finding makes the notion of the unified self theoretically gratuitous. Mischel fills in this thesis by outlining various cognitive heuristic strategies that encourage us to be oblivious to the diversity of context-dependent character traits actually present in ourselves and others. Goffman (1959) and writers in the "dramaturgical school" of social analysis also argue that there is no core person underlying the various context-dependent personalities we occupy in life.

Second, privacy may serve functions in addition to withholding information others would regard as discrediting. For example, some of the positions discussed earlier argue that privacy is important in regulating and maintaining diverse relationships and a sense of oneself as a person. Politically and socially, recognition of privacy interests functions to provide individuals with a part of their life unregulated and unobserved by persons with objective and external perspectives. This kind of freedom from constraints allows people to seek meaning on the basis of inner values. Additionally, one may wish to keep certain information private because of the role such information plays in one's life. Some information may be regarded as special, and consequently properly or respectfully revealed only in a context in which it will be appreciated with the kind of meaning it has for the person it concerns. Revelations of this information in other contexts may strike one as defiling, devaluing, and diminishing significant aspects of oneself. (Henry James's expression "pollution" is apt here.) A detailed response to these presuppositions is covered in Ferdinand Schoeman's paper entitled "Privacy and Intimate Information" [Chapter 17 of this volume].

NOTES

I am indebted to Patrick Hubbard, Linda Weingarten, Jonathan Sinclair-Wilson, Hugh Wilder, Judith Jarvis Thomson, and Sara Schechter-Schoeman for extensive critical and supportive comments on earlier versions of this essay. This interpretative essay is an adaptation of a paper forthcoming in *The American Philosophical Quarterly*.

1 While a number of authors have devoted whole essays to the definition of privacy, I have chosen not to include such in this anthology because the issues addressed are adequately reviewed in some of the essays included, which are more broadly focused.

2 Another way in which the coherence and distinctiveness issue may arise in one's thinking is to question whether privacy concerns as they arise in criminal law and privacy concerns as they arise in tort law raise fundamentally different kinds of concerns. The papers represented in this collection represent both sides of this disagreement.

REFERENCES

Arendt, Hannah. 1958. *The Human Condition*. Chicago: University of Chicago Press.

Benn, Stanley I. 1971. Privacy, freedom and respect for persons. In *Nomos XIII: Privacy*, J. R. Pennock and J. W. Chapman, eds. New York: Atherton Press, pp. 1–26.

Benn, Stanley I. 1978. Protection and limitation of privacy. *Australian Law Journal* 52: 601–12, 686–92.

Bloustein, Edward. 1964. Privacy as an aspect of human dignity: an answer to Dean Prosser. *New York University Law Review* 39: 962–1007.

Davis, Frederick. 1959. What do we mean by "right to privacy?" *South Dakota Law Review* 4: 1–24.

Flaherty, David. 1972. *Privacy in Colonial New England*. Charlottesville: University of Virginia Press.

Fontane, Theodor. 1976. *Effi Briest*. New York: Penguin.

Fried, Charles. 1968. Privacy. *Yale Law Journal* 77: 475–93.

Gavison, Ruth. 1980. Privacy and the limits of law. *Yale Law Journal* 89: 421–71.

Gerety, Tom. 1977. Redefining privacy. *Harvard Civil Rights – Civil Liberties Law Review* 12: 233–96.

Gerstein, Robert. 1970. Privacy and self-incrimination. *Ethics* 80: 87–101.

1978. Intimacy and privacy. *Ethics* 89: 76–81.

1979. Demise of Boyd: self-incrimination and private papers in the Burger court. *UCLA Law Review* 27: 343–97.

1982. California's constitutional right to privacy: the development of the protection of private life. *Hastings Constitutional Law Quarterly* 9: 385–427.

Godkin, E. L. 1890. Rights of the citizen, part IV – to his own reputation. *Scribner's Magazine* 8: 58–67.

Goffman, Erving. 1959. *The Presentation of Self in Everyday Life*. Garden City: Doubleday.

Gross, Hyman. 1967. The concept of privacy. *New York University Law Review* 42: 34–54.

1971. Privacy and autonomy. In *Nomos XIII: Privacy*, J. R. Pennock and J. W. Chapman, eds. New York: Atherton Press, pp. 169–81.

Henkin, Louis. 1974. Privacy and autonomy. *Columbia Law Review* 74: 1410–33.

James, Henry. 1886. *The Bostonians*. New York: Macmillan.

1888. *The Reverberator*. New York: Macmillan.

1944. The death of the lion. In *Stories of Writers and Artists*, F. O. Mattheissen, ed. New York: New Directions.

1946. The private life. In *Fourteen Stories by Henry James*, David Garnett, ed. London: Rupert Hart-Davis.

Kalven, Harry, Jr. 1966. Privacy in tort law – were Warren and Brandeis wrong? *Law and Contemporary Problems* 31: 326–41.

Landynski, Jacob. 1966. *Search and Seizure and the Supreme Court: A Study in Constitutional Interpretation*. Baltimore: Johns Hopkins University Press.

Lasson, Nelson. 1937. *The History and Development of the Fourth Amendment to the United States Constitution*. Baltimore: Johns Hopkins University Press.

MacIntyre, Alasdair. 1981. *Beyond Virtue*. Notre Dame, Indiana: University of Notre Dame Press.

Mischel, Walter. 1968. *Personality and Assessment*. New York: John Wiley and Sons, Inc.

Murphy, Robert. 1964. Social distance and the veil. *American Anthropologist* 66: 1257–74.

O'Brien, David. 1979. *Privacy, Law and Public Policy*. New York: Praeger Special Studies.

Parker, Richard. 1974. A definition of privacy. *Rutgers Law Review* 27: 275–96.

Posner, Richard. 1978. An economic theory of privacy. *Regulation* (May/June): 19–26.

1978. The right of privacy. *Georgia Law Review* 12: 393–422.

Prosser, William. 1960. Privacy. *California Law Review* 48: 383–423.

Rachels, James. 1975. Why privacy is important. *Philosophy and Public Affairs* 4: 323–33.

Reiman, Jeffrey. 1976. Privacy, intimacy, and personhood. *Philosophy and Public Affairs* 6: 26–44.

Simmel, Georg. 1950. *The Sociology of Georg Simmel,* Kurt Wolff, ed. Glencoe: Free Press.

Schoeman, Ferdinand. 1983. Privacy and intimate information. In *The Philosophical Dimensions of Privacy: An Anthology,* Ferdinand Schoeman, ed. Cambridge: Cambridge University Press.

Stephen, James Fitzjames. 1873. *Liberty, Equality and Fraternity.* New York: Henry Hold and Co.

Taylor, Telford. 1964. *Two Studies in Constitutional Interpretation.* Columbus: The Ohio State University Press.

Thomson, Judith Jarvis. 1975. The right to privacy. *Philosophy and Public Affairs.* 4: 295–314.

Warren, Samuel, and Brandeis, Louis. 1890. The right to privacy. *Harvard Law Review* 4: 193–220.

Wasserstrom, Richard. 1978. Privacy: some arguments and assumptions. In *Philosophical Law,* Richard Bronough, ed. Westport: Greenwood Press.

Westin, Alan. 1970. *Privacy and Freedom.* New York: Atheneum Press.

2

Social distance and the veil[1]

ROBERT F. MURPHY

The company scatters, the lights go out, the song dies, the guitars grow
silent, as they approach the habitations of man. Put on your masks; you
are again among your brothers.

José Rizal in *Noli Me Tangere*

This is an essay on the means by which man promotes the establishment of social relationships and the maintenance of social interaction
through aloofness, removal, and reserve. It attempts, on one level, to
present a functional interpretation of a curious Tuareg custom, but,
in a more general sense, the paper undertakes an exposition of certain
dialectical processes in social life.

The question I have asked of a body of field data is very simply:
why do Tuareg males cover their faces so completely that only areas
around the eyes and nose may be seen? We will come back to this
matter in greater detail, but, for introductory purposes, my answer
is that by doing so, they are symbolically introducing a form of distance
between their selves and their social others. The veil, though providing
neither isolation nor anonymity, bestows facelessness and the idiom
of privacy upon its wearer and allows him to stand somewhat aloof
from the perils of social interaction while remaining a part of it.

Social distance

It is not my purpose to become involved in a general exegesis on the
subject of social distance, privacy and reserve, and I wish in these
prefatory comments only to inform the reader of the theoretical
framework within which I am operating. This study rests heavily on
ideas first advanced by Georg Simmel, especially upon his delineation
of self-revelation and self-restraint as necessary qualities of all social

relationships, rather than as mutually exclusive categories applying to some relationships as opposed to others. For Simmel, distance was inversely related to the amount of knowledge of each other available to actors. This knowledge can never approximate completeness, however, for he stresses that the sphere of knowledge is determined by the type of relationship and, more important, that the actor's self-revelations are filtered to produce what he calls "a teleologically determined non-knowledge of one another" (1950:312). An area of privacy, then, is maintained by all, and reserve and restraint are common, though not constant, factors in all social relationships. Society could not perdure if people knew too much of one another, and one may also ask, following Simmel, if the individual could endure as a social person under the burden of complete self-awareness.

Further writing on the subject of social distance rests only on a part of Simmel's work and has tended to emphasize distance as an inverse function of affect. Shibutani, in a recent work, sees social distance to lie along an axis between "sentiments" and "conventional norms" (1961:382), a usage closely related to Bogardus' criterion of "the degrees of sympathetic understandings" that obtain between persons or groups (1938:462). Distance scaling using these standards has been extensively applied to certain problems in modern industrial society, and generations of undergraduates have answered questionnaires oriented towards data on rate and kind of interaction between groups and on preferences of propinquity. Of central concern is the axis between antipathy and affection, as expressed in marriage, residence, and other choices. Norms regulating interactions between groups in our own society may thus be ascertained, but the social anthropologist would be hard put to derive comparable results by asking a Tiv if he would live next to his mother's brother. Or marry a father's brother's daughter. I would suggest that recent sociological writing on social distance has often departed from Simmel's original work and is more reflective of Western society than interpretative of Society. Knowledge of the other does not necessarily involve sentiment, nor is the expression of sentiment always based upon knowledge. Quite the opposite is often the case in ordinary life, and to Simmel knowledge was more closely related to penetration of the identity and intrusion into closed areas.

Since Simmel, the requirement of privacy in society has been discussed by such writers as Park and Burgess (1924:231) and more recently by Merton in his treatment of role segregation (Merton 1957:374–376). Merton notes the dilemma imposed by the assumption of multiple roles and the fact that the members of the actor's

various role sets have differing and sometimes contradictory expectations of him. He then proceeds to the self-evident proposition that,
if these expectations are to be maintained and conformity to the role
model assured, the actor must insulate these various activities and
sometimes the role sets and sub-sets themselves. In short, if social
interaction is to be made possible, a public life must be at one and
the same time a private life.

In many types of role, this separation is assured by a restriction of
information within the confines of the role set. The doctor takes care
to give minimal information about his profession to the patient (and
often minimal information on the patient's ailment), and the husband-
wife set guards its intimacies with jealousy. This imposition of distance
on the parameters of the role set does more than make other roles
possible, for it promotes the solidarity of the relationship itself. In
this sense, many role sets are effective secret societies. Just as the
impersonator of a god must wear a mask to erase his other *roles*—for
everybody surely knows who he *is*—the actor in the profane situation
must stylize his impersonation of the moment in such a way that he
can be at some future moment one of the many other persons he is
thought to be.

The above discussion takes us finally to the problem of the individual identity and the concept of the self. Goffman (1956) has written
eloquently on the person as a sacred object, a bearer of demeanor
and a recipient of deference, and argues that the individual's sense
of worth and significance is threatened by his vulnerability and pen-
etrability. These sources of weakness arise, of course, out of the fact
that we are of necessity social beings and, of equal necessity, require
some stable definition of ourselves if we are to effectively interact with
social others. Beyond this, the self is the object of our own attachment,
and identity is by its nature conservative. One of the great human
dilemmas, following George Herbert Mead (1934), derives from the
premise that the concept of the self is bestowed upon us by society
and through social interaction. But these very processes are at one
and the same time testing this identity and working to change it;
senescence and altered circumstance, then, conspire in an erosion of,
and sometimes assault upon, the ego. Interaction is threatening by
definition, and reserve, here seen as an aspect of distance, serves to
provide partial and temporary protection to the self.

Beyond the above strictures on identity, the expression of distance
in one form or another promotes autonomy of action (cf. Merton
1957:375). That the privacy obtained makes other roles more viable
has already been discussed, but reserve in the playing of one particular
role is also an essential ingredient of interaction. Here the actor allows

the other enough cues so that the game may go on, but withholds sufficient stimuli so that his further course of action cannot be fully predicted. This not only gives him flexibility, but by decreasing the show of emotional attachment to the means and also the end of action he is not trapped into commitment. More simply, and elegantly, this is what is known as "playing it cool."

Of central importance in this paper, the display of distance in social relationships is crucial in settings of ambivalence and ambiguity. Here flexibility and autonomy are essential because the outcome of the transaction cannot be predicted, because contrary interests are involved or because of some special indeterminacy in the situation. We joke with the person who is in the midst of radical status change, just as many peoples do with a cross-cousin. A senior affine may not always be avoided, but he is generally accorded some patterned and stylized treatment. And the person about whom we know little is treated with constraint and reserve if absence of embarrassment is to be assured; this is the converse of Simmel's measure of distance by knowledge of the other.

It would follow from the above that the expression of distance would occur just as commonly, if not more so, in our intimate associations as in our more marginal ones. Where knowledge of the other is minimal, the actor need know only that he is dealing with the butcher, the baker, or some *other* social *thing*. The actor gives socially and personally nothing more than the situation requires for accomplishment of a task. On the other hand, as the sphere of knowledge increases, the defenses about certain residual private spheres must be correspondingly strengthened. It is these intimate relationships, commonly the most affect-laden and central to the life of the individual, most difficult to maintain, and most ambivalent, which are most demanding of expressions of distance, however elusive and subtle these may be. This was best expressed by Simmel in the concluding lines of his famous discussion of marriage (1950:329):

The fertile depth of relations suspects and honors something even more ultimate behind every ultimateness revealed; it daily challenges us to reconquer even secure possessions. But this depth is only the reward for that tenderness and self-discipline which, even in the most intimate relation that comprises the total individual, respects his inner private property, and allows the right to question to be limited by the right to secrecy.

This is the real meaning of Simmel's use of knowledge as a measure of distance, for he understood well that familiarity, carried too far, breeds threat as well as contempt.

In summary, social distance is here viewed as a pervasive factor in human relationships and the necessary corollary of association. The more common usage of the term sees it as a spacing between individuals and groups, determinative of rate of interaction and reinforced by consciously felt attitudes. This gross, structural sense of the term is but one expression of the general phenomenon of distance, however, and I have briefly noted its manifestation as privacy and reserve in small scale interaction settings, as well as its relevance for the sociology of identity.

The intensity and form of distance, as well as its areas of occurrence, are variant and a function of social systems. It is inadequate to comment merely that distance mechanisms are found in society, and we must also inquire into the symbolic means of its expressions and the relationship of these symbols to other cultural factors. And given my, by no means original (cf. Radcliffe-Brown 1952:90–116), hypothesis that distance may be found pronouncedly in ambivalent relationships, we must search out those sectors of the social system and analyze the function of distance in maintaining the social order. Finally, just as the territorial requirements of different species of animals vary, it might be that human spacing, accomplished by symbolic, cultural means, is similarly different from one society to another. We will pursue this inquiry and seek the structural reasons for such variation.

The Tuareg

Even in the eyes of the experienced and well-traveled anthropologist, the Tuareg are a strange and exotic people. The French appellation of "les hommes bleus" is most appropriate, for in their finest robes of indigo-dyed cotton, and with blue veils falling from the bridge of the nose to below the chin, little shows of them except hands, feet and the area around their eyes. Even the small exposed sections of skin have a blue tinge, the result of the dye rubbing off the cloth, and the overall impression given by one of the fully armed warriors is almost awesome. No accurate census exists for the Tuareg but their numbers are estimated at about a quarter of a million. Their language is one of the Hamitic group, and it is closely related to the Berber of the Mediterranean littoral. This is their genetic affinity also, and the Tuareg are basically a Caucasoid people of Mediterranean type, though there has been a good deal of admixture, especially among the Sudanese and Sahelian Tuareg, with the Negroid peoples who live in their midst and to the south. There is no single, unified Tuareg tribe, and when we speak of them as an entity it is only to signify a people having common characteristics of race, language, and custom, as distinguished from their neighbors. There are deep and lasting enmities between different political federations of Tuareg, and, as should be expected, there are significant differences in dialect and culture throughout their vast territory. This area covers a large section of the Territoire des Oases in southern Algeria, and the northern parts of Mali and Niger. There is a slight extension of Tuareg into Libya, and their caravans reach Haute Volta, Nigeria, Chad, Morocco and other African countries. Though some Tuareg are sedentarized in Saharan oases or in farming communities of the northern Sudan, most are nomadic pastoralists, tending flocks of camels, sheep, goats, and in their southern extension, cattle. They are usually identified as dwellers of the Sahara desert, but the large majority of the population lives outside this forbidding and impoverished zone, tending their flocks in the richer pastures of the northern Sudan and the Sahel, the belt of savannah between the Sudan and the true desert.

The southeastern Tuareg of the Tanout and Agades districts, among whom I worked, are aligned in a number of major tribal confederations based on regional contiguity and traditional amity. These functioned mainly in time of war and today have diminished political significance. The component tribes of these federations are territory holding units under a chief whose powers are limited by traditional Tuareg egalitarianism and the countervailing power of the notables of the tribe. These tribes are commonly further divided into sub-tribes, each of which is under the leadership of a lesser chief and has a territorial locus. Both tribe and sub-tribe are conceived to be descent groups, the members of which acknowledge a common ancestry, but the mutual kinship of their members is putative and no genealogies of any depth or comprehensiveness are kept except in chiefly lines. Below the sub-tribe is the fundamental unit of Tuareg society, the *iriwan*, or house, which consists of some 50 to several hundred people who reside about a well to which they hold rights and who pasture their herds in the surrounding land. The name of each iriwan is taken from the name of its leader, who is acknowledged as the most notable member of the group, and as at the levels of segmentation of tribe and sub-tribe, it is a local-political-kin group. Kin ties are demonstrably closer in the iriwan than at higher levels, however, and its members feel themselves to share close bonds of consanguinity and, as we will see, affinity.

In addition to the differentiation of the population along tribal lines, Tuareg society is divided into three distinct and endogamic classes. The true Tuareg consist of the politically dominant noble tribes, or *imajaren,* and their vassals, or *imrad.* Each noble tribe exacts tribute and fealty from one or more vassal tribes, both noble and vassal tribes acting as corporate entities in their interrelations. The members of each class hold property individually in slaves, or *iklen,* who act as herdsmen and servants for their masters. The slaves are of Saharan and Sudanese Negroid origin, but most cannot trace their ancestry beyond slave status among the Tuareg. In language and in most aspects of their culture they are much like their masters, despite certain differences which are not the subject of this paper. Tuareg stratification has broken down in recent years, for French colonial rule loosened the political hold of the nobles over their vassal tribes, and many members of the slave class have been manumitted in accordance with government policy. But even where the traditional ties have been severed, the classes remain distinct as status groups, and membership in one class or another is the single most important criterion of a Tuareg's worth and standing.

The Tuareg, like their neighbors on all sides, are Moslem. They are noted, however, as infamous and unregenerate back-sliders who observe neither proper law nor custom, who misperform the ritual postures in prayer, fail to make ablutions, eat and drink during the fasting days of Ramadan, and who have few of the wise and holy in their ranks. Despite the best Tuareg efforts to simulate orthodoxy in the presence of their censurious neighbors, these charges are substantially true.

One of their most obvious points of heterodoxy is in the treatment of their women. The Tuareg woman enjoys privileges unknown to her sex in most Moslem societies. She is not kept in seclusion nor is she diffident about expressing her opinions publicly, though positions of formal leadership are in the hands of the men. Frequently beautiful and commonly mercurial in temperament, she places little value upon pre-marital chastity, stoutly defends the institution of monogamy after marriage, maintains the right to continue to see her male friends, and secures a divorce merely by demanding it—and she is allowed to keep the children. The shock of early Arab travelers at this state of affairs is understandable and was aggravated by the fact that the men were veiled and the women were not.

The high status of the Tuareg women is linked to their traditional matrilineality. Among many Tuareg tribes, especially those in the southern part of the territory, matrilineality has disappeared or become severely attenuated and has been replaced by a patrilineal mode of descent or a bilateral one. In the traditional system, still in force in many tribes, group membership is determined matrilineally and office passes through the male sibling group and then to the eldest son of the eldest sister. Tuareg matrilineality is, however, a curious institution and should not be equated with the rule as we usually know it. Most rules of unilineal descent are, of course, associated with a corresponding rule that marriage is exogamic to the descent group, but among the Tuareg the group is endogamic. There is a decided preference among the Tuareg for cousin marriage of all types. In addition to the Koranic preference for the daughter of the father's brother, it is considered good to marry the daughter of the mother's brother or sister, and the father's sister's daughter also is an acceptable partner.[2] Despite these preferences, marriages are usually not between first cousins, and the ideal of cousin marriage should be looked on as the ultimate idiom of a more general preference for endogamy. This pertains first to the local-political-kin group, or iriwan, which is an in-marrying unit as well as the most close-knit aggregation of kinsmen. After the iriwan, marriage is preferentially endogamic in the sub-tribe, the tribe, and the tribal confederation, in that order. Tuareg marriage preferences should be borne closely in mind because they are highly pertinent to our discussion of veiling practices. For present purposes, however, it should be noted that endogamy vitiates the rule of descent by making it an academic point in an in-marriage, inasmuch as both mother and father belong to the same group and so also will the children. And, more important, the setting of the boundaries of the kin group by endogamy rather than exogamy makes the Tuareg social system unique and typologically different from most other systems of kinship. The veiling of the men is a most strange custom, but it occurs in a most strange and baffling society. We will now turn to our attempt to impose rationality upon the bizarre.

The social uses of the veil

The Tuareg veil, or *legelmoust* in the Air Tuareg dialect, is the distinguishing characteristic of dress of this people. The standard Tuareg raiment consists of an underrobe and a flowing outer garment that extends from shoulders to ankles. The underrobe is sleeveless, but the outer garb has loose wide sleeves ideal for carrying the long daggers that are worn in sheaths strapped to the arm. These robes are either blue or white; some Tuareg affect a blue outer garment and a white inner one, while others adopt the opposite mode. Still others wear either all blue or all white. The more expensive cloth is the blue, and it is quite common for a man to wear various mixtures of blue and white for ordinary dress but to reserve an all blue ensemble for festive occasions. The most expensive item of dress, however, is the blue turban and veil, a long bolt of cloth that is made up of narrow strips of cloth sewn together. This special cloth is made and dyed in Nigeria and a good specimen may cost well over twenty-five dollars, a large sum of money to most Tuareg. A Tuareg who cannot afford this price, or who simply wishes a veil for everyday use, will generally use a bolt of ordinary white or blue cloth, but it is worn in much the same manner as the expensive kind. The art of putting on the veil is not easily mastered but, quite simply, the cloth is wrapped about the head to form a low turban and the end is then brought across the face, the top of the cloth falling across the nose and the bottom hanging well below the chin. The resultant effect is that the only part of the face showing is the area across the plane of the eyes. Raised to its extreme height, only a narrow slit is left open and even the eyes can barely be seen. There are situational differences in the actual attitude of the veil and the amount of face that the wearer exposes, but this is a key part of my analysis and will be discussed more fully below.

Whatever may be the precise position of the veil in different social settings, the most striking fact is that it is worn almost continually. The veil is worn when at home or traveling, during the evening or the day, when eating and smoking, and some even sleep veiled. That this is not simply a casual mode of costume is manifest when one watches a group of Tuareg men eating. Whether using spoons or their fingers, or drinking milk from a calabash, the veil is not lowered for the food to be passed to the mouth; rather, the proper Tuareg carefully raises the veil enough to enable him to eat but not far enough for his mouth to be seen. The occasional Tuareg who lowers his veil to eat reveals his low status as either a slave or a member of a vassal tribe—a member of a noble tribe does not expose his mouth. The veil has even inhibited the diffusion of that most pervasive habit, smoking. An occasional Tuareg would accept a proffered cigarette and proceed to smoke it by holding it gingerly under the veil—it was suspenseful to watch them light it. Most, however, take tobacco mixed with lime, and pack this mixture in their cheek or behind the lower lip, thus eliminating the obvious dangers of smoking. The constancy of veil wearing was once impressed upon me when I encountered in Kano, Nigeria, a rather deviant and renegade young Tuareg who was flamboyantly dressed in yellow plastic shoes, blue shorts, a checked sport shirt—and the turban and veil. It is not only the hallmark of the Tuareg but their most unchanging item of clothing.

Such a unique custom has not been without its interpreters, and I will give and discuss a few of the more common, and obvious, reasons advanced for veiling. Most explanations have been of the 'origin' type, though my prefatory remarks indicate that mine is quite clearly of a structural and functional kind. Even these origin theories, however, indicate that the custom persists for the same obvious utility that it had in its incipience, and it is worthwhile and pertinent to consider them. The first, of course, is that the veil keeps out the sand and dust of the desert and steppes. It does indeed do this, and during the dry season Kanuri, Hausa, Teda, and other traders commonly wrap the ends of their turbans across their mouths and noses while on caravan, much in the manner of the American cowboy driving a herd to market. But the Tuareg also wear their veils during the rainy season when there is little dust, and when sitting within the confines of their huts. Moreover, the veil is not worn until a youth approaches the manly state, at about the age of seventeen, and it is exactly the unveiled youths, and slaves, who do much of the dusty work of herding. It should also be remembered that the women go unveiled whatever the atmospheric condition; in fact, women only pull their shawls across the lower parts of their faces when expressing reserve and modesty.

The French explorer, Henri Duveyrier, noted and refuted this argument in 1864 and raised also the question of whether the veil disguised the Tuareg from their enemies (Duveyrier 1864:391–2). The ethnographer can only agree with his observation that the Tuareg recognize each other despite the veils and that this explanation is beside the point. I might add, however, that the Tuareg wear the veil highest and conceal their faces most completely when among many of those who are closest to them and know quite well who they are; they are sometimes most lax in the wearing of the veil when among non-Tuareg, exactly those from whom they could conceal their identity most successfully by veiling.

The Tuareg can probably recognize others among their range of acquaintances as rapidly and at as great a distance as Europeans, for they use a broad range of means of identification other than the face. First, every Tuareg affects a slightly different style of dress by varying the colors of the various items of apparel and individualizing the mode of wearing them. Second, the Tuareg are even more sensitized to the common criteria of identity given by stature and body set than are we, and they use a series of other cues from the exposed parts of the body. One Tuareg claimed that, though he had left home as an unveiled boy and returned five years later veiled, his sister recognized him by his feet. Even the non-Tuareg accustoms himself to these forms of recognition, as was forceably brought home to me on one occasion when a Tuareg friend approached me for the first time unveiled and I failed to recognize him. The source of my confusion is evident; he had disguised himself by adding facial cues rather than subtracting them.

The question of identification raises a series of interesting problems, for face reading and mouthwork are virtually absent among the Tuareg as media of communication. The first months of field ethnography among a totally unfamiliar people are disturbing to the anthropologist because of his inability to accurately assay the meaning of both verbal and non-verbal responses from his subjects. Among the Tuareg, these difficulties are aggravated by the fact that entire zones around the nose, mouth, chin, and throat, from which he is so accustomed to make inferences about the subjective state of the other, are concealed to him. He notes that the Tuareg is not a mouth-watcher, but rather an eye-watcher and that during interaction his eyes are fixed by the steady stare of his respondent. On one occasion, I countered this by wearing dark glasses, but my Tuareg friends retaliated by the same technique and succeeded in totally effacing themselves. Everything is watched and used as a cue. The position of the eyelids, the lines and wrinkles of the eyes and nose, the set of the body, and the tone of voice are all part of the Tuareg's gestalt of the situation, and the outsider must adapt himself to this and learn to control these stimuli in himself and observe them in the other if he is to correctly interpret the behavior of his subjects. It would be a mistake then to assume that the veiling practice, among a people who are accustomed to the continual wearing of the veil, *totally* conceals the disposition of the actor to a certain course of action: quite clearly, this would be the negation of social interaction. Rather, this curious article of apparel cuts down the total range of stimuli that can be emitted and received and makes for a diffuseness of Ego's behavioral stance. Beyond this, and perhaps of greater importance, by concealing the primary communication zone of the mouth region the Tuareg decreases his vulnerability to others by *symbolically* removing himself from the interaction; he becomes less labile before the world. It is their quality of remoteness that strikes the outside observer, and it is congruent with the Tuareg's own expressed feelings of exposure and defenselessness when he is unveiled.

It is exactly the feeling of openness and the corresponding sentiment of shame expressed by the Tuareg as their reason for wearing the veil which is our principal clue to an understanding of the custom. When asked to explain the usage, the Tuareg informant will simply say that it would be shameful to show his mouth among his people. This sense of shame suggests that the veil is connected with privacy and withdrawal, and these sentiments are consistent with the comments at the outset of this article upon the nature of social distance.

It suggests also that the exposure of the mouth is a violation of the moral order, a transgression that lowers the prestige of the offender and his own self-esteem. The restrictions surrounding the use of the veil are rigid and highly formalized, and we can well infer that they impinge upon vital areas of social life.

The place of the veil in the social system is best seen in its specific, situational uses, and variation in style according to the mood and situation of the wearer is vividly described by Henri Lhote (1955: 308–9):

The style of wearing the veil, of placing the different parts about the head, may vary from one tribe to another and some individuals give their preference, according to personal taste, to certain local styles. . . . But beside these different fashions, there is also the turn, the knack which makes it more or less elegant. Similarly there is a psychology of the veil; by the way in which it is set, one can gain an idea of the mood of the wearer just as among us the angle of the cap or hat permits analogous deductions. There is the reserved and modest style used when one enters a camp where there are women, the elegant and *recherchée* style for going to courting parties, the haughty manner of warriors conscious of their own importance, like the whimsy of the blustering vassal or slave. There is also the detached and lax fashion of the jovial fellow, the good chap, or the disordered one of the unstable man of irritable character. The veil may also express a transient sentiment. For example, *it is brought up to the eyes before women or prestigeful persons, while it is a sign of familiarity when it is lowered.* To laugh from delight with a joke, the Tuareg will lift up the lower part of his veil very high on his nose, and, in case of irritation, will tighten it like a chin strap to conceal his anger. [Italics mine]

The veil, then, is not a fixed article of clothing to be worn either uniformly or relaxedly. Most Tuareg are continually adjusting and readjusting the veil, changing the height at which it is worn, tugging on the lower part of it, tightening its ends beneath the turban, and straightening its folds. The observer soon notes that, though there is a certain element of random primping involved, the different individuals in a group will readjust their veils as the tone of relationships subtly shifts or persons enter or leave the setting.

The Tuareg are notable for their haughty and arrogant demeanor. They walk with a long swagger and hold their heads high with dignity and aloofness; even when mounted atop a camel they hardly deign to incline their heads to a pedestrian. The veils promote this atmosphere of mystery and apartness, and the Tuareg whether in town or in his native desert has often been remarked upon for his penchant for appearing the master of all he surveys. That the cold, long look through a slit of cloth impresses the foreigner is indisputable and is used to this end, but it is exactly when in the presence of the outsider with whom he is on familiar terms that the Tuareg is most relaxed in his veiling. This was most manifest when I encountered them in Nigeria, well outside of their proper territory. In these circumstances, they would frequently allow the veil to fall below the nose, but still covering the mouth, and others would occasionally allow their mouths to show. The first reaction of our little children to the veils was, of course, to pull them down, which provoked only indulgent laughter from the Tuareg. Despite the strictures on covering the mouth, it evidently mattered least when in our house and especially before little children, who, after all, hardly have social identities. Distance requirements were not so rigorously observed in our case because we were outside the social system, nor were those familiar with us attempting to impress us with the haughty bearing that they often assume toward the sedentary Sudanese populations. Besides, differences of custom and language were already so great that we could not intrude too closely upon their identities.

Many of those who were most lax in their veiling were members of the inferior vassal tribes or of the slave class. The slaves also go veiled, but through a kind of implicit sumptuary restriction on dress, they are much more slack about the position of the veil than are the Caucasoid nobles and vassals. Slaves commonly go about their work with their veils below their chins or at least across the chin. On other occasions, a slave may wear his veil under the nose but covering the mouth and, even when placed across the nose it generally rides well below the bridge. Vassals, as a rule, wear their veils much above the level of the slaves but do not take quite the care that the nobles do. The occasional vassal who affects the high and tight veil is usually attempting to improve his status.

Among all segments of the Tuareg population, the veil is worn higher when confronting a person of power and influence. The Tuareg do not prostrate themselves before a chief, as is the custom among their Hausa neighbors, but they do elevate their veils to the bridge of the nose. The person of higher status will usually keep his veil at a somewhat lower level, though its actual height depends much on the amount of deference due the other. On the other hand, veils may be worn at the level of the tip of the nose or below it by a companionable group of young men, especially when they are outside of camp precincts.

Variations in veiling usage are found not only at fixed positions within the status hierarchy but at relative ones such as in the dyadic relationships given within the kinship system. This is most clearly seen, and the distance setting usage of the veil best demonstrated, in affinal relationships (cf. Nicolaisen 1961:114). The Tuareg speak of proper decorum toward the parents of the wife and, to a lesser extent, the siblings of the latter as being based on the observation of both shame (*tekeraki*) and respect (*isimrarak*). A man shows this, among other ways, through avoidance of the name of his father-in-law, which he generally accomplishes by calling him *amrar*, or 'leader,' in reference to the father-in-law's position as head of his own household, or through teknonymy. The latter usage is most commonly expressed by addressing the father-in-law as the father of one of his sons, as for example "aba 'n Ibrahim." The mother-in-law's name is also taboo, but the Tuareg generally refrains from addressing her by a title, inasmuch as he commonly does not have as much contact with her as he does with the wife's father. There is some tribal variation in the extension of these taboos to the siblings of the father-in-law and mother-in-law, but such avoidance pertains in most of the southeastern Tuareg tribes.

Conduct toward the senior affines is characterized by general restraint and self-effacement. During the courtship period, the Tuareg does not take food or drink when visiting in the house of the intended or possible bride, for commensality among the Tuareg, as among most peoples, symbolizes the closing of distance and the establishment of solidary bonds. This form of avoidance is maintained even after marriage, though the groom has more frequent occasion to contact his father-in-law on matters of business. Similarly, the bride observes greater avoidance of the father-in-law, but here there is a further normative component to the relationship, for the bride commonly will draw her shawl over her head and across the lower part of her face when in his presence. Thus the female has occasion to approximate the veiling practice when observing distance in a highly specific and intensive form. This, I might mention, is the nearest any Tuareg woman comes to the Near Eastern purdah, one aspect of which entails the veiling of the woman's face in compliance with Sura 4 of the Koran, which says of good women: "They guard their unseen parts because Allah has guarded them."

It is, then, all the more interesting to observe that the Tuareg men are most strict with their veils when in the presence of the father-in-law or the mother-in-law, for, in addition to other signs of respect and avoidance, the son-in-law is careful to adjust the veil so that only a very narrow aperture is left open, and the eyes are hooded and left in shadow. At this point, we are no longer dealing with an analytic statement of the relationship of veiling to social distance, but with a

48 ROBERT F. MURPHY

concrete, conscious motivation, for the Tuareg state that reserve and shame are the essence of conduct toward the senior affine and that they partially express this with the veil. Beyond the aspect of ceremonial avoidance, it would seem that there is another component closely related to this symbolism, that of maintenance of the dignity of the actor—by his symbolic withdrawal from the threatening situation vis-à-vis the superordinate, Ego is also furthering the maintenance of his self image. This is manifest in the fact that the veil is also worn high when courting, and very special care is given at the formalized courting sessions, or *ahals*. On the latter occasions, the young suitors conduct themselves with great dignity; the veils are worn very high and close and a full retinue of retainers accompany the young men, if they are sufficiently wealthy. But avoidance, in the physical sense, could hardly be the function, either latent or manifest, of the veil at such times, for Tuareg courting frequently culminates in sexual activity. Rather, the young man attempts to communicate to the girl his own worth and standing and, concomitantly, through standing somewhat aloof, maintains his command over a rather critical situation in which the prognosis of success is never certain.[3]

The above data suggest that there are two aspects to distance: the external dialogue and the internal dialogue; the actor maintaining the interaction situation and Ego maintaining ego. Perhaps this is best illustrated by the fact that the veil is now worn by men at two phases in the life cycle—when they have no status, as in the case of minors, and when they have too much status, as in the case of the *hajji*. The latter is the honorific term applied by most Moslems to persons who have made the pilgrimage to Mecca, and this status signifies that the occupant of it has gained religious merit and, with it, secular prestige. But beyond this the *hajji* is a person who has partaken of the sacred and by so doing has absorbed it as part of his identity. Among the southeastern Tuareg it is quite common for such men—and they are relatively few in number—to permanently divest themselves of the veil, for dignity and esteem are theirs by right. Moreover, a Pilgrim need show no shame or respect before others: his very status is adequate to guarantee him distance. It will be remembered, however, that even very powerful chiefs wear the veil, suggesting that there is a further quality to the divestment of the veil than that of sheer prestige. What then is this difference between the Pilgrim and the Chief? It is simply this: though the latter may have more power and influence than the former, the status of the chief is secular and that of the pilgrim is sacred. The symbolism of the veil, then, belongs to the realm of the sacred in social relations, and I would suggest that this is why the secular chief continues to wear it while the holder of status of pilgrim does not. That the veil is best understood in terms of Durkheim's concept of the sacred and that its use conforms to ritual has already been suggested by the form and protocol surrounding it. I will develop this point further in the conclusion of this essay.

Social structure and the veil

It would perhaps belabor the point to inquire further into the functions of the veil as a maker of symbolic distance, and I wish to turn to its structural setting. Granted the premise that the Tuareg veil is a distance setting device, why do the Tuareg need such a device? If distance is a component of all social relations and is essentially a part of sociation, as was maintained at the outset of this article, then why do not all peoples wear veils? Granted that all humans present a facade of sorts to society, the proper question is why do the Tuareg go to such extremes? After all, these people *really* wear veils. To answer this question, we must return to the subject of Tuareg social structure and explore certain aspects of it in some detail, for the veil has been seen to be a part of the ritual apparatus of the society and must have a meaning within the social system itself.

It will be remembered that the Tuareg social units are preferentially endogamic, from the local groups settled about the wells to larger tribal aggregations, and that the boundaries of these groups are set by in-marriage and not by exogamy as is common is most societies having extended kin groupings. Among the Tuareg this yields a rather distinct spatial juxtaposition of role players. Almost every type of residence possibility is known among the Tuareg. Though couples are not normally neolocal, it is not unknown for a family to move to residence among a group in which they have no close kinsmen but where certain concrete advantages await them. Duolocality also occurs, at least among the Kel Oui tribes south of the Air massif, and the couple in the early years of their marriage resorts periodically to life with the families of both bride and groom. Most Tuareg, however, profess to a norm of patrilocality, though they admit freely that the alternative of matrilocal residence, especially in the initial phase of marriage, is also common. To summarize, despite the professed patrilocality, there is considerable variation in residence alternatives, and no local-political-kin group yields a uniform composition in terms of types of kin. It should, however, be reemphasized that the rule of endogamy does determine a majority of marriages—and to the extent that marriages are endogamic the above residence choices become an academic matter. A Taureg may well state that he resides with his own kin, but further questions will reveal that his wife's relatives indeed reside in the same group. Under conditions of residence near the affines, however, it is common to observe avoidance through placing the hut at some distance from that of the wife's parents. In a humorous mood, one said to me: "We don't want them to hear the noises we make at night." Wherever they camp, the fact remains that life among one's consanguines is quite commonly life among the affines, and, further, they are the same people.

This takes us to a very real, and sometimes overlooked, aspect of most societies having unilineal descent: rules of group and local exogamy function primarily to define the boundaries between the conceptually antithetical, and complementary, principles of incorporation and alliance and the social groups based upon these principles. This segregation is impossible in a society such as Tuareg, for one's in-laws are at one and the same time members of one's kin group. This situation is compounded by the fact that, despite the nominal matrilineality discussed above, the Tuareg actually reckon their ties of kinship bilaterally; in this way they differ from the Arab Bedouin who also practice kin and local group endogamy but suppress the resulting diffuseness of cross-cutting relationships through a formal ideology of patrilineality. Lacking such an ideology, the Tuareg recognize and trace ties through both lines and further insist upon regarding all members of local-political aggregations at whatever level as co-descendants from some common ancestor. This, combined with endogamy, results in a multitude of ties through which any two people in one of the iriwan groups can trace relationship in several ways. In most of the Tuareg groupings the shallowness of genealogies allows kin ties to remain diffuse and unspecified except with very close relatives, thus giving some protection from the possible role conflicts inherent in the cross-cutting ties. But these relationships remain ambivalent for this very reason, and bonds of incorporation and solidarity within the social units are charged also with the antithesis and opposition of affinality and alliance.

My thesis, then, is that given this ambiguity and ambivalence of relationships, this immanence of role conflict, the Tuareg veil functions to maintain a diffuse and generalized kind of distance between the actor and those who surround him socially and physically. By the symbolic removal of a portion of his identity from the interaction situation, the Tuareg is allowed to act in the presence of conflicting interests and uncertainty. The social distance set in some societies by joking and respect or avoidance behavior towards certain specific categories of relatives is accomplished here through the veil. It is, however, difficult to maintain specific differentiation of kin roles given their dual character, and the expression of distance is generalized in varying degree to all one's fellows. It is, therefore, for sound structural reasons that the Tuareg is most mindful of the attitude of his veil exactly when he is among his own.

That women do not wear veils is another manifestation of the very simple and universal fact that the differences between the sexes go beyond biology, a cause for wonder to those who, for example, point out that father's sister's child marriage is quite common in patrilineal societies (with asymmetrical cross-cousin marriage)—for women. The Tuareg woman is also placed in a situation of ambiguity vis-à-vis her kin, but, despite her rather high prestige in this society, she is not a public figure and does not operate in as wide a social context as does the man. The quality of her social relationships is not so instrumental as that of the man. It is repetitive to stress that kinship relations are political relations in a society of this kind, and the Tuareg woman is not a significant political actor in the formal sense.

Conclusions

In this paper, I have taken the single item of the Tuareg veil, and through an analysis of its operation in the social system, I have attempted to say something general on the subject of social distance. I have argued, following Simmel, that social distance pervades all social relationships though it may be found in varying degrees in different relationships and in different societies. I take this as axiomatic, for inasmuch as social conduct implies limitations upon range of expectable behavior and closures upon other relations and behavior, the actor must insulate large portions of his social existence. This is done through withholding knowledge of his course and commitment in the action situation, and it is concretely accomplished through distance setting mechanisms—the privacy and withdrawal of the social person is a quality of life in society. That he withholds himself while communicating and communicates through removal is not a contradiction in terms but a quality of all social interaction.

Pursuing the well-established premise that distance is to be found most strongly in those relationships that are most difficult but which must be perpetuated, I have examined the custom of veiling among the Tuareg and have concluded that it functions to maintain a generalized distance. This is manifest in the specific use of the veil, as for example in association with senior affines, and we have seen that the more delicate of social interaction situations requires the greatest distance and removal of the actors. Further, the use of the veil has been interpreted as being ritualistic in nature, not only because of the protocol and punctiliousness surrounding its use but because it concerns itself with something "sacred." The sense of the sacred is seen here in the sentiments of shame and pollution that surround the hidden region of the mouth and derives, I believe, from the very delicacy of Tuareg social relations, from the fact that maintenance of the social system is deeply connected with the maintenance of a high degree of social distance. Though this sacred quality is found suffused through all societies and all social action, and though all social *conduct* is in a sense ritual, certain characteristics of the Tuareg social order cause it to be more pronounced here. I found this quality to lie in some aspects of marriage, descent, and residence practices, one result of which is that there is no segregation of bonds of locality, affinality, and kin group membership. From this there proceeds an ambiguity of role complementarity that is partially resolved by the maintenance of diffuse distance towards all others. Beyond this, there is a complete overlap, both in the real situation and in the formal, jural sense, of ties of descent and the antithetical relations of alliance. While it would be incorrect to say that the Tuareg solves the potentiality of role conflict by physical avoidance, he certainly promotes this resolution by distance. In so doing, two things are accomplished. First, the setting of distance in relations with a broad range of others removes the actor from the interaction situation sufficiently that he diminishes his commitment to a specific course of action. This allows for flexibility and viability in social situations that are not highly defined by the kinship system. Second, given the particularly threatening quality of the interaction situation, the actor is enabled to maintain autonomy and self-esteem. In a very real sense, he is in hiding.

The above analysis is directed to the question raised earlier as to whether distance, in general, varies from one society to another, and, if so, what are the structural concomitants of this distance. Briefly, I find the answer to lie in the immanence of role conflict. I also queried the forms of symbolism that are involved in distance maintenance, and I deem this to be the more difficult problem. Though I do not wish to go into the psychological bases of the symbolism, I would call the attention of the reader to the fact that distance setting techniques are quite commonly associated with the eyes and the mouth. The extreme case of this is perhaps the masked ball, which, in its more earthy traditional form, allowed maximum latitude and freedom of behavior by totally effacing at least the area of the eyes. Other examples that come to mind from our own culture are the averted eyes of the Victorian maiden, who also was wont to demurely cover her mouth with a fan. That this is not simply a rather passé European trait was brought home to me when doing research in an Amazonian Indian group in which the definition of a wanton woman is one who looks directly at men and laughs openly without placing her hand over her mouth (Murphy 1962:50). In contemporary society such a means of defense and withdrawal is often achieved by wearing dark glasses. Sun glasses and tinted glasses are almost badges of office among West African emirs and Near Eastern potentates, and they have also become items of prestige in other parts of the world. They are commonly used in Latin America, where, indoors and out, heavily tinted glasses are the hallmark of the prestigeful as well as those aspiring to status, for they bestow the aloofness and distance that has always been the prerogative of the high in these lands.

The literature of Freudian psychology gives extensive documentation to the female symbolism of the mouth, its vulnerability to penetration, and to the unconscious association between the eyes and the male generative powers; it is not surprising to find that it is these areas that are defended most often in social interaction. Beyond this, these are the areas of the body by which we most actively communicate with others and from which we emit the cues that guide those with whom we interact. But there is more to social distance than the simple symbolism involved in the non-use of the eye and mouth regions. It is well established that distance of a kind can also be set by the use of humor and that there may be involved heavy and expressive use of the eyes and mouth for communication on these occasions. I would state that the single binding and unifying characteristic of all distance techniques is constancy of demeanor. This may take the form of a constant kind of behavior in a specific social situation, be it joking with one's cross-cousin, the showing of respect to one's father-in-law, or the even observance of business etiquette. The actor achieves a refuge by submergence in his social identity and, through uniformity of behavior, discloses the least of himself, while maintaining his social relationships.

The kind of social distance that is best known to us, be it under the rubric of joking, reserve, avoidance, or antipathy, is that which obtains between certain categories of role players and which is part of expected behavior in specific interaction settings. This I would term *role specific distance,* as opposed to the kind of diffuse social distance connected with the Tuareg veil. The latter I classify as *generalized distance,* for it is not only characteristic of a series of specific relationships but tends to pervade social interaction in its entirety. Often identified as a basic personality trait and attributed to ontogeny, it is seen here as a requirement of the social system as a whole. Role specific distance is manifested at certain nodal points in any social system, but generalized distance varies from one society to another depending upon the total configuration of the social system. It can be seen in the husband who treats his wife with the same polite consideration and affection which he accords to all ladies, and it can be seen in the Tuareg behind his veil. I will conclude by reminding the reader that it was a novelist, and not the social scientist, who told us that the uniform affability and the evenly distributed backslapping of the middle-class American were the loneliest of all gestures. But this aloneness is not the tragedy and dilemma of our place and time only, for alienation is the natural condition of social man.

NOTES

1 This article emerges from fieldwork carried out among the Tuareg during 1959–60. The research was supported by a Foreign Area Training Fellowship, granted by the Ford Foundation, and by the Social Science Research Council, which awarded me a Faculty Research Fellowship for the period 1957–60. I wish to acknowledge my gratitude to these organizations and to the Research Committee and the Institute of Social Sciences of the University of California, Berkeley, for their generous support. Several colleagues have been of assistance to me in the formulation of this paper, but I am particularly indebted to Dr. Erving Goffman for his stimulation and criticism.

2 Briggs (1960:128) states that among the northern Tuareg of the Hoggar massif marriage is prohibited with first cousins and with members of the same "camp community or fraction," which I assume to be the iriwan. This may well be an area difference, but my informants expressed a normative preference for such unions, and actual genealogies and censuses showed large numbers of marriages within the iriwan. On the other hand, only a small percentage of marriages were with actual first cousins, though they did occur. To pursue these points would carry us into a full analysis of Tuareg marriage and kinship, which is beyond the scope of the present essay and the subject of a future article.

3 Nicolaisen, in his important paper on Tuareg magic and religion (1961), also recognizes that a proper understanding of the veil must be sought in the social system. He notes that the veil is always worn in a high position when confronting a stranger, especially a female, a status that must be distinguished from that of the friend or acquaintance who is but marginally involved in the society. This is consistent with my previous remarks on the

function of social distance, here expressed in hauteur and reserve, in situations that are not readily definable nor their outcomes easily predictable.

REFERENCES

Bogardus, Emory S. 1938. Social distance and its practical implications. Journal of Sociology and Social Research 22:462–476.

Briggs, L. C. 1960. Tribes of the Sahara. Harvard University Press, Cambridge, Mass.

Duveyrier, H. 1864. Les Touaregs du nord. Paris, Challamel.

Goffman, Erving. 1956. The nature of deference and demeanor. American Anthropologist 58:473–502.

Lhote, Henri. 1955. Les Touaregs du Hoggar. Paris, Payot.

Mead, George H. 1934. Mind, self and society. Chicago, University of Chicago Press.

Merton, Robert K. 1957. Social theory and social structure. Glencoe, Ill., The Free Press.

Murphy, R. F. 1962. Deviance and social control II: Coleta. Kroeber Anthropological Society Papers, no. 27:49–54.

Nicolaisen, Johannes. 1961. Essai sur la religion et la magie touarègues. Folk 3:113–62.

Park, Robert E. and Ernest W. Burgess. 1924. Introduction to the science of sociology. Chicago, University of Chicago Press.

Radcliffe-Brown, A. R. 1952. Structure and function in primitive society. Glencoe, Ill., The Free Press.

Shibutani, Tamotsu. 1961. Society and personality. Englewood Cliffs, N.J., Prentice-Hall, Inc.

Simmel, Georg. 1950. The sociology of Georg Simmel (K. H. Wolff, trans.), Glencoe, Ill., The Free Press.

3

The origins of modern claims to privacy

ALAN WESTIN

Privacy in the animal world

Man likes to think that his desire for privacy is distinctively human, a function of his unique ethical, intellectual, and artistic needs. Yet studies of animal behavior and social organization suggest that man's need for privacy may well be rooted in his animal origins, and that men and animals share several basic mechanisms for claiming privacy among their own fellows. Within the past year these points have been in two excellent books for the general reader that report recent findings in biology, ecology, and anthropology—Edward Hall's *The Hidden Dimension*[1] and Robert Ardrey's *The Territorial Imperative*.[2] Thus we begin our analysis of man's patterns of privacy at the chronological starting point—man's evolutionary heritage.

One basic finding of animal studies is that virtually all animals seek periods of individual seclusion or small-group intimacy. This is usually described as the tendency toward territoriality, in which an organism lays private claim to an area of land, water, or air and defends it against intrusion by members of its own species.[3] A meadow pipit chases fellow pipits away from a private space of six feet around him. Except during nesting time, there is only one robin on a bush or branch. The three-spined stickleback guards an invisible water wall around him and attacks any other stickleback that swims into his territory. Antelopes in African fields and dairy cattle in an American farmyard space themselves to establish individual territory.[4] For species in which the female cannot raise the young unaided, nature has created the "pair bond," linking temporarily or permanently a male and a female who demand private territory for the unit during breeding time.[5] Studies of territoriality have even shattered the romantic notion that when robins sing or monkeys shriek, it is solely for the

Alan F. Westin, "The Origins of Modern Claims to Privacy," from *Privacy and Freedom*. Copyright © 1967 The Association of the Bar of the City of New York. Reprinted with the permission of Atheneum Publishers.

"animal joy of life." Actually, it is often a defiant cry for privacy, given within the borders of the animal's private territory to warn off possible intruders.[6]

These territorial patterns have been found by scientists to serve a cluster of important purposes. They ensure propagation of the species by regulating density to available resources. They enhance selection of "worthy males" and provide breeding stations for animals that require male assistance in raising the young. They also provide a physical frame of reference for group activity such as learning, playing, and hiding, and provide contact for group members against the entry of intruders. The parallels between territory rules in animal life and trespass concepts in human society are obvious: in each, the organism lays claim to private space to promote individual well-being and small-group intimacy.

Animals and man also share elaborate distance-setting mechanisms to define territorial spacing of individuals in the group. The distance set between one non-contact animal and another (illustrated by the spacing of birds on a telephone wire) has been called "personal distance."[7] Among species such as birds and apes, there are rules of "intimate distance" regulating the space held between mates or between parents and their young.[8] "Social distance" links members of the animal group to one another and sets off the group from others,[9] while "flight distance" is the point of approach at which an animal will flee from an intruder of another species.[10] Though man has eliminated flight distance as a regular mechanism of his social life, Hall's studies indicate that man sets basically the same kinds of personal, intimate, and social distance in his interpersonal relationships as do mammals in the animal world.[11] In addition, man still relies heavily on his "animal" or physical senses—touch, taste, smell, sight, and hearing—to define his daily boundaries of privacy. What is considered "too close" a contact and therefore an "invasion of privacy" in human society will often be an odor, a noise, a visual intrusion, or a touch; the mechanism for defining privacy in these situations is sensory.

Ecological studies have demonstrated that animals also have minimum needs for private space without which the animal's survival will be jeopardized. Since overpopulation can impede the animal's ability to smell, court, or be free from constant defensive reactions, such a condition upsets the social organization of the animal group. The animals may then kill each other to reduce the crowding, or they may engage in mass suicidal reductions of the population, as with lemmings and rabbits.[12] Experiments with spacing rats in cages showed that even rats need time and space to be alone.[13] When rats were deliberately crowded in cages, patterns of courting, nest building, rearing the young, social hierarchies, and territorial taboos were disrupted. Aggression and fighting increased and sexual conduct became more sadistic. Experiments also showed that wild rat populations would stabilize at about 150 when the rats were placed in an open quarter-acre pen, even though the females there could have produced 50,000 progeny in the test period. However, if rats are given individual quarters in pens two feet square, 5,000 rats could thrive in the same area, and 50,000 in the same space in eight-inch cages. This suggests that when private space is provided, density does not necessarily produce social disorganization or diseases. Studies of crowding in many animals other than rats indicate that disruption of social relationships through overlapping personal distances aggravates all forms of pathology within a group and causes the same diseases in animals that overcrowding does in man—"high blood pressure, circulatory diseases, and heart disease."[14]

Crowding in animals can also produce what has been called "biochemical die-off." For example, a deer herd on an island near the coast of Maryland had increased gradually to 300, about one deer to an acre. Food was adequate for all, and there was no evidence of infection. Yet between 1958 and 1959 more than two thirds of the deer simply died, in apparently fine physical health. A study of the "die-off" concluded that crowding had created such metabolic stress that an endocrine reaction set in, producing a process of natural selection and reducing the population.[15]

A final parallel between animal and human societies is the need for social stimulation which exists in animals alongside their needs for privacy. As Ardrey has written:

In species after species natural selection has encouraged social mechanisms which seem ultimately to exist for no reason other than to provide conditions for antagonism and conflict and excitement. We may comprehend the evolutionary necessity for bringing together a breeding community. . . . But why must it live in a dense, disturbing, challenging, competing, squabbling, argumentative mass? If it is not to avoid boredom, then why must the animal demand for privacy stand cheek-by-jowl with the urge to plunge into the largest available crowd?[16]

Even though food supplies are adequate for living in seclusion, even though natural enemies may be manageable alone, and even though pairs could have their sex and family activities alone, animals consistently return to the group after being apart. The work of leading scientists such as Darling,[17] Fisher,[18] and Wynne-Edwards[19] shows that it is not security per se that brings animals of the same species together, but a desire for the stimulation of their fellows.

What the animal studies demonstrate is that virtually all animals have need for the temporary individual seclusion or small-unit intimacy that constitute two of the core aspects of privacy. Animals also need the stimulation of social encounters among their own species. As a result, the animal's struggle to achieve a balance between privacy and participation provides one of the basic processes of animal life. In this sense, the quest for privacy is not restricted to man alone, but arises in the biological and social processes of all life.

Privacy in the primitive world

Even though man shares some needs for privacy with most animals, the dominant anthropological "lesson" about privacy seems to be that our contemporary norms of privacy are "modern" and "advanced" values largely absent from primitive societies of the past and present. For example, Dorothy Lee, whose work as a cultural anthropologist has focused on the relation between freedom and culture in various societies, has drawn a sharp contrast between privacy in American society and interpersonal life among the Tikopia of Polynesia.[20] In child rearing, Americans concentrate on teaching the child to be "himself" and "self-dependent," preparing him for his individual struggle in life and also giving the mother important privacy during child rearing.

Now the child grows up needing time to himself, a room of his own, freedom of choice, freedom to plan his own time and his own life. . . . He will spend his wealth installing private bathrooms in his house, buying a private car, a private yacht, private woods and a private beach, which he will then people with his privately chosen society. The need for privacy is an imperative one in our society, recognized by official bodies of our government.[21]

Life among the Tikopia, Mrs. Lee notes, with their greater emphasis on social rather than individual values, produces very different practices.

[T]he Tikopia help the self to be continuous with its society [rather than separate from it]. . . . They find it good to sleep side by side crowding each other, next to their children or their parents or their brothers and sisters, mixing sexes and generations; and if a widow finds herself alone in her one-room house, she may adopt a child or a brother to allay her intolerable privacy. . . .

Work among the Tikopia is also socially conceived and structured; and if a man has to work alone, he will probably try to take a little child along. In our culture, the private office is a mark of status, an ideal; and a man has really arrived when he can even have a receptionist to guard him from any social intrusion without his private consent.[22]

Margaret Mead's famous study of Samoa deals with another society in which the basic American concepts of privacy are unknown.[23] In the Samoan house there are no walls, and only mosquito netting separates the sleeping quarters of the married couples, children, and old folks. Adults wear little clothing and children none. Bathing in the sea is performed without clothes. The beaches are used openly as latrines. No privacy is claimed or provided for the processes of birth and death; even the children stand about watching these moments of intimacy. In all these areas, Dr. Mead notes, "there is no privacy and no sense of shame." In Samoa, "little is mysterious, . . . little forbidden."

To give one last example from another area of the world, Livingston Jones has written of the Tlingit Indians of North America:

There are no skeletons tucked away in native families, for the acts of one are familiar to all the others. Privacy is hardly known among them. It cannot be maintained very well under their system of living, with families bunched together. . . . The Tlingit's bump of curiosity is well developed and any thing out of the ordinary, as an accident, a birth, a death or a quarrel never fails to draw a crowd. . . . They walk in and out of one another's homes without knocking on the door. A woman may be in the very act of changing her garments when Mr. Quakish steps in unannounced to visit her husband. This does not embarrass her in the least. She proceeds as if no one had called.[24]

One could compile a long list of societies, primitive and modern, that neither have nor would admire the norms of privacy found in American culture—norms which some Americans regard as "natural" needs of all men living in society. Yet this circumstance does not prove that there are no universal needs for privacy and no universal processes for adjusting the values of privacy, disclosure, and surveillance within each society. It suggests only that each society must be studied in its own terms, focusing sensitively on social customs to see whether there are norms of privacy called by other names, and recognizing all the difficulties in making cross-cultural comparisons. The analysis must also recognize the fact that there are psychological ways of achieving privacy for the individual or the family as well as physical arrangements, ways which are crucial in those societies where communal life makes solitude or intimacy impossible within the living areas.

Most of the work on cultural universals has been based on studies of about 200 to 300 non-literate societies, providing us with a fairly representative cross-section of the 3,000 to 4,000 people with distinctive cultures who have lived on the earth.[25] Based on the leading general works of anthropology and sociology, a survey of the major ethnographic studies, and the relevant categories of the Human Relations Area Files at Yale University, I suggest that there are four general aspects of privacy which apply to men living together in virtually every society that has been systematically examined.

Individual and group norms of privacy in primitive societies

Needs for individual and group privacy and resulting social norms are present in virtually every society. Encompassing a vast range of activities, these needs affect basic areas of life for the individual, the intimate family group, and the community as a whole. Privacy norms for the society are established in each of these three areas. The individual seeks privacy, as well as companionship, in his daily interactions with others; limits are set to maintain a degree of distance at certain crucial times in his life. The family-household unit also institutes limitations on both members of the unit and outsiders to protect various activities within the household. Finally, significant rituals and ceremonies in the larger community are also protected by customs which prescribe privacy for these rites within the group. As we will see, the norms vary, but the functions which privacy performs are crucial for each of these three areas of social life.

Anthropological studies have shown that the individual in virtually every society engages in a continuing personal process by which he seeks privacy at some times and disclosure or companionship at other times. This part of the individual's basic process of interaction with those around him is usually discussed by social scientists under the terms "social distance" and "avoidance rules."[26] Although it is obviously affected by the cultural patterns of each society, the process is adjusted in its finer degrees by each individual himself. A sensitive discussion of this distance-setting process has been contributed recently by Robert F. Murphy of Columbia University.[27] Murphy noted that the use of "reserve and restraint" to provide "an area of privacy" for the individual in his relations with others represents a "common, though not constant" factor in "all social relationships." Indeed, Murphy says, it is one of the key "dialectical processes in social life." The reason for the universality of this process is that individuals have conflicting roles to play in any society; to play these different roles with different persons, the individual must present a different "self" at various times.[28] Restricting information about himself and his emotions is a crucial way of protecting the individual in the stresses and strains of this social interaction. Murphy also notes that creating social distance is especially important in the individual's intimate relations, perhaps even more so than in his casual ones. Precisely because the intimate relationships are the most emotional and ambivalent for the individual, they are "most demanding of expressions of distance, however elusive and ambivalent these may be."

Murphy's work among the Tuareg tribes of North Africa, where men veil their faces and constantly adjust the veil to changing interpersonal relations, provides a particularly visual example of the distance-setting process. Murphy concluded that the Tuareg veil is a symbolic realization of the need for privacy in every society. "The social distance set in some societies by joking and respect or avoidance behavior toward certain specific categories of relatives is accomplished here through the veil." The eyes and the mouth are instruments that "expose" the individual and diminish his psychological privacy; thus Tuareg men shield the eyes and mouth. Murphy notes that the Tuareg custom is only a more physical and exaggerated rendition of the privacy-protecting "masks" found in many societies, such as the use of the fan by women to cover the mouth and eyes when establishing their relations with men, or the use of dark glasses today among high personages in the Near and Middle East, Latin America, or Hollywood.

Examples of distance-setting techniques and avoidance rules from other primitive societies could be presented at length. The point is that kinship rules and interaction norms present individuals with a need to restrict the flow of information about themselves to others and to adjust these regulations constantly in contacts with others. This need is fundamental to individual behavior with intimates, casual acquaintances, and authorities.

The claim to individual privacy gives rise to some other limits on interpersonal disclosure. Virtually all societies have rules for concealment of the female genitals, and restrictions on the time and manner of female genital exposure; only a handful of societies practice complete nudity.[29] Though Murdock lists "modesty about natural functions" as a trait found in all societies,[30] the openness with which people in most nonliterate societies engage in evacuation makes this a "public" affair in contrast to modern norms in a society like the United States. Similarly, the individual's moments of birth, illness, and death are considered taboo and are secluded from general view in many societies,[31] but as some peoples conduct these affairs in casual view, they cannot be considered universal matters of privacy.

Needs for privacy do appear in the intimacy of sexual relations (the "pair territory" discussed by Ardrey). There are only a few exceptions to the norm that men and women will seek seclusion for performance of the sexual act. In their survey of sexual patterns in 190 societies, Ford and Beach note that "human beings in general prefer to copulate under conditions of privacy."[32] Only in a few cultures, such as the Formosan and among Yap natives of the Pacific, is the sexual act performed openly in public. Even here, Formosans will not have intercourse if children are present, and Yapese couples are generally secluded when intercourse takes place, though they do not seem to mind the presence of other persons who may come on the scene.[33]

The location of sexual intercourse in various societies sheds further light on norms of privacy in society. Where the household contains a nuclear family (husband, wife, and their children), or where it includes various other relatives but furnishes physical arrangements that provide opportunities for privacy, the sexual act takes place within the household. But where the household is crowded, or when there are communal households of large numbers of families sharing the dwelling, the sexual act is usually performed outside, so that privacy can be obtained, in bush, field, forest, or beach.[34]

As A. R. Holmberg wrote in describing the situation of the Sirionó Indians of eastern Bolivia:

Much more intercourse takes place in the bush than in the house. The principal reason for this is that privacy is almost impossible to obtain within the hut where as many as fifty hammocks may be hung in the confined space of five hundred square feet. Moreover, the hammock of a man and his wife hangs not three feet from that of the former's mother-in-law. Furthermore, young children commonly sleep with the father and mother, so that there may be as many as four or five people crowded together in a single hammock. In addition to these frustrating circumstances, people are up and down most of the night, quieting children, cooking, eating, urinating, and defecating. . . . Consequently intercourse is indulged in more often in some secluded nook in the forest.[35]

Norms of privacy are also found in the family-household settings of primitive life. Whether the primitive household is nuclear or extended, most societies have rules limiting free entry into the house by non-residents, as well as rules governing the outsider's conduct once he enters.[36] Even in those societies where entry is fairly free, there will usually be rules limiting what a person may touch or where he may go within the house. There will also be norms limiting family conversation or acts performed while the outsiders are present.

Clearly there is less privacy for the individual or pair in an extended household than in the nuclear one, based on the criterion that more people see and exercise influence over each other's behavior in the extended household. But even here there are usually rules of avoidance, based on the kinship system, to govern who speaks to whom and which relatives may be in the same room with each other. These avoidance rules have the effect of ensuring certain levels of psychological privacy in the midst of crowding.[37] Restricting the flow of information about oneself in an extended household is often accomplished by covering the face, averting the eyes, going to one's mat, or facing the wall. The respect given to these claims to withhold information are part of the way social structure is defined in all societies.[38] Writing of the Papago, whose households contain ten or more people living and sleeping in a one-room house, R. M. Underhill notes that their avoidance rules are such that "they maneuver without touching one another where Europeans, who have more privacy, are continually doing so."[39]

The subtlety with which norms of privacy operate in the household has been described in a paper by Clifford Geertz comparing household-privacy practices in two Indonesian societies, Bali and Java.

In Java people live in small, bamboo-walled houses, each of which almost always contains a single nuclear family—i.e. mother, father, and unmarried children. Once in a while an aged grandparent may be present, but almost never anyone else. The houses face the street with a cleared front yard in front of them. There are no walls or fences around them, the house walls are thinly and loosely woven, and there are commonly not even doors. Within the house people wander freely just about any place any time, and even outsiders wander in fairly freely almost any time during the day and early evening. In brief, privacy in our terms is about as close to nonexistent as it can get. You may walk freely into a room where a man or woman is stretched out (clothed, of course) sleeping. You may enter from the rear of the house as well as from the front with hardly more warning than a greeting announcing your presence. Except for the bathing enclosure (where people change their clothes) no place is really private, and that is open above the shoulders and below the knees. . . . The Javanese have literally almost no defense against the outside world of a physical sort.

The result is that their defenses are mostly psychological. Relationships even within the household are very restrained; people speak softly, hide their feelings and even in the bosom of a Javanese family you have the feeling that you are in the public square and must behave with appropriate decorum. Javanese shut people out with a wall of etiquette (patterns of politeness are very highly developed), with emotional restraint, and with a general lack of candor in both speech and behavior. It is not, in short, that the Javanese do not wish or value privacy; but merely that because they put up no physical or social barriers against the physical ingress of outsiders into their household life they must put up psychological ones and surround themselves with social barriers of a different sort. Thus, there is really no sharp break between public and private in Java: people behave more or less the same in private as they do in public—in a manner we would call stuffy at best—and maintain the privacy of their personal life by the same means as they deal with others in their public life. . . .

Now, in Bali people live in houseyards surrounded by high stone walls into which you enter by a narrow, half blocked-off doorway. Inside such a yard lives some form of what anthropologists call a patrilineal extended family. Such a family may consist of from one to a dozen or so nuclear families of the Javanese sort whose heads are related patrilineally: i.e. father, his two married sons, his two married brothers, *his* father, and the unmarried children of these; or a set of cousins with their families who are sons of two brothers, etc. . . .

In contrast to Java, nonkinsmen almost never enter one's houseyard (except on ceremonial occasions, etc. when they are invited to do so). Within the yard one is in one's castle and other people know better than to push their way in (if they wish to see you they will send a child to fetch you, etc.). Other patrilineal relatives of yours may come around in the early evening to gossip and in some cases a close friend or two may do so, but except for these when you are in your houseyard you are free of the public. Only your immediate family is around.[40]

While the emotional atmosphere of a Javanese house is "stuffy," Geertz said, the Balinese house is marked by "a tremendous warmth, humor, [and] openness. . . . As soon as the Balinese steps through the doorway to the street and the public square, market and temples beyond, however, he becomes more or less like the Javanese."

Privacy for certain group ceremonies is another characteristic of primitive societies. One major example involves the rites of passage, by which girls and boys, as they come of age, are withdrawn from the whole group, go into seclusion, participate in special ceremonies, and then re-enter as "adults." At the first onset of menstruation, for instance, girls in most societies go to secluded places away from the village for periods ranging from several days to several months; in the privacy of this all-female society (men are forbidden to visit the area), the girls receive sexual instruction and marriage information from older women. A similar secluded period for boys in many societies involves subjecting the youths to ordeals designed to test their manhood; after these ceremonies the boys are given sexual instruction.[41]

Margaret Mead suggests that the enforcement of privacy for the ceremonies of various sub-groups in the community rests on the feeling that the presence of "spectators" would affect the psychological feeling of unity and belonging of the participants. Speaking of the night dances among the Samoans, which usually end in openly promiscuous relations, Mead writes:

[C]hildren and old people are excluded, as non-participants whose presence as uninvolved spectators would have been indecent. This attitude toward non-participants characterised all emotionally charged events, a women's weaving bee which was of a formal, ceremonial nature, a house-building, [and] a candlenut burning.[42]

Whatever the reasons given, virtually every society holds ceremonies for special groups from which various segments of the whole tribe or community will be barred—ceremonies for warrior males, cult members, women, and the like. Strict sanctions are imposed on invasion of the privacy of these occasions. In addition, there are taboos forbidding anyone other than priests or some special elite from entering sacred quarters or going to sacred places.[43]

Privacy and isolation

The ways in which human beings perceive their situation when they are alone, in a state of privacy, is another important area in which to compare primitive and modern aspects of privacy. The data suggest that fear of isolation leads individuals in human societies to believe that they are never wholly alone, even when they are in physical solitude. Especially in pre-literate societies, men are convinced that they are in the presence and under the observation of supernatural forces, some protecting the individual, some threatening or tempting him, and some simply watching to judge him for a future purpose, perhaps his fate after death.[44] "The longing to communicate with the supernatural" has been said to be "common to all races of mankind."[45] It arises from such factors as the need for protection, the desire for identity, and spiritual longings. Both the idea of being watched and the need to communicate are found in contemporary Judeo-Christian, Moslem, Hindu, and Buddhist systems as much as in the beliefs of primitive peoples about ancestors, spirits, witches, and gods.

In primitive societies a man who was truly alone when he was away from fellow humans was a man in terrible peril, since hostile spirits were believed to be all around—in the bodies of animals, in trees or rocks, in shadows, and even in the air.[46] While primitive man follows various taboos and performs various rituals to avoid offending or disturbing such spirits, they remain all about him, and his prime protection lies in the friendly spirits that go with him and protect him if he retains their favor.[47]

Whatever the manner in which the individual establishes initial contact with the spirits or gods,[48] he will seek privacy in order to communicate with his guardian spirits. Among primitive peoples, this situation usually rests on fear that enemies would locate his spiritual guardian and appropriate it or cause it to go away.[49] In modern societies, periods of seclusion, whether for minutes or days, are assumed to be essential to create the contemplative and holy mood for religious communication. Thus when man seeks to reach his guardian spirit, he seeks privacy—usually by physical solitude in forest, beach, or church but also by psychological isolation through self-induced trance or reverie, or even dreams,[50] if the individual cannot escape the physical presence of others.

The significant point is that men in most organized societies have a belief that they are watched by gods or spirits even when they are physically alone, and that personal communication with guardian spirits requires either physical or psychological privacy if it is to be most effective.

Curiosity and surveillance

The third element of privacy that seems universal is a tendency on the part of individuals to invade the privacy of others, and of society to engage in surveillance to guard against anti-social conduct. At the individual level, this is based upon the propensity for curiosity that lies in each individual, from the time that as a child he seeks to explore his environment to his later conduct as an adult in wanting to know more than he learns casually about what is "really" happening to others.[51] Again, this is not a phenomenon restricted to man. Studies of monkeys have shown that even when experiments take away such possible motivations as hunger, fear, sex, comfort, and the like, monkeys will actively take things apart, poke their fingers into holes, and exercise active curiosity.[52] Though the degree to which action will be taken to satisfy human curiosity varies according to cultural and personality factors, men and women in all primitive societies try to find out what has been happening to members of their own family, other villagers, other tribal members, and so forth. Gossip, which is only a particular way of obtaining private information to satisfy curiosity, seems to be found in all societies. People want to know what others are doing, especially the great and the powerful, partly as a means of gauging their own performances and desires and partly as a means of vicarious experience, for by satisfying curiosity the individual experiences a sense of pleasure from knowing about exciting or awesome behavior in others.

It has been noted that the tendency to curiosity varies widely among individual members of any society. William McDougal has written that "these differences are apt to be increased during the course of life, the impulse growing weaker for lack of use in those in whom it is innately weak, stronger through exercise in those in whom it is innately strong. In men of the latter type it may become the main source of intellectual energy and effort."[53] And, of course, each society can encourage or discourage such curiosity in its members.

The conduct just described might be called simple curiosity, the day-to-day inquisitiveness or search for explanations that is usually acceptable or even considered beneficial in most societies. There is also "anti-social" curiosity, the phenomenon that takes place when curiosity leads individuals to break the taboos of their society and penetrate the sacred worlds. This is the well-known "insatiable" craving to discover the secret things—to watch the forbidden ceremonies, visit the forbidden places, eat the forbidden fruit, utter the forbidden names. Some persons will take great risks to satisfy this craving.

The commonness of this phenomenon (and the need to control it) is illustrated by the myths in many societies about men and women who have lost precious things, or destroyed themselves, or injured their community because they did not control their curiosity. Western society's cautionary tales of Lot's wife, Pandora opening the box, Eve tasting the apple, Bluebeard's wives opening the forbidden room, Orpheus looking back to Hades, Psyche almost losing Cupid, and others,[54] all have their primitive counterparts, as in the Australian bush myth that death came to mankind because a woman went to a tabooed tree.[55] When normal curiosity is placed alongside the desire of some members of society to penetrate the secrets, it becomes clear that the notion of societies in which people happily "mind their own business" and "let everyone alone" is a fantasy of some libertarian's imagination, not the condition of men in either primitive or modern societies.

Curiosity is only half of the privacy-invading phenomenon, the "individual" half. There is also the universal process of surveillance by authorities to enforce the rules and taboos of the society. Any social system that creates norms—as all human societies do—must have mechanisms for enforcing those norms. Since those who break the rules and taboos must be detected, every society has mechanisms of watching conduct, investigating transgressions, and determining "guilt."

In these processes each society sets socially approved machinery for penetrating the privacy of individuals or groups in order to protect personal and group rights and enforce the society's rules and taboos. Society also requires certain acts to be done in the presence of others, in recognition that visibility itself provides a powerful method of enforcing social norms.[56]

The importance of recognizing this "social" half of the universal privacy-invading process is similar to the recognition of individual curiosity—it reminds us that every society which wants to protect its rules and taboos against deviant behavior must have enforcement machinery. Until a society appears in which every individual obeys every rule and taboo and there is no ambiguity to create choices and tensions, there will be family heads, group leaders, religious authorities, and tribal-national authorities who will engage in surveillance to see that private conduct stays within a socially determined degree of conformity with the rules and taboos of that culture. Any discussion of privacy must recognize this fact.

Privacy and the movement from primitive to modern societies

Finally, the anthropological literature suggests that the movement from primitive to modern societies increases both the physical and psychological opportunities for privacy by individuals and family units and converts these opportunities into choices of values in the socio-political realm. Some anthropologists, such as John Honigmann, have expressed this concept in terms of an increase in the scale of life.

Increase of scale . . . though necessarily involving greater centralization produces not less but more freedom in personal relations. . . . The freedom of a primitive man is limited at every point by the pressure of neighbors and kinsmen, living and dead, from whom he cannot escape. He has little privacy. His position in society is largely fixed by sex, age, and blood. The freedom of the civilized man from neighbors and kinsmen, and from the immediate past, is much greater than that of the primitive; not only does he live relatively aloof in his house, but he can escape the living by moving.[57]

The developments associated with the rise of modern industrial societies—such as the nuclear family living in individual households, urbanization and the anonymity of city life, mobility in work and residence, the weakening of religious authority over individuals—all provide greater situations of physical and psychological privacy than do the milieu and belief-systems of primitive man. But modern societies have also brought developments that work against the achievement of privacy: density and crowding of populations; large bureaucratic organizational life; popular moods of alienation and insecurity that can lead to desires for new "total" relations; new instruments of physical, psychological, and data surveillance, as discussed in this book; and the modern state, with its military, technological, and propaganda capacities to create and sustain an Orwellian control of life. This suggests that the achievement of privacy for individuals, families, and groups in modern society has become a matter of freedom rather than the product of necessity.

Privacy in Western history: the struggle to limit surveillance by authorities

The point just made is illustrated concretely by the evolution of Western political and social institutions from Greek and Roman antiquity to the contemporary era.[58] This development has been marked by two competing traditions. One, associated primarily with phenomena like the democratic city-state in ancient Greece, English Protestantism and common-law traditions, and American constitutionalism and property concepts, has been a trend to place limits on the surveillance powers of governmental, religious, and economic authorities in the interest of privacy for individuals, families, and certain social groups in each society. A competing tradition in Western history, associated with societies such as Sparta, the Roman Empire, the medieval Church, and the continental nation-state, continued very broad powers of surveillance for governmental, economic, and religious authorities. The socio-political balance of the former tradition expanded, in each society, the opportunities of individuals and groups to enjoy substantial opportunities for privacy as that was conceived in the particular era. The socio-political balance in the second tradition created a restrictive setting and instilled a competing set of values in its citizenry. Of course, the two traditions sometimes competed within particular societies, as alternative trends, but it is remarkable how constant the dominant themes have been.

It is beyond the scope of this brief summary to describe how the leading elites, general citizens, and the poor and unfree in each of the Western societies studied conceived of privacy, enjoyed or had none of it, and balanced the values of privacy, disclosure, and surveillance in their civic life. The point that can be made, however, is that no society with a reputation for providing liberty in its own time failed to provide limits on the surveillance power of authorities. In this sense, American society in the 1970's faces the task of keeping this tradition meaningful when technological change promises to give public and private authorities the physical power to do what a combination of physical and socio-legal restraints had denied to them as part of our basic social system.

NOTES

1 Edward T. Hall, *The Hidden Dimension* (New York, 1966).
2 Robert Ardrey, *The Territorial Imperative* (New York, 1966).
3 See H. E. Howard, *Territory in Bird Life* (London, 1920); W. C. Allee, *The Social Life of Animals* (Boston, 1958); C. R. Carpenter, "Territoriality: A Review of Concepts and Problems," in A. Roe and G. G. Simpson (eds.), *Behavior and Evolution* (New Haven, Conn., 1958); H. Hediger, "The Evolution of Territorial Behavior," in S. L. Washburn (ed.), *Social Life of Early Man* (New York, 1961); V. C. Wynne-Edwards, *Animal Dispersion in Relation to Social Behavior* (New York, 1962).
4 Ardrey, *op. cit.*, 158–59, 94–100, 178–83.
5 *Ibid.*, 87–88.
6 *Ibid.*, 95.
7 Hall, *op. cit.*, 15, 16–37.
8 *Ibid.*, 120.
9 Hall, *op. cit.*, 13–14.
10 *Ibid.*, 10–14.
11 *Ibid.*, 39–70.
12 *Ibid.*, 17.
13 John B. Calhoun, "A 'Behavioral Sink,' " in E. L. Bliss (ed.), *Roots of Behavior* (New York, 1962), Ch. 22; "Population Density and Social Pathology," 206 *Scientific American*, 139–46 (1962); Hall, *op. cit.*, 21–29.
14 H. L. Ratcliffe and R. L. Snyder, "Patterns of Disease, Controlled Populations, and Experimental Design," 26 *Circulation*, 1352–57 (1962); Hall, *op. cit.*, 175.
15 John J. Christian, "Factors in Mass Mortality of a Herd of Sika Deer (*Cervus nippon*)," 1 *Chesapeake Science*, 79–95 (1960); Hall, *op. cit.*, 17–19.
16 Ardrey, *op. cit.*, 162.
17 F. F. Darling, "Social Behavior and Survival," 69 *Auk*, 183–91 (1952).
18 J. Fisher, "Evolution and Bird Sociality," in J. Huxley *et al.* (eds.), *Evolution as a Process* (London, 1954).
19 Wynne-Edwards, *op. cit.*
20 Dorothy Lee, *Freedom and Culture* (Englewood Cliffs, N.J., 1959), 31–32.
21 *Ibid.*, 74–75.
22 *Ibid.*
23 Margaret Mead, *Coming of Age in Samoa* (Mentor ed., New York, 1949), 82–85.
24 Livingston F. Jones, *A Study of the Tlingets of Alaska* (New York, 1914), 58.

25 See George P. Murdock, "The Universals of Culture," in E. A. Hoebel, J. D. Jennings, and E. R. Smith (eds.), *Readings in Anthropology* (New York, 1955), 4–5; G. P. Murdock, *Outline of World Cultures* (3rd ed., rev., New Haven, Conn., 1963).

26 There is a large literature on avoidance and social distance. Perhaps the leading work is that of Georg Simmel. See *The Sociology of Georg Simmel*, tr. and ed. by Kurt Wolff (New York, 1950).

27 Robert F. Murphy, "Social Distance and the Veil," 66 *American Anthropologist*, 1257–74 (1964).

28 For a discussion of the idea of "self" as present in all societies, though very differently conceived and integrated, see Gardner Murphy, "Social Motivation," in Gardner Lindzey (ed.), *Handbook of Social Psychology* (Cambridge, Mass., 1954), vol. 1, 601–31.

29 Clellan S. Ford and Frank A. Beach, *Patterns of Sexual Behavior* (paperback ed., New York, 1951), 102–104.

30 Murdock, in Hoebel *et al.*, *op. cit.*, 5. See also J. W. M. Whiting and I. L. Child, *Child Training and Personality* (New Haven, Conn., 1953), 84–86, 116.

31 See references and discussion in Sigmund Freud, *Totem and Taboo* (New York, 1950), 27–29, 33.

32 Ford and Beach, *op. cit.*, 92. See also 77–79, 81–83, 196. This is not a characteristic of animal sexual behavior. "A desire for privacy during sexual intercourse seems confined to human beings. Male-female pairs of other animal species appear to be quite unaffected by the presence of other individuals and to mate quite as readily in a crowd as when alone" (*ibid.*, 80).

33 *Ibid.*, 77.

34 *Ibid.*, 77–80.

35 A. R. Holmberg, *The Siriono* (unpublished Ph.D. dissertation, Yale, 1946), 183; quoted in *ibid.*, 78.

36 See, for example, references to the QuKan, in M1, J.25, 3033, Human Relations Area Files, Yale University; W. E. Freeman, "The Family Systems of the Iban of Borneo," in Jack Goody, ed., *Cambridge Papers in Social Anthropology*, No. 1, 1552 London (1958), 52; Aurel Krause, *The Tlingit Indians* (New York, 1956), 112.

37 William J. Goode, *The Family* (Englewood Cliffs, N.J., 1964), 53–54; Beatrice Blackwood, *Both Sides of the Buka Passage* (Oxford, 1935), 22–23.

38 Murphy, *op. cit.*, 1274.

39 R. M. Underhill, "Social Organization of the Papago Indians," 30 *Columbia University Contributions of Anthropology*, 119.

40 Dr. Geertz's paper was delivered informally at a seminar on privacy conducted by members of the Center for Advanced Study in the Behavioral Sciences, Stanford, Calif., in 1959. Quoted by permission of Dr. Geertz.

41 Arnold van Gennep, *The Rites of Passage* (Chicago, 1960), 180–83, 183–85.

42 Mead, *op. cit.*, 85.
43 See Georg Simmel, "The Sociology of Secrecy and Secret Societies," 11 *American Journal of Sociology*, 441 (1906); Hutton Webster, *Primitive Secret Societies* (New York, 1908); Camilla H. Wedgwood, "The Nature and Functions of Secret Societies," I *Oceania*, 129 (1930); George Schwab, *The Tribes of the Liberian Hinterland* (Cambridge, Mass., 1947); George Harley, *Notes on the Poro in Liberia* (Cambridge, Mass., 1941).
44 See William W. Howells, *The Heathens: Primitive Man, and His Religions* (New York, 1948), Ch. 10; Robert H. Lowie, *Primitive Religion* (New York, 1924); E. Vogt and W. Lessa (eds.), *Reader in Comparative Religion* (New York, 1965).
45 Edwin H. Gomes, *Seventeen Years Among the Sea Dyaks of Borneo* (1911), 204.
46 For an outstanding discussion, see Frederica de Laguna, "Tlingit Ideas About the Individual," 10 *Southwestern Journal of Anthropology*, 180–81, 189 (1954). See also Edward Sapir, "The Life of a Nootka Indian," 28 *Queen's Quarterly*, 232–243, 351–367 (1921).
47 See de Laguna, *op. cit.*, 180.
48 For examples of the "ordeal of privacy," see James, *op. cit.*, 204–205; F. E. Williams, *Orokaiva Magic* (London, 1928), 81–82; Robert H. Lowie, *Indians of the Plains* (New York, 1954); James Swan, *Three Years Residence in Washington Territory* (New York, 1857), 62–63.
49 See, for example, P. Drucker, "The Northern and Central Nootka Tribes," *Bulletin of the Bureau of American Ethnology*, 185 (1951); Swan, *op. cit.*, 61; Elizabeth Colson, *The Makah Indians* (Manchester, Eng., 1953), 48.
50 F. E. Williams, *op. cit.*
51 D. E. Berlyne, *Conflict, Arousal, and Curiosity* (New York, 1960).
52 H. F. Harlow, "Learning Motivated by a Manipulation Drive," 40 *Journal of Experimental Psychology*, 228 (1950).
53 W. McDougal, *An Introduction to Social Psychology* (London, 1908), 49–50.
54 For discussions of the curiosity theme, see Thomas Bulfinch, *Bulfinch's Mythology* (New York, 1947), 80–89; Alexander S. Murray, *Manual of Mythology* (1895), 282–83.
55 Lewis Spence, *An Introduction to Mythology* (New York, 1931), 150.
56 See Robert K. Merton, *Social Theory and Social Structure* (rev. ed., Glencoe, Ill., 1957), 355.
57 John J. Honigmann, *The World of Man* (New York, 1959), 154. Of course there are areas in which some primitive societies set sharp privacy norms that have not been carried over into modern industrial societies. In the culture of the Eskimo, the individual's name is private. To ask it is an intrusion, for to utter the name is to give it life and run risks of sickness and death. Among Australian tribes the new name a youth receives on entering manhood is taboo and must be kept secret. See Freud, *op. cit.*, 33. For an example of the difficulties one anthropologist had in learning names among the Nuer, see E. E. Evans-Pritchard, *The Nuer* (Oxford, 1960), 12–13.

58 For a full treatment of the historical basis of privacy in the West, see Alan
   F. Westin, *Privacy in Western History* (New York, 1967). See also Edward
   Shils, "Privacy: Its Constitution and Vicissitudes," 31 *Law and Contemporary
   Problems* (Spring, 1966), 281.

4

The right to privacy
[The implicit made explicit]

SAMUEL D. WARREN AND LOUIS D. BRANDEIS

> It could be done only on principles of private justice, moral fitness, and
> public convenience, which, when applied to a new subject, make common
> law without a precedent; much more when received and approved by
> usage.
>
> Willes, J., in Millar v. Taylor, 4 Burr. 2303, 2312.

That the individual shall have full protection in person and in property is a principle as old as the common law; but it has been found
necessary from time to time to define anew the exact nature and extent
of such protection. Political, social, and economic changes entail the
recognition of new rights, and the common law, in its eternal youth,
grows to meet the demands of society. Thus, in very early times, the
law gave a remedy only for physical interference with life and property, for trespasses *vi et armis*. Then the "right to life" served only to
protect the subject from battery in its various forms; liberty meant
freedom from actual restraint; and the right to property secured to
the individual his lands and his cattle. Later, there came a recognition
of man's spiritual nature, of his feelings and his intellect. Gradually
the scope of these legal rights broadened; and now the right to life
has come to mean the right to enjoy life,—the right to be let alone;
the right to liberty secures the exercise of extensive civil privileges;
and the term "property" has grown to comprise every form of possession—intangible, as well as tangible.

Thus, with the recognition of the legal value of sensations, the
protection against actual bodily injury was extended to prohibit mere
attempts to do such injury; that is, the putting another in fear of such
injury. From the action of battery grew that of assault.[1] Much later
there came a qualified protection of the individual against offensive
noises and odors, against dust and smoke, and excessive vibration.
The law of nuisance was developed.[2] So regard for human emotions
soon extended the scope of personal immunity beyond the body of
the individual. His reputation, the standing among his fellow-men,
was considered, and the law of slander and libel arose.[3] Man's family

relations became a part of the legal conception of his life, and the alienation of a wife's affections was held remediable.[4] Occasionally the law halted,—as in its refusal to recognize the intrusion by seduction upon the honor of the family. But even here the demands of society were met. A mean fiction, the action *per quod servitium amisit*, was resorted to, and by allowing damages for injury to the parents' feelings, an adequate remedy was ordinarily afforded.[5] Similar to the expansion of the right to life was the growth of the legal conception of property. From corporeal property arose the incorporeal rights issuing out of it; and then there opened the wide realm of intangible property, in the products and processes of the mind,[6] as works of literature and art,[7] goodwill,[8] trade secrets, and trade-marks.[9]

This development of the law was inevitable. The intense intellectual and emotional life, and the heightening of sensations which came with the advance of civilization, made it clear to men that only a part of the pain, pleasure, and profit of life lay in physical things. Thoughts, emotions, and sensations demanded legal recognition, and the beautiful capacity for growth which characterizes the common law enabled the judges to afford the requisite protection, without the interposition of the legislature.

Recent inventions and business methods call attention to the next step which must be taken for the protection of the person, and for securing to the individual what Judge Cooley calls the right "to be let alone."[10] Instantaneous photographs and newspaper enterprise have invaded the sacred precincts of private and domestic life; and numerous mechanical devices threaten to make good the prediction that "what is whispered in the closet shall be proclaimed from the housetops." For years there has been a feeling that the law must afford some remedy for the unauthorized circulation of portraits of private persons;[11] and the evil of the invasion of privacy by the newspapers, long keenly felt, has been but recently discussed by an able writer.[12] The alleged facts of a somewhat notorious case brought before an inferior tribunal in New York a few months ago,[13] directly involved the consideration of the right of circulating portraits; and the question whether our law will recognize and protect the right to privacy in this and in other respects must soon come before our courts for consideration.

Of the desirability—indeed of the necessity—of some such protection, there can, it is believed, be no doubt. The press is overstepping in every direction the obvious bounds of propriety and of decency. Gossip is no longer the resource of the idle and of the vicious, but has become a trade, which is pursued with industry as well as effrontery. To satisfy a prurient taste the details of sexual relations are spread broadcast in the columns of the daily papers. To occupy the indolent, column upon column is filled with idle gossip, which can only be procured by intrusion upon the domestic circle. The intensity and complexity of life, attendant upon advancing civilization, have rendered necessary some retreat from the world, and man, under the refining influence of culture, has become more sensitive to publicity, so that solitude and privacy have become more essential to the individual; but modern enterprise and invention have, through invasions upon his privacy, subjected him to mental pain and distress, far greater than could be inflicted by mere bodily injury. Nor is the harm wrought by such invasions confined to the suffering of those who may be made the subjects of journalistic or other enterprise. In this, as in other branches of commerce, the supply creates the demand. Each crop of unseemly gossip, thus harvested, becomes the seed of more, and, in direct proportion to its circulation, results in a lowering of social standards and of morality. Even gossip apparently harmless, when widely and persistently circulated, is potent for evil. It both belittles and perverts. It belittles by inverting the relative importance of things, thus dwarfing the thoughts and aspirations of a people. When personal gossip attains the dignity of print, and crowds the space available for matters of real interest to the community, what wonder that the ignorant and thoughtless mistake its relative importance. Easy of comprehension, appealing to that weak side of human nature which is never wholly cast down by the misfortunes and frailties of our neighbors, no one can be surprised that it usurps the place of interest in brains capable of other things. Triviality destroys at once robustness of thought and delicacy of feeling. No enthusiasm can flourish, no generous impulse can survive under its blighting influence.

It is our purpose to consider whether the existing law affords a principle which can properly be invoked to protect the privacy of the individual; and, if it does, what the nature and extent of such protection is.

Owing to the nature of the instruments by which privacy is invaded, the injury inflicted bears a superficial resemblance to the wrongs dealt with by the law of slander and of libel, while a legal remedy for such injury seems to involve the treatment of mere wounded feelings, as a substantive cause of action. The principle on which the law of defamation rests, covers, however, a radically different class of effects from those for which attention is now asked. It deals only with damage to reputation, with the injury done to the individual in his external relations to the community, by lowering him in the estimation of his fellows. The matter published of him, however widely circulated, and however unsuited to publicity, must, in order to be actionable, have a direct tendency to injure him in his intercourse with others, and even if in writing or in print, must subject him to the hatred, ridicule, or contempt of his fellow-men,—the effect of the publication upon his estimate of himself and upon his own feelings not forming an essential element in the cause of action. In short, the wrongs and correlative rights recognized by the law of slander and libel are in their nature material rather than spiritual. That branch of the law simply extends the protection surrounding physical property to certain of the conditions necessary or helpful to worldly prosperity. On the other hand, our law recognizes no principle upon which compensation can be granted for mere injury to the feelings. However painful the mental effects upon another of an act, though purely wanton or even malicious, yet if the act itself is otherwise lawful, the suffering inflicted is *damnum absque injuria*. Injury of feelings may indeed be taken account of in ascertaining the amount of damages when attending what is recognized as a legal injury;[14] but our system, unlike the Roman law, does not afford a remedy even for mental suffering which results from mere contumely and insult, from an intentional and unwarranted violation of the "honor" of another.[15]

It is not however necessary, in order to sustain the view that the common law recognizes and upholds a principle applicable to cases of invasion of privacy, to invoke the analogy, which is but superficial, to injuries sustained, either by an attack upon reputation or by what the civilians called a violation of honor; for the legal doctrines relating to infractions of what is ordinarily termed the common-law right to intellectual and artistic property are, it is believed, but instances and applications of a general right to privacy, which properly understood afford a remedy for the evils under consideration.

The common law secures to each individual the right of determining, ordinarily, to what extent his thoughts, sentiments, and emotions shall be communicated to others.[16] Under our system of government, he can never be compelled to express them (except when upon the witness-stand); and even if he has chosen to give them expression, he generally retains the power to fix the limits of the publicity which shall be given them. The existence of this right does not depend upon the particular method of expression adopted. It is immaterial whether it be by word[17] or by signs,[18] in painting,[19] by sculpture, or in music.[20] Neither does the existence of the right depend upon the nature or value of the thought or emotion, nor upon the excellence of the means of expression.[21] The same protection is accorded to a casual letter or an entry in a diary and to the most valuable poem or essay, to a botch or daub and to a masterpiece. In every such case the individual is entitled to decide whether that which is his shall be given to the public.[22] No other has the right to publish his productions in any form, without his consent. This right is wholly independent of the material on which, or the means by which, the thought, sentiment, or emotion is expressed. It may exist independently of any corporeal being, as in words spoken, a song sung, a drama acted. Or if expressed on any material, as a poem in writing, the author may have parted with the paper, without forfeiting any proprietary right in the composition itself. The right is lost only when the author himself communicates his production to the public,—in other words, publishes it.[23] It is entirely independent of the copyright laws, and their extension into the domain of art. The aim of those statutes is to secure to the author, composer, or artist the entire profits arising from publication; but the common-law protection enables him to control absolutely the act of publication, and in the exercise of his own discretion, to decide whether there shall be any publication at all.[24] The statutory right is of no value, *unless* there is a publication; the common-law right is lost *as soon as* there is a publication.

What is the nature, the basis, of this right to prevent the publication of manuscripts or works of art? It is stated to be the enforcement of a right of property,[25] and no difficulty arises in accepting this view, so long as we have only to deal with the reproduction of literary and artistic compositions. They certainly possess many of the attributes of ordinary property: they are transferable; they have a value; and publication or reproduction is a use by which that value is realized. But where the value of the production is found not in the right to take the profits arising from publication, but in the peace of mind or the relief afforded by the ability to prevent any publication at all, it is difficult to regard the right as one of property, in the common acceptation of that term. A man records in a letter to his son, or in his diary, that he did not dine with his wife on a certain day. No one into whose hands those papers fall could publish them to the world, even if possession of the documents had been obtained rightfully; and the prohibition would not be confined to the publication of a copy of the letter itself, or of the diary entry; the restraint extends also to a publication of the contents. What is the thing which is protected? Surely, not the intellectual act of recording the fact that the husband did not dine with his wife, but that fact itself. It is not the intellectual product, but the domestic occurrence. A man writes a dozen letters to different people. No person would be permitted to publish a list of the letters written. If the letters or the contents of the diary were protected as literary compositions, the scope of the protection afforded should be the same secured to a published writing under the copyright law. But the copyright law would not prevent an enumeration of the letters, or the publication of some of the facts contained therein. The copyright of a series of paintings or etchings would prevent a reproduction of the paintings as pictures; but it would not prevent a publication of a list or even a description of them.[26] Yet in the famous case of Prince Albert *v.* Strange, the court held that the common-law rule prohibited not merely the reproduction of the etchings which the plaintiff and Queen Victoria had made for their own pleasure, but also "the publishing (at least by printing or writing), though not by copy or resemblance, a description of them, whether more or less limited or summary, whether in the form of a catalogue or otherwise."[27] Likewise, an unpublished collection of news possessing no element of a literary nature is protected from piracy.[28]

That this protection cannot rest upon the right to literary or artistic property in any exact sense, appears the more clearly when the subject-matter for which protection is invoked is not even in the form of intellectual property, but has the attributes of ordinary tangible property. Suppose a man has a collection of gems or curiosities which he keeps private: it would hardly be contended that any person could publish a catalogue of them, and yet the articles enumerated are certainly not intellectual property in the legal sense, any more than a collection of stoves or of chairs.[29]

The belief that the idea of property in its narrow sense was the basis of the protection of unpublished manuscripts led an able court to refuse, in several cases, injunctions against the publication of private letters, on the ground that "letters not possessing the attributes of literary compositions are not property entitled to protection;" and that it was "evident the plaintiff could not have considered the letters as of any value whatever as literary productions, for a letter cannot be considered of value to the author which he never would consent to have published."[30] But these decisions have not been followed,[31] and it may now be considered settled that the protection afforded by the common law to the author of any writing is entirely independent of its pecuniary value, its intrinsic merits, or of any intention to publish the same, and, of course, also, wholly independent of the material, if any, upon which, or the mode in which, the thought or sentiment was expressed.

Although the courts have asserted that they rested their decisions

on the narrow grounds of protection to property, yet there are rec-
ognitions of a more liberal doctrine. Thus in the case of Prince Albert
v. Strange, already referred to, the opinions both of the Vice-
Chancellor and of the Lord Chancellor, on appeal, show a more or
less clearly defined perception of a principle broader than those which
were mainly discussed, and on which they both placed their chief
reliance. Vice-Chancellor Knight Bruce referred to publishing of a
man that he had "written to particular persons or on particular subjects" as an instance of possibly injurious disclosures as to private
matters, that the courts would in a proper case prevent; yet it is
difficult to perceive how, in such a case, any right of property, in the
narrow sense, would be drawn in question, or why, if such a publication would be restrained when it threatened to expose the victim
not merely to sarcasm, but to ruin, it should not equally be enjoined,
if it threatened to embitter his life. To deprive a man of the potential
profits to be realized by publishing a catalogue of his gems cannot *per
se* be a wrong to him. The possibility of future profits is not a right
of property which the law ordinarily recognizes; it must, therefore,
be an infraction of other rights which constitutes the wrongful act,
and that infraction is equally wrongful, whether its results are to
forestall the profits that the individual himself might secure by giving
the matter a publicity obnoxious to him, or to gain an advantage at
the expense of his mental pain and suffering. If the fiction of property
in a narrow sense must be preserved, it is still true that the end
accomplished by the gossip-monger is attained by the use of that which
is another's, the facts relating to his private life, which he has seen fit
to keep private. Lord Cottenham stated that a man "is entitled to be
protected in the exclusive use and enjoyment of that which is exclusively his," and cited with approval the opinion of Lord Eldon, as
reported in a manuscript note of the case of Wyatt *v.* Wilson, in 1820,
respecting an engraving of George the Third during his illness, to
the effect that "if one of the late king's physicians had kept a diary
of what he heard and saw, the court would not, in the king's lifetime,
have permitted him to print and publish it;" and Lord Cottenham
declared, in respect to the acts of the defendants in the case before
him, that "privacy is the right invaded." But if privacy is once recognized as a right entitled to legal protection, the interposition of the
courts cannot depend on the particular nature of the injuries resulting.

These considerations lead to the conclusion that the protection afforded to thoughts, sentiments, and emotions, expressed through the
medium of writing or of the arts, so far as it consists in preventing

publication, is merely an instance of the enforcement of the more general right of the individual to be let alone. It is like the right not to be assaulted or beaten, the right not to be imprisoned, the right not to be maliciously prosecuted, the right not to be defamed. In each of these rights, as indeed in all other rights recognized by the law, there inheres the quality of being owned or possessed—and (as that is the distinguishing attribute of property) there may be some propriety in speaking of those rights as property. But, obviously, they bear little resemblance to what is ordinarily comprehended under that term. The principle which protects personal writings and all other personal productions, not against theft and physical appropriation, but against publication in any form, is in reality not the principle of private property, but that of an inviolate personality.[32]

If we are correct in this conclusion, the existing law affords a principle which may be invoked to protect the privacy of the individual from invasion either by the too enterprising press, the photographer, or the possessor of any other modern device for recording or reproducing scenes or sounds. For the protection afforded is not confined by the authorities to those cases where any particular medium or form of expression has been adopted, nor to products of the intellect. The same protection is afforded to emotions and sensations expressed in a musical composition or other work of art as to a literary composition; and words spoken, a pantomime acted, a sonata performed, is no less entitled to protection than if each had been reduced to writing. The circumstance that a thought or emotion has been recorded in a permanent form renders its identification easier, and hence may be important from the point of view of evidence, but it has no significance as a matter of substantive right. If, then, the decisions indicate a general right to privacy for thoughts, emotions, and sensations, these should receive the same protection, whether expressed in writing, or in conduct, in conversation, in attitudes, or in facial expression.

It may be urged that a distinction should be taken between the deliberate expression of thoughts and emotions in literary or artistic compositions and the casual and often involuntary expression given to them in the ordinary conduct of life. In other words, it may be contended that the protection afforded is granted to the conscious products of labor, perhaps as an encouragement to effort.[33] This contention, however plausible, has, in fact, little to recommend it. If the amount of labor involved be adopted as the test, we might well find that the effort to conduct one's self properly in business and in domestic relations had been far greater than that involved in painting a picture or writing a book; one would find that it was far easier to express lofty sentiments in a diary than in the conduct of a noble life. If the test of deliberateness of the act be adopted, much casual correspondence which is now accorded full protection would be excluded from the beneficent operation of existing rules. After the decisions denying the distinction attempted to be made between those literary productions which it was intended to publish and those which it was not, all considerations of the amount of labor involved, the degree of deliberation, the value of the product, and the intention of publishing must be abandoned, and no basis is discerned upon which the right to restrain publication and reproduction of such so-called literary and artistic works can be rested, except the right to privacy, as a part of the more general right to the immunity of the person,—the right to one's personality.

It should be stated that, in some instances where protection has been afforded against wrongful publication, the jurisdiction has been asserted, not on the ground of property, or at least not wholly on that ground, but upon the ground of an alleged breach of an implied contract or of a trust or confidence.

Thus, in Abernethy v. Hutchinson, 3 L. J. Ch. 209 (1825), where the plaintiff, a distinguished surgeon, sought to restrain the publication in the "Lancet" of unpublished lectures which he had delivered at St. Bartholomew's Hospital in London, Lord Eldon doubted whether there could be property in lectures which had not been reduced to writing, but granted the injunction on the ground of breach of confidence, holding "that when persons were admitted as pupils or otherwise, to hear these lectures, although they were orally delivered, and although the parties might go to the extent, if they were able to do so, of putting down the whole by means of short-hand, yet they could do that only for the purposes of their own information, and could not publish, for profit, that which they had not obtained the right of selling."

In Prince Albert v. Strange, 1 McN. & G. 25 (1849), Lord Cottenham, on appeal, while recognizing a right of property in the etchings which of itself would justify the issuance of the injunction, stated, after discussing the evidence, that he was bound to assume that the possession of the etchings by the defendant had "its foundation in a breach of trust, confidence, or contract," and that upon such ground also the plaintiff's title to the injunction was fully sustained.

In Tuck v. Priester, 19 Q. B. D. 639 (1887), the plaintiffs were owners of a picture, and employed the defendant to make a certain number of copies. He did so, and made also a number of other copies for himself, and offered them for sale in England at a lower price. Subsequently, the plaintiffs registered their copyright in the picture, and then brought suit for an injunction and damages. The Lords Justices differed as to the application of the copyright acts to the case, but held unanimously that independently of those acts, the plaintiffs were entitled to an injunction and damages for breach of contract.

In Pollard v. Photographic Co., 40 Ch. Div. 345 (1888), a photographer who had taken a lady's photograph under the ordinary circumstances was restrained from exhibiting it, and also from selling copies of it, on the ground that it was a breach of an implied term in the contract, and also that it was a breach of confidence. Mr. Justice North interjected in the argument of the plaintiff's counsel the inquiry: "Do you dispute that if the negative likeness were taken on the sly, the person who took it might exhibit copies?" and counsel for the plaintiff answered: "In that case there would be no trust or consideration to support a contract." Later, the defendant's counsel argued that "a person has no property in his own features; short of doing what is libellous or otherwise illegal, there is no restriction on the photographer's using his negative." But the court, while expressly finding a breach of contract and of trust sufficient to justify its interposition, still seems to have felt the necessity of resting the decision also upon a right of property,[34] in order to bring it within the line of those cases which were relied upon as precedents.[35]

This process of implying a term in a contract, or of implying a trust (particularly where the contract is written, and where there is no established usage or custom), is nothing more nor less than a judicial declaration that public morality, private justice, and general convenience demand the recognition of such a rule, and that the publication under similar circumstances would be considered an intolerable abuse. So long as these circumstances happen to present a contract upon which such a term can be engrafted by the judicial mind, or to supply relations upon which a trust or confidence can be erected, there may be no objection to working out the desired protection through the doctrines of contract or of trust. But the court can hardly stop there. The narrower doctrine may have satisfied the demands of society at a time when the abuse to be guarded against could rarely have arisen without violating a contract or a special confidence; but now that modern devices afford abundant opportunities for the perpetration of such wrongs without any participation by the injured party, the protection granted by the law must be placed upon a broader foundation. While, for instance, the state of the photographic art was such that one's picture could seldom be taken without his consciously "sitting" for the purpose, the law of contract or of trust might afford the prudent man sufficient safeguards against the improper circulation of his portrait; but since the latest advances in photographic art have rendered it possible to take pictures surreptitiously, the doctrines of contract and of trust are inadequate to support the required protection, and the law of tort must be resorted to. The right of property in its widest sense, including all possession, including all rights and privileges, and hence embracing the right to an inviolate personality, affords alone that broad basis upon which the protection which the individual demands can be rested.

Thus, the courts, in searching for some principle upon which the publication of private letters could be enjoined, naturally came upon the ideas of a breach of confidence, and of an implied contract; but it required little consideration to discern that this doctrine could not afford all the protection required, since it would not support the court in granting a remedy against a stranger; and so the theory of property in the contents of letters was adopted.[36] Indeed, it is difficult to conceive on what theory of the law the casual recipient of a letter, who proceeds to publish it, is guilty of a breach of contract, express or implied, or of any breach of trust, in the ordinary acceptation of that term. Suppose a letter has been addressed to him without his solicitation. He opens it, and reads. Surely, he has not made any contract; he has not accepted any trust. He cannot, by opening and reading the letter, have come under any obligation save what the law declares; and, however expressed, that obligation is simply to observe the legal right of the sender, whatever it may be, and whether it be called his right of property in the contents of the letter, or his right to privacy.[37]

A similar groping for the principle upon which a wrongful publication can be enjoined is found in the law of trade secrets. There, injunctions have generally been granted on the theory of a breach of contract, or of an abuse of confidence.[38] It would, of course, rarely happen that any one would be in the possession of a secret unless confidence had been reposed in him. But can it be supposed that the court would hesitate to grant relief against one who had obtained his knowledge by an ordinary trespass,—for instance, by wrongfully looking into a book in which the secret was recorded, or by eavesdropping? Indeed, in Yovatt v. Winyard, 1 J. & W. 394 (1820), where an injunction was granted against making any use of or communicating certain recipes for veterinary medicine, it appeared that the defendant, while in the plaintiff's employ, had surreptitiously got access to his book of recipes, and copied them. Lord Eldon "granted the injunction, upon the ground of there having been a breach of trust and confidence;" but it would seem to be difficult to draw any sound legal distinction between such a case and one where a mere stranger wrongfully obtained access to the book.[39]

We must therefore conclude that the rights, so protected, whatever their exact nature, are not rights arising from contract or from special trust, but are rights as against the world; and, as above stated, the principle which has been applied to protect these rights is in reality not the principle of private property, unless that word be used in an extended and unusual sense. The principle which protects personal writings and any other productions of the intellect or of the emotions, is the right to privacy, and the law has no new principle to formulate when it extends this protection to the personal appearance, sayings, acts, and to personal relation, domestic or otherwise.[40]

If the invasion of privacy constitutes a legal *injuria,* the elements for demanding redress exist, since already the value of mental suffering, caused by an act wrongful in itself, is recognized as a basis for compensation.

The right of one who has remained a private individual, to prevent his public portraiture, presents the simplest case for such extension; the right to protect one's self from pen portraiture, from a discussion by the press of one's private affairs, would be a more important and far-reaching one. If casual and unimportant statements in a letter, if handiwork, however inartistic and valueless, if possessions of all sorts are protected not only against reproduction, but against description and enumeration, how much more should the acts and sayings of a man in his social and domestic relations be guarded from ruthless publicity. If you may not reproduce a woman's face photographically without her consent, how much less should be tolerated the reproduction of her face, her form, and her actions, by graphic descriptions colored to suit a gross and depraved imagination.

The right to privacy, limited as such right must necessarily be, has already found expression in the law of France.[41]

It remains to consider what are the limitations of this right to privacy, and what remedies may be granted for the enforcement of the right. To determine in advance of experience the exact line at which the dignity and convenience of the individual must yield to the demands of the public welfare or of private justice would be a difficult task; but the more general rules are furnished by the legal analogies already developed in the law of slander and libel, and in the law of literary and artistic property.

1. The right to privacy does not prohibit any publication of matter which is of public or general interest.

In determining the scope of this rule, aid would be afforded by the analogy, in the law of libel and slander, of cases which deal with the qualified privilege of comment and criticism on matters of public and general interest.[42] There are of course difficulties in applying such a rule, but they are inherent in the subject-matter, and are certainly no greater than those which exist in many other branches of the law,— for instance, in that large class of cases in which reasonableness or unreasonableness of an act is made the test of liability. The design of the law must be to protect those persons with whose affairs the community has no legitimate concern, from being dragged into an undesirable and undesired publicity and to protect all persons, whatsoever; their position or station, from having matters which they may properly prefer to keep private, made public against their will. It is the unwarranted invasion of individual privacy which is reprehended, and to be, so far as possible, prevented. The distinction, however, noted in the above statement is obvious and fundamental. There are persons who may reasonably claim as a right, protection from the notoriety entailed by being made the victims of journalistic enterprise. There are others who, in varying degrees, have renounced the right to live their lives screened from public observation. Matters which men of the first class may justly contend, concern themselves alone, may in those of the second be the subject of legitimate interest to their fellow-citizens. Peculiarities of manner and person, which in the ordinary individual should be free from comment, may acquire a public importance, if found in a candidate for political office. Some further discrimination is necessary, therefore, than to class facts or deeds as public or private according to a standard to be applied to the fact or deed *per se*. To publish of a modest and retiring individual that he suffers from an impediment in his speech or that he cannot spell correctly, is an unwarranted, if not an unexampled, infringement of his rights, while to state and comment on the same characteristics found in a would-be congressman could not be regarded as beyond the pale of propriety.

The general object in view is to protect the privacy of private life, and to whatever degree and in whatever connection a man's life has ceased to be private, before the publication under consideration has been made, to that extent the protection is to be withdrawn.[43] Since, then, the propriety of publishing the very same facts may depend wholly upon the person concerning whom they are published, no fixed formula can be used to prohibit obnoxious publications. Any rule of liability adopted must have in it an elasticity which shall take account of the varying circumstances of each case,—a necessity which unfortunately renders such a doctrine not only more difficult of application, but also to a certain extent uncertain in its operation and easily rendered abortive. Besides, it is only the more flagrant breaches of decency and propriety that could in practice be reached, and it is not perhaps desirable even to attempt to repress everything which the nicest taste and keenest sense of the respect due to private life would condemn.

In general, then, the matters of which the publication should be repressed may be described as those which concern the private life, habits, acts, and relations of an individual, and have no legitimate connection with his fitness for a public office which he seeks or for which he is suggested, or for any public or quasi public position which he seeks or for which he is suggested, and have no legitimate relation to or bearing upon any act done by him in a public or quasi public capacity. The foregoing is not designed as a wholly accurate or exhaustive definition, since that which must ultimately in a vast number of cases become a question of individual judgment and opinion is incapable of such definition; but it is an attempt to indicate broadly the class of matters referred to. Some things all men alike are entitled to keep from popular curiosity, whether in public life or not, while others are only private because the persons concerned have not assumed a position which makes their doings legitimate matters of public investigation.[44]

2. The right to privacy does not prohibit the communication of any matter, though in its nature private, when the publication is made under circumstances which would render it a privileged communication according to the law of slander and libel.

Under this rule, the right to privacy is not invaded by any publication made in a court of justice, in legislative bodies, or the committees of those bodies; in municipal assemblies, or the committees of such assemblies, or practically by any communication made in any other public body, municipal or parochial, or in any body quasi public, like the large voluntary associations formed for almost every purpose of benevolence, business, or other general interest; and (at least in many jurisdictions) reports of any such proceedings would in some measure be accorded a like privilege.[45] Nor would the rule prohibit any publication made by one in the discharge of some public or private duty, whether legal or moral, or in conduct of one's own affairs, in matters where his own interest is concerned.[46]

3. The law would probably not grant any redress for the invasion of privacy by oral publication in the absence of special damage.

The same reasons exist for distinguishing between oral and written publications of private matters, as is afforded in the law of defamation by the restricted liability for slander as compared with the liability for libel.[47] The injury resulting from such oral communications would ordinarily be so trifling that the law might well, in the interest of free speech, disregard it altogether.[48]

4. The right to privacy ceases upon the publication of the facts by the individual, or with his consent.

This is but another application of the rule which has become familiar in the law of literary and artistic property. The cases there decided establish also what should be deemed a publication,—the important principle in this connection being that a private communication of circulation for a restricted purpose is not a publication within the meaning of the law.[49]

5. The truth of the matter published does not afford a defence. Obviously this branch of the law should have no concern with the truth or falsehood or the matters published. It is not for injury to the individual's character that redress or prevention is sought, but for injury to the right of privacy. For the former, the law of slander and libel provides perhaps a sufficient safeguard. The latter implies the right not merely to prevent inaccurate portrayal of private life, but to prevent its being depicted at all.[50]

6. The absence of "malice" in the publisher does not afford a defence.

Personal ill-will is not an ingredient of the offence, any more than in an ordinary case of trespass to person or to property. Such malice is never necessary to be shown in an action for libel or slander at common law, except in rebuttal of some defence, *e.g.,* that the occasion rendered the communication privileged, or, under the statutes in this State and elsewhere, that the statement complained of was true. The invasion of the privacy that is to be protected is equally complete and equally injurious, whether the motives by which the speaker or writer was actuated are, taken by themselves, culpable or not; just as the damage to character, and to some extent the tendency to provoke a breach of the peace, is equally the result of defamation without regard to the motives leading to its publication. Viewed as a wrong to the individual, this rule is the same pervading the whole law of torts, by which one is held responsible for his intentional acts, even though they are committed with no sinister intent; and viewed as a wrong to society, it is the same principle adopted in a large category of statutory offences.

The remedies for an invasion of the right of privacy are also suggested by those administered in the law of defamation, and in the law of literary and artistic property, namely:—

1. An action of tort for damages in all cases.[51] Even in the absence of special damages, substantial compensation could be allowed for injury to feelings as in the action of slander and libel.
2. An injunction, perhaps a very limited class of cases.[52]

It would doubtless be desirable that the privacy of the individual should receive the added protection of the criminal law, but for this, legislation would be required.[53] Perhaps it would be deemed proper to bring the criminal liability for such publication within narrower limits; but that the community has an interest in preventing such invasions of privacy, sufficiently strong to justify the introduction of such a remedy, cannot be doubted. Still, the protection of society must come mainly through a recognition of the rights of the individual. Each man is responsible for his own acts and omissions only. If he condones what he reprobates, with a weapon at hand equal to his defence, he is responsible for the results. If he resists, public opinion will rally to his support. Has he then such a weapon? It is believed that the common law provides him with one, forged in the slow fire of the centuries, and to-day fitly tempered to his hand. The common law has always recognized a man's house as his castle, impregnable, often, even to its own officers engaged in the execution of its commands. Shall the courts thus close the front entrance to constituted authority, and open wide the back door to idle or prurient curiosity?

NOTES

1 Year Book, Lib. Ass., folio 99, pl. 60 (1348 or 1349), appears to be the first reported case where damages were recovered for a civil assault.
2 These nuisances are technically injuries to property; but the recognition

of the right to have property free from interference by such nuisances involves also a recognition of the value of human sensations.

3 Year Book, Lib. Ass., folio 177, pl. 19 (1356), (2 Finl. Reeves Eng. Law, 395) seems to be the earliest reported case of an action for slander.

4 Winsmore *v.* Greenbank, Willes, 577 (1745).

5 Loss of service is the gist of the action; but it has been said that "we are not aware of any reported case brought by a parent where the value of such services was held to be the measure of damages." Cassoday, J., in Lavery *v.* Crooke, 52 Wis. 612, 623 (1881). First the fiction of constructive service was invented; Martin *v.* Payne, 9 John. 387 (1812). Then the feelings of the parent, the dishonor to himself and his family, were accepted as the most important element of damage. Bedford *v.* McKowl, 3 Esp. 119 (1800); Andrews *v.* Askey, 8 C. & P. 7 (1837); Phillips *v.* Hoyle, 4 Gray, 568 (1855); Phelin *v.* Kenderdine, 20 Pa. St. 354 (1853). The allowance of these damages would seem to be a recognition that the invasion upon the honor of the family is an injury to the parent's person, for ordinarily mere injury to parental feelings is not an element of damage, *e.g.*, the suffering of the parent in case of physical injury to the child. Flemington *v.* Smithers, 2 C. & P. 292 (1827); Black *v.* Carrolton R. R. Co., 10 La. Ann. 33 (1855); Covington Street Ry. Co. *v.* Packer, 9 Bush, 455 (1872).

6 "The notion of Mr. Justice Yates that nothing is property which cannot be earmarked and recovered in detinue or trover, may be true in an early stage of society, when property is in its simple form, and the remedies for violation of it also simple, but is not true in a more civilized state, when the relations of life and the interests arising therefrom are complicated." Erle, J., in Jefferys *v.* Boosey, 4 H. L. C. 815, 869 (1854).

7 Copyright appears to have been first recognized as a species of private property in England in 1558. Drone on Copyright, 54, 61.

8 Gibblett *v.* Read, 9 Mod. 459 (1743), is probably the first recognition of goodwill as property.

9 Hogg *v.* Kirby, 8 Ves. 215 (1803). As late as 1742 Lord Hardwicke refused to treat a trade-mark as property for infringement upon which an injunction could be granted. Blanchard *v.* Hill, 2 Atk. 484.

10 Cooley on Torts, 2d ed., p. 29.

11 8 Amer. Law Reg. N.S. 1 (1869); 12 Wash. Law Rep. 353 (1884); 24 Sol. J. & Rep. 4 (1879).

12 Scribner's Magazine, July, 1890. "The Rights of the Citizen: To his Reputation," by E. L. Godkin, Esq., pp. 65, 67.

13 Marion Manola *v.* Stevens & Myers, N.Y. Supreme Court, "New York Times" of June 15, 18, 21, 1890. There the complainant alleged that while she was playing in the Broadway Theatre, in a role which required her appearance in tights, she was, by means of a flash light, photographed surreptitiously and without her consent, from one of the boxes by defendant Stevens, the manager of the "Castle in the Air" company, and

defendant Myers, a photographer, and prayed that the defendants might be restrained from making use of the photograph taken. A preliminary injunction issued *ex parte*, and a time was set for argument of the motion that the injunction should be made permanent, but no one then appeared in opposition.

14 Though the legal value of "feelings" is now generally recognized, distinctions have been drawn between the several classes of cases in which compensation may or may not be recovered. Thus, the fright occasioned by an assault constitutes a cause of action, but fright occasioned by negligence does not. So fright coupled with bodily injury affords a foundation for enhanced damages; but, ordinarily, fright unattended by bodily injury cannot be relied upon as an element of damages, even where a valid cause of action exists, as in trespass *quare clausum fregit*. Wyman v. Leavitt, 71 Me. 227; Canning v. Williamstown, 1 Cush. 451. The allowance of damages for injury to the parents' feelings, in case of seduction, abduction of a child (Stowe v. Heywood, 7 All. 118), or removal of the corpse of child from a burial-ground (Meagher v. Driscoll, 99 Mass. 281), are said to be exceptions to a general rule. On the other hand, injury to feelings is a recognized element of damages in actions of slander and libel, and of malicious prosecution. These distinctions between the cases, where injury to feelings does and where it does not constitute a cause of action or legal element of damages, are not logical, but doubtless serve well as practical rules. It will, it is believed, be found, upon examination of the authorities, that wherever substantial mental suffering would be the natural and probable result of the act, there compensation for injury to feelings has been allowed, and that where no mental suffering would ordinarily result, or if resulting, would naturally be but trifling, and, being unaccompanied by visible signs of injury, would afford a wide scope for imaginative ills, there damages have been disallowed. The decisions on this subject illustrate well the subjection in our law of logic to common-sense.

15 "Injuria, in the narrower sense, is every intentional and illegal violation of honour, *i.e.*, the whole personality of another." "Now an outrage is committed not only when a man shall be struck with the fist, say, or with a club, or even flogged, but also if abusive language has been used to one." Salkowski, Roman Law, p. 668 and p. 669, n. 2.

16 "It is certain every man has a right to keep his own sentiments, if he pleases. He has certainly a right to judge whether he will make them public, or commit them only to the sight of his friends." Yates, J., in Millar v. Taylor, 4 Burr. 2303, 2379 (1769).

17 Nicols v. Pitman, 26 Ch. D. 374 (1884).

18 Lee v. Simpson, 3 C. B. 871, 881; Daly v. Palmer, 6 Blatchf. 256.

19 Turner v. Robinson, 10 Ir. Ch. 121; s.c. ib. 510.

20 Drone on Copyright, 102.

21 "Assuming the law to be so, what is its foundation in this respect? It is not, I conceive, referable to any consideration peculiarly literary. Those with whom our common law originated had not probably among their

many merits that of being patrons of letters; but they knew the duty and necessity of protecting property, and with that general object laid down rules providently expansive,—rules capable of adapting themselves to the various forms and modes of property which peace and cultivation might discover and introduce.

"The produce of mental labor, thoughts and sentiments, recorded and preserved by writing, became, as knowledge went onward and spread, and the culture of man's understanding advanced, a kind of property impossible to disregard, and the interference of modern legislation upon the subject, by the stat. 8 Anne, professing by its title to be 'For the encouragement of learning,' and using the words 'taken the liberty,' in the preamble, whether it operated in augmentation or diminution of the private rights of authors, having left them to some extent untouched, it was found that the common law, in providing for the protection of property, provided for their security, at least before general publication by the writer's consent." Knight Bruce, V. C., in Prince Albert *v.* Strange, 2 DeGex & Sm. 652, 695 (1849).

22 "The question, however, does not turn upon the form or amount of mischief or advantage, loss or gain. The author of manuscripts, whether he is famous or obscure, low or high, has a right to say of them, if innocent, that whether interesting or dull, light or heavy, saleable or unsaleable, they shall not, without his consent, be published." Knight Bruce, V. C., in Prince Albert *v.* Strange, 2 DeGex & Sm. 652, 694.

23 Duke of Queensberry *v.* Shebbeare, 2 Eden, 329 (1758); Bartlett *v.* Crittenden, 5 McLean, 32, 41 (1849).

24 Drone on Copyright, pp. 102, 104; Parton *v.* Prang, 3 Clifford, 537, 548 (1872); Jefferys *v.* Boosey, 4 H. L. C. 815, 867, 962 (1854).

25 "The question will be whether the bill has stated facts of which the court can take notice, as a case of civil property, which it is bound to protect. The injunction cannot be maintained on any principle of this sort, that if a letter has been written in the way of friendship, either the continuance or the discontinuance of the friendship affords a reason for the interference of the court." Lord Eldon in Gee *v.* Pritchard, 2 Swanst. 402, 413 (1818).

"Upon the principle, therefore, of protecting property, it is that the common law, in cases not aided or prejudiced by statute, shelters the privacy and seclusion of thought and sentiments committed to writing, and desired by the author to remain not generally known." Knight Bruce, V. C., in Prince Albert *v.* Strange, 2 DeGex & Sm. 652, 695.

"It being conceded that reasons of expediency and public policy can never be made the sole basis of civil jurisdiction, the question, whether upon any ground the plaintiff can be entitled to the relief which he claims, remains to be answered; and it appears to us that there is only one ground upon which his title to claim, and our jurisdiction to grant, the relief, can be placed. We must be satisfied, that the publication of private letters, without the consent of the writer, is an invasion of an exclusive right of property which remains in the writer, even when the letters have been sent to, and are still in the possession of his correspondent." Duer, J., in Woolsey, *v.* Judd, 4 Duer, 379, 384 (1855).

26 "A work lawfully published, in the popular sense of the term, stands in this respect, I conceive, differently from a work which has never been in that situation. The former may be liable to be translated, abridged, analyzed, exhibited in morsels, complimented, and otherwise treated, in a manner that the latter is not.

"Suppose, however,—instead of a translation, an abridgment, or a review,—the case of a catalogue,—suppose a man to have composed a variety of literary works ('innocent,' to use Lord Eldon's expression), which he has never printed or published, or lost the right to prohibit from being published,—suppose a knowledge of them unduly obtained by some unscrupulous person, who prints with a view to circulation a descriptive catalogue, or even a mere list of the manuscripts, without authority or consent, does the law allow this? I hope and believe not. The same principles that prevent more candid piracy must, I conceive, govern such a case also.

"By publishing of a man that he has written to particular persons, or on particular subjects, he may be exposed, not merely to sarcasm, he may be ruined. There may be in his possession returned letters that he had written to former correspondents, with whom to have had relations, however harmlessly, may not in after life be a recommendation; or his writings may be otherwise of a kind squaring in no sort with his outward habits and worldly position. There are callings even now in which to be convicted of literature, is dangerous, though the danger is sometimes escaped.

"Again, the manuscripts may be those of a man on account of whose name alone a mere list would be matter of general curiosity. How many persons could be mentioned, a catalogue of whose unpublished writings would, during their lives or afterwards, command a ready sale!" Knight Bruce, V. C., in Prince Albert *v.* Strange, 2 DeGex & Sm. 652, 693.

27 "A copy or impression of the etchings would only be a means of communicating knowledge and information of the original, and does not a list and description of the same? The means are different, but the object and effect are similar; for in both, the object and effect is to make known to the public more or less of the unpublished work and composition of the author, which he is entitled to keep wholly for his private use and pleasure, and to withhold altogether, or so far as he may please, from the knowledge of others. Cases upon abridgments, translations, extracts, and criticisms of published works have no reference whatever to the present question; they all depend upon the extent of right under the acts respecting copyright, and have no analogy to the exclusive rights in the author of unpublished compositions which depend entirely upon the common-law right of property." Lord Cottenham in Prince Albert *v.* Strange, 1 McN. & G. 23, 43 (1849). "Mr. Justice Yates, in Millar *v.* Taylor, said, that an author's case was exactly similar to that of an inventor of a new

mechanical machine; that both original inventions stood upon the same
footing in point of property, whether the case were mechanical or literary,
whether an epic poem or an orrery; that the immorality of pirating another man's invention was as great as that of purloining his ideas. Property
in mechanical works or works of art, executed by a man for his own
amusement, instruction, or use, is allowed to subsist, certainly, and may,
before publication by him, be invaded, not merely by copying, but by
description or by catalogue, as it appears to me. A catalogue of such works
may in itself be valuable. It may also as effectually show the bent and turn
of the mind, the feelings and taste of the artist, especially if not professional, as a list of his papers. The portfolio or the studio may declare as
much as the writing-table. A man may employ himself in private in a
manner very harmless, but which, disclosed to society, may destroy the
comfort of his life, or even his success in it. Every one, however, has a
right, I apprehend, to say that the produce of his private hours is not
more liable to publication without his consent, because the publication
must be creditable or advantageous to him, than it would be in opposite
circumstances."

"I think, therefore, not only that the defendant here is unlawfully
invading the plaintiff's rights, but also that the invasion is of such a kind
and affects such property as to entitle the plaintiff to the preventive
remedy of an injunction; and if not the more, yet, certainly, not the less,
because it is an intrusion,—an unbecoming and unseemly intrusion,—an
intrusion not alone in breach of conventional rules, but offensive to that
inbred sense of propriety natural to every man,—if intrusion, indeed, fitly
describes a sordid spying into the privacy of domestic life,—into the home
(a word hitherto sacred among us), the home of a family whose life and
conduct form an acknowledged title, though not their only unquestionable
title, to the most marked respect in this country." Knight Bruce, V. C.,
in Prince Albert *v.* Strange, 2 DeGex & Sm. 652, 696, 697.

28 Kiernan *v.* Manhattan Quotation Co., 50 How. Pr. 194 (1876).
29 "The defendants' counsel say, that a man acquiring a knowledge of another's property without his consent is not by any rule or principle which
a court of justice can apply (however secretly he may have kept or en-
deavored to keep it) forbidden without his consent to communicate and
publish that knowledge to the world, to inform the world what the property is, or to describe it publicly, whether orally, or in print or writing.

"I claim, however, leave to doubt whether, as to property of a private
nature, which the owner, without infringing on the right of any other,
may and does retain in a state of privacy, it is certain that a person who,
without the owner's consent, express or implied, acquires a knowledge of
it, can lawfully avail himself of the knowledge so acquired to publish
without his consent a description of the property.

"It is probably true that such a publication may be in a manner or relate
to property of a kind rendering a question concerning the lawfulness of
the act too slight to deserve attention. I can conceive cases, however, in

which an act of the sort may be so circumstanced or relate to property such, that the matter may weightily affect the owner's interest or feelings, or both. For instance, the nature and intention of an unfinished work of an artist, prematurely made known to the world, may be painful and deeply prejudicial against him; nor would it be difficult to suggest other examples. . . .

"It was suggested that, to publish a catalogue of a collector's gems, coins, antiquities, or other such curiosities, for instance, without his consent, would be to make use of his property without his consent; and it is true, certainly, that a proceeding of that kind may not only as much embitter one collector's life as it would flatter another,—may be not only an ideal calamity,—but may do the owner damage in the most vulgar sense. Such catalogues, even when not descriptive, are often sought after, and sometimes obtain very substantial prices. These, therefore, and the like instances, are not necessarily examples merely of pain inflicted in point of sentiment or imagination; they may be that, and something else beside." Knight Bruce, V. C., in Prince Albert *v.* Strange, 2 DeGex & Sm. 652, 689, 690.

30 Hoyt *v.* Mackenzie, 3 Barb. Ch. 320, 324 (1848); Wetmore *v.* Scovell, 3 Edw. Ch. 515 (1842). See Sir Thomas Plumer in 2 Ves. & B. 19 (1813).

31 Woolsey *v.* Judd, 4 Duer, 379, 404 (1855). "It has been decided, fortunately for the welfare of society, that the writer of letters, though written without any purpose of profit, or any idea of literary property, possesses such a right of property in them, that they cannot be published without his consent, unless the purposes of justice, civil or criminal, require the publication." Sir Samuel Romilly, *arg.,* in Gee *v.* Pritchard, 2 Swanst. 402, 418 (1818). But see High on Injunctions, 3d ed, § 1012, *contra.*

32 "But a doubt has been suggested, whether mere private letters, not intended as literary compositions, are entitled to the protection of an injunction in the same manner as compositions of a literary character. This doubt has probably arisen from the habit of not discriminating between the different rights of property which belong to an unpublished manuscript, and those which belong to a published book. The latter, as I have intimated in another connection, is a right to take the profits of publication. The former is a right to control the act of publication, and to decide whether there shall be any publication at all. It has been called a right of property; an expression perhaps not quite satisfactory, but on the other hand sufficiently descriptive of a right which, however incorporeal, involves many of the essential elements of property, and is at least positive and definite. This expression can leave us in no doubt as to the meaning of the learned judges who have used it, when they have applied it to cases of unpublished manuscripts. They obviously intended to use it in no other sense, than in contradistinction to the mere interests of feeling, and to describe a substantial right of legal interest." Curtis on Copyright, pp. 93, 94.

The resemblance of the right to prevent publication of an unpublished manuscript to the well-recognized rights of personal immunity is found in the treatment of it in connection with the rights of creditors. The right to prevent such publication and the right of action for its infringement, like the cause of action for an assault, battery, defamation, or malicious prosecution, are not assets available to creditors.

"There is no law which can compel an author to publish. No one can determine this essential matter of publication but the author. His manuscripts, however valuable, cannot, without his consent, be seized by his creditors as property." McLean, J., in Bartlett *v.* Crittenden, 5 McLean, 32, 37 (1849).

It has also been held that even where the sender's rights are not asserted, the receiver of a letter has not such property in it as passes to his executor or administrator as a salable asset. Eyre *v.* Higbee, 22 How. Pr. (N.Y.) 198 (1861).

"The very meaning of the word 'property' in its legal sense is 'that which is peculiar or proper to any person; that which belongs exclusively to one.' The first meaning of the word from which it is derived—*proprius*—is 'one's own.' " Drone on Copyright, p. 6.

It is clear that a thing must be capable of identification in order to be the subject of exclusive ownership. But when its identity can be determined so that individual ownership may be asserted, it matters not whether it be corporeal or incorporeal.

33 "Such then being, as I believe, the nature and the foundation of the common law as to manuscripts independently of Parliamentary additions and subtractions, its operation cannot of necessity be confined to literary subjects. That would be to limit the rule by the example. Wherever the produce of labor is liable to invasion in an analogous manner, there must, I suppose, be a title to analogous protection or redress." Knight Bruce, V. C., in Prince Albert *v.* Strange, 2 DeGex & Sm. 652, 696.

34 "The question, therefore, is whether a photographer who has been employed by a customer to take his or her portrait is justified in striking off copies of such photograph for his own use, and selling and disposing of them, or publicly exhibiting them by way of advertisement or otherwise, without the authority of such customer, either express or implied. I say 'express or implied,' because a photographer is frequently allowed, on his own request, to take a photograph of a person under circumstances in which a subsequent sale by him must have been in the contemplation of both parties, though not actually mentioned. To the question thus put, my answer is in the negative, that the photographer is not justified in so doing. Where a person obtains information in the course of a confidential employment, the law does not permit him to make any improper use of the information so obtained; and an injunction is granted, if necessary, to restrain such use; as, for instance, to restrain a clerk from disclosing his master's accounts, or an attorney from making known his client's affairs, learned in the course of such employment. Again, the law is clear that a breach of contract, whether express or implied, can be restrained by

injunction. In my opinion the case of the photographer comes within the principles upon which both these classes of cases depend. The object for which he is employed and paid is to supply his customer with the required number of printed photographs of a given subject. For this purpose the negative is taken by the photographer on glass; and from this negative copies can be printed in much larger numbers than are generally required by the customer. The customer who sits for the negative thus puts the power of reproducing the object in the hands of the photographer; and in my opinion the photographer who uses the negative to produce other copies for his own use, without authority, is abusing the power confidentially placed in his hands merely for the purpose of supplying the customer; and further, I hold that the bargain between the customer and the photographer includes, by implication, an agreement that the prints taken from the negative are to be appropriated to the use of the customer only." Referring to the opinions delivered in Tuck v. Priester, 19 Q. B. D. 639, the learned justice continued: "Then Lord Justice Lindley says: 'I will deal first with the injunction, which stands, or may stand, on a totally different footing from either the penalties or the damages. It appears to me that the relation between the plaintiffs and the defendant was such that, whether the plaintiffs had any copyright or not, the defendant has done that which renders him liable to an injunction. He was employed by the plaintiffs to make a certain number of copies of the picture, and that employment carried with it the necessary implication that the defendant was not to make more copies for himself, or to sell the additional copies in this country in competition with his employer. Such conduct on his part is a gross breach of contract and a gross breach of faith, and, in my judgment, clearly entitles the plaintiffs to an injunction whether they have a copyright in the picture or not.' That case is the more noticeable, as the contract was in writing; and yet it was held to be an implied condition that the defendant should not make any copies for himself. The phrase 'a gross breach of faith' used by Lord Justice Lindley in that case applies with equal force to the present, when a lady's feelings are shocked by finding that the photographer she has employed to take her likeness for her own use is publicly exhibiting and selling copies thereof." North, J., in Pollard v. Photographic Co., 40 Ch. D. 345, 349–352 (1888).

"It may be said also that the cases to which I have referred are all cases in which there was some right of property infringed, based upon the recognition by the law of protection being due for the products of a man's own skill or mental labor; whereas in the present case the person photographed has done nothing to merit such protection, which is meant to prevent legal wrongs, and not mere sentimental grievances. But a person whose photograph is taken by a photographer is not thus deserted by the law; for the Act of 25 and 26 Vict., c. 68, s.1, provides that when the negative of any photograph is made or executed for or on behalf of another person for a good or valuable consideration, the person making or executing the same shall not retain the copyright thereof, unless it is expressly reserved to him by agreement in writing signed by the person for or on whose behalf the same is so made or executed; but the copyright shall belong to the person for or on whose behalf the same shall have been made or executed.

"The result is that in the present case the copyright in the photograph is in one of the plaintiffs. It is true, no doubt, that sect. 4 of the same act provides that no proprietor of copyright shall be entitled to the benefit of the act until registration, and no action shall be sustained in respect of anything done before registration; and it was, I presume, because the photograph of the female plaintiff has not been registered that this act was not referred to by counsel in the course of the argument. But, although the protection against the world in general conferred by the act cannot be enforced until after registration, this does not deprive the plaintiffs of their common-law right of action against the defendant for his breach of contract and breach of faith. This is quite clear from the cases of Morison *v.* Moat [9 Hare, 241] and Tuck *v.* Priester [19 Q. B. D. 629] already referred to, in which latter case the same act of Parliament was in question." Per North, J., ibid. p. 352.

This language suggests that the property right in photographs or portraits may be one created by statute, which would not exist in the absence of registration; but it is submitted that it must eventually be held here, as it has been in the similar cases, that the statute provision becomes applicable only when there is a publication, and that before the act of registering there is property in the thing upon which the statute is to operate.

35 Duke of Queensberry *v.* Shebbeare, 2 Eden, 329; Murray *v.* Heath, 1 B. & Ad. 804; Tuck *v.* Priester, 19 Q. B. D. 629.

36 See Mr. Justice Story in Folsom *v.* Marsh, 2 Story, 100, 111 (1841):—

"If he [the recipient of a letter] attempt to publish such letter or letters on other occasions, not justifiable, a court of equity will prevent the publication by an injunction, as a breach of private confidence or contract, or of the rights of the author; and *a fortiori,* if he attempt to publish them for profit; for then it is not a mere breach of confidence or contract, but it is a violation of the exclusive copyright of the writer. . . . The general property, and the general rights incident to property, belong to the writer, whether the letters are literary compositions, or familiar letters, or details of facts, or letters of business. The general property in the manuscripts remains in the writer and his representatives, as well as the general copyright. *A fortiori,* third persons, standing in no privity with either party, are not entitled to publish them, to subserve their own private purposes of interest, or curiosity, or passion."

37 "The receiver of a letter is not a bailee, nor does he stand in a character analogous to that of a bailee. There is no right to possession, present or future, in the writer. The only right to be enforced against the holder is a right to prevent publication, not to require the manuscript from the

holder in order to a publication of himself." Per Hon. Joel Parker, quoted in Grigsby v. Breckenridge, 2 Bush. 480, 489 (1867).

38 In Morison v. Moat, 9 Hare, 241, 255 (1851), a suit for an injunction to restrain the use of a secret medical compound, Sir George James Turner, V. C., said: "That the court has exercised jurisdiction in cases of this nature does not, I think, admit of any question. Different grounds have indeed been assigned for the exercise of that jurisdiction. In some cases it has been referred to property, in others to contract, and in others, again, it has been treated as founded upon trust or confidence,—meaning, as I conceive, that the court fastens the obligation on the conscience of the party, and enforces it against him in the same manner as it enforces against a party to whom a benefit is given, the obligation of performing a promise on the faith of which the benefit has been conferred; but upon whatever grounds the jurisdiction is founded, the authorities leave no doubt as to the exercise of it."

39 A similar growth of the law showing the development of contractual rights into rights of property is found in the law of goodwill. There are indications, as early as the Year Books, of traders endeavoring to secure to themselves by contract the advantages now designated by the term "goodwill," but it was not until 1743 that goodwill received legal recognition as property apart from the personal covenants of the traders. See Allan on Goodwill, pp. 2, 3.

40 The application of an existing principle to a new state of facts is not judicial legislation. To call it such is to assert that the existing body of law consists practically of the statutes and decided cases, and to deny that the principles (of which these cases are ordinarily said to be evidence) exist at all. It is not the application of an existing principle to new cases, but the introduction of a new principle, which is properly termed judicial legislation.

But even the fact that a certain decision would involve judicial legislation should not be taken as conclusive against the propriety of making it. This power has been constantly exercised by our judges, when applying to a new subject principles of private justice, moral fitness, and public convenience. Indeed, the elasticity of our law, its adaptability to new conditions, the capacity for growth, which has enabled it to meet the wants of an ever changing society and to apply immediate relief for every recognized wrong, have been its greatest boast.

"I cannot understand how any person who has considered the subject can suppose that society could possibly have gone on if judges had not legislated, or that there is any danger whatever in allowing them that power which they have in fact exercised, to make up for the negligence or the incapacity of the avowed legislator. That part of the law of every country which was made by judges has been far better made than that part which consists of statutes enacted by the legislature." 1 Austin's Jurisprudence, p. 224.

The cases referred to above show that the common law has for a century and a half protected privacy in certain cases, and to grant the further protection now suggested would be merely another application of an existing rule.

41 Loi Relative à la Presse. 11 Mai 1868.

"11. Toute publication dans un écrit périodique relative à un fait de la vie privée constitue une contravention punie d'un amende de cinq cent francs.

"La poursuite ne pourra être exercée que sur la plainte de la partie interessée." Riviére, Codes Francais et Lois Usuelles. App. Code Pen., p. 20.

42 See Campbell *v.* Spottiswoode, 3 B. & S. 769, 776; Henwood *v.* Harrison, L. R. 7 C. P. 606; Gott *v.* Pulsifer, 122 Mass. 235.

43 "Nos moeurs n'admettent pas la prétention d'enlever aux investigations de la publicité les actes qui relèvent de la vie publique, et ce dernier mot ne doit pas être restreint à la vie officielle ou à celle du fonctionnaire. Tout homme qui appelle sur lui l'attention ou les regards du publique, soit par une mission qu'il a reçue ou qu'il se donne, soit par le rôle qu'il s'attribue dans l'industrie, les arts, le theâtre, etc., ne peut plus invoquer contre la critique ou l'exposé de sa conduite d'autre protection que les lois qui repriment la diffamation et l'injure." Circ. Mins. Just., 4 Juin, 1868. Rivière Codes Français et Lois Usuelles, App. Code Pen. 20 n (b).

44 "Celui-la seul a droit au silence absolu qui n'a pas expressément ou in-directment provoqué ou authorisé l'attention, l'approbation ou le blâme." Circ. Mins. Just., 4 Juin, 1868. Rivière Codes Français et Lois Usuelles, App. Code Pen. 20 n (b).

The principle thus expressed evidently is designed to exclude the wholesale investigations into the past of prominent public men with which the American public is too familiar, and also, unhappily, too well pleased; while not entitled to the "silence *absolu*" which less prominent men may claim as their due, they may still demand that all the details of private life in its most limited sense shall not be laid bare for inspection.

45 Wason *v.* Walters, L. R. 4 Q. B. 73; Smith *v.* Higgins, 16 Gray, 251; Barrows *v.* Bell, 7 Gray, 331.

46 This limitation upon the right to prevent the publication of private letters was recognized early:—

"But, consistently with this right [of the writer of letters], the persons to whom they are addressed may have, nay, must, by implication, possess, the right to publish any letter or letters addressed to them, upon such occasions, as require, or justify, the publication or public use of them; but this right is strictly limited to such occasions. Thus, a person may justifiably use and publish, in a suit at law or in equity, such letter or letters as are necessary and proper, to establish his right to maintain the suit, or defend the same. So, if he be aspersed or misrepresented by the writer, or accused of improper conduct, in a public manner, he may publish such parts of such letter or letters, but no more, as may be necessary to vindicate his

character and reputation, or free him from unjust obloquy and reproach."
Story, J., in Folsom *v.* Marsh, 2 Story, 100, 110, 111 (1841).

The existence of any right in the recipient of letters to publish the same
has been strenuously denied by Mr. Drone; but the reasoning upon which
his denial rests does not seem satisfactory. Drone on Copyright, pp. 136–
139.

47 Townshend on Slander and Libel, 4th ed., § 18; Odgers on Libel and
Slander, 2d ed., p. 3.

48 "But as long as gossip was oral, it spread, as regards any one individual,
over a very small area, and was confined to the immediate circle of his
acquaintances. It did not reach, or but rarely reached, those who knew
nothing of him. It did not make his name, or his walk, or his conversation
familiar to strangers. And what is more to the purpose, it spared him the
pain and mortification of knowing that he was gossipped about. A man
seldom heard of oral gossip about him which simply made him ridiculous,
or trespassed on his lawful privacy, but made no positive attack upon his
reputation. His peace and comfort were, therefore, but slightly affected
by it." E. L. Godkin, "The Rights of the Citizen: To his Reputation."
Scribner's Magazine, July, 1890, p. 66.

Vice-Chancellor Knight Bruce suggested in Prince Albert *v.* Strange,
2 DeGex & Sm. 652, 694, that a distinction would be made as to the right
of privacy of works of art between an oral and a written description or
catalogue.

49 See Drone on Copyright, pp. 121, 289, 290.

50 Compare the French law.

"En prohibant l'envahissement de la vie privée, sans qu'il soit nêcessaire
d'établir l'intention criminelle, la loi a entendue interdire toute discussion
de la part de la défense sur la vérité des faits. Le remède eut été pire que
le mal, si un débat avait pu s'engager sur ce terrain." Circ. Mins. Just., 4
Juin, 1868. Rivière Code Français et Lois Usuelles, App. Code Penn. 20
n(a).

51 Comp. Drone on Copyright, p. 107.

52 Comp. High on Injunctions, 3d ed., § 1015; Townshend on Libel and
Slander, 4th ed., §§ 417a–417d.

53 The following draft of a bill has been prepared by William H. Dunbar,
Esq., of the Boston bar, as a suggestion for possible legislation:—

"Section 1. Whoever publishes in any newspaper, journal, magazine,
or other periodical publication any statement concerning the private life
or affairs of another, after being requested in writing by such other person
not to publish such statement or any statement concerning him, shall be
punished by imprisonment in the State prison not exceeding five years,
or by imprisonment in the jail not exceeding two years, or by fine not
exceeding one thousand dollars; provided, that no statement concerning
the conduct of any person in, or the qualifications of any person for, a
public office or position which such person holds, has held, or is seeking
to obtain, or for which such person is at the time of such publication a

candidate, or for which he or she is then suggested as a candidate, and no statement of or concerning the acts of any person in his or her business, profession, or calling, and no statement concerning any person in relation to a position, profession, business, or calling, bringing such person prominently before the public, or in relation to the qualifications for such a position, business, profession, or calling of any person prominent or seeking prominence before the public, and no statement relating to any act done by any person in a public place, nor any other statement of matter which is of public and general interest, shall be deemed a statement concerning the private life or affairs of such person within the meaning of this act.

"Sect. 2. It shall not be a defence to any criminal prosecution brought under section 1 of this act that the statement complained of is true, or that such statement was published without a malicious intention; but no person shall be liable to punishment for any statement published under such circumstances that if it were defamatory the publication thereof would be privileged."

5

Privacy
[A legal analysis]

WILLIAM L. PROSSER

In the year 1890 Mrs. Samuel D. Warren, a young matron of Boston, which is a large city in Massachusetts, held at her home a series of social entertainments on an elaborate scale. She was the daughter of Senator Bayard of Delaware, and her husband was a wealthy young paper manufacturer, who only the year before had given up the practice of law to devote himself to an inherited business. Socially Mrs. Warren was among the élite; and the newspapers of Boston, and in particular the *Saturday Evening Gazette,* which specialized in "blue blood" items, covered her parties in highly personal and embarrassing detail. It was the era of "yellow journalism," when the press had begun to resort to excesses in the way of prying that have become more or less commonplace today;[1] and Boston was perhaps, of all of the cities in the country, the one in which a lady and a gentleman kept their names and their personal affairs out of the papers. The matter came to a head when the newspapers had a field day on the occasion of the wedding of a daughter, and Mr. Warren became annoyed.[2] It was an annoyance for which the press, the advertisers and the entertainment industry of America were to pay dearly over the next seventy years.

Mr. Warren turned to his recent law partner, Louis D. Brandeis, who was destined not to be unknown to history. The result was a noted article, *The Right to Privacy,*[3] in the *Harvard Law Review,* upon which the two men collaborated. It has come to be regarded as the outstanding example of the influence of legal periodicals upon the American law. In the Harvard Law School class of 1877 the two authors had stood respectively second and first, and both of them were gifted with scholarship, imagination, and ability. Internal evidences of style, and the probabilities of the situation, suggest that the writing, and perhaps most of the research, was done by Brandeis; but

© California Law Review 1960. Reprinted from *California Law Review* 48: 338–423, 1960.

it was undoubtedly a joint effort, to which both men contributed their ideas.

Piecing together old decisions in which relief had been afforded on the basis of defamation, or the invasion of some property right,[4] or a breach of confidence or an implied contract,[5] the article concluded that such cases were in reality based upon a broader principle which was entitled to separate recognition. This principle they called the right to privacy; and they contended that the growing abuses of the press made a remedy upon such a distinct ground essential to the protection of private individuals against the outrageous and unjustifiable infliction of mental distress. This was the first of a long line of law review discussions of the right of privacy,[6] of which this is to be yet one more. With very few exceptions,[7] the writers have agreed, expressly or tacitly, with Warren and Brandeis.

The article had little immediate effect upon the law. The first case to allow recovery upon the independent basis of the right of privacy was an unreported decision[8] of a New York trial judge, when an actress very scandalously, for those days, appeared upon the stage in tights, and the defendant snapped her picture from a box, and was enjoined from publishing it. This was followed by three reported cases in New York,[9] and one in a federal court in Massachusetts,[10] in which the courts appeared to be quite ready to accept the principle. Progress was brought to an abrupt halt, however, when the Michigan court flatly rejected the whole idea, in a case[11] where a brand of cigars was named after a deceased public figure. In 1902 the question reached the Court of Appeals of New York, in the case of *Roberson v. Rochester Folding Box Co.*[12] in which the defendant made use of the picture of a pulchritudinous young lady without her consent to advertise flour, along with the legend, "The Flour of the Family." One might think that the feebleness of the pun might have been enough in itself to predispose the court in favor of recovery; but in a four-to-three decision, over a most vigorous dissent, it rejected Warren and Brandeis and declared that the right of privacy did not exist, and that the plaintiff was entitled to no protection whatever against such conduct. The reasons offered were the lack of precedent, the purely mental character of the injury, the "vast amount of litigation" that might be expected to ensue, the difficulty of drawing any line between public and private figures, and the fear of undue restriction of the freedom of the press.

The immediate result of the *Roberson* case was a storm of public disapproval, which led one of the concurring judges to take the unprecedented step of publishing a law review article in defense of the decision.[13] In consequence the next New York Legislature enacted a statute[14] making it both a misdemeanor and a tort to make use of the name, portrait or picture of any person for "advertising purposes or for the purposes of trade" without his written consent. This act remains the law of New York, where there have been upwards of a hundred decisions dealing with it. Except as the statute itself limits the extent of the right, the New York decisions are quite consistent with the common law as it has been worked out in other states, and they are customarily cited in privacy cases throughout the country.

Three years later the supreme court of Georgia had much the same question presented in *Pavesich v. New England Life Insurance Co.*,[15] when the defendant's insurance advertising made use of the plaintiff's name and picture, as well as a spurious testimonial from him. With the example of New York before it, the Georgia court in turn rejected the *Roberson* case, accepted the views of Warren and Brandeis, and recognized the existence of a distinct right of privacy. This became the leading case.

For the next thirty years there was a continued dispute as to whether the right of privacy existed at all, as the courts elected to follow the *Roberson* or the *Pavesich* case. Along in the thirties, with the benediction of the *Restatement of Torts*,[16] the tide set in strongly in favor of recognition, and the rejecting decisions began to be overruled. At the present time the right of privacy, in one form or another, is declared to exist by the overwhelming majority of the American courts. It is recognized in Alabama,[17] Alaska,[18] Arizona,[19] California,[20] Connecticut,[21] the District of Columbia,[22] Florida,[23] Georgia,[24] Illinois,[25] Indiana,[26] Iowa,[27] Kansas,[28] Kentucky,[29] Louisiana,[30] Michigan,[31] Mississippi,[32] Missouri,[33] Montana,[34] Nevada,[35] New Jersey,[36] North Carolina,[37] Ohio,[38] Oregon,[39] Pennsylvania,[40] South Carolina,[41] Tennessee,[42] and West Virginia.[43] It will in all probability be recognized in Delaware[44] and Maryland,[45] where a federal and a lower court have accepted it; and also in Arkansas,[46] Colorado,[47] Massachusetts,[48] Minnesota,[49] and Washington,[50] where the courts at least have refrained from holding that it does not exist, but the decisions have gone off on other grounds. It is recognized in a limited form by the New York statute,[51] and by similar acts adopted in Oklahoma,[52] Utah,[53] and Virginia.[54]

At the time of writing the right of privacy stands rejected only by a 1909 decision in Rhode Island,[55] and by more recent ones in Nebraska,[56] Texas,[57] and Wisconsin,[58] which have said that any change in the old common law must be for the legislature, and which have not gone without criticism.

In nearly every jurisdiction the first decisions were understandably preoccupied with the question whether the right of privacy existed at all, and gave little or no consideration to what it would amount to if it did. It is only in recent years, and largely through the legal writers, that there has been any attempt to inquire what interests are we protecting, and against what conduct. Today, with something over three hundred cases in the books, the holes in the jigsaw puzzle have been largely filled in, and some rather definite conclusions are possible.

What has emerged from the decisions is no simple matter. It is not one tort, but a complex of four. The law of privacy comprises four distinct kinds of invasion of four different interests of the plaintiff, which are tied together by the common name, but otherwise have almost nothing in common except that each represents an interference with the right of the plaintiff, in the phrase coined by Judge Cooley,[59] "to be let alone." Without any attempt to exact definition, these four torts may be described as follows:

1. Intrusion upon the plaintiff's seclusion or solitude, or into his private affairs.
2. Public disclosure of embarrassing private facts about the plaintiff.
3. Publicity which places the plaintiff in a false light in the public eye.
4. Appropriation, for the defendant's advantage, of the plaintiff's name or likeness.

It should be obvious at once that these four types of invasion may be subject, in some respects at least, to different rules; and that when what is said as to any one of them is carried over to another, it may not be at all applicable, and confusion may follow.

The four may be considered in detail, in order.

I. Intrusion

Warren and Brandeis, who were concerned with the evils of publication, do not appear to have had in mind any such thing as intrusion upon the plaintiff's seclusion or solitude. Nine years before their article was published there had been a Michigan case[60] in which a young man had intruded upon a woman in childbirth, and the court, invalidating her consent because of fraud, had allowed recovery without specifying the ground, which may have been trespass or battery. In retrospect, at least, this was a privacy case. Others have followed, in which the defendant has been held liable for intruding into the plaintiff's home,[61] his hotel room,[62] and a woman's stateroom on a steamboat,[63] and for an illegal search of her shopping bag in a store.[64] The privacy action which has been allowed in such cases will evidently overlap, to a considerable extent at least, the action for trespass to land or chattels.

The principle was, however, soon carried beyond such physical intrusion. It was extended to eavesdropping upon private conversations by means of wire tapping[65] and microphones;[66] and there are three decisions,[67] the last of them aided by a Louisiana criminal statute, which have applied the same principle to peering into the windows of a home. The supreme court of Ohio, which seems to be virtually alone among our courts in refusing to recognize the independent tort of the intentional infliction of mental distress by outrageous conduct,[68] has accomplished the same result[69] under the name of privacy, in a case where a creditor hounded the debtor for a considerable length of time with telephone calls at his home and his place of employment.[70] The tort has been found in the case of unauthorized prying into the plaintiff's bank account,[71] and the same principle has been used to invalidate a blanket subpoena duces tecum requiring the production of all of his books and documents,[72] and an illegal compulsory blood test.[73]

It is clear, however, that there must be something in the nature of prying or intrusion, and mere noises which disturb a church congregation,[74] or bad manners, harsh names and insulting gestures in public,[75] have been held not to be enough. It is also clear that the intrusion must be something which would be offensive or objectionable to a reasonable man, and that there is no tort when the landlord stops by on Sunday morning to ask for the rent.[76]

It is clear also that the thing into which there is prying or intrusion must be, and be entitled to be, private. The plaintiff has no right to complain when his pre-trial testimony is recorded,[77] or when the police, acting within their powers, take his photograph, fingerprints or measurements,[78] or when there is inspection and public disclosure of corporate records which he is required by law to keep and make available.[79] On the public street, or in any other public place, the plaintiff has no right to be alone, and it is no invasion of his privacy to do no more than follow him about.[80] Neither is it such an invasion to take his photograph in such a place,[81] since this amounts to nothing more than making a record, not differing essentially from a full written description, of a public sight which any one present would be free to see. On the other hand, when he is confined to a hospital bed,[82] and in all probability when he is merely in the seclusion of his home, the making of a photograph without his consent is an invasion of a private right, of which he is entitled to complain.

It appears obvious that the interest protected by this branch of the tort is primarily a mental one. It has been useful chiefly to fill in the gaps left by trespass, nuisance, the intentional infliction of mental distress, and whatever remedies there may be for the invasion of constitutional rights.

II. Public disclosure of private facts

Because of its background of personal annoyance from the press, the article of Warren and Brandeis was primarily concerned with the second form of the tort, which consists of public disclosure of embarrassing private facts about the plaintiff. Actually this was rather slow to appear in the decisions. Although there were earlier instances,[83] in which other elements were involved, its first real separate application was in a Kentucky case[84] in 1927, in which the defendant put up a notice in the window of his garage announcing to the world that the defendant owed him money and would not pay it. But the decision which has become the leading case, largely because of its spectacular facts, is *Melvin v. Reid,*[85] in California in 1931. The plaintiff, whose original name was Gabrielle Darley, had been a prostitute, and the defendant in a sensational murder trial. After her acquittal she had abandoned her life of shame, become rehabilitated, married a man named Melvin, and in a manner reminiscent of the plays of Arthur Wing Pinero, had led a life of rectitude in respectable society, among friends and associates who were unaware of her earlier career. Seven years afterward the defendant made and exhibited a motion picture, called "The Red Kimono," which enacted the true story, used the name of Gabrielle Darley, and ruined her new life by revealing her past to the world and her friends. Relying in part upon a vague constitutional provision that all men have the inalienable right of "pursuing and obtaining happiness," which has since disappeared from the California cases, the court held that this was an actionable invasion of her right of privacy.

Other decisions have followed, involving the use of the plaintiff's name in a radio dramatization of a robbery of which he was the victim,[86] and publicity given to his debts,[87] to medical pictures of his anatomy,[88] and to embarrassing details of a woman's masculine characteristics, her domineering tendencies, her habits of profanity, and incidents of her personal conduct toward her friends and neighbors.[89] Some limits, at least, of this branch of the right of privacy appear to be fairly well marked out, as follows:

First, the disclosure of the private facts must be a public disclosure, and not a private one. There must be, in other words, publicity. It is an invasion of the right to publish in a newspaper that the plaintiff does not pay his debts,[90] or to post a notice to that effect in a window on the public street[91] or cry it aloud in the highway;[92] but, except for one decision of a lower Georgia court which was reversed on other grounds,[93] it has been agreed that it is no invasion to communicate that fact to the plaintiff's employer,[94] or to any other individual, or even to a small group,[95] unless there is some breach of contract, trust or confidential relation which will afford an independent basis for relief.[96] Warren and Brandeis[97] thought that the publication would have to be written or printed unless special damage could be shown; and there have been decisions[98] that the action will not lie for oral publicity; but the growth of radio alone has been enough to make this obsolete,[99] and there now can be little doubt that writing is not required.[100]

Second, the facts disclosed to the public must be private facts, and not public ones. Certainly no one can complain when publicity is given to information about him which he himself leaves open to the public eye, such as the appearance of the house in which he lives, or to the business in which he is engaged. Thus it has been held that a public school teacher has no action for a compulsory disclosure of her war work and other outside activities.[101]

Here two troublesome questions arise. One is whether any individual, by appearing upon the public highway or in any other public place, makes his appearance public, so that any one may take and publish a picture of him as he is at the time. What if an utterly obscure citizen, reeling along drunk on the main street, is snapped by an enterprising reporter, and the picture given to the world? Is his privacy invaded? The cases have been much involved with the privilege of reporting news and other matters of public interest,[102] and for that reason cannot be regarded as very conclusive; but the answer appears to be that it is not. The decisions indicate that anything visible in a public place may be recorded and given circulation by means of a photograph, to the same extent as by a written description,[103] since this amounts to nothing more than giving publicity to what is already public and what any one present would be free to see.[104] Outstanding is the California case[105] in which the plaintiff, photographed while embracing his wife in the market place, was held to have no action when the picture was published. It has been contended[106] that when an individual is thus singled out from the public scene, and undue attention is focused upon him, there is an invasion of his private rights; and there is one New York decision to that effect.[107] It was, however, later explained upon the basis of the introduction of an element of fiction into the accompanying narrative.[108]

On the other hand, it seems clear that when a picture is taken surreptitiously, or over the plaintiff's objection, in a private place,[109] or one already made is stolen,[110] or obtained by bribery or other inducement of breach of trust,[111] the plaintiff's appearance which is thus made public is at the time still a private thing, and there is an invasion of a private right, for which an action will lie.

The other question is as to the effect of the fact that the matter made public is already one of public record. If the record is a confidential one, not open to public inspection, as in the case of income tax returns,[112] it is not public, and there can be no doubt that there is an invasion of privacy. But it has been held that no one is entitled to complain when there is publication of his recorded date of birth or his marriage,[113] or his military service record;[114] and the same must certainly be true of his admission to the bar or to the practice of medicine, or the fact that he is driving a taxicab. The difficult question is as to the effect of lapse of time, and the extent to which forgotten records, as for example of a criminal conviction, may be dredged up in after years and given more general publicity. As in the case of news,[115] with which the problem may be inextricably interwoven, it has been held that the memory of the events covered by the record, such as a criminal trial,[116] can be revived as still a matter of legitimate public interest. But there is the leading case of *Melvin v. Reid*,[117] which held that the unnecessary use of the plaintiff's name, and the revelation of her history to new friends and associates, introduced an element which was in itself a transgression of her right of privacy. The answer may be that the existence of a public record is a factor of a good deal of importance, which will normally prevent the matter from being private, but that under some special circumstances it is not necessarily conclusive.

Third, the matter made public must be one which would be offensive and objectionable to a reasonable man of ordinary sensibilities.[118] All of us, to some extent, lead lives exposed to the public gaze or to the public inquiry, and complete privacy does not exist in this world except for the eremite in the desert. Any one who is not a hermit must expect the more or less casual observation of his neighbors and the passing public as to what he is and does, and some reporting of his daily activities. The ordinary reasonable man does not take offense at mention in a newspaper of the fact that he has returned from a visit, or gone camping in the woods, or that he has given a party at his house for his friends; and very probably Mr. Warren would never have had any action for the reports of his daughter's wedding. The law of privacy is not intended for the protection of any shrinking soul who is abnormally sensitive about such publicity.[119] It is quite a different matter when the details of sexual relations are spread before the public gaze,[120] or there is highly personal portrayal of his intimate private characteristics or conduct.[121]

Here the outstanding case is *Sidis v. F-R Publishing Corporation*.[122] The plaintiff, William James Sidis, had been an infant prodigy, who had graduated from Harvard at sixteen, and at the age of eleven had lectured to eminent mathematicians on the fourth dimension. When he arrived at adolescence he underwent some unusual psychological change, which brought about a complete revulsion toward mathematics, and toward the publicity he had received. He disappeared, led an obscure life as a bookkeeper, and occupied himself in collecting street car transfers, and studying the lore of the Okamakammessett Indians. The *New Yorker* magazine sought him out, and published a not unsympathetic account of his career, revealing his present whereabouts and activities. The effect upon Sidis was devastating, and the article unquestionably contributed to his early death. The case involved the privilege of reporting on matters of public interest;[123] but the decision that there was no cause of action rested upon the ground that there was nothing in the article which would be objectionable to any normal person. When this case is compared with *Melvin v. Reid*,[124] with its revelation of the past of a prostitute and a murder defendant, what emerges is something in the nature of a "mores" test,[125] by which there will be liability only for publicity given to those things which the customs and ordinary views of the community will not tolerate.

This branch of the tort is evidently something quite distinct from intrusion. The interest protected is that of reputation, with the same overtones of mental distress that are present in libel and slander. It is in reality an extension of defamation, into the field of publications that do not fall within the narrow limits of the old torts, with the elimination of the defense of truth.[126] As such, it has no doubt gone far to remedy the deficiencies of the defamation actions, hampered as they are by technical rules inherited from ancient and long forgotten jurisdictional conflicts, and to provide a remedy for a few real and serious wrongs that were not previously actionable.

III. False light in the public eye

The third form of invasion of privacy, which Warren and Brandeis again do not appear to have had in mind at all, consists of publicity that places the plaintiff in a false light in the public eye. It seems to have made its first appearance in 1816, when Lord Byron succeeded in enjoining the circulation of a spurious and inferior poem attributed to his pen.[127] The principle frequently, over a good many years, has made a rather nebulous appearance in a line of decisions[128] in which falsity or fiction has been held to defeat the privilege of reporting news and other matters of public interest, or of giving further publicity to already public figures. It is only in late years that it has begun to receive any independent recognition of its own.

One form in which it occasionally appears, as in Byron's case, is that of publicity falsely attributing to the plaintiff some opinion or utterance.[129] A good illustration of this might be the fictitious testimonial used in advertising,[130] or the Oregon case[131] in which the name of the plaintiff was signed to a telegram to the governor urging political action which it would have been illegal for him, as a state employee, to advocate. More typical are spurious books and articles, or ideas expressed in them, which purport to emanate from the plaintiff.[132] In the same category are the unauthorized use of his name as a candidate for office,[133] or to advertise for witnesses of an accident,[134] or the entry of an actor, without his consent, in a popularity contest of an embarrassing kind.[135]

Another form in which this branch of the tort frequently has made its appearance is the use of the plaintiff's picture to illustrate a book or an article with which he has no reasonable connection. As remains to be seen,[136] public interest may justify a use for appropriate and pertinent illustration. But when the face of some quite innocent and unrelated citizen is employed to ornament an article on the cheating propensities of taxi drivers,[137] the negligence of children,[138] profane love,[139] "man hungry" women,[140] juvenile delinquents,[141] or the peddling of narcotics,[142] there is an obvious innuendo that the article applies to him, which places him in a false light before the public, and which is actionable.

Still another form in which the tort occurs is the inclusion of the plaintiff's name, photograph and fingerprints in a public "rogues' gallery" of convicted criminals, when he has not in fact been convicted of any crime.[143] Although the police are clearly privileged to make such a record in the first instance, and to use it for any legitimate purpose pending trial,[144] or even after conviction,[145] the element of false publicity in the inclusion among the convicted goes beyond the privilege.

The false light need not necessarily be a defamatory one, although it very often is,[146] and a defamation action will also lie. It seems clear, however, that it must be something that would be objectionable to the ordinary reasonable man under the circumstances, and that, as in the case of disclosure,[147] the hypersensitive individual will not be protected.[148] Thus minor and unimportant errors in an otherwise accurate biography, as to dates and place, and incidents of no significance, do not entitle the subject of the book to recover,[149] nor does the erroneous description of the plaintiff as a cigarette girl when an inquiring photographer interviews her on the street.[150] Again, in all probability, something of a "mores" test must be applied.

The false light cases obviously differ from those of intrusion, or disclosure of private facts. The interest protected is clearly that of reputation, with the same overtones of mental distress as in defamation. There is a resemblance to disclosure; but the two differ in that one involves truth and the other lies, one private or secret facts and the other invention. Both require publicity. There has been a good deal of overlapping of defamation in the false light cases, and apparently either action, or both, will very often lie. The privacy cases do go considerably beyond the narrow limits of defamation, and no doubt have succeeded in affording a needed remedy in a good many instances not covered by the other tort.

It is here, however, that one disposed to alarm might express the greatest concern over where privacy may be going. The question may well be raised, and apparently still is unanswered, whether this branch of the tort is not capable of swallowing up and engulfing the whole law of public defamation; and whether there is any false libel printed, for example, in a newspaper, which cannot be redressed upon the alternative ground. If that turns out to be the case, it may well be asked, what of the numerous restrictions and limitations which have hedged defamation about for many years, in the interest of freedom of the press and the discouragement of trivial and extortionate claims? Are they of so little consequence that they may be circumvented in so casual and cavalier a fashion?

IV. Appropriation

There is little indication that Warren and Brandeis intended to direct their article at the fourth branch of the tort, the exploitation of attributes of the plaintiff's identity. The first decision[151] had relied upon breach of an implied contract, where a photographer who had taken the plaintiff's picture proceeded to put it on sale; and this is still one basis upon which liability continues to be found.[152] By reason of its early appearance in the *Roberson* case,[153] and the resulting New York statute,[154] this form of invasion has bulked rather large in the law of privacy. It consists of the appropriation, for the defendant's benefit or advantage, of the plaintiff's name or likeness.[155] Thus in New York, as well as in many other states, there are a great many decisions in which the plaintiff has recovered when his name[156] or picture,[157] or other likeness,[158] has been used without his consent to advertise the defendant's product, or to accompany an article sold,[159] to add luster to the name of a corporation,[160] or for other business purposes.[161] The statute in New York,[162] and the others patterned after it[163] are limited by their terms to use for advertising or for "purposes of trade," and for that reason must be somewhat more narrow in their scope than the common law of the other states;[164] but in general, there has been no significant difference in their application in the field that they cover.

It is the plaintiff's name as a symbol of his identity that is involved here, and not his name as a mere name. There is, as a good many thousand John Smiths can bear witness, no such thing as an exclusive right to the use of any name. Unless there is some tortious use made of it, any one can be given or assume any name he likes.[165] The Kabotznicks may call themselves Cabots, and the Lovelskis become the Lowells, and the ancient proper Bostonian houses can do nothing about it but grieve. Any one may call himself Dwight D. Eisenhower, Henry Ford, Nelson Rockefeller, Eleanor Roosevelt, or Willie Mays, without any liability whatever. It is when he makes use of the name to pirate the plaintiff's identity for some advantage of his own, as by impersonation to obtain credit or secret information,[166] or by posing as the plaintiff's wife,[167] or providing a father for a child on a birth certificate,[168] that he becomes liable. It is in this sense that "appropriation" must be understood.

On this basis, the question before the courts has been first of all whether there has been appropriation of an aspect of the plaintiff's identity. It is not enough that a name which is the same as his is used in a novel,[169] a comic strip,[170] or the title of a corporation,[171] unless the context or the circumstances,[172] or the addition of some other element,[173] indicate that the name is that of the plaintiff. It seems clear that a stage or other fictitious name can be so identified with the plaintiff that he is entitled to protection against its use.[174] On the other hand, there is no liability for the publication of a picture of his hand, leg and foot,[175] his dwelling house,[176] his automobile,[177] or his dog,[178] with nothing to indicate whose they are. Nor is there any liability when the plaintiff's character, occupation, and the general outline of his career, with many real incidents in his life, are used as the basis for a figure in a novel who is still clearly a fictional one.[179]

Once the plaintiff is identified, there is the further question whether the defendant has appropriated the name or likeness for his own advantage. Under the statutes this must be a pecuniary advantage; but the common law is very probably not so limited.[180] The New York courts were faced very early with the obvious fact that newspapers and magazines, to say nothing of radio, television and motion pictures, are by no means philanthropic institutions, but are operated for profit. As against the contention that everything published by these agencies must necessarily be "for purposes of trade," they were compelled to hold that there must be some closer and more direct connection, beyond the mere fact that the newspaper is sold; and that the presence of advertising matter in adjacent columns does not make any difference.[181] Any other conclusion would undoubtedly have been an unconstitutional interference with the freedom of the press.[182] Accordingly, it has been held that the mere incidental mention of the plaintiff's name in a book[183] or a motion picture[184] or even in a commentary upon news which is part of an advertisement,[185] is not an invasion of his privacy; nor is the publication of a photograph[186] or a newsreel[187] in which he incidentally appears.

This liberality toward the publishers was brought to an abrupt termination, however, when cases began to appear in which false statements were made. It was held quite early in New York[188] that the publication of fiction concerning a man is a use of his name for purposes of trade, and that in such a case the mere sale of the article is enough in itself to provide the commercial element. It follows that when the name or the likeness is accompanied by false statements about the plaintiff,[189] or he is placed in a false light before the public,[190] there is such a use. The result of this rule for the encouragement of accuracy in the press is that the New York court has in fact recognized and applied the third form of invasion of privacy[191] under a statute which was directed only at the fourth.

It seems sufficiently evident that appropriation is quite a different matter from intrusion, disclosure of private facts, or a false light in the public eye. The interest protected is not so much a mental as a proprietary one, in the exclusive use of the plaintiff's name and likeness as an aspect of his identity. It seems quite pointless to dispute over whether such a right is to be classified as "property."[192] If it is not, it is at least, once it is protected by the law, a right of value upon which the plaintiff can capitalize by selling licenses. Its proprietary nature is clearly indicated by a decision of the Second Circuit[193] that an exclusive license has what has been called a "right of publicity,"[194] which entitles him to enjoin the use of the name or likeness by a third person. Although this decision has not yet been followed,[195] it would seem clearly to be justified.

V. Common features

Judge Biggs has described the present state of the law of privacy as "still that of a haystack in a hurricane."[196] Disarray there certainly is; but almost all of the confusion is due to a failure to separate and distinguish these four forms of invasion, and to realize that they call for different things. Typical is the bewilderment which a good many members of the bar have expressed over the holdings in the two *Gill* cases in California. Both of them involved publicity given to the same photograph, taken while the plaintiff was embracing his wife in the Farmers' Market in Los Angeles. In one of them,[197] which involved only the question of disclosure by publishing the picture, it was held that there was nothing private about it, since it was a part of the public scene in a public place. In the other,[198] which involved the use of the picture to illustrate an article on the right and the wrong kind of love, with the innuendo that this was the wrong kind, liability was found for placing the plaintiff in a false light in the public eye. The two conclusions were based entirely upon the difference between the two branches of the tort.

Taking them in order—intrusion, disclosure, false light, and appropriation—the first and second require the invasion of something secret, secluded or private pertaining to the plaintiff; the third and fourth do not. The second and third depend upon publicity, while the first does not, nor does the fourth, although it usually involves it. The third requires falsity or fiction; the other three do not. The fourth involves a use for the defendant's advantage, which is not true of the rest. Obviously this is an area in which one must treat warily and be on the lookout for bogs. Nor is the difficulty decreased by the fact that quite often two or more of these forms of invasion may be found in the same case, and quite conceivably all four.[199]

There has nevertheless been a good deal of consistency in the rules that have been applied to the four disparate torts under the common name. As to any one of the four, it is agreed that the plaintiff's right is a personal one, which does not extend to the members of his family,[200] unless, as is obviously possible,[201] their own privacy is invaded along with his. The right is not assignable;[202] and while the cause of action may[203] or may not[204] survive after his death, according to the survival rules of the particular state, there is no common law right of action for a publication concerning one who is already dead.[205] The statutes of Oklahoma, Utah and Virginia,[206] however, expressly provide for such an action. It seems to be generally agreed that the right of privacy is one pertaining only to individuals, and that a corporation[207] or a partnership[208] cannot claim it as such, although either may have an exclusive right to the use of its name, which may be protected upon some other basis such as that of unfair competition.[209]

So far as damages are concerned, there is general agreement that the plaintiff need not plead or prove special damages,[210] and that in this respect the action resembles one for libel or slander per se. The difficulty of measuring the damages is no more reason for denying relief here than in a defamation action.[211] Substantial damages may be awarded for the presumed mental distress inflicted, and other probable harm, without proof.[212] If there is evidence of special damage, such as resulting illness, or unjust enrichment of the defendant,[213] or harm to the plaintiff's own commercial interests,[214] it can be recovered. Punitive damages can be awarded upon the same basis as in other torts, where a wrongful motive or state of mind appears,[215] but not in cases where the defendant has acted innocently, as for example in the belief that the plaintiff has given his consent.[216]

At an early stage of its existence, the right of privacy came into head-on collision with the constitutional guaranty of freedom of the press. The result was the slow evolution of a compromise between the two. Much of the litigation over privacy has been concerned with this compromise, which has involved two closely related, special and limited privileges arising out of the rights of the press.[217] One of these is the privilege of giving further publicity to already public figures. The other is that of giving publicity to news, and other matters of public interest. The one primarily concerns the person to whom publicity is given; the other the event, fact or other subject-matter. They are, however, obviously only different phases of the same thing.

VI. Public figures and public interest

A public figure has been defined as a person who, by his accomplishments, fame, or mode of living, or by adopting a profession or calling which gives the public a legitimate interest in his doings, his affairs, and his character, has become a "public personage."[218] He is, in other words, a celebrity—one who by his own voluntary efforts has succeeded in placing himself in the public eye. Obviously to be included in this category are those who have achieved at least some degree of reputation[219] by appearing before the public, as in the case of an actor,[220] a professional baseball player,[221] a pugilist,[222] or any other entertainer.[223] The list is, however, broader than this. It includes public officers,[224] famous inventors[225] and explorers,[226] war heroes[227] and even ordinary soldiers,[228] an infant prodigy,[229] and no less a personage than the Grand Exalted Ruler of a lodge.[230] It includes, in short, any one who has arrived at a position where public attention is focused upon him as a person. It seems clear, however, that such public stature must already exist before there can be any privilege arising out of it, and that the defendant, by directing attention to one who is obscure and unknown, cannot himself create a public figure.[231]

Such public figures are held to have lost, to some extent at least, their right of privacy. Three reasons are given, more or less indiscriminately, in the decisions: that they have sought publicity and consented to it, and so cannot complain of it; that their personalities and their affairs already have become public, and can no longer be regarded as their own private business; and that the press has a privilege, guaranteed by the Constitution, to inform the public about those who have become legitimate matters of public interest. On one or another of these grounds, and sometimes all, it is held that there is no liability when they are given additional publicity, as to matters reasonably within the scope of the public interest which they have aroused.[232]

The privilege of giving publicity to news, and other matters of public interest, arises out of the desire and the right of the public to know what is going on in the world, and the freedom of the press and other agencies of information to tell them. "News" includes all events and items of information which are out of the ordinary humdrum routine, and which have "that indefinable quality of information which arouses public attention."[233] To a very great extent the press, with its experience or instinct as to what its readers will want, has succeeded in making its own definition of news. A glance at any morning newspaper will sufficiently indicate the content of the term. It includes homicide[234] and other crimes,[235] arrests[236] and police raids,[237] suicides,[238] marriages[239] and divorces,[240] accidents,[241] a death from the use of narcotics,[242] a woman with a rare disease,[243] the birth of a child to a twelve year old girl,[244] the filing of a libel suit,[245] a report to the police concerning the escape of a black panther,[246] the reappearance of one supposed to have been murdered years ago,[247] and undoubtedly many other similar matters of genuine, if more or less deplorable, popular appeal.[248]

The privilege of enlightening the public is not, however, limited to the dissemination of news in the sense of current events. It extends also to information or education, or even entertainment and amusement,[249] by books, articles, pictures, films and broadcasts concerning interesting phases of human activity in general,[250] and the reproduction of the public scene as in newsreels and travelogues.[251] In determining where to draw the line the courts have been invited to exercise nothing less than a power of censorship over what the public may be permitted to read; and they have been understandably liberal in allowing the benefit of the doubt.

Caught up and entangled in this web of news and public interest are a great many people who have not sought publicity, but indeed, as in the case of the accused criminal, have tried assiduously to avoid it. They have nevertheless lost some part of their right of privacy. The misfortunes of the frantic woman whose husband is murdered before her eyes,[252] or the innocent bystander who is caught in a raid on a cigar store and mistaken by the police for the proprietor,[253] can be broadcast to the world, and they have no remedy. Such individuals become public figures[254] for a season; and "until they have reverted to the lawful and unexciting life led by the great bulk of the community, they are subject to the privileges which publishers have to satisfy the curiosity of the public as to their leaders, heroes, villains and victims."[255] The privilege extends even to identification and some reasonable depiction of the individual's family,[256] although there must certainly be limits as to their own private lives into which the publisher cannot go.[257]

What is called for, in short, is some logical connection between the plaintiff and the matter of public interest. The most extreme cases of the privilege are those in which the likeness of an individual is used to illustrate a book or an article on some general topic, rather than any specific event. Where this is appropriate and pertinent, as where the picture of a strikebreaker is used to illustrate a book on strikebreaking,[258] or that of a Hindu illusionist is employed to illustrate an article on the Indian rope trick,[259] it has been held that there is no liability, since the public interest justifies any invasion of privacy. On the other hand, where the illustration is not pertinent, and a connection is suggested which does not exist, as where the face of an honest taxi driver appears in connection with an article on the cheating practices of the trade,[260] or the picture of a decent model illustrates one on "man hungry" women,[261] the plaintiff is placed in a false light, and may recover on that basis. The difference is well brought out by two cases in California and New York. In one of them[262] a photograph of the plaintiff arguing with a would-be suicide on a bridge was held properly used to illustrate an article on suicide. In the other[263] the picture of a boy in the slums, taken while he was innocently talking baseball on the street, was used with an article about juvenile delinquency, entitled "Gang Boy," and he was allowed to recover.

VII. Limitations

It is clear, however, that the public figure loses his right of privacy only to a limited extent,[264] and that the privilege of reporting news and matters of public interest is likewise limited. The decisions indicate very definitely that both privileges apply only to one branch of the tort, that of disclosure of private facts about the individual. The famous motion picture actress who "vants to be alone"[265] unquestionably has as much right as any one else to be free from intrusion into her home or her bank account; and so has the individual whose divorce is the sensation of the day.[266] The celebrity can undoubtedly complain of the appropriation of his name or likeness for purposes of advertising, or the sale of a product,[267] and so can the victim of an accident.[268] It was once held that even the Emperor of Austria had a right to object when his name was bestowed on an insurance company.[269] And while it seems to be agreed that the courts are not arbiters of taste, and the fact that a publication is morbid, gruesome, lurid, sensational, immoral, and altogether cheap and despicable will not forfeit the privilege,[270] it is also clear that either the public figure[271] or the man in the news[272] can maintain an action when false or fictitious statements are published about him, or when his picture is used with an innuendo which places him in a false light before the public.[273]

But even as to the disclosure of private facts, it appears that there must be some rather undefined limits upon these privileges. Warren and Brandeis[274] thought that even a celebrity was entitled to his private life, and that he would become a public figure only as to matters already public and those which directly bore upon them. The development of the law has not been so narrow. It has recognized a legitimate public curiosity about the personalities of celebrities, and about a great deal of otherwise private and personal information concerning them. Their biographies can be written,[275] and their life histories and their characters set forth before the world in unflattering detail. Discreditable facts about them can be exposed.[276] And as our newspapers demonstrate daily, the public can be treated to an enormous amount of petty gossip as to what they eat for breakfast, wear, read, do with their spare time, or say to their friends.

Some boundaries, however, still remain; and one may venture the guess that the private sex relations of actresses and baseball players, to say nothing of inventors and the victims of automobile accidents, are still not in the public domain.[277] As some evidence of popular feeling in such matters, one might look to the statutes in several states[278] prohibiting the public disclosure of the names of victims of sex crimes. The private letters, even of celebrities, cannot be published without their consent;[279] and the good Prince Albert was once held to have an action when his private etchings were exhibited to all comers.[280] An excellent illustration of the privacy of a public figure is a case[281] in a trial court in Los Angeles, not officially reported, in which the actor Kirk Douglas, after engaging in some undignified antics before a home motion picture camera for his friends, was held to have a cause of action when the film was put upon public exhibition.

Very probably there is some rough proportion to be looked for, between the importance of the public figure or the man in the news, and of the occasion for the public interest in him, and the nature of the private facts revealed. Perhaps there is very little in the way of information about the President of the United States, or any candidate for that high office,[282] that is not a matter of legitimate public concern; but when a mere member of the armed forces is in question, the line is drawn at his military service, and those things that more or less directly bear upon it.[283] And no doubt the defendant in a spectacular murder trial which draws national attention can expect a good deal less in the way of privacy than an ordinary citizen who is arrested for ignoring a parking ticket. But thus far there is very little in the cases to indicate just where such lines are to be drawn.

One troublesome question, which cannot be said to have been fully resolved, is that of the effect of lapse of time, during which the plaintiff has returned to obscurity. There can be no doubt that one quite legitimate function of the press is that of educating or reminding the public as to past history, and that the recall of former public figures, the revival of past events that once were news, can properly be a matter of present public interest. If it is only the event itself which is recalled, without the use of the plaintiff's name, there seems to be no doubt that even a great lapse of time does not destroy the privilege.[284] Most of the cases have held that even the use of his name[285] or likeness[286] is not enough in itself to lead to liability. Thus a luckless prosecuting attorney who once made the mistake of allowing himself to be photographed with his arm around a noted criminal was held to have no remedy when the picture was republished fifteen years later in connection with a story of the criminal's career.[287] Such decisions indicate that once a man has become a public figure, or news, he remains a matter of legitimate recall to the public mind to the end of his days. There is, however, *Melvin v. Reid*,[288] in which it was held that the use of the name of a former prostitute and murder defendant made the publisher liable when a motion picture narrated her story; and there are a few other cases[289] that look in the same direction. One may speculate that the real reason for the decision in the *Melvin* case was not the use of the name in connection with past history, but the disclosure of the plaintiff's whereabouts and identity, which were no part of the revived "news," or perhaps that the explanation lay in the shocking enormity of the revelation of a woman's past when she was trying to lead a decent life, and that again something in the nature of a "mores" test is to be applied. There is, however, almost nothing in the cases to throw any satisfactory light upon such speculations. All that can be said is that there appear to be situations in which ancient history cannot safely be revived.

VIII. Defenses

Next in order are the various defenses to the claim of invasion of privacy. It is clear first of all that the truth of the matter published does not arise in the cases of intrusion, and can be no defense to the appropriation of name or likeness, nor to the public disclosure of private facts.[290] It may, however, be in issue where the third form of the tort is involved, that of putting the plaintiff in a false light in the public eye,[291] and to that extent it has some limited importance, and cannot be entirely ruled out.

Chief among the available defenses is that of the plaintiff's consent to the invasion, which will bar his recovery as in the case of any other tort.[292] It may be given expressly, or by conduct, such as posing for a picture with knowledge of the purposes for which it is to be used,[293] or industriously seeking publicity of the same kind.[294] A gratuitous consent can be revoked at any time before the invasion;[295] but if the agreement is a matter of contract it is normally irrevocable, and there is no liability for any publicity or appropriation within its terms.[296] But if the actual invasion goes beyond the contract, fairly construed, as by alteration of the plaintiff's picture,[297] or publicity materially differing in kind or in extent from that contemplated,[298] the consent is not effective to avoid liability. The statutes[299] all require that the consent be given in writing. As against the contention that this can still be "waived" by consent given orally, the rule which has emerged in New York is that the oral consent will not bar the cause of action, but is to be taken into account in mitigation of damages.[300]

Other defenses have appeared only infrequently. Warren and Brandeis[301] thought that the action for invasion of privacy must be subject to any privilege which would justify the publication of libel or slander, reasoning that that which is true should be no less privileged than that which is false. There is still no reason to doubt this conclusion, since the absolute privilege of a witness,[302] and the qualified one to report the filing of a nominating petition for office[303] or the pleadings in a civil suit[304] have both been recognized. The privilege of the defendant to protect or further his own legitimate interests has appeared in a case or two, where a telephone company has been permitted to monitor calls,[305] and the defendant was allowed to make use of the plaintiff's name in insuring his wife without his consent.[306] It has been held that where uncopyrighted literature is in the public domain, and the defendant is free to publish it, the name of the plaintiff may be used to indicate its authorship,[307] and that when the plaintiff has designed dresses for the defendant it is no invasion of his privacy to disclose his connection with the product in advertising.[308]

The conflict of laws, so far as the right of privacy is concerned, is in the same state of bewildered confusion as that which surrounds the law of defamation. The writer has attempted to deal with it elsewhere,[309] and will not repeat it here.

Conclusion

It is evident from the foregoing that, by the use of a single word supplied by Warren and Brandeis, the courts have created an independent basis of liability, which is a complex of four distinct and only loosely related torts; and that this has been expanded by slow degrees to invade, overlap, and encroach upon a number of other fields. So far as appears from the decisions, the process has gone on without any plan, without much realization of what is happening or its significance, and without any consideration of its dangers. They are nonetheless sufficiently obvious, and not to be overlooked.

One cannot fail to be aware, in reading privacy cases, of the extent to which defenses, limitations and safeguards established for the protection of the defendant in other tort fields have been jettisoned, disregarded, or ignored. Taking intrusion first, the gist of the wrong is clearly the intentional infliction of mental distress, which is now in itself a recognized basis of tort liability.[310] Where such mental disturbance stands on its own feet, the courts have insisted upon extreme outrage, rejecting all liability for trivialities, and upon genuine and serious mental harm, attested by physical illness, or by the circumstances of the case. But once "privacy" gets into the picture, and the fact of the intrusion is added, such guarantees apparently are no longer required. No doubt the cases thus far have been sufficiently extreme; but the question may well be raised whether there are not some limits, and whether, for example, a lady who insists upon sunbathing in the nude in her own back yard should really have a cause of action for her humiliation when the neighbors examine her with appreciation and binoculars.

The public disclosure of private facts, and putting the plaintiff in a false light in the public eye, both concern the interest in reputation, and move into the field occupied by defamation. Here, as a result of some centuries of conflict, there have been jealous safeguards thrown about the freedom of speech and of the press, which are now turned on the left flank. Gone is the defense of truth, and the defendant is held liable for the publication of entirely accurate statements of fact, without any wrongful motive. Gone also is the requirement of special damage where what is said is not libel or slander "per se"—which, however antiquated and unreasonable the rigid categories may be, has at least served some useful purpose in the discouragement of trivial and extortionate claims. Gone even is the need for any defamatory innuendo at all, since the publication of nondefamatory facts, or of even laudatory fiction concerning the plaintiff, may be enough. The retraction statutes, with their provision for demand upon the defendant, and the limitation to proved special damage if a demand is not made or is complied with, are circumvented; and so are the statutes requiring the filing of a bond for costs before a defamation action can be begun. These are major inroads upon a right to which there has always been much sentimental devotion in our land; and they have gone almost entirely unremarked. Perhaps more important still is the extent to which, under any test of "ordinary sensibilities," or the "mores" of the community as to what is acceptable and proper, the courts, although cautiously and reluctantly, have accepted a power of censorship over what the public may be permitted to read, extending very much beyond that which they have always had under the law of defamation.

As for the appropriation cases, they create in effect, for every individual, a common law trade name, his own, and a common law trade mark in his likeness. They confer upon him rights much more extensive than those which any corporation engaged in business can expect under the law of unfair competition. These rights are subject to the verdict of a jury. And there has been no hint that they are in any way affected by any of the limitations which have been considered necessary and desirable in the ordinary law of trade marks and trade names.

This is not to say that the developments in the law of privacy are wrong. Undoubtedly they have been supported by genuine public demand and lively public feeling, and made necessary by real abuses on the part of defendants who have brought it all upon themselves. It is to say rather that it is high time that we realize what we are doing, and give some consideration to the question of where, if anywhere, we are to call a halt.

All this is a most marvelous tree to grow from the wedding of the daughter of Mr. Samuel D. Warren. One is tempted to surmise that she must have been a very beautiful girl. Resembling, perhaps, that fabulous creature, the daughter of a Mr. Very, a confectioner in Regent Street, who was so wondrous fair that her presence in the shop caused three or four hundred people to assemble every day in the street before the window to look at her, so that her father was forced to send her out of town, and counsel was led to inquire whether she might not be indicted as a public nuisance.[311] This was the face that launched a thousand lawsuits.

NOTES

1 "The press is overstepping in every direction the obvious bounds of propriety and of decency. Gossip is no longer the resource of the idle and of the vicious, but has become a trade, which is pursued with industry as well as effrontery. To satisfy a prurient taste the details of sexual relations are spread broadcast in the columns of the daily papers. To occupy the indolent, column upon column is filled with idle gossip, which can only be procured by intrusion upon the domestic circle. The intensity and complexity of life, attendant upon advancing civilization, have rendered necessary some retreat from the world, and man, under the refining influence of culture, has become more sensitive to publicity, so that solitude and privacy have become more essential to the individual; but modern enterprise and invention have, through invasions upon his privacy, subjected him to mental pain and distress, far greater than could be inflicted by mere bodily injury." Warren and Brandeis, *The Right to Privacy*, 4 Harv. L. Rev. 193, 196 (1890).

2 Mason, Brandeis, A Free Man's Life 70 (1946).

3 4 Harv. L. Rev. 193 (1890).

4 Woolsey v. Judd, 4 Duer (11 N.Y. Super.) 379, 11 How. Pr. 49 (N.Y.1855) (publication of private letters); Gee v. Pritchard, 2 Swans. 402, 36 Eng. Rep. 670 (1818) (same); Prince Albert v. Strange, 2 De G. & Sm. 652, 41

Eng. Rep. 1171, 1 Mac. & G. 25, 64 Eng. Rep. 293 (1849) (exhibition of etchings and publication of catalogue).

5 Yovatt v. Winyard, 1 Jac. & W. 394, 37 Eng. Rep. 425 (1820) (publication of recipes surreptitiously obtained by employee); Abernethy v. Hutchinson, 3 L.J. Ch. 109 (1825) (publication of lectures to class of which defendant was a member); Pollard v. Photographic Co., 40 Ch. D. 345 (1888) (publication of plaintiff's picture made by defendant).

6 Larremore, *The Law of Privacy*, 12 Colum. L. Rev. 693 (1912); Ragland, *The Right of Privacy*, 17 Ky. L.J. 101 (1929); Winfield, *Privacy*, 47 L.Q. Rev. 23 (1931); Green, *The Right of Privacy*, 27 Ill. L. Rev. 237 (1932); Kacedan, *The Right of Privacy*, 12 B.U.L. Rev. 353, 600 (1932); Dickler, *The Right of Privacy*, 70 U.S.L. Rev. 435 (1936); Harper & McNeely, *A Reexamination of the Basis for Liability for Emotional Distress*, [1938] Wis. L. Rev. 426; Nizer, *The Right of Privacy*, 39 Mich. L. Rev. 526 (1941); Feinberg, *Recent Developments in the Law of Privacy*, 48 Colum. L. Rev. 713 (1948); Ludwig, *"Peace of Mind" in 48 Pieces vs. Uniform Right of Privacy*, 32 Minn. L. Rev. 734 (1948); Yankwich, *The Right of Privacy*, 27 Notre Dame Law. 429 (1952); Daims, *What Do We Mean by "Right to Privacy,"* 4 S.D.L. Rev. 1 (1959).

Also Notes in 8 Mich. L. Rev. 221 (1909); 12 Colum. L. Rev. 1 (1912); 43 Harv. L. Rev. 297 (1929); 7 N.C.L. Rev. 435 (1929); 26 Ill. L. Rev. 63 (1931); 81 U. Pa. L. Rev. 324 (1933); 33 Ill. L. Rev. 87 (1938); 13 So. Cal. L. Rev. 81 (1939); 15 Temp. L.Q. 148 (1941); 25 Minn. L. Rev. 619 (1941); 30 Cornell L.Q. 398 (1945); 48 Colum. L. Rev. 713 (1948); 15 U. Chi. L. Rev. 926 (1948); 6 Ark. L. Rev. 459 (1952); 38 Va. L. Rev. 117 (1952); 28 Ind. L.J. 179 (1953); 27 Miss. L.J. 256 (1956); 44 Va. L. Rev. 1303 (1958); 31 Miss. L.J. 191 (1960).

The foreign law is discussed in Gutteridge, *The Comparative Law of the Right to Privacy*, 47 L.Q. Rev. 203 (1931); Walton, *The Comparative Law of the Right to Privacy*, 47 L.Q. Rev. 219 (1960).

7 O'Brien, *The Right of Privacy*, 2 Colum. L. Rev. 437 (1902); Lisle, *The Right of Privacy (A Contra View)*, 19 Ky. L.J. 137 (1931); Notes, 2 Colum. L. Rev. 437 (1902); 64 Albany L.J. 428 (1902); 29 Law Notes 64 (1925); 43 Harv. L. Rev. 297 (1929); 26 Ill. L. Rev. 63 (1931).

8 Manela v. Stevens (N.Y. Sup. Ct. 1890), in N.Y. Times, June 15, 18, 21, 1890.

9 Mackenzie v. Soden Mineral Springs Co., 27 Abb. N. Cas. 402, 18 N.Y.S. 240 (Sup. Ct. 1891) (use of name of physician in advertising patent medicine enjoined); Marks v. Jaffa, 6 Misc. 290, 26 N.Y.S. 908 (Super. Ct. N.Y. City 1893) (entering actor in embarrassing popularity contest); Schuyler v. Curtis, 147 N.Y. 434, 42 N.E. 22 (1895) (erection of statue as memorial to deceased; relief denied only because he was dead).

10 Corliss v. E. W. Walker Co., 64 Fed. 280 (D. Mass. 1894) (portrait to be inserted in biographical sketch of plaintiff; relief denied because he was a public figure).

11 Atkinson v. John E. Doherty & Co., 121 Mich. 372, 80 N.W. 285 (1899).

The man was dead, and in any case a public figure; and on either ground the same decision would probably result today. See *infra*, text at notes 205, 218–32.

12 171 N.Y. 538, 64 N.E. 442 (1902).

13 O'Brien, *The Right of Privacy*, 2 Colum. L. Rev. 437 (1902).

14 N.Y. Sess. Laws 1903, ch. 132, §§ 1–2. Now, as amended in 1921, N.Y. Civ. Rights Law, §§ 50–51. Held constitutional in Rhodes v. Sperry & Hutchinson Co., 193 N.Y. 223, 85 N.E. 1097 (1908), *aff'd*, 220 U.S. 502 (1911). See generally, Hofstadter, The Development of the Right of Privacy in New York (1954).

15 122 Ga. 190, 50 S.E. 68 (1905).

16 Restatement, Torts § 867 (1939).

17 Smith v. Doss, 251 Ala. 250, 37 So. 2d 118 (1948); Birmingham Broadcasting Co. v. Bell, 259 Ala. 656, 68 So. 2d 314 (1953), *later appeal*, 266 Ala. 266, 96 So. 2d 263 (1957).

18 Smith v. Suratt, 7 Alaska 416 (1926).

19 Reed v. Real Detective Pub. Co., 63 Ariz. 294, 162 P.2d 133 (1945).

20 Melvin v. Reid, 112 Cal. App. 285, 197 Pac. 91 (1931); Kerby v. Hal Roach Studios, 53 Cal. App. 2d 207, 127 P.2d 577 (1942); Stryker v. Republic Pictures Corp., 108 Cal. App. 2d 191, 238 P.2d 670 (1951); Gill v. Curtis Pub. Co., 38 Cal. 2d 273, 239 P.2d 630 (1952); Linehan v. Linehan, 134 Cal. App. 2d 250, 285 P.2d 326 (1955); Fairfield v. American Photocopy Equipment Co., 138 Cal. App. 2d 82, 291 P.2d 194 (1955).

21 Korn v. Rennison, 156 A.2d 476 (Conn. Super. 1959).

22 Peay v. Curtis Pub. Co., 78 F. Supp. 305 (D.D.C. 1948).

23 Cason v. Baskin, 155 Fla. 198, 20 So. 2d 243 (1944), *second appeal*, 159 Fla. 31, 30 So. 2d 635 (1947); and see Jacova v. Southern Radio & Television Co., 83 So. 2d 34 (Fla. 1955).

24 Pavesich v. New England Life Ins. Co., 122 Ga. 190, 50 S.E. 68 (1905); Bazemore v. Savannah Hospital, 171 Ga. 257, 155 S.E. 194 (1930); McDaniel v. Atlanta Coca Cola Bottling Co., 60 Ga. App. 92, 2 S.E.2d 810 (1939); Walker v. Whittle, 83 Ga. App. 445, 64 S.E.2d 87 (1951); Gouldman-Taber Pontiac, Inc. v. Zerbst, 96 Ga. App. 48, 99 S.E.2d 475 (1957).

25 Eick v. Perk Dog Food Co., 347 Ill. App. 293, 106 N.E.2d 742 (1952); Annerino v. Dell Pub. Co., 17 Ill. App.2d 205, 149 N.E.2d 761 (1958).

26 Continental Optical Co. v. Reed, 119 Ind. App. 643, 86 N.E.2d 306 (1949). See also Estill v. Hearst Pub. Co., 186 F.2d 1017 (7th Cir. 1951).

27 Bremmer v. Journal-Tribune Co., 247 Iowa 817, 76 N.W.2d 762 (1956).

28 Kunz v. Allen, 102 Kan. 883, 172 Pac. 532 (1918). See also Johnson v. Boeing Airplane Co., 175 Kan. 275, 262 P.2d 808 (1953).

29 Foster-Milburn Co. v. Chinn, 134 Ky. 424, 120 S.W. 364 (1909); Douglas v. Stokes, 149 Ky. 506, 149 S.W. 849 (1912); Brents v. Morgan, 221 Ky. 765, 299 S.W. 967 (1927); Rhodes v. Graham, 238 Ky. 225, 37 S.W.2d 46 (1931); Trammell v. Citizens News Co., 285 Ky. 529, 148 S.W.2d 708 (1941).

30 Itzkovitch v. Whitaker, 115 La. 479, 39 So. 499 (1905); Schwartz v. Ed-
    rington, 133 La. 235, 62 So. 660 (1913); Hamilton v. Lumbermen's Mut.
    Cas. Co., 82 So. 2d 61 (La. App. 1955); Souder v. Pendleton Detectives,
    88 So. 2d 716 (La. App. 1956).
31 Pallas v. Crowley, Milner & Co., 322 Mich. 411, 33 N.W.2d 911 (1948).
32 Martin v. Dorton, 210 Miss. 668, 50 So. 2d 391 (1951). See Note, 27 Miss.
    L.J. 256 (1956).
33 Munden v. Harris, 153 Mo. App. 652, 134 S.W. 1076 (1911); Barber v.
    Time, Inc., 348 Mo. 1199, 159 S.W.2d 291 (1942); State *ex rel.* Clemens
    v. Witthaus, 228 S.W.2d 4 (Mo. 1950); Biederman's of Springfield, Inc.
    v. Wright, 322 S.W.2d 892 (Mo. 1959).
34 Welsh v. Pritchard, 125 Mont. 517, 241 P.2d 816 (1952).
35 Norman v. City of Las Vegas, 64 Nev. 38, 177 P.2d 442 (1947).
36 Vanderbilt v. Mitchell, 72 N.J. Eq. 910, 67 Atl. (Ct. Err. & App. 1907);
    Edison v. Edison Polyform Mfg. Co., 73 N.J. Eq. 136, 67 Atl. 392 (Ch.
    1907); Frey v. Dixon, 141 N.J. Eq. 481, 58 A.2d 86 (Ch. 1948); Ettore v.
    Philco Television Broadcasting Co., 229 F.2d 481 (3d Cir. 1956).
37 Flake v. Greensboro News Co., 212 N.C. 780, 195 S.E. 55 (1938).
38 Friedman v. Cincinnati Local Joint Exec. Board, 6 Ohio Supp. 276, 20
    Ohio Op. 472 (C.P. 1941); Housh v. Peth, 165 Ohio St. 35, 133 N.E.2d
    340 (1956).
39 Hinish v. Meier & Frank Co., 166 Ore. 482, 113 P.2d 438 (1941).
40 Clayman v. Bernstein, 38 Pa. D. & C. 543 (C.P. 1940); Bennett v. Norban,
    396 Pa. 94, 151 A.2d 476 (1959); Aquino v. Bulletin Co., 154 A.2d 422
    (Pa. Super. 1959); Jenkins v. Dell Pub. Co., 251 F.2d 447 (3d Cir. 1958).
41 Holloman v. Life Ins. Co. of Va., 192 S.C. 454, 7 S.E.2d 169 (1940);
    Meetze v. Associated Press, 230 S.C. 330, 95 S.E.2d 606 (1956); Frith v.
    Associated Press, 176 F. Supp. 671 (E.D.S.C. 1959).
42 Langford v. Vanderbilt University, 199 Tenn. 389, 287 S.W.2d 32 (1956).
43 Roach v. Harper, 105 S.E.2d 564 (W. Va. 1958); Sutherland v. Kroger
    Co., 110 S.E.2d 716 (W. Va. 1959).
44 Miller v. National Broadcasting Co., 157 F. Supp. 240 (D. Del. 1957).
45 Graham v. Baltimore Post Co. (Baltimore Super. Ct. 1932), reported in
    22 Ky. L.J. 108 (1933).
46 Mabry v. Kettering, 89 Ark. 551, 117 S.W. 746 (1909), *second appeal,* 92
    Ark. 81, 122 S.W. 115 (1909).
47 Fitzsimmons v. Olinger Mortuary Ass'n, 91 Colo. 544, 17 P.2d 535 (1932);
    McCreery v. Miller's Grocerteria Co., 99 Colo. 499, 64 P.2d 803 (1936).
    In the last named case the dissent indicates that an opinion recognizing
    the right of privacy was written, but withdrawn.
48 Marek v. Zanol Products Co., 298 Mass. 1, 9 N.E.2d 393 (1937); Thayer
    v. Worcester Post Pub. Co., 284 Mass. 160, 187 N.E. 292 (1933); Themo
    v. New England Newspaper Pub. Co., 306 Mass. 54, 27 N.E.2d 753 (1940).
    In Wright v. R.K.O. Radio Pictures, 55 F. Supp. 639 (D. Mass. 1944), the
    court considered that the state had rejected the right of privacy; but in

Kelley v. Post Pub. Co., 327 Mass. 275, 98 N.E.2d 286 (1951), the question was said to be still open. See also Hazlitt v. Fawcett Publications, 116 F. Supp. 538 (D. Conn. 1953).

49 Berg. v. Minneapolis Star & Tribune Co. 79 F. Supp. 957 (D. Minn. 1948). See also Hazlitt v. Fawcett Publications, 116 F. Supp. 538 (D. Conn. 1953).

50 In Hillman v. Star Pub. Co., 64 Wash. 691, 117 Pac. 594 (1911), the right of privacy was rejected, and said to be a matter for legislation. In State ex rel. La Follette v. Hinkle, 131 Wash. 86, 229 Pac. 317 (1924), it was apparently recognized; but in Lewis v. Physicians & Dentists Credit Bureau, 27 Wash. 2d 267, 177 P.2d 896 (1947), the question was said to be still open in Washington. See also Hazlitt v. Fawcett Publications, 116 F. Supp. 538 (D. Conn. 1953).

Writers have added South Dakota and Wyoming. Davis, *What Do We Mean by "Right to Privacy,"* 4 S.D.L. Rev. 1 (1959), considers that rather vague constitutional provisions in South Dakota will lead to recognition of the right; and the Note, 11 Wyo. L.J. 184 (1957), believes that the same result may follow on the basis of the Wyoming constitutional provision that truth is a defense to libel.

51 See *supra,* note 14.

52 Okla. Stat. Ann. tit. 21, §§ 839–40 (1958). Before the statute there were numerous indications that Oklahoma would recognize the right of privacy without it. Bartholomew v. Workman, 197 Okl. 267, 169 P.2d 1012 (1946); McKinzie v. Huckaby, 112 F. Supp. 642 (W.D. Okl. 1953); Lyles v. State, 330 P.2d 734 (Okl. Cr. 1958); Paramount Pictures v. Leader Press, 24 F. Supp. (W.D. Okl. 1938), *rev'd on other grounds* in 106 F.2d 229 (10th Cir. 1939); Banks v. King Features Syndicate, 30 F. Supp. 352 (S.D.N.Y. 1939, Oklahoma law); Hazlitt v. Fawcett Publications, 116 F. Supp. 538 (D. Conn. 1953, Oklahoma law). The Note in 10 Okl. L. Rev. 353 (1957), considers that there is still some doubt as to whether the common law right may not be recognized, in addition to the statutory one. The New York statute has been held to be exclusive. Kimmerle v. New York Evening Journal Co., 262 N.Y. 99, 186 N.E. 217 (1933).

53 Utah Code Ann. §§ 76–4–8 and 76–4–9 (1953).

54 Va. Code Ann. § 8–650 (1957). See Notes, 38 Va. L. Rev. 117 (1952); 44 Va. L. Rev. 1303 (1958).

55 Henry v. Cherry & Webb, 30 R.I. 13, 73 Atl. 97 (1909).

56 Brunson v. Ranks Army Store, 161 Neb. 519, 73 N.W.2d 803 (1955). See also Schnieding v. American Farmers Mut. Ins. Co., 138 F. Supp. 167 (D. Neb. 1955).

57 Milner v. Red River Valley Pub. Co., 249 S.W.2d 227 (Tex. Civ. App. 1952); McCullagh v. Houston Chronicle Pub. Co., 211 F.2d 4 (5th Cir. 1954). See Seavey, *Can Texas Courts Protect Newly Discovered Interests,* 31 Texas L. Rev. 309 (1953).

58 Judevine v. Benzies-Montanye Fuel & Warehouse Co., 222 Wis. 512, 269 N.W. 295 (1936); State *ex rel.* Distenfeld v. Neelen, 255 Wis. 214, 38

N.W.2d 703 (1949); see Note, [1952] Wis. L. Rev. 507. The last decision, in Yoeckel v. Samonig, 272 Wis. 430, 75 N.W.2d 925 (1956), involved a particularly outrageous invasion, when the defendant intruded into a ladies' rest room, photographed the plaintiff there, and exhibited the picture to patrons in a restaurant. The court bowed to the fact that a bill providing for the right of privacy had failed to pass in the last legislature. The case is nevertheless an atrocity.

59 Cooley, Torts 29 (2d ed. 1888).
60 De May v. Roberts, 46 Mich. 160, 9 N.W. 146 (1881).
61 Young v. Western & A. R. Co., 39 Ga. App. 761, 148 S.E. 414 (1929) (search without warrant); Walker v. Whittle, 83 Ga. App. 445, 64 S.E.2d 87 (1951) (entry without legal authority to arrest husband); Welsh v. Pritchard, 125 Mont. 517, 241 P.2d 816 (1952) (landlord moving in on tenant).
62 Newcomb Hotel Co. v. Corbett, 27 Ga. App. 365, 108 S.E. 309 (1921).
63 Byfield v. Candler, 33 Ga. App. 275, 125 S.E. 905 (1924).
64 Sutherland v. Kroger Co., 110 S.E.2d 716 (W. Va. 1959).
65 Rhodes v. Graham, 238 Ky. 225, 37 S.W.2d 46 (1931).
66 McDaniel v. Atlanta Coca Cola Bottling Co., 60 Ga. App. 92, 2 S.E.2d 810 (1939); Roach v. Harper, 105 S.E.2d 564 (W. Va. 1958). The same conclusion was reached, on the basis of a criminal statute, in People v. Trieber, 28 Cal. 2d 657, 163 P.2d 492, 171 P.2d 1 (1946).
67 Moore v. New York Elevated R. Co., 130 N.Y. 523, 29 N.E. 997 (1892) (looking into windows from elevated railway; plaintiff compensated under eminent domain); Pritchett v. Board of Commissioners of Knox County, 42 Ind. App. 3, 85 N.E. 32 (1908) (relief on the basis of nuisance); Souder v. Pendleton Detectives, 88 So. 2d 716 (La. App. 1956) (spying into windows).

This topic gave rise to a possible nomination for the all-time prize law review title, in the Note, *Crimination of Peeping Toms and Other Men of Vision,* 5 Ark. L. Rev. 388 (1951).

68 Bartow v. Smith, 149 Ohio St. 301, 78 N.E.2d 735 (1948).
69 *Cf.* Duty v. General Finance Co., 154 Tex. 16, 273 S.W.2d 64 (1954).
70 House v. Path, 165 Ohio St. 35, 133 N.E.2d 340 (1956), *affirming* 99 Ohio App. 485, 135 N.E.2d 440 (1955). *Accord,* on the ground of "nuisance," Wiggins v. Moskins Credit Clothing Store, 137 F. Supp. 764 (E.D.S.C. 1956).
71 Brex v. Smith, 104 N.J. Eq. 386, 146 Atl. 34 (Ch. 1929); Zimmerman v. Wilson, 81 F.2d 847 (3d Cir. 1936).
72 Frey v. Dixon, 141 N.J. Eq. 481, 58 A.2d 86 (Ch. 1948); State *ex rel.* Clemens v. Whitthaus, 228 S.W.2d 4 (Mo. 1950) (court order).
73 Bednarik v. Bednarik, 18 N.J. Misc. 633, 16 A.2d 80 (Ch. 1940). *Cf.* Hawkins v. Kuhne, 153 App. Div. 216, 137 N.Y.S. 1090 (1912), *aff'd,* 208 N.Y. 555, 101 N.E. 1104 (1913) (illegal photographing and measuring by police called an "assault").

74 Owens v. Henman, 1 W. & S. 548, 37 Am. Dec. 481 (Pa. 1841).
75 Lisowski v. Jaskiewicz, 76 Pa. D & C. 79 (C.P. 1950); Christie v. Greenleaf, 78 Pa. D. & C. 191 (C.P. 1951).
76 Horstman v. Newman, 291 S.W.2d 567 (Ky. 1956).
77 Gotthelf v. Hillcrest Lumber Co., 280 App. Div. 668, 116 N.Y.S.2d 873 (1952).
78 Voelker v. Tyndall, 226 Ind. 43, 75 N.E.2d 548 (1947); McGovern v. Van Riper, 140 N.J. Eq. 341, 54, A.2d 469 (Ch. 1947), affirming 137 N.J. Eq. 548, 45 A.2d 842 (Ct. Err. & App. 1946), which reversed 137 N.J. Eq. 24, 43 A.2d 514 (Ch. 1945); State ex rel. Mavity v. Tyndall, 224 Ind. 364, 66 N.E.2d 755 (1946); Bartletta v. McFeeley, 107 N.J. Eq. 141, 152 Atl. 17 (Ch. 1930), aff'd, 109 N.J. Eq. 241, 156 Atl. 658 (Ct. Err. & App. 1931); Fernicola v. Keenan, 136 N.J. Eq. 9, 39 A.2d 851 (Ch. 1944); Norman v. City of Las Vegas, 64 Nev. 38, 177 P.2d 442 (1947); Mabry v. Kettering, 89 Ark. 551, 117 S.W. 746 (1909), second appeal, 92 Ark. 81, 122 S.W. 115 (1909); Hodgeman v. Olson, 86 Wash. 615, 150 Pac. 1122 (1915); cf. Sellers v. Henry, 329 S.W.2d 214 (Ky. 1959). As to the use made of police photographs, see infra, text at notes 143–45.

In Anthony v. Anthony, 9 N.J. Super. 411, 74 A.2d 919 (Ch. 1950), a compulsory blood test in a paternity suit was held to be justified, and not to invade any right of privacy.

Such cases, of course, usually turn on constitutional rights.
79 Bowles v. Misle, 64 F. Supp. 835 (D. Neb. 146); United States v. Alabama Highway Express Co., 46 F. Supp. 450 (D. Ala. 1942); Alabama State Federation of Labor v. McAdory, 246 Ala. 1, 13 So. 2d 810 (1944).
80 Chappell v. Stewart, 82 Md. 323, 33 Atl. 542 (1896). Cf. McKinzie v. Huckaby, 112 F. Supp. 642 (W.D. Okl. 1953), where the defendant, calling at the plaintiff's home, brought along a policeman, who remained outside in the car.

In Schultz v. Frankfort Marine, Accident & Plate Glass Ins. Co., 151 Wis. 537, 139 N.W. 386 (1913), "rough shadowing" which was visible to onlookers, was held to be actionable as slander.
81 Gill v. Hearst Pub. Co., 40 Cal. 2d 224, 253 P.2d 441 (1953); Berg v. Minneapolis Star & Tribune Co., 79 F. Supp. 957 (D. Minn. 1948) (courtroom); Lyles v. State, 330 P.2d 734 (Okl. Cr. 1958) (television in court). Cf. Gautier v. Pro-Football, Inc., 304 N.Y. 354, 107 N.E.2d 485 (1952); Sports & General Press Agency v. "Our Dogs" Pub. Co., [1916] 2 K.B. 880; and cases cited infra, note 104. See Fitzpatrick, Unauthorized Photographs, 20 Geo. L.J. 134 (1932). In United States v. Gugel, 119 F. Supp. 897 (E.D. Ky. 1954), the right to take such pictures was said to be protected by the Constitution of the United States.

The same type of reasoning, that the record does not differ from a written report, was applied to the recording of a private telephone conversation between plaintiff and defendant, in Chaplin v. National Broadcasting Co., 15 F.R.D. 134 (S.D.N.Y. 1953).

As to publication, see *infra*, text at notes 102–08.

In Friedman v. Cincinnati Local Joint Executive Board, 6 Ohio Supp. 276, 20 Ohio Op. 473 (C.P. 1941), a labor union which had taken pictures of customers crossing a picket line was enjoined from making use of them for purposes of retaliation.

82 Barber v. Time, Inc. 348 Mo. 1199, 159 S.W.2d 291 (1942). *Cf.* Clayman v. Bernstein, 38 Pa. D. & C. 543 (C.P. 1940) (picture of semi-conscious patient taken by physician).

83 Douglas v. Stokes, 149 Ky. 506, 149 S.W. 849 (1912) (publication of picture by photographer, breach of implied contract); Thompson v. Adelberg & Berman, 181 Ky. 487, 205 S.W. 558 (1918) (publication of debt, libel); Feeney v. Young, 191 App. Div. 501, 181 N.Y.S. 481 (1920) (exhibition of pictures of caesarian operation, breach of trust and implied contract); Peed v. Washington Times, 55 Wash. L. Rep. 182 (D.C. 1927) (publication of stolen picture).

84 Brents v. Morgan, 221 Ky. 765, 229 S.W. 967 (1927). "Dr. W. R. Morgan owes an account here of $49.67. And if promises would pay an account this account would have been settled long ago. This account will be advertised as long as it remains unpaid."

85 112 Cal. App. 285, 297 Pac. 91 (1931).

86 Mau v. Rio Grande Oil, Inc., 28 F. Supp. 845 (N.D. Cal. 1939).

87 Trammell v. Citizens News Co., Inc., 285 Ky. 529, 148 S.W.2d 708 (1941); Biederman's of Springfield, Inc. v. Wright, 322 S.W.2d 892 (Mo. 1959). *Cf.* Bennett v. Norban, 396 Pa. 94, 151 A.2d 476 (1959).

In Maysville Transit Co. v. Ort, 296 Ky. 524, 177 S.W.2d 369 (1944), it was held that a corporation had no right of privacy, but that there could be recovery for disclosure of its tax returns on the basis of violation of a statute.

88 Banks v. King Features Syndicate, 30 F. Supp. 352 (S.D.N.Y. 1939) (Oklahoma law; newspaper publication of X-rays of woman's pelvic region); Griffin v. Medical Society, 11 N.Y.S.2d 109 (Sup. Ct. 1939) (publication in medical journal of pictures of plaintiff's deformed nose); Feeney v. Young, 191 App. Div. 501, 181 N.Y.S. 481 (1920) (public exhibition of films of caesarian operation). *Cf.* Clayman v. Bernstein, 38 Pa. D & C. 543 (C.P. 1940) (doctor enjoined from using pictures of facial disfigurement taken while patient was semiconscious).

89 Cason v. Baskin, 155 Fla. 198, 20 So. 2d 243 (1945), *second appeal*, 159 Fla. 31, 30 So.2d 635 (1947).

90 Trammell v. Citizens News Co., 285 Ky. 529, 148 S.W.2d 708 (1941). *Cf.* Thompson v. Adelberg & Berman, Inc., 181 Ky. 487, 205 SW. 558 (1918).

91 Brents v. Morgan, 221 Ky. 765, 299 S.W. 967 (1927).

92 Bennett v. Norban, 396 Pa. 94, 151 A.2d 476 (1959). *Cf.* Biederman's of Springfield, Inc. v. Wright, 322 S.W.2d 892 (Mo. 1959) (public restaurant).

93 Gouldman-Taber Pontiac, Inc. v. Zerbst, 96 Ga. App. 48, 99 S.E.2d 475

134   WILLIAM L. PROSSER

(1957), *reversed in* 213 Ga. 682, 100 S.E.2d 881 (1957), on the ground that the communication was privileged.
94 Patton v. Jacobs, 118 Ind. App. 358, 78 N.E.2d 789 (1948); Voneye v. Turner, 240 S.W.2d 588 (Ky. 1951); Lucas v. Moskins Stores, 262 S.W.2d 679 (Ky. 1953); Hawley v. Professional Credit Bureau, Inc., 345 Mich. 500, 76 N.W.2d 835 (1956); Lewis v. Physicians & Dentists Credit Bureau, 27 Wash. 2d 267, 177 P.2d 896 (1947). *Cf.* Davis v. General Finance & Thrift Corp., 80 Ga. App. 708, 57 S.E.2d 225 (1950) (telegram to plaintiff); Perry v. Moskins Stores, 249 S.W.2d 812 (Ky. 1952) (postcard to plaintiff).
95 Gregory v. Bryan-Hunt Co., 295 Ky. 345, 174 S.W.2d 510 (1943) (oral accusation of theft). On the other hand, in Kerby v. Hal Roach Studios, 53 Cal. App.2d 207, 127 P.2d 577 (1942), the distribution of a letter to a thousand persons was held, without discussion, to make it public.
96 Berry v. Moench, 8 Utah 2d 191, 331 P.2d 814 (1958); *cf.* Simonsen v. Swenson, 104 Neb. 224, 177 N.W. 831 (1920); and see Note, 43 Minn. L. Rev. 943 (1959).
97 Warren and Brandeis, *The Right to Privacy*, 4 Harv. L. Rev. 193, 217 (1890).
98 Martin v. F.I.Y. Theatre Co., 10 Ohio Op. 338 (Ohio C.P. 1938); Gregory v. Bryan-Hunt Co., 295 Ky. 345, 174 S.W.2d 510 (1943); Pangallo v. Murphy, 243 S.W.2d 496 (Ky. 1951); Lewis v. Physicians & Dentists Credit Bureau, 27 Wash. 2d 267, 177 P.2d 896 (1947).
99 Mau v. Rio Grande Oil, Inc., 28 F. Supp. 845 (N.D. Cal. 1939) (radio); Strickler v. National Broadcasting Co., 167 F. Supp. 68 (S.D. Cal. 1958) (television); Binns v. Vitagraph Co. of America, 210 N.Y. 51, 103 N.E. 1108 (1913) (motion picture); Donohue v. Warner Bros. Pictures, 194 F.2d 6 (10th Cir. 1952) (same); Ettore v. Philco Television Broadcasting Co., 229 F.2d 481 (3d Cir. 1956) (motion picture film on television).
100 Bennett v. Norban, 396 Pa. 94, 151 A.2d 476 (1959); Biederman's of Springfield, Inc. v. Wright, 322 S.W.2d 892 (Mo. 1959); Linehan v. Linehan, 134 Cal. App. 2d 250, 285 P.2d 326 (1955).
101 Reed v. Orleans Parish Schoolboard, 21 So. 2d 895 (La. App. 1945). Compare the cases of disclosure of corporate records, *supra* note 79.
102 See *infra*, text at notes 218–63.
103 In Chaplin v. National Broadcasting Co., 15 F.R.D. 134 (S.D.N.Y. 1953), the same reasoning was applied to the broadcast of a recorded private telephone conversation between plaintiff and defendant. The case looks wrong, since one element, the sound of Chaplin's voice, was not then public, and was expected to be private to the recipient.
104 Sports & General Press Agency v. "Our Dogs" Pub. Co., [1916] 2 K.B. 880; Humiston v. Universal Film Mfg. Co., 189 App. Div. 467, 178 N.Y.S. 752 (1919); Merle v. Sociological Research Film Corp., 166 App. Div. 376, 152 N.Y.S. 829 (1915); Berg v. Minneapolis Star & Tribune Co., 79 F. Supp. 957 (D. Minn. 1948) (courtroom); Lyles v. State, 330 P.2d

734 (Okl. Cr. 1958) (television in courtroom). *Cf.* Gautier v. Pro-Football, Inc., 304 N.Y. 354, 107 N.E.2d 485 (1952) (football game); Jacova v. Southern Radio & Television Co., 83 So. 2d 34 (Fla. 1955) (cigar store raid).

It may be suggested, however, that a man may still be private in a public place. Suppose that a citizen responds to a call of nature in the bushes in a public park?

105 Gill v. Hearst Pub. Co., 40 Cal. 2d 224, 253 P.2d 441 (1953).

106 Note, 44 Va. L. Rev. 1303 (1958).

107 Blumenthal v. Picture Classics, 235 App. Div. 570, 257 N.Y.S. 800 (1932), *aff'd,* 261 N.Y. 504, 185 N.E. 713 (1933).

108 In Sarat Lahiri v. Daily Mirror, 162 Misc. 776, 295 N.Y.S. 382 (Sup. Ct. 1937).

109 Barber v. Time, Inc., 348 Mo. 1199, 159 S.W.2d 291 (1942) (hospital bed). *Cf.* Clayman v. Bernstein, 38 Pa. D. & C. 543 (C.P. 1940) (picture of semi-conscious patient taken by physician).

110 Peed v. Washington Times, 55 Wash. L. Rep. 182 (D.C. 1927).

In Metter v. Los Angeles Examiner, 35 Cal. App. 2d 304, 95 P.2d 491 (1939), the newspaper appears to have gotten away with a great deal. After plaintiff's wife had committed suicide, the screen of his kitchen window was forced open, and a photograph of his wife disappeared from his table. The same day the same photograph appeared in the paper. The court considered that there was no evidence that the defendant had stolen it. The actual decision can be justified, however, on the ground that the woman was dead. See *infra,* text at note 205.

111 Bazemore v. Savannah Hospital, 171 Ga. 257, 155 S.E. 194 (1930) (picture of deformed child born to plaintiff, obtained from hospital attendants). *Cf.* Douglas v. Stokes, 149 Ky. 506, 149 S.W. 849 (1912) (breach of implied contract by photographer).

112 *Cf.* Maysville Transit Co. v. Ort, 296 Ky. 524, 177 S.W.2d 369 (1944); Munzer v. Blaisdell, 183 Misc. 773, 49 N.Y.S.2d 915 (Sup. Ct. 1944), *aff'd,* 269 App. Div. 970, 58 N.Y.S.2d 360 (1945) (records of mental institution); Sellers v. Henry, 329 S.W.2d 214 (Ky. 1959) (police photograph; liability dependent upon use).

113 Meetze v. Associated Press, 230 S.C. 330, 95 S.E.2d 606 (1956).

114 Stryker v. Republic Pictures Corp., 108 Cal. App. 2d 191, 238 P.2d 670 (1951); Continental Optical Co. v. Reed, 119 Ind. App. 643, 86 N.E.2d 306 (1949).

In Thompson v. Curtis Pub. Co., 193 F.2d 953 (3d Cir. 1952), a patent obtained by the plaintiff was held to be a public matter, "as fully as a play, a book, or a song."

115 See *infra,* text at notes 285–88.

116 Bernstein v. National Broadcasting Co., 129 F. Supp. 817 (D.D.C. 1955), *aff'd,* 232 F.2d 369 (D.C. Cir. 1956) (murder trial used in broadcast); Smith v. National Broadcasting Co., 138 Cal. App. 2d 807, 292 P.2d 600

(1956) (false report to police of escape of black panther). In both cases the name of the plaintiff was not used.

117 112 Cal. App. 285, 297 Pac. 91 (1931) (see *supra*, text at note 85). *Accord*, Mau v. Rio Grande Oil, Inc., 28 F. Supp. 845 (N.D. Cal. 1939); and see cases cited in the preceding note. The Melvin and Mau cases were explained on the basis of the use of the name in the Smith case.

118 Reed v. Real Detective Pub. Co., 63 Ariz. 294, 162 P.2d 133 (1945); Davis. v. General Finance & Thrift Corp., 80 Ga. App. 708, 57 S.E.2d 225 (1950); Gill v. Hearst Pub. Co. 40 Cal. 2d 224, 253 P.2d 441 (1953); Samuel v. Curtis Pub. Co., 122 F. Supp. 327 (N.D. Cal. 1954).

119 Meetze v. Associated Press, 230 S.C. 330, 95 S.E.2d 606 (1956) (report of birth of child to girl twelve years old).

120 Garner v. Triangle Publications, 97 F. Supp. 546 (S.D.N.Y. 1951). *Cf.* Myers v. U.S. Camera Pub. Corp., 9 Misc. 2d 765, 167 N.Y.S.2d 771 (N.Y. City Ct. 1957) (nude full body photograph of model); Feeney v. Young, 191 App. Div. 501, 181 N.Y.S. 481 (1920) (exhibition of film of caesarian operation); Banks v. King Features Syndicate, 30 F. Supp. 352 (S.D.N.Y. 1939) (X-rays of woman's pelvic region).

121 Cason v. Baskin, 155 Fla. 198, 20 So. 2d 243 (1944), *second appeal*, 159 Fla. 31, 30 So. 2d 635 (1947). *Cf.* Stryker v. Republic Pictures Corp., 108 Cal. App. 2d 191, 238 P.2d 670 (1951).

122 113 F.2d 806 (2d Cir. 1940), *affirming* 34 F. Supp. 19 (S.D.N.Y. 1938).

123 See *infra*, text at notes 218–63.

124 See *supra*, text at note 85.

125 Suggested by the lower court in Sidis v. F–R Pub. Corp., 34 F. Supp. 19 (S.D.N.Y. 1938).

126 See *infra*, text at note 290.

127 Lord Byron v. Johnston, 2 Mer. 29, 35 Eng. Rep. 851 (1816).

128 See *infra*, text at notes 260–63, 271–73.

129 See Wigmore, *The Right Against False Attribution of Belief or Utterance*, 4 Ky. L.J. No. 8, p. 3 (1916).

130 *Cf.* Pavesich v. New England Life Ins. Co., 122 Ga. 190, 50 S.E. 68 (1905); Manger v. Kree Institute of Electrolysis, 233 F.2d 5 (2d Cir. 1956); Foster-Milburn Co. v. Chinn, 134 Ky. 424, 120 S.W. 364 (1909); Fairfield v. American Photocopy Equipment Co., 138 Cal. App. 2d 82, 291 P.2d 194 (1955).

131 Hinish v. Meier & Frank Co., 166 Ore. 482, 113 P.2d 438 (1941). *Accord*, Schwartz v. Edrington, 133 La. 235, 62 So. 660 (1913) (continued circulation of petition after plaintiff had withdrawn his signature).

132 D'Altomonte v. New York Herald Co., 154 App. Div. 453, 139 N.Y.S. 200 (1913), *modified*, however, as not within the New York statute, in 208 N.Y. 596, 102 N.E. 1101 (1913) (authorship of absurd travel story); Hogan v. A. S. Barnes & Co., 114 U.S.P.Q. 314 (Pa. C.P. 1957) (book on golf purporting to give information from plaintiff about his game).

133 State *ex rel.* La Follette v. Hinkle, 131 Wash. 86, 229 Pac. 317 (1924).

134 Hamilton v. Lumbermen's Mutual Cas. Co., 82 So. 2d 61 (La. App. 1955).
135 Marks v. Jaffa, 6 Misc. 290, 26 N.Y.S. 908 (Super. Ct. N.Y. City 1893).
136 *Infra,* text at notes 258–59.
137 Peay v. Curtis Pub. Co., 78 F. Supp. 305 (D.D.C. 1948).
138 Leverton v. Curtis Pub. Co., 192 F.2d 974 (3d Cir. 1951).
139 Gill v. Curtis Pub. Co., 38 Cal. 2d 273, 239 P.2d 630 (1952).
140 Martin v. Johnson Pub. Co., 157 N.Y.S.2d 409 (Sup. Ct. 1956). *Accord,* Semler v. Ultem Publications, 170 Misc. 551, 9 N.Y.S.2d 319 (N.Y. City Ct. 1938) (pictures of model in sensational sex magazine); Russell v. Marboro Books, 18 Misc.2d 166, 183 N.Y.S.2d 8 (Sup. Ct. 1959) (picture of model used in bawdy advertisement for bed sheets).
141 Metzger v. Dell Pub. Co., 207 Misc. 182, 136 N.Y.S.2d 888 (Sup. Ct. 1955).
    More doubtful is Callas v. Whisper, Inc., 198 Misc. 829 (1950), *affirmed,* 278 App. Div. 974, 105 N.Y.S.2d 1001 (1951), where the picture of a minor, obtained by fraudulent representations, was used as background in a night club, with the innuendo that she was in a disreputable place. It was held that she had no cause of action. The facts, however, are by no means entirely clear from the summary of the pleading.
142 Thompson v. Close-Up, Inc., 277 App. Div. 848, 98 N.Y.S.2d 300 (1950).
143 Itzkovitch v. Whitaker, 115 La. 479, 39 So. 499 (1950); and see Downs v. Swann, 111 Md. 53, 73 Atl. 653 (1909); State *ex rel.* Mavity v. Tyndall, 224 Ind. 364, 66 N.E.2d 755 (1946); Norman v. City of Las Vegas, 64 Nev. 38, 177 P.2d 442 (1947). *Cf.* Vanderbilt v. Mitchell, 72 N.J. Eq. 910, 67 Atl. 97 (Ct. Err. & App. 1907) (birth certificate naming plaintiff as father of child).
144 Mabry v. Kettering, 89 Ark. 551, 117 S.W. 746 (1909), *second appeal,* 92 Ark. 81, 122 S.W. 115 (1909); State *ex rel.* Mavity v. Tyndall, 224 Ind. 364, 66 N.E.2d 755 (1946); Norman v. City of Las Vegas, 64 Nev. 38, 177 P.2d 442 (1947); Bartletta v. McFeeley, 107 N.J. Eq. 141, 152 Atl. 17 (Ch. 1930), *affirmed,* 109 N.J. Eq. 241, 156 Atl. 658 (Ct. Err. & App. 1931); McGovern v. Van Riper, 140 N.J. Eq. 341, 54 A.2d 469 (Ch. 1947); Downs v. Swann, 111 Md. 53, 73 Atl. 653 (1909).
145 Hodgeman v. Olsen, 86 Wash. 615, 150 Pac. 1122 (1915) (convict); Fernicola v. Keenan, 136 N.J. Eq. 9, 39 A.2d 851 (Ch. 1944).
146 *Cf.* Bennett v. Norban, 396 Pa. 94, 151 A.2d 476 (1959) (accusation of theft upon the street); Linehan v. Linehan, 134 Cal. App. 2d 250, 285 P.2d 326 (1955) (public accusation that plaintiff was not the lawful wife of defendant's ex-husband); D'Altomonte v. New York Herald, 154 App. Div. 453, 139 N.Y.S. 200 (1913), *modified,* 208 N.Y. 596, 102 N.E. 1101 (1913) (imputing authorship of absurd travel story); Peay v. Curtis Pub. Co., 78 F. Supp. 305 (D.D.C. 1948) (imputing cheating practices to taxi driver); Martin v. Johnson Pub. Co., 157 N.Y.S.2d 409 (Sup. Ct. 1956) (use of picture with article on "man hungry" women); Russell v. Marboro

Books, 18 Misc. 2d 166, 183 N.Y.S.2d 8 (Sup. Ct. 1959) (picture used in bawdy advertisement).
147 See *supra*, text at notes 118–25.
148 In Strickler v. National Broadcasting Co., 167 F. Supp. 68 (S.D. Cal. 1958), it was left to the jury to decide whether fictitious details of plaintiff's conduct in an airplane crisis, as portrayed in a broadcast, would be objectionable to a reasonable man.
149 Koussevitzky v. Allen, Towne & Heath, 188 Misc. 479, 68 N.Y.S.2d 779 (Sup. Ct.), *aff'd*, 272 App. Div. 759, 69 N.Y.S.2d 432 (1947).
150 Middleton v. News Syndicate Co., 162 Misc. 516, 295 N.Y.S. 120 (Sup. Ct. 1937).
  It would appear, however, that this was carried entirely too far in Jones v. Herald Post Co., 230 Ky. 227, 18 S.W.2d 972 (1929). There was a newspaper report of the murder of plaintiff's husband in her presence, and false and sensational statements were attributed to her, that she had fought with the criminals, and would have killed them if she could.
151 Pollard v. Photographic Co., 40 Ch. D. 345 (1888).
152 Holmes v. Underwood & Underwood, 225 App. Div. 360, 233 N.Y.S. 153 (1929); Klug v. Sheriffs, 129 Wis. 468, 109 N.W. 656 (1906); Fitzsimmons v. Olinger Mortuary Ass'n, 91 Colo. 544, 17 P.2d 535 (1932); McCreery v. Miller's Grocerteria Co., 99 Colo. 499, 64 P.2d 803 (1936); Bennett v. Gusdorf, 101 Mont. 39, 53 P.2d 91 (1935).
153 *Supra*, text at note 12.
154 *Supra*, note 14.
155 It is not impossible that there might be appropriation of the plaintiff's identity, as by impersonation, without the use of either his name or his likeness, and that this would be an invasion of his right of privacy. No such case appears to have arisen.
156 Mackenzie v. Soden Mineral Springs Co., 27 Abb. N. Cas. 402, 18 N.Y.S. 240 (Sup. Ct. 1891); Eliot v. Jones, 66 Misc. 95, 120 N.Y.S. 989 (Sup. Ct. 1910), *aff'd*, 140 App. Div. 911, 125 N.Y.S. 1119 (1910); Thompson v. Tillford, 152 App. Div. 928, 137 N.Y.S. 523 (1912); Brociner v. Radio Wire Television, Inc., 15 Misc.2d 843, 183 N.Y.S.2d 743 (Sup. Ct. 1959) (use in union drive for membership held advertising); Birmingham Broadcasting Co. v. Bell, 259 Ala. 656, 68 So. 2d 314 (1953), *later appeal*, 266 Ala. 266, 96 So. 2d 263 (1957); Kerby v. Hal Roach Studios, 53 Cal. App.2d 207, 127 P.2d 577 (1942); Fairfield v. American Photocopy Equipment Co., 138 Cal. App. 2d 82, 291 P.2d 194 (1955).
  In the cases cited in the next note, the plaintiff's name accompanied the picture.
157 Fisher v. Murray M. Rosenberg, Inc., 175 Misc. 370, 23 N.Y.S.2d 677 (Sup. Ct. 1940); Russell v. Marboro Books, 18 Misc. 2d 166, 183 N.Y.S.2d 8 (Sup. Ct. 1959); Flores v. Mosler Safe Co., 7 N.Y.2d 276, 164 N.E.2d 853 (1959), *affirming* 7 App. Div. 2d 226; 182 N.Y.S.2d 126 (1959); Korn v. Rennison, 156 A.2d 476 (Conn. Super. 1959); Pavesich v. New England

Life Ins. Co., 122 Ga. 190, 50 S.E. 68 (1905); Colgate-Palmolive Co. v.
Tullos, 219 F.2d 617 (5th Cir. 1955) (Georgia law); Eick v. Perk Dog
Food Co., 347 Ill. App. 293, 106 N.E.2d 742 (1952); Continental Optical
Co. v. Reed, 119 Ind. App. 643, 86 N.E.2d 306 (1949); Kunz v. Allen,
102 Kan. 883, 172 Pac. 532 (1918); Foster-Milburn Co. v. Chinn, 134
Ky. 424, 120 S.W. 364 (1909); Pallas v. Crowley, Milner & Co., 322 Mich.
411, 33 N.W.2d 911 (1948); Munden v. Harris, 153 Mo. App. 652, 134
S.W. 1076 (1911); Flake v. Greensboro News Co., 212 N.C. 780, 195
S.E. 55 (1938).
158 Young v. Greneker Studios, 175 Misc. 1027, 26 N.Y.S.2d 357 (Sup. Ct.
1941) (manikin). In Freed v. Loew's, Inc., 175 Misc. 616, 24 N.Y.S.2d
679 (Sup. Ct. 1940), an artist used the plaintiff's figure as a base, but
improved it, and it was held not to be a "portrait or picture" within the
New York statute. But in Loftus v. Greenwich Lithographing Co., 192
App. Div. 251, 182 N.Y.S. 428 (1920), the artist used the plaintiff's
picture in designing a poster, but made some changes, and the result
was held not to fall within the statute. The difference between the two
cases may have been one of the extent of the resemblance.
159 Neyland v. Home Pattern Co., 65 F.2d 363 (2d Cir. 1933) (patterns);
Lane v. F. W. Woolworth Co., 171 Misc. 66, 11 N.Y.S.2d 199 (Sup. Ct.
1939), *aff'd*, 256 App. Div. 1065, 12 N.Y.S.2d 352 (1939) (lockets); McNulty
v. Press Pub. Co., 136 Misc. 833, 241 N.Y.S. 29 (Sup. Ct. 1930) (cartoon
containing photograph); Jansen v. Hilo Packing Co., 202 Misc. 900, 118
N.Y.S.2d 162 (Sup. Ct. 1952), *aff'd*, 282 App. Div. 935, 125 N.Y.S.2d
648 (1952) (popcorn); Miller v. Madison Square Garden Corp., 176 Misc.
714, 28 N.Y.S.2d 811 (Sup. Ct. 1941) (booklet sold at bicycle races).
　　Also, of course, when there is an unauthorized sale of the picture
itself. Kunz v. Boselman, 131 App. Div. 288, 115 N.Y.S. 650 (1909);
Wyatt v. James McCreery Co., 126 App. Div. 650, 111 N.Y.S. 86 (1908);
Holmes v. Underwood & Underwood, 225 App. Div. 360, 233 N.Y.S.
153 (1929).
160 Von Thodorovich v. Franz Josef Beneficial Ass'n, 154 Fed. 911 (E.D.
Pa. 1907); Edison v. Edison Polyform Mfg. Co., 73 N.J. Eq. 136, 67 Atl.
392 (Ch. 1907). *Cf.* U.S. Life Ins. Co. v. Hamilton, 238 S.W.2d 289 (Tex.
Civ. App. 1951), where the use of an employee's name on company
letterhead after termination of his employment was said not to invade
his right of privacy (not recognized in Texas), but was held to be actionable anyway.
161 Hogan v. A. S. Barnes Co., 114 U.S.P.Q. 314 (1957) (book); Binns v.
Vitagraph Co. of America, 210 N.Y. 51, 103 N.E. 1108 (1913) (motion
picture); Redmond v. Columbia Pictures Corp., 277 N.Y. 707, 14 N.E.2d
636 (1938), *affirming* 253 App. Div. 708, 1 N.Y.S.2d 643 (same); Stryker
v. Republic Pictures Corp., 108 Cal. App. 2d 191, 238 P.2d 670 (1951)
(same); Ettore v. Philco Television Broadcasting Co., 229 F.2d 481 (3d
Cir. 1956) (motion picture exhibited on television); Almind v. Sea Beach

Co., 78 Misc. 445, 139 N.Y.S. 559 (Sup. Ct. 1912), aff'd, 157 App. Div. 927, 142 N.Y.S. 1106 (1913) (picture of plaintiff entering or leaving street car used to teach other passengers how to do it).

In Donahue v. Warner Bros. Pictures, 194 F.2d 6 (10th Cir. 1952), it was held that a motion picture, based upon the life of a deceased celebrity but partly fictional, and using his name, came within the Utah statute. But in Donahue v. Warner Bros. Pictures Distributing Corp., 2 Utah 2d 256, 272 P.2d 177 (1954), the state court rejected this decision, and indicated that the statute was to be limited to the use of name or likeness in advertising, or the sale of "some collateral commodity." The effect of this is to nullify the federal decision.

162 Supra, text at note 14.
163 In Oklahoma, Utah, and Virginia. See supra notes 52–54.
164 See, as illustrations of possible differences: Cardy v. Maxwell, 9 Misc.2d 329, 169 N.Y.S.2d 547 (Sup. Ct. 1957) (use of name and publicity to extort money not a commercial use within the statute); Hamilton v. Lumbermen's Mutual Cas. Co., 82 So. 2d 61 (La. App. 1955) (advertising in name of plaintiff for witnesses of accident); State ex rel. La Follette v. Hinkle, 131 Wash. 86, 229 Pac. 317 (1924) (use of name as candidate for office by political party). See also the cases cited infra, notes 167 and 168.
165 Du Boulay v. Du Boulay, L.R. 2 P.C. 430 (1869); Cowley v. Cowley, [1901] A.C. 450; Brown Chemical Co. v. Meyer, 139 U.S. 540 (1891); Smith v. United States Casualty Co., 197 N.Y. 420, 90 N.E. 947 (1910); Baumann v. Baumann, 250 N.Y. 382, 165 N.E. 819 (1929); Bartholomew v. Workman, 197 Okla. 267, 169 P.2d 1012 (1946).
166 "While I know of no instance, it can safely be assumed that should A, by the use of B's name, together with other characteristics of B, successfully impersonate B, and thereby obtain valuable recognition or benefits from a third person, a suit by B against A could be maintained." Green, The Right of Privacy, 27 Ill. L. Rev. 237, 243–44 (1932).

Three years after these words were published, recovery was allowed in such a case. Goodyear Tire & Rubber Co. v. Vandergriff, 52 Ga. App. 662, 184 S.E. 452 (1936), in which defendant, impersonating plaintiff's agent, obtained confidential information from dealers about tire prices.
167 Burns v. Stevens, 236 Mich. 443, 210 N.W. 482 (1926). Contra, Baumann v. Baumann, 250 N.Y. 382, 165 N.E. 819 (1929); but cf. Niver v. Niver, 200 Misc. 993, 111 N.Y.S.2d 889 (Sup. Ct. 1951).
168 Vanderbilt v. Mitchell, 71 N.J. Eq. 910, 67 Atl. 97 (Ct. Err. & App. 1907).
169 Swacker v. Wright, 154 Misc. 822, 277 N.Y.S. 296 (Sup. Ct. 1935); People v. Charles Scribner's Sons, 205 Misc. 818, 130 N.Y.S.2d 514 (N.Y. City Magis. Ct. 1954).
170 Nebb v. Bell Syndicate, 41 F. Supp. 929 (S.D.N.Y. 1941).
171 Pfaudler v. Pfaudler Co., 114 Misc. 477, 186 N.Y.S. 725 (Sup. Ct. 1920).
172 In Uproar Co. v. National Broadcasting Co., 8 F. Supp. 358 (D. Mass.

1934), *affirmed as modified,* 81 F.2d 373 (1st Cir. 1936), the comedian Ed Wynn published, in pamphlet form, humorous skits which he had performed on the radio, in which he made frequent mention of "Graham." It was held that the public would reasonably understand this to refer to Graham McNamee, a radio announcer who had been his foil.

In Kerby v. Hal Roach Studios, 53 Cal. App. 2d 207, 127 P.2d 577 (1942), defendant, advertising a motion picture, made use of the name Marion Kerby, which was signed to a letter apparently suggesting an assignation. Plaintiff, an actress named Marion Kerby, was the only person of that name listed in the city directory and the telephone book. She had in fact a large number of telephone calls about the letter. It was held that it might reasonably be understood to refer to her.

In Krieger v. Popular Publications, 167 Misc. 5, 3 N.Y.S.2d 480 (Sup. Ct. 1938), a complaint alleging that the plaintiff was a professional boxer, and that the defendant had appropriated his name by publishing a story about such a boxer of the same name, which appeared more than a hundred times in twenty pages, was held sufficient to state a cause of action.

On the other hand, in Levey v. Warner Bros. Pictures, 57 F. Supp. 40 (S.D.N.Y. 1944), the plaintiff, whose name was Mary, was the divorced first wife of the actor George M. Cohan. The defendant made a motion picture of his life, in which the part of the wife, named Mary, was played by an actress. The part was almost entirely fictional, and there was no mention of the divorce. It was held that this could not reasonably be understood to be a portrayal of the plaintiff.

In such cases the test appears to be that usually applied in cases of defamation, as to whether a reasonable man would understand the name to identify the plaintiff. Compare Harrison v. Smith, 20 L.T.R. (n.s.) 713 (1869); Clare v. Farrell, 70 F. Supp. 276 (D. Minn. 1947); Macfadden's Publications v. Turner, 95 S.W.2d 1027 (Tex. Civ. App. 1936); Landau v. Columbia Broadcasting System, 205 Misc. 357, 128 N.Y.S.2d 254 (Sup. Ct. 1954); Newton v. Grubb, 155 Ky. 479, 159 S.W. 994 (1913).

173 Mackenzie v. Soden Mineral Springs Co., 27 Abb. N. Cas. 402, 18 N.Y.S. 240 (Sup. Ct. 1891) (signature); Orsini v. Eastern Wine Corp., 190 Misc. 235, 73 N.Y.S.2d 426 (Sup. Ct. 1947), *aff'd,* 273 App. Div. 947, 78 N.Y.S.2d 224 (1948), *appeal denied,* 273 App. Dov. 996, 79 N.Y.S.2d 870 (1948) (plaintiff's coat of arms).

174 The only cases have involved construction of the New York statute, as to the use of the plaintiff's "name." In Davis v. R.K.O. Radio Pictures, 16 F. Supp. 195 (S.D.N.Y. 1936), where a clairvoyant made use of the name "Cassandra," it was held that this was limited to genuine names. In Gardella v. Log Cabin Products Co., 89 F.2d 891 (2d Cir. 1937), a trade mark case, a dictum disagreed, and said that the statute would cover a stage name. In People v. Charles Scribner's Sons, 205 Misc. 818, 130 N.Y.S.2d 514 (N.Y. City Magis. Ct. 1954), it was said that there was

no protection of an "assumed" name, and doubt as to a "stage name." In the unreported case of Van Duren v. Fawcett Publications, No. 13114, S.D. Cal. 1952, the court regarded the *Davis* case as controlling New York law, and disregarded the *Gardella* case as dictum.

Apart from statutory language, however, it is suggested that the text statement is correct. The suggestion, for example, that Samuel L. Clemens would have a cause of action when that name was used in advertising, but not for the use of "Mark Twain," fully speaks for itself.

175 Brewer v. Hearst Pub. Co., 185 F.2d 846 (7th Cir. 1950). *Cf.* Sellers v. Henry, 329 S.W.2d 214 (Ky. 1959), and Waters v. Fleetwood, 212 Ga. 161, 91 S.E.2d 344 (1956), where there were photographs of unidentifiable dead bodies.

176 Rozhon v. Triangle Publications, 230 F.2d 359 (7th Cir. 1956). In accord is the unreported case of Cole v. Goodyear Tire & Rubber Co., App. Dept. Superior Court, San Francisco, Calif., Nov. 21, 1955.

177 Branson v. Fawcett Publications, 124 F. Supp. 429 (E.D. Ill. 1954).

178 Lawrence v. Ylla, 184 Misc. 807, 55 N.Y.S.2d 343 (Sup. Ct. 1945).

179 Toscani v. Hersey, 271 App. Div. 445, 65 N.Y.S.2d 814 (1946). *Cf.* Bernstein v. National Broadcasting Co., 129 F. Supp. 817 (D.D.C. 1955), *aff'd,* 232 F.2d 369 (D.C. Cir. 1956); Miller v. National Broadcasting Co., 157 F. Supp. 240 (D. Del. 1957); Levey v. Warner Bros. Pictures, 57 F. Supp. 40 (S.D.N.Y. 1944).

180 See, for example, State *ex rel.* La Follette v. Hinkle, 131 Wash. 86, 229 Pac. 317 (1924) (use of name as candidate by political party); Hinish v. Meier & Frank Co., 166 Ore. 482, 113 P.2d 438 (1941) (name signed to telegram urging governor to veto a bill); Schwartz v. Edrington, 133 La. 235, 62 So. 660 (1913) (name signed to petition); Vanderbilt v. Mitchell, 72 N.J. Eq. 910, 67 Atl. 97 (Ct. Err. & App. 1907) (birth certificate naming plaintiff as father); Burns v. Stevens, 236 Mich. 443, 210 N.W. 482 (1926) (posing as plaintiff's common law wife).

181 Colyer v. Richard K. Fox Pub. Co., 162 App. Div. 297, 146 N.Y.S. 999 (1914).

182 See Donahue v. Warner Bros. Picture Distributing Corp., 2 Utah 2d 256, 272 Pac. 177 (1954).

183 Damron v. Doubleday, Doran & Co., 133 Misc. 302, 231 N.Y.S. 444 (Sup. Ct. 1928), *aff'd,* 226 App. Div. 796, 234 N.Y.S. 773 (1929); Shubert v. Columbia Pictures Corp., 189 Misc. 734, 72 N.Y.S.2d 851 (Sup. Ct. 1947), *aff'd,* 274 App. Div. 571, 80 N.Y.S.2d 724 (1948), *appeal denied,* 274 App. Div. 880, 83 N.Y.S.2d 233 (1948).

184 Stillman v. Paramount Pictures Corp., 1 Misc.2d 108, 147 N.Y.S.2d 504 (Sup. Ct. 1956), *aff'd,* 2 App. Div. 2d 18, 153 N.Y.S.2d 190 (1956), *appeal denied,* 2 App. Div.2d 886, 157 N.Y.S.2d 899 (1956).

185 Wallach v. Bacharach, 192 Misc. 979, 80 N.Y.S.2d 37 (Sup. Ct. 1948), *aff'd,* 274 App. Div. 919, 84 N.Y.S.2d 894 (1948).

In accord is O'Brien v. Pabst Sales Co., 124 F.2d 167 (5th Cir. 1941), where the court refused to find a commercial use in the publication of the pictures of an all-American football team on a calendar advertising the defendant's beer, with no suggestion that the team endorsed it.

186 Dallessandro v. Henry Holt & Co., 4 App. Div.2d 470, 166 N.Y.S.2d 805 (1957) (plaintiff's photograph while conversing with a priest who was the subject of the book).

187 Humiston v. Universal Film Mfg. Co., 189 App. Div. 467, 178 N.Y.S. 752 (1919); Merle v. Sociological Research Film Corp., 166 App. Div. 376, 152 N.Y.S. 829 (1915) (picture of plaintiff's factory showing his name).

188 Binns v. Vitagraph Co. of America, 147 App. Div. 783, 132 N.Y.S. 237 (1911), *aff'd,* 210 N.Y. 51, 103 N.E. 1108 (1913).

189 Holmes v. Underwood and Underwood, 225 App. Div. 360, 233 N.Y.S. 153 (1929); Sutton v. Hearst Corp., 277 App. Div. 155, 98 N.Y.S.2d 233 (1950), *appeal denied,* 297 App. Div. 873, 98 N.Y.S.2d 589 (1950); Garner v. Triangle Publications, 97 F. Supp. 546 (S.D.N.Y. 1951).

190 Semler v. Ultem Publications, 170 Misc. 551, 9 N.Y.S.2d 319 (N.Y. City Ct. 1938); Thompson v. Close-Up, Inc., 277 App. Div. 848, 98 N.Y.S.2d 300 (1950); Metzger v. Dell Pub. Co., 207 Misc. 182, 136 N.Y.S.2d 888 (Sup. Ct. 1955); Martin v. Johnson Pub. Co., 157 N.Y.S.2d 409 (Sup. Ct. 1956). These were all cases involving the use of plaintiff's picture to illustrate articles with which he had no connection.

191 *Supra,* text at notes 126–50.

192 See Rhodes v. Sperry & Hutchinson Co., 193 N.Y. 223, 85 N.E. 1097 (1908); Gautier v. Pro-Football, Inc. 304 N.Y. 354, 107 N.E.2d 485 (1952); Mau v. Rio Grande Oil, Inc., 28 F. Supp. 845 (N.D. Cal. 1939); Hull v. Curtis Pub. Co., 182 Pa. Super. 86, 125 A.2d 644 (1956); Metter v. Los Angeles Examiner, 35 Cal. App. 2d 304, 95 P.2d 491 (1939); Ludwig, *"Peace of Mind" in 48 pieces vs. Uniform Right of Privacy,* 32 Minn. L. Rev. 734 (1948).

193 Haelan Laboratories v. Topps Chewing Gum, Inc., 202 F.2d 866 (2d Cir. 1953), *reversing* Bowman Gum Co. v. Topps Chewing Gum, Inc., 103 F. Supp. 944 (E.D.N.Y. 1952).

194 Nimmer, *The Right of Publicity,* 19 Law & Contemp. Prob. 203 (1954); Notes, 62 Yale L.J. 1123 (1953); 41 Geo. L.J. 583 (1953).

195 The "right of publicity" was held not to exist in California in Strickler v. National Broadcasting Co., 167 F. Supp. 68 (S.D. Cal. 1958). It was rejected in Pekas Co. v. Leslie, 52 N.Y.L.J. 1864 (Sup. Ct. 1915).

It appears to have been foreshadowed when relief was granted on other grounds in Uproar Co. v. National Broadcasting Co., 8 F. Supp. 358 (D. Mass. 1934), *modified* in 81 F.2d 373 (1st Cir. 1936); Liebig's Extract of Meat Co. v. Liebig Extract Co., 180 Fed. 68 (2d Cir. 1910). See also Madison Square Garden Corp. v. Universal Pictures Co., 255 App. Div. 459, 7 N.Y.S.2d 845 (1938).

196 In Ettore v. Philco Television Broadcasting Co., 229 F.2d 481 (3d Cir. 1956).
197 Gill v. Hearst Pub. Co., 40 Cal. 2d 224, 253 P.2d 441 (1953). The complaint alleged the publication of the picture in connection with the article involved in the other case, but failed to plead that the defendant had authorized it. A demurrer was sustained, but the plaintiff was permitted to amend.
198 Gill v. Curtis Pub. Co., 38 Cal. 2d 273, 239 P.2d 630 (1952).
199 *E.g.,* the defendant breaks into the plaintiff's home, steals his photograph, and publishes it with false statements about the plaintiff in his advertising.
200 Murray v. Gast Lithographic & Engraving Co., 8 Misc. 36, 28 N.Y.S. 271 (N.Y.C.P. 1894); Rozhon v. Triangle Publications, 230 F.2d 359 (7th Cir. 1956); Waters v. Fleetwood, 212 Ga. 161, 91 S.E.2d 344 (1956); Bremmer v. Journal-Tribune Co., 247 Iowa 817, 76 N.W.2d 762 (1956); Kelley v. Johnson Pub. Co., 160 Cal. App. 2d 718, 325 P.2d 659 (1958). See also the cases cited *infra,* note 202.
201 Walker v. Whittle, 83 Ga. App. 445, 64 S.E.2d 87 (1951) (intrusion into home to arrest husband). See Coverstone v. Davies, 38 Cal. 2d 315, 239 P.2d 876 (1952); Smith v. Doss, 251 Ala. 250, 37 So. 2d 118 (1948); and *cf.* Bazemore v. Savannah Hospital, 171 Ga. 257, 155 S.E. 195 (1930); Douglas v. Stokes, 149 Ky. 506, 149 S.W. 849 (1912).
202 Hanna Mfg. Co. v. Hillerich & Bradsby Co., 78 F.2d 763 (5th Cir. 1939); Wyatt v. Hall's Portrait Studios, 71 Misc. 199, 128 N.Y.S. 247 (Sup. Ct. 1911); Murray v. Gast Lithographic & Engraving Co., 8 Misc. 36, 28 N.Y.S. 271 (N.Y.C.P. 1894); Rhodes v. Sperry & Hutchinson Co., 193 N.Y. 223, 85 N.E. 1097 (1908). *Cf.* Von Thodorovich v. Franz Josef Beneficial Ass'n, 154 Fed. 911 (E.D. Pa. 1907) (Austrian diplomat cannot maintain action on behalf of Emperor of Austria).
203 Reed v. Real Detective Pub. Co., 63 Ariz. 294, 162 P.2d 133 (1945).
204 Wyatt v. Hall's Portrait Studios, 71 Misc. 199, 128 N.Y.S. 247 (Sup. Ct. 1911); Lunceford v. Wilcox, 88 N.Y.S.2d 225 (N.Y. City Ct. 1949).
205 Schuyler v. Curtis, 147 N.Y. 434, 42 N.E. 22 (1895); *In re* Hart's Estate, 193 Misc. 884, 83 N.Y.S.2d 635 (Surr. Ct. 1948); Schumann v. Loew's, Inc., 199 Misc. 38, 102 N.Y.S.2d 572 (Sup. Ct. 1951), *aff'd,* 135 N.Y.S.2d 361 (Sup. Ct. 1954); Rozhon v. Triangle Publications, 230 F.2d 359 (7th Cir. 1956); Abernathy v. Thornton, 263 Ala. 496, 83 So. 2d 235 (1955); Metter v. Los Angeles Examiner, 35 Cal. App. 2d 304, 95 P.2d 491 (1939); Kelly v. Johnson Pub. Co., 160 Cal. App. 2d 718, 325 P.2d 659 (1958); James v. Screen Gems, Inc., 174 Cal. App. 2d 650, 344 P.2d 799 (1959); Kelley v. Post Pub. Co., 327 Mass. 275, 98 N.E.2d 286 (1951); Bartholomew v. Workman, 197 Okl. 267, 169 P.2d 1012 (1946). *Cf.* Atkinson v. John E. Doherty & Co., 121 Mich. 372, 80 N.W. 285 (1899).

As in the case of living persons, however, a publication concerning one who is dead may invade the separate right of privacy of surviving relatives. See the last three cases cited *supra* and note 198.

206 *Supra,* notes 52–54. See Donahue v. Warner Bros. Pictures, 194 F.2d 6 (10th Cir. 1952); Donahue v. Warner Bros. Pictures Distributing Corp., 2 Utah 2d 256, 272 P.2d 177 (1954).

207 Jaggard v. R. H. Macy & Co., 176 Misc. 88, 26 N.Y.S.2d 829 (Sup. Ct. 1941), *aff'd,* 265 App. Div. 15, 37 N.Y.S.2d 570 (1942); Shubert v. Columbia Pictures Corp., 189 Misc. 734, 72 N.Y.S.2d 851 (Sup. Ct. 1947), *aff'd,* 274 App. Div. 571, 80 N.Y.S.2d 724 (1948), *appeal denied,* 274 App. Div. 880, 83 N.Y.S.2d 233 (1948); Maysville Transit Co. v. Ort, 296 Ky. 524, 177 S.W.2d 369 (1944); United States v. Morton, 338 U.S. 632 (1950).

208 Rosenwasser v. Ogoglia, 172 App. Div. 107, 158 N.Y.S. 56 (1916).

209 Vassar College v. Loose-Wiles Biscuit Co., 197 Fed. 982 (W.D. Mo. 1912).

210 Reed v. Real Detective Pub. Co., 63 Ariz. 294, 162 P.2d 133 (1945); Fairfield v. American Photocopy Equipment Co., 138 Cal. App. 2d 82, 291 P.2d 194 (1955); Cason v. Baskin, 155 Fla. 198, 20 So. 2d 243 (1945); Pavesich v. New England Life Ins. Co., 122 Ga. 190, 50 S.E. 68 (1905); Kunz v. Allen, 102 Kan. 883, 172 Pac. 532 (1918); Foster-Milburn Co. v. Chinn, 134 Ky. 424, 120 S.W. 364 (1909); Munden v. Harris, 153 Mo. App. 652, 134 S.W. 1076 (1911); Flake v. Greensboro News Co., 212 N.C. 780, 195 S.E. 55 (1938).

211 Brents v. Morgan, 221 Ky. 765, 299 S.W. 967 (1927); Rhodes v. Graham, 238 Ky. 225, 37 S.W.2d 46 (1951); Hinish v. Meier & Frank Co., 166 Ore. 482, 113 P.2d 438 (1941); Fairfield v. American Photocopy Equipment Co., 138 Cal. App. 2d 82, 291 P.2d 194 (1955).

212 Pavesich v. New England Life Ins. Co., 122 Ga. 190, 50 S.E. 68 (1905); Sutherland v. Kroger Co, 110 S.E.2d 716 (W. Va. 1959). In Cason v. Baskin, 159 Fla. 31, 30 So. 2d 635 (1947), where there was evidence that the plaintiff had suffered no great distress, and had gained weight, the recovery was limited to nominal damages.

213 Bunnell v. Keystone Varnish Co., 254 App. Div. 885, 5 N.Y.S.2d 415 (1938), *affirming* 167 Misc. 707, 4 N.Y.S.2d 601 (Sup. Ct. 1938).

214 Continental Optical Co. v. Reed, 119 Ind. App. 643, 86 N.E.2d 306 (1949); Manger v. Kree Institute of Electrolysis, 233 F.2d 5 (2d Cir. 1956); Hogan v. A. S. Barnes & Co., Inc., 114 U.S.P.Q. 314 (Pa. C.P. 1957). Likewise, the fact that the plaintiff has benefited in his profession by the publicity may be considered in mitigation, and may reduce his recovery to nominal damages. Harris v. H. W. Gossard Co., 194 App. Div. 688, 185 N.Y.S. 861 (1921).

215 Munden v. Harris, 153 Mo. App. 652, 134 S.W. 1076 (1911); Hinish v. Meier & Frank Co., 166 Ore. 482, 113 P.2d 438 (1941); Welsh v. Pritchard, 125 Mont. 517, 241 P.2d 816 (1952).

216 Fisher v. Murray M. Rosenberg, Inc. 175 Misc. 370, 23 N.Y.S.2d 677 (Sup. Ct. 1940); Barber v. Time, Inc., 348 Mo. 1199, 159 S.W.2d 291

(1942). But in Myers v. U.S. Camera Pub. Corp., 9 Misc. 2d 765, 167 N.Y.S.2d 771 (N.Y. City Ct. 1957), punitive damages were allowed where the defendant "knew or should have known."

In Harlow v. Buno Co., 36 Pa. D.& C. 101 (C.P. 1939), the fact that the defendant had acted in good faith under a forged consent was held to defeat the action entirely. This appears to be wrong. *Cf.* Kerby v. Hal Roach Studios, 53 Cal. App. 2d 207, 127 P.2d 577 (1942), where the defendant made use of the plaintiff's name without even being aware of her existence.

217 In Themo v. New England Newspaper Pub. Co., 306 Mass. 54, 27 N.E.2d 753 (1940), it was said that these privileges are not technically defenses, and the absence of a privileged occasion must be pleaded and proved by the plaintiff. This is the only case found bearing on the question; but it may be doubted that other jurisdictions will agree.

218 Cason v. Baskin, 159 Fla. 31, 30 So. 2d 635, 638 (1947).

219 The question of degree has not been discussed in the cases. In Kerby v. Hal Roach Studios, 53 Cal. App. 2d 207, 127 P.2d 577 (1942), the plaintiff was an actress, concert singer and monologist, so obscure that the defendant's studio had never heard of her. She was allowed to recover for appropriation of her name and a false light before the public, without mention of whether she was a public figure, which obviously would have made no difference in the decision. It may be suggested that even an obscure entertainer may be a public figure to some limited extent, but that the field in which she may be given further publicity may be more narrowly limited. See *infra*, text at notes 282–84.

220 Paramount Pictures v. Leader Press, 24 F. Supp. 1004 (W.D. Okl. 1938), *reversed on other grounds* in 106 F.2d 229 (10th Cir. 1939); Chaplin v. National Broadcasting Co., 15 F.R.D. 134 (S.D.N.Y. 1953).

221 Ruth v. Educational Films, 194 App. Div. 893, 184 N.Y.S. 948 (1920); see Jansen v. Hilo Packing Co., 202 Misc. 900, 118 N.Y.S.2d 162 (Sup. Ct. 1952), *aff'd*, 282 App. Div. 935, 125 N.Y.S.2d 648 (1953). *Cf.* O'Brien v. Pabst Sales Co., 124 F.2d 167 (5th Cir. 1941) (all-American football player).

222 Jeffries v. New York Evening Journal Pub. Co., 67 Misc. 570, 124 N.Y.S. 780 (Sup. Ct. 1910); Cohen v. Marx, 94 Cal. App. 2d 704, 211 P.2d 320 (1950); Oma v. Hillman Periodicals, 281 App. Div. 240, 118 N.Y.S.2d 720 (1953).

223 Colyer v. Richard K. Fox Pub. Co., 162 App. Div. 297, 146 N.Y.S. 999 (1914) (high diver); Koussevitzky v. Allen, Towne & Heath, 188 Misc. 479, 68 N.Y.S.2d 779 (Sup. Ct. 1947), *aff'd*, 272 App. Div. 759, 69 N.Y.S.2d 432 (1947) (symphony conductor); Gavrilov v. Duell, Sloan & Pierce, 84 N.Y.S.2d 320 (Sup. Ct. 1948) (dancer); Redmond v. Columbia Pictures Corp., 277 N.Y. 707, 14 N.E.2d 636 (1938), *affirming* 253 App. Div. 708, 1 N.Y.S.2d 643 (trick shot golfer). *Cf.* Gautier v. Pro-Football, Inc., 304 N.Y. 354, 107 N.E.2d 485 (1952) (performing animal act at

football game); Goelet v. Confidential, Inc., 5 App. Div.2d 226, 171 N.Y.S.2d 223 (1958) (unspecified).
224 Martin v. Dorton, 210 Miss. 668, 50 So. 2d 391 (1951) (sheriff); Hull v. Curtis Pub. Co., 182 Pa. Super. 86, 125 A.2d 644 (1956) (arrest by policeman).
225 Corliss v. E. W. Walker Co., 64 Fed. 280 (D. Mass. 1894). *Cf.* Thompson v. Curtis Pub. Co., 193 F.2d 953 (3d Cir. 1952).
226 Smith v. Suratt, 7 Alaska 416 (1926).
227 Stryker v. Republic Pictures Corp., 108 Cal. App. 2d 191, 238 P.2d 670 (1951). *Accord,* Molony v. Boy Comics Publishers, 277 App. Div. 166, 98 N.Y.S.2d 199 (1950), *reversing* 188 Misc. 450, 65 N.Y.S.2d 173 (Sup. Ct. 1946) (hero in disaster).
228 See Continental Optical Co. v. Reed, 119 Ind. App. 643, 86 N.E.2d 306 (1949).
229 Sidis v. F-R Pub. Corp., 113 F.2d 806 (2d Cir. 1940), *affirming* 34 F. Supp. 19 (S.D.N.Y. 1938).
230 Wilson v. Brown, 189 Misc. 79, 73 N.Y.S.2d 587 (Sup. Ct. 1947).
231 Cason v. Baskin, 155 Fla. 198, 20 So. 2d 243 (1945), *second appeal,* 159 Fla. 31, 30 So. 2d 635 (1947). A book, *Cross Creek,* which became a best seller, was written about the back woods people of Florida, and an obscure local woman was described in embarrassing personal detail. It was held that she did not become a public figure.
232 See cases cited *supra,* notes 221–31.
233 Sweenek v. Pathe News, 16 F. Supp. 746, 747 (E.D.N.Y. 1936).
234 Jones v. Herald Post Co., 230 Ky. 227, 18 S.W.2d 972 (1929); Bremmer v. Journal-Tribune Co., 247 Iowa 817, 76 N.W.2d 762 (1956); Waters v. Fleetwood, 212 Ga. 161, 91 S.E.2d 344 (1956); Jenkins v. Dell Pub. Co., 143 F. Supp. 953 (W.D. Pa. 1956), *aff'd,* 251 F.2d 447 (3d Cir. 1958); Bernstein v. National Broadcasting Co., 129 F. Supp. 817 (D.D.C. 1955), *aff'd,* 232 F.2d 369 (D.C. Cir. 1956).
235 Elmhurst v. Pearson, 153 F.2d 467 (D.C. Cir. 1946) (sedition); Miller v. National Broadcasting Co., 157 F. Supp. 240 (D. Del. 1957) (robbery); Hillman v. Star Pub. Co., 64 Wash. 691, 117 Pac. 594 (1911) (mail fraud).
236 Frith v. Associated Press, 176 F. Supp. 671 (E.D.S.C. 1959) (mob action); Coverstone v. Davies, 38 Cal. 2d 315, 239 P.2d 876 (1952) ("hot-rod" race); Hull v. Curtis Pub. Co., 182 Pa. Super. 86, 125 A.2d 644 (1956).
237 Jacova v. Southern Radio & Television Co., 83 So. 2d 34 (Fla. 1955). *Cf.* Schnabel v. Meredith, 378 Pa. 609, 107 A.2d 860 (1954).
238 Metter v. Los Angeles Examiner, 35 Cal. App. 2d 304, 95 P.2d 491 (1939); and see Samuel v. Curtis Pub. Co., 122 F. Supp. 327 (N.D. Cal. 1954).
239 Aquino v. Bulletin Co., 154 A.2d 422, 190 Pa. Super. 528 (1959).
240 Berg v. Minneapolis Star & Tribune Co., 79 F. Supp. 957 (D. Minn. 1948); Aquino v. Bulletin Co., 154 A.2d 422, 190 Pa. Super. 528 (1959).
241 Kelley v. Post Pub. Co., 327 Mass. 275, 98 N.E.2d 286 (1951). *Cf.* Strickler

v. National Broadcasting Co., 167 F. Supp. 68 (S.D. Cal. 1958) (crisis in airplane).

242 Rozhon v. Triangle Publications, 230 F.2d 539 (7th Cir. 1956). *Cf.* Abernathy v. Thornton, 263 Ala. 496, 83 So. 2d 235 (1955) (death of criminal paroled for federal offense).

243 See Barber v. Time, Inc., 348 Mo. 1199, 159 S.W.2d 291 (1942).

244 Meetze v. Associated Press, 230 S.C. 330, 95 S.E.2d 606 (1956).

245 Langford v. Vanderbilt University, 199 Tenn. 389, 287 S.W.2d 32 (1956).

246 Smith v. National Broadcasting Co., 138 Cal. App. 2d 807, 292 P.2d 600 (1956).

247 Smith v. Doss, 251 Ala. 250, 37 So. 2d 118 (1948).

248 See, as to unspecified news, Moser v. Press Pub. Co., 59 Misc. 78, 109 N.Y.S. 963 (Sup. Ct. 1908); Themo v. New England Newspaper Pub. Co., 306 Mass. 54, 27 N.E.2d 753 (1940).

249 Ruth v. Educational Films, 194 App. Div. 893, 184 N.Y.S. 948 (1920) (baseball); Sweenek v. Pathe News, 16 F. Supp. 746 (E.D.N.Y. 1936) (group of fat women reducing with novel and comical apparatus); and see Jenkins v. Dell Pub. Co., 143 F. Supp. 953 (W.D. Pa. 1956), *aff'd,* 251 F.2d 447 (3d Cir. 1958).

250 People *ex rel.* Stern v. Robert M. McBride & Co., 159 Misc. 5, 288 N.Y.S. 501 (N.Y. City Magis. Ct. 1936) (strike-breaking); Kline v. Robert M. McBride & Co., 170 Misc. 974, 11 N.Y.S.2d 674 (Sup. Ct. 1939) (same); Samuel v. Curtis Pub. Co., 122 F. Supp. 327 (N.D. Cal. 1954) (suicide); Hogan v. A.S. Barnes Co., 114 U.S.P.Q. 314 (Pa. C.P. 1957) (golf); Oma v. Hillman Periodicals, 281 App. Div. 240, 118 N.Y.S.2d 720 (1953) (boxing); Delinger v. American News Co., 6 App. Div.2d 1027, 178 N.Y.S.2d 231 (1958) (muscular development and virility).

251 Humiston v. Universal Film Mfg. Co., 189 App. Div. 467, 178 N.Y.S. 752 (1919). *Cf.* Gill v. Hearst Pub. Co., 40 Cal. 2d 224, 253 P.2d 441 (1953) (market place); Berg v. Minneapolis Star & Tribune Co., 79 F. Supp. 957 (D. Minn. 1948) (photograph in courtroom); Lyles v. State, 330 P.2d 734 (Okl. Cr. 1958) (television in courtroom); Middleton v. News Syndicate Co., 162 Misc. 516, 295 N.Y.S. 120 (Sup. Ct. 1937) ("inquiring photographer" on the street).

252 Jones v. Herald Post Co., 230 Ky. 227, 18 S.W.2d 972 (1929).

253 Jacova v. Southern Radio & Television Co., 83 So. 2d 34 (Fla. 1955).

254 In theory the privilege as to public figures is to depict the person, while that as to news is to report the event. In practice the two often become so merged as to be inseparable. See, for example, Elmhurst v. Pearson, 153 F.2d 467 (D.D.C. 1946) (place of employment of defendant in sedition trial); Martin v. Dorton, 210 Miss. 668, 50 So. 2d 391 (1951) (mass meeting complaining of conduct of sheriff); Stryker v. Republic Pictures Corp., 108 Cal. App.2d 191, 238 P.2d 670 (1951) (military career of war hero); Molony v. Boy Comics Publishers, 277 App. Div. 166, 98 N.Y.S.2d 119 (1950), *reversing* 188 Misc. 450, 65 N.Y.S.2d 173 (Sup. Ct. 1946)

(conduct of hero in disaster). The outstanding example in our time has been the popular interest in Charles A. Lindbergh, after he flew the Atlantic.

255 Restatement, Torts § 867, comment *c* (1939).

256 Smith v. Doss, 251 Ala. 250, 37 So. 2d 118 (1948) (family of man who disappeared, was believed murdered, died, and his body was brought home); Coverstone v. Davies, 38 Cal. 2d 315, 239 P.2d 876 (1952) (father of boy arrested for "hot-rod" race); Kelly v. Post Pub. Co., 327 Mass. 275, 98 N.E.2d 286 (1951) (parents of girl killed in accident); Aquino v. Bulletin Co., 190 Pa. Super. 528, 154 A.2d 422 (1959) (parents of girl secretly married and then divorced); Jenkins v. Dell Pub. Co., 143 F. Supp. 952 (W.D. Pa. 1956), *aff'd*, 251 F.2d 447 (3d Cir. 1958) (family of boy kicked to death by hoodlums); Hillman v. Star Pub. Co., 64 Wash. 691, 117 Pac. 594 (1911) (son of man arrested for mail fraud). *Cf.* Milner v. Red River Valley Pub. Co., 249 S.W.2d 227 (Tex. Civ. App. 1952) (family of man killed in accident).

257 Such a limitation is indicated in Martin v. New Metropolitan Fiction, 139 Misc. 290, 248 N.Y.S. 359 (Sup. Ct. 1931), *aff'd*, 234 App. Div. 904, 254 N.Y.S. 1015 (1931), where a mother, attending her son's criminal trial, was depicted as broken-hearted in a news story. On the pleadings, the court refused to dismiss because it could not say that evidence could not be produced which would go beyond the privilege.

258 People *ex rel.* Stern v. Robert M. McBride & Co., 159 Misc. 5, 288 N.Y.S. 501 (N.Y. City Magis. Ct. 1936); Kline v. Robert M. McBride & Co., 170 Misc. 974, 11 N.Y.S.2d 674 (Sup. Ct. 1939).

259 Sarat Lahiri v. Daily Mirror, 162 Misc. 776, 295 N.Y.S. 382 (Sup. Ct. 1937). *Accord*, Delinger v. American News Co., 6 App. Div. 2d 1027, 178 N.Y.S.2d 231 (1958) (physical training instructor, article on relation of muscular development and virility); Dallessandro v. Henry Holt & Co., 4 App. Div. 2d 470, 166 N.Y.S.2d 805 (1957) (picture of plaintiff conversing with priest who was subject of book); Oma v. Hillman Periodicals, 281 App. Div. 240, 118 N.Y.S.2d 720 (1953) (boxer, article on boxing); Gavrilov v. Duell, Sloan & Pierce, 84 N.Y.S.2d 320 (Sup. Ct. 1948), *aff'd*, 276 App. Div. 826, 93 N.Y.S.2d 715 (dancer, book on dancing).

260 Peay v. Curtis Pub. Co., 78 F. Supp. 305 (D.D.C. 1948).

261 Martin v. Johnson Pub. Co., 157 N.Y.S.2d 409 (Sup. Ct. 1956). For other examples, see *supra* notes 137–42.

262 Samuel v. Curtis Pub. Co., 122 F. Supp. 327 (N.D. Cal. 1954).

263 Metzger v. Dell Pub. Co., 207 Misc. 182, 136 N.Y.S.2d 888 (Sup. Ct. 1955).

264 Discussed in Spiegel, *Public Celebrity v. Scandal Magazine—The Celebrity's Right to Privacy*, 30 So. Cal. L. Rev. 280 (1957).

265 Attributed to Greta Garbo.

266 This seems to be clear from the cases holding that the publication of stolen or surreptitiously obtained pictures is actionable, even though the

plaintiff is "news." See *supra* notes 109–11.

267 Eliot v. Jones, 66 Misc. 95, 120 N.Y.S. 989 (Sup. Ct. 1910), *aff'd*, 140 App. Div. 911, 125 N.Y.S. 1119 (1910) (name of president of Harvard used to sell books); Lane v. F. W. Woolworth Co., 171 Misc. 66, 11 N.Y.S.2d 199 (Sup. Ct. 1939), *aff'd*, 256 App. Div. 1065, 12 N.Y.S.2d 352 (1939) (picture of actress sold in lockets); Birmingham Broadcasting Co. v. Bell, 259 Ala. 656, 68 So. 2d 314 (1953), *later appeal*, 69 So. 2d 263 (Ala. 1957) (name of sports broadcaster used to advertise program with which he had no connection); Continental Optical Co. v. Reed, 119 Ind. App. 643, 86 N.E.2d 306 (1949) (picture of soldier used to advertise optical goods); Jansen v. Hilo Packing Co., 202 Misc. 900, 118 N.Y.S.2d 162 (Sup. Ct. 1952), *aff'd*, 282 App. Div. 935, 125 N.Y.S.2d 648 (1953) (picture of baseball player sold with popcorn). *Cf.* Kerby v. Hal Roach Studios, 53 Cal. App. 2d 207, 127 P.2d 577 (1942) (name of actress used to advertise motion picture); State *ex rel.* La Follette v. Hinkle, 131 Wash. 86, 229 Pac. 317 (1924) (use of name of politician as candidate by political party).

268 Flores v. Mosler Safe Co., 7 N.Y.2d 276, 164 N.E.2d 853 (1959), *affirming* 7 App. Div. 2d 226, 182 N.Y.S.2d 126 (1959) (picture and news story of man who accidentally set a fire used to advertise safes).

269 Von Thodorovich v. Franz Josef Beneficial Ass'n, 154 Fed. 911 (E.D. Pa. 1907). *Accord*, Edison v. Edison Polyform Mfg. Co., 73 N.J. Eq. 136, 67 Atl. 392 (Ch. 1907) (Thomas Edison).

270 Goelet v. Confidential, Inc., 5 App. Div. 2d 226, 171 N.Y.S.2d 223 (1958); Bremmer v. Journal-Tribune Pub. Co., 247 Iowa 817, 76 N.W.2d 762 (1956); Jenkins v. Dell Pub. Co., 143 F. Supp. 953 (W.D. Pa. 1956), *aff'd*, 251 F.2d 447 (3d Cir. 1958); Aquino v. Bulletin Co., 190 Pa. Super. 528, 154 A.2d 422 (1959); Waters v. Fleetwood, 212 Ga. 161, 91 S.E.2d 344 (1956).

Two cases sometimes cited to the contrary, Douglas v. Stokes, 149 Ky. 506, 149 S.W. 849 (1912), and Bazemore v. Savannah Hospital, 171 Ga. 257, 155 S.E. 194 (1930), are apparently to be explained on the basis of pictures obtained by inducing breach of trust.

It may nevertheless be suggested that there must be some as yet undefined limits of common decency as to what can be published about anyone; and that a photograph of indecent exposure, for example, can never be legitimate "news."

271 Hazlitt v. Fawcett Publications, 116 F. Supp. 539 (D. Conn. 1953) (fictional account of stunt driver, tried for homicide); Sutton v. Hearst Corp., 277 App. Div. 155, 98 N.Y.S.2d 233 (1950), *appeal denied*, 277 App. Div. 873, 98 N.Y.S.2d 589 (1950) (fictional story about turret gunner); Hogan v. A. S. Barnes Co., 114 U.S.P.Q. 314 (Pa. C.P. 1957) (book purporting to give information from plaintiff about his golf game); Stryker v. Republic Pictures Corp., 108 Cal. App. 2d 191, 238 P.2d 670 (1951) (fiction in motion picture about war hero); Binns v. Vitagraph

Co. of America, 147 App. Div. 783, 132 N.Y.S. 237 (1911), *aff'd,* 210 N.Y. 51, 103 N.E. 1108 (1913) (fiction in motion picture about radio operator hero); Donahue v. Warner Bros. Pictures, 194 F.2d 6 (10th Cir. 1952) (fiction in motion picture about entertainer); D'Altomonte v. New York Herald Co., 154 App. Div. 953, 139 N.Y.S. 200 (1913), *modified* as not within the New York statute in 208 N.Y. 596, 102 N.E. 1101 (1913) (authorship of absurd story attributed to well known writer). See also the last two cases cited *supra,* note 167.

272 Garner v. Triangle Publications, 97 F. Supp. 546 (S.D.N.Y. 1951) (fiction added to murder story); Reed v. Real Detective Pub. Co., 63 Ariz. 294, 162 P.2d 133 (1945) (false statements in story of crime); Annerino v. Dell Pub. Co., 11 Ill. App. 2d 205, 149 N.E.2d 761 (1958) (fiction in account of murder of plaintiff's husband); Strickler v. National Broadcasting Co., 167 F. Supp. 68 (S.D. Cal. 1958) (false details in story of plaintiff's conduct in airplane crisis); Aquino v. Bulletin Co., 190 Pa. Super. 528, 154 A.2d 422 (1959) (reporter of secret marriage and subsequent divorce drew on his imagination).

273 See the cases of pictures used to illustrate articles, *supra,* notes 137–42.

274 "In general, then, the matters of which the publication should be repressed may be described as those which concern the private life, habits, acts and relations of an individual, and have no legitimate connection with his fitness for a public office which he seeks or for which he is suggested, and have no legitimate relation to or bearing upon any act done by him in a public or quasi public capacity." Warren and Brandeis, *The Right to Privacy,* 4 Harv. L. Rev. 193, 215 (1890).

275 Jeffries v. New York Evening Journal Co., 67 Misc. 570, 124 N.Y.S. 780 (Sup. Ct. 1910); Koussevitzky v. Allen, Towne & Heath, 188 Misc. 479, 68 N.Y.S.2d 779 (1947), *aff'd,* 272 App. Div. 759, 69 N.Y.S.2d 432 (1947). *Cf.* Corliss v. E. W. Walker Co., 64 Fed. 280 (D. Mass. 1894).

276 Smith v. Suratt, 7 Alaska 416 (1926) (Dr. Cook).

277 *Cf.* Garner v. Triangle Publications, 97 F. Supp. 546 (S.D.N.Y. 1951) (relations, partly fictional, between participants in murder).

278 For example, Fla. Stat. § 794.03 (1957); Wis. Stat. Ann. § 942.02 (1958).

279 Pope v. Curl, 2 Atk. 341, 26 Eng. Rep. 608 (1741); Roberts v. McKee, 29 Ga. 161 (1859); Woolsey v. Judd, 4 Duer 379 (11 N.Y. Super. 1855); Denis v. Leclerc, 1 Mart. (o.s.) 297 (La. 1811); Baker v. Libbie, 210 Mass. 599, 97 N.E. 109 (1912). Usually this has been put upon the ground of a property right in the letter itself, or literary property in its contents. See Note, 44 Iowa L. Rev. 705 (1959).

280 Prince Albert v. Strange, 1 Mac. & G. 25, 64 Eng. Rep. 293 (1848), *aff'd,* 2 De. G. & Sm. 652, 41 Eng. Rep. 1171 (1849).

281 Douglas v. Disney Productions, reported in Los Angeles Daily Journal Rep., Dec. 31, 1956, p. 27, col. 3.

282 Witness the disclosure, in the election of 1884, of Grover Cleveland's parentage of an illegitimate child, many years before.

283 Stryker v. Republic Pictures Corp., 108 Cal. App.2d 191, 238 P.2d 670
    (1951); and see Continental Optical Co. v. Reed, 119 Ind. App. 643, 86
    N.E.2d 306 (1949).

284 Bernstein v. National Broadcasting Co., 129 F. Supp. 817 (D.D.C. 1955),
    aff'd, 232 F.2d 369 (D.C. Cir. 1956) (murder and trial); Smith v. National
    Broadcasting Co., 138 Cal. App. 2d 807, 282 P.2d 600 (1956) (false report
    to police of escape of black panther).

285 Cohen v. Marx, 94 Cal. App. 2d 704, 211 P.2d 320 (1950) (pugilist, ten
    years); Sidis v. F-R Pub. Corp., 113 F.2d 806 (2d Cir. 1940), affirming
    34 F. Supp. 19 (S.D.N.Y. 1938) (infant prodigy, seven years); Schnabel
    v. Meredith, 378 Pa. 609, 107 A.2d 860 (1954) (slot machines found on
    plaintiff's premises, six months).

286 Jenkins v. Dell Pub. Co., 143 F. Supp. 953 (W.D. Pa. 1956), aff'd, 251
    F.2d 447 (3d Cir. 1958) (family of murdered boy, three months). Accord,
    as to pictures illustrating articles, Samuel v. Curtis Pub. Co., 122 F. Supp.
    327 (N.D. Cal. 1954) (arguing with suicide, twenty-two months); and see
    Leverton v. Curtis Pub. Co., 192 F.2d 974 (3d Cir. 1951) (child struck
    by car, two years).

287 Estill v. Hearst Pub. Co., 186 F.2d 1017 (7th Cir. 1951).
    The case of Smith v. Doss, 251 Ala. 250, 37 So. 2d 118 (1948), where
    a man who had disappeared and was believed to have been murdered
    died in a distant state, and his body was brought back to town, is probably
    to be distinguished on the basis that the later event was itself "news,"
    and so justified the revival of the story.

288 112 Cal. App. 285, 297 Pac. 91 (1931).
    The report of the case leaves the facts in some doubt. It came up on
    the plaintiff's pleading, which alleged that the defendant made use of
    the plaintiff's maiden name of Gabrielle Darley, and that "by the pro-
    duction and showing of the picture, friends of appellant learned for the
    first time of the unsavory incidents of her early life." It is difficult to see
    how this was accomplished, unless the picture also revealed her present
    identity under her married name of Melvin. At least the allegation is
    not to be ignored in interpreting the case.

289 Mau v. Rio Grande Oil, Inc., 28 F. Supp. 845 (N.D. Cal. 1939) (radio
    dramatization of robbery); and see the cases cited supra, note 284.
    In Barber v. Time, Inc., 348 Mo. 1199, 159 S.W.2d 291 (1942), the
    court laid stress upon the "unnecessary" use of the name in even a current
    report, concerning a woman suffering from a rare disease. The decision,
    however, appears rather to rest upon the intrusion of taking her picture
    in bed in a hospital.

290 Brents v. Morgan, 221 Ky. 765, 299 S.W. 967 (1927); Melvin v. Reid,
    112 Cal. App. 285, 297 Pac. 91 (1931); Mau v. Rio Grande Oil, Inc., 28
    F. Supp. 845 (N.D. Cal. 1939); Barber v. Time, Inc., 348 Mo. 1199, 159
    S.W.2d 291 (1942); Cason v. Baskin, 155 Fla. 198, 20 So. 2d 243 (1945),
    second appeal, 159 Fla. 31, 30 So. 2d 635 (1947); Themo v. New England
    Newspaper Pub. Co., 306 Mass. 54, 27 N.E.2d 753 (1940).

291 See *supra*, text at notes 127–50.
292 Grossman v. Frederick Bros. Acceptance Corp., 34 N.Y.S.2d 785 (Sup. Ct., App. T. 1942) (written consent a complete defense under the New York statute); Jenkins v. Dell Pub. Co., 143 F. Supp. 953 (W.D. Pa. 1956), *aff'd*, 250 F.2d 447 (3d Cir. 1958); Reitmeister v. Reitmeister, 162 F.2d 691 (2d Cir. 1947); Tanner-Brice Co. v. Sims, 174 Ga. 13, 161 S.E. 819 (1931).
   In Porter v. American Tobacco Co., 140 App. Div. 871, 125 N.Y.S. 710 (1910), it was held that consent must be pleaded and proved as a defense.
293 Gill v. Hearst Pub. Co., 40 Cal. 2d 224, 253 P.2d 441 (1953); Thayer v. Worcester Post Co., 284 Mass. 160, 187 N.E. 292 (1933); Wendell v. Conduit Machine Co., 74 Misc. 201, 133 N.Y.S. 758 (Sup. Ct. 1911); Johnson v. Boeing Airplane Co., 175 Kan. 275, 262 P.2d 808 (1953).
294 In O'Brien v. Pabst Sales Co., 124 F.2d 167 (5th Cir. 1941), the fact that the plaintiff had gone to great lengths to get himself named as an all-American football player was held to prevent any recovery for publicity given to him in that capacity. *Cf.* Gautier v. Pro-Football, Inc., 304 N.Y. 354, 107 N.E.2d 485 (1952) (television broadcast of performing animal act at football game).
   See also Schmieding v. American Farmers Mut. Ins. Co., 138 F. Supp. 167 (D. Neb. 1955), where the plaintiff failed to object to continued use of his rubber-stamp signature after termination of his employment.
295 Garden v. Parfumerie Rigaud, 151 Misc. 692, 271 N.Y.S. 187 (Sup. Ct. 1933); State *ex rel.* La Follette v. Hinkle, 131 Wash. 86, 229 Pac. 317 (1924).
296 Lillie v. Warner Bros. Pictures, 139 Cal. App. 724, 34 P.2d 835 (1934) (motion picture contract includes use of "shorts"); Long v. Decca Records, 76 N.Y.S.2d 133 (Sup. Ct. 1947) (contract to make records held to include use of name and picture in advertising); Fairbanks v. Winik, 119 Misc. 809, 198 N.Y.S. 299 (Sup. Ct. 1922) (motion picture actor surrenders right to use of film); Wendell v. Conduit Machine Co., 74 Misc. 201, 133 N.Y.S. 758 (Sup. Ct. 1911) (use of employee's picture in business after termination of employment); Marek v. Zanol Products Co., 298 Mass. 1, 9 N.E.2d 393 (1937) (contract consent to use of name); Sharaga v. Sinram Bros., 275 App. Div. 967, 90 N.Y.S.2d 705 (1949) (use of salesman's name after termination of employment); Johnson v. Boeing Airplane Co., 175 Kan. 275, 262 P.2d 808 (1953) (consent to picture in house organ held to include national publication).
   In Bell v. Birmingham Broadcasting Co., 263 Ala. 355, 82 So. 2d 345 (1955), it was held that a custom of giving consent was proper evidence bearing on the interpretation of the contract.
297 *Cf.* Manger v. Kree Institute of Electrolysis, 233 F.2d 5 (2d Cir. 1956) (letter altered to make it testimonial); Myers v. Afro-American Pub. Co., 168 Misc. 429, 5 N.Y.S.2d 223 (Sup. Ct. 1938), *aff'd*, 255 App. Div. 838,

7 N.Y.S.2d 662 (1938) (consent to use of semi-nude picture on condition that nudity be covered up).

298 Ettore v. Philco Television Broadcasting Co., 229 F.2d 481 (3d Cir. 1956) (motion picture contract held not to include use of the film on television, subsequently developed); Colgate-Palmolive Co. v. Tullos, 219 F.2d 617 (5th Cir. 1955) (use of employee's picture in advertising after termination of employment); Sinclair v. Postal Tel. & Cable Co., 72 N.Y.S.2d 841 (Sup. Ct. 1935) (picture of actor putting him in undignified light); Russell v. Marboro Books, 18 Misc. 2d 166, 183 N.Y.S.2d 8 (Sup. Ct. 1959) (picture of model used in bawdy advertisement of bed sheets).

299 *Supra,* notes 14, 52–54. It has been held that the consent of an infant is ineffective under the New York statute and that of the parent must be obtained. Semler v. Ultem Publications, 170 Misc. 551, 9 N.Y.S.2d 319 (N.Y. City Ct. 1938); Wyatt v. James McCreery Co., 126 App. Div. 650, 111 N.Y.S. 86 (1908).

300 Buschelle v. Conde Nast Publications, 173 Misc. 674, 19 N.Y.S.2d 129 (Sup. Ct. 1940); Hammond v. Crowell Pub. Co., 253 App. Div. 205, 1 N.Y.S.2d 728 (1938); Miller v. Madison Square Garden Corp., 176 Misc. 714, 28 N.Y.S.2d 811 (Sup. Ct. 1941) (reduced to nominal damages); Lane v. F. W. Woolworth Co., 171 Misc. 66, 11 N.Y.S.2d 199 (Sup. Ct. 1939), *aff'd,* 256 App. Div. 1065, 12 N.Y.S.2d 352 (1939); Harris v. H. W. Gossard Co., 194 App. Div. 688, 185 N.Y.S. 861 (1921).

301 Warren and Brandeis, *The Right to Privacy,* 4 Harv. L. Rev. 193, 216 (1890).

302 Application of Tiene, 19 N.J. 149, 115 A.2d 543 (1955).

303 Johnson v. Scripps Pub. Co., 18 Ohio Op. 372 (C.P. 1940).

304 Langford v. Vanderbilt University, 199 Tenn. 389, 287 S.W.2d 32 (1956). *Cf.* Lyles v. State, 330 P.2d 734 (Okl. Cr. 1958) (television in courtroom); Berg v. Minneapolis Star & Tribune Co., 79 F. Supp. 957 (D. Minn. 1948) (photograph taken in courtroom).

305 Schmukler v. Ohio-Bell Tel. Co., 116 N.E.2d 819 (Ohio C.P. 1953). *Accord,* People v. Appelbaum, 277 App. Div. 43, 97 N.Y.S.2d 807 (1950), *aff'd,* 301 N.Y. 738, 95 N.E.2d 410 (1950) (subscriber tapping his own telephone to protect his interests). *Cf.* Davis v. General Finance & Thrift Co., 80 Ga. App. 708, 57 S.E.2d 225 (1950) (creditor's telegram to debtor threatening suit); Gouldman-Taber Pontiac, Inc. v. Zerbst, 213 Ga. 682, 100 S.E.2d 881 (1957) (creditor's complaint to debtor's employer).

306 Holloman v. Life Ins. Co. of Va., 192 S.C. 454, 7 S.E.2d 169 (1940).

307 Ellis v. Hurst, 70 Misc. 122, 128 N.Y.S. 144 (Sup. Ct. 1910); Shostakovitch v. Twentieth-Century Fox Film Corp., 196 Misc. 67, 80 N.Y.S.2d 575 (Sup. Ct. 1948), *aff'd,* 275 App. Div. 692, 87 N.Y.S.2d 430 (1949).

   Cf. White v. William G. White Co., 160 App. Div. 709, 145 N.Y.S. 743 (1914), where the plaintiff's sale of a corporation bearing his name was held to convey the right to continue to use it.

308 Brociner v. Radio Wire Television, Inc., 15 Misc. 2d 843, 183 N.Y.S.2d 743 (Sup. Ct. 1959).

309 Prosser, *Interstate Publication*, 51 Mich. L. Rev. 959 (1953), reprinted in Prosser, Selected Topics on the Law of Torts 70–134 (1953).

310 Discussed at length in Prosser, *Insult and Outrage*, 44 Calif. L. Rev. 40 (1956).

311 Reported in a note to Rex v. Carlisle, 6 Car. & P. 636, 172 Eng. Rep. 1397 (1834).

6

Privacy as an aspect of
human dignity
An Answer to Dean Prosser

EDWARD J. BLOUSTEIN

I. Introduction

Three-quarters of a century have passed since Warren and Brandeis published their germinal article, "The Right of Privacy."[1] In this period many hundreds of cases, ostensibly founded upon the right to privacy, have been decided,[2] a number of statutes expressly embodying it have been enacted,[3] and a sizeable scholarly literature has been devoted to it.[4] Remarkably enough, however, there remains to this day considerable confusion concerning the nature of the interest which the right to privacy is designed to protect. The confusion is such that in 1956 a distinguished federal judge characterized the state of the law of privacy by likening it to a "haystack in a hurricane."[5] And, in 1960, the dean of tort scholars wrote a comprehensive article on the subject which, in effect, repudiates Warren and Brandeis by suggesting that privacy is not an independent value at all but rather a composite of the interests in reputation, emotional tranquility and intangible property.[6]

My purpose in this article is to propose a general theory of individual privacy which will reconcile the divergent strands of legal development—which will put the straws back into the haystack. The need for such a theory is pressing. In the first place, the disorder in the cases and commentary offends the primary canon of all science that a single general principle of explanation is to be preferred over a congeries of discrete rules. Secondly, the conceptual disarray has had untoward effects on the courts; lacking a clear sense of what interest or interests are involved in privacy cases has made it difficult to arrive at a judicial consensus concerning the elements of the wrong or the nature of the defenses to it. Thirdly, analysis of the interest

© New York University Law Review, 1964. Reprinted from *New York University Law Review* 39: 962–1007, 1964.

involved in the privacy cases is of utmost significance because in our own day scientific and technological advances have raised the spectre of new and frightening invasions of privacy.[7] Our capacity as a society to deal with the impact of this new technology depends, in part, on the degree to which we can assimilate the threat it poses to the settled ways our legal institutions have developed for dealing with similar threats in the past.

The concept of privacy has, of course, psychological, social and political dimensions which reach far beyond its analysis in the legal context;[8] I will not deal with these, however, except incidentally. Nor do I pretend to give anything like a detailed exposition of the requirements for relief and the character of the available defenses in the law of privacy. Nor will my analysis touch on privacy problems of organizations and groups. My aim is rather the more limited one of discovering in the welter of cases and statutes the interest or social value which is sought to be vindicated in the name of individual privacy.

I propose to accomplish this by examining in some detail Dean Prosser's analysis of the tort of privacy and by then suggesting the conceptual link between the tort and the other legal contexts in which privacy finds protection. My reasons for taking this route rather than another, for concentrating initially on the tort cases and Dean Prosser's analysis of them, are that privacy began its modern history as a tort and that Dean Prosser is by far the most influential contemporary exponent of the tort. Warren and Brandeis who are credited with "discovering" privacy thought of it almost exclusively as a tort remedy. However limited and inadequate we may ultimately consider such a remedy, the historical development in the courts of the concept of privacy stems from and is almost exclusively devoted to the quest for such a civil remedy. We neglect it, therefore, only at the expense of forsaking the valuable insights which seventy-five years of piecemeal common law adjudication can provide.

The justification for turning my own search for the meaning of privacy around a detailed examination of Dean Prosser's views on the subject is simply that his influence on the development of the law of privacy begins to rival in our day that of Warren and Brandeis.[9] His concept of privacy is alluded to in almost every decided privacy case in the last ten years or so,[10] and it is reflected in the current draft of the Restatement of Torts.[11] Under these circumstances, if he is mistaken, as I believe he is, it is obviously important to attempt to demonstrate his error and to attempt to provide an alternative theory.

II. Dean Prosser's analysis of the privacy cases

Although it is not written in the style of an academic exposé of a legal myth, Dean Prosser's 1960 article on privacy has that effect; although he does not say it in so many words, the clear consequence of his view is that Warren and Brandeis were wrong, and their analysis of the tort of privacy a mistake. For, after examining the "over three hundred cases in the books,"[12] in which a remedy has ostensibly been sought for the same wrongful invasion of privacy, he concludes that, in reality, what is involved "is not one tort, but a complex of four."[13] A still more surprising conclusion is that these four torts involve violations of "four different interests,"[14] none of which, it turns out, is a distinctive interest in privacy.[15]

The "four distinct torts" which are discovered in the cases are described by Dean Prosser as follows:

1. Intrusion upon the plaintiff's seclusion or solitude, or into his private affairs.
2. Public disclosure of embarrassing facts about the plaintiff.
3. Publicity which places the plaintiff in a "false light" in the public eye.
4. Appropriation, for the defendant's advantage, of the plaintiff's name or likeness.[16]

The interest protected by each of these torts is: in the intrusion cases, the interest in freedom from mental distress,[17] in the public disclosure and "false light" cases, the interest in reputation,[18] and in the appropriation cases, the proprietary interest in name and likeness.[19]

Thus, under Dean Prosser's analysis, the much vaunted and discussed right to privacy is reduced to a mere shell of what it has pretended to be. Instead of a relatively new, basic and independent legal right protecting a unique, fundamental and relatively neglected interest, we find a mere application in novel circumstances of traditional legal rights designed to protect well-identified and established social values. Assaults on privacy are transmuted into a species of defamation, infliction of mental distress and misappropriation. If Dean Prosser is correct, there is no "new tort" of invasion of privacy, there are rather only new ways of committing "old torts." And, if he is right, the social value or interest we call privacy is not an independent one, but is only a composite of the value our society places on protecting mental tranquility, reputation and intangible forms of property.

III. Dean Prosser's analysis appraised

A. Consistency with the Warren and Brandeis analysis

One way of testing Dean Prosser's analysis and of illuminating the concept of privacy itself, is to compare it with the Warren-Brandeis article.[20] Did those learned authors propose a "new tort" or merely a new name for "old torts"?

We may begin by noting the circumstances which stimulated the writing of the article. "On January 25, 1883," Brandeis' biographer writes,

Warren had married Miss Mabel Bayard, daughter of Senator Thomas Francis Bayard, Sr. They set up housekeeping in Boston's exclusive Back Bay section and began to entertain elaborately. The *Saturday Evening Gazette*, which specialized in "blue blood items" naturally reported their activities in lurid detail. This annoyed Warren who took the matter up with Brandeis. The article was the result.[21]

The article itself presents an intellectualized and generalized account of the plight of the Warrens beleaguered by the yellow journalism of their day.

Instantaneous photographs and newspaper enterprise have invaded the sacred precincts of private and domestic life; and numerous mechanical devices threaten to make good the prediction that "what is whispered in the closet shall be proclaimed from the house tops."[22]
The press is overstepping in every direction the obvious bounds of propriety and of decency. Gossip is no longer the resource of the idle and of the vicious, but has become a trade, which is pursued with industry as well as effrontery. To satisfy a prurient taste the details of sexual relations are spread broadcast in the columns of the daily papers. To occupy the indolent, column upon column is filled with idle gossip, which can only be procured by intrusion upon the domestic circle.[23]

Thus, Warren and Brandeis were disturbed by lurid newspaper gossip concerning private lives. But what, in their view, made such gossip wrongful? What value or interest did such gossip violate to give it a tortious character? How, in other words, were people hurt by such gossip?

On more than one occasion in their article, they allude to the "distress" which "idle gossip" in newspapers causes. "[M]odern enterprise and invention," they write, "have, through invasions . . . [of man's] privacy, subjected him to mental pain and distress, far greater than could be inflicted by mere bodily injury."[24] And they mention "the suffering of those who may be made the subjects of journalistic or other enterprise."[25]

These allusions to mental distress seem to afford support for Dean Prosser's view that, in one of its aspects, at least, the right to privacy protects against intentionally inflicted emotional trauma; that the gravamen of an action for the invasion of privacy is really hurt feelings.[26] Such a conclusion, however, cannot be justified by the Warren and Brandeis article because, in fact, they expressly disown it. They point out that, although "a legal remedy for . . . [invasion of privacy] seems to involve the treatment of mere wounded feelings,"[27] the law affords no remedy for "mere injury to feelings. However painful the mental effects upon another of an act, though purely wanton or even malicious, yet if the act is otherwise lawful the suffering inflicted is without legal remedy."[28] And they then go on to distinguish invasion of privacy as "a legal *injuria*" or "act wrongful in itself" from "mental suffering" as a mere element of damages.[29]

Thus, in Warren and Brandeis' view, idle gossip about private affairs may well cause mental distress, but this is not what makes it wrongful; the mental distress is, for them, parasitic of an independent tort, the invasion of privacy. Nor did they believe, as evidently Dean Prosser believes, that "public disclosure of private facts" constitutes a species of defamation and an injury to reputation.[30]

"The principle on which the law of defamation rests," they say, "covers . . . a radically different class of effects from those for which attention is now asked."[31] Defamation concerns "injury done to the individual in his external relations to the community," injury to the estimation in which others hold him; the wrong involved in defamation is "material."[32] The invasion of privacy, by contrast, involves a "spiritual" wrong, an injury to a man's "estimate of himself" and an assault upon "his own feelings."[33] Moreoever, invasion of privacy does not rest upon falsity as does defamation; the right to privacy exists not only "to prevent inaccurate portrayal of private life, but to prevent its being depicted at all."[34]

The third interest or value which Warren and Brandeis examine as the possible basis of the wrongfulness of newspaper gossip concerning private lives is a proprietary or property interest. Here as well, their conclusion is the negative one that, although the invasion of privacy may involve, on occasion, a misappropriation of something of pecuniary value, this is not the essence of the wrong.

This conclusion is the more striking because the legal precedents upon which they rely for the erection of a right to privacy are cases enforcing so-called common law property rights in literary and artistic works and cases involving trade secrets.[35] It is also a strong argument against Dean Prosser's identification of a "distinct" tort of appropriation of name or likeness as involving the protection of a proprietary interest[36] because, although they primarily concentrate on publicity cases, they expressly take account of the cases involving an unconsented use of a photographic likeness.[37]

Warren and Brandeis announce at the outset of their article that they believe that "the legal doctrines relating to infraction of what is ordinarily termed the common-law right to *intellectual and artistic property*" can, "properly understood," provide "a remedy for the evils under consideration."[38] They distinguish, however, between the common law protection of such property and that secured by forms of copyright statutes. The common law right allows a man "to control absolutely the act of publication, and in the exercise of his own discretion, to decide whether there shall be any publication at all."[39] The statutory right, by contrast, aims "to secure to the author, composer or artist the entire profits arising from publication."[40]

This distinction between the purposes of common law and statutory protection of literary and artistic property provides, in the Warren and Brandeis analysis, a key to the underlying significance of common law rights to literary and artistic property. They are really nothing but "instances and applications of a general right to privacy"[41] because "the value of the production [of a work subject to *common law* property right] is found not in the right to take the profits arising from publication, but in the peace of mind or the relief afforded by the ability to prevent any publication at all."[42] This being so, "it is difficult to regard the [common law] right as one of property."[43]

It is admitted that the courts which erected the legal remedy which "secures to each individual the right of determining, ordinarily, to what extent his thoughts, sentiments, and emotions shall be communicated to others,"[44] had, for the most part, "asserted that they rested their decisions on the narrow grounds of protection of property."[45] Yet, according to Warren and Brandeis, no thing of pecuniary value, no right of property "in the narrow sense," is to be found at issue in many of the cases. The concept of "property" was put forward by the courts as a fiction to rationalize a form of legal relief which was really founded on other grounds of policy. In other words, what we mean by saying there is common law property in literary and artistic works is not that violation of the right involves destruction or appropriation of something of monetary value but rather only that the law affords a remedy for the violation.[46]

In sum, as far as Warren and Brandeis were concerned, newspaper gossip about private lives was not a wrong because it destroyed character, caused mental distress, or constituted a misappropriation of property—a taking of something of pecuniary value. Although the yellow journalism which feeds luridly upon the details of private lives may incidentally accomplish each of these results, they are not the essence of the wrong. Mrs. Warren's reputation could have been completely unaffected, her equanimity entirely unruffled, and her fortune wholly undisturbed; the publicity about her and her husband would nevertheless be wrongful, nevertheless be in violation of an interest which the law should protect.

What then is the basis of the wrong? Unfortunately, the learned authors were not as successful in describing the interest violated by publicity concerning private lives as in saying what it was not. This explains, in part, the fact that after hundreds of cases enforcing Warren and Brandeis' "right to privacy," Dean Prosser, Harper and James,[47] the Restatement of Torts,[48] and other learned authorities[49] predicate the right on bases expressly rejected by Warren and Brandeis.

Warren and Brandeis obviously felt that the term "privacy" was in itself a completely adequate description of the interest threatened by an untrammeled press; man, they said, had a right to his privacy, a right to be let alone, and this was, for them, a sufficient description of the interest with which they were concerned. This right, although violated by publication of information about a person's life and character, much in the same way the right to reputation is violated, is not the same as the right to reputation. Nor is the interest in being let alone like that of being protected against attempts to inflict mental trauma, even though distress is the frequent accompaniment of intrusions on privacy. And, although the common law property right to literary and artistic products is an instance of the right to privacy, privacy is not to be confused with something of pecuniary value.

Warren and Brandeis went very little beyond thus giving "their right" and "their interest" a name and distinguishing it from other rights or interests. It is only in asides of characterization and passing attempts at finding a verbal equivalent of the principle of privacy that we may find any further clues to the interest or value they sought to protect. Thus, at one point they remark, as I have indicated above, that, unlike reputation which is a "material" value, privacy is a "spiritual" one.[50] And they make repeated suggestions that the invasion of privacy, in some way, involves man's mentality,[51] that it involves an "effect upon . . . [a man's] estimate of himself and upon his own feelings."[52]

The most significant indication of the interest they sought to protect, however, is in their statement that "the principle which protects personal writings and all other personal productions ... against publication in any form is in reality not the principle of private property, but that of *inviolate personality*."[53] I take the principle of "inviolate personality" to posit the individual's independence, dignity and integrity; it defines man's essence as a unique and self-determining being. It is because our Western ethico-religious tradition posits such dignity and independence of will in the individual that the common law secures to a man "literary and artistic property"—the right to determine "to what extent his thoughts, sentiments, emotions shall be communicated to others."[54] The literary and artistic property cases led Warren and Brandeis to the concept of privacy because, for them, it would have been inconsistent with a belief in man's individual dignity and worth to refuse him the right to determine whether his artistic and literary efforts should be published to the world. He would be less of a man, less of a master over his own destiny, were he without this right.

Thus, I believe that what provoked Warren and Brandeis to write their article was a fear that a rampant press feeding on the stuff of private life would destroy individual dignity and integrity and emasculate individual freedom and independence. If this is so, Dean Prosser's analysis of privacy stands clearly at odds with "the most influential law review article ever published," one which gave rise to a "new tort,"[55] not merely to a fancy name for "old torts."

As I have already indicated,[56] Dean Prosser's analysis of the privacy cases is remarkable for two propositions; the first, that there is not a single tort of the invasion of privacy, but rather "four distinct torts"; the second, that there is no distinctive single value or interest which these "distinct torts" protect and that, in fact, they protect three different interests, no one of which can properly be denominated an interest in privacy. I have considerable doubt that the cases support either of these conclusions.

B. *The intrusion cases*

This category of cases comprises instances in which a defendant has used illegal or unreasonable means to discover something about the plaintiff's private life.[57] Included in the category, thus, is a case in which a defendant was an unwanted spectator to the plaintiff giving birth to her child.[58] The Michigan court, writing nine years before Warren and Brandeis, declared the wrong was actionable in tort because "to the plaintiff the occasion was a most sacred one and no one had a right to intrude unless invited or because of some real and pressing necessity."[59]

Another illustrative case is *Rhodes v. Graham*,[60] where the defendant tapped the plaintiff's telephone wires without authorization. In upholding the cause of action for damages the court declared that "the evil incident to the invasion of the privacy of the telephone is as great as that accompanied by unwarranted publicity in newspapers and by other means of a man's private affairs."[61] In still another case of the same type, where a home was illegally entered, a cause of action for damages was upheld on the theory of a violation of state constitutional search and seizure provisions.[62]

What interest or value is protected in these cases? Dean Prosser's answer is that "the gist of the wrong [in the intrusion cases] is clearly the intentional infliction of mental distress."[63]

The fact is, however, that in no case in this group is mental distress said by the court to be the basis or gravamen of the cause of action. Moreover, all but one of these decisions predate the recognition in the jurisdictions concerned of a cause of action for intentionally inflicted mental distress[64] and, in most instances, the lines of authority relied upon in the intrusion cases are quite different from those relied upon in the mental distress cases.[65]

Furthermore, special damages in the form of "severe emotional distress" is recognized by Dean Prosser[66] and other authorities[67] as a requisite element of the cause of action for intentionally inflicted emotional distress. Yet, many of the cases allowing recovery for an intrusion expressly hold that special damages are not required.[68] Except in a small number of the cases of this group, there does not even seem to have been an allegation of mental illness or distress, certainly not an allegation of serious mental illness. And even in one of the rare cases in which serious mental distress was alleged, the court expressly says that recovery would be available without such an allegation.[69]

The most important reason, however, for disputing Dean Prosser's thesis in regard to the intrusion cases is that, in my judgment, he neglects the real nature of the complaint; namely that the intrusion is demeaning to individuality, is an affront to personal dignity. A woman's legal right to bear children without unwanted onlookers does not turn on the desire to protect her emotional equanimity, but rather on a desire to enhance her individuality and human dignity. When the right is violated she suffers outrage or affront, not necessarily mental trauma or distress. And, even where she does undergo anxiety or other symptoms of mental illness as a result, these consequences themselves flow from the indignity which has been done to her.

The fundamental fact is that our Western culture defines individuality as including the right to be free from certain types of intrusions. This measure of personal isolation and personal control over the conditions of its abandonment is of the very essence of personal freedom and dignity, is part of what our culture means by these concepts. A man whose home may be entered at the will of another, whose conversation may be overheard at the will of another, whose marital and familial intimacies may be overseen at the will of another, is less of a man, has less human dignity, on that account. He who may intrude upon another at will is the master of the other and, in fact, intrusion is a primary weapon of the tyrant.[70]

I contend that the gist of the wrong in the intrusion cases is not the intentional infliction of mental distress but rather a blow to human dignity, an assault on human personality. Eavesdropping and wiretapping, unwanted entry into another's home, may be the occasion and cause of distress and embarrassment but that is not what makes these acts of intrusion wrongful. They are wrongful because they are demeaning of individuality, and they are such whether or not they cause emotional trauma.

This view of the gravamen of the wrong of intrusion finds support in cases in which courts have expressly rested the right to recover damages for the intrusion on violation of constitutional prohibitions against search and seizure.[71] To be sure, these cases do not say that an unwanted intrusion strikes at one's dignity and offends one's individuality. But the suggestion of this constitutional basis of the right to damages is a step in that direction; at the very least, the cases contradict the view that mental distress is the gist of the action.

Cases in which some form of relief other than damages is sought for an intrusion violating the constitutional prohibition against unreasonable searches and seizures are even closer to the point. The Supreme Court of the United States has declared plainly that the fourth amendment to the federal constitution is designed to protect against intrusions into privacy and that the underlying purpose of such protection is the preservation of individual liberty.[72] These cases represent, it seems to me, a recognition that unreasonable intrusion is a wrong because it involves a violation of constitutionally protected liberty of the person.

Thus, from the early *Boyd* case[73] to the recent case of *Silverman v. United States*,[74] the Supreme Court has made clear that the "Fourth Amendment gives a man the right to retreat into his own home and there be free from unreasonable governmental intrusion"[75] and that this right is of "the very essence of constitutional liberty and security."[76] "The Fourth Amendment," the Court has declared, "forbids every search that is unreasonable and is construed to safeguard the right of privacy."[77] Moreover, the Court has proclaimed that "the security of one's privacy against arbitrary intrusion by the police . . . is basic to a free society."[78]

In all of these cases, the intruder was an agent of government and, without doubt, the forms of relief available against a government officer are to be distinguished from those available against intrusions by a private person.[79] This is not to say, however, that intrusion is a different wrong when perpetrated by an FBI agent and when perpetrated by a next door neighbor; nor is it to say that the gist of the wrong is different in the two cases. The threat to individual liberty is undoubtedly greater when a policeman taps a telephone than when an estranged spouse does, but a similar wrong is perpetrated in both instances. Thus, the conception of privacy generated by the fourth amendment cases may rightly be taken, I would urge, as being applicable to any instance of intrusion even though remedies under the fourth amendment are not available in all such instances.

Brandeis' dissent in the *Olmstead* case[80] is especially instructive in this regard.[81] In that case—decided before the enactment of Section 605 of the Federal Communications Act—the federal government had gained evidence of a violation of the Prohibition Act by tapping a telephone, and the defendant sought to preclude use of the evidence on the theory that it was gained in violation of the fourth amendment. The majority of the Court held that, since the wiretap did not involve a trespass, there was no violation of the fourth amendment and, therefore, the evidence so obtained was legally admissible. Brandeis and Holmes dissented.

It is apparent from Brandeis' dissent that, in the almost forty years which had passed since he had written his article on privacy, he had become as concerned about the evils of unbridled intrusion upon private affairs as he had once been about the evils of unreasonable publicity concerning private affairs. He had also begun to look upon the evils of wiretapping, eavesdropping and the like in the same perspective in which he regarded those attendant upon lurid journalistic exposés of private life.

Modesty seems to have kept him from citing his article, but he nevertheless "lifts" phrases out of it almost verbatim,[82] and the underlying conceptual scheme is identical. The article was written to thwart threats posed to privacy by "recent inventions and business methods,"[83] by "numerous mechanical devices";[84] the dissent is directed against "far-reaching means of invading privacy"[85] occasioned by "discovery and invention."[86] The article seeks to move the common law in the direction of protecting "man's spiritual nature,"[87] in the direction of recognizing "thoughts, emotions and sensations"[88] as objects of legal protection; the dissent attempts to enlarge the sphere of constitutionally protected liberty so as to encompass "man's spiritual nature," and so as "to protect Americans in their beliefs, their thoughts, their emotions and their sensations."[89]

The parallelism between the privacy article and the *Olmstead* dissent is so close as to suggest strongly that Brandeis believed, at the time he wrote his dissent, that the fourth amendment was intended to protect the very principle of "inviolate personality" which he had earlier suggested was the principle underlying the common law right to privacy.[90] More recently, Justice Murphy of the Supreme Court has made this conceptual identification explicit. In his dissent in the *Goldman* case, he said that the "right of personal privacy [is] guaranteed by the Fourth Amendment" and in describing the right he relied upon the Warren-Brandeis article, as well as numerous tort cases.[91] The dissents of Brandeis and Murphy—and it should be noted that in each of these cases the Court divided over the scope of the protection of the fourth amendment rather than the analysis of the social value it embodies—provide authoritative support for believing that the social interest underlying the "intrusion cases" is that of liberty of the person, the same interest protected by the fourth amendment.

C. The public disclosure cases

The second group of privacy cases to which Dean Prosser addresses himself is that in which there is a public disclosure of facts concerning a person's private life.[92] Typically, these cases involve a newspaper story, a film, or a magazine article about some aspect of a person's private life. Two of the leading cases are *Melvin v. Reid*[93] and *Sidis v. F-R Publishing Corp.*[94] In the former case, the defendant had made a motion picture using the plaintiff's maiden name and depicting her as a prostitute who had been involved in a sensational murder trial. The scandalous and sensational behavior shown in the film took place many years before it was made and, when the picture was released, the plaintiff was living a conventionally respectable life. The California court upheld a cause of action for the violation of the plaintiff's right to privacy, relying upon the Warren-Brandeis article and upon a provision of the California constitution guaranteeing the "inalienable rights" of "enjoying and defending life and liberty; acquiring, possessing, and protecting property; and pursuing and obtaining safety and happiness."[95]

In the *Sidis* case, the New Yorker magazine had published a "profile" of a young man who, years before, had been an infant prodigy, well known to the public, but who, at the time of the article, had retired of his own will and desire into a life of obscurity and seclusion. The article, although true and not unfriendly, was "merciless in its dissection of intimate details of its subject's personal life"[96] and the court plainly indicated that Sidis' privacy had been invaded.[97] Recovery was nevertheless denied. Relying on a suggestion in the Warren-Brandeis article that "the interest of the individual in privacy must inevitably conflict with the interest of the public in news," the court concluded that, since Sidis was a "public figure," the "inevitable conflict" had to be resolved in favor of the public interest in news.[98]

After discussing *Melvin v. Reid*, the *Sidis* case and dozens of others like them, Dean Prosser concludes that "this branch of the tort is evidently something quite distinct from intrusion" and that the interest protected in these cases "is that of reputation."[99] As I have shown above, this analysis is completely at odds with that of Warren and Brandeis.[100] It is also, I believe, at odds with the cases.

What Warren and Brandeis urged, even before the decision of any of the public disclosure cases, about the differences between privacy and defamation makes eminent good sense in the light of the cases themselves,[101] and Dean Prosser nowhere attempts to meet it. The public disclosure cases rest on a "radically different principle" than the defamation cases because the former class of cases involves an affront to "inviolate personality" while the latter class of cases involves an impairment of reputation.[102] Moreover, the one class of cases rests on unreasonable publicity, the other on falsity. The right to privacy exists not only "to prevent inaccurate portrayal of private life, but to prevent its being depicted at all."[103]

To be sure, *Melvin v. Reid*[104] and many other of the cases of this type contain express allegations of loss of reputation, of being exposed to public contempt, obloquy, ridicule and scorn as a result of the public disclosure. To my mind, however, such allegations are only incidental to the real wrong complained of, which is the intrusion on privacy, and this wrong, as the *Sidis* case[105] makes apparent, is made out even if the public takes a sympathetic rather than a hostile view of the facts disclosed. What the plaintiffs in these cases complain of is not that the public has been led to adopt a certain attitude or opinion concerning them—whether true or false, hostile or friendly—but rather that some aspect of their life has been held up to public scrutiny at all. In this sense, the gravamen of the complaint here is just like that in the intrusion cases; in effect, the publicity constitutes a form of intrusion, it is as if 100,000 people were suddenly peering in, as through a window, on one's private life.

When a newspaper publishes a picture of a newborn deformed child,[106] its parents are not disturbed about any possible loss of reputation as a result. They are rather mortified and insulted that the world should be witness to their private tragedy. The hospital and the newspaper have no right to intrude in this manner upon a private life. Similarly, when an author does a sympathetic but intimately detailed sketch of someone, who up to that time had only been a face in the crowd,[107] the cause for complaint is not loss of reputation but that a reputation was established at all. The wrong is in replacing personal anonymity by notoriety, in turning a private life into a public spectacle.

The cases in which undue publicity was given to a debt[108] and in which medical pictures were published[109] are founded on a similar wrong. The complaint is not that people will take a different attitude towards the plaintiff because he owes a debt or has some medical deformity—although they might do so—but rather that publicity concerning these facets of private life represents an imposition upon and an affront to the plaintiff's human dignity.

The essential difference between the cause of action for invasion of privacy by public disclosures and that for defamation is exhibited forcefully by examining how the fact of publication fits into each of the actions. In defamation, publication to even one person is sufficient to make out the wrong.[110] In privacy, unless the information was gained by wrongful prying or unless its communication involves a breach of confidence or the violation of an independent duty, some form of mass publication is a requisite of the action. As Dean Prosser himself points out, citing cases in support,

It is an invasion of the right [of privacy] to publish in a newspaper that the plaintiff does not pay his debts, or to post a notice to that effect in a window on the public street or cry it aloud in the highway; but except for one decision of a lower Georgia court which was reversed on other grounds, it has been agreed that it is no invasion to communicate that fact to the plaintiff's employer, or to any other individual, or even to a small group, unless there is some breach of contract, trust or confidential relation which will afford an independent basis for relief.[111]

What at first seem like exceptions to the requirement of mass publication in privacy are easily explained. Where private information is wrongfully gained and subsequently communicated, the wrong is made out independently of the communication. Communication in such a case, whether to one person or many, is not of the essence of the wrong and only goes to enhance damages. This, then, is not an exception to the rule of mass communication at all. Where, however, a person chooses to give another information of a personal nature on the understanding it will be held private and the confidence is broken, publication is indeed a requisite of recovery and even limited publication is sufficient to support the action. But the wrong here is not the disclosure itself, but rather the disclosure in violation of a relationship of confidence. Disclosure, whether to one person or many, is equally wrongful as a breach of the condition under which the information was initially disclosed.

It is in cases where public disclosure of personal and intimate facts is made without any breach of confidence that the rule of mass disclosure applies in full force. Why should it make a difference in such cases—other than in the amount of damages recoverable, as it does in defamation actions—whether a statement is published to one or many? Why should it make a difference in determining if an invasion of privacy is made out whether I tell a man's employer he owes me money or whether I shout it from the rooftops? In defamation, a statement is either actionable or not depending upon its subject matter and irrespective of the extent of publication. Why should actionability in privacy sometimes depend upon the extent of publication?

The reason is simply that defamation is founded on loss of reputation while the invasion of privacy is founded on an insult to individuality. A person's reputation may be damaged in the minds of one man or many. Unless there is a breach of a confidential relationship, however, the indignity and outrage involved in disclosure of details of a private life, only arise when there is a massive disclosure, only when there is truly a disclosure to the public.

If a woman who had always lived a life of rectitude were called a prostitute, she could succeed in defamation even if the charge had been made to only one individual. The loss of the respect of that single individual is the wrong complained of. However, absent a breach of confidentiality, if a respectable woman who had once been a prostitute was described as such to a single friend or small group of friends, no cause of action would lie, no matter how radically her friends' opinions changed as a result. The wrong in the public disclosure cases is not in changing the opinions of others, but in having facts about private life made public. The damage is to an individual's self-respect in being made a public spectacle.

The gravamen of a defamation action is engendering a false opinion about a person, whether in the mind of one other person or many people. The gravamen in the public disclosure cases is degrading a person by laying his life open to public view. In defamation a man is robbed of his reputation; in the public disclosure cases it is his individuality which is lost.

It is admitted that no court has expressed such a view of the series of cases Dean Prosser identifies as public disclosure cases.[112] But then no court has adopted Dean Prosser's view of these cases either. The analysis I offer is, however—as I showed above—suggested by the Warren-Brandeis article.[113] Moreover, it finds support in the fact that *Melvin v. Reid*, one of the leading cases of this type, relied upon a constitutional provision guaranteeing life, liberty and happiness.[114] Even if this suggestion of a constitutional conceptual basis for privacy is considered "vague,"[115] it nevertheless points away from reputation and towards personal dignity and integrity as the gist of the wrong.

Further support for this analysis of the public disclosure cases is found in the fact that it brings these cases into the same framework of theory as the intrusion cases. Many of the intrusion cases rely upon the authority of the public disclosure cases and vice versa.[116] If Dean Prosser were correct, such reliance would be mistaken or, at the least, misleading. All else being equal, a theory of the intrusion and public disclosure cases which explains their interdependence and provides a single rationale for them is, I suggest, to be preferred. Physical intrusion upon a private life and publicity concerning intimate affairs are simply two different ways of affronting individuality and human dignity. The difference is only in the means used to threaten the protected interest.

Consider the childbirth situation involved in the *De May* case,[117] discussed above. The cause of action there, it will be recalled, was based upon the defendant's having been an unwanted and unauthorized spectator to the plaintiff's birth pangs. To the Michigan court, this was a defilement of what was "sacred."[118] But the same sense of outrage, of defilement of what was "sacred," would have ensued if the defendant had been authorized to witness the birth of the plaintiff's child and had subsequently described the scene in detail in the public press. An unwanted report in a newspaper of the delivery room scene, including the cries of anguish and delight, the sometimes abusive, sometimes profane, sometimes loving comments voiced under sedation and the myriad other intimacies of childbirth, would be an insult and an affront of the same kind as an unauthorized physical intrusion upon the scene. The publicity would constitute the same sort of blow to our moral sensibility as the intrusion.

The parallelism which can be constructed in the *De May* case cannot be constructed in all of the intrusion and publicity cases. Sometimes public disclosure of what is seen or overheard can be offensive and, perhaps, actionable even though the intrusion itself may not be, as, for example, where a reporter "crashes" a private social gathering. Sometimes the details of private life which are publicly reported are not subject to being seen or overheard in a secret or unauthorized fashion at all, as in the case of a debt or a sordid detail of someone's past which is recorded in a public record. However, the fact that public disclosure of information might be actionable even though gaining the information by physical intrusion might not be, or vice versa, is not a ground for believing that the interest protected in each instance is different. The only thing it proves is that publicity concerning personal affairs and physical intrusions upon private life may each be the cause of personal indignity and degradation in ways the other cannot.

The underlying identity of interest in these two branches of the tort was lost sight of, I would suggest, because menacing technological means for intruding upon privacy developed at a later period than threateneing forms of public disclosure. Lurid journalism became a fact of American life before the "private eye," the "bug" and the "wiretap." At the time Warren and Brandeis wrote, the common neighborhood snoop was not a sufficient cause for public concern to arouse their interest and the uncommon snoop who uses electronic devices had not yet made his appearance. This possibly explains why their article neglects the three earliest forms of protection against physical intrusions upon privacy, the action in trespass quare clausum fregit, "peeping tom" statutes[119] and the fourth amendment.[120] However, by the time Brandeis wrote his dissent in the *Olmstead* case,[121] involving a telephone wiretap, the technology of intrusion had developed to the point where he saw that it presented the same threat to individuality as did lurid journalism. As I have already indicated,[122] Brandeis then drew the necessary consequences for his theory of privacy.

Another aspect of our social history which teaches us something about the gravamen of the public disclosure cases is that Warren and Brandeis did not write their article until 1890, when the American metropolitan press had turned to new forms of sensational reporting and when the social pattern of American life had begun to be set by the mores of the metropolis instead of the small town. A number of writers have recently pointed out that gossip about the private affairs of others is surely as old as human society and that the small town gossip spread the intimacies of one's life with the same energy, skill and enthusiasm as the highest paid reporter of the metropolitan press.[123]

Why then did it take "recent inventions" and "numerous mechanical devices," the advent of yellow journalism where "gossip . . . has become a trade,"[124] to awaken Warren and Brandeis to the need for the right to privacy?

Although the distinction should not be drawn too sharply—the mythology of ruralism is already too deeply embedded—the small town gossip did not begin to touch human pride and dignity in the way metropolitan newspaper gossip mongering does. Resources of isolation, retribution, retraction and correction were very often available against the gossip but are not available to anywhere near the same degree, against the newspaper report. The whispered word over a back fence had a kind of human touch and softness while newsprint is cold and impersonal. Gossip arose and circulated among neighbors, some of whom would know and love or sympathize with the person talked about. Moreover, there was a degree of mutual interdependence among neighbors which generated tolerance and tended to mitigate the harshness of the whispered disclosure.

Because of this context of transmission, small town gossip about private lives was often liable to be discounted, softened and put aside. A newspaper report, however, is spread abroad as part of a commercial enterprise among masses of people unknown to the subject of the report and on this account it assumes an imperious and unyielding influence. Finally, for all of these reasons and others as well, the gossip was never quite believed or was grudgingly and surreptitiously believed, while the newspaper tends to be treated as the very fount of truth and authenticity, and tends to command open and unquestioning recognition of what it reports.

Thus, only with the emergence of newspapers and other mass means of communication did degradation of personality by the public disclosure of private intimacies become a legally significant reality. The right to sue for defamation has ancient origins because reputation could be put in peril by simple word of mouth or turn of the pen. The right to privacy in the form we know it, however, had to await the advent of the urbanization of our way of life including, as an instance, the institutionalization of mass publicity, because only then was a significant and everyday threat to personal dignity and individuality realized.

D. *The use of name or likeness*

The third "distinct tort" involving a "distinct interest" which Dean Prosser isolates turns on the commercial exploitation of a person's name or likeness.[125] This group of cases is designed, he says, to protect an interest which "is not so much a mental as a proprietary one, in the exclusive use of the plaintiff's name and likeness as an aspect of identity."[126]

In 1902, a flour company circulated Abigail Roberson's photograph, without her consent, as part of an advertising flier and, as a result, she was "greatly humiliated by the scoffs and jeers of persons who recognized her face and picture . . . and her good name had been attacked, causing her great distress and suffering in body and mind."[127] The New York Court of Appeals, in a 4 to 3 decision, refused recovery because they could find no legal precedent for Warren and Brandeis' right to privacy, on which Abigail relied.[128] To succeed, the majority indicated, the plaintiff in such a case had to prove either "a breach of trust or that plaintiff had a property right in the subject of litigation which the court could protect,"[129] and here the plaintiff could show neither.

Three years after the *Roberson* case was decided the same issue came before the Georgia Supreme Court which reached the opposite result. In *Pavesich v. New England Life Ins. Co.*,[130] the plaintiff's photograph was used, without his consent, in a newspaper advertisement for life insurance, which proclaimed to the world that Pavesich had bought life insurance and was the better man for it. There was no suggestion in the case that the plaintiff sought to vindicate a proprietary interest, that he sought recompense for the commercial value of the use of his name; since he was not well known, the use of his name or picture could hardly command even a fraction of the cost of the lawsuit. Nor did Pavesich claim, as the plaintiff in the *Roberson* case did, that he suffered severe nervous shock as a result of the publication.

The basis of recovery in the case was rather "a trespass upon Pavesich's right of privacy."[131] Relying heavily on the Warren-Brandeis article, the Georgia court recognized the right as derivative of natural law and "guaranteed . . . by the constitutions of the United States and State of Georgia, in those provisions which declare that no person shall be deprived of liberty except by due process of law."[132] The use of the photograph, declared the court, was an "outrage":

The knowledge that one's features and form are being used for such a purpose and displayed in such places as such advertisements are often liable to be found brings not only the person of an extremely sensitive nature, but even the individual of ordinary sensibility, to a realization that his liberty has been taken away from him, and as long as the advertiser uses him for these purposes, he cannot be otherwise than conscious of the fact that he is, for the time being, under the control of another, and that he is no longer free, and that he is in reality a slave without hope of freedom, held to service by a merciless master; and if a man of true instincts, or even of ordinary sensibilities, no one can be more conscious of his complete enthrallment than he is.[133]

The *Paveisch* case has probably been cited more often than any other case in the history of the development of the right to privacy, and it has been cited not only in cases involving use of name or likeness but also in the so-called intrusion cases,[134] and the public disclosure cases.[135] To my mind, *Pavesich* and the other use of name or likeness cases are no different in the interest they seek to protect than the intrusion and public disclosure cases. That interest is not, as Dean Prosser suggests,[136] a "proprietary one," but rather the interest in preserving individual dignity.

The use of a personal photograph or a name for advertising purposes has the same tendency to degrade and humiliate as has publishing details of personal life to the world at large; in the *Pavesich* court's words, the use of a photograph for commercial purposes brings a man "to a realization that his liberty has been taken away from him" and "that he is no longer free."[137] Thus, a young girl whose photograph was used to promote the sale of dog food complained of "humiliation," "loss of respect and admiration" and co-incident "mental anguish," and the Illinois court which upheld her cause of action cited the Illinois constitutional guarantee of life, liberty and pursuit of happiness as the basis of recovery.[138] Similarly, where a lawyer's name was used for the purposes of advertising photocopy equipment,[139] where a young woman's picture in a bathing suit was used to advertise a slimming product,[140] or where the plaintiff's photograph was used to advertise Doan's pills,[141] the wrong complained of was mortification, humiliation and degradation rather than any pecuniary or property loss.

The only difference between these cases and the public disclosure cases is the fact that the sense of personal affront and indignity is provoked by the association of name or likeness with a commercial product rather than by publicity concerning intimacies of personal life. In the public disclosure cases what is demeaning to individuality is being made a public spectacle by disclosure of private intimacies. In these cases what is demeaning and humiliating is the commercialization of an aspect of personality.

One possible cause for confusion concerning the interest which underlies these cases is that the use of name or likeness is held to be actionable in many of the cases precisely because it is a use for commercial or trade purposes. This seems to suggest that the value or interest threatened is a proprietary or commercial one. Such a conclusion is mistaken, however, because, in the first place, as I noted above, the name or likeness which is used in most instances has no true commercial value, or it has a value which is only nominal and hardly worth the lawsuit. In fact, it has been held that general rather than special damages are recoverable and this, in itself, is a refutation of the conclusion that the interest concerned is a proprietary one.[142]

In the second place, the conclusion that the plaintiff seeks to vindicate a proprietary right in these cases overlooks the true role of the allegation that the plaintiff's name or picture was used commercially. The reason that the commercial use of a personal photograph is actionable, while—under many circumstances, such as where consent to publication is implied from the fact the photograph was taken in a public place—the use of the same photograph in a news story would not be,[143] is that it is the very commercialization of a name or photograph which does injury to the sense of personal dignity. As one court has stated, "the right protected is the right to be protected against the commercial exploitation of one's personality."[144]

No man wants to be "used" by another against his will, and it is for this reason that commercial use of a personal photograph is obnoxious. Use of a photograph for trade purposes turns a man into a commodity and makes him serve the economic needs and interest of others. In a community at all sensitive to the commercialization of human values, it is degrading to thus make a man part of commerce against his will.[145]

Another reason which has possibly led Dean Prosser and others[146] to the conclusion that the interest involved in the use of name or likeness cases is a proprietary one, is that in some few of the cases,[147] the plaintiffs are well known figures whose name or photograph does indeed command a commercial price. In these cases, as Judge Frank has pointed out, the plaintiffs, "far from having their feelings bruised through public exposure of their likenesses, would feel sorely deprived if they no longer received money for authorizing advertisements, popularizing their countenances, displayed in newspapers, magazines, busses, trains and subways."[148]

The conclusion to be drawn from such cases, however, is simply that, under special circumstances, as where the plaintiff is a public figure, the use of his likeness or name for commercial purposes involves the appropriation of a thing of value. But it is important to note that, in this respect, such cases are distinguishable from cases like *Pavesich*[149] and *Eick*,[150] for instance, where the plaintiff had no public renown. In other words, the use of a name or likeness only involves an appropriation of a thing of value in a limited class of cases where the plaintiff is known to the public and where his name or likeness commands a price.

Some have said that in such cases a "right of publicity" rather than a right of privacy is involved.[151] It is a mistake, however, to conclude from these "right of publicity" cases that all the cases involving commercial use of name or likeness are founded on a proprietary interest.[152] Moreover, the very characterization of these cases as involving a "right to publicity" disguises the important fact that name and likeness can only begin to command a commercial price in a society which recognizes that there is a right to privacy, a right to control the conditions under which name and likeness may be used. Property becomes a commodity subject to be bought and sold only where the community will enforce an individual's right to maintain use and possession of it as against the world. Similarly, unless an individual has a right to prevent another from using his name or likeness commercially, even where the use of that name or likeness has no commercial value, no name or likeness could ever command a price.

Thus, there is really no "right to publicity"; there is only a right, under some circumstances, to command a commercial price for abandoning privacy. Every man has a right to prevent the commercial exploitation of his personality, not because of its commercial worth, but because it would be demeaning to human dignity to fail to enforce such a right. A price can be had in the market place by some men for abandoning it, however. If a commercial use is made of an aspect of the personality of such a man without his consent, he has indeed suffered a pecuniary loss, but the loss concerned is the price he could command for abandoning his right to privacy. The so-called "right to publicity" is merely a name for the price for which some men can sell their right to maintain their privacy.

Undoubtedly, there will be cases in which the publication of a name or likeness without consent is a boon and not a burden. Rather than suffering humiliation and degradation as a result, the beautiful but unknown girl pictured on the cover of a nationally circulated phonograph record might be delighted at having been transfigured into a modern Cinderella. Suddenly, she is a national figure, glowing in the limelight, and her picture and name have become sought after commodities as a result. Has privacy been violated when there is no personal sense of indignity and the commercial values of name or likeness have been enhanced rather than diminished?

I believe that in such a case there is an invasion of privacy, although it is obviously not one which will be sued on and not one which is liable to evoke community sympathy or command anything but a

nominal jury award. The case is very much like one in which a physician successfully treats a patient but is held liable for the technical
tort of battery because the treatment extended beyond the consent.[153]
However beneficent the motive, or successful the result, the "touching" is considered wrongful. As I view the matter, using a person's
name or likeness for a commercial purpose without consent is a wrongful exercise of dominion over another even though there is no subjective sense of having been wronged, even, in fact, if the wrong was
subjectively appreciated, and even though a commercial profit might
accrue as a result. This is so because the wrong involved is the objective
diminution of personal freedom rather than the infliction of personal
suffering or the misappropriation of property.

I agree with Dean Prosser that, in one sense, it is "quite pointless
to dispute over whether such a right is to be classified as 'property' ";[154]
as Warren and Brandeis long ago pointed out, there is a sense in
which there inheres "in all . . . rights recognized by the law . . . the
quality of being owned or possessed—and (as that is the distinguishing
attribute of property) there may be some propriety in speaking of
those rights as property."[155]

But in one sense it is very important, as Warren and Brandeis saw,
to decide whether the right to damages for the commercial use of
name or likeness is called a property right. The importance resides
in finding the common ground between the use of name and likeness
cases, the public disclosure cases and the intrusion cases. In Dean
Prosser's view the interest vindicated in each of these classes of cases
is a different one. In my view the interest protected in each is the
same, it is human dignity and individuality or, in Warren and Brandeis' words, "inviolate personality."

E. The "false light" cases

The fourth and final distinct group of cases which Dean Prosser identifies within the overall rubric of privacy are cases which he describes
as involving "publicity falsely attributing to the plaintiff some opinion
or utterance,"[156] cases in which "the plaintiff's picture [is used] to
illustrate a book or an article with which he has no reasonable
connection"[157] or in which "the plaintiff's name, photograph and fingerprints [are included] in a public 'rogues' gallery' of convicted criminals, when he has not in fact been convicted of any crime."[158] He says
these cases all involve reputation and "obviously differ from those of
intrusion, or disclosure of private facts [or appropriation]."[159]

I agree with Dean Prosser that all of these cases involve reputation, but I am persuaded, though he is not, that they also involve the assault on individual personality and dignity which is characteristic of all the other privacy cases. The slur on reputation is an aspect of the violation of individual integrity.

Two California cases in which Mr. and Mrs. Gill sued for damages illustrate the point. They were photographed embracing in their place of business and the photograph was used in two different articles in the public press on the subject of love. In one of the articles, the photograph was used to illustrate the "wrong kind of love" consisting "wholly of sexual attraction and nothing else." In the other article, the photograph was used without any particular portion of the text referring to it. The plaintiffs succeeded against the publisher who characterized their love as being of the "wrong kind,"[160] but their complaint was dismissed as against the other publisher.[161]

The use of a photograph taken in a public place and published without comment in a news article could not be considered offensive to personal dignity because consent to such a publication, to the abandonment of privacy, is implied from the fact the Gills embraced in public. Use of the same photograph accompanied by false and derogatory comment is another matter, however. Although the comment may not be defamatory and, therefore, not actionable as such, when combined with the public exploitation of the photograph, it turns the otherwise inoffensive publication into one which is an undue and unreasonable insult to personality. It is the combination of false and stigmatic comment on character with public exhibition of the photograph which constitutes the actionable wrong.

Publishing a photograph in a "false light" serves the same function in constituting the wrong as does a use of the photograph for advertising purposes. The picture of Mr. and Mrs. Gill embracing could no more be used to cast aspersions on the character of their love than it could be used to advertise the aphrodisiac effects of a perfume. In both instances, such publicity "violates the ordinary decencies"[162] and impinges on their right to maintain their identity as individuals. (Significantly, the California District Court of Appeals which upheld the Gills' action cited a section of the California constitution guaranteeing the right to pursue and gain happiness[163] which is almost identical to the section of the Georgia constitution cited in the *Pavesich* case,[164] involving an unauthorized use of a photograph for advertising purposes.)

The use of a name in a "false light" is actionable for the same reasons as the use of a name for a commercial purpose. The "false light" in which the name is used makes the use wrongful for the same reason that the use of the name for advertising purposes does. And, in fact, many of the cases which Dean Prosser cites as actionable for "falsely attributing to the plaintiff some opinion or utterance"[165]—including the leading *Pavesich* case[166]—are cases in which a name has been used for advertising purposes.

I suspect that the reason which leads Dean Prosser to distinguish the "false light" cases from the use of name and likeness cases is that, as I indicated above,[167] he mistakenly regards the latter group of cases as turning on a proprietary interest in name or likeness. If you believe the use for advertising purposes of a photograph of two ordinary people embracing is wrongful because it violates their pecuniary interest in their name or likeness, you will regard the use of the same photograph in a "false light"—illustrating a depraved kind of love-making, for instance—as involving a fundamentally different kind of wrong. However, once it is recognized that the use of a name for advertising purposes is wrongful because it is an affront to personal dignity,[168] the underlying similarity between the advertising and "false light" cases becomes apparent. The "false light" and the advertising use are merely two different means of publishing a person's name or likeness so as to offend his dignity as an individual.

There is a recent tendency in the law of defamation which has extended the interest protected by that cause of action beyond the traditional reaches of character to include aspects of personal humiliation and degradation.[169] The cases pointing in this direction are those, for instance, in which recovery in libel has been allowed to a man whose published photograph represented him as grossly deformed[170] and in which recovery was allowed for publishing a photograph of an English sports amateur so as to suggest that he was commercially advertising chocolate.[171] These cases, it has been said, "have made it possible to reach certain indecent violations of privacy by means of the law of libel, on the theory that any writing is a libel that discredits the plaintiff in the minds of any considerable and respectable class in the community though no wrongdoing or bad character is imputed to him."[172]

This tendency in the law of defamation is consistent with, is, in fact, the counterpart of, the growth of the "false light" category of recovery in the law of privacy. It strongly suggests that the law of privacy may provide a valuable avenue or development for the law of defamation.[173] In this sense, however, it is the law of privacy which helps explain the defamation cases, rather than vice versa, as Dean Prosser suggests.

IV. Privacy in non-tort contexts

Besides introducing four principles to explain the tort cases involving privacy where one will suffice, Dean Prosser's analysis also has the unfortunate consequence that it makes impossible the reconciliation of privacy in tort and non-tort contexts. If privacy in tort is regarded as an amalgam of the infliction of emotional distress, defamation and misappropriation, it is impossible to find any common link between the tort cases and various forms of protection of privacy which are found in constitutions, statutes and common law rules which do not involve tort claims.

Actually, however, there is a common thread of principle and an identical interest or social value which runs through the tort cases as well as the other forms of legal protection of privacy. Thus, for instance, as I have already shown,[174] the fourth amendment to the federal constitution erects a barrier against unreasonable governmental entries into a man's home or searches of his person, and the Supreme Court has indicated on many occasions that this protection is of the very essence of constitutional liberty and security.[175] If the gravamen of intrusion as a tort is said to be the intentional infliction of emotional distress, the conceptual link between the tort and the fourth amendment is lost. But if the intrusion cases in tort are regarded as involving a blow to human dignity or an injury to personality, their relation to the constitutional protection of the fourth amendment becomes apparent.

The difference between the *De May* case,[176] involving an unauthorized witness to childbirth, and the *Silverman* case,[177] involving the use of a "spike" microphone in a criminal investigation to overhear a conversation in a home, is that the former involved an intrusion by a private person and a tort remedy was sought, while the latter involved an intrusion by a government agent and the remedy sought was the suppression of the use of the fruits of the intrusion. But the underlying wrong in both instances was the same; the act complained of was an affront to the individual's independence and freedom. A democratic state which values individual liberty can no more tolerate an intrusion on privacy by a private person than by an officer of government and the protections afforded in tort law, like those afforded under the Constitution, are designed to protect this same value.

A similar analysis may also be made of the public disclosure cases, the use of name or likeness cases and the "false light" cases. In these cases the individual's dignity has been subject to challenge just as it was in the *Silverman* case, the *De May* case and the other intrusion cases. Respect for individual liberty not only commands protection against intruders into a person's home but also against making him a public spectacle by undue publicity concerning his private affairs or degrading him by commercializing his name or likeness or using it in a "false light." Each of these wrongs constitutes an intrusion on personality, an attack on human dignity.

It is true, of course, that the fourth amendment only protects against invasions of privacy perpetrated by state or federal officers.[178] This does not mean, however, that the wrong against which the amendment was erected is different from that which is involved where one private citizen intrudes upon another's home or subjects his person to an unwarranted search. Moreover, each state has a search and seizure provision comparable to that of the fourth amendment[179] and, in some states at least, it has been held that the provision applies to private persons.[180]

Thus, the protection which the fourth amendment secures against the enforcement of the criminal law by means of unreasonable searches and seizures involves the same underlying interest as that secured by the right of privacy in tort law. Although there are undoubtedly other considerations of policy involved in the fourth amendment cases,[181] they, like the tort cases, are intended to preserve individual dignity.

This same value is also enforced in numerous statutes which make intrusions on privacy a crime. The oldest of such are the so-called "peeping tom" statutes, which make it a misdemeanor to peer into the window of another's home.[182] The introduction of new means of "peeping," of electronic means of eavesdropping, has brought forth modern versions of the older "peeping tom" statutes. The Federal Communications Act makes it a crime to listen in to a telephone conversation without consent by tapping the telephone and subsequently disclosing what is heard.[183] And in New York, Illinois and Nevada it is a crime to eavesdrop "by means of instrument" on any conversation, telephonic or otherwise, or even to possess eavesdropping equipment.[184]

These statutes are obviously aimed at the same wrong against which the common law intrusion cases discussed above are directed.[185] Some of them provide for a civil remedy as well as a criminal penalty and thereby expressly enlarge the tort right to privacy.[186] Some courts have engrafted a civil remedy on the criminal prohibition, using the criminal statute—as is frequently done in the law of tort[187]—to define the wrong for which recompense in damages may be sought.[188]

Thus, for instance, in *Reitmaster v. Reitmaster,*[189] the defendants had
violated the provisions against wiretapping in Section 605 of the Federal Communications Act and the plaintiff sued for damages. Although a jury verdict in favor of the defendant based on a finding of
consent was affirmed, Judge Learned Hand, writing for the Second
Circuit Court of Appeals, plainly indicated that a civil suit for damages
would lie for a breach of Section 605. He said:

> Although the Act does not expressly create any civil liability, we can see no
> reason why the situation is not within the doctrine which, in the absence of
> contrary implications, construes a criminal statute, enacted for the benefit of
> a specified class, as creating a civil right in members of the class, although
> the only express sanctions are criminal.[190]

Such judicial creation of a civil remedy on the basis of the criminal
wrong of wiretapping or eavesdropping, read together with the eavesdropping statutes which expressly provide coordinate civil and criminal remedies,[191] proves the identity of interest behind the civil and
criminal remedies. It also provides an added reason for disputing
Dean Prosser's contention[192] that the wrong in such intrusion cases is
the intentional infliction of mental distress; if it were, the civil remedy
would only be available on a showing of such distress, but, in fact,
there is no such requirement. Finally, it should be noted that the
theory expressed by Judge Hand in *Reitmaster* would provide an easy
avenue for extending the civil right of privacy in New York, where
it is a creature of a statute which limits recovery of damages to the
use of name or likeness for purposes of trade or advertising.[193]

Another important class of statutes which are intended to protect
against degradation of individuality are those which prohibit the disclosure of confidential information of various sorts. Thus, for instance, we are all required by law to divulge a great deal of information—
of a personal as well as of a business nature—to the United States
Government for the purpose of the census.[194] But all such information
is made confidential by statute and unauthorized disclosure of it is a
crime.[195] Although it is not as comprehensive, a similar prohibition
against disclosure of data concerning personal lives and business affairs given for purposes of tax collection is to be found in the Internal
Revenue Code.[196] And, in Title 18 of the United States Code, there
is a broad prohibition, backed by criminal penalty, against disclosure
by a federal officer of a wide range of confidential information concerning the operation of businesses.[197]

Similar statutes are to be found in state law. New York, for example,
has a provision in its Public Officer's Law, which is not enforced by

a criminal penalty, forbidding any public officer from disclosing confidential information acquired in the course of his official duties.[198] In the Penal Law, there are provisions making it a crime for an employee of a telegraph or telephone company to divulge information gained in the course of his employment.[199] In another section of the Penal Law, disclosure by an election officer or poll watcher of the name of the candidate for whom a person has voted is made a misdemeanor.[200] In the Social Welfare Law, publication of the names of people receiving or applying for public assistance is made a crime, and all information obtained by and communications to a public welfare official, as well as all records of abandoned or delinquent children, are made confidential.[201]

The same pattern of protection is found in still other New York statutes. Thus, the Correction Law contains provisions intended to preserve the confidential character of criminal identification records and statistics.[202] The General Business Law forbids an employee of a licensed private investigator to divulge information gathered by his employer.[203] The Civil Rights Law forbids the publication of testimony taken in private by certain state investigative agencies.[204] And, finally, the Education Law forbids soliciting, receiving or giving information concerning persons applying for vocational rehabilitation training.[205]

This brief survey of federal and New York State statutes regulating disclosure of confidential information is not, of course, intended to be exhaustive. My purpose is rather to demonstrate by these statutes— and it should be noted that there are undoubtedly untold administrative regulations on the federal and state level which have a similar purport—that the same impetus which moved the common law courts to erect a civil cause of action founded on public disclosure of aspects of private life[206] also provoked action by the national and state legislatures intending to serve the same purpose.

Following Warren and Brandeis' lead, the common law courts responded to the threat posed to privacy by lurid journalism and demeaning advertising. Legislatures have responded to threats to personal dignity which were not yet manifest when Warren and Brandeis wrote. It was only after the turn of the century that the telephone and telegraph became instruments of everyday life, used to confide personal intimacies and business secrets. Unless some security could be found against people illicitly breaking in upon these private communications and divulging what was learned, an important area of private life would be subject to degrading public scrutiny, and public confidence in these instruments of communication would be destroyed. Section 605 of the Federal Communications Act[207] and various state statutes[208] were intended to prevent this consequence. Whether they were successful or not is, of course, another question.

Another avenue for impairing the privacy of our lives—again one which only became a cause for public concern after Warren and Brandeis wrote—was the increasing accumulation of information about each of us which finds its way into government records and files. Of course, the very fact that a government agency requires such information under the compulsion of law,[209] whether for the purposes of providing social welfare benefits, taking the census, or collecting taxes, is itself an intrusion upon our persons. Most of us have agreed, however, that the social benefit to be gained in these instances require the information to be given and that the ends to be achieved are worth the price of diminished privacy.

But this tacit agreement is founded upon an assumption that information given for one purpose will not be used for another.[210] We are prepared to tell the tax collector and the census taker what they need to know, but we are not prepared to have them make a public disclosure of what they have learned. The intrusion is tolerable only if public disclosure of the fruits of the intrusion is forbidden. This explains why many of the statutes which require us to tell something about ourselves to a government agency contain an express provision against disclosure of such information.[211] It also explains why there are general provisions prohibiting disclosure of information of a personal nature gained in an official capacity.[212] Again, I note that my purpose here is not to comment upon the effectiveness of these anti-disclosure statutes; it is only to describe their broad aims.

The parallelism between the intrusion and the disclosure statutes, on the one hand, and the intrusion and disclosure tort cases, on the other, illuminates, I believe, the common conceptual character of privacy which runs through all of them. Intrusion and public disclosure are merely alternative forms of injury to individual freedom and dignity. The common law courts provide civil relief against turning a man's private life into a public spectacle as well as against impairing his private intimacies by intruding upon them.[213] Similarly, legislatures have been impelled to prevent both eavesdropping *and* divulgence[214] or, where the intrusion is socially sanctioned, as in the census and tax fields, disclosure for other than sanctioned purposes. The disclosure provisions of the statutes, like the tort disclosure cases, preserve dignity by restricting publicity, by assuring a man that his life is not the open and indiscriminate object of all eyes. And, as the comparable tort cases do in relation to the tort intrusion cases, the statutory disclosure provisions complement the statutory intrusion provisions by making a man secure in his person, not only against prying eyes and ears, but against the despair of being the subject of public scrutiny and knowledge.

V. Conclusion: the invasion of privacy as an affront to human dignity

Dean Prosser has described the privacy cases in tort as involving "not one tort, but a complex of four,"[215] as "four disparate torts under . . . [a] common name."[216] And he believes that the reason the state of the law of privacy is "still that of a haystack in a hurricane," as Chief Judge Biggs said in *Ettore v. Philco Television Broadcasting Co.*,[217] is that we have failed to "separate and distinguish" these four torts.[218]

I believe to the contrary that the tort cases involving privacy are of one piece and involve a single tort. Furthermore, I believe that a common thread of principle runs through the tort cases, the criminal cases involving the rule of exclusion under the fourth amendment, criminal statutes prohibiting peeping toms, wiretapping, eavesdropping, the possession of wiretapping and eavesdropping equipment, and criminal statutes or administrative regulations prohibiting the disclosure of confidential information obtained by government agencies.

The words we use to identify and describe basic human values are necessarily vague and ill-defined. Compounded of profound human hopes and longings on the one side and elusive aspects of human psychology and experience on the other, our social goals are more fit to be pronounced by prophets and poets than by professors. We are fortunate, then, that some of our judges enjoy a touch of the prophet's vision and the poet's tongue.

Before he ascended to the bench, Justice Brandeis had written that the principle which underlies the right to privacy was "that of an inviolate personality."[219] Some forty years later, in the *Olmstead* case,[220] alarmed by the appearance of new instruments of intrusion upon "inviolate personality," he defined the threatened interest more fully.

The makers of our Constitution undertook to secure conditions favorable to the pursuit of happiness. They recognized the significance of man's spiritual nature, of his feeling and of his intellect. . . . They sought to protect Americans in their beliefs, their thoughts, their emotions and their sensations. They conferred as against the government, the right to be let alone—the most comprehensive of rights and the right most valued by civilized men.[221]

Other Justices of our Supreme Court have since repeated, elucidated and expanded upon this attempt to define privacy as an aspect of the pursuit of happiness.[222]

More obscure judges, writing in the more mundane context of tort law, have witnessed this same connection. In two of the leading cases in the field, *Melvin v. Reid*[223] and *Pavesich v. New England Life Ins. Co.*[224]—one a so-called public disclosure case, the other a so-called appropriation or "false light" case—the right to recovery was founded upon the state constitutional provision insuring the pursuit of happiness.[225] Judge Cobb, writing in *Pavesich*, declared:

> An individual has a right to enjoy life in any way that may be most agreeable and pleasant to him, according to his temperament and nature, provided that in such enjoyment he does not invade the rights of his neighbor or violate public law or policy. The right of personal security is not fully accorded by allowing an individual to go through his life in possession of all his members and his body unmarred; nor is his right to personal liberty fully accorded by merely allowing him to remain out of jail or free from other physical restraints. . . .
>
> Liberty includes the right to live as one will, so long as that will does not interfere with the rights of another or of the public. One may desire to live a life of seclusion; another may desire to live a life of publicity; still another may wish to live a life of privacy as to certain matters and of publicity as to others. . . . Each is entitled to a liberty of choice as to his manner of life, and neither an individual nor the public has a right to arbitrarily take away from him his liberty.[226]

Some may find these judicial visions of the social goal embodied in the right to privacy vague and unconvincing. I find them most illuminating. Unfortunately, the law's vocabulary of mind is exceedingly limited. Our case law too often speaks of distress, anguish, humiliation, despair, anxiety, mental illness, indignity, mental suffering, and psychosis without sufficient discrimination of the differences between them. Justice Brandeis and Judge Cobb help us see, however, that the interest served in the privacy cases is in some sense a spiritual interest rather than an interest in property or reputation. Moreover, they also help us understand that the spiritual characteristic which is at issue is not a form of trauma, mental illness or distress, but rather individuality or freedom.

An intrusion on our privacy threatens our liberty as individuals to do as we will, just as an assault, a battery or imprisonment of our person does. And just as we may regard these latter torts as offenses "to the reasonable sense of personal dignity,"[227] as offensive to our concept of individualism and the liberty it entails, so too should we regard privacy as a dignitary tort.[228] Unlike many other torts, the harm caused is not one which may be repaired and the loss suffered is not one which may be made good by an award of damages. The injury is to our individuality, to our dignity as individuals, and the legal remedy represents a social vindication of the human spirit thus threatened rather than a recompense for the loss suffered.

What distinguishes the invasion of privacy as a tort from the other torts which involve insults to human dignity and individuality is merely the means used to perpetrate the wrong. The woman who is indecently petted[229] suffers the same indignity as the woman whose birth pangs are overseen.[230] The woman whose photograph is exhibited for advertising purposes[231] is degraded and demeaned as surely as the woman who is kept aboard a pleasure yacht against her will.[232] In all of these cases there is an interference with individuality, an interference with the right of the individual to do what he will. The difference is in the character of the interference. Whereas the affront to dignity in the one category of cases is affected by physical interference with the person, the affront in the other category of cases is affected, among other means, by physically intruding on personal intimacy and by using techniques of publicity to make a public spectacle of an otherwise private life.

The man who is compelled to live every minute of his life among others and whose every need, thought, desire, fancy or gratification is subject to public scrutiny, has been deprived of his individuality and human dignity. Such an individual merges with the mass. His opinions, being public, tend never to be different; his aspirations, being known, tend always to be conventionally accepted ones; his feelings, being openly exhibited, tend to lose their quality of unique personal warmth and to become the feelings of every man. Such a being, although sentient, is fungible; he is not an individual.

The conception of man embodied in our tradition and incorporated in our Constitution stands at odds to such human fungibility. And our law of privacy attempts to preserve individuality by placing sanctions upon outrageous or unreasonable violations of the conditions of its sustenance. This, then, is the social value served by the law of privacy, and it is served not only in the law of tort, but in numerous other areas of the law as well.

To be sure, this identification of the interest served by the law of privacy does not of itself "solve" any privacy problems; it does not furnish a ready-made solution to any particular case of a claimed invasion of privacy. In the first place, not every threat to privacy is of sufficient moment to warrant the imposition of civil liability or to evoke any other form of legal redress. We all are, and of necessity must be, subject to some minimum scrutiny of our neighbors as a very condition of life in a civilized community. Thus, even having identified the interest invaded, we are left with the problem whether, in the particular instance, the intrusion was of such outrageous and unreasonable character as to be made actionable.

Secondly, even where a clear violation of privacy is made out, one must still face the question whether it is not privileged or excused by some countervailing public policy or social interest. The most obvious such conflicting value is the public interest in news and information which, of necessity, must sometimes run counter to the individual's interest in privacy.[233] Again, identification of the nature of the privacy interest does not resolve the conflict of values, except insofar as it makes clear at least one of the elements which is to be weighed in the balance.

One may well ask, then, what difference it makes whether privacy is regarded as involving a single interest, a single tort, or four? What difference whether the tort of invasion of privacy is taken to protect the dignity of man and whether this same interest is protected in non-tort privacy contexts?

The study and understanding of law, like any other study, proceeds by way of generalization and simplification. To the degree that relief in the law courts under two different sets of circumstances can be explained by a common rule or principle, to that degree the law has achieved greater unity and has become a more satisfying and useful tool of understanding. Conceptual unity is not only fulfilling in itself, however; it is also an instrument of legal development.

Dean Prosser complains of "the extent to which defenses, limitations and safeguards established for the protection of the defendant in other tort fields have been jettisoned, disregarded, or ignored" in the privacy cases.[234] Because he regards intrusion as a form of the infliction of mental distress, it comes as a surprise and cause for concern that the courts, in the intrusion cases, have not insisted upon "genuine and serious mental harm," the normal requirement in the mental distress cases.[235] Because he believes the public disclosure cases and the "false light" cases involve injury to reputation, he is alarmed that the courts in these cases have jettisoned numerous safeguards—the defense of truth and the requirement, in certain cases, of special damages, for instance—which were erected in the law of defamation to preserve a proper balance between the interest in reputation and the interest in a free press.[236] And because he conceives of the use of name and likeness cases as involving a proprietary interest in name or likeness comparable to a common law trade name or trademark, he is puzzled that there has been "no hint" in these cases "of any of the limitations which have been considered necessary and desirable in the ordinary law of trade-marks and trade names."[237]

The reason for Dean Prosser's concern and puzzlement in each instance is based on his prior identification of the interest the tort remedy serves. If the intrusion cases serve the purpose of protecting emotional tranquility, certain legal consequences concerning necessary allegations and defenses appropriate to the protection of that interest seem to follow. The same is true for the other categories of cases as well. If he is mistaken in his identification of the interest involved in the privacy cases, however, the development of the tort will take—actually, as I have shown above, it has already taken—an entirely different turn, and will have entirely different dimensions.

The interest served by the remedy determines the nature of the cause of action and the available defenses because it enters into the complex process of weighing and balancing of conflicting social values which courts undertake in affording remedies. Therefore, my suggestion that all of the tort privacy cases involve the same interest in preserving human dignity and individuality has important consequences for the development of the tort. If this, rather than emotional tranquility, reputation or the monetary value of a name or likeness is involved, courts will be faced by the need to compromise and adjust an entirely different set of values, values more similar to those involved in battery, assault and false imprisonment cases than in mental distress, defamation and misappropriation cases.

The identification of the social value which underlies the privacy cases will also help to determine the character of the development of new legal remedies for threats posed by some of the aspects of modern technology. Criminal statutes which are intended to curb the contemporary sophisticated electronic forms of eavesdropping and evidentiary rules which forbid the disclosure of the fruits of such eavesdropping can only be assimilated to the common law forms of protection against intrusion upon privacy if the social interest served by the common law is conceived of as the preservation of individual dignity. These statutes are obviously not designed to protect against forms of mental illness or distress and to so identify the interest involved in the common law intrusion cases is to rob the argument for eavesdropping statutes of a valuable source of traditional common law analysis.

A similar argument may be made concerning other contemporary tendencies in the direction of stripping the individual naked of his human dignity by exposing his personal life to public scrutiny. The personnel practices of government and large-scale corporate enterprise increasingly involve novel forms of investigation of personal lives. Extensive personal questionnaires, psychological testing and, in some instances, the polygraph have been used to delve deeper and deeper into layers of personality heretofore inaccessible to all but a lover, an intimate friend or a physician. And the information so gathered is very often stored, correlated and retrieved by electronic machine techniques. The combined force of the new techniques for uncovering personal intimacies and the new techniques of electronic use of this personal data threatens to uncover inmost thoughts and feelings never even "whispered in the closet" and to make them all too easily available "to be proclaimed from the housetops."[238]

The character of the problems posed by psychological testing, the polygraph and electronic storage of personal data can better be grasped if seen in the perspective of the common law intrusion and disclosure cases. The interest threatened by these new instruments is the same as that which underlies the tort cases. The feeling of being naked before the world can be produced by having to respond to a questionnaire or psychological test as well as by having your bedroom open to prying eyes and ears. And the fear that a private life may be turned into a public spectacle is greatly enhanced when the lurid facts have been reduced to key punches or blips on a magnetic tape accessible, perhaps, to any clerk who can throw the appropriate switch.

This is not to say, of course, that the same adjustments of conflicting values which have been made in the tort privacy cases can be assumed to apply without modification to resolve the questions of public policy raised by the use of sophisticated electronic eavesdropping equipment, psychological techniques of probing the individual psyche or the electronic data processing equipment. Nor is to say that the expansion of the tort remedy will provide a satisfactory legal or social response to these new problems. It is rather only to say that, in both instances, community concern for the preservation of the individual's dignity is at issue and that the legal tradition associated with resolving the one set of problems is available for us in resolving the other.

NOTES

1 Warren & Brandeis, The Right of Privacy, 4 Harv. L. Rev. 193 (1890) [hereinafter cited as Warren & Brandeis].
2 See, e.g., Annot., 138 A.L.R. 22 (1942); Annot., 168 A.L.R. 446 (1947); Annot., 14 A.L.R.2d 750 (1950).

3 N.Y. Civ. Rights Law §§ 50–51; Okla. Stat. Ann. tit. 30, §§ 839–40 (1951); Utah Code Ann. §§ 76–4–7, 76–4–9 (1953); Va. Code Ann. § 8–650 (1950).

4 E.g., Feinberg, Recent Developments in the Law of Privacy, 48 Colum. L. Rev. 713 (1948); Green, Right of Privacy, 27 Ill. L. Rev. 237 (1932); Lisle, Right of Privacy (A Contra View), 19 Ky. L.J. 137 (1931); Nizer, Right of Privacy: A Half Century's Developments, 39 Mich. L. Rev. 526 (1941); O'Brien, The Right of Privacy, 2 Colum. L. Rev. 437 (1902); Winfield, Privacy, 47 L.Q. Rev. 23 (1931); Yankwich, Right of Privacy: Its Development, Scope and Limitations, 27 Notre Dame Law. 499 (1952).

5 Ettore v. Philco Television Broadcasting Co., 229 F.2d 481 (3d Cir. 1956) (Biggs, C.J.).

6 Prosser, Privacy, 48 Calif. L. Rev. 383 (1960) [hereinafter cited as Prosser, Privacy].

7 See, e.g., Brenton, The Privacy Invaders (1964); Dash, Knowlton & Schwartz, The Eavesdroppers (1959); Gross, The Brain Watchers (1962); Packard, The Naked Society (1964); Big Brother 7074 Is Watching You, Popular Science, March 1963; 1410 Is Watching You, Time, Aug. 1963; Hearings Before the Subcommittee on the Use of Polygraphs as "Lie Detectors" By the Federal Government of the House Committee on Government Operations, 88th Cong., 2d Sess., pt. 3 (1964).

8 See, e.g., Arendt, The Human Condition (1958); Hoffer, The True Believer: Thoughts on the Nature of Mass Movements (1951); Orwell, 1984 (1949).

9 Dean Wade, writing in the Virginia Law Weekly Dicta, Oct. 8, 1964, p. 1, col. 1, described the influence of Dean Prosser in this fashion:

> Another event took place some four years ago which may quickly bring the state of the law to maturity, and may also modify the habit of referring to the Warren-Brandeis article as both the origin and the true description of the nature of the right [to privacy]. This was the publication by William L. Prosser of an article entitled very simply *Privacy*, in 48 California Law Review 383, in August 1960.

10 See, e.g., Norris v. Moskin Stores, Inc., 272 Ala. 174, 176, 132 So. 2d 321, 323 (1961); Gill v. Curtis Publishing Co., 38 Cal. 2d 273, 239 P.2d 630 (1952); Carlisle v. Fawcett Publishing, Inc., 201 Cal. App. 2d 733, 734, 20 Cal. Rptr. 405, 411 (Dist. Ct. App. 1962); Werner v. Times-Mirror Co., 193 Cal. App. 2d 111, 118, 14 Cal. Rptr. 208, 214 (Dist. Ct. App. 1961); Felly v. Johnson Publishing Co., 160 Cal. App. 2d 718, 720, 325 P.2d 659, 661 (Dist. Ct. App. 1959); Barbieri v. News Journal Publishing Co., 189 A.2d 773, 774 (Del. 1963); McAndrews v. Roy, 131 So. 2d 256, 261 (Fla. 1961); Harms v. Miami Daily News, Inc., 127 So. 2d 715, 717 (Fla. 1961); Ford Motor Co. v. Williams, 108 Ga. App. 21, 29–30 nn.6 & 7, 132 S.E.2d 206, 211 nn.6 & 7 (1964); Peterson v. Idaho First Nat'l Bank, 83 Idaho 578, 583, 367 P.2d 284, 287 (1961); Yoder v. Smith, 253 Iowa 506, 507, 112 N.W.2d 862 (1962); Bremmer v. Journal-Tribune Publishing Co., 247 Iowa 817, 821, 76 N.W.2d 762, 764 (1956); Carr v. Watkins, 227 Md. 578, 583, 585–86, 177 A.2d 841, 843, 845–46 (1962);

Hawley v. Professional Credit Bureau, 245 Mich. 500, 514, 325 P.2d 659, 671 (1956); Hubbard v. Journal Publishing Co., 67 N.M. 473, 475, 368 P.2d 147, 148–49 (1961); Spahn v. Messner, Inc., 43 Misc.2d 219, 221, 250 N.Y.S.2d 529, 532 (Sup. Ct. 1964).

11 "[T]here is every reason to expect that when the second edition of the Restatement on Torts is completed and adopted by the American Law Institute, [Dean Prosser's] analysis will be substituted for the very generalized treatment now to be found in section 867." Wade, supra note 9. Dean Prosser, it should be noted, is the Reporter for the Restatement of the Law Second, Torts, and Dean Wade is one of his advisers.

12 Prosser, Privacy 388.

13 Id. at 389.

14 Ibid. Actually, Dean Prosser subsequently identifies only three distinct interests since, in his view, both the public disclosure and the "false light" cases involve the same interest in reputation. See note 18 infra and accompanying text.

15 Prosser, Privacy 389–407, 422–23.

16 Id. at 389.

17 Id. at 392, 422.

18 Id. at 398, 401, 422–23; see note 14 supra.

19 Id. at 406, 423.

20 Warren & Brandeis.

21 Mason, Brandeis: A Free Man's Life 70 (1960).

22 Warren & Brandeis 195.

23 Id. at 196.

24 Ibid.

25 Ibid.

26 It should be noted, however, that Dean Prosser regards the Warren & Brandeis article as devoted primarily to one of the four torts he identifies, namely to "public disclosure of embarrassing facts," and he regards the interest invaded in this tort as being that of reputation. Prosser, Privacy 392.

27 Warren & Brandeis 197.

28 Ibid.

29 Id. at 197–98, 213.

30 Prosser, Privacy 398, 422–23.

31 Warren & Brandeis 197.

32 Ibid.

33 Ibid.

34 Id. at 218.

35 E.g., id. at 198–205, 211–12.

36 Prosser, Privacy 406, 423.

37 See e.g., Warren & Brandeis 195, 208, 210, 214.

38 Id. at 198. (Emphasis added.)

39 Id. at 200.

40 Ibid.

41 Id. at 198.
42 Id. at 200.
43 Ibid.
44 Id. at 198.
45 Id. at 204.
46 I omit extended discussion of the theory that common law literary and artistic property rights rest on theories of breach of contract or breach of trust. Warren and Brandeis found here, as with the "property theory," that a fiction of sorts was involved, that courts implied a term of contract or a condition of trust as a form of "judicial declaration that public morality, private justice, and general convenience demand the recognition of . . . [the] rule [proscribing publication]." Warren & Brandeis 210.
47 Harper & James, Torts § 9.6 (1956).
48 Restatement, Torts § 867 (1939).
49 See, e.g., Davis, What Do We Mean by "Right of Privacy"?, 4 S.D.L. Rev. 1 (1959); Green, The Right of Privacy, 27 Ill. L. Rev. 237 (1932); Pound, Interests or Personality, 28 Harv. L. Rev. 343 (1915).
50 See text accompanying notes 32 & 33 supra.
51 See, e.g., Warren & Brandeis 196.
52 Id. at 197.
53 Id at 205. (Emphasis added.)
54 Id. at 198.
55 Gregory & Kalven, Cases on Torts 883 (1959).
56 See text accompanying notes 13–19 supra.
57 For the relevant cases, see Prosser, Privacy 389–90 nn.60–73.
58 De May v. Roberts, 46 Mich. 160, 9 N.W. 146 (1881).
59 Id. at 165, 9 N.W. at 149.
60 238 Ky. 225, 37 S.W.2d 46 (1931).
61 Id. at 228–29, 37 S.W.2d at 47.
62 Young v. Western & A.R. Co., 39 Ga. App. 761, 766–67, 148 S.E. 414, 417 (1929).
63 Prosser, Privacy 422.
64 The exception is West Virginia. Roach v. Harper, 143 W. Va. 869, 105 S.E.2d 564 (1958); Monteleone v. Cooperative Transit Co., 128 W. Va. 340, 36 S.E.2d 475 (1945) (dictum).
65 In at least two instances, however, courts have cited privacy cases for the proposition that there may be recovery for mental suffering without physical impact or physical injury. State Rubbish Collector Ass'n v. Siliznoff, 38 Cal.2d 330, 240 P.2d 282 (1952); Kuhr Bros. v. Spakas, 89 Ga. App. 885, 81 S.E.2d 491 (1954).
66 Prosser, Insult and Outrage, 44 Calif. L. Rev. 40, 43 (1956). See also, Prosser, Privacy 422.
67 See, e.g., Sams v. Eccles, 11 Utah 2d 289, 358 P.2d 344 (1961); Margruder, Mental and Emotional Disturbances in the Law of Torts, 49 Harv. L. Rev. 1033 (1936); Restatement, Torts § 46 (Supp. 1948).

68 E.g., Young v. Western & A.R. Co., 39 Ga. App. 761, 148 S.E. 414 (1929); Rhodes v. Graham, 238 Ky. 225, 228, 37 S.W.2d 46, 47 (1931); Welsh v. Pritchard, 125 Mont. 517, 525, 241 P.2d 816, 820 (1959); Sutherland v. Kroger Co., 144 W. Va. 673, 684–85, 110 S.E.2d 716, 724 (1959); Roach v. Harper, 143 W. Va. 869, 877, 105 S.E.2d 564, 568 (1958).

69 Young v. Western & A.R. Co., supra note 68.

70 See Arendt, The Human Condition (1958); Hoffer, The True Believer: Thoughts on the Nature of Mass Movements (1951); Orwell, 1984 (1949).

71 Young v. Western & A.R. Co., 39 Ga. App. 761, 148 S.E. 414 (1929); cf. Walker v. Whittle, 83 Ga. App. 445, 64 S.E.2d 87 (1951).

72 See, e.g., Silverman v. United States, 365 U.S. 505 (1961); Wolf v. Colorado, 338 U.S. 25 (1949); United States v. Lefkowitz, 285 U.S. 452 (1932); Gouled v. United States, 255 U.S. 298 (1921); Boyd v. United States, 116 U.S. 616 (1886); Lopez v. United States, 373 U.S. 427, 439 (1963) (Brennan, Douglas, and Goldberg, JJ., dissenting); Poe v. Ullman, 367 U.S. 497, 549–50 (1961) (Harlan, J., dissenting); OnLee v. United States, 343 U.S. 747, 763 (1952) (Douglas, J., dissenting); Goldman v. United States, 316 U.S. 129, 136–37 (1942) (Murphy, J., dissenting); Olmstead v. United States, 277 U.S. 438, 469, 476–79 (1928) (Brandeis, J., dissenting); cf. Public Utilities Comm'n v. Pollak, 343 U.S. 451, 467 (1952) (Douglas J., dissenting).

73 Boyd v. United States, note 72 supra.

74 365 U.S. 505 (1961).

75 Id. at 511.

76 Boyd v. United States, 116 U.S. 616, 630 (1886).

77 United States v. Lefkowitz, 285 U.S. 452, 464 (1932).

78 Wolf v. Colorado, 338 U.S. 25, 27 (1949).

79 See, e.g., Burdeau v. McDowell, 256 U.S. 465 (1921); Imboden v. People, 46 Colo. 142, 90 Pac. 608 (1907); Sackler v. Sackler, 16 App. Div.2 d 423, 229 N.Y.S.2d 61 (2d Dep't 1962), aff'd 15 N.Y.S.2d 40, 255 N.Y.S.2d 83 (1964); Sutherland v. Kroger, 110 S.E.2d 716 (W. Va. 1959); Note, 72 Yale L.J. 1062 (1963).

80 277 U.S. 438, 471 (1928).

81 It might be noted in passing that Dean Prosser's analysis of privacy neglects this phase of Brandeis' thinking on the subject.

82 E.g., compare, "Discovery and invention have made it possible for the Government, by means far more effective than stretching upon the rack, to obtain disclosure in court of *what is whispered in the closet,*" 277 U.S. at 473, with "numerous mechanical devices threaten to make good the prediction that *'what is whispered in the closet'* shall be proclaimed from the housetops." Warren & Brandeis 195. (Emphasis added.) Also compare

The makers of our Constitution . . . *recognized* the significance of *man's spiritual nature, of his feelings and of his intellect.* They knew that *only part of the pain, pleasure* and satisfactions of life are to be found in material things. They sought to *protect Americans in their beliefs, their thoughts, their emotions and their sensations,*

277 U.S. at 478, with

> Later, there came a recognition [in the law] of *man's spiritual nature, of his feelings and his intellect.* . . . [It was] made . . . clear to men that *only part of the pain, pleasure and profit of life lay in physical things. Thoughts, emotions, and sensations demanded legal recognition.* . . . The common law *secures to each individual the right of determining, ordinarily, to what extent his thoughts, sentiments, and emotions shall be communicated to others.*

Warren & Brandeis 193, 195, 198. (Emphasis added.)

83 Warren & Brandeis 195.
84 Ibid.
85 277 U.S. at 473.
86 Ibid.
87 Warren & Brandeis 193.
88 Id. at 195.
89 277 U.S. at 478.
90 Ibid.
91 316 U.S. at 136–37. It should be noted that Justice Murphy cites so-called "intrusion cases," "public disclosure cases," and "appropriation cases," as defining the right protected by the fourth amendment, without distinguishing between them conceptually.
92 See cases cited in Prosser, Privacy 392–93 nn.83–89.
93 112 Cal. App. 285, 297 Pac. 91 (Dist. Ct. App. 1931).
94 113 F.2d 806 (2d Cir. 1940).
95 112 Cal. App. at 291, 297 Pac. at 93.
96 113 F.2d at 807.
97 Id. at 811.
98 Id. at 809.
99 Prosser, Privacy 398, 422.
100 See text accompanying notes 30–34 supra.
101 This is not accidental of course, since most, if not all, of these cases rely on Warren and Brandeis' analysis.
102 Warren & Brandeis 197; cf. Themo v. New England Newspaper Publishing Co., 306 Mass. 54, 27 N.E.2d 753 (1940).
103 Warren & Brandeis 218.
104 112 Cal. App. 285, 297 Pac. 91 (Dist. Ct. App. 1931).
105 113 F.2d 806 (2d Cir. 1940).
106 Bazemore v. Savannah Hosp., 171 Ga. 257, 155 S.E. 194 (1930); Douglas v. Stokes, 149 Ky. 506, 149 S.W. 849 (1912).
107 Cason v. Baskin, 155 Fla. 198, 20 So. 2d 243 (1944).
108 Trammell v. Citizen's News Co., 285 Ky. 529, 148 S.W.2d 708 (1941); Brederman's of Springfield, Inc. v. Wright, 322 S.W.2d 892 (Mo. 1941).
109 Banks v. King Features Syndicate, 30 F. Supp. 353 (S.D.N.Y. 1939); Feeney v. Young, 191 App. Div. 501, 181 N.Y. Supp. 481 (2d Dep't 1920); Griffin v. Medical Soc'y, 11 N.Y.S.2d 109 (Sup Ct. 1939).
110 Prosser, Torts 597 (2d ed. 1955).

111 Prosser, Privacy 393–94.
112 But see the discussion of Pavesich v. New England Life Ins. Co., 122 Ga. 190, 50 S.E. 68 (1905) in text accompanying notes 130–33 infra.
113 See text accompanying notes 53–54 supra.
114 112 Cal. App. 285, 291, 297 Pac. 91, 93 (Dist. Ct. App. 1931).
115 Dean Prosser states that reliance on this "vague constitutional provision . . . has since disappeared from the California cases." Prosser, Privacy 392–93. The suggestion of a constitutional ground for the privacy cases was reaffirmed by the California District Court of Appeals in Gill v. Curtis Publishing Co., 231 P.2d 565 (Dist. Ct. App. 1951), twenty years after Melvin v. Reid, supra note 114, was decided. But in the opinion of the California Supreme Court in the same case six months later, no mention is made of the constitutional basis of the right. Gill v. Curtis Publishing Co., 38 Cal. 2d 273, 239 P.2d 630 (1952).
116 See, e.g., McDaniel v. Atlanta Coca-Cola Bottling Co., 60 Ga. App. 92, 2 S.E.2d 810 (1939); Pritchett v. Board of Comm'rs, 42 Ind. App. 3, 85 N.E. 32 (1908); Rhodes v. Graham, 238 Ky. 225, 37 S.W.2d 46 (1931); Roach v. Harper, 143 W. Va. 869, 105 S.E.2d 564 (1958).
117 46 Mich. 160, 9 N.W. 146 (1881).
118 Id. at 165, 9 N.W. at 149.
119 See, e.g., La. Rev. Stat. Ann § 14:284 (1950); N.Y. Pen. Law § 721; Bishop, Criminal Law §§ 1122–24 (9th ed. 1923); 4 Blackstone, Commentaries § 168(6) (Cooley ed. 1889); Wharton, Criminal Law and Procedure § 1718 (12th ed. 1932).
120 See notes 72–91 supra and accompanying text.
121 See note 72 supra.
122 See text accompanying notes 80–89 supra.
123 Hicks, The Limits of Privacy, The American Scholar, Spring 1959, p. 185; Ruebhausen, Book Review, N.Y.L.J. Vol. 151, No. 106, p. 4 (May 29, 1964).
124 Warren & Brandeis 195–96.
125 Illustrative cases are set out in Prosser, Privacy 401–06.
126 Prosser, Privacy 406.
127 Roberson v. Rochester Folding Box Co., 171 N.Y. 538, 542–43, 64 N.E. 442, 448 (1902) (dissenting opinion).
128 Id. at 543, 64 N.E. at 443.
129 Id. at 550, 64 N.E. at 445.
130 122 Ga. 190, 50 S.E. 68 (1905).
131 Id. at 222, 50 S.E. at 81. Actually, the case could have been decided, but was not, on the narrow ground that the publication involved a breach of trust by one Adams, a photographer who had taken Pavesich's picture.
132 Id. at 197, 50 S.E. at 71.
133 Id. at 220, 50 S.E. at 80.
134 See note 116 supra.
135 See, e.g., Bazemore v. Savannah Hosp., 117 Ga. 257, 155 S.E. 194 (1930);

Brents v. Morgan, 221 Ky. 765, 299 S.W. 967 (1927); Housch v. Peth, 165 Ohio St. 35, 133 N.E.2d 340 (1956).
136 Prosser, Privacy 406.
137 Pavesich v. New England Life Ins. Co., 122 Ga. 190, 220, 50 S.E. 68, 80 (1905).
138 Eick v. Perk Dog Food Co., 347 Ill. App. 293, 106 N.E.2d 742 (1952).
139 Fairfield v. American Photocopy Equip. Co., 138 Cal. App. 2d 82, 291 P.2d 194 (Dist. Ct. App. 1955).
140 Flake v. Greensboro News Co., 212 N.C. 780, 195 S.E. 55 (1938).
141 Foster-Milburn Co. v. Chinn, 134 Ky. 424, 120 S.W. 364 (1909).
142 See, e.g., Fairfield v. American Photocopy Equip. Co., 138 Cal. App. 2d 82, 291 P.2d 194 (Dist. Ct. App. 1955); Eick v. Perk Dog Food Co., 347 Ill. App. 293, 106 N.E.2d 742 (1952); Kunz v. Allen, 102 Kan. 883, 172 Pac. 532 (1918); Foster-Milburn Co. v. Chinn, supra note 141; Munden v. Harris, 153 Mo. App. 652, 134 S.W. 1076 (1911); Flake v. Greensboro News Co., 212 N.C. 780, 195 S.E. 55 (1938); State ex. rel. La Follette v. Hinkle, 131 Wash. 86, 229 Pac. 317 (1924).
143 See, e.g., Berg v. Minneapolis Star & Tribune Co., 79 F. Supp. 957 (D. Minn. 1948); Gill v. Hearst Publishing Co., 40 Cal. 2d 224, 253 P.2d 441 (1953); Lyles v. State, 330 P.2d 734 (Okla. Crim. 1958).
144 Hill v. Hayes, 18 App. Div. 2d 485, 488, 240 N.Y.S.2d 286, 290 (1st Dep't 1963). See also Birmingham Broadcasting Co. v. Bell, 266 Ala. 266, 96 So. 2d 263 (1957); Gautier v. Pro-Football, 304 N.Y. 354, 358, 107 N.E.2d 485, 487–88 (1952); Spahn v. Messner, Inc., 43 Misc. 2d 219, 226, 250 N.Y.S.2d 529, 537 (Sup. Ct. 1964).
145 Dean Wade, in Virginia Law Weekly Dicta, Oct. 8, 1964, p. 1, col. 1, has suggested that these appropriation cases really involve "an action for unjust enrichment which the defendant has wrongfully obtained." This view was presented and rejected in Birmingham Broadcasting Co. v. Bell, 259 Ala. 656, 661, 68 So. 2d 314, 319 (1953), on the ground that commercial use of name or likeness did not fit any of the well-defined categories of recovery in quasi-contract. Moreover, the measure of recovery in the cases is not "what defendant may have gained, nor what plaintiff may have lost, but the recovery is as for other forms of tort." Id. at 662, 68 So. 2d at 320.
146 See, e.g., Nimmer, The Right of Publicity, 19 Law & Contemp. Prob. 203 (1954); Note, 62 Yale L.J. 1123 (1953).
147 Uproar Co. v. National Broadcasting Co., 8 F. Supp. 358 (D. Mass. 1934); Birmingham Broadcasting Co. v. Bell, 259 Ala. 656, 68 So. 2d 314 (1953); cf. Haelan Labs., Inc. v. Topps Chewing Gum, Inc., 202 F.2d 866 (2d Cir.), cert. denied, 346 U.S. 816 (1953); Gautier v. Pro-Football, Inc., 304 N.Y. 354, 107 N.E.2d 485 (1952) (Desmond, J. concurring); Spahn v. Messner, Inc., 43 Misc. 2d 219, 226, 250 N.Y.S.2d 529, 537 (Sup. Ct. 1964).
148 Haelan Labs, Inc. v. Topps Chewing Gum, Inc., supra note 147, at 868; Gautier v. Pro-Football, Inc., supra note 147, at 361, 107 N.E.2d at 489.

149 See Pavesich v. New England Life Ins. Co., 122 Ga. 190, 50 S.E. 68 (1905).
150 See Eick v. Perk Dog Food Co., 347 Ill. App. 293, 106 N.E.2d 742 (1952).
151 See authorities cited supra note 146; cf. Haelan Labs., Inc. v. Topps Chewing Gum, Inc., 202 F.2d 866 (2d Cir. 1953).
152 See Prosser, Privacy 406–07.
153 Cf. Mohr v. Williams, 95 Minn. 261, 263, 104 N.W. 12, 16 (1905); Prosser, Torts 83–84 (2d ed. 1955).
154 Prosser, Privacy 406.
155 Warren & Brandeis 205.
156 Prosser, Privacy 398.
157 Id. at 399.
158 Ibid.
159 Id. at 400, 422–23.
160 Gill v. Curtis Publishing Co., 38 Cal. 2d 273, 239 P.2d 630 (1952).
161 Gill v. Hearst Publishing Co., 40 Cal. 2d 224, 253 P.2d 441 (1953). Leave to amend the complaint was granted.
162 Gill v. Curtis Publishing Co., 38 Cal. 2d 273, 239 P.2d 630 (1952).
163 Gill v. Curtis Publishing Co., 231 P.2d 565 (Dist. Ct. App. 1951). But see note 115 supra.
164 Pavesich v. New England Life Ins. Co., 122 Ga. 190, 203, 50 S.E. 68, 73 (1905).
165 Prosser, Privacy 398.
166 See note 112 supra.
167 See notes 136–52 supra and accompanying text.
168 See text accompanying notes 137–41 supra.
169 See Wade, Defamation and the Right of Privacy, 15 Vand. L. Rev. 1093 (1963).
170 Burton v. Crowell Publishing Co., 82 F.2d 154 (2d Cir. 1936).
171 Tolley v. J.S. Fry & Sons Ltd., [1931] A.C. 333.
172 Themo v. New England Publishing Co., 306 Mass. 54, 55, 27 N.E.2d 753, 754 (1940).
173 Wade, supra note 169, at 1094–95.
174 See text accompanying notes 72–91 supra.
175 See, e.g., Silverman v. United States, 365 U.S. 505 (1961), and cases cited in note 72 supra.
176 DeMay v. Roberts, 46 Mich. 160, 9 N.W. 146 (1881).
177 Silverman v. United States, 365 U.S. 505 (1961).
178 See note 79 supra.
179 Frankfurter, J., dissenting in Monroe v. Pape, 365 U.S. 167, 209 (1961), sets forth a complete list of these state search and seizure provisions.
180 See, e.g., Lebel v. Swincicki, 354 Mich. 427, 93 N.W.2d 281 (1958); Young v. Western & A.R. Co., 39 Ga. App. 761, 148 S.E. 414 (1929). But see Sutherland v. Kroger Co., 144 W. Va. 673, 683, 110 S.E.2d 716, 723 (1959).
181 One of them, at least, was mentioned by Brandeis in his dissent in the

Olmstead case: "If government becomes a lawbreaker, it breeds contempt for law." 277 U.S. 438, 485 (1928).

182 See authorities cited supra note 119.

183 48 Stat. 1103–04 (1934), 47 U.S.C. § 605 (1958).

184 See Ill. Stat. Ann. ch. 38, §§ 14–1 to 14–7 (1961); Nev. Rev. Stat. § 200.650 (1957); N.Y. Pen. Law § 738. It should be noted that, under the New York statutes, evidence gained by means of illegal eavesdropping is inadmissible in a civil suit. See N.Y.C.P.L.R. § 4506.

185 See note 116 supra and accompanying text.

186 Ill. Stat. Ann. ch. 38, §§ 14–1 to 14–7 (1961); cf. Pa. Stat. Ann. tit. 72, § 2443 (1958).

187 See, e.g., Martin v. Herzog, 228 N.Y. 164, 126 N.E. 814 (1920); Thayer, Public Wrong and Private Action, 27 Harv. L. Rev. 317 (1914).

188 See, e.g., Pugach v. Dollinger, 277 F.2d 739 (2d Cir. 1960), aff'd, 365 U.S. 458 (1961); Reitmaster v. Reitmaster, 162 F.2d 691 (2d Cir. 1947); United States v. Goldstein, 120 F.2d 485 (2d Cir. 1941); Newfield v. Ryan, 91 F.2d 700 (5th Cir. 1937); McDaniel v. Atlanta Coca-Cola Bottling Co., 60 Ga. App. 92, 2 S.E.2d 810 (1939); Sander v. Pendleton Detectives, 88 So. 2d 716 (La. Ct. App. 1956); cf. People v. Trieber, 163 P.2d 492 (Cal. Dist. Ct. App. 1945).

189 See note 188 supra.

190 Id. at 694.

191 See Ill. Stat. Ann. ch. 38, §§ 14–1 to 14–7 (1961); cf. Pa. Stat. Ann. tit. 72, § 2443 (1958).

192 See text accompanying note 63 supra.

193 See N.Y. Civ. Rights Law §§ 50–51 (1948). See also, e.g., Gautier v. Pro-Football, 304 N.Y. 354, 107 N.E.2d 485 (1952); Kimmerle v. New York Evening J., 262 N.Y. 99, 186 N.E. 217 (1933).

194 Census Act, 13 U.S.C. §§ 221–24 (1954); cf. Hearings on the "Confidentiality of Census Reports" Before the House Committee on Post Office and Civil Service, 87th Cong., 2d Sess. (1962).

195 Census Act, 13 U.S.C. §§ 8, 9, 214 (1954).

196 Fed. Tax Reg. § 301.6l03(a) (1964).

197 18 U.S.C. § 1905 (1948).

198 N.Y. Pub. Officers Law § 74.

199 N.Y. Pen. Law §§ 553, 554, 734(1).

200 N.Y. Pen. Law § 762.

201 N.Y. Soc. Welfare Law §§ 136, 372, 258(2). These provisions are evidently mandated by § 402(a)(8) of the federal Social Security Act. See Pennsylvania Dep't of Pub. Assistance, People in Need 88–90 (1947).

202 N.Y. Correc. Law § 615, 616 (2i)(3).

203 N.Y. Gen. Bus. Law § 82.

204 N.Y. Civ. Rights Law § 73(8).

205 N.Y. Educ. Law § 1007.

206 See text accompanying notes 92–98 supra.

207 48 Stat. 1103–04 (1934), 47 U.S.C. § 605 (1958).

208 The earliest New York provisions, limited to telephone and telegraphic eavesdropping, were to be found in §§ 552–54 of the Penal Law. They have, for the most part, since been superseded by the broader provisions against eavesdropping cited in note 184 supra.

209 See, e.g., notes 181 & 188 supra.

210 This "condition" is stated very broadly for the purposes of my main argument. It should be noted, however, that, for instance, income tax information given to one federal agency is available, under certain conditions, to other governmental agencies and to state governments. 26 C.F.R. §§ 301.6103(a)–(1)(f)(1961), 301.6103(b) (1961), 301.6103(d). To what degree this is true of other government records is not known. A provocative case in this regard is St. Regis Paper Co. v. United States, 368 U.S. 208 (1961), in which the Supreme Court upheld the right of the Federal Trade Commission to subpoena a copy of a report submitted to the Census Bureau, even though the Commission was forbidden by statute to obtain the report directly from the Census Bureau.

211 See notes 195, 196, 201, & 205 supra.

212 See notes 197, 198, 200, 201, 202, & 204 supra.

213 See text accompanying notes 57–62, 92–98 supra.

214 The federal crime under § 605 of the Communications Act requires divulgence to make out any violation. Pugach v. Klein, 193 F. Supp. 630 (S.D.N.Y. 1961). The state prohibitions against eavesdropping are generally distinct from those against divulgence. See note 184 supra.

215 Prosser, Privacy 389.

216 Id. at 408.

217 229 F.2d 481 (3d Cir. 1956).

218 Prosser, Privacy 407. See also notes 181 & 188 supra.

219 Warren & Brandeis 205.

220 Olmstead v. United States, 277 U.S. 438 (1928).

221 Id. at 478.

222 See, e.g., Poe v. Ullman, 367 U.S. 497, 522 (1961) (dissenting opinion of Harlan, J.); Public Util. Comm'n v. Pollak, 343 U.S. 451, 467 (1952) (dissenting opinion of Douglas, J.); Goldman v. United States, 316 U.S. 129, 136 (1942) (dissenting opinion of Murphy, J.).

223 112 Cal. App. 285, 297 Pac. 91 (Dist. Ct. App. 1931).

224 122 Ga. 190, 50 S.E. 68 (1905).

225 112 Cal. App. 285, 297 Pac. 91 (Dist. Ct. App. 1931); 122 Ga. 190, 50 S.E. 68 (1905).

226 122 Ga. 190, 195–96, 50 S.E. 68, 70 (1905).

227 The phrase is used in the Restatement of Torts to describe an "offensive battery," i.e., one not involving bodily harm. Restatement, Torts § 18 (1934).

228 Gregory and Kalven describe privacy as a dignitary tort in the index to their casebook, but seem to treat it as within the mental distress category in the text. See Gregory & Kalven, Cases on Torts 883–99, 1307 (1959).

229 Hatchett v. Blacketer, 162 Ky. 266, 172 S.W. 533 (1915).

230 DeMay v. Roberts, 46 Mich. 160, 9 N.W. 146 (1881).

231 Flake v. Greensboro News Co., 212 N.C. 780, 195 S.E. 55 (1938).

232 Whittaker v. Sanford, 110 Me. 77, 85 Atl. 399 (1912).

233 See, e.g., Sidis v. F-R Publishing Corp., 113 F.2d 806, 809 (2d Cir. 1940); Hubbard v. Journal Publishing Co., 69 N.M. 473, 475, 368 P.2d 147, 148 (1962); Franklin, A Constitutional Problem in Privacy Protection: Legal Inhibitions on Reporting of Fact, 16 Stan. L. Rev. 107 (1963).

234 Prosser, Privacy 422.

235 Ibid.

236 Id. at 422–23.

237 Id. at 423.

238 For a description of the threat, see the authorities cited in note 7 supra.

7

Privacy
[A moral analysis]

CHARLES FRIED

Privacy has become the object of considerable concern. The purely fortuitous intrusions inherent in a compact and interrelated society have multiplied. The more insidious intrusions of increasingly sophisticated scientific devices into previously untouched areas, and the burgeoning claims of public and private agencies to personal information, have created a new sense of urgency in defense of privacy. The intensity of the debates about electronic eavesdropping and the privilege against self-incrimination are but two examples of this urgency.

The purpose of this essay is not to add yet another concrete proposal, nor even to call attention to yet another intrusion upon privacy. Rather I propose to examine the foundations of the right of privacy— the reasons why men feel that invasions of that right injure them in their very humanity.

I

To bring out the special quality of the concern over privacy I shall first put a not entirely hypothetical proposal, which should serve to isolate from restrictions and intrusions in general whatever is peculiar about invasions of privacy.

There are available today electronic devices to be worn on one's person which emit signals permitting one's exact location to be determined by a monitor some distance away.[1] These devices are so small as to be entirely unobtrusive: other persons cannot tell that a subject is "wired," and even the subject himself—if he could forget the initial installation—need be no more aware of the device than of a small bandage. Moreover, existing technology can produce devices

capable of monitoring not only a person's location, but other significant facts about him: his temperature, pulse rate, blood pressure, the
alcoholic content of his blood, the sounds in his immediate environment—*e.g.*, what he says and what is said to him—and perhaps in the
not too distant future even the pattern of his brain waves. The suggestion has been made, and is being actively investigated, that such
devices might be employed in the surveillance of persons on probation
or parole.

Probation leaves an offender at large in the community as an alternative to imprisonment, and parole is the release of an imprisoned
person prior to the time that all justification for supervising him and
limiting his liberty has expired. Typically, both probation and parole
are granted subject to various restrictions. Most usually the proba-
tioner or parolee is not allowed to leave a prescribed area. Also common are restrictions on the kinds of places he may visit—bars, pool
halls, brothels, and the like—or the persons he may associate with,
and on the activities he may engage in. The most common restriction
of the latter sort is a prohibition on drinking, but sometimes probation
and parole have been revoked for "immorality"—that is, intercourse
with a person other than a spouse. There are also affirmative conditions, such as a requirement that the subject work regularly in an
approved employment, maintain an approved residence or report
regularly to correctional, social, or psychiatric personnel. Failure to
abide by such conditions is thought to endanger the rehabilitation of
the subject and to identify him as a poor risk.

Now the application of personal monitoring to probation and parole
is obvious. Violations of any one of the conditions and restrictions
could be uncovered immediately by devices using present technology
or developments of it; by the same token, a wired subject assured of
detection would be much more likely to obey. Although monitoring
is admitted to be unusually intrusive, it is argued that this particular
use of monitoring is entirely proper, since it justifies the release of
persons who would otherwise remain in prison, and since surely there
is little that is more intrusive and unprivate than a prison regime.
Moreover, no one is obliged to submit to monitoring: an offender
may decline and wait in prison until his sentence has expired or until
he is judged a proper risk for parole even without monitoring. Proponents of monitoring suggest that seen in this way monitoring of
offenders subject to supervision is no more offensive than the monitoring on an entirely voluntary basis of epileptics, diabetics, cardiac
patients and the like.

II

Much of the discussion about this and similar (though perhaps less futuristic) measures has proceeded in a fragmentary way to catalogue the disadvantages they entail: the danger of the information falling into the wrong hands, the opportunity presented for harassment, the inevitable involvement of persons as to whom no basis for supervision exists, the use of the material monitored by the government for un-authorized purposes, the danger to political expression and association, and so on.[2] Such arguments are often sufficiently compelling, but situations may be envisaged where they are overridden. The monitoring case in some of its aspects is such a situation. And yet one often wants to say the invasion of privacy is wrong, intolerable, although each discrete objection can be met. The reason for this, I submit, is that privacy is much more that just a possible social technique for assuring this or that substantive interest. Such analyses of the value of privacy often lead to the conclusion that the various substantive interests may after all be protected as well by some other means, or that if they cannot be protected quite as well, still those other means will do, given the importance of our reasons for violating privacy. It is just because this instrumental analysis makes privacy so vulnerable that we feel impelled to assign to privacy some intrinsic significance. But to translate privacy to the level of an intrinsic value might seem more a way of cutting off analysis than of carrying it forward. In this essay I hope to show that it is possible to discuss what it means to accord to privacy such a high status and to show why the value of privacy should be recognized.

It is my thesis that privacy is not just one possible means among others to insure some other value, but that it is necessarily related to ends and relations of the most fundamental sort: respect, love, friendship and trust. Privacy is not merely a good technique for furthering these fundamental relations; rather without privacy they are simply inconceivable. They require a context of privacy or the possibility of privacy for their existence. To make clear the necessity of privacy as a context for respect, love, friendship and trust is to bring out also why a threat to privacy seems to threaten our very integrity as persons. To respect, love, trust, feel affection for others and to regard ourselves as the objects of love, trust and affection is at the heart of our notion of ourselves as persons among persons, and privacy is the necessary atmosphere for these attitudes and actions, as oxygen is for combustion.

III

The conception of privacy as a necessary context for love, friendship and trust depends on a complex account of these concepts, and they in turn depend on the more general notions of morality, respect and personality. If my sketch of this underlying perspective leaves the reader full of doubts and queries, I draw comfort from the fact that a more elaborate presentation of this system is in progress.[3] I only hope that the sketch I give here has sufficient coherence to lay the basis for the discussion of privacy which is the primary concern of this essay.

Love, friendship and trust are not just vague feelings or emotions; they each comprise a system of dispositions, beliefs and attitudes which are organized according to identifiable principles. Though love, friendship and trust differ from each other, they each build on a common conception of personality and its entitlements. This conception is a moral conception of the basic entitlements and duties of persons in regard to each other, and the structure of that conception is articulated by what I call the principle of morality and the correlative attitude of respect.

The view of morality upon which my conception of privacy rests is one which recognizes basic rights in persons, rights to which all are entitled equally, by virtue of their status as persons. These rights are subject to qualification only in order to ensure equal protection of the same rights in others. In this sense, the view is Kantian; it requires recognition of persons as ends, and forbids the overriding of their most fundamental interests for the purpose of maximizing the happiness or welfare of all. It has received contemporary exposition in the work of John Rawls, who—summing up the fundamental interests of persons in the term "liberty"—has formulated the maxim that social institutions must be framed so as to entitle each person to the maximum liberty compatible with a like liberty for all.[4]

The principle of morality does not purport to represent the highest value in a person's economy of values and interests. It necessarily assumes that persons have a variety of substantive values and interests and it is consistent with a large range of ethical systems which rank these values and interests in many different ways. It functions rather as a constraint upon systems and orderings of values and interests, demanding that whatever their content might be, they may be pursued only if and to the extent that they are consistent with an equal right of all persons to a similar liberty to pursue their interests, whatever they might be. Thus the principle of morality, far from representing a complete system of values, establishes only the equal liberty of each

person to define and pursue his values free from undesired impinge-
ments by others. The principle of morality establishes not a complete
value system but the basic entitlements of persons vis-à-vis each other.[5]
   Correlative to this view of morality—and indeed to any view which
recognizes moral entitlements in persons—is the concept of respect.[6]
Respect is the attitude which is manifested when a person observes
the constraints of the principle of morality in his dealings with another
person, and thus respects the basic rights of the other. Respect is also
an attitude which may be taken in part as defining the concept of a
person: persons are those who are obliged to observe the constraints
of the principle of morality in their dealings with each other,[7] and
thus to show respect towards each other.[8] Self-respect is, then, the
attitude by which a person believes himself to be entitled to be treated
by other persons in accordance with the principle of morality.
   The principle of morality and its correlative, respect, lie at the
bottom of our conception of justice and fair play, as moral philosophers have convincingly argued. Perhaps less obviously, they play an
important part in our concepts of love, friendship and trust.[9] It is my
thesis that an essential part of the morality which underlies these
relations is the constraint of respect for the privacy of all, by state and
citizen alike.

IV

There can be no thought of counting on an accepted core of meaning
in developing the concept of love. What I say about love therefore
cannot be taken as expressing a synthesis of all that has plausibly been
thought and said on the subject. Nevertheless an important tradition
of thought about love holds that it is a necessary feature of that
emotion that the beloved person be valued for his own sake, and not
on account of some attribute or product.[10] This aspect of love corresponds to the respect which we are obligated to accord each other.
But morality requires impartial respect; love, surely, is not so impartial. The respect required by morality is a necessary condition for love;
it is not sufficient. The further element in love is a spontaneous relinquishment of certain entitlements of one's own to the beloved, a
free and generous relinquishment inspired by a regard which goes
beyond impartial respect. But a sense of freedom and generosity
depends—logically depends—on a sense of the secure possession of
the claims one renounces and the gifts one bestows. I shall argue that
the nature of the gifts of love and friendship is such that privacy is
necessary to provide one important aspect of security.
   This account has emphasized the necessity to love of a voluntary

relinquishment of rights. But love is not, of course, so negative nor so one-sided. Persons love, hoping to be loved in return, and thus the fulfilled form of the relationship is one of mutual relinquishment of entitlement, but not simply of relinquishment. The fulfilled form is the mutual relinquishment of rights in favor of new, shared interests which the lovers create and value as the expression of their relationship. Thus love is an active and creative relationship not only of reciprocal relinquishment but reciprocal support as well. The structure of this reciprocal relationship is complex and elusive,[11] and I shall not analyze it further here. For present purposes it is sufficient to see that the gift, the relinquishment, is logically prior to the relationship which requires it; and if privacy is necessary to the first, it is necessary to the second.

Friendship differs from love largely in the degree of absorption in the relationship and of the significance which the relationship has in the total economy of a person's life and interests. Allowing for these differences of degree, love and friendship are close in that they have a similar relation to the more general concepts of morality and respect. And that similar relation is all that I propose here concerning friendship.

Intuitively, trust is an attitude of expectation about another person. But it would be a mistake to see it as simply a recognition of a disposition in another and a reliance that he will act in accordance with that disposition.[12] To be sure, we have expressions such as "trust him to do *that*," where "*that*" may be a vile deed which we know to be in character for that person, or perhaps a fit of sneezing during a grand evening at the opera on the part of a person given to sneezing when in close proximity to perfumed ladies. But these usages are ironical. Although trust has to do with reliance on a disposition of another person, it is reliance on a disposition of a special sort: the disposition to act morally, to deal fairly with others, to live up to one's undertakings, and so on. Thus to trust another is first of all to expect him to accept the principle of morality in his dealings with you, to respect your status as a person, your personality.

Trust, like love and friendship, is in its central sense a *relation:* it is reciprocal. Fairness does not require that we sacrifice our interests for the sake of those who are not willing to show us a similar forbearance. Thus as to those who do not accept morality, who are wicked and deceitful, the occasion for trust does not arise. We do not trust them, and they have no reason to trust us in the full sense of a relationship of mutual expectation, for our posture towards them is not one of cooperative mutual forbearance but of defensive watchfulness. Thus not only can a thoroughly untrustworthy person not be trusted; he cannot trust others, for he is disabled from entering into the relations of voluntary reciprocal forbearance for mutual advantage which trust consists of. At most an untrustworthy person can predict more or less accurately how another will behave, but the behavior he predicts will not arise out of a relation of mutual respect which each party has for the personality of the other and a reciprocal willingness to work together according to the constraints of morality.

Trust is like love and friendship in that it is a "free" relationship. Morality does not require that we enter into relations of trust with our fellow men. But trust differs from love or friendship in that it is not always a relation we seek simply for its own sake. It is more functional. Persons build relations on trust in part because such relations are useful to accomplish other ends. (In a sense love and friendship are needed for the pursuit of ends too, but they are ends that arise out of the relationship itself, and are shared in it.) However, the other ends never dominate entirely: they may be attainable without genuine trust, and the recourse to trust is then an independent and concurrent affirmation of respect for human personality. So, whether as individuals or as states, we conduct our business when we can on the basis of trust, not just because it is more efficient to do so—it may not be— but because we value the relations built on trust for their own sake. Finally, trust is also less intrusive than love or friendship. Trust can be limited to the particular matter at hand, and does not imply a disposition to seek more and more mutually shared ends. Thus, one can trust persons for whom one has neither love nor liking, although friendship and love imply, at least in the standard cases, trust as well.

V

Privacy is closely implicated in the notions of respect and self-respect, and of love, friendship and trust. Quite apart from any philosophical analysis this is intuitively obvious. In this section I shall try to make the connection explicit. In general it is my thesis that in developed social contexts love, friendship and trust are only possible if persons enjoy and accord to each other a certain measure of privacy.

It is necessary at the outset to sharpen the intuitive concept of privacy. As a first approximation, privacy seems to be related to secrecy, to limiting the knowledge of others about oneself. This notion must be refined. It is not true, for instance, that the less that is known about us the more privacy we have. Privacy is not simply an absence of information about us in the minds of others; rather it is the *control* we have over information about ourselves.

To refer for instance to the privacy of a lonely man on a desert island would be to engage in irony. The person who enjoys privacy is able to grant or deny access to others. Even when one considers private situations into which outsiders could not possibly intrude, the context implies some alternative situation where the intrusion is possible. A man's house may be private, for instance, but that is because it is constructed—with doors, windows, window shades—to allow it to be made private, and because the law entitles a man to exclude unauthorized persons. And even the remote vacation hide-away is private just because one resorts to it in order—in part—to preclude access to unauthorized persons.

Privacy, thus, is control over knowledge about oneself. But it is not simply control over the quantity of information abroad; there are modulations in the quality of the knowledge as well. We may not mind that a person knows a general fact about us, and yet feel our privacy invaded if he knows the details. For instance, a casual acquaintance may comfortably know that I am sick, but it would violate my privacy if he knew the nature of the illness. Or a good friend may know what particular illness I am suffering from, but it would violate my privacy if he were actually to witness my suffering from some symptom which he must know is associated with the disease.[13]

VI

There are reasons other than its relation to love, friendship and trust why we value privacy. Most obviously, privacy in its dimension of control over information is an aspect of personal liberty. Acts derive their meaning partly from their social context—from how many people know about them and what the knowledge consists of.[14] A reproof administered out of the hearing of third persons may be an act of kindness, but if administered in public it becomes cruel and degrading. Thus, for instance, if a man cannot be sure that third persons are not listening—if his privacy is not secure—he is denied the freedom to do what he regards as an act of kindness.

Besides giving us control over the context in which we act, privacy has a more defensive role in protecting our liberty. We may wish to do or say things not forbidden by the restraints of morality, but which are nevertheless unpopular or unconventional. If we thought that our every word and deed were public, fear of disapproval or more tangible retaliation might keep us from doing or saying things which we would do or say if we could be sure of keeping them to ourselves or within a circle of those who we know approve or tolerate our tastes.[15]

For these important reasons, among others, men would value privacy even if there were nothing in the world called love, friendship or trust. These reasons support the familiar arguments for the right of privacy. Yet they leave privacy with less security than we feel it deserves; they leave it vulnerable to arguments that a particular invasion of privacy will secure to us other kinds of liberty which more than compensate for what is lost. To present privacy then, only as an aspect of or an aid to general liberty, is to miss some of its most significant differentiating features. The value of title to control of some information about ourselves is more nearly absolute than that. For privacy is the necessary context for relationships which we would hardly be human if we had to do without—the relationships of love, friendship and trust.

Love and friendship, as analyzed here, involve the initial respect for the rights of others which morality requires of everyone. They further involve the voluntary and spontaneous relinquishment of *something* between friend and friend, lover and lover. The title to information about oneself conferred by privacy provides the necessary something. To be friends or lovers persons must be intimate to some degree with each other. But intimacy is the sharing of information about one's actions, beliefs, or emotions which one does not share with all, and which one has the right not to share with anyone. By conferring this right, privacy creates the moral capital which we spend in friendship and love.

The entitlements of privacy are not just one kind of entitlement among many which a lover can surrender to show his love. Love or friendship can be partially expressed by the gift of other rights—gifts of property or of service. But these gifts, without the intimacy of shared private information, cannot alone constitute love or friendship. The man who is generous with his possessions, but not with himself, can hardly be a friend, nor—and this more clearly shows the necessity of privacy for love—can the man who, voluntarily or involuntarily, shares everything about himself with the world indiscriminately.

Privacy is essential to friendship and love in another respect besides providing what I call "moral capital." The rights of privacy are among those basic entitlements which men must respect in each other; and mutual respect is the minimal precondition for love and friendship.

Privacy also provides the means for modulating those degrees of friendship which fall short of love. Few persons have the emotional resources to be on the most intimate terms with all their friends. Privacy grants the control over information which enables us to maintain degrees of intimacy. Thus even between friends the restraints of privacy apply; since friendship implies a *voluntary* relinquishment of private information, one will not wish to know what his friend or lover has not chosen to share with him. The rupture of this balance by a third party—the state perhaps—thrusting information concerning one friend upon another might well destroy the limited degree of intimacy the two have achieved.

Finally, there is a more extreme case where privacy serves not to save something which will be "spent" on a friend, but to keep it from all the world. There are thoughts whose expression to a friend or lover would be a hostile act, though the entertaining of them is completely consistent with friendship or love. That is because these thoughts, prior to being given expression, are mere unratified possibilities for action. Only by expressing them do we adopt them, choose them as part of ourselves, and draw them into our relations with others.[16] Now a sophisticated person knows that a friend or lover must entertain thoughts which if expressed would be wounding, and so—it might be objected—why should he attach any significance to their actual expression? In a sense the objection is well taken. If it were possible to give expression to these thoughts and yet make clear to ourselves and to others that we do not thereby ratify, adopt them as our own, it might be that in some relations at least another could be allowed complete access to us. But this possibility is not a very likely one.[17] Thus this most complete form of privacy is perhaps also the most basic, as it is necessary not only to our freedom to define our relations to others but also to our freedom to define ourselves.[18] To be deprived of this control not only over what we do but over who we are is the ultimate assault on liberty, personality, and self-respect.

Trust is the attitude of expectation that another will behave according to the constraints of morality. Insofar as trust is only instrumental to the more convenient conduct of life, its purposes could be as well served by cheap and efficient surveillance of the person upon whom one depends. One does not trust machines or animals; one takes the fullest economically feasible precautions against their going wrong. Often, however, we choose to trust people where it would be safer to take precautions—to watch them or require a bond from them. This must be because, as I have already argued, we value the relation of trust for its own sake. It is one of those relations, less inspiring than love or friendship, but also less tiring, through which we express our humanity.

There can be no trust where there is no possibility of error. More specifically, a man cannot know that he is trusted unless he has a right to act without constant surveillance so that he knows he can betray the trust. Privacy confers that essential right. And since, as I have argued, trust in its fullest sense is reciprocal, the man who cannot be trusted cannot himself trust or learn to trust. Without privacy and the possibility of error which it protects that aspect of his humanity is denied to him.

VII

The previous sections have explored the meaning of the concept of privacy and the significance of privacy to the notion of personality and to the relations of love, trust and friendship which are inseparable from it. The conclusions have been abstract and entirely general. But the concrete expressions of privacy in particular societies and cultures differ enormously. It remains to be shown why such differences both are to be expected and are entirely consistent with the general conceptions I have put forward.

In concrete situations and actual societies, control over information about oneself, like control over one's bodily security or property, can only be relative and qualified. As is true for property or bodily security, the control over privacy must be limited by the rights of others. And as in the cases of property and bodily security, so too with privacy the more one ventures into the outside, the more one pursues one's other interests with the aid of, in competition with, or even in the presence of others, the more one must risk invasions of privacy. Moreover, as with property and personal security, it is the business of legal and social institutions to define and protect the right of privacy which emerges intact from the hurly-burly of social interactions. Now it would be absurd to argue that these concrete definitions and protections, differing as they do from society to society, are or should be strict derivations from general principles, the only legitimate variables being differing empirical circumstances (such as, for instance, differing technologies or climatic conditions). The delineation of standards must be left to a political and social process the results of which will accord with justice if two conditions are met: (1) the process itself is just, that is the interests of all are fairly represented; and (2) the outcome of the process protects basic dignity and provides moral capital for personal relations in the form of absolute title to at least some information about oneself.[19]

The particular areas of life which are protected by privacy will be conventional at least in part, not only because they are the products of political processes, but also because of one of the reasons we value privacy. Insofar as privacy is regarded as moral capital for relations of love, friendship and trust, there are situations where what kinds of information one is entitled to keep to oneself is not of the first importance. The important thing is that there be *some* information which is protected.[20] Convention may quite properly rule in determining the particular areas which are private.

Convention plays another more important role in fostering privacy and the respect and esteem which it protects; it designates certain areas, intrinsically no more private than other areas, as symbolic of the whole institution of privacy, and thus deserving of protection beyond their particular importance. This apparently exaggerated respect for conventionally protected areas compensates for the inevitable fact that privacy is gravely compromised in any concrete social system: it is compromised by the inevitably and utterly just exercise of rights by others, it is compromised by the questionable but politically sanctioned exercise of rights by others, it is compromised by conduct which society does not condone but which it is unable or unwilling to forbid, and it is compromised by plainly wrongful invasions and aggressions. In all this hurly-burly there is a real danger that privacy might be crushed altogether, or what would be as bad, that any venture outside the most limited area of activity would mean risking an almost total compromise of privacy.

Given these threats to privacy in general, social systems have given symbolic importance to certain conventionally designated areas of privacy. Thus in our culture the excretory functions are shielded by more or less absolute privacy, so much so that situations in which this privacy is violated are experienced as extremely distressing, as detracting from one's dignity and self-esteem.[21] But there does not seem to be any reason connected with the principles of respect, esteem and the like why this would have to be so, and one can imagine other cultures in which it was not so, but where the same symbolic privacy was attached to, say, eating and drinking.[22] There are other more subtly modulated symbolic areas of privacy, some of which merge into what I call substantive privacy (that is, areas where privacy does protect substantial interests). The very complex norms of privacy about matters of sex and health are good examples.

An excellent, very different sort of example of a contingent, symbolic recognition of an area of privacy as an expression of respect for personal integrity is the privilege against self-incrimination and the associated doctrines denying officials the power to compel other kinds of information without some explicit warrant. By according the privilege as fully as it does, our society affirms the extreme value of the individual's control over information about himself. To be sure, prying into a man's personal affairs by asking questions of others or by observing him is not prevented by the privilege. Rather it is the point of the privilege that a man cannot be forced to make public information about himself. Thereby his sense of control over what others know of him is significantly enhanced, even if other sources of the same information exist. Without his cooperation, the other sources are necessarily incomplete, since he himself is the only ineluctable witness to his own present life, public or private, internal or manifest. And information about himself which others have to give out is in one sense information over which he has already relinquished control.

The privilege is contingent and symbolic. It is part of a whole structure of rules by which there is created an institution of privacy sufficient to the sense of respect, trust and intimacy. It is contingent in that it cannot, I believe, be shown that some particular set of rules is necessary to the existence of such an institution of privacy. It is symbolic because the exercise of the privilege provides a striking expression of society's willingness to accept constraints on the pursuit of valid, perhaps vital interests in order to recognize the right of privacy and the respect for the individual that privacy entails. Conversely, a proceeding in which compulsion is brought to bear on an individual to force him to make revelations about himself provides a striking and dramatic instance of a denial of title to control information about oneself, to control the picture we would have others have of us.[23] In this sense such a procedure quite rightly seems profoundly humiliating.[24] Nevertheless it is not clear to me that a system is unjust which sometimes allows such an imposition.

In calling attention to the symbolic aspect of some areas of privacy I do not mean to minimize their importance. On the contrary, they are highly significant as expressions of respect for others in a general situation where much of what we do to each other may signify a lack of respect or at least presents no occasion for expressing respect. That this is so is shown not so much in the occasions where these symbolic constraints are observed, for they are part of our system of expectations, but where they are violated.[25] Not only does a person feel his standing is gravely compromised by such symbolic violations, but also those who wish to degrade and humiliate others often choose just such symbolic aggressions and invasions on the assumed though conventional area of privacy.

VIII

Let us return now to the concrete problem of electronic monitoring to see whether the foregoing elucidation of the concept of privacy will help to establish on firmer ground the intuitive objection that monitoring is an intolerable violation of privacy. Let us consider the more intrusive forms of monitoring where not only location but conversations and perhaps other data are monitored.

Obviously such a system of monitoring drastically curtails or eliminates altogether the power to control information about oneself. But, it might be said, this is not a significant objection if we assume the monitored data will go only to authorized persons—probation or parole officers—and cannot be prejudicial so long as the subject of the monitoring is not violating the conditions under which he is allowed to be at liberty. But this retort misses the importance of privacy as a context for all kinds of relations, from the most intense to the most casual. For all of these may require a context of some degree of intimacy, and intimacy is made impossible by monitoring.

It is worth being more precise about this notion of intimacy. Monitoring obviously presents vast opportunities for malice and misunderstanding on the part of authorized personnel. For that reason the subject has reason to be constantly apprehensive and inhibited in what he does. There is always an unseen audience, which is the more threatening because of the possibility that one may forget about it and let down his guard, as one would not with a visible audience. But even assuming the benevolence and understanding of the official audience, there are serious consequences to the fact that no degree of true intimacy is possible for the subject. Privacy is not, as we have seen, just a defensive right. It rather forms the necessary context for the intimate relations of love and friendship which gives our lives much of whatever affirmative value they have. In the role of citizen or fellow worker, one need reveal himself to no greater extent than is necessary to display the attributes of competence and morality appropriate to those relations. In order to be a friend or lover one must reveal far more of himself. Yet where any intimate revelation may be heard by monitoring officials, it loses the quality of exclusive intimacy required of a gesture of love or friendship. Thus monitoring, in depriving one of privacy, destroys the possibility of bestowing the gift of intimacy, and makes impossible the essential dimension of love and friendship.

Monitoring similarly undermines the subject's capacity to enter into relations of trust. As I analyzed trust, it required the possibility of error on the part of the person trusted. The negation of trust is constant surveillance—such as monitoring—which minimizes the possibility of undetected default. The monitored parolee is denied the sense of self-respect inherent in being trusted by the government which has released him. More important, monitoring prevents the parolee from entering into true *relations* of trust with persons in the outside world. An employer, unaware of the monitoring, who entrusts a sum of money to the parolee cannot thereby grant him the sense of responsibility and autonomy which an unmonitored person in the same position would have. The parolee in a real—if special and ironical—sense, cannot be trusted.

Now let us consider the argument that however intrusive monitoring may seem, surely prison life is more so. In part, of course, this will be a matter of fact. It may be that even a reasonably secure and well-run prison will allow prisoners occasions for conversation among themselves, with guards, or with visitors, which are quite private. Such a prison regime would in this respect be less intrusive than monitoring. Often prison regimes do not allow even this, and go far toward depriving a prisoner of any sense of privacy: if the cells have doors, these may be equipped with peep-holes. But there is still an important difference between this kind of prison and monitoring: the prison environment is overtly, even punitively unprivate. The contexts for relations to others are obviously and drastically different from what they are on the "outside." This, it seems to me, itself protects the prisoner's human orientation where monitoring only assails it. If the prisoner has a reasonably developed capacity for love, trust and friendship and has in fact experienced ties of this sort, he is likely to be strongly aware (at least for a time) that prison life is a drastically different context fom the one in which he enjoyed those relations, and this awareness will militate against his confusing the kinds of relations that can obtain in a "total institution" like a prison with those of freer social settings on the outside.

Monitoring, by contrast, alters only in a subtle and unobtrusive way—though a significant one—the context for relations. The subject *appears* free to perform the same actions as others and to enter the same relations, but in fact an important element of autonomy, of control over one's environment is missing: he cannot be private. A prisoner can adopt a stance of withdrawal, of hibernation as it were, and thus preserve his sense of privacy intact to a degree. A person subject to monitoring by virtue of being in a free environment, dealing with people who expect him to have certain responses, capacities and dispositions, is forced to make at least a show of intimacy to the persons he works closely with, those who would be his friends, and so on. They expect these things of him, because he is assumed to have the capacity and disposition to enter into ordinary relations with them. Yet if he does—if, for instance, he enters into light banter with slight sexual overtones with the waitress at the diner where he eats regularly[26]—

he has been forced to violate his own integrity by being forced to reveal to his official monitors even so small an aspect of his private personality, the personality he wishes to reserve for persons towards whom he will make some gestures of intimacy and friendship. Theoretically, of course, a monitored parolee might adopt the same attitude of withdrawal that a prisoner does, but in fact that too would be a costly and degrading experience. He would be tempted, as in prison he would not be, to "give himself away" and to act like everyone else, since in every outward respect he seems like everyone else. Moreover, by withdrawing, the person subject to monitoring would risk seeming cold, unnatural, odd, inhuman to the very people whose esteem and affection he craves. In prison the circumstances dictating a reserved and tentative facade are so apparent to all that adopting such a facade is no reflection on the prisoner's humanity.

Finally, the insidiousness of a technique which forces a man to betray himself in this humiliating way or else seem inhuman is compounded when one considers that the subject is also forced to betray others who may become intimate with him. Even persons in the overt oppressiveness of a prison do not labor under the burden of this double betrayal.

As against all of these considerations, there remains the argument that so long as monitoring depends on the consent of the subject, who feels it is preferable to prison, to close off this alternative in the name of a morality so intimately concerned with liberty is absurd. This argument may be decisive; I am not at all confident that the alternative of monitored release should be closed off. My analysis does show, I think that it involves costs to the prisoner which are easily overlooked, that on inspection it is a less desirable alternative than might at first appear. Moreover, monitoring presents systematic dangers to potential subjects as a class. Its availability as a compromise between conditional release and continued imprisonment may lead officials who are in any doubt whether or not to trust a man on parole or probation to assuage their doubts by resorting to monitoring.

The seductions of monitored release disguise not only a cost to the subject but to society as well. The discussion of trust should make clear that unmonitored release is a very different experience from monitored release, and so the educational and rehabilitative effect of unmonitored release is also different. Unmonitored release affirms in a far more significant way the relations of trust between the convicted criminal and society which the criminal violated by his crime and which we should now be seeking to reestablish. But trust can only arise, as any parent knows, through the experience of being trusted.

IX

The discussion of privacy in this essay has explored the meaning and significance of the concept. It reveals privacy as that aspect of social order by which persons control access to information about themselves. How this control is granted to individuals and the means for bringing about the social structures which express the notion of privacy have not been of direct concern. Clearly many of the social structures by which persons express their respect for the privacy of others are informal and implicit. The sanctions for violating the expectations set up by these structures, if they exist at all, are often subtle and informal too. But legal rules also play a large part in establishing the social context of privacy. These rules guarantee to a person the claim to control certain areas, his home, perhaps his telephone communications, etc., and back this guarantee with enforceable sanctions. Now these legal norms are more or less incomprehensible without some understanding of what kind of a situation is sought to be established with their aid. Without this understanding we cannot sense the changing law they demand in changing circumstances.

What is less obvious is that law is not just an instrument for protecting privacy; it is an essential element, in our culture, of the institution itself. The concept of privacy requires, as we have seen, a sense of control and a justified, acknowledged power to control aspects of one's environment. But in most developed societies the only way to give a person the full measure of both the sense and the fact of control is to give him a legal title to control. A legal right to control is control which is the least open to question and argument; it is the kind of control we are most serious about. As we have seen, privacy is not just an absence of information abroad about ourselves; it is a feeling of security in control over that information. By using the public, impersonal and ultimate institution of law to grant persons this control, we at once put the right to control as far beyond question as we can and at the same time show how seriously we take that right.

NOTES

1 For a discussion of these devices and the legal issues to which they give rise, see Note, *Anthropotelemetry: Dr. Schwitzgebel's Machine* 80 Harv. L. Rev. 403 (1966).
2 The literature on privacy is enormous. A. Westin, Privacy and Freedom (1967), provides an exhaustive bibliography as well as a critical review of

the literature. In addition, Part One of that book presents a sensitive general theory of privacy much along the lines of the present article. Of particular interest also is the symposium on privacy in 31 Law & Contemp. Prob. 251–435 (1966).

For an example of the fragmentary approach referred to in the text, as applied to one manifestation of privacy, the privilege against self-incrimination, see McNaughton, *The Privilege Against Self-Incrimination: Its Constitutional Affectation, Raison d'Etre and Miscellaneous Implications,* 51 J. Crim. L.C. & P.S. 138 (1960). Dean Prosser takes this fragmentary approach to the right of privacy as recognized by tort law. *See* Prosser, *Privacy,* 48 Calif. L. Rev. 383 (1960). And he has been criticized for it. Bloustein, *Privacy as an Aspect of Human Dignity: An Answer to Dean Prosser,* 39 N.Y.U.L. Rev. 962 (1964).

3 For a preliminary statement of the larger scheme, see Fried, *Reason and Action,* 11 Natural L.F. 13 (1966).

4 The ethical system I sketch here is essentially Kantian. Different aspects of it are expressed in I. Kant, Foundations of the Metaphysics of Morals (L. Beck transl. 1959) and in I. Kant, Metaphysical Elements of Justice (J. Ladd transl. 1965). For a discussion of the use of the term morality to apply primarily to the principles governing the relations of persons with each other *see* Falk, *Morality, Self and Others,* and Frankena, *Recent Conceptions of Morality,* in Morality and the Language of Conduct (H. Castañeda & G. Nakhnikian eds. 1963). Much of what I say derives, however, not from Kant, but more directly from the writings of John Rawls, who in his published and unpublished work has developed a comprehensive system of concepts and principles. In addition to the published articles (*Legal Obligation and the Duty of Fair Play,* in Law and Philosophy 3 (S. Hook ed. 1964); *The Sense of Justice,* 72 Phil. Rev. 281 (1963); *Constitutional Liberty and the Concept of Justice,* in Nomos VI, Justice 98 (C. Friedrich & J. Chapman eds. 1963); *Justice as Fairness,* 67 Phil. Rev. 164 (1958), I have profited greatly from an opportunity to read Professor Rawls' unpublished chapters on justice and his lectures on Kant and Hegel. *See also* Hart, *Are There Natural Rights?,* 64 Phil. Rev. 175 (1955).

5 For a discussion see Fried, *Natural Law and the Concept of Justice,* 74 Ethics 237, 250 (1964).

6 The concept of respect is also Kantian. I. Kant, Critique of Practical Reason 76–84 (L. Beck transl. 1956). The best recent discussion of this concept of respect and its relation to personality is J. Piaget, The Moral Judgment of the Child (M. Gabain transl. 1948). An excellent and fundamental illustration of the importance of respect in human relations is Hegel's dialectic of the master and the slave, discussed in 2 J. Plamenatz, Man and Society 154–56, 188–92 (1963).

7 The condition is sufficient, not necessary, since children, lunatics, and some others are also to be considered persons. All persons are entitled to the respect of other persons.

8 *See generally* Piaget, *supra* note 6; Rawls, *The Sense of Justice, supra* note 4.

9 For a discussion of the relationship between these concepts and the principle of morality see Rawls, *The Sense of Justice, supra* note 4. Although my account differs from Rawls' in some respects, it is based on his.

10 *Cf.* Aristotle, Nicomachean Ethics bk. 8, chs. 2–3.

11 For an excellent discussion see M. Scheler, The Nature of Sympathy, especially ch. 7 (P. Heath transl. 1954).

12 For a brilliant sociological analysis of trust, which seems perhaps to overemphasize this aspect of trust, see Garfinkel, *A Conception of, and Experiments with, "Trust" as a Condition of Stable Concerted Actions*, in Motivation and Social Interaction 187 (O. Harvey ed. 1963).

13 These modulations are explored with great subtlety and a wealth of concrete illustrations in E. Goffman, Behavior in Public Places (1963); E. Goffman, Encounters (1961); E. Goffman, The Presentation of Self in Everyday Life (1959).

14 The writings of Erving Goffman, *supra* note 13, are replete with illustrations of the connections between context and relations among persons.

15 *Cf.* Schwartz, *On Current Proposals to Legalize Wire Tapping*, 103 U. Pa. L. Rev. 157, 157–58, 161–65 (1954).

16 *Compare* M. Montaigne, *De la Solitude*, in Essais, ch. 38, with J. P. Sartre, Being and Nothingness pt. 2 (H. Barnes transl. 1956).

17 Perhaps it is, after all, one of the functions of psychoanalysis to provide such a possibility.

18 Erving Goffman has suggested to me in conversation that new methods of data storage and retrieval pose a threat to privacy in that it is possible to make readily accessible information about a person's remote and forgotten past. This means a person is unable to change his own and others' definitions of him as readily as once may have been the case.

19 *Cf.* Rawls, *Legal Obligation and the Duty of Fair Play, supra* note 4.

20 Thus, for instance, so long as the mails are still private, wire tapping may not be so severe an imposition, particularly if people do not in any case consider telephone conversations as necessarily private.

21 There is another form of mortification in total institutions; beginning with admission a kind of contaminative exposure occurs. On the outside, the individual can hold objects of self-feeling—such as his body, his immediate actions, his thoughts, and some of his possessions—clear of contact with alien and contaminating things. But in total institutions these territories of the self are violated; the boundary that the individual places between his being and the environment is invaded and the embodiments of self profaned. . . . "New audiences not only learn discreditable facts about oneself that are ordinarily concealed but are also in a position to perceive some of these facts directly. Prisoners and mental patients cannot prevent their visitors from seeing them in humiliating circumstances. Another example is the shoulder patch of ethnic identification worn by concentration-camp inmates. Medical and security examinations often expose the inmate physically, sometimes to persons of both sexes; a similar exposure follows from collective sleeping arrangements and doorless toilets.

An extreme here, perhaps, is the situation of a self-destructive mental patient who is stripped naked for what is felt to be his own protection and placed in a constantly lit seclusion room, into whose Judas window any person passing on the ward can peer. In general, of course, the inmate is never fully alone; he is always within sight and often earshot of someone, if only his fellow inmates. Prison cages with bars for walls fully realize such exposure." E. Goffman, Asylums 23–25 (1961) (footnotes omitted).

22 *See generally* A. Westin, Privacy and Freedom ch. 1 (1967). It is apparently traditional for the commanding officer of a naval vessel to eat alone.

23 The struggle between Thomas More and King Henry VIII's officers to compel More to state his views on Henry's claims to ecclesiastical supremacy provides an example of how this aspect of privacy is linked to conceptions of personal integrity. *See* R. Chambers, Thomas More (1935).

24 It is just because the privilege bears this relation to the notion of personal integrity, at once intimate and symbolic, that criticisms which examine it as a tool for accomplishing this or that other purpose—*e.g.*, 6–7 J.Bentham, *Rationale of Judicial Evidence,* in The Works of Jeremy Bentham (J. Bowring ed. 1843); McNaughton, *supra* note 2—seem so unanswerable yet one feels they somehow miss the point.

25 Erving Goffman gives numerous examples of subtle, implicit norms, of whose pervasive and powerful hold on us we are quite unaware until they are violated. E. Goffman, Behavior in Public Places (1963).

26 *Cf.* E. Goffman, Encounters 37–45 (1961).

8

Privacy, freedom, and respect for persons

STANLEY I. BENN

When your mind is set on mating
It is highly irritating
To see an ornithologist below:
Though it may be nature-study,
To a bird it's merely bloody
Awful manners. Can't he see that he's *de trop!*
                    from A.N.L. Munby's "Bird Watching"

Introduction

If two people retire to the privacy of the bushes, they go where they
expect to be unobserved. What they do is done *privately*, or *in private*,
if they are not actually seen doing it. Should they later advertise or
publish what they were about, what *was* private would then become
public knowledge. Or they may have been mistaken in thinking their
retreat private—they may have been in full view of passersby all the
time. One's *private affairs*, however, are private in a different sense.
It is not that they are kept out of sight or from the knowledge of
others that makes them private. Rather, they are matters that it would
be inappropriate for others to try to find out about, much less report
on, without one's consent; one complains if they are publicized precisely because they are private. Similarly, a private room remains
private in spite of uninvited intruders, for, unlike the case of the
couple in the bushes, falsifying the expectation that no one will intrude
is not a logically sufficient ground for saying that something private
in this sense is not private after all.

"Private" used in this second, immunity-claiming[1] way is both norm-
dependent and norm-invoking. It is norm-dependent because *private
affairs* and *private rooms* cannot be identified without some reference
to norms. So any definition of the concept "private affairs" must
presuppose the existence of *some* norms restricting unlicensed observation, reporting, or entry, even though no norm in particular is

necessary to the concept. It is norm-invoking in that one need say no more than "This is a private matter" to claim that anyone not invited to concern himself with it ought to stay out of it. That is why the normative implications of "Private" on a letter or a notice board do not need to be spelled out.[2]

The norms invoked by the concept are not necessarily immunity-conferring, however; one can imagine cultures, for instance, in which they would be prohibitive, where to say that someone had done something in private would be to accuse him of acting inappropriately—perhaps cutting himself off from a collective experience and cheating others of their right to share in it. Or again, "privacy" might apply mandatorily; that is, anything private *ought* to be kept from the knowledge of others. This is rather the sense of the somewhat old-fashioned phrase "private parts," referring not to parts of the body that one might keep unseen if one chose, but to parts that one had a duty to keep out of sight. In our culture, sexual and excretory acts are private not merely in the sense that performers are immune from observation but also in the sense that some care ought to be taken that they are not generally observed. Thus, liberty to publicize, that is, to license scrutiny and publicity, whether generally or to a select public, is commonly but by no means necessarily associated with the right to immunity from observation.

The norms invoked by the concept of privacy are diverse, therefore, not only in substance but also in logical form; some grant immunities, some are prohibitive, some are mandatory. There may be cultures, indeed, with no norm-invoking concept of privacy at all, where *nothing* is thought properly immune from observation and anything may be generally displayed. It might still be possible, of course, to seek out private situations where one would not be observed, but it would never be a ground of grievance either that an action was or was not open for all to see or that someone was watching. But whatever the possible diversity, some privacy claims seem to rest on something a bit more solid than mere cultural contingency. The first objective of this paper is to explore the possibility that some minimal right to immunity from uninvited observation and reporting is required by certain basic features of our conception of a person.

The general principle of privacy and respect for persons

The umbrella "right to privacy" extends, no doubt, to other claims besides the claims not to be watched, listened to, or reported upon without leave, and not to have public attention focused upon one uninvited. It is these particular claims, however, that I have primarily in mind in this paper. It deals, therefore, with a cluster of immunities which, if acknowledged, curb the freedom of others to do things that are generally quite innocent if done to objects other than persons, and even to persons, if done with their permission. There is nothing intrinsically objectionable in observing the world, including its inhabitants, and in sharing one's discoveries with anyone who finds them interesting; and this is not on account of any special claims, for instance, for scientific curiosity, or for a public interest in the discovery of truth. For I take as a fundamental principle in morals a general liberty to do whatever one chooses unless someone else has good reasons for interfering to prevent it, reasons grounded either on the freedom of others or on some other moral principle such as justice or respect for persons or the avoidance of needless pain. The onus of justification, in brief, lies on the advocate of restraint, not on the person restrained. The present question, then, is whether any moral principle will provide a quite general ground for a prima facie claim that B should not observe and report on A unless A agrees to it. Is there a principle of privacy extending immunity to inquiry of all human activities, to be overridden only by special considerations, like those suggested? Or is it rather that there is a general freedom to inquire, observe, and report on human affairs as on other things, unless a special case can be made out for denying it with respect to certain activities that are *specifically* private?

My strategy, then, is to inquire, first, whether anyone is entitled, prima facie, to be private if he chooses, irrespective of what he is about: would the couple in the bushes have grounds for complaint if they discovered someone eavesdropping on their discussion of, say, relativity theory? Second, whether or not such grounds exist, can any rational account be given (that is, an account not wholly dependent on conventional norms) of "private affairs," the area in which uninvited intrusions are judged *particularly* inappropriate?

The former, more sweeping claim may appear at first sight extravagant, even as only a prima facie claim. Anyone who wants to remain unobserved and unidentified, it might be said, should stay at home or go out only in disguise. Yet there is a difference between happening to be seen and having someone closely observe, and perhaps record, what one is doing, even in a public place. Nor is the resentment that some people feel at being watched necessarily connected with fears of damaging disclosures in the Sunday papers or in a graduate thesis in social science. How reasonable is it, then, for a person to resent being treated much in the way that a birdwatcher might treat a redstart?

Putting the case initially at this rather trivial level has the advantage of excluding two complicating considerations. In the first place, I have postulated a kind of intrusion (if that is what it is) which does no obvious damage. It is not like publishing details of someone's sex life and ruining his career. Furthermore, what is resented is not being watched *tout court,* but being watched without leave. If observation as such were intrinsically or even consequentially damaging, it might be objectionable even if done with consent. In the present instance, consent removes all ground for objection. In the second place, by concentrating on simple unlicensed observation, I can leave aside the kind of interference with which Mill was mainly concerned in the essay *On Liberty,* namely, anything that prevents people doing, in their private lives, something they want to do, or that requires them to do what they do not want to do.[3] Threatening a man with penalties, or taking away his stick, are ways of preventing his beating his donkey; but if he stops simply because he is watched, the interference is of a different kind. He could continue if he chose; being observed affects his action only by changing his perception of it. The observer makes the act impossible only in the sense that the actor now sees it in a different light. The intrusion is not therefore obviously objectionable as an interference with freedom of action. It is true that there are special kinds of action—any that depend upon surprise, for example— that could be made objectively impossible merely by watching and reporting on them; but my present purpose is to ask whether a *general* case can be made out, not one that depends on special conditions of that kind.

Of course, there is always a danger that information may be used to harm a man in some way. The usual arguments against wiretapping, bugging, a National Data Center, and private investigators rest heavily on the contingent possibility that a tyrannical government or unscrupulous individuals might misuse them for blackmail or victimization. The more one knows about a person, the greater one's power to damage him. Now it may be that fears like this are the only reasonable ground for objecting *in general* to being watched. I might suspect a man who watches my house of "casing the joint." But if he can show me he intends no such thing, and if there is no possibility of his observations being used against me in any other way, it would seem to follow that I could have no further reasonable ground for objecting. Eliza Doolittle resents Professor Higgins's recording her speech in Covent Garden because she believes that a girl of her class subject to so close a scrutiny is in danger of police persecution: "You dunno what it means to me. They'll take away my character and drive me on the streets for speaking to gentlemen."[4] But the resentment of the bystanders is excited by something else, something intrinsic in Higgins's performance, not merely some possible consequence of his ability to spot their origins by their accents: "See here: what call have you to know about people what never offered to meddle with you? . . . You take us for dirt under your feet, don't you? Catch you taking liberties with a gentleman!" What this man resents is surely that Higgins fails to show a proper respect for persons; he is treating people as objects or specimens—like "dirt"—and not as subjects with sensibilities, ends, and aspirations of their own, morally responsible for their own decisions, and capable, as mere specimens are not, of reciprocal relations with the observer. This failure is, of course, precisely what Eliza, in her later incarnation as Higgins's Galatea, complains of too. These resentments suggest a possible ground for a prima facie claim not to be watched, at any rate in the same manner as one watches a thing or an animal. For this is "to take liberties," to act impudently, to show less than a proper regard for human dignity.

Finding oneself an object of scrutiny, as the focus of another's attention, brings one to a new consciousness of oneself, as something seen through another's eyes. According to Sartre, indeed, it is a necessary condition for knowing oneself *as* anything at all that one should conceive oneself as an object of scrutiny.[5] It is only through the regard of the other that the observed becomes aware of himself as an object, knowable, having a determinate character, in principle predictable. His consciousness of pure freedom as subject, as originator and chooser, is at once assailed by it; he is fixed *as something*—with limited probabilities rather than infinite, indeterminate possibilities. Sartre's account of human relations is of an obsessional need to master an unbearable alien freedom that undermines one's belief in one's own; for Ego is aware of Alter not only as a fact, an object in his world, but also as the subject of a quite independent world of Alter's own, wherein Ego himself is mere object. The relationship between the two is essentially hostile. Each, doubting his own freedom, is driven to assert the primacy of his own subjectivity. But the struggle for mastery, as Sartre readily admits, is a self-frustrating response; Alter's reassurance would be worthless to Ego unless it were freely given, yet the freedom to give it would at once refute it.

What Sartre conceived as a phenomenologically necessary dilemma, however, reappears in R. D. Laing's *The Divided Self*[6] as a characteristically schizoid perception of the world, the response of a personality denied free development, trying to preserve itself from domination by hiding away a "real self" where it cannot be absorbed or overwhelmed. The schizoid's problem arises because he cannot believe fully in his own existence as a person. He may *need* to be observed in order to be convinced that he exists, if only in the world of another; yet, resenting the necessity to be what the other perceives him as, he may try at the same time to hide. His predicament, like Sartre's, may seem to him to arise not from the *manner* of his being observed, but to be implicit in the very relation of observer and observed.

Sartre, however, does not show why the awareness of others as subjects must evoke so hostile a response. Even if it were true that my consciousness of my own infinite freedom is shaken by my being made aware that in the eyes of another I have only limited possibilities, still if I am not free, it is not his regard that confines me; it only draws my attention to what I was able formerly to disregard. And if I *am* free, then his regard makes no real difference. And if there is a dilemma here, may I not infer from it that the Other sees me too as a subject, and has the same problem? Could this not be a bond between us rather than a source of resentment, each according the other the same dignity as subject?

It is because the schizoid cannot believe in himself as a person, that he cannot form such a bond, or accept the respectful regard of another. So every look is a threat or an insult. Still, without question, there are ways of looking at a man that do diminish him, that provide cause for offense as real as any physical assault. But, of course, that cannot be a reason either for hiding or for going around with one's eyes shut. Yet it does suggest that if, like a doctor, one has occasion to make someone an object of scrutiny and study, or like a clinician the topic for a lecture, the patient will have grounds for resentment if the examiner appears insensible to the fact that it is a person he is examining, a subject to whom it makes a difference that he is observed, who will also have a view about what is discovered or demonstrated, and will put his own value upon it.

It would be a mistake to think that the only objection to such examination is that an incautious observer could cause damage to a sensitive person's mental state, for that could be avoided by watching him secretly. To treat a man without respect is not to injure him—at least, not in *that* sense; it is more like insulting him. Nor is it the fact of scrutiny as such that is offensive, but only unlicensed scrutiny, which may in fact do no damage at all, yet still be properly resented as an impertinence.

I am suggesting that a general principle of privacy might be grounded on the more general principle of respect for persons. By a *person* I understand a subject with a consciousness of himself as agent, one who is capable of having projects, and assessing his achievements in relation to them. To *conceive* someone as a person is to see him as actually or potentially a chooser, as one attempting to steer his own course through the world, adjusting his behavior as his apperception of the world changes, and correcting course as he perceives his errors. It is to understand that his life is for him a kind of enterprise like one's own, not merely a succession of more or less fortunate happenings, but a record of achievements and failures; and just as one cannot describe one's own life in these terms without claiming that what happens is important, so to see another's in the same light is to see that for him at least this must be important. Professor Higgins's offense was to be insensitive to this fact about other people. Of course, one may have a clinical interest in people as projectmakers without oneself attaching any importance to their projects. Still, if one fails to see how their aims and activities could be important for them, one has not properly understood what they are about. Even so, it requires a further step to see that recognizing another as engaged on such an enterprise makes a claim on oneself. To *respect* someone as a person is to concede that one ought to take account of the way in whch his enterprise might be affected by one's own decisions. By the principle of respect for persons, then, I mean the principle that every human being, insofar as he is qualified as a person, is entitled to this minimal degree of consideration.

I do not mean, of course, that someone's having some attitude toward *anything* I propose to do is alone sufficient for his wishes to be a relevant consideration, for he will certainly have attitudes and wishes about actions of mine that do not affect his enterprise at all. B's dislike of cruelty to animals is not in itself a reason why A should stop beating his donkey. It is not enough that B will be gratified if he can approve A's action, and disappointed if not; it is the conception of B as a chooser, as engaged in an active, creative enterprise, that lays an obligation of respect upon A, not the conception of him as *suffering* gratifications and disappointments. This can be a ground for sympathetic joy or pity, but not respect. B's attitudes are considerations relevant for A's decisions only if what A does will make a difference to the conditions under which B makes *his* choices, either denying him an otherwise available option (which would be to interfere with his freedom of action) or changing the significance or meaning for B of acts still open to him. B may disapprove of A's watching C or listening to his conversation with D, but B's own conditions of action—what I have called B's enterprise—remain unaffected. On the other hand, if C knows that A is listening, A's intrusion alters C's consciousness of himself, and his experienced relation to his world.

Formerly self-forgetful, perhaps, he may now be conscious of his opinions as candidates for A's approval or contempt. But even without self-consciousness of this kind, his immediate enterprise—the conversation with D—may be changed for him merely by the fact of A's presence. I am not postulating a private conversation in the sense of one about personal matters; what is at issue is the change in the way C apprehends his own performance—the topic makes no difference to this argument. A's uninvited intrusion is an impertinence because he treats it as of no consequence that he may have effected an alteration in C's perception of himself and of the nature of his performance.[7] Of course, no *damage* may have been done; C may actually enjoy performing before an enlarged audience. But C's wishes in the matter must surely be a relevant consideration (as B's are not), and in the absence of some overriding reason to the contrary, if C were inclined to complain, he has legitimate grounds.

The underpinning of a claim not to be watched without leave will be more general if it can be grounded in this way on the principle of respect for persons than on a utilitarian duty to avoid inflicting suffering. That duty may, of course, reinforce the claim in particular instances. But respect for persons will sustain an objection even to secret watching, which may do no actual harm at all. Covert observation—spying—is objectionable because it deliberately deceives a person about his world, thwarting, for reasons that *cannot* be his reasons, his attempts to make a rational choice. One cannot be said to respect a man as engaged on an enterprise worthy of consideration if one knowingly and deliberately alters his conditions of action, concealing the fact from him. The offense is different in this instance, of course, from A's open intrusion on C's conversation. In that case, A's attentions were liable to affect C's enterprise by changing C's perception of it; he may have felt differently about his conversation with D, even to the extent of not being able to see it as any longer the same activity, knowing that A was now listening. In the present instance, C is unaware of A. Nevertheless, he is wrong because the significance to him of his enterprise, assumed unobserved, is deliberately falsified by A. He may be in a fool's paradise or a fool's hell; either way, A is making a fool of him. Suppose that in a situation in which he might be observed, there is no reason why he should not choose to act privately (for instance, he is doing nothing wrong); then for anyone to watch without his knowledge is to show disrespect not only for the privacy that may have been his choice, but, by implication, for him, as a chooser. I can well imagine myself freely consenting to someone's watching me at work, but deeply resenting anyone's doing so without my knowledge—as though it didn't matter whether I liked it or not. So a policeman may treat suspected criminals like this only if there are good grounds for believing that there is an overriding need to frustrate what they are about, not because they have no rights as persons to privacy. Psychiatrists may be entitled to treat lunatics like this—but only to the extent that being incapable of rational choice, they are defective as persons. (Even so, their interests, if not their wishes, will be limiting considerations.)

The close connection between the general principle of privacy and respect for persons may account for much of the resentment evoked by the idea of a National Data Center, collating all that is known about an individual from his past contacts with government agencies. Much has been made, of course—and no doubt rightly—of the dangers of computerized data banks, governmental or otherwise. The information supplied to and by them may be false; or if true, may still put a man in a false light, by drawing attention, say, to delinquencies in his distant past that he has now lived down. And even the most conforming of citizens would have reason for dread if officials came to regard their computers as both omniscient and infallible. A good deal of legislative invention has been exercised, accordingly, in seeking safeguards against the abuse of information power. Yet for some objectors at least it altogether misses the point. It is not just a matter of a fear to be allayed by reassurances, but of a resentment that anyone—even a thoroughly trustworthy official—should be able at will to satisfy any curiosity, without the knowledge let alone the consent of the subject. For since what others know about him can radically affect a man's view of himself, to treat the collation of personal information about him as if it raised purely technical problems of safeguards against abuse is to disregard his claim to consideration and respect as a person.

I have argued so far as though the principle of respect for persons clearly indicated what a man might reasonably resent. This needs some qualification. If someone stares at my face, I cannot help seeing his gaze as focused on me. I am no less self-conscious if I catch him scrutinizing the clothes I am wearing. But would it be reasonable to resent scrutiny of a suit I am not wearing—one I have just given, perhaps, to an old folks' home? Or of my car outside my home? Or in the service station? Granted that I can reasonably claim immunity from the uninvited attentions of observers and reporters, what is to count for this purpose as *me*? As I suggested above, it cannot be sufficient that I do not *want* you to observe something; for the principle of respect to be relevant, it must be something about my own person that is in question, otherwise the principle would be so wide that a mere wish of mine would be a prima facie reason for everyone to refrain from observing and reporting on anything at all. I do not make something a part of me merely by having feelings about it. The principle of privacy proposed here is, rather, that any man who desires that he *himself* should not be an object of scrutiny has a reasonable prima facie claim to immunity. But the ground is not in the mere fact of his desiring, but in the relation between himself as an object of scrutiny and as a conscious and experiencing subject. And it is clearly not enough for a man to *say* that something pertains to him as a person and therefore shares his immunity; there must be reasons for saying so.

What could count as a reason? The very intimate connection between the concepts of *oneself* and *one's body* (about which philosophers have written at length) would seem to put that much beyond question (though some schizoids' perception of the world would suggest that dissociation even of these concepts is possible). Beyond that point, however, cultural norms cannot be ignored. In a possessive individualist culture, in which a man's property is seen as an extension of his personality, as an index to his social standing, a measure of his achievements, or an expression of his taste, to look critically on his clothes or his car is to look critically on him. In other cultures, the standards might well be different. The notion we have of our own extension, of the outer limits of our personalities—those events or situations in respect of which we feel pride or shame—is unquestionably culture-variant; consequently, the application even of a quite general principle of privacy will be affected by culturally variant norms—those regarding family, say, or property.

Applying the general principle

Allow that the principle of respect for persons will underpin a general principle of privacy; even so, it would amount only to a prima facie ground for limiting the freedom of others to observe and report at will. It would place on them a burden of justification but it would not override any special justification. The principle might be thought quite inadequate, for instance, to sustain on its own a case for legal restraints; the protection of privacy is less important, perhaps, than the danger to political freedom from legal restrictions on reporting. It might be argued that in every case it is for the press to show what reasonable public interest publicity would serve. But so uncertain a criterion could result in an overtimorous press. The courts have been properly wary of recognizing rights that might discourage if not disable the press from publicizing what *ought* to be exposed.

General principles do not *determine* solutions to moral problems of this kind. They indicate what needs to be justified, where the onus of justification lies, and what can count as a justification. So to count as an overriding consideration, an argument must refer to some further principle. Consider the difficult case of the privacy of celebrities. According to a learned American judge, the law "recognizes a legitimate public curiosity about the personalities of celebrities, and about a great deal of otherwise private and personal information about them."[8] But is all curiosity equally legitimate, or must there be something about the kind of celebrity that legitimizes special kinds of curiosity? Is there no difference between, say, a serious historian's curiosity about what (and who) prompted President Johnson's decision not to run a second time and that to which the Sunday gossip columnists appeal? If a person is in the public eye for some performance that he intends to be public or that is in its nature public—like conducting an orchestra—this may, as a matter of fact, make "human interest stories" about him more entertaining and exciting than similar stories about an unknown. But the fact that many people enjoy that kind of entertainment is no reason at all for overriding the principle of privacy; for though there is a presumptive liberty to do whatever there is no reason for not doing, there is no general claim to have whatever one enjoys. To treat even an entertainer's life simply as material for entertainment is to pay no more regard to him as a person than to an animal in a menagerie. Of course, anyone who indiscriminately courts publicity, as some entertainers do, can hardly complain if they are understood to be offering a general license. But merely to be a celebrity—even a willing celebrity—does not disable someone from claiming the consideration due to a person. Admittedly, it opens up a range of special claims to information about him, to override his general claim to privacy. Candidates for appointment to the Supreme Court must expect some public concern with their business integrity. Or—a rather different case—because an eminent conductor participates in a public activity with a public tradition, anyone choosing conducting as a profession must expect that his musical experience, where he was trained, who has influenced his interpretations, will be matters of legitimate interest to others concerned as he is with music. But this is not a warrant for prying into other facts about him that have nothing to do with his music: his taste in wines, perhaps, or women. The principle of privacy would properly give way in one area, but it would

stand in any other to which the special overriding grounds were irrelevant. For the principle itself is not limited in its application; it
constitutes a prima facie claim in respect to *anything* a man does.

"Private affairs" and personal ideals

To claim immunity on the ground that an inquiry is an intrusion into
one's *private affairs* is to make an argumentative move of a quite different kind. For this concept entrenches the privacy of certain special
areas far more strongly than the mere presumptive immunity of the
general principle. To justify such an intrusion, one has to have not
merely a reason, but one strong enough to override special reasons
for *not* intruding. So while the interests of phonetic science might
justify Professor Higgins's impertinence in Covent Garden, they would
not be good enough reasons for bugging Eliza's bedroom.

The activities and experiences commonly thought to fall within this
special private area are diverse and largely culture-dependent. Some
seem to have no rational grounds at all. For instance, why should the
bodily functions that in our culture are appropriately performed in
solitude include defecation but not eating? Of course, so long as certain acts are assigned to this category anyone who has internalized
the social norms will experience a painful embarrassment if seen doing
them; embarrassment, indeed, is the culturally appropriate response
in a society with the concept of *pudenda,* and anyone not showing it
may be censured as brazen or insensitive. But though this furnishes
a kind of rational interest in privacy of this kind, its rationale depends
on a conventional norm that may itself be wholly irrational.

Not all areas of privacy are like this, however; others are closely
related to ideals of life and character which would be difficult, perhaps
impossible, to achieve were privacy not safeguarded. The liberal individualist tradition has stressed, in particular, three personal ideals,
to each of which corresponds a range of "private affairs." The first
is the ideal of personal relations; the second, the Lockian ideal of the
politically free man in a minimally regulated society; the third, the
Kantian ideal of the morally autonomous man, acting on principles
that he accepts as rational.

The privacy of personal relations

By personal relations, I mean relations between persons that are considered valuable and important at least as much because of the quality

of each person's attitude to another as for what each does to, or for, another.

All characteristically human relations—I mean relations of a kind that could not exist between stones or wombats—involve some element, however small, of role-expectancy. We structure our relations with others according to an understanding of *what* they are and what accordingly is due to them and from them. That may exhaust some relations: if the railway booking clerk gives me the correct ticket in exchange for my fare, he has fulfilled his function. Moreover, the point of the relationship calls for no more than this; the grating that separates us, with just space enough to push through a ticket or a coin, appropriately symbolizes it. One cannot be indifferent to his performance, but one need not attend to his personality.

The relation between father and son, or husband and wife, is necessarily more than this, or if in a given instance it is not, then that instance is defective. Here, too, there are role-expectancies, but each particular set of related persons will fulfill them in a different way. There is room for being a father in this or in that manner. Moreover, only a part of what it is to be a father has been met when the specified duties of the role have been fulfilled. Beyond that, the value of the relation depends on a personal understanding between the parties, and on whether, and how, they care about one another. Father and son might be meticulous in the performance of the formal duties of their roles, but if they are quite indifferent to each other, the relationship is missing its point. The relationship between friends or lovers is still less role-structured than family relations, though even here there are conventional patterns and rituals—gifts on ritual occasions, forms of wooing, etc. But they are primarily symbols: their main point is to communicate a feeling or an attitude, to reassure, perhaps, or make a proposal. And though they could be gone through even if the feeling did not really exist, such a performance would surely be a pretense or a deception, and therefore parasitic on the primary point.

Personal relations can of course be of public concern; children may need to be protected, for instance, from certain kinds of corrupting relations with adults. But while it may be possible and desirable to prevent such relations altogether, there is little that third parties can do to regulate or reshape them. By inducing the booking clerk to do his job more efficiently, or passengers to state their destinations more clearly, the railway staff controller can improve the relation between them. But this is because he can keep them up to the mark—they are all interested exclusively in role-performance, and each can have a clear notion of the standard that the other's performance should reach. But friends can be kept up to the mark only by one another. There is no "mark" that anyone outside could use to assess them, for friendship is not confined by role requirements.[9]

To intrude on personal relations of this kind may be very much worse than useless. Of course, people do take their troubles to others, to friends or marriage counselors for guidance and advice. But this is to invite the counselor to become, in a small way perhaps, a party to the relationship—or rather, to enter into a relationship with him, the success of which depends on his resolve to keep it a purely second-order relationship, demanding of him a sensitive and reticent understanding of the first. Personal relations are exploratory and creative; they survive and develop if they are given care and attention; they require continuous adjustment as the personalities of the parties are modified by experience, both of one another and of their external environment. Such relationships are, in their nature, private. They could not exist if it were not possible to create excluding conditions. One cannot have a personal relation with all comers, nor carry on personal conversations under the same conditions as an open seminar.[10]

If we value personal relations, then, we must recognize these at least as specifically private areas. And since the family and the family home are the focal points of important and very generally significant personal relations, these must be immune from intrusion, at least beyond the point at which minimal public role requirements are satisfied. A father who regularly beats the children insensible cannot claim, of course, that intrusion could only spoil his personal relations. But while the public is properly concerned that there should be no cruelty, exploitation, or neglect, these are only the minimal conditions for personal relations. The rest are the private business of the parties.

Preoccupation with privacy—in particular with the privacy of family relations—has been criticized by some writers, however, as an unhealthy feature of post-Renaissance bourgeois society. Consider Edmund Leach's strictures:

In the past, kinsfolk and neighbors gave the individual continuous moral support throughout his life. Today the domestic household is isolated. The family looks inward upon itself; there is an intensification of emotional stress between husband and wife, and parents and children. The strain is greater than most of us can bear. Far from being the basis of the good society, the family, with its narrow privacy and tawdry secrets, is the source of all our discontents.[11]

Paul Halmos, too, speaks of "a hypertrophied family devotion and family insularity," arising from the attempt by contemporary man "to transcend his solitude. . . ."

[He] may finally negate his apartness in an obsessional affirmation of family ties. . . . Friendship and companionship, when manifestly present in the marital couple, is regarded as an instance of great virtue even when it is equally manifestly absent in all other relationships. Furthermore, the nepotistic solidarity of the family is another symptom of the contemporary attitude according to which the world is hostile and dangerous and the family is the only solid rock which is to be protected against all comers.[12]

The insistence on the private area is, in this view, either a symptom or a contributory cause of a pathological condition. But to concede this diagnosis need not weaken the argument I am advancing for the right of exclusion, for it may imply only that in modern society we seek personal relations with too few people, the ones we succeed in forming being overtaxed in consequence by the emotional weight they are forced to bear.

Halmos concedes the value and importance of the personal relations between lovers and "the composed intimacy and companionship of man and wife," admitting these as properly and necessarily exclusive: "Such retreat and privacy may vary according to cultural standards but they are on the whole universal among mankind and not infrequent among animals."[13] It is not clear, however, how much value Halmos attaches to personal relations in general. It may be that men suffer least from neurotic maladjustments in communities like the kibbutz, where everyone feels the security and comfortable warmth of acceptance by a peer group, without the tensions of too-personalized individual attachments. But the children of the kibbutz have been found by some observers defective as persons, precisely because their emotional stability has been purchased at the cost of an incapacity to establish deep personal relations. Perhaps we have to choose between the sensitive, human understanding that we achieve only by the cultivation of our relations within a confined circle and the extrovert assurance and adjustment that a *Gemeinschaft* can confer. However this may be, to the extent that we value the former, we shall be committed to valuing the right of privacy.

Though personal relations need some freedom from interference, different kinds of interference would affect them differently. An extreme kind is to attempt to participate—to turn, for instance, a relation *à deux* into one *à trois*. It is not evident, however, that the attentions of the observer and reporter are necessarily so objectionable. A strong-minded couple might pursue their own course undisturbed under the eyes of a reasonably tactful and self-effacing paying guest. Of course, the uncommitted observer makes most of us self-conscious and inhibited—we do not find it as easy to express our feelings for one another spontaneously, to produce the same kind of mutually sensitive and responsive relations, in full view of a nonparticipant third party, as we do in private. I do not know, however, whether this is a psychologically necessary fact about human beings, or only a culturally conditioned one. Certainly, personal relations are not impossible in places where people live perforce on top of one another. But they call for a good deal of tact and goodwill from the bystanders; there is some evidence that in such conditions, people develop psychological avoidance arrangements—a capacity for not noticing, and a corresponding confidence in not being noticed—that substitute for physical seclusion.[14]

The importance of personal relations suggests a limit to what can be done by antidiscrimination laws. Whatever the justification for interfering with the freedom to discriminate in, say, hiring workers, there are some kinds of choice where a man's reasons for his preferences and antipathies are less important than that he has them. If the personal relations of a home are valued, its constituent members must be left free to decide who can be accepted into it, for example, as a lodger. Club membership might be different. True, we join clubs to cultivate personal relations, like friendships; but we do not expect to enter into such relations with every member. The mere presence in the clubroom of people whom one would not invite to join one's circle of intimates need not endanger the relations within that circle. Nevertheless, if the club's members are, in general, antipathetic to a particular group, to deny them the right of exclusion may create tensions defeating the end for which the club exists.

Of course, merely having prejudices gives no man a right to discriminate unfairly and irrationally in all his relations at whatever cost to the personal dignity of the outsider; insofar as the relations can be specified in terms of role-performances, it is reasonable to demand that discriminations be based only on relevant differences. But to the degree that the point of the relationship has built into it a quality of life depending on reciprocal caring, it qualifies as an area of privacy, and therefore as immune from regulation. (There may be overriding reasons, in times of racial tension and hostility, for discouraging the formation of exclusive clubs, whose rules can only appear inflammatory. But this is to adduce further special reasons against privacy, overriding reasons for it based on the value of personal relations.)

The privacy of the free citizen

The second personal ideal to which privacy is closely related is that of the free man in a minimally regulated society, a way of life where, first, the average individual is subject only within reasonable and legally safeguarded limits to the power of others, and, second, where the requirements of his social roles still leave him considerable breadth of choice in the way he lives. The first of these considerations, the one that has received most attention in the polemical literature on privacy, I have referred to already. The dossier and the computer bank threaten us with victimization and persecution by unscrupulous, intolerant, or merely misunderstanding officials. But these misgivings might be set at rest, at least in principle, by institutional safeguards and assurances. More fundamental is the second consideration, which depends on a conceptual distinction between the private and the official.

The judge's pronouncements on the bench have public significance; though he may not be easily called to account, still there is an important sense in which he has a public responsibility. What he says in his home or in his club—even on matters of law—is another matter; it has no official standing and no official consequences. Of course, if he happens also to be club secretary, what he says about other members in *this* official capacity is not "his own private affair"; but conversely, the members might resist a police inquiry into its secretary's statements as an interference with the club's private affairs. What is official and what is private depends, therefore, on the frame of reference. But for there to be privacy of this kind at all the distinction between official and nonofficial must be intelligible. Admittedly, we may all have some public (that is, official) roles as voters, taxpayers, jurymen, and so on. But we distinguish what we do as family men, shopkeepers, and club treasurers from such public functions. A private citizen, unlike a public official, has no *special* official roles, just as a private member of Parliament, not being a minister, has no special official function in Parliament.

This conception of privacy is closely bound up with the liberal ideal. The totalitarian claims that everything a man is and does has significance for society at large. He sees the state as the self-conscious organization of society for the well-being of society; the social significance of our actions and relations overrides any other. Consequently, the public or political universe is all inclusive, *all* roles are public, and every function, whether political, economic, or artistic, can be interpreted as involving a public responsibility.

The liberal, on the other hand, claims not merely a private capacity—an area of action in which he is not responsible to the state for what he does so long as he respects certain minimal rights of others; he claims further that this is the residual category, that the onus is on anyone who claims he is accountable. How he does his job may affect the gross national product, and not only his own slice of it. But he will grant that this is socially significant only in the same way that a drought is, for that too can have serious economic consequences. He may consent to public manipulation of the environment of private choices, by subsidies or customs duties, for instance, as he may agree to cloud-seeding to break a drought, but he resists the suggestion that every citizen should be held publicly responsible for his economic choices as though he were a public servant or the governor of the central bank.

This ideal of the private citizen provides no very precise criteria for distinguishing the private realm; it is rather that no citizen other than actual employees of the administration can be held culpable—even morally culpable—for any action as a failure in public duty unless special grounds can be shown why this is a matter in which he may not merely please himself. Of course, there will be duties associated with roles he has voluntarily assumed—as husband, employee, and so on—but such responsibilities are of his own choosing, not thrust upon him, like his public roles of juror, or taxpayer.

Just as the privacy of personal relations may be invoked to rationalize an obsessive preoccupation with the restricted family, to the exclusion of all other human concern, so the privacy of the free citizen may be invoked to rationalize a selfish economic individualism. One critic, H. W. Arndt, has written that

The cult of privacy seems specifically designed as a defence mechanism for the protection of anti-social behaviour. . . . The cult of privacy rests on an individualist conception of society, not merely in the innocent and beneficial sense of a society in which the welfare of individuals is conceived as the end of all social organisation, but in the more specific sense of "each for himself and the devil take the hindmost." . . . An individualist of this sort sees "the Government" where we might see "the public interest," and this Government will appear to him often as no more than one antagonist in the battle of wits which is life—or business.[15]

There is room for a good deal of disagreement about the extent to which considerations like those of general economic well-being, social equality, or national security justify pressing back the frontiers of the private, to hold men responsible for the way they conduct their daily business. For the liberal, however, every step he is forced to take in that direction counts as a retreat from an otherwise desirable state of affairs, in which because men may please themselves what they are about is no one's business but their own.

Privacy and personal autonomy

The third personal ideal is that of the independently minded individual, whose actions are governed by principles that are his own. This does not mean, of course, that he has concocted them out of nothing, but that he subjects his principles to critical review, rather than taking them over unexamined from his social environment. He is the man who resists social pressures to conform if he has grounds for uneasiness in doing the conformist thing.

Much has been made of the need for privacy, as a safeguard against conformism. Hubert Humphrey has written:

We act differently if we believe we are being observed. If we can never be sure whether or not we are being watched and listened to, all our actions will be altered and our very character will change.[16]

Senator Edward V. Long deplores the decline in spontaneity attendant on a situation where "because of this diligent accumulation of facts about each of us, it is difficult to speak or act today without wondering if the words or actions will reappear 'on the record.' "[17]

It is not only the authorities we fear. We are all under strong pressure from our friends and neighbors to live up to the roles in which they cast us. If we disappoint them, we risk their disapproval, and what may be worse, their ridicule. For many of us, we are free to be ourselves only within that area from which observers can legitimately be excluded. We need a sanctuary or retreat, in which we can drop the mask, desist for a while from projecting on the world the image we want to be accepted as ourselves, an image that may reflect the values of our peers rather than the realities of our natures. To remain sane, we need a closed environment, open only to those we trust, with whom we have an unspoken understanding that whatever is revealed goes no farther.

Put in this way, however, the case for privacy begins to look like a claim to the conditions of life necessary only for second-grade men in a second-grade society. For the man who is truly independent— the autonomous man—is the one who has the strength of mind to resist the pressure to believe with the rest, and has the courage to act on his convictions. He is the man who despises bad faith, and refuses to be anything or to pretend to be anything merely because the world casts him for the part. He is the man who does not hesitate to stand and be counted. That sort of man can be greatly inconvenienced by the world's clamor—but he *does* what lesser men claim that they are not free to do. "There is no reason," writes Senator Long, "why conformity must be made an inescapable part of the American dream. Excessive pressures can and must be prevented: there must be preserved in each individual a sphere of privacy that will allow his personality to bloom and thrive."[18] One wonders, however, whether the Senator has drawn the right moral. Excessive pressures can be prevented not merely by allowing an individual to hide, but by tolerating the heresy he is not afraid to publish. Socrates did not ask to be allowed to teach philosophy in private. Senator Long quotes a speech of Judge Learned Hand, with apparent approval: "I believe that community is already in process of dissolution . . . when faith in the eventual supremacy of reason has become so timid that we dare not enter our convictions in the open lists to win or lose."[19] But the moral of that sentiment is that preoccupation with the need for a private retreat is a symptom of social sickness.

Of course, there are not many like Socrates in any society; not many have the knowledge of what they are, the virtue to be content with what they know, and the courage to pretend to be nothing else. For the rest of us, the freedom we need is the freedom to be something else—to be ourselves, to do what we think best, in a small, protected sea, where the winds of opinion cannot blow us off course. We cannot learn to be autonomous save by practicing independent judgment. It is important for the moral education of children that at a certain stage they should find the rules porous—that sometimes they should be left to decide what is best to do. Not many of us perhaps have gone so far along the road to moral maturity that we can bear unrelenting exposure to criticism without flinching.

This last stage of my argument brings me back to the grounds for the general principle of privacy, to which I devoted the first half of this paper. I argued that respect for someone as a person, as a chooser, implied respect for him as one engaged on a kind of self-creative enterprise, which could be disrupted, distorted, or frustrated even by so limited an intrusion as watching. A man's view of what he does may be radically altered by having to see it, as it were, through another man's eyes. Now a man has attained a measure of success in his enterprise to the degree that he has achieved autonomy. To the same degree, the importance to him of protection from eavesdropping and Peeping Toms diminishes as he becomes less vulnerable to the judgments of others, more reliant on his own (though he will still need privacy for personal relations, and protection from the grosser kinds of persecution).

This does not weaken the ground for the general principle, however, for this was not a consequentialist ground. It was not that allowing men privacy would give them a better chance to be autonomous. It was rather that a person—anyone potentially autonomous—was worthy of respect on that account; and that if such a person wanted to pursue his enterprise unobserved, he was entitled, unless there were overriding reasons against it, to do as he wished. The argument there was in terms of respect for the enterprise as such, irrespective of the chances of success or failure in any particular instance. In this last section, I have suggested a further, reinforcing argument for privacy as a condition necessary, though to a progressively diminishing degree, if that enterprise is to succeed.

NOTES

1 I do not use "immunity" in this paper in the technical Hohfeldian sense. Where it is not used in a simple descriptive sense, I intend that a person shall be understood to be immune from observation if he has grounds for complaint should anyone watch him; an activity is immune if it is not appropriate for unauthorized persons to watch it.

2 Of course, though "Someone has been reading my private letters" is enough to state a protest, it need not be well founded; the letters may not really qualify as private, or even if they are, there may be other conditions overriding the implicit claim to immunity.

3 W. L. Weinstein's illuminating contribution to this volume, "The Private and the Free: A Conceptual Inquiry," is mainly concerned with Mill's questions; I shall touch on them only indirectly.

4 G. B. Shaw, *Pygmalion*, Act I.

5 See J.-P. Sartre, *L'être et le néant* (Paris, 1953), Part 3, "Le pour-autrui."

6 Harmondsworth, England, 1965.

7 Of course, there are situations, such as in university common rooms, where there is a kind of conventional general license to join an ongoing conversation. A railway compartment confers a similar license in Italy, but not in England. In such situations, if one does not wish to be listened to, one stays silent.

8 See W. L. Prosser, "Privacy," *California Law Review*, 48 (1960), 416–417.

9 "According to the newspaper *Szabad Nép*, some members of the Communist Party in Hungary have not a single working man among their friends, and they are censured in a way that implies that they had better quickly make

a friend of a worker or it will be the worse for them" (*The Times* [London], July 20, 1949, quoted by P. Halmos, *Solitude and Privacy* [London, 1952], p. 167).

10 Charles Fried has argued that privacy is logically prior to love and friendship, since a necessary feature of these concepts is a "sharing of information about one's actions, beliefs, or emotions which one does not share with all, and which one has the right not to share with anyone. By conferring this right, privacy creates the moral capital which we spend in friendship and love" ("Privacy," in G. Hughes, ed., *Law, Reason, and Justice* [New York, 1969], p. 56).

11 E. Leach, *A Runaway World*, The 1967 Reith Lectures (London, 1968), p. 44.

12 P. Halmos, *Solitude and Privacy* (London, 1952), pp. 121–122.

13 Halmos, *Solitude and Privacy*, p. 121. The standpoint Halmos adopts may be inferred from the following passage: "While . . . the material needs of man . . . have been increasingly satisfied, since the Industrial Revolution, the bio-social needs have been more and more neglected. Culture, a fortuitous expression of the basic principia of life, rarely favoured man's pacific, creative gregariousness . . ." p. 51.

14 See A. F. Westin, *Privacy and Freedom* (New York, 1967), p. 18, for references to evidence of this point.

15 H. W. Arndt, "The Cult of Privacy," *Australian Quarterly*, XXI: 3 (September 1949), 69, 70–71.

16 Foreword to Edward V. Long, *The Intruders* (New York, 1967), p. viii.

17 *Ibid.*, p. 55.

18 *Ibid.*, p. 62.

19 *Ibid.*, p. 63.

9

Privacy and self-incrimination

ROBERT S. GERSTEIN

Introduction

The privilege against self-incrimination embodied in the Fifth
Amendment is under attack again.[1] This in itself is not surprising.
All of the rights set out in the Bill of Rights are limitations on the will
of the majority, and they are bound to be resented if they are effective.
But the attack on this privilege is of a rather different character from
those made on the other rights and privileges. It is more persistent,
emanates from more respectable sources, and calls forth a rather more
equivocal and ineffectual defense.

Much of the reason for this seems to lie in history. The privilege
is, to a great extent, a victim of its own early popularity. It became a
rallying point in seventeenth-century England, and, to a degree, in
seventeenth- and eighteenth-century America, in large part for reasons which had little to do with its intrinsic merit or lack of it. It was
seized upon because it just happened to be a handy means to shield
some very popular people against some very unpopular laws. Anything, no matter how badly supported by reasoning, might have served
as well.[2] Thus, it became established as part of our legal tradition
without ever having been subjected to a thorough examination. Levy
seems wholly justified in saying that "by 1776 the principle . . . was
simply taken for granted and so deeply accepted that its constitutional
expression had the mechanical quality of a ritualistic gesture in favor
of a self-evident truth needing no explanation."[3] A privilege with such
an origin will remain in a healthy state only if it continues to be
regarded as self-evident as it develops over time. But this has not been
the case with the privilege against self-incrimination. Many have ceased
to see it as a self-evident truth and have begun to question it. An
effort has been made to bolster it with a variety of justifications, but
none of them seems wholly satisfying.[4] Nor have the lines drawn to
limit the principle's applicability responded to any self-evident scheme.

© The University of Chicago Press, 1970. Reprinted from *Ethics* 80: 87–101, 1970.

Many of the limitations and extensions which have developed in recent years remain without any well-thought-out basis in principle. In such a situation, it is not surprising that the attack has been particularly effective.

Any defense of the privilege must be founded on a clearly articulated justification for its existence. It must be a justification which will form a solid basis for the core of the privilege as we now know it, while offering criteria for a soundly rationalized redrawing of the boundaries for its applicability. All of the purported rationales must be culled through in order to see which are sound and which are not, and those which seem sound must then be further explored and developed, both separately and in relation to each other.[5]

The first thing that becomes clear in this process is that there are a number of relatively sound justifications for the privilege and that they do not fit together very nicely into any sort of pattern. They share a roughly common core but make for very different configurations beyond the core area, each including cases within its reach which would be excluded by others.

Of all these various lines of reasoning, three seem to me to have real force: the argument that the privilege is necessary to the maintenance of an efficient and genuinely "accusatorial" system of criminal justice,[6] the argument that it is profoundly cruel and inhumane to require a man to take part in his own undoing,[7] and the argument that a compelled confession is a serious invasion of privacy.[8] It is immediately apparent that this is a rather diverse set. The first justification involves the privilege as an instrument for the achievement of other goals, not as an end in itself, while the others point to its intrinsic value. Further, the justifications do not by any means all cover the same ground. For example, the argument from the need to maintain an accusatory system would only apply where there was some danger of prosecution, but the privacy argument would be effective even where there was immunity from prosecution.[9] In this and other important areas, a consideration of the privilege in the light of all of the various arguments put forward to support it brings to light a complex skein of relationships which must be disentangled before sound judgments can be made. The decision to grant the privilege or not must rest on a separate consideration of the extent to which each of these rationales is applicable under the particular circumstances. The case for allowing the privilege would be strongest where all of these purposes would be served by its application. It would be weaker where only one or two of them were served, particularly if they were only tangentially relevant.[10]

I do not here intend to develop a complete analysis of the privilege along these lines. I propose only to analyze one of these three justifications which seem to me to form the major supports of the privilege. It is the one which I regard as lying at the core of the feeling behind the privilege, but which has received the least careful attention from its analysts: the argument that the privilege is needed to protect privacy. I would like to attempt an analysis of this rather vague notion, and then to see whether it can be used to shed new light on some of the inconsistencies and ambiguities which currently becloud the development of the privilege.

I

An analysis of the role which the privacy argument plays in self-incrimination must be founded on a careful consideration of the concept of privacy itself. Fried's recent article on the subject offers a solid basis for such a consideration.[11] His first point is that the right of privacy has intrinsic and not merely instrumental value. "Privacy is not just one possible means among others to insure some other value . . . it is necessarily related to ends and relations of the most fundamental sort: respect, love, friendship and trust. Privacy is not merely a good technique for furthering these fundamental relations; rather without privacy they are simply inconceivable."[12]

He points out that "privacy is not simply an absence of information about us in the minds of others; rather it is the *control* we have over information about ourselves."[13] He goes on to show that this control, this capacity to modulate the amount of information about ourselves known to others according to our esteem for them and our relationship to them, is essential to the existence of relationships of love, friendship, and trust.[14] "To be friends or lovers, persons must be intimate to some degree with each other. But intimacy is the sharing of information about one's actions, beliefs, or emotions which one does not share with all, and which one has a right not to share with anyone. By conferring this right, privacy creates moral capital which we spend in friendship and love."[15]

Any compulsory self-incrimination will quite obviously be an involuntary relinquishment of control over information about himself by the person involved. Does this mean, without more, that compulsory self-incrimination is a violation of the right of privacy and that the privilege is therefore a necessary corollary of the right? The answer must be that it does not. If privacy is a constitutional right it is immediately apparent that it cannot be an absolute right. Govern-

ments have always compelled people to disclose some sorts of information about themselves, and it is hard to see how they could get
along effectively without the ability to do so. If the argument for
privacy is made so broadly as to sweep away tax returns, accident
reports, and the capacity to compel testimony on personal matters in
civil cases, for example, it must surely be rejected. The right of privacy
cannot be understood as embodying the rule that "privacy may never
be violated."

The alternative is to look at the right of privacy not as an absolute
rule but as a principle[16] which would establish privacy as a value of
great significance, not to be interfered with lightly by governmental
authority. Whenever an interference with privacy is proposed, the
government ought to have the burden of showing that interference
to that extent is justified by a clearly preponderant governmental
interest on the other side. If the individual is being asked to relinquish
control over information of relatively little personal significance, then
it would not take a terribly weighty governmental interest to overcome
it. If, on the other hand, the information is of such a kind that control
over it would have profound significance for the individual, then it
would take very powerful societal needs to justify the demand that it
be relinquished, and there are some sorts of information which have
such great significance to the individual that we would under no
circumstances require him to give up his control over it.[17]

If we examine the problem of the privilege against compulsory self-
incrimination in this context, we are immediately confronted with
what seems to be a highly paradoxical situation. People who are not
accused of any crime may be required, for example, to testify as to
personal matters as witnesses in civil trials. The societal interest in
having information in these cases is regarded as sufficient to overcome
the witness's right to control over information which might otherwise
be regarded as entirely private. Yet when we are dealing with people
who are presumably guilty of crime, we decide that their right to
exclusive control over the information about the offenses which they
committed is allowed to stand even in the face of the important societal
interest in the detection and punishment of crime. Why is the right
of the guilty given preference over the right of the innocent? A criminal act is generally an unjust invasion of the interests of another. A
person whose actions invade another's interests would apparently have
a far weaker moral claim to exclusive control over the information
he has about those actions than one who has not. Yet we find him
being treated with special solicitude.[18] We must go further to find a
justification for respecting the right of privacy in this case.

Fried offers an explanation for this apparent paradox. He regards the law of self-incrimination as "an example of a contingent symbolic recognition of an area of privacy as an expression of respect for personal integrity."[19]

Fried points out that the authorities can require others to disclose information about an individual accused of crime. But information which others have gained about the individual through his words to them, and his actions insofar as they have been visible to them, is indeed information "over which he has already relinquished control."[20] The idea of the privilege is not that the government be kept from finding out any information about the accused but rather "that a man cannot be forced to make public information about himself. Thereby his sense of control over what others know of him is significantly enhanced, even if other sources of the same information exist."[21]

This may be part of the explanation for this privilege. But if the privilege can only be supported as a symbolic recognition of privacy, then it is hard to see how it has lasted this long, and it seems implausible that it will not crumble in the face of the attacks currently being made upon it. The problem is that, if it is a symbol, it is a very costly one. Of course we give the greatest possible symbolic recognition to privacy when we grant it added protection in the very area where society has a strong countervailing interest and where any moral claim to such protection seems to have been forfeited. But how long will our society continue to revere such a symbol once the facts become clear?[22] If this is all there is to the privacy argument, it is hard to believe that it will withstand the current attacks upon the privilege.

But I think there is more to the privacy argument than this. I think we are dealing here with a special sort of information, a sort of information which it is particularly important for the individual to be able to control.

I am thinking about what is likely to be involved in a confession beyond the bare recital of facts about the crime: the admission of wrongdoing, the self-condemnation, the revelation of remorse. I would argue that a man ought to have absolute control over the making of such revelations as these. They have generally been regarded as a matter between a man and his conscience or his God, very much as have been religious opinions. This, it seems to me, is a very important part of what lies behind the privilege against self-incrimination. It is a dimension which is suggested by such words as these, by Fortas: "A man may be punished, even put to death, by the state; but . . . he should not be made to prostrate himself before its majesty. *Mea culpa* belongs to a man and his God. It is a plea that cannot be exacted from free men by human authority."[23]

It is not the disclosure of the facts of the crime, but the mea culpa, the public admission of the private judgment of self-condemnation, that seems to be of real concern.

I am not suggesting that such a revelation is involved in the confession of every person who is guilty of violating any section of the penal code. There are people who could commit any offense without moral compunction, and there are some offenses included in the penal code which almost anyone could commit without much trouble to his conscience. What I am thinking about is violations in the core area of criminal law, violations which involve serious injury to the interests of others and therefore serious immorality, committed by one of the vast majority of people for whom the criminal law is designed: people who to one degree or another feel themselves to be part of the same moral community with those whose interests they have injured, and who therefore see the violation as a moral issue.[24] In these central cases we can assume that the kind of expression of self-condemnation with which we are concerned will be an expressed or implied part of the confession, and it is, I believe, for these cases that the privilege against self-incrimination, and the other guarantees of fair procedure for the criminal, were chiefly designed.

What, then, is it that gives this kind of revelation its peculiarly private character?

What is first of all involved is, I believe, the special character of the individual's judgments of himself. Winch has pointed out that the moral decisions of agents, the decisions about "what I ought to do," or "what I ought to have done," at least when they are difficult decisions involving a conflict of obligations, are indeed of a very special sort.[25] Unlike our general judgments on moral issues and our judgments of the actions of others, they are not really "universalizable." I do not necessarily, when I say "I ought [or ought not] to have done that," commit myself to saying that anyone else in relevantly similar circumstances ought (or ought not) to have done the same thing. This is because what is involved in finding out what the right (or wrong) thing for me to have done involves more than knowing the relevant circumstances and the general principles of morality. It involves coming to know something about myself; something which I can find out about by careful consideration of the nature of my own moral character and inclinations.

Winch uses the example of Captain Vere's decision that he ought to condemn Billy Budd in Melville's novel, *Billy Budd*. Winch considers what he would have done in that situation and tells us that

> I believe that I could not have acted as did Vere; and by the "could not" I do not mean "should not have the nerve to," but that I should have found it morally impossible to condemn a man "innocent before God" under such circumstances. In reaching this decision I do not think that I should appeal to any considerations over and above those to which Vere himself appeals. It is just that I think I should find the considerations connected with Billy Budd's peculiar innocence too powerful to be overridden by the appeal to military duty.[26]

Winch makes it clear, however, that this does not lead him to decide that Vere acted wrongly. This is because his decision, and the moral decisions of agents in general, rest finally on "something about oneself, rather than anything one can speak of as holding universally."[27]

It is this self-knowledge which is revealed to the public in the process of self-incrimination; what is involved is the laying bare of the innermost recesses of conscience. And this is done in the most poignant case, the case of self-condemnation.[28] I would assert that this is one of the peculiarly private sorts of information over which the individual should be allowed to retain full control. The courts quite rightly put upon the convict the publicly displayed stigma of publicly determined guilt. But it ought not be be able to force him to make public the judgment by which he has condemned himself in conscience. He ought to be able to keep his mea culpa for his God, or for those to whom he feels bound by trust and affection.[29]

Each of us knows from experience that such admissions are very generally kept private and made only to those to whom the person involved is closest. They seem to be the prime example of disclosures which are kept from the outside world as a whole, while frequently forming a part of the basis of relationships of love and of trust. We also know that confession has played a major role in religious experience.

Self-condemnation has traditionally had its setting within the profoundly personal area of religious experience, and its private character has been emphasized in this context. True confession was, at least in the early church, the product of a wholly spontaneous and profound personal awareness of the sinful character of the individual's actions, an awareness which had an enormous emotional impact upon him. Thus Aquinas is quoted as describing it as the greatest suffering which can be endured. It involves, in this view, a total change of heart and way of life.[30] The motive of the penitent is profoundly important, and a confession motivated by fear of disgrace or temporal punishment was at one time thought to be invalid. It was regarded as essential that the penitent be motivated by a hatred of his sin and a desire for a new life.[31] It seems quite clearly to be a matter in which the compulsion of the state can properly play no part.

So personal was confession in the early church, indeed, that at first apparently secret confession of the individual to God was all that was thought necessary.[32] Confession before the whole body of the congregation was also in use, but in discussions of this the close bonds of love within the church are emphasized, and it is pointed out that the person confessing should feel that "the Church and Christ are in each of the brethren, and he is humbling himself not before them but before Christ."[33] Later, of course, the secrecy of confession to the priest replaces both of these earlier practices, and again the especially private character of confession is emphasized.[34]

It is of course obvious that the secrecy and trust which will be present in relationships of love and religious faith must be there before most people willingly disclose themselves to the extent required in a true and deeply felt confession. What has been less obvious, but becomes apparent upon consideration, is the extent to which the existence of relationships of love, confidence, and religious feeling depends upon their being the setting for such confession. One would not have the "moral capital" needed to invest in a full relationship with the Catholic church, or with a loved one, if one were by some means always compelled immediately to expose all of one's wrongdoing to public view.[35] Relations of confidence will not work if there is nothing of importance to confide.[36]

It should be emphasized, then, that the argument is by no means that the degree of self-disclosure involved in confession is in itself a bad thing. Indeed there is a good deal of reason to believe that it is a very good thing, and a very important thing for the individual. It is of course a commonplace of religion that confession and repentance are a medicine for the soul. They are the source of God's forgiveness.[37] Further it has been argued quite cogently that a capacity for self-disclosure is not only a symptom of a healthy personality but a means to achieve it. The point is that it is impossible to know oneself and to grow as a person unless one has the opportunity to *be* and *act* oneself to at least some other person or people.[38]

But this should not lead one to believe that there is nothing wrong with *compulsory* self-incrimination; quite the contrary is the case. First of all, it is voluntary confession which has this value, not compulsory.[39] Then, too, the sort of self-disclosure that seems to be essential to health is not the baring of one's soul before the whole world but exposure

to a few in the context of trust and warmth established by love, friendship, or religious faith, while the facade of one's role remains intact
for all others.[40] Further, the very fact that confession has such significance for the internal life of the individual is a strong argument
against allowing the authorities involved with the criminal law to use
coercion in order to get it. It is wrong to use this as a means of
convicting people for very much the same reasons that it is wrong to
use compulsory psychological conditioning directed at reforming the
criminal as a part of the punishment of those who are convicted.[41]
Such an approach may be thought to be more humane than the more
traditional concept of punishment, but, as Louch pointed out:

> To act humanely requires not just an environment or method of a certain
> kindliness, it requires also a special attitude on the part of the judge, jailor,
> or therapist. A person must be thought to be in rightful possession of his
> desires, needs, and beliefs, however much we may wish him to change them
> or give them up, or however deeply we feel them wrong or bad. We may
> attempt to argue and persuade; and with major breaches of the legal code
> we may be forced to confine him for his actions. But we do not subject him
> to devices that will insure that his actions will be no more than automatic
> responses to our commands. This, however, is the promise of a truly scientific
> therapy.[42]

The criminal process necessarily involves enormous invasions of
privacy, but it can still be a perfectly appropriate way of dealing with
the person who is regarded as a fully responsible free agent who has
done something wrong. This is not true, however, of treatment which
probes the conscience and seeks directly to change the internal processes of the personality. Such treament is inconsistent with the treatment of the individual as a responsible agent. It denies him the right
to set his own conscience in order. He may of course seek help if he
chooses; he may even put himself under a religious discipline which
involves the obligation to confess. But all of this is for him to determine
for himself. The processes by which a man comes to know himself,
by which his conscience is formed and he is brought to come to terms
with it, ought not to be forced.[43]
While it is true that the early history of the privilege suggests that
it took root mainly because it was a useful instrument in the struggle
for religious liberty, some early proponents did put forward arguments very much like the one developed here. There is, for example,
this striking passage in the attack on the ex officio oath, written by
Cartwright and other Puritan leaders, in the late sixteenth century:

> Much more is it equall that a mans owne private faults should remayne private
> to God and him selfe till the lord discover them. And in regard of this righte

consider howe the lord ordained wittnesses whereby the magistrate should seeke into the offenses of his subjects and not by oathe to rifle the secretts of theare hearts.[44]

Such statements as this do make it look as if this was a factor in the development of the privilege, though not so well articulated as the concern for religious liberty, or the sense that it is inhuman to require a man to be the instrument of his own punishment. But my major interest here is not historical. I have not been so much concerned with showing that the justification I am setting forth was a major historical factor in the development of the privilege as with establishing its soundness and significance for the present.

II

I would now like to undertake a consideration of some of the problems involved in delimiting the precise scope of the privilege in the light of the reasoning developed in the previous section. In some cases the lines which have been drawn by the Supreme Court gain new validity under such scrutiny; in others, they are cast into doubt. In each case it must, of course, be remembered that the rationale developed here may be only one of a number of reasons for applying the privilege and that they may not all point in the same direction.

One critical point at which a rather questionable limitation on the privilege would gain significant support from the privacy argument involves the testimonial-nontestimonial evidence distinction. *Schmerber v. California*[45] contains the major reaffirmation of the distinction to be found in the opinions of the Supreme Court in recent years. Yet a careful examination of Justice Brennan's opinion in that case offers almost nothing in the way of a justification of it.

The *Schmerber* case involved the constitutionality of the use, in evidence, of a blood sample taken from the defendant without his consent.[46] Justice Brennan's opinion bases the decision that such use does not violate the prohibition against compelled self-incrimination on the finding that the evidence is not testimonial in nature.[47] But Brennan admits that he has some difficulty squaring this decision with the rationale of the privilege as he understands it. "If the scope of the privilege coincided with the complex of values it helps to protect," he wrote, "we might be obliged to conclude that the privilege was violated."[48]

Brennan gets his statement of the "complex of values" to be protected by the privilege from the opinion of the court in *Miranda*, where they are summed up in "one overriding thought: the constitutional foundation underlying the privilege is the respect a government—state or federal—must accord to the dignity and integrity of its citizens. To maintain a 'fair state-individual balance,' to require the government 'to shoulder the entire load,' . . . to respect the inviolability of the human personality, our accusatory system of criminal justice demands that the government seeking to punish an individual produce the evidence against him by its own independent labors, rather than by the cruel, simple expedient of compelling it from his own mouth."[49]

There is the suggestion here that it might be possible to show that a single concept, the concept of the "dignity and integrity" of the citizen, unifies all of the policies used to support the privilege and might indeed be found to unify the whole constitutional structure of civil rights and liberties into a coherent "scheme of ordered liberty."[50] But this is only a suggestion, and what we in fact get in the language that follows is no more than a pasting together of bits and pieces of the various policies into a typically vague and rhetorical declaration.

Having accepted this broad and imprecise formulation, Brennan assumes that the case before him would fall within its general area of operation.[51] When he decides that, in spite of this, the privilege does not apply here, he can find no other reason for doing so than the fact that "history and a long line of authorities" have limited its application to cases of testimonial evidence.[52] We might surmise that what really lies behind the division is the feeling that the broad-ranging radiations of the policy behind the privilege must at some point be limited to accommodate the needs of law enforcement and that, lacking any clear guidance from principle on where the line ought to be drawn, it is just as well to leave it where it has already been drawn, though arbitrarily, by history. But we are not given even this much of an explanation by Justice Brennan.

The opinion as it stands in fact seems to deserve the criticism made of it by Justice Black in dissent. Brennan has taken a section of the Bill of Rights, which has generally been construed quite liberally, and given it "a construction that would generally be considered too narrow and technical even in the interpretation of an ordinary commercial contract."[53] Surely a major limitation of an important part of the Bill of Rights ought to have more than history to support it. The point was made by Holmes in a well-known passage: "It is revolting to have no better reason for a rule of law than that it was so laid down in the time of Henry IV."[54]

The privacy argument developed here would, however, put the limitation of the privilege to testimonial evidence on a much firmer foundation. The personal revelations with which it is concerned could only come out in some form of speech or writing by the individual involved. Such other sorts of personal evidence as fingerprints and bloodtests could not possibly come within the ambit of the policy of privacy as it has been understood here.

Of course, the other policies behind the privilege would be applicable in the *Schmerber* case, as they would be in cases involving fingerprints and the line-up. If the policy of avoiding the cruelty involved in requiring a man to lend a hand in his own undoing is to be rigorously applied, and if the process of ridding criminal procedure of all elements which do not fit into the accusatorial framework is carried to its drily logical extreme, then all such forms of compelled cooperation by the defendant must be forbidden.[55] But if it is felt, as the court obviously does feel, that these policies have a force which is less than absolutely overwhelming and that they may at times be overcome by the opposing need for an efficient system of crime control, then it becomes crucially important that the privacy argument extends only to cases of communication and no further. The testimonial-nontestimonial line ceases to be arbitrary and becomes a meaningful limit between the core area of the privilege, in which all three of the guiding policies combine to support it, and the periphery, where only two of the policies are relevant and one is wholly absent.

In fact, the particular privacy interest with which we are concerned here would be present only in cases in which there was a full confession, or something close to it. It would not, for example, have direct relevance in those cases in which a man's testimony is used against him to the extent of providing clues which might lead the police to evidence of his guilt. This does not mean, however, that we ought necessarily to follow Wigmore's advice[56] and end the long tradition of extending the privilege to such cases.[57] Not only would the other two important policies behind the privilege point toward a continuation of this broader coverage, it might even be necessary to the complete security of the privacy interest itself. The line to be drawn between questioning which would elicit a full or partial confession and questioning which would only give clues, will in practice be a fine one. The core area might be satisfactorily secure in this case only if we allow the privilege in periphery as well.[58] This would, however, be an area in which more flexibility in the decision to grant or withhold the privilege would, obviously, be acceptable.

Another area of considerable difficulty in the application of the privilege is that of required records and reports.[59] We are dealing here with situations in which the government requires that the citizen divulge information about himself which is (at least purportedly) unrelated to criminal prosecution but which, under the particular circumstances, turns out to be incriminating.

The first point to make here is that the fact that we are dealing with written rather than verbal statements does not make a great deal of difference. To consider the clearest case, it is true that there would be some difference between the degree of humiliation and anguish experienced by a man who made a confession orally in court and that felt by a man who had his written confession read out before the court in his presence; but the difference would surely be marginal. The disclosure of a written document can be just as serious a violation of privacy as the enforcement of a duty to speak.[60]

The question is, just how private is the written document in question? If the information in the report or record is of a sort which the person involved would readily and regularly disclose to anyone with whom he would normally come into contact, and which he now seeks to withhold from the government just because he doesn't want to be punished for the offenses it reveals, there is no significant privacy interest to be considered. If, on the other hand, the information is of a sort which would normally be kept private and revealed only in the context of a confidential relationship, if the individual is being required, for example, to keep a private diary and reveal it to the government so that it can be examined for expressions of self-incrimination, then the privacy interest is very strong.[61]

The Supreme Court has in fact drawn lines in this area which seem to accord quite closely with the privacy approach, though the grounds for drawing them have not been articulated with any degree of clarity. The *Shapiro*[62] case, which had previously been regarded as the ruling decision in the field, had been read by many as holding that the privilege could never be used to block production of any records which the government required a person to keep.[63] So understood, the doctrine of *Shapiro* would in fact nullify the privilege to the extent that the government required people to keep records of their activities, as Justice Jackson warned in dissent.[64] But the effect of *Shapiro* was severely limited in the recent case of *Marchetti* v. *United States*.[65]

The *Marchetti* opinion does not contain any extended critique of the doctrine of *Shapiro,* rather it turns on the factual distinctions between the two. The court finds it "unnecessary for present purposes to pursue in detail the question . . . of what 'limits . . . the government cannot constitutionally exceed in requiring the keeping of records.' It is enough that there are significant points of difference between the situations here and in *Shapiro*."[66]

The differences between the two cases are in fact very large. Shapiro was required to keep, and disclose records of his business which he would normally have kept in any case, in order to facilitate the enforcement of OPA regulations.[67] Marchetti, a resident of a state in which gambling was illegal, was required, by a federal tax statute, to register as a gambler and then to keep records of his gambling activities for official inspection.[68] The court discussed these differences in terms of three major factors. First, it was pointed out that the records required in *Shapiro*, unlike those in *Marchetti*, were of a sort "customarily kept" by the person involved. Second, the records in *Marchetti* could in no sense have been thought to have such "public aspects" as might be present in the records of a business covered by a system of price control. Finally, the *Shapiro* case involved the regulation of lawful business, while the statute in *Marchetti* was carefully designed to apply to illegal activity,[69] the major forms of lawful gambling being omitted from its coverage.[70]

All of these considerations point to the need to protect privacy in one case but not in the other. The implications of all of them taken together is, I think, that while Shapiro was asked to disclose information which he would normally be willing to make generally available, Marchetti was being asked to reveal what he would otherwise make known only to himself and his closest confederates. To the extent that the privilege against self-incrimination is understood as a ban on forcing people to make public disclosure of information about themselves which they would otherwise keep confidential, it would be applicable in *Marchetti* and not in *Shapiro*.[71]

A related aspect of the *Marchetti* case which raises rather different problems is the provision of the statute which, in effect, requires anyone who intends to gamble to register as a gambler. Previous cases had held that this sort of "prospective" incrimination does not come under the privilege because it involves only the expression of the intention to commit a crime and not the confession of a crime which has already been committed.[72] The court in *Marchetti* rejects this reasoning and finds the privilege applicable because registration does clearly "enhance the likelihood of their prosecution for future acts."[73]

The privacy approach developed here suggests a different analysis and a different basis for deciding that the privilege should apply. The particular privacy interest with which we have been dealing is obviously not present here. This cannot be a matter of compelling someone to make a public condemnation of himself for a crime he has committed, for no crime has yet been committed. What we do have here, however, is compulsion used to get a public revelation of the intention to commit a crime, and this surely involves serious problems of invasion of privacy as well. In fact, it apparently involves almost the same sort of disclosure of the self as the admission of the crime. A serious moral judgment of one's own character is implied in both cases, though the sense of self-degradation may not be as severe in the case of the admission of the intention as in the case of the admission of the act.[74] Indeed, the invasion of privacy is in other respects more serious in the prospective case, as the person involved has not yet revealed himself in overt action.

The perspective developed here would have its greatest impact in those cases where the privilege has not been allowed because there is no danger of prosecution arising from the confession. The absence of this danger would have no effect whatsoever on the relevance of the privacy argument.[75] Unlike the other arguments, it retains its force in the face of acquittal, conviction, pardon, or grant of immunity. The invasion of privacy is there whether there is any danger of punishment or not. It is indeed in the dissents from the prevailing doctrine that a grant of immunity defeats the privilege that the privacy argument is most likely to be expressed, as it was, for example, by Justice Douglas in his Ullman dissent:

The guarantee against self-incrimination contained in the Fifth Amendment is not only a protection against conviction and prosecution but a safeguard of conscience and human dignity and freedom of expression as well. My view is that the Framers put it well beyond the power of Congress to *compel* anyone to confess his crimes. The evil to be guarded against was partly self-accusation under legal compulsion. But that was only a part of the evil. The conscience and dignity of man were also involved.[76]

The case of the person who has already been convicted of a crime may be of particular concern in this respect. There is evidence that a convict who has confessed and shown contrition may receive more favorable treatment from the authorities in sentencing and parole decisions.[77] Far from being a matter wholly outside the ambit of the privilege, this is perhaps the clearest possible violation of the privacy interest we are considering, involving, as Professor Mansfield points out, "penetration into the mind and personality and suggesting notorious practices in other political systems."[78] In the case of a person accused of a crime, the purpose of the authorities in compelling a confession is simply to get the facts, and the expression of self-condemnation and contrition which is likely to accompany the facts is generally no more than an unintended consequence of that effort. But in the case of a person who has been convicted, the whole purpose is to get that expression of self-contempt; the invasion of privacy is not incidental to some other governmental purpose, it is the point of the exercise. Governmental authority is being used for the express purpose of shaping the conscience of the individual. Nothing could be more repugnant to the principle with which we are concerned.

Conclusion

It may be that the Fifth Amendment will survive the attacks now being made upon it, even if the case in its favor remains in its current questionable state. The civil libertarians who have made the fight to save it will then probably breathe a sigh of relief and accomplishment, secure in the feeling that they have done their job well in helping to retain an ancient and rather obscure part of that machinery which, whatever else might be said for or against it, at least makes it harder for the authorities to get people convicted of crimes. But this seems to me in fact to be a very short-sighted view. What it misses is the fact that the punishment of people who intentionally injure the rights of others is an inseparable part of a society of free men, and that the deprivation of liberty to which the victim of a crime is subjected is at least as serious as that involved in jailing the criminal. It is fraudulent to retain a piece of this due process machinery in the name of civil liberty unless we have a good reason for doing so. If we do not, we may in fact be perpetuating a situation in which the liberty of the citizen considered from the broadest perspective is the loser.

It is because of this that I believe it is incumbent upon us to give good reasons whenever we introduce or maintain in existence a principle of law which does make it harder to convict people, and particularly if it gives more favorable treatment to the presumptively guilty than to the presumptively innocent. I have tried here to develop a good reason for retaining the privilege against self-incrimination, which is admittedly a guilty man's privilege. I have tried to show that the privilege, at least in its core application, is a necessary part of a system of criminal law which is based on a respect for individual dignity. If that is so, then it is worth fighting for.

NOTES

1 See, e.g., Judge Friendly's proposal to amend the Fifth Amendment (*New York Times*, November 10, 1968, sec. 1, p. 73). The classic attack is contained in J. Bentham, "A Rationale of Judicial Evidence," quoted in John H. Wigmore, *Evidence*, 10 vols. (3d ed.; Boston: Little, Brown & Co., 1940), 8:305–7 (hereafter cited as Wigmore).

2 See L. W. Levy, *Origins of the Fifth Amendment* (New York: Oxford University Press, 1968).

3 Ibid., p. 430.

4 See the enumeration in Wigmore, *Evidence,* ed. J. T. McNaughton (rev. ed.; Boston: Little, Brown, & Co., 1961), 8:310–17 (hereafter cited as McNaughton).

5 Important efforts in this direction include Wigmore (n. 1 above), pp. 305–18; McNaughton (n. 4 above), pp. 310–18; Bernard D. Meltzer, "Required Records, the McCarran Act, and the Privilege against Self-Incrimination," *University of Chicago Law Review* 18 (1951): 687; Robert B. McKay, "Self-Incrimination and the New Privacy," in *Supreme Court Review,* ed. P. B. Kurland (Chicago: University of Chicago Press, 1967), p. 193.

6 See Wigmore (n. 1 above), p. 312; McNaughton (n. 4 above), p. 317; Meltzer (n. 5 above); McKay (n. 5 above), p. 209. Bentham attacks this as the "fox hunter's reason" (quoted in Wigmore [n. 1 above], p. 305).

7 See Levy (n. 2 above), pp. 159 and 170, for vivid examples of this approach in the early development of the privilege. See, also, e.g., David W. Louisell, "Criminal Discovery and Self-Incrimination," *California Law Review* 53 (1965): 89, 95. This is Bentham's "old woman's reason" (quoted in Wigmore [n. 1 above], p. 305).

8 See, e.g., McKay (n. 5 above), esp. pp. 210–14.

9 Ibid., and also pp. 14–26.

10 Meltzer's "Required Records . . ." (n. 5 above) and John Mansfield's "The Albertson Case: Conflict between the Privilege against Self-Incrimination and the Government's Need for Information" (in *Supreme Court Review,* ed. P. B. Kurland [Chicago: University of Chicago Press, 1966]) are both careful and sensitive efforts to track down the implications of current approaches to the privilege in its specific applications.

11 Charles Fried, "Privacy," *Yale Law Journal* 77 (1968): 475. See, also, A. F. Westin, *Privacy and Freedom* (New York: Atheneum Publishers, 1967), esp. pp. 52–63.

12 Fried (n. 11 above), p. 477.

13 Ibid., p. 482.

14 Ibid., pp. 478–85.

15 Ibid., p. 484.

16 On the distinction between rules and principles, see Ronald Dworkin, "The Model of Rules," *University of Chicago Law Review* 35 (1967): 14.

17 This is true, e.g., of religious beliefs (see Rule 30, *Uniform Rules of Evidence*).

18 See "Note, a Reexamination of the Fifth Amendment as Applied to Federal Registration of Gamblers: U.S. v. Costello," *UCLA Law Review* 14 (1967): 947, 954–56.

19 Fried (n. 11 above), p. 488.

20 Ibid.

21 Ibid.

22 Surely Mansfield (n. 10 above), p. 108, is right in asserting that this preference for the guilty is a likely source of dissatisfaction with the privilege.

23 Abe Fortas, "The Fifth Amendment: Nemo Tenetur Prodere Seipsum," *Cleveland Bar Association Journal* 25 (1954): 91, 98–100.
24 For development of this view of the criminal law, see Henry M. Hart, "The Aims of the Criminal Law," *Law and Contemporary Problems* (1958), p. 401; Herbert Morris, "Punishment for Thoughts," *Monist* 49 (1965): 342, 371–73.
25 Peter Winch, "The Universalizability of Moral Judgments," *Monist* 49 (1965): 196.
26 Ibid., p. 208.
27 Ibid., p. 212.
28 The answer to those who object to the privilege because it protects the privacy of the guilty more than that of the innocent lies here: we are dealing with a sort of privacy which is special to guilty men.
29 McNaughton (n. 4 above), p. 316, briefly considers a similar argument but rejects it because it only covers cases involving full confessions of serious crimes. I have attempted to answer this criticism on p. [250] above.
30 Henry Charles Lea, *A History of Auricular Confessions and Indulgences in the Latin Church* (Philadelphia: Lea Bros., 1896), pp. 5–6.
31 See ibid., 2:3–72.
32 See ibid., 1:168–226.
33 Ibid., 1:174–75.
34 See ibid., 1:168–226.
35 Mansfield (n. 10 above), pp. 129 ff., discusses such a hypothetical practice. See Levy (n. 2 above), p. 47, for a historical example of something very like it.
36 Fried (n. 11 above).
37 See Lea (n. 30 above), 1:76–105.
38 See Sidney Marshall Jourard, "Healthy Personality and Self-Disclosure," *Mental Hygiene* 43 (1959): 499. See, also, Erving Goffman, *The Presentation of Self in Everyday Life* (New York: Doubleday & Co., Anchor Books, 1959).
39 See Walter Fisher, "The Fifth Amendment and Forced Confession," *Christian Century* 71 (1954): 945.
40 See Goffman (n. 38 above).
41 See A. R. Louch, "Scientific Discovery and Legal Charge," *Monist* 49 (1965): 485.
42 Ibid., pp. 498–99.
43 See Mansfield (n. 10 above), p. 113, for a practical example of such a practice.
44 Levy (n. 2 above), p. 177.
45 U.S. Supreme Court Reports, ser. 384, p. 757.
46 Ibid., pp. 758–59.
47 Ibid., p. 765.
48 Ibid., p. 762.

49 Ibid., quoting Miranda v. Arizona, U.S. Supreme Court Reports (1966), ser. 384, p. 460.

50 Palko v. Connecticut, U.S. Supreme Court Reports (1937), ser. 302, pp. 324–25 (J. Cardozo).

51 Schmerber v. California (n. 45 above), p. 762.

52 Ibid., pp. 762–63.

53 Ibid., p. 777.

54 Oliver Wendell Holmes, "The Path of the Law," *Harvard Law Review* (1897), pp. 457, 469.

55 Meltzer (n. 5 above), p. 692.

56 Wigmore (n. 1 above), p. 359.

57 Counselman v. Hitchcock, U.S. Supreme Court Reports (1892), ser. 142, p. 547.

58 See McNaughton (n. 4 above), p. 372.

59 See, generally, Mansfield (n. 10 above) for a penetrating analysis of the problems in this area.

60 Ibid., pp. 135–37.

61 See "Note, Required Information and the Privilege against Self-Incrimination," *Columbia Law Review* 65 (1965): 681, 694–95.

62 U.S. Supreme Court Reports (1948), ser. 335, p. 1.

63 McKay (n. 5 above), pp. 215–17.

64 U.S. Supreme Court Reports (1948), ser. 335, pp. 70–71.

65 Supreme Court Reporter (1968), ser. 88, p. 697. See, also, Grosso v. United States, Supreme Court Reporter (1968), ser. 88, p. 709; and Haynes v. United States, Supreme Court Reporter (1968), ser. 88, p. 722.

66 Supreme Court Reporter (1968), ser. 88, p. 707.

67 U.S. Supreme Court Reports (1948), ser. 335, pp. 3–5.

68 Supreme Court Reporter, ser. 88, pp. 699–702.

69 Ibid., p. 707.

70 Ibid., p. 699.

71 See n. 61 above.

72 United States v. Kahringer, U.S. Supreme Court Reports (1953), ser. 345, p. 22; United States v. Lewis (1955), ser. 348, p. 419.

73 Supreme Court Reporter (1968), ser. 88, p. 706.

74 See Mansfield (n. 10 above), p. 152.

75 See McKay (n. 5 above), pp. 230–31.

76 Ullmann v. United States, U.S. Supreme Court Reports (1956), ser. 350, p. 440.

77 See Robert O. Dawson, "The Decision to Grant or Deny Parole: A Study of Parole Criteria in Law and Practice," *Washington University Law Quarterly* (1966), p. 243; also Mansfield (n 10 above), p. 111. See, also, Conway v. California Adult Authority, certiorari granted, U.S. Law Week, ser. 37, p. 3275 (U.S. January 28, 1969) (no. 211 misc.), is a case now before the Supreme Court in which this issue is raised.

78 While Mansfield (n. 10 above) assumes that such a case does not come

under the privilege as currently understood, he does regard it as falling within "earlier, broader notions of the privilege . . . which shielded against self-disgrace even when there was no danger of conviction" (p. 111). In support of this view, that the privilege was at one time applied to cases of self-infamation, see Levy (n. 2 above), pp. 317–18; for the opposite view, see Wigmore (n. 1 above), p. 327.

10

Intimacy and privacy

ROBERT S. GERSTEIN

Intimacy and privacy seem to go together. The vast majority of us seek isolation from outsiders for our experiences of intimacy and regard it as indecent for others to intrude upon them.

Why should this be so? A number of reasons suggest themselves. For one thing, people may simply not want to be distracted, any more than they do when they are involved in anything that is important and engrossing. For another, there may be things about the way they act in their intimate relationships which they want to hide because these would discredit them in the eyes of others. Then there is the fact that intimate relationships have as an important part of their content the exclusive sharing among the intimates of things about themselves that no one else knows. The nature of the intimate relationship itself would naturally make up an important part of this exclusive stock of information. To allow outsiders to come in and find out about every detail of intimacy would therefore be seriously to impoverish the "moral capital" upon which the relationship can draw for its sustenance.[1]

I shall argue that the relationship between privacy and intimacy runs deeper than this. Specifically, I shall argue that a fuller analysis will show that intimate relationships simply could not exist if we did not continue to insist on privacy for them.[2]

I

An experience of intimacy is first of all an experience of a relationship in which we are deeply engrossed. It is an experience so intense that it wholly shapes our consciousness and action. We do not understand ourselves to be choosing to do this or that, or to be looking here or there as we choose. Rather, whatever we do, whatever we see, is a product of the experience in which we are taking part.

The experience in its most striking form is well described in the literature on religious ecstasy.[3] "These powers being united and gathered together and immersed and inflamed in Me, the body loses its feeling, so that the seeing eye sees not, and the hearing ear hears not. . . .[4] The soul neither sees nor distinguishes by seeing. . . .[5] There is no sense of anything: only fruition without understanding what that may be the fruition of which is granted. The senses are all occupied in this fruition in such a way, that not one of them is at liberty so as to be able to attend to anything else, whether outward or inward."[6]

It is not that the person is suddenly blinded or struck deaf, but that "the senses are occupied in this fruition. . . ." Nor is it simply that he suddenly finds himself looking at or hearing something, rather than consciously directing his attention to it. He does not find himself at all, but loses himself in the experience.

The awareness involved in having such an experience is very different from the awareness we gain from observation. When we observe we turn our attention toward things in order to learn about them. We turn them over to walk around them in order to examine their various aspects and find out what we want to know about them. What we mean by "observation" is perceiving things while maintaining our independence of them. We may observe understandingly, even sympathetically, but we must remain somewhat aloof from that which we are observing. If we lose ourselves in the experience, we relinquish our role as observers and become participants. We cease to be free to look around as we like to find out what we want to know; we see what the internal dynamic of the experience directs us to see, and we see it in the context of meaning established by the experience.

On the other hand, we cannot continue to be immersed in the experience of intimacy if we begin to observe ourselves or other things around us. We become aware of ourselves as observers separate from the object of observation. The fragile unity of the experience is broken. The intensity with which such experiences involve us shields us to some extent from such distraction, but once it occurs the experience dissolves. We cannot at the same time be lost in an experience and be observers of it. We can, of course, continue to understand its nature even after we cease to be immersed in it. One who has been lost in the intimate communion of prayer can, when he becomes self-consciously aware of what he is doing, continue to understand what true prayer is about, just as the outsider could. But now he is observing, considering, and appraising his own actions from the point of view of his understanding of prayer. In this sense even the person who observes himself at prayer is a kind of outsider as compared with the person who loses himself in prayer. The praying man's own appearance and actions have now become objects of observation for him.

For while he was lost in prayer these things were not objects of observation, either for himself or for any other. They were not intended to be seen, interpreted, and appraised. There was no question of whether they appeared to be appropriate expressions of prayer or not. It was not their function to "appear" to be anything to anyone. They were simply the spontaneous manifestations of intimate communion.

This is not to say that the observer could not come upon someone lost in prayer and see that his gestures and words relate to his own very intense experience of prayer. It is, rather, to make the point that there is a great difference between the way we experience our own actions when we intend them to be observed and understood by others and the way we relate to them when we are immersed in intimacy. When we intend our actions to be observed our sense of them is very much of the same sort as that of the observers. We watch ourselves to see what sort of a point our actions appear to be making, just as they watch us in order to get the point. This is even true of those cases in which we intend to be observed only by ourselves (as where we rehearse in front of a mirror before a public performance). In that case we can protest that our right to privacy is violated if someone breaks in on us, but the injury done is not the same as if we were lost in some form of intimate communion. Even if we meant the performance to be seen by no one else, at least we meant it to be seen. We intended our actions to be objects of observation, to express something to an audience, even though we have limited that audience to ourselves.

II

What are the implications of this distinction between observation and intimate communion for the claim to privacy for intimate relationships?

First of all, it is clear that anyone who intrudes uninvited on the intimacy of another person interferes with his autonomy in a very serious way. It is prima facie wrong to observe a person against his will at any time, because it violates his autonomous right to decide whether he will be observed or not.[7] But the wrong is far greater where the victim of the invasion was submerged in an intimate relationship and therefore did not intend to be observed at all, even by himself. Not only has the enlargement of his audience been forced upon him, but a fundamental change in the nature of his actions as well.

But this only gives us a strong argument for insisting that people ought to have a right not to be observed in such cases if they choose. The question is, Why would they choose to keep out the observer? I shall argue that they must choose to keep him out because having the experience of intimacy depends on their doing so.

When I have been involved in intimate communion and then am made suddenly aware that I am being observed, I also am suddenly brought to an awareness of my own actions as objects of observation. Where before I had the sense of my actions only as they flowed immediately from the development of the intimate relationship, I am now drawn into seeing them as they represent that relationship to the eye of the observer.

The temptation now to appraise the appearance I make, and to change my actions so that they will reflect to the observer what I would like them to, would certainly be very strong. To do this would obviously be to kill the spontaneity which is essential to intimacy. But even if I resisted this temptation, I would still be pulled out of the experience into the perspective from which meaning is to be read off from appearances. No longer would I experience the relationship from within; I would have become an observer of it. All possibility of spontaneous development would have been swallowed up in this consciousness of myself which has been forced upon me by the intrusion.

But the damage done by breaking in upon intimate communion may go far beyond the immediate disruption. At least in some important cases, the invasion can be deeply destructive of the relationship which underlies the particular moment of intimacy that is broken in upon. These are cases in which there is potentially a serious contradiction between the significance the intimacy has for the relationship out of which it grows and the meaning that the outsider could be expected to read off from it.

I understand intimacy to be characterized not only by its intensity, but also by the significance it has for those caught up in it. We would not call an encounter, no matter how intense, "intimate" if the people involved in it were simply using each other. An intimate relationship is one we value for its own sake. When we are intensely involved in it everything we do flows from it and is shaped by the meaning it has for us. The relationship is not a vehicle to be used for the things we want to do; rather, the things we do within the relationship are vehicles for its spontaneous expression.

In the example of sexual love, then, the love relationship shapes the sexual experience. Sexual pleasure in itself is subordinated to, and given a new significance by, the love relationship. Each caress and response is a spontaneous expression and development of the meaning the relationship has for us.

But genuine intimacy in sexual relationships is a very fragile thing. The problem is that they can so easily degenerate into self-indulgence. There is always the temptation to use the relationship for selfish satisfaction, destroying the context of intimacy. It is this temptation which forms the background against which the problem of the outsider must be seen. An awareness of the eye of the outsider imposes upon us an awareness of the externally observable, physical side of sexuality in isolation from the context of intimacy within which it could otherwise be a part of the natural growth of the relationship. To tolerate the intrusion is to use the vantage point of the outsider as a means to selfish exploitation and thus to degrade the relationship.[8] Resistance to the invasion of the outsider is therefore an important part of the defense against our own tendency to self-indulgence.

This is by no means to say that every outsider is a voyeur, or that anyone who tolerates an audience for his sexual relations necessarily has base motivations. It is simply to say that, when we feel the eye of the outsider upon us, the physical side of sexuality is transformed into an object of observation and uprooted from the wholeness of intimacy. Instead of being a heightened experience of the love relationship, the sexual encounter then becomes an attack upon it, an indulgence in the selfish satisfactions of using the body of another.

Scheler develops this point in his discussion of the functions of sexual shame. He argues that it is one of the functions of sexual shame to distract the lovers' attention from the sexual organs so that the way will be open for the experience of genuine intimacy. It is precisely our natural desire to indulge ourselves by focusing our attention on our physical sexuality that makes this so necessary. So, too, the natural inclination of the uninvolved observer to focus his attention on the sexual organs, and draw the eyes of the lovers there along with his own, makes it essential that he be excluded. It also makes it essential that these "private parts" in fact be kept private outside of the context of the intimate experience. We clothe ourselves because we must resist the temptation to join with others in the sensual indulgence of focusing our eyes on our physical sexuality. We must resist this, at least some of the time, if we are to develop a sense of ourselves beyond self-indulgence, a sense of ourselves which we can then bring to our intimate relationships with others.[9]

The same sort of thing may occur with religious ceremonies. Prayer, ritual sacrifice, dancing—all of these are physical means for the manifestation of the spiritual relationship experienced by the participant. Seen from outside, these ceremonials may be picturesque, grotesque, or very beautiful. From within, their significance derives purely from their religious meaning. This means that there will always be the threat of the degeneration of the religious act into a mere form, a hollow shell with nothing but its surface attractiveness to give it value. Again, the need to deal with this threat from within makes it necessary to resist observation from without. The presence of the onlooker, if it is not met with resistance, makes those involved in the ceremony accomplices in a concentration on the surface of things at the expense of inner meaning.[10]

Beyond this there is another sense in which the eye of the observer is destructive of intimacy. The observer is always using the outward appearance of intimacy in one way or another. In the most objectionable case he is exploiting it, disregarding the meaning it has for the participants, and taking voyeuristic pleasure in having others expose themselves before him. On the other hand, the use he makes of it might appear to be more morally neutral or even admirable. He might be watching out of detached and idle curiosity. He might be looking on in an effort to gain a sympathetic understanding of this type of intimate communion.

But in each case he is making use of the outward appearance of those involved in intimacy. Whether it is used as a means to sensual satisfaction or as a means to learn about the experience, it is still being used. And this is an affront to the relationship of which it is an intrinsic part. The physical manifestation of intimacy is consecrated to the relationship of which it is a natural outgrowth, and to turn it into a tool to be used to some end is to demean the relationship. The lovers may well feel that they are being exploited and degraded even if the onlooker has the greatest understanding and sympathy; the religious person may well feel a sense of desecration whenever what was to function purely as part of the expression of a relationship between himself and his God is made use of by others—even as a means of learning about that relationship.

Conclusion

I have tried to show that the connection between privacy and intimacy is a very deep one. For the reasons I have suggested, it seems to me that intimacy simply could not exist unless people had the opportunity for privacy. Excluding outsiders and resenting their uninvited intrusions are essential parts of having an intimate relationship.

Of course, excluding outsiders is not all there is to having an intimate relationship. The presence of outsiders is only one of the things which might make the growth of intimacy impossible; there are many others. We can and do often feel that we are ourselves outsiders observing the relationships in which we are involved, even when we are completely alone.

Most people probably believe, in fact, that it is a good idea for us to look at our relationships from the point of view of the outside observer sometimes. Self-consciousness is not in itself a bad thing, it is simply something we must get rid of for a time if we are to lose ourselves in intimacy, and we cannot do that unless we can have privacy.

NOTES

1 Charles Fried, "Privacy," *Yale Law Journal* 77 (1968): 475–93.
2 The analysis that follows owes much to Max Scheler, "Über Scham und Schamgefuhl," *Schriften aus dem Nachlass*, vol. 1 (Bern, 1957).
3 The examples are drawn from Margharita Laski, *Ecstasy: A Study of Some Secular and Religious Experiences* (Bloomington, Ind., 1961).
4 Quoted from Saint Catherine of Siena in ibid., p. 425.
5 Quoted from Plotinus in ibid., p. 426.
6 Quoted from Saint Teresa of Avila in ibid., p. 430.
7 See Stanley Benn, "Privacy, Freedom, and Respect for Persons," in *Privacy*, ed. J. R. Pennock and J. W. Chapman (New York, 1971).
8 I think this is the point Erving Goffman is making when he writes about "contaminative exposure" of the self and particularly of ". . . the individual's close relationship to significant others" (*Asylums: Essays on the Social Situation of Mental Patients and Other Inmates* [New York, 1961], p.31).
9 Scheler, 1:134–44.
10 Margaret Mead writes of the exclusion of outsiders from ceremonial events in Samoa, because their "presence as uninvolved spectators would be indecent. This attitude toward non-participants characterized all emotionally charged events" (*Coming of Age in Samoa* [New York, 1949], p.85).

11

The right to privacy

JUDITH JARVIS THOMSON

I

Perhaps the most striking thing about the right to privacy is that nobody seems to have any very clear idea what it is. Consider, for example, the familiar proposal that the right to privacy is the right "to be let alone." On the one hand, this doesn't seem to take in enough. The police might say, "We grant we used a special X-ray device on Smith, so as to be able to watch him through the walls of his house; we grant we trained an amplifying device on him so as to be able to hear everything he said; but we let him strictly alone: we didn't touch him, we didn't even go near him—our devices operate at a distance." Anyone who believes there is a right to privacy would presumably believe that it has been violated in Smith's case; yet he would be hard put to explain precisely how, if the right to privacy is the right to be let alone. And on the other hand, this account of the right to privacy lets in far too much. If I hit Jones on the head with a brick I have not let him alone. Yet, while hitting Jones on the head with a brick is surely violating some right of Jones', doing it should surely not turn out to violate his right to privacy. Else, where is this to end? Is *every* violation of a right a violation of the right to privacy?

It seems best to be less ambitious, to begin with at least. I suggest, then, that we look at some specific, imaginary cases in which people would say, "There, in that case, the right to privacy has been violated," and ask ourselves precisely why this would be said, and what, if anything, would justify saying it.

II

But there is a difficulty to be taken note of first. What I have in mind is that there may not be so much agreement on the cases as I implied.

Judith Jarvis Thomson, "The Right to Privacy," *Philosophy & Public Affairs* 4(4) (Summer):295–314, 1975. Copyright © 1975 by Princeton University Press. Reprinted by permission of Princeton University Press.

Suppose that my husband and I are having a fight, shouting at each other as loud as we can; and suppose that we have not thought to close the windows, so that we can easily be heard from the street outside. It seems to me that anyone who stops to listen violates no right of ours; stopping to listen is at worst bad, Not Nice, not done by the best people. But now suppose, by contrast, that we are having a quiet fight, behind closed windows, and cannot be heard by the normal person who passes by; and suppose that someone across the street trains an amplifier on our house, by means of which he can hear what we say; and suppose that he does this in order to hear what we say. It seems to me that anyone who does this does violate a right of ours, the right to privacy, I should have thought.

But there is room for disagreement. It might be said that in neither case is there a violation of a right, that both are cases of mere bad behavior—though no doubt worse behavior in the second case than in the first, it being very much naughtier to train amplifiers on people's houses than merely to stop in the street to listen.

Or, alternatively, it might be said that in both cases there is a violation of a right, the right to privacy in fact, but that the violation is less serious in the first case than in the second.

I think that these would both be wrong. I think that we have in these two cases, not merely a difference in degree, but a difference in quality: that the passerby who stops to listen in the first case may act badly, but violates no one's rights, whereas the neighbor who uses an amplifier in the second case does not merely act badly but violates a right, the right to privacy. But I have no argument for this. I take it rather as a datum in this sense: it seems to me there would be a mark against an account of the right to privacy if it did not yield the conclusion that these two cases do differ in the way I say they do, and moreover explain why they do.

But there is one thing perhaps worth drawing attention to here: doing so may perhaps diminish the inclination to think that a right is violated in both cases. What I mean is this. There is a familiar account of rights—I speak now of rights generally, and not just of the right to privacy—according to which a man's having a right that something shall not be done to him just itself consists in its being the case that anyone who does it to him acts badly or wrongly or does what he ought not do. Thus, for example, it is said that to have a right that you shall not be killed or imprisoned just itself consists in its being the case that if anyone does kill or imprison you, he acts badly, wrongly, does what he ought not do. If this account of rights were correct, then my husband and I would have a right that nobody shall stop in the street and listen to our loud fight, since anyone who does stop in the street and listen acts badly, wrongly, does what he ought not do. Just as we have a right that people shall not train amplifiers on the house to listen to our quiet fights.

But this account of rights is just plain wrong. There are many, many things we ought not do to people, things such that if we do them to a person, we act badly, but which are not such that to do them is to violate a right of his. It is bad behavior, for example to be ungenerous and unkind. Suppose that you dearly love chocolate ice cream but that, for my part, I find that a little of it goes a long way. I have been given some and have eaten a little, enough really, since I don't care for it very much. You then, looking on, ask, "May I have the rest of your ice cream?" It would be bad indeed if I were to reply, "No, I've decided to bury the rest of it in the garden." I ought not do that; I ought to give it to you. But you have no right that I give it to you, and I violate no right of yours if I do bury the stuff.

Indeed, it is possible that an act which is not a violation of a right should be a far worse act than an act which is. If you did not merely want the ice cream but needed it, for your health perhaps, then my burying it would be monstrous, indecent, though still, of course, no violation of a right. By contrast, if you snatch it away, steal it, before I can bury it, then while you violate a right (the ice cream is mine, after all), your act is neither monstrous nor indecent—if it's bad at all, it's anyway not very bad.

From the point of view of conduct, of course, this doesn't really matter: bad behavior is bad behavior, whether it is a violation of a right or not. But if we want to be clear about *why* this or that bit of bad behavior is bad, then these distinctions do have to get made and looked into.

III

To return, then, to the two cases I drew attention to, and which I suggest we take to differ in this way: in one of them a right is violated, in the other not. It isn't, I think, the fact that an amplifying device is used in the one case, and not in the other, that is responsible for this difference. On the one hand, consider someone who is deaf: if he passes by while my husband and I are having a loud fight at an open window and turns up his hearing-aid so as to be able to hear us, it seems to me he no more violates our right to privacy than does one who stops to listen and can hear well enough without a hearing-aid. And on the other hand, suppose that you and I have to talk over some personal matters. It is most convenient to meet in the park, and we do so, taking a bench far from the path since we don't want to be overheard. It strikes a man to want to know what we are saying to each other in that heated fashion, so he creeps around in the bushes behind us and crouches back of the bench to listen. He thereby violates the right to privacy—fully as much as if he had stayed a hundred yards away and used an amplifying device to listen to us.

IV

The cases I drew attention to are actually rather difficult to deal with, and I suggest we back away from them for a while and look at something simpler.

Consider a man who owns a pornographic picture. He wants that nobody but him shall ever see the picture—perhaps because he wants that nobody shall know that he owns it, perhaps because he feels that someone else's seeing it would drain it of power to please. So he keeps it locked in his wall-safe, and takes it out to look at only at night or after pulling down the shades and closing the curtains. We have heard about his picture, and we want to see it, so we train our X-ray device on the wall-safe and look in. To do this is, I think, to violate a right of his—the right to privacy, I should think.

No doubt people who worry about violations of the right to privacy are not worried about the possibility that others will look at their *possessions*. At any rate, this doesn't worry them very much. That it is not nothing, however, comes out when one thinks on the special source of discomfort there is if a burglar doesn't go straight for the TV set and the silver, and then leave, but if he stops for a while just to look at things—e.g. at your love letters or at the mound of torn socks on the floor of your closet. The trespass and the theft *might* swamp everything else; but they might not: the burglar's merely looking around in that way might make the episode feel worse than it otherwise would have done.

So I shall suppose that we do violate this man's right to privacy if we use an X-ray device to look at the picture in his wall-safe. And now let us ask how and why.

To own a picture is to have a cluster of rights to respect of it. The cluster includes, for example, the right to sell it to whomever you like, the right to give it away, the right to tear it, the right to look at it. These rights are all "positive rights": rights to do certain things to or in respect of the picture. To own a picture is also to have certain "negative rights" in respect of it, that is, rights that others shall not do certain things to it—thus, for example, the right that others shall not sell it or give it away or tear it.

Does owning a picture also include having the negative right that others shall not look at it? I think it does. If our man's picture is good pornography, it would be pretty mingy of him to keep it permanently hidden so that nobody but him shall ever see it—a nicer person would let his friends have a look at it too. But he is within his rights to hide it. If someone is about to tear his picture, he can snatch it away: it's his, so he has a right that nobody but him shall tear it. If someone is about to look at his picture, he can snatch it away or cover it up: it's his, so he has a right that nobody but him shall look at it.

It is important to stress that he has not merely the right to snatch the picture away in order that nobody shall tear it, he has not merely the right to do everything he can (within limits) to prevent people from tearing it, he has also the right that nobody *shall* tear it. What I have in mind is this. Suppose we desperately want to tear his picture. He locks it in his wall-safe to prevent us from doing so. And suppose we are so eager that we buy a penetrating long-distance picture-tearer: we sit quietly in our apartment across the street, train the device on the picture in the wall-safe, press the button—and lo! we have torn the picture. The fact that he couldn't protect his picture against the action of the device doesn't make it all right that we use it.

Again, suppose that there was a way in which he could have protected his picture against the action of the device: the rays won't pass through platinum, and he could have encased the picture in platinum. But he would have had to sell everything else he owns in order to pay for the platinum. The fact he didn't do this does not make it all right for us to have used the device.

We all have a right to do what we can (within limits) to secure our belongings against theft. I gather, however, that it's practically impossible to secure them against a determined burglar. Perhaps only hiring armed guards or sealing the house in solid steel will guarantee that our possessions cannot be stolen; and perhaps even these things won't work. The fact (if it's a fact) that we can't guarantee our belongings against theft; the fact (if it's a fact) that though we can, the cost of doing so is wildly out of proportion to the value of the things, and therefore we don't; neither of these makes it all right for the determined burglar to walk off with them.

Now I said that if a man owns a picture he can snatch it away or he can cover it up to prevent anyone else from *looking* at it. He can also hide it in his wall-safe. But I think he has a right, not merely to do what he can (within limits) to prevent it from being looked at: he has a right that it shall not be looked at—just as he has a right that it shall not be torn or taken away from him. That he has a right that it shall not be looked at comes out, I think, in this way: if he hides it in his wall-safe, and we train our X-ray device on the wall-safe and look in, we have violated a right of his in respect of it, and the right is surely the right that it shall not be looked at. The fact that he couldn't protect his picture against the action of an X-ray device which enables us to look at it doesn't make it all right that we use the X-ray device to look at it—just as the fact that he can't protect his picture against the action of a long-distance picture-tearing device which enables us to tear his picture doesn't make it all right that we use the device to tear it.

Compare, by contrast, a subway map. You have no right to take it off the wall or cover it up: you haven't a right to do whatever you can to prevent it from being looked at. And if you do cover it up, and if anyone looks through the covering with an X-ray device, he violates no right of yours: you do not have a right that nobody but you shall look at it—it's not *yours*, after all.

Looking at a picture doesn't harm it, of course, whereas tearing a picture does. But this doesn't matter. If I use your toothbrush I don't harm it; but you, all the same, have a right that I shall not use it.

However, to have a right isn't always to claim it. Thus, on any view to own a picture is to have (among other rights) the right that others shall not tear it. Yet you might want someone else to do this and therefore (1) invite him to, or (2) get him to whether he wants to or not—e.g. by carefully placing it where he'll put his foot through it when he gets out of bed in the morning. Or again, while not positively wanting anyone else to tear the picture, you might not care whether or not it is torn, and therefore you might simply (3) let someone tear it—e.g. when, out of laziness, you leave it where it fell amongst the things the children are in process of wrecking. Or again still, you might positively want that nobody shall tear the picture and yet in a fit of absent-mindedness (4) leave it in some place such that another person would have to go to some trouble if he is to avoid tearing it, or (5) leave it in some place such that another person could not reasonably be expected to know that it still belonged to anybody.

Similarly, you might want someone else to look at your picture and therefore (1) invite him to, or (2) get him to whether he wants to or not. Or again, while not positively wanting anyone else to look at the picture, you might not care whether or not it is looked at, and therefore you might simply (3) let it be looked at. Or again still, you might positively want that nobody shall look at the picture, and yet in a fit of absent-mindedness (4) leave it in some place such that another person would have to go to some trouble if he is to avoid looking at it (at least, avert his eyes) or (5) leave it in some place such that another person could not reasonably be expected to know that it still belonged to anybody.

In all of these cases, it is permissible for another person on the one hand to tear the picture, on the other to look at it: no right of the owner's is violated. I think it fair to describe them as cases in which, though the owner had a right that the things not be done, he *waived* the right: in cases (1), (2), and (3) intentionally, in cases (4) and (5) unintentionally. It is not at all easy to say under what conditions a man has waived a right—by what acts of commission or omission and in what circumstances. The conditions vary, according as the right is more or less important; and while custom and convention, on the one hand, and the cost of securing the right, on the other hand, play very important roles, it is not clear precisely what roles. Nevertheless there plainly is such a thing as waiving a right; and given a man has waived his right to a thing, we violate no right of his if we do not accord it to him.

There are other things which may bring about that although a man had a right to a thing, we violate no right of his if we do not accord it to him: he may have transferred the right to another or he may have forfeited the right or he may still have the right, though it is overridden by some other, more stringent right. (This is not meant to be an exhaustive list.) And there are also some circumstances in which it is not clear what should be said. Suppose someone steals your picture and invites some third party (who doesn't know it's yours) to tear it or look at it; or suppose someone takes your picture by mistake, thinking it's his, and invites some third party (who doesn't know it's yours) to tear it or look at it; does the *third* party violate a right of yours if he accepts the invitation? A general theory of rights should provide an account of all of these things.

It suffices here, however, to stress one thing about rights: a man may have had a right that we shall not do a thing, he may even still have a right that we shall not do it, consistently with its being the case that we violate no right of his if we go ahead.

If this is correct, we are on the way to what we want. I said earlier that when we trained our X-ray device on the man's wall-safe in order to have a look at his pornographic picture, we violate a right of his, the right to privacy, in fact. It now turns out (if I am right) that we violated a property right of his, specifically the negative right that others shall not look at the picture, this being one of the (many) rights which his owning the picture consists of. I shall come back a little later to the way in which these rights interconnect.

V

We do not, of course, care nearly as much about our possessions as we care about ourselves. We do not want people looking at our torn socks; but it would be much worse to have people watch us make faces at ourselves in the mirror when we thought no one was looking or listen to us while we fight with our families. So you might think I have spent far too much time on that pornographic picture.

But in fact, if what I said about pornographic pictures was correct, then the point about ourselves comes through easily enough. For if we have fairly stringent rights over our property, we have very much more stringent rights over our own persons. None of you came to possess your knee in exactly the way in which you came to possess your shoes or your pornographic pictures: I take it you neither bought nor inherited your left knee. And I suppose you could not very well sell your left knee. But that isn't because it isn't yours to sell—some women used to sell their hair, and some people nowadays sell their blood—but only because who'd buy a used left knee? For if anyone wanted to, you are the only one with a right to sell yours. Again, it's a nasty business to damage a knee; but you've a right to damage yours, and certainly nobody else has—its being your left knee includes your having the right that nobody else but you shall damage it. And, as I think, it also includes your having the right that nobody else shall touch it or look at it. Of course you might invite somebody to touch or look at your left knee; or you might let someone touch or look at it; or again still, you might in a fit of absent-mindedness leave it in some place such that another person would have to go to some trouble if he is to avoid touching or looking at it. In short, you might waive your right that your left knee not be touched or looked at. But that is what doing these things would be: waiving a right.

I suppose there are people who would be deeply distressed to learn that they had absent-mindedly left a knee uncovered, and that somebody was looking at it. Fewer people would be deeply distressed to learn that they had absent-mindedly left their faces uncovered. Most of us wouldn't, but Moslem women would; and so might a man whose face had been badly disfigured, in a fire, say. Suppose you woke up one morning and found that you had grown fangs or that you no longer had a nose; you might well want to claim a right which most of us so contentedly waive: the right that your face not be looked at. That we have such a right comes out when we notice that if a man comes for some reason or another to want his face not to be looked at, and if he therefore keeps it covered, and if we then use an X-ray device in order to be able to look at it through the covering, we violate a right of his in respect of it, and the right we violate is surely the right that his face shall not be looked at. Compare again, by contrast, a subway map. No matter how much you may want a subway map to not be looked at, if we use an X-ray device in order to be able to look at it through the covering you place over it, we violate no right of yours: you do not have a right that nobody but you shall look at it—it is not *yours*, after all.

Listening, I think, works in the same way as looking. Suppose you are an opera singer, a great one, so that lots of people want to listen to you. You might sell them the right to listen. Or you might invite them to listen or let them listen or absent-mindedly sing where they cannot help but listen. But if you have decided you are no longer willing to be listened to; if you now sing only quietly, behind closed windows and carefully sound-proofed walls; and if somebody trains an amplifier on your house so as to be able to listen, he violates a right, the right to not be listened to.

These rights—the right to not be looked at and the right to not be listened to[1]—are analogous to rights we have over our property. It sounds funny to say we have such rights. They are not mentioned when we give lists of rights. When we talk of rights, those that come to mind are the grand ones: the right to life, the right to liberty, the right to not be hurt or harmed, and property rights. Looking at and listening to a man do not harm him, but neither does stroking his left knee harm him, and yet he has a right that it shall not be stroked without permission. Cutting off all a man's hair while he's asleep will not harm him, nor will painting his elbows green; yet he plainly has a right that these things too shall not be done to him. These un-grand rights seem to be closely enough akin to be worth grouping together under one heading. For lack of a better term, I shall simply speak of "the right over the person," a right which I shall take to consist of the un-grand rights I mentioned, and others as well.

When I began, I said that if my husband and I are having a quiet fight behind closed windows and cannot be heard by the normal person who passes by, then if anyone trains an amplifier on us in order to listen he violates a right, the right to privacy, in fact. It now turns out (if I am right) that he violates our right to not be listened to, which is one of the rights included in the right over the person.

I had said earlier that if we use an X-ray device to look at the pornographic picture in a man's wall-safe, we violate his right to privacy. And it then turned out (if I was right) that we violated the right that others shall not look at the picture, which is one of the rights which his owning the picture consists in.

It begins to suggest itself, then, as a simplifying hypothesis, that the right to privacy is itself a cluster of rights, and that it is not a distinct cluster of rights but itself intersects with the cluster of rights which the right over the person consists in and also with the cluster of rights which owning property consists in. That is, to use an X-ray device to look at the picture is to violate a right (the right that others shall not look at the picture) which is both one of the rights which the right to privacy consists in and also one of the rights which property-owner-ship consists in. Again, that to use an amplifying device to listen to us is to violate a right (the right to not be listened to) which is both one of the rights which the right to privacy consists in and also one of the rights which the right over the person consists in.

Some small confirmation for this hypothesis comes from the other listening case. I had said that if my husband and I are having a loud fight, behind open windows, so that we can easily be heard by the normal person who passes by, then if a passerby stops to listen, he violates no right of ours, and so in particular does not violate our right to privacy. Why doesn't he? I think it is because, though he listens to us, we have *let* him listen (whether intentionally or not), we have waived our right to not be listened to—for we took none of the conventional and easily available steps (such as closing the windows and lowering our voices) to prevent listening. But this would only be an explanation if waiving the right to not be listened to were waiving the right to privacy, or if it were at least waiving the only one among the rights which the right to privacy consists in which might plausibly be taken to have been violated by the passerby.

But for further confirmation, we shall have to examine some further violations of the right to privacy.

VI

The following cases are similar to the ones we have just been looking at. (a) A deaf spy trains on your house a bugging device which pro-duces, not sounds on tape, but a typed transcript, which he then reads. (Cf. footnote 1.) (b) A blind spy trains on your house an X-ray device which produces, not views of you, but a series of bas-relief panels, which he then feels. The deaf spy doesn't listen to you, the blind spy doesn't look at you, but both violate your right to privacy just as if they did.

It seems to me that in both cases there is a violation of that same right over the person which is violated by looking at or listening to a person. You have a right, not merely that you not be looked at or listened to but also that you not have your words transcribed, and that you not be modeled in bas-relief. These are rights that the spies violate, and it is these rights in virtue of the violation of which they violate your right to privacy. Of course, one may waive these rights: a teacher presumably waives the former when he enters the classroom, and a model waives the latter when he enters the studio. So these cases seem to present no new problem.

VII

A great many cases turn up in connection with information.

I should say straightaway that it seems to me none of us has a right over any fact to the effect that that fact shall not be known by others. You may violate a man's right to privacy by looking at him or listening to him; there is no such thing as violating a man's right to privacy by simply knowing something about him.

Where our rights in this area do lie is, I think here: we have a right that certain steps shall not be taken to find out facts, and we have a right that certain uses shall not be made of facts. I shall briefly say a word about each of these.

If we use an X-ray device to look at a man in order to get personal information about him, then we violate his right to privacy. Indeed, we violate his right to privacy whether the information we want is personal or impersonal. We might be spying on him in order to find out what he does all alone in his kitchen at midnight; or we might be spying on him in order to find out how to make puff pastry, which we already know he does in the kitchen all alone at midnight; either way his right to privacy is violated. But in both cases, the simplifying hypothesis seems to hold: in both cases we violate a right (the right to not be looked at) which is both one of the rights which the right to privacy consists in and one of the rights which the right over the person consists in.

What about torturing a man in order to get information? I suppose that if we torture a man in order to find out how to make puff pastry, then though we violate his right to not be hurt or harmed, we do not violate his right to privacy. But what if we torture him to find out what he does in the kitchen all alone at midnight? Presumably in that case we violate both his right to not be hurt or harmed and his right to privacy—the latter, presumably, because it was personal information we tortured him to get. But here too we can maintain the simplifying hypothesis: we can take it that to torture a man in order to find out personal information is to violate a right (the right to not be tortured to get personal information) which is both one of the rights which the right to privacy consists in and one of the rights which the right to not be hurt or harmed consists in.

And so also for extorting information by threat: if the information is not personal, we violate only the victim's right to not be coerced by threat; if it is personal, we presumably also violate his right to privacy—in that we violate his right to not be coerced by threat to give personal information, which is both one of the rights which the right to privacy consists in and one of the rights which the right to not be coerced by threat consists in.

I think it a plausible idea, in fact, that doing something to a man to get personal information from his is violating his right to privacy only if doing that to him is violating some right of his not identical with or included in the right to privacy. Thus writing a man a letter asking him where he was born is no violation of his right to privacy: writing a man a letter is no violation of any right of his. By contrast, spying on a man to get personal information is a violation of the right to privacy, and spying on a man for any reason is a violation of the right over the person, which is not identical with or included in (though it overlaps) the right to privacy. Again, torturing a man to get personal information is presumably a violation of the right to privacy, and torturing a man for any reason is a violation of the right not to be hurt or harmed, which is not identical with or included in (though it overlaps) the right to privacy. If the idea is right, the simplifying hypothesis is trivially true for this range of cases. If a man has a right that we shall not do such and such to him, then he has a right that we shall not do it to him in order to get personal information from him. And his right that we shall not do it to him in order to get personal information from him is included in both his right that we shall not do it to him, and (if doing it to him for this reason is violating his right to privacy) his right to privacy.

I suspect the situation is the same in respect of uses of information. If a man gives us information on the condition we shall not spread it, and we then spread it, we violate his right to confidentiality, whether the information is personal or impersonal. If the information is personal, I suppose we also violate his right to privacy—by virtue of violating a right (the right to confidentiality in respect of personal information) which is both one of the rights which the right to privacy consists in and one of the rights which the right to confidentiality consists in. The point holds whether our motive for spreading the information is malice or profit or anything else.

Again, suppose I find out by entirely legitimate means (e.g. from a third party who breaks no confidence in telling me) that you keep a pornographic picture in your wall-safe; and suppose that, though I know it will cause you distress, I print the information in a box on the front page of my newspaper, thinking it newsworthy: Professor Jones of State U. Keeps Pornographic Picture in Wall-Safe! Do I violate your right to privacy? I am, myself, inclined to think not. But if anyone thinks I do, he can still have the simplifying hypothesis: he need only take a stand on our having a right that others shall not cause us distress, and then add that what is violated here is the right to not be caused distress by the publication of personal information, which is one of the rights which the right to privacy consists in, and one of the rights which the right to not be caused distress consists in. Distress, after all, is the heart of the wrong (if there is a wrong in such a case): a man who positively wants personal information about himself printed in newspapers, and therefore makes plain he wants it printed, is plainly not wronged when newspapers cater to his want.

(My reluctance to go along with this is not due to a feeling that we have no such right as the right to not be caused distress: that we have such a right seems to me a plausible idea. So far as I can see, there is nothing special about physical hurts and harms; mental hurts and harms are hurts and harms too. Indeed, they may be more grave and long-lasting than the physical ones, and it is hard to see why we should be thought to have rights against the one and not against the other. My objection is, rather, that even if there is a right to not be caused distress by the publication of personal information, it is mostly, if not always, overridden by what seems to me a more stringent right, namely the public's right to a press which prints any and all information, personal or impersonal, which it deems newsworthy; and thus that in the case I mentioned no right is violated, and hence, a fortiori, the right to privacy is not violated.)[2]

VIII

The question arises, then, whether or not there are *any* rights in the right to privacy cluster which aren't also in some other right cluster. I suspect there aren't any, and that the right to privacy is everywhere overlapped by other rights. But it's a difficult question. Part of the difficulty is due to it's being (to put the best face on it) unclear just what is in this right to privacy cluster. I mentioned at the outset that there is disagreement on cases; and the disagreement becomes even more stark as we move away from the kinds of cases I've so far been drawing attention to which seem to me to be the central, core cases.

What should be said, for example, of the following?

(a) The neighbors make a terrible racket every night. Or they cook foul-smelling stews. Do they violate my right to privacy? Some think yes, I think not. But even if they do violate my right to privacy, perhaps all would be well for the simplifying hypothesis since their doing this is presumably a violation of another right of mine, roughly, the right to be free of annoyance in my house.

(b) The city, after a city-wide referendum favoring it, installs loud-speakers to play music in all the buses and subways. Do they violate my right to privacy? Some think yes, I think not. But again perhaps all is well: it is if those of us in the minority have a right to be free of what we (though not the majority) regard as an annoyance in public places.

(c) You are famous, and photographers follow you around, every-where you go, taking pictures of you. Crowds collect and stare at you. Do they violate your right to privacy? Some think yes, I think not: it seems to me that if you do go out in public, you waive your right to not be photographed and looked at. But of course you, like the rest of us, have a right to be free of (what anyone would grant was) annoyance in public places; so in particular, you have a right that the photographers and crowds not press in too closely.

(d) A stranger stops you on the street and asks, "How much do you weigh?" Or an acquaintance, who has heard of the tragedy, says, "How terrible you must have felt when your child was run over by that delivery truck!"[3] Or a cab driver turns around and announces, "My wife is having an affair with my psychoanalyst." Some think that your right to privacy is violated here; I think not. There is an element of coercion in such cases: the speaker is trying to force you into a re-lationship you do not want, the threat being your own embarrassment at having been impolite if you refuse. But I find it hard to see how we can be thought to have a right against such attempts. Of course the attempt may be an annoyance. Or a sustained series of such at-tempts may become an annoyance. (Consider, for example, an ac-quaintance who takes to stopping at your office *every morning* to ask if you slept well.) If so, I suppose a right *is* violated, namely, the right against annoyances.

(e) Some acquaintances of yours indulge in some very personal gossip about you.[4] Let us imagine that all of the information they share was arrived at without violation of any right of yours, and that none of the participants violates a confidence in telling what he tells. Do they violate a right of yours in sharing the information? If they do, there is trouble for the simplifying hypothesis, for it seems to me there is no right not identical with, or included in, the right to privacy cluster which they could be thought to violate. On the other hand, it seems to me they *don't* violate any right of yours. It seems to me we simply do not have rights against others that they shall not gossip about us.

(f) A state legislature makes it illegal to use contraceptives. Do they violate the right to privacy of the citizens of that state? No doubt certain techniques for enforcing the statute (e.g., peering into bedroom windows) would be obvious violations of the right to privacy; but is there a violation of the right to privacy in the mere enacting of the statute—in addition to the violations which may be involved in enforcing it? I think not. But it doesn't matter for the simplifying hypothesis if it is: making a kind of conduct illegal is infringing on a liberty, and we all of us have a right that our liberties not be infringed in the absence of compelling need to do so.

IX

The fact, supposing it a fact, that every right in the right to privacy cluster is also in some other right cluster does not by itself show that the right to privacy is in any plausible sense a "derivative" right. A more important point seems to me to be this: the fact that we have a right to privacy does not explain our having any of the rights in the right to privacy cluster. What I have in mind is this. We have a right to not be tortured. Why? Because we have a right to not be hurt or harmed. I have a right that my pornographic picture shall not be torn. Why? Because it's mine, because I own it. I have a right to do a somersault now. Why? Because I have a right to liberty. I have a right to try to preserve my life. Why? Because I have a right to life. In these cases we explain the having of one right by appeal to the having of another which includes it. But I don't have a right to not be looked at because I have a right to privacy; I don't have a right that no one shall torture me in order to get personal information about me because I have a right to privacy; one is inclined, rather, to say that it is because I have *these* rights that I have a right to privacy.

This point, supposing it correct, connects with what I mentioned at the outset: that nobody seems to have any very clear idea what the right to privacy is. We are confronted with a cluster of rights—a cluster with disputed boundaries—such that most people think that to violate at least any of the rights in the core of the cluster is to violate the right to privacy; but what have they in common other than their being rights such that to violate them is to violate the right to privacy? To violate these rights is to not let someone alone? To violate these rights is to visit indignity on someone? There are too many acts in the course of which we do not let someone alone, in the course of which we give affront to dignity, but in the performing of which we do not violate anyone's right to privacy. That we feel the need to find something in common to all of the rights in the cluster and, moreover, feel we haven't yet got it in the very fact that they *are* all in the cluster, is a consequence of our feeling that one cannot explain our having any of the rights in the cluster in the words: "Because we have a right to privacy."

But then if, as I take it, every right in the right to privacy cluster is also in some other right cluster, there is no need to find the that-which-is-in-common to all rights in the right to privacy cluster and no need to settle disputes about its boundaries. For if I am right, the right to privacy is "derivative" in this sense: it is possible to explain in the case of each right in the cluster how come we have it without ever once mentioning the right to privacy. Indeed, the wrongness of every violation of the right to privacy can be explained without ever once mentioning it. Someone tortures you to get personal information from you, and you have that right because you have the right to not be hurt or harmed—and it is because you have this right that what he does is wrong. Someone looks at your pornographic picture in your wall-safe? He violates your right that your belongings not be looked at, and you have that right because you have ownership rights—and it is because you have them that what he does is wrong. Someone uses an X-ray device to look at you through the walls of your house? He violates your right to not be looked at, and you have that right because you have rights over your person analogous to the rights you have over your property—and it is because you have these rights that what he does is wrong.

In any case, I suggest it is a useful heuristic device in the case of any purported violation of the right to privacy to ask whether or not the act is a violation of any other right, and if not whether the act *really* violates a right at all. We are still in such deep dark in respect of rights that any simplification at all would be well worth having.[5]

NOTES

I am grateful to the members of the Society for Ethical and Legal Philosophy for criticisms of the first draft of this paper. Alan Sparer made helpful criticisms of a later draft.

1 In "A Definition of Privacy," *Rutgers Law Review*, 1974, p. 281, Richard B. Parker writes:

> The definition of privacy defended in this article is that *privacy is control over when and by whom the various parts of us can be sensed by others.* By "sensed," is meant simply seen, heard, touched, smelled, or tasted. By "parts of us," is meant the parts of our bodies, our voices, and the products of our bodies. "Parts of us" also includes objects very closely associated with us. By "closely associated" is meant primarily what is spatially associated. The objects which are "parts of us" are objects we usually keep with us or locked up in a place accessible only to us.

The right to privacy, then, is presumably the right to this control. But I find this puzzling, on a number of counts. First, why *control?* If my neighbor invents an X-ray device which enables him to look through walls, then I should imagine I thereby lose control over who can look at me: going home and closing the doors no longer suffices to prevent others from doing so. But my right to privacy is not violated until my neighbor actually does train the device on the wall of my house. It is the actual looking that violates it, not the acquisition of power to look. Second, there *are* other cases. Suppose a more efficient bugging device is invented: instead of tapes, it produces neatly typed transcripts (thereby eliminating the middlemen). One who reads those transcripts does not *hear* you, but your right to privacy is violated just as if he does.

On the other hand, this article is the first I have seen which may be taken to imply (correctly, as I think) that there are such rights as the right to not be looked at and the right to not be listened to. And in any case, Professor Parker's interest is legal rather than moral: he is concerned to find a definition which will be useful in legal contexts. (I am incompetent to estimate how successful he is in doing this.)

I am grateful to Charles Fried for drawing my attention to this article.
2 It was Warren and Brandeis, in their now classic article, "The Right to Privacy," *Harvard Law Review*, 1890, who first argued that the law ought to recognize wrongs that are (they thought) committed in cases such as these. For a superb discussion of this article, see Harry Kalven, Jr., "Privacy in Tort Law—Were Warren and Brandeis Wrong?" *Law and Contemporary Problems*, Spring 1966.
3 Example from Thomas Nagel.
4 Example from Gilbert Harman.
5 Frederick Davis' article, "What Do We Mean by 'Right to Privacy'?" *South Dakota Law Review*, Spring 1959, concludes, in respect of tort law, that

> If truly fundamental interests are accorded the protection they deserve, no need to champion a right to privacy arises. Invasion of privacy is, in reality, a complex of more fundamental wrongs. Similarly, the individual's interest in privacy itself, however real, is derivative and a state better vouchsafed by protecting more immediate rights [p. 20]. . . . Indeed, one can logically argue that the concept of a right to privacy was never required in the first place, and that its whole history is an illustration

of how well-meaning but impatient academicians can upset the normal development of the law by pushing it too hard [p. 230].

I am incompetent to assess this article's claims about the law, but I take the liberty of warmly recommending it to philosophers who have an interest in looking further into the status and nature of the right to privacy.

12

Why privacy is important

JAMES RACHELS

According to Thomas Scanlon, the first element of a theory of privacy should be "a characterization of the special interest we have in being able to be free from certain kinds of intrusions." Since I agree that is the right place to begin, I shall begin there. Then I shall comment briefly on Judith Jarvis Thomson's proposals.

I

Why, exactly, is privacy important to us? There is no one simple answer to this question, since people have a number of interests that may be harmed by invasions of their privacy.

(a) Privacy is sometimes necessary to protect people's interests in competitive situations. For example, it obviously would be a disadvantage to Bobby Fischer if he could not analyze the adjourned position in a chess game in private, without his opponent learning his results.

(b) In other cases someone may want to keep some aspect of his life or behavior private simply because it would be embarrassing for other people to know about it. There is a splendid example of this in John Barth's novel *End of the Road*. The narrator of the story, Jake Horner, is with Joe Morgan's wife, Rennie, and they are approaching the Morgan house where Joe is at home alone:

"Want to eavesdrop?" I whispered impulsively to Rennie. "Come on, it's great! See the animals in their natural habitat."

Rennie looked shocked. "What for?"

"You mean you never spy on people when they're alone? It's wonderful! Come on, be a sneak! It's the most unfair thing you can do to a person."

James Rachels, "Why Privacy is Important," *Philosophy & Public Affairs* 4(4) (Summer):323–33, 1975. Copyright © 1975 by Princeton University Press. Reprinted by permission of Princeton University Press.

"You disgust me, Jake!" Rennie hissed. "He's just reading. You don't know Joe at all, do you?"

"What does that mean?"

"*Real* people aren't any different when they're alone. No masks. What you see of them is authentic."

. . . . Quite reluctantly, she came over to the window and peeped in beside me.

It is indeed the grossest of injustices to observe a person who believes himself to be alone. Joe Morgan, back from his Boy Scout meeting, had evidently intended to do some reading, for there were books lying open on the writing table and on the floor beside the bookcase. But Joe wasn't reading. He was standing in the exact center of the bare room, fully dressed, smartly executing military commands. About *face*! Right *dress*! 'Ten-*shun*! Parade *rest*! He saluted briskly, his cheeks blown out and his tongue extended, and then proceeded to cavort about the room—spinning, pirouetting, bowing, leaping, kicking. I watched entranced by his performance, for I cannot say that in my strangest moments (and a bachelor has strange ones) I have surpassed him. Rennie trembled from head to foot.[1]

The scene continues even more embarrassingly.

(c) There are several reasons why medical records should be kept private, having to do with the consequences to individuals of facts about them becoming public knowledge. "The average patient doesn't realize the importance of the confidentiality of medical records. Passing out information on venereal disease can wreck a marriage. Revealing a pattern of alcoholism or drug abuse can result in a man's losing his job or make it impossible for him to obtain insurance protection."[2]

(d) When people apply for credit (or for large amounts of insurance or for jobs of certain types) they are often investigated, and the result is a fat file of information about them. Now there is something to be said in favor of such investigations, for business people surely do have the right to know whether credit-applicants are financially reliable. The trouble is that all sorts of other information goes into such files, for example, information about the applicant's sex-life, his political views, and so forth. Clearly it is unfair for one's application for credit to be influenced by such irrelevant matters.

These examples illustrate the variety of interests that may be protected by guaranteeing people's privacy, and it would be easy to give further examples of the same general sort. However, I do not think that examining such cases will provide a complete understanding of the importance of privacy, for two reasons.

First, these cases all involve relatively unusual sorts of situations, in

which someone has something to hide or in which information about
a person might provide someone with a reason for mistreating him
in some way. Thus, reflection on these cases gives us little help in
understanding the value which privacy has in *normal* or *ordinary* situations. By this I mean situations in which there is nothing embarrassing or shameful or unpopular in what we are doing, and nothing
ominous or threatening connected with its possible disclosure. For
example, even married couples whose sex-lives are normal (whatever
that is), and so who have nothing to be ashamed of, by even the most
conventional standards, and certainly nothing to be blackmailed about,
do not want their bedrooms bugged. We need an account of the value
which privacy has for us, not only in the few special cases but in the
many common and unremarkable cases as well.

Second, even those invasions of privacy that *do* result in embarrassment or in some specific harm to our other interests are objectionable on other grounds. A woman may rightly be upset if her credit-
rating is adversely affected by a report about her sexual behavior
because the use of such information is unfair; however, she may also
object to the report simply because she feels—as most of us do—that
her sex-life is *nobody else's business.* This, I think, is an extremely important point. We have a "sense of privacy" which is violated in such
affairs, and this sense of privacy cannot adequately be explained merely
in terms of our fear of being embarrassed or disadvantaged in one
of these obvious ways. An adequate account of privacy should help
us to understand what makes something "someone's business" and
why intrusions into things that are "none of your business" are, as
such, offensive.

These considerations lead me to suspect that there is something
important about privacy which we shall miss if we confine our attention to examples such as (a), (b), (c), and (d). In what follows I will
try to bring out what this something is.

II

I want now to give an account of the value of privacy based on the
idea that there is a close connection between our ability to control
who has access to us and to information about us, and our ability to
create and maintain different sorts of social relationships with different people. According to this account, privacy is necessary if we
are to maintain the variety of social relationships with other people
that we want to have, and that is why it is important to us. By a "social
relationship" I do not mean anything especially unusual or technical;

I mean the sort of thing which we usually have in mind when we say of two people that they are friends or that they are husband and wife or that one is the other's employer.

The first point I want to make about these relationships is that, often, there are fairly definite patterns of behavior associated with them. Our relationships with other people determine, in large part, how we act toward them and how they behave toward us. Moreover, there are *different* patterns of behavior associated with different relationships. Thus a man may be playful and affectionate with his children (although sometimes firm), businesslike with his employees, and respectful and polite with his mother-in-law. And to his close friends he may show a side of his personality that others never see— perhaps he is secretly a poet, and rather shy about it, and shows his verse only to his best friends.

It is sometimes suggested that there is something deceitful or hypocritical about such differences in behavior. It is suggested that underneath all the role-playing there is the "real" person, and that the various "masks" that we wear in dealing with some people are some sort of phony disguise that we use to conceal our "true" selves from them. I take it that this is what is behind Rennie's remark, in the passage from Barth, that, "*Real* people aren't any different when they're alone. No masks. What you see of them is authentic." According to this way of looking at things, the fact that we observe different standards of conduct with different people is merely a sign of dishonesty. Thus the cold-hearted businessman who reads poetry to his friends is "really" a gentle poetic soul whose businesslike demeanor in front of his employees is only a false front; and the man who curses and swears when talking to his friends, but who would never use such language around his mother-in-law, is just putting on an act for her.

This, I think, is quite wrong. Of course the man who does not swear in front of his mother-in-law may be just putting on an act so that, for example, she will not disinherit him, when otherwise he would curse freely in front of her without caring what she thinks. But it may be that his conception of how he ought to behave with his mother-in-law is very different from his conception of how he may behave with his friends. Or it may not be appropriate for him to swear around *her* because "she is not that sort of person." Similarly, the businessman may be putting up a false front for his employees, perhaps because he dislikes his work and has to make a continual, disagreeable effort to maintain the role. But on the other hand he may be, quite comfortably and naturally, a businessman with a certain conception of how it is appropriate for a businessman to behave; and this conception is compatible with his also being a husband, a father, and a friend, with different conceptions of how it is appropriate to behave with his wife, his children, and his friends. There need be nothing dishonest or hypocritical in any of this, and neither side of his personality need be the "real" him, any more than any of the others.

It is not merely accidental that we vary our behavior with different people according to the different social relationships that we have with them. Rather, the different patterns of behavior are (partly) what define the different relationships; they are an important part of what makes the different relationships what they are. The relation of friendship, for example, involves bonds of affection and special obligations, such as the duty of loyalty, which friends owe to one another; but it is also an important part of what it means to have a friend that we welcome his company, that we confide in him, that we tell him things about ourselves, and that we show him sides of our personalities which we would not tell or show to just anyone.[3] Suppose I believe that someone is my close friend, and then I discover that he is worried about his job and is afraid of being fired. But, while he has discussed this situation with several other people, he has not mentioned it at all to me. And then I learn that he writes poetry, and that this is an important part of his life; but while he has shown his poems to many other people, he has not shown them to me. Moreover, I learn that he behaves with his other friends in a much more informal way than he behaves with me, that he makes a point of seeing them socially much more than he sees me, and so on. In the absence of some special explanation of his behavior, I would have to conclude that we are not as close as I had thought.

The same general point can be made about other sorts of human relationships: businessman to employee, minister to congregant, doctor to patient, husband to wife, parent to child, and so on. In each case, the sort of relationship that people have to one another involves a conception of how it is appropriate for them to behave with each other, and what is more, a conception of the kind and degree of knowledge concerning one another which it is appropriate for them to have. (I will say more about this later.) I do not mean to imply that such relationships are, or ought to be, structured in exactly the same way for everyone. Some parents are casual and easy-going with their children, while others are more formal and reserved. Some doctors want to be friends with at least some of their patients; others are businesslike with all. Moreover, the requirements of social roles may vary from community to community—for example, the role of wife may not require exactly the same sort of behavior in rural Alabama as it does in New York or New Guinea. And, the requirements of social roles may change: the women's liberation movement is making an attempt to redefine the husband-wife relationship. The examples that I have been giving are drawn, loosely speaking, from contemporary American society; but this is mainly a matter of convenience. The only point that I want to insist on is that *however* one conceives one's relations with other people, there is inseparable from that conception an idea of how it is appropriate to behave with and around them, and what information about oneself it is appropriate for them to have.

The point may be underscored by observing the new types of social institutions and practices sometimes make possible new sorts of human relationships, which in turn make it appropriate to behave around people, and to say things in their presence, that would have been inappropriate before. "Group therapy" is a case in point. Many psychological patients find the prospect of group therapy unsettling, because they will have to speak openly to the group about intimate matters. They sense that there is something inappropriate about this: one simply does not reveal one's deepest feelings to strangers. Our aspirations, our problems, our frustrations and disappointments are things that we may confide to our husbands and wives, our friends, and perhaps to some others—but it is out of the question to speak of such matters to people that we do not even know. Resistance to this aspect of group therapy is overcome when the patients begin to think of each other not as strangers but as *fellow members of the group.* The definition of a kind of relation between them makes possible frank and intimate conversation which would have been totally out of place when they were merely strangers.

All of this has to do with the way that a crucial part of our lives— our relations with other people—is organized, and as such its importance to us can hardly be exaggerated. Thus we have good reason to object to anything that interferes with these relationships and makes it difficult or impossible for us to maintain them in the way that we want to. Conversely, because our ability to control who has access to us, and who knows what about us, allows us to maintain the variety of relationships with other people that we want to have, it is, I think, one of the most important reasons why we value privacy.

First, consider what happens when two close friends are joined by a casual acquaintance. The character of the group changes; and one of the changes is that conversation about intimate matters is now out of order. Then suppose these friends could *never* be alone; suppose there were always third parties (let us say casual acquaintances or strangers) intruding. Then they could do either of two things. They could carry on as close friends do, sharing confidences, freely expressing their feelings about things, and so on. But this would mean violating their sense of how it is appropriate to behave around casual acquaintances or strangers. Or they could avoid doing or saying anything which they think inappropriate to do or say around a third party. But this would mean that they could no longer behave with one another in the way that friends do and further that, eventually, they would no longer *be* close friends.

Again, consider the differences between the way that a husband and wife behave when they are alone and the way they behave in the company of third parties. Alone, they may be affectionate, sexually intimate, have their fights and quarrels, and so on; but with others, a more "public" face is in order. If they could never be alone together, they would either have to abandon the relationship that they would otherwise have as husband and wife or else behave in front of others in ways they now deem inappropriate.[4]

These considerations suggest that we need to separate our associations, at least to some extent, if we are to maintain a system of different relationships with different people. Separation allows us to behave with certain people in the way that is appropriate to the sort of relationship we have with them, without at the same time violating our sense of how it is appropriate to behave with, and in the presence of, others with whom we have a different kind of relationship. Thus, if we are to be able to control the relationships that we have with other people, we must have control over who has access to us

We now have an explanation of the value of privacy in ordinary situations in which we have nothing to hide. The explanation is that, even in the most common and unremarkable circumstances, we regulate our behavior according to the kinds of relationships we have with the people around us. If we cannot control who has access to us, sometimes including and sometimes excluding various people, then we cannot control the patterns of behavior we need to adopt (this is one reason why privacy is an aspect of liberty) or the kinds of relations with other people that we will have. But what about our feeling that certain facts about us are "simply nobody else's business"? Here, too, I think the answer requires reference to our relationships with people. If someone is our doctor, then it literally is his business to keep track of our health; if someone is our employer, then it literally is his business to know what salary we are paid; our financial dealings literally are the business of the people who extend us credit; and so on.

In general, a fact about ourselves is someone's business if there is a specific social relationship between us which entitles them to know. We are often free to choose whether or not to enter into such relationships, and those who want to maintain as much privacy as possible will enter them only reluctantly. What we cannot do is accept such a social role with respect to another person and then expect to retain the same degree of privacy relative to him that we had before. Thus, if we are asked how much money we have in the bank, we cannot say, "It's none of your business," to our banker, to prospective creditors, or to our spouses, because their relationships with us do entitle them to know. But, at the risk of being boorish, we could say that to others with whom we have no such relationship.

<h1 style="text-align:center">III</h1>

Thomson suggests, "as a simplifying hypothesis, that the right to privacy is itself a cluster of rights, and that it is not a distinct cluster of rights but itself intersects with the cluster of rights which the right over the person consists of, and also with the cluster of rights which owning property consists of." This hypothesis is "simplifying" because it eliminates the right to privacy as anything distinctive.

"The right over the person" consists of such "un-grand" rights as the right not to have various parts of one's body looked at, the right not to have one's elbow painted green, and so on. Thomson understands these rights as analogous to property rights. The idea is that our bodies are *ours* and so we have the same rights with respect to them that we have with respect to our other possessions.

But now consider the right not to have various parts of one's body looked at. Insofar as this is a matter of *privacy*, it is not simply analogous to property rights; for the kind of interest we have in controlling who looks at what parts of our bodies is very different from the interest we have in our cars or fountain pens. For most of us, physical intimacy is a part of very special sorts of personal relationships. Exposing one's knee or one's face to someone may not count for us as physical intimacy, but exposing a breast, and allowing it to be seen and touched, does. Of course the details are to some extent a matter of social convention; that is why it is easy for us to imagine, say, a Victorian woman for whom an exposed knee would be a sign of intimacy. She would be right to be distressed at learning that she had absent-mindedly left a knee uncovered and that someone was looking at it— if the observer was not her spouse or her lover. By dissociating the body from ideas of physical intimacy, and the complex of personal relationships of which such intimacies are a part, we can make this "right over the body" seem to be nothing more than an un-grand kind of property right; but that dissociation separates this right from the matters that make *privacy* important.

Thomson asks whether it violates your right to privacy for acquaintances to indulge in "very personal gossip" about you, when they got the information without violating your rights, and they are not violating any confidences in telling what they tell. (See part VIII, case (e), in Thomson's paper.) She thinks they do not violate your right to privacy, but that if they do "there is trouble for the simplifying hypothesis."

This is, as she says, a debatable case, but if my account of why privacy is important is correct, we have at least some reason to think that your right to privacy can be violated in such a case. Let us fill in some details. Suppose you are recently divorced, and the reason your marriage failed is that you became impotent shortly after the wedding. You have shared your troubles with your closest friend, but this is not the sort of thing you want everyone to know. Not only would it be humiliating for everyone to know, it is none of their business. It is the sort of intimate fact about you that is not appropriate for strangers or casual acquaintances to know. But now the gossips have obtained the information (perhaps one of them innocently overheard your discussion with your friend; it was not his fault, so he did not violate your privacy in the hearing, but then you did not know he was within earshot) and now they are spreading it around to everyone who knows you and to some who do not. Are they violating your right to privacy? I think they are. If so, it is not surprising, for the interest involved in this case is just the sort of interest which the right to privacy typically protects. Since the right that is violated in this case is not also a property right, or a right over the person, the simplifying hypothesis fails. But this should not be surprising, either, for if the right to privacy has a different *point* than these other rights, we should not expect it always to overlap with them. And even if it did always overlap, we could still regard the right to privacy as a distinctive sort of right in virtue of the special kind of interest it protects.

NOTES

1 John Barth, *End of the Road* (New York, 1960), pp. 57–58.
2 Dr. Malcolm Todd, President of the A.M.A., quoted in the *Miami Herald*, 26 October 1973, p. 18-A.

3 My view about friendship and its relation to privacy is similar to Charles
   Fried's view in his book *An Anatomy of Values* (Cambridge, Mass., 1970).
4 I found this in a television program-guide in the *Miami Herald*, 21 October
   1973, p.17:

> "I think it was one of the most awkward scenes I've ever done," said actress Brenda
> Benet after doing a romantic scene with her husband, Bill Bixby, in his new NBC-
> TV series, "The Magician."
> "It was even hard to kiss him," she continued. "It's the same old mouth, but it
> was terrible. I was so abnormally shy; I guess because I don't think it's anybody's
> business. The scene would have been easier had I done it with a total stranger because
> that would be real acting. With Bill, it was like being on exhibition."

I should stress that, on the view that I am defending, it is *not* "abnormal
shyness" or shyness of any type that is behind such feelings. Rather, it is
a sense of what is appropriate with and around people with whom one has
various sorts of personal relationships. Kissing *another actor* in front of the
camera crew, the director, and so on, is one thing; but kissing *one's husband*
in front of all these people is quite another thing. What made Ms. Benet's
position confusing was that her husband *was* another actor, and the behavior that was permitted by the one relationship was discouraged by the
other.

13

Privacy, intimacy, and personhood

JEFFREY H. REIMAN

The Summer 1975 issue of *Philosophy & Public Affairs* featured three
articles on privacy, one by Judith Jarvis Thomson, one by Thomas
Scanlon in response to Thomson, and one by James Rachels in response to them both.[1] Thomson starts from the observation that "the
most striking thing about the right to privacy is that nobody seems to
have any very clear idea what it is" (p. 295) and goes on to argue that
nobody should have one—a very clear idea, that is. Her argument is
essentially that all the various protections to which we feel the right
to privacy entitles us are already included under other rights, such
as "the cluster of rights which the right over the person consists in
and also . . . the cluster of rights which owning property consists in"
(p. 306). After a romp through some exquisitely fanciful examples,
she poses and answers some questions about some of the kinds of
"invasions" we would likely think of as violations of the right to privacy:

> Someone looks at your pornographic picture in your wall-safe? He violates
> your right that your belongings not be looked at, and you have that right
> because you have ownership rights—and it is because you have them that
> what he does is wrong. Someone uses an X-ray device to look at you through
> the walls of your house? He violates your right not to be looked at, and you
> have that right because you have rights over your person analogous to the
> rights you have over your property—and it is because you have these rights
> that what he does is wrong [p. 313].

From this she concludes that the right to privacy is "derivative,"
and therefore that "there is no need to find the that-which-is-in-common to all rights in the right to privacy cluster and no need to settle
disputes about its boundaries" (p. 313). In other words, we are right
not to have any very clear idea about what the right is, and we ought

not spin our wheels trying to locate some unique "something" that is protected by the right to privacy. Now I think Thomson is wrong about this—and, incidentally, so do Scanlon and Rachels, although I am inclined to believe they think so for the wrong reasons.

Thomson's argument is a large non sequitur balanced on a small one. She holds that the right to privacy is "derivative" in the sense that each right in the cluster of rights to privacy can be explained by reference to another right and thus without recourse to the right to privacy. This is the little non sequitur. The easiest way to see this is to recognize that it is quite consistent with the notion that the other rights (that is, the rights over one's person and one's property) are— in whole or in part—expressions of the right to privacy, and thus *they* are "derivative" from *it*. If all the protections we include under the right to privacy were specified in the Fourth and Fifth Amendments, this would hardly prove that the right to privacy is "derivative" from the right to be secure against unreasonable search or seizure and the privilege against self-incrimination. It would be just as plausible to assert that this is evidence that the Fourth and Fifth Amendment protections are "derivative" from the right to privacy.[2]

Now all of this would amount to mere semantics, and Professor Thomson could define "derivative" however she pleased, if she didn't use this as an argument against finding (indeed, against even looking for) the "that-which-is-in-common" to the cluster of rights in the right to privacy. This is the large non sequitur. Even if the right were derivative in the sense urged by Thomson, it would not follow that there is nothing in common to all the protections in the right-to-privacy cluster, or that it would be silly to try to find what they have in common. Criminology is probably derivative from sociology and psychology and law and political science in just the way that Thomson holds privacy rights to be derivative from rights to person and property. This hardly amounts to a reason for not trying to define the unifying theme of criminological studies—at least a large number of criminologists do not think so.[3] In other words, even if privacy rights were a grab-bag of property and personal rights, it might still be revealing, as well as helpful, in the resolution of difficult moral conflicts to determine whether there is anything unique that this grab-bag protects that makes it worthy of distinction from the full field of property and personal rights.

I shall argue that there is indeed something unique protected by the right to privacy. And we are likely to miss it if we suppose that what is protected is just a subspecies of the things generally safeguarded by property rights and personal rights. And if we miss it, there may come a time when we think we are merely limiting some personal or property right in favor of some greater good, when in fact we are really sacrificing something of much greater value.

At this point, I shall leave behind all comments on Thomson's paper, since if I am able to prove that there is something unique and uniquely valuable protected by the right to privacy, I shall take this as refutation of her view. It will serve to clarify my own position, however, to indicate briefly what I take to be the shortcomings of the responses of Scanlon and Rachels to Thomson.

Scanlon feels he has refuted Thomson by finding the "special interests" which are the "common foundation" for the right(s) to privacy. He says:

> I agree with Thomson that the rights whose violation strikes us as invasion of privacy are many and diverse, and that these rights do not derive from any single overarching right to privacy. I hold, however, that these rights have a common foundation in the special interests that we have in being able to be free from certain kinds of intrusions. The most obvious examples of such offensive intrusions involve observation of our bodies, our behavior or our interactions with other people (or overhearings of the last two), but while these are central they do not exhaust the field [p. 315].

Now on first glance, it is certainly hard to dispute this claim. But it is nonetheless misleading. Scanlon's position is arresting and appears true because it rests on a tautology, not unlike the classic "explanation" of the capacity of sedatives to induce sleep by virtue of their "dormative powers." The right to privacy *is* the right "to be free from certain kinds of (offensive) intrusions." Scanlon's position is equivalent to holding that the common foundation of our right to privacy lies in our "privatistic interests."

In sum, Scanlon announces that he has found the common element in rights to privacy: rights to privacy protect our special interest in privacy! Thomson could hardly deny this, although I doubt she would find it adequate to answer the questions she raised in her essay. What Scanlon has not told us is *why* we have a special interest in privacy, that is, a special interest in being free from certain kinds of intrusions; and *why* it is a legitimate interest, that is, an interest of sufficient importance to warrant protection by our fellow citizens.[4] I suspect that this is the least that would be necessary to convince Thomson that there is a common foundation to privacy rights.

James Rachels tries to provide it. He tries to answer precisely the questions Scanlon leaves unanswered. He asks, "Why, exactly, is privacy important to us?" (p. 323). He starts his answer by categorizing some of the interests we might have in privacy and finds that they basically have to do with protecting our reputations or the secrecy of our plans or the like. Rachels recognizes, however, that

reflection on these cases gives us little help in understanding the value which privacy has in *normal* or *ordinary* situations. By this I mean situations in which there is nothing embarrassing or shameful or unpopular in what we are doing, and nothing ominous or threatening connected with its possible disclosure. For example, even married couples whose sex-lives are normal (whatever that is), and so who have nothing to be ashamed of, by even the most conventional standards, and certainly nothing to be blackmailed about, do not want their bedrooms bugged [p. 325].

In other words, Rachels recognizes that if there is a unique interest to be protected by the right(s) to privacy, it must be an interest simply in being able to limit other people's observation of us or access to information about us—even if we have certain knowledge that the observation or information would not be used to our detriment or used at all. Rachels tries to identify such an interest and to point out why it is important.

His argument is this. Different human relationships are marked— indeed, in part, constituted—by different degrees of sharing personal information. One shares more of himself with a friend than with an employer, more with a life-long friend than with a casual friend, more with a lover than an acquaintance. He writes that "*however* one conceives one's relations with other people, there is inseparable from that conception an idea of how it is appropriate to behave with and around them, and what information about oneself it is appropriate for them to have" (pp. 328–329). It is "an important part of what it means to have a friend that we welcome his company, that we confide in him, *that we tell him things about ourselves, and that we show him sides of our personalities which we would not tell or show to just anyone*" (pp. 327–328, my emphasis). And therefore, Rachels concludes, "because our ability to control who has access to us, and who knows what about us, allows us to maintain the variety of relationships with other people that we want to have, it is, I think, one of the most important reasons why we value privacy" (p. 329).

Rachels acknowledges that his view is similar to that put forth by Charles Fried in *An Anatomy of Values*. Since, for our purposes, we can regard these views as substantially the same, and since they amount to an extremely compelling argument about the basis of our interest in privacy, it will serve us well to sample Fried's version of the doctrine. He writes that privacy is the necessary context for relationships which we would hardly be human if we had to do without—the relationships of love, friendship, and trust.

Love and friendship . . . involve the voluntary and spontaneous relinquishment of something between friend and friend, lover and lover. The title to information about oneself conferred by privacy provides the necessary something. To be friends or lovers persons must be intimate to some degree with each other. Intimacy is the sharing of information about one's actions, beliefs or emotions, which one does not share with all, and which one has the right not to share with anyone. By conferring this right, privacy creates the moral capital which we spend in friendship and love.[5]

The Rachels-Fried theory is this. Only because we are able to withhold personal information about—and forbid intimate observation of—ourselves from the rest of the world, can we give out the personal information—and allow the intimate observations—to friends and/or lovers, that constitute intimate relationships. On this view, intimacy is both signaled and constituted by the sharing of information and allowing of observation *not shared with or allowed to the rest of the world.* If there were nothing about myself that the rest of the world did not have access to, I simply would not have anything to give that would mark off a relationship as intimate. As Fried says,

The man who is generous with his possessions, but not with himself, can hardly be a friend, nor—and this more clearly shows the necessity of privacy for love—can the man who, voluntarily or involuntarily, shares everything about himself with the world indiscriminately.[6]

Presumably such a person cannot enter into a friendship or a love because he has literally squandered the "moral capital" which is necessary for intimate emotional investment in another.

Now I find this analysis both compelling and hauntingly distasteful. It is compelling first of all because it fits much that we ordinarily experience. For example, it makes jealousy understandable. If the value—indeed, the very reality—of my intimate relation with you lies in your sharing with me what you don't share with others, then if you do share it with another, what I have is literally decreased in value and adulterated in substance. This view is also compelling because it meets the basic requirement for identifying a compelling interest at the heart of privacy. That basic requirement is, as I have already stated, an important interest in simply being able to restrict information about, and observation of, myself regardless of what may be done with that information or the results of that observation.

The view is distasteful, however, because it suggests a market con-

ception of personal intimacy. The value and substance of intimacy—
like the value and substance of my income—lies not merely in what
I have but essentially in what others do *not* have. The reality of my
intimacy with you is constituted not simply by the quality and intensity
of what we share, but by its unavailability to others—in other words,
by its scarcity. It may be that our personal relations are valuable to
us because of their exclusiveness rather than because of their own
depth or breadth or beauty. But it is not clear that this is necessary.
It may be a function of the historical limits of our capacity for empathy
and feeling for others. It may be a function of centuries of accultur-
ation to the nuclear family with its narrow intensities. The Rachels-
Fried thesis, however, makes it into a logical necessity by asserting
that friendship and love *logically* imply exclusiveness and narrowness
of focus.

As compelling as the Rachels-Fried view is then, there is reason to
believe it is an example of the high art of ideology: the rendering of
aspects of our present possessive market-oriented world into the eternal forms of logical necessity. Perhaps the tip-off lies precisely in the
fact that, on their theory, jealousy—the most possessive of emotions—
is rendered rational. All of this is not itself an argument against the
Rachels-Fried view, but rather an argument for suspicion. However,
it does suggest an argument against that view.

I think the fallacy in the Rachels-Fried view of intimacy is that it
overlooks the fact that what constitutes intimacy is not merely the
sharing of otherwise withheld information, but the context of caring
which makes the sharing of personal information significant. One
ordinarily reveals information to one's psychoanalyst that one might
hesitate to reveal to a friend or lover. That hardly means one has an
intimate relationship with the analyst. And this is not simply because
of the asymmetry. If two analysts decided to psychoanalyze one another alternately—the evident unwisdom of this arrangement aside—
there is no reason to believe that their relationship would necessarily
be the most intimate one in their lives, even if they revealed to each
other information they withheld from everyone else, lifelong friends
and lovers included. And this wouldn't be changed if they cared about
each other's well-being. What is missing is that particular kind of
caring that makes a relationship not just personal but intimate.

The kind of caring I have in mind is not easily put in words, and
so I shall claim no more than to offer an approximation. Necessary
to an intimate relationship such as friendship or love is a reciprocal
desire to share present and future intense and important experiences
together, not merely to swap information. Mutual psychoanalysis is

not love or even friendship so long as it is not animated by this kind
of caring. This is why it remains localized in the office rather than
tending to spread into other shared activities, as do love and friendship. Were mutual psychoanalysis animated by such caring it might
indeed be part of a love or friendship—but then the "prime mover"
of the relationship would not be the exchange of personal information. It would be the caring itself.

   In the context of a reciprocal desire to share present and future
intense and important experiences, the revealing of personal information takes on significance. The more one knows about the other,
the more one is able to understand how the other experiences things,
what they mean to him, how they feel to him. In other words the
more each knows about the other, the more they are able to really
share an intense experience instead of merely having an intense experience alongside one another. The revealing of personal information then is not what constitutes or powers the intimacy. Rather it
deepens and fills out, invites and nurtures, the caring that powers the
intimacy.

   On this view—in contrast to the Rachels-Fried view—it is of little
importance who has access to personal information about me. What
matters is who cares about it and to whom I care to reveal it. Even if
all those to whom I am indifferent and who return the compliment
were to know the intimate details of my personal history, my capacity
to enter into an intimate relationship would remain unhindered. So
long as I could find someone who did not just want to collect data
about me, but who cared to know about me in order to share my
experience with me and to whom I cared to reveal information about
myself so that person could share my experience with me, and vice
versa, I could enter into a meaningful friendship or love relationship.

   On the Rachels-Fried view, it follows that the significance of sexual
intimacy lies in the fact that we signal the uniqueness of our love
relationships by allowing our bodies to be seen and touched by the
loved one in ways that are forbidden to others. But here too, the
context of caring that turns physical contact into intimacy is overlooked. A pair of urologists who examine each other are no more
lovers than our reciprocating psychoanalysts. What is missing is the
desire to share intense and important experiences. And to say this is
to see immediately the appropriateness of sexual intimacy to love: in
sexual intimacy one is literally and symbolically stripped of the ordinary masks that obstruct true sharing of experience. This happens
not merely in the nakedness of lovers but even more so in the giving
of themselves over to the physical forces in their bodies. In surren-

dering the ordinary restraints, lovers allow themselves to be what they truly are—at least as bodies—intensely and together. (Recall Sartre's marvelous description of the *caress*.)[7] If this takes place in the context of caring—in other words if people are making love and not just fucking—their physical intimacy is an expression and a consummation of that caring. It is one form of the authentic speech of loving.

Finally, on this view—in contrast to the Rachels-Fried view—the unsavory market notion of intimacy is avoided. Since the content of intimacy is caring, rather than the revealing of information or the granting of access to the body usually withheld from others, there is no necessary limit to the number of persons one can be intimate with, no logical necessity that friendship or love be exclusive. The limits rather lie in the limits of our capacity to care deeply for others, and of course in the limits of time and energy. In other words it may be a fact—for us at this point in history, or even for all prople at all points in history—that we can only enter into a few true friendships and loves in a lifetime. But this is not an inescapable logical necessity. It is only an empirical fact of our capacity, one that might change and might be worth trying to change. It might be a fact that we are unable to disentangle love from jealousy. But this, too, is not an a priori truth. It is rather an empirical fact, one that might change if fortune brought us into a less possessive, less exclusive, less invidious society.

This much is enough, I think, to cast doubt on the relationship between privacy and friendship or love asserted by Rachels and Fried. It should also be enough to refute their theory of the grounds on which the right to privacy rests. For if intimacy *may* be a function of caring and not of the yielding of otherwise withheld information, their claim to have established the *necessity* of privacy for important human relationships must fall. I think, however, that there is another equally fundamental ground for rejecting their position: it makes the right to individual privacy "derivative" from the right to social (that is, interpersonal) relationships. And I mean "derivative" in a much more irreversible way than Thomson does.

On the Rachels-Fried view, my right to parade around naked alone in my house free from observation by human or electronic peeping toms, is not a fundamental right. It is derived from the fact that without this right, I could not meaningfully reveal my body to the loved one in that exclusive way that is necessary to intimacy on the Rachels-Fried view. This strikes me as bizarre. It would imply that a person who had no chance of entering into social relations with others, say a catatonic or a perfectly normal person legitimately sentenced to life imprisonment in solitary confinement, would thereby have no ground for a right to privacy. This must be false, because it seems that if there is a right to privacy it belongs to individuals regardless of whether they are likely to have friends or lovers, regardless of whether they have reason to amass "the moral capital which we spend in friendship and love." What this suggests is that even if the Rachels-Fried theory of the relationship of privacy and intimacy were true, it would not give us a fundamental interest that can provide the foundation for a right to privacy for all human individuals. I believe, however, that such a fundamental interest can be unearthed. Stanley I. Benn's theory of the foundation of privacy comes closer to the view which I think is ultimately defensible.

Benn attempts to base the right to privacy on the principle of respect for persons. He too is aware that utilitarian considerations—for example, prevention of harm that may result from misuse of personal information—while important, are not adequate to ground the right to privacy.

The underpinning of a claim not to be watched without leave will be more general if it can be grounded in this way on the principle of respect for persons than on a utilitarian duty to avoid inflicting suffering. That duty may, of course, reinforce the claim in particular instances. But respect for persons will sustain an objection even to secret watching, which may do no actual harm at all. Covert observation—spying—is objectionable because it deliberately deceives a person about his world [that is, it transforms the situation he thinks is unobserved into one which is observed], thwarting, for reasons that *cannot* be his reasons, his attempts to make a rational choice. One cannot be said to respect a man as engaged on an enterprise worthy of consideration if one knowingly and deliberately alters his conditions of action, concealing the fact from him. The offense is different in this instance, of course, from A's open intrusion on C's conversation. In that case, A's attentions were liable to affect C's enterprise by changing C's perception of it; he may have felt differently about his conversation with D, even to the extent of not being able to see it as any longer the same activity, knowing that A was now listening.[8]

Benn's view is that the right to privacy rests on the principle of respect for persons as choosers. Covert observation or unwanted overt observation deny this respect because they transform the actual conditions in which the person chooses and acts, and thus make it impossible for him to act in the way he set out to act, or to choose in the way he thinks he is choosing.

This too is a compelling analysis. I shall myself argue that the right to privacy is fundamentally connected to personhood. However, as it stands, Benn's theory gives us too much—and though he appears to know it, his way of trimming the theory to manageable scale is not very helpful. Benn's theory gives us too much because it appears to establish a person's right never to be observed when he thought he wasn't being observed, and never to be overtly observed when he didn't wish it. This would give us a right not to have people look at us from their front windows as we absent-mindedly stroll along, as well as a right not to be stared in the face. To deal with this, Benn writes,

it cannot be sufficient that I do not *want* you to observe something; for the principle of respect to be relevant, it must be something about my own person that is in question, otherwise the principle would be so wide that a mere wish of mine would be a prima facie reason for everyone to refrain from observing and reporting on anything at all. I do not make something a part of me merely by having feelings about it. The principle of privacy proposed here is, rather, that any man who desires that he *himself* should not be an object of scrutiny has a reasonable claim to immunity.[9]

Benn goes on to say that what is rightly covered by this immunity are one's body and those things, like possessions, which the conventions of a culture may cause one to think of as part of one's identity.

But this begs the question. Benn has moved from the principle that respect for me as a person dictates that I am entitled not to have the conditions in which I choose altered by unknown or unwanted observation, to the principle that I am entitled to have those things (conventionally) bound up with my identity exempt from unknown or unwanted observation. But the first principle does not entail the second, because the second principle is not merely a practical limitation on the first; it is a moral limitation. It asserts that it is wrong (or at least, significantly worse) to have the conditions in which I choose altered, when things closely bound up with my identity are concerned. But this follows only if the first principle is conjoined with another that holds that the closer something is to my identity, the worse it is for others to tamper with it. But this is after all just an abstract version of the right to privacy itself. And since Benn has not shown that it follows from the principle of respect for persons as choosers, his argument presupposes what he seeks to establish. It is quite strictly a *petitio principii.*

In sum then, though we have moved quite a bit further in the direction of the foundation of privacy, we have still not reached our destination. What we are looking for is a fundamental interest, connected to personhood, which provides a basis for a right to privacy to which all human beings are entitled (even those in solitary con-

finement) and which does not go so far as to claim a right never to
be observed (even on crowded streets). I proceed now to the consideration of a candidate for such a fundamental interest.

Privacy is a social practice. It involves a complex of behaviors that
stretches from refraining from asking questions about what is none
of one's business to refraining from looking into open windows one
passes on the street, from refraining from entering a closed door
without knocking to refraining from knocking down a locked door
without a warrant.

Privacy can in this sense be looked at as a very complicated social
ritual. But what is its point? In response I want to defend the following
thesis. *Privacy is a social ritual by means of which an individual's moral title
to his existence is conferred.* Privacy is an essential part of the complex
social practice by means of which the social group recognizes—and
communicates to the individual—that his existence is his own. And
this is a precondition of personhood. To be a person, an individual
must recognize not just his actual capacity to shape his destiny by his
choices. He must also recognize that he has an exclusive moral right
to shape his destiny. And this in turn presupposes that he believes
that the concrete reality which he is, and through which his destiny
is realized, belongs to him in a moral sense.

And if one takes—as I am inclined to—the symbolic interactionist
perspective which teaches that "selves" are created in social interaction
rather than flowering innately from inborn seeds, to this claim is
added an even stronger one: privacy is necessary to the creation of
selves[10] out of human beings, since a self is at least in part a human
being who regards his existence—his thoughts, his body, his actions—
as his *own*.

Thus the relationship between privacy and personhood is a twofold
one. First, the social ritual of privacy seems to be an essential ingredient in the process by which "persons" are created out of prepersonal
infants. It conveys to the developing child the recognition that his
body to which he is uniquely "connected" is a body over which he has
some exclusive moral rights. Secondly, the social ritual of privacy
confirms, and demonstrates respect for, the personhood of already
developed persons. I take the notion of "conferring title to one's
existence" to cover both dimensions of the relationship of privacy to
personhood: the original bestowal of title and the ongoing confirmation. And of course, to the extent that we believe that the creation
of "selves" or "persons" is an ongoing social process—not just something which occurs once and for all during childhood—the two dimensions become one: privacy is a condition of the original and
continuing creation of "selves" or "persons."

To understand the meaning of this claim, it will be helpful to turn to Erving Goffman's classic study, "On the Characteristics of Total Institutions."[11] Goffman says of total institutions that "each is a natural experiment on what can be done to the self."[12] The goal of these experiments is *mortification of the self*, and in each case total deprivation of privacy is an essential ingredient in the regimen. I have taken the liberty of quoting Goffman at length, since I think his analysis provides poignant testimony to the role that elimination of privacy plays in destruction of the self. And thus conversely, he shows the degree to which the self *requires* the social rituals of privacy to exist.

There is another form of mortification in total institutions; beginning with admission a kind of contaminative exposure occurs. On the outside, the individual can hold objects of self-feeling—such as his body, his immediate actions, his thoughts, and some of his possessions—clear of contact with alien and contaminating things. But in total institutions *these territories of the self are violated.* . . .
There is, first, a violation of one's informational preserve regarding self. During admission, facts about the inmate's social statuses and past behavior—especially discreditable facts—are collected and recorded in a dossier available to staff. . . .
New audiences not only learn discreditable facts about oneself that are ordinarily concealed but are also in a position to perceive some of these facts directly. Prisoners and mental patients cannot prevent their visitors from seeing them in humiliating circumstances. Another example is the shoulder-patch of ethnic identification worn by concentration-camp inmates. Medical and security examinations often expose the inmate physically, sometimes to persons of both sexes; a similar exposure follows from collective sleeping arrangements and doorless toilets. . . . In general, of course, the inmate is never fully alone; he is always within sight and often earshot of someone, if only his fellow inmates. Prison cages with bars for walls fully realize such exposure.[13]

That social practices which penetrate "the private reserve of the individual"[14] are effective means to mortify the inmate's self—that is, literally, to kill it off—suggests (though it doesn't prove) that privacy is essential to the creation and maintenance of selves. My argument for this will admittedly be speculative. However, in view of the fact that it escapes the shortcomings of the views we have already analyzed, fits Goffman's evidence on the effects of deprivation of privacy, fulfills the requirement that it be a fundamental human interest worthy of protection, provides the basis for a right to privacy to which all human beings are entitled, and yet does not claim a right never to be observed, I think it is convincing.

If I am sitting with other people, how do I know this body which is connected to the thoughts I am having is *mine* in the moral sense? That is, how do I know that I have a unique moral right to this body? It is not enough to say that it is connected to my consciousness, since that simply repeats the question or begs the question of what makes these thoughts *my* consciousness. In any event, connection to my consciousness is a factual link, not a moral one. In itself it accounts for why I am not likely to confuse the events in this body (mine) with events in that body (yours). It does not account for the moral title which gives me a unique right to control the events in this body which I don't have in respect to the events in that body.

Ownership in the moral sense presupposes a social institution. It is based upon a complex social practice. A social order in which bodies were held to belong to others or to the collectivity, and in which individuals grew up believing that their bodies were not theirs from a moral point of view, is conceivable. To imagine such an order does not require that we deny that for each body only one individual is able to feel or move it. Such a social order is precisely what Goffman portrays in his description of total institutions and it might be thought of as displaying the ultimate logic of totalitarianism. Totalitarianism is the political condition that obtains when a state takes on the characteristics of a total institution. For a society to exist in which individuals do not own their bodies, what is necessary is that people not be treated as if entitled to control what the bodies they can feel and move do, or what is done to those bodies—in particular that they not be treated as if entitled to determine when and by whom that body is experienced.[15]

This suggests that there are two essential conditions of moral ownership of one's body. The right to do with my body what I wish, and the right to control when and by whom my body is experienced. This in turn reflects the fact that things can be appropriated in two ways: roughly speaking, actively and cognitively. That is, something is "mine" to the extent that I have the power to use it, to dispose of it as I see fit. But additionally there is a way in which something becomes "mine" to the extent that I know it. What I know is "my" knowledge; what I experience is "my" experience. Thus, it follows that if an individual were granted the right to control his bodily movements although always under observation, he might develop some sense of moral ownership of his physical existence.[16] However, that ownership would surely be an impoverished and partial one compared to what we take to be contained in an individual's title to his existence. This is because it would be ownership only in one of the two dimensions of appropriation, the active. Ownership, in the sense we know it, requires control over cognitive appropriation as well. It requires that the individual have control over whether or not his physical existence becomes part of someone else's experience. That is, it requires that the individual be treated as entitled to determine when and by whom his concrete reality is experienced. Moral ownership in the full sense requires the social ritual of privacy.

As I sit among my friends, I know this body is mine because first of all, unlike any other body present, I believe—and my friends have acted and continue to act as if they believe—that I am entitled to do with this body what I wish. Secondly, but also essential, I know this body is mine because unlike any other body present, I have in the past taken it outside of the range of anyone's experience but my own, I can do so now, and I expect to be able to do so in the future. What's more, I believe—and my friends have acted and continue to act as if they believe—that it would be wrong for anyone to interfere with my capacity to do this. In other words, they have and continue to treat me according to the social ritual of privacy. And since my view of myself is, in important ways, a reflection of how others treat me, I come to view myself as the kind of entity that is entitled to the social ritual of privacy. That is, I come to believe that this body is mine in the moral sense.

I think the same thing can be said about the thoughts of which I am aware. That there are thoughts, images, reveries and memories of which only I am conscious does not make them mine in the moral sense—any more than the cylinders in a car belong to it just because they are in it. This is why ascribing ownership of my body to the mere connection with my consciousness begs the question. Ownership of my thoughts requires a social practice as well. It has to do with learning that I can control when, and by whom, the thoughts in my head will be experienced by someone other than myself and learning that I am entitled to such control—that I will not be forced to reveal the contents of my consciousness, even when I put those contents on paper. The contents of my consciousness become mine because they are treated according to the ritual of privacy.

It may seem that this is to return full circle to Thomson's view that the right to privacy is just a species of the rights over person and property. I would argue that it is more fundamental. The right to privacy is the right to the existence of a social practice which makes it possible for me to think of this existence as *mine.* This means that it is the right to conditions necessary for me to think of myself as the kind of entity for whom it would be meaningful and important to claim personal and property rights. It should also be clear that the

JEFFREY H. REIMAN

ownership of which I am speaking is surely more fundamental than property rights. Indeed, it is only when I can call this physical existence mine that I can call objects somehow connected to this physical existence mine. That is, the transformation of physical possession into ownership presupposes ownership of the physical being I am. Thus the right to privacy protects something that is presupposed by both personal and property rights. Thomson's recognition that there is overlap should come as no surprise. The conclusion she draws from the existence of this overlap is, however, unwarranted. Personal and property rights presuppose an individual with title to his existence—and privacy is the social ritual by which that title is conferred.

The right to privacy, then, protects the individual's interest in becoming, being, and remaining a person. It is thus a right which *all* human individuals possess—even those in solitary confinement. It does not assert a right never to be seen even on a crowded street. It is sufficient that I can control whether and by whom my body is experienced in some significant places and that I have the real possibility of repairing to those places. It is a right which protects my capacity to enter into intimate relations, not because it protects my reserve of generally withheld information, but because it enables me to make the commitment that underlies caring as *my* commitment uniquely conveyed by *my* thoughts and witnessed by *my* actions.

NOTES

I am grateful to the editors of *Philosophy & Public Affairs* for many helpful comments and suggestions which have aided me in clarifying and communicating the views presented here.

1 Judith Jarvis Thomson, "The Right to Privacy," Thomas Scanlon, "Thomson on Privacy," and James Rachels, "Why Privacy is Important," *Philosophy & Public Affairs* 4, no. 4 (Summer 1975): 295–333. Unless otherwise indicated, page numbers in the text refer to this issue.

2 This reversibility of "derivative"-ness is to be found in Justice Douglas' historic opinion on the right to privacy in Griswold v. State of Connecticut. He states there that "specific guarantees in the Bill of Rights have penumbras, formed by emanations from those guarantees that help give them life and substance." The right of privacy, he goes on to say, is contained in the penumbras of the First, Third, Fourth, Fifth, and Ninth Amendment guarantees. Surely the imagery of penumbral emanations suggests that the right to privacy is "derivative" from the rights protected in these amendments. But later Douglas states that the Court is dealing "with a right of privacy older than the Bill of Rights," which along with other language he

uses, suggests that the rights in the Bill of Rights are meant to give reality to an even more fundamental right, the right to privacy, 381 U.S. 479, 85 S. Ct. 1678 (1965).

3 See for instance, Herman and Julia Schwendinger, "Defenders of Order or Guardians of Human Rights?" *Issues in Criminology* 5, no. 2 (Summer 1970); 123–157, especially the section entitled "The Thirty-Year-Old Controversy," pp. 123–129.

4 I think it is fair to say that Scanlon makes no claim to answer these questions in his essay.

5 Charles Fried, *An Anatomy of Values: Problems of Personal and Social Choice* (Cambridge, Mass., 1970), p. 142. It might be thought that in lifting Fried's analysis of privacy out of his book, I have lifted it out of context and thus done violence to his theory. Extra weight is added to this objection by the recognition that when Fried speaks about love in his book (though not in the chapter relating privacy to love), he speaks of something very like the caring that I present as a basis for refuting his view. For instance Fried writes that, "There is rather a creation of love, a middle term, which is a new pattern or system of interests which both share and both value, in part at least just because it is shared" (ibid., p. 79). What is in conflict between us then is not recognition of this or something like this as an essential component of the love relationship. The conflict rather lies in the fact that I argue that recognition of this factor undermines Fried's claim that *privacy* is *necessary* for the very existence of love relationships.

6 Ibid., p. 142.

7 "The Other's flesh did not exist explicitly for me since I grasped the Other's body in situation; neither did it exist for her since she transcended it toward her possibilities and toward the object. The caress causes the Other to be born as flesh for me and for herself . . . , the caress reveals the flesh by stripping the body of its action, by cutting it off from the possibilities which surround it; the caress is designed to uncover the web of inertia beneath the action—i.e., the pure 'being-there'—which sustains it. . . . The caress is designed to cause the Other's body to be born, through pleasure, for the Other—and for myself. . . ." Jean-Paul Sartre, *Being and Nothingness*, trans. Hazel E. Barnes (New York, 1956), p. 390.

8 Stanley I. Benn, "Privacy, Freedom, and Respect for Persons," in Richard Wasserstrom, ed., *Today's Moral Problems* (New York, 1975), p. 8.

9 Ibid., p. 10.

10 For purposes of this discussion, we can take "self" and "person" as equivalent. I use them both insofar as they refer to an individual who recognizes that he *owns* his physical and mental reality in the sense that he is morally entitled to realize his destiny through it, and thus that he has at least a strong presumptive moral right not to have others interfere with his self-determination.

11 Erving Goffman, *Asylums* (New York, 1961), pp. 1–124.

12 Ibid., p. 12.

13 Ibid., pp. 23–25; my emphasis.

14 Ibid., p. 29.

15 Macabre as it may sound, a world in which the body that I can feel and move *is distinct from* the body that I own *is* conceivable. Imagine, for example, a world of 365 people each born on a different day of the year, in which each person has complete access to the body of the person whose birthday is the day after his.

16 I am indebted to Professor Phillip H. Scribner for pointing this out to me.

14

Privacy
Some arguments and assumptions

RICHARD A. WASSERSTROM

In this paper I examine some issues involving privacy—issues with
which the legal system of the United States has had and continues to
have a good deal of concern. What I am interested in is the nature
of privacy and the reasons why it might be thought important. The
issues I consider have been of particular interest in recent years as
changes in technology have made new ways to interfere with privacy
possible. For this reason, too, I am primarily concerned with the ways
in which government and other powerful institutions can and do
interfere with privacy, for it is these institutions that tend to have the
sophisticated instruments most at their disposal.

I consider first some distinctions that I think it important to make
among different kinds of cases that involve privacy. I then consider
in some detail one plausible set of arguments for the value of privacy.
These arguments help to explain why the law protects privacy in some
of the ways it does and to provide a possible justification for continuing
to do so. Some of the arguments are not without their problems,
however. And in the final section of the article I raise certain questions
about them and indicate the key issues that require additional exploration before any satisfactory justification can be developed.

It is apparent that there are a number of different claims that can
be made in the name of privacy. A number—and perhaps all—of
them involve the question of the kind and degree of control that a
person ought to be able to exercise in respect to knowledge or the
disclosure of information about himself or herself. This is not all there
is to privacy, but it is surely one central theme.

It is also true that information about oneself is not all of the same
type. As a result control over some kinds may be much more important
than control over others. For this reason, I want to start by trying to
identify some of the different types of information about oneself over

which persons might desire to retain control, and I will describe the situations in which this information comes into being. To do this, I will consider four rather ordinary situations and look at the ways they resemble one another and differ from one another.

I

The cases I have in mind are these.

1. It is midafternoon and I am sitting in a chair resting. As I close my eyes and look inward, I become aware of numerous ideas running through my mind, of various emotions and feelings, and of a variety of bodily sensations—an itch on my scalp, a slight pain in my side, and so on.
2. I am in a closed telephone booth, no one is standing near the booth, and I am talking in a normal voice into the telephone. I have called my travel agent to find out what time there are flights to Chicago so that I can make a reservation for a trip.
3. I am in the bedroom of my home with my wife. We are both undressed, lying on the bed, having sexual intercourse.
4. I am considering hiring a research assistant for the summer. If I wish to, I dial a special number on the telephone and a few days later receive in the mail a computer printout consisting of a profile of the prospective assistant—her age, marital status, arrest record, if any, grades at school, income, as well as a summary of how she has spent her time over the past few years.

The first kind of case is that of the things that are going on within a person's head or body—especially, though, a person's head: his or her mental state. One thing that is significant about my dreams, my conscious thoughts, hopes, fears, and desires is that the most direct, the best, and often the only evidence for you of what they are consists in my deliberately revealing them to you. To be sure, my nonverbal behavior may give an observer a clue as to what is going on in my mind. If, for example, I have a faraway look in my eyes you may infer that I am daydreaming about something and not paying very much attention to you. In addition there is, no doubt, a more intimate and even conceptual connection between observable behavior and certain states of feeling. If I am blushing that may mean that I am embarrassed. If I am talking very fast that may lead you to infer correctly that I am excited or nervous. It is also sometimes the case that I will not know my own thoughts and feelings and that by saying what I think they are, a skilled observer listening to me and watching me as

I talk can tell better than can I what is really going on inside my head. This may be one way to describe what can take place during psychotherapy.

But even taking all of these qualifications into account, it still remains the case that the only way to obtain very detailed and accurate information about what I am thinking, fearing, imagining, desiring, or hating and how I am experiencing it is for me to tell you or show you. If I do not, the ideas and feeling remain within me and in some sense, at least, known only to me. Because people cannot read other people's minds, these things about me are known only to me in a way in which other things are not unless I decide to disclose them to you.

What about things that are going on in my body? In some respects the situation is similar to that of my thoughts and in some respects different. There are things that are going on in my body that are like my thoughts, fears, and fantasies. If I have a slight twinge of pain in my left big toe, there is no way for anyone else to know that unless I choose to disclose it. Of course, if the toe is swollen and red and if I grimace whenever I put any weight on it, an observer could doubtless infer correctly that I was experiencing pain there. But in many other cases the only evidence would be my verbal report.

There are other things about my body concerning which this privileged position does not obtain. Even though they are my ribs, I cannot tell very well what they look like; even though it is my blood, I cannot tell with any precision how much alcohol is there. A person looking through a fluoroscope at my ribs or at an x-ray of them can tell far better than I can (just from having them as my ribs or from looking down at my chest) what they look like. A trained technician looking at a sample of my blood in combination with certain chemicals can determine far better than I can (just from it being *my* blood) what the alcohol content is or whether I am anemic.

So there are some facts about my body that I know in a way others logically cannot know them, that can be known to others only if I disclose them by telling what they are. There are other facts about my body that cannot be known by others in the way I know them but that can be inferred from observation of my body and my behavior. And there are still other kinds of facts about my body that I do not know and that can be learned, if at all, only by someone or something outside of myself.

The second kind of case was illustrated by an imagined telephone conversation from a phone booth with my travel agent to make the reservations for a trip. Another case of the same type is this: I am in the dining room of my house, the curtains are drawn, and I am eating dinner with my wife. In both of these cases it is the setting that makes the behavior distinctive and relevant for our purposes. In the example of the reservations over the telephone, the substance of my conversation with my travel agent is within my control if it is the case that no one is in a position to overhear (at my end) what I am saying to him, that no one is listening in along the way, and that only one person, the travel agent, is in a position to hear what I am telling him. It is less within my control, of course, than is information about my mental state, not yet revealed to anyone, because the agent can choose to reveal what I have told him.

In the second case—that of eating dinner in my dining room—knowledge of what I am eating and how I am eating is in the control of my wife and me if it is correct that no one else is in a position to observe us as we are eating. We might want to describe both of these cases as cases of things being done *in private* (although this is a very weak sense of private)—meaning that they were done in a setting in which there did not appear to be anyone other than the person to whom I was talking or with whom I was eating who was in a position to hear what was being said or to see what was being eaten at the time the behavior was taking place. Both of these are to be contrasted with the third example given earlier.

Instead of eating dinner with my wife in the dining room, we are having sexual intercourse in the bedroom. Or, instead of talking to my travel agent, imagine that I call my lawyer to discuss the terms of my will with her. Both of these things are being done in private in the same sense in which the discussion with the travel agent and the dinner with my wife were private. But these have an additional quality not possessed by the earlier two examples. While I expect that what I tell my lawyer is not being overheard by anyone else while I am telling her, I also reasonably expect that she will keep in confidence what I tell her. The conversation is private in the additional respect that the understanding is that it will not be subsequently disclosed to anyone without my consent. It is a private kind of communication. That is not the case with my phone reservations for Chicago. Absent special or unusual circumstances (for example, telling the agent that I do not want anyone to know when I am going to Chicago), I have no particular interest in retaining control over disclosure of this fact.

Similarly, having intercourse with my wife is private in the additional respect that it is the sort of intimate thing that is not appropriately observed by others or discussed with them—again, absent special or unusual circumstances. In addition to being done in private, it, too, is a private kind of thing. It is in this respect unlike the dinner we had together. There is no expectation on my part that what I ate or how I ate it will not be discussed with others by my wife.

The most obvious and the important connection between the idea of doing something in private and doing a private kind of thing is that we typically do private things only in situations where we reasonably believe that we are doing them in private. That we believe we are doing something in private is often a condition that has to be satisfied before we are willing to disclose an intimate fact about ourselves or to perform an intimate act. I would probably make my airplane reservations even in a crowded travel agency where there were lots of people who could overhear what I was saying. The telephone was a convenient way to make the reservations. But the fact that I was making them in a setting that appeared to be private was not important to me. It did not affect what I disclosed to the agent. Thus, even if I had suspected that my agent's telephone was tapped so that someone unknown to us both overheard our conversation, I would probably have made the reservation. In the case of my conversation with my lawyer, however, it was the belief that the conversation was in a private setting that made me willing to reveal a private kind of information. If someone taped my discussion with my lawyer, he injured me in a way that is distinguishable on this basis alone from the injury, if any, done to me by taping my conversation with the travel agent. That is to say, he got me to do or to reveal something that I would not have done or revealed if they had not hidden his presence from me.

It should be evident, too, that there are important similarities, as well as some differences, between the first and third cases—between my knowledge of my own mental state and my disclosure of intimate or otherwise confidential information to those to whom I choose to disclose it. These can be brought out by considering what it would be like to live in a society whose technology permitted an observer to gain access to the information in question.

II

Suppose existing technology made it possible for an outsider in some way to look into or monitor another's mind. What, if anything, would be especially disturbing or objectionable about that?

To begin with, there is a real sense in which we have far less control over when we shall have certain thoughts and what their content will be than we have over, for example, to whom we shall reveal them and to what degree. Because our inner thoughts, feelings, and bodily sensations are so largely beyond our control, I think we would feel appreciably more insecure in our social environment than we do at present were it possible for another to "look in" without our consent to see what was going on in our heads.

This is so at least in part because many, although by no means all, of our uncommunicated thoughts and feelings are about very intimate matters. Our fantasies and our fears often concern just those matters that in our culture we would least choose to reveal to anyone else. At a minimum we might suffer great anxiety and feelings of shame were the decisions as to where, when, and to whom we disclose not to be wholly ours. Were access to our thoughts possible in this way, we would see ourselves as creatures who are far more vulnerable than we are now.

In addition, there is a more straightforward worry about accountability for our thoughts and feelings. As I mentioned, they are often not within our control. For all of the reasons that we ought not hold people accountable for behavior not within their control, we would not want the possibility of accountability to extend to uncommunicated thoughts and feelings.

Finally, one rather plausible conception of what it is to be a person carries with it the idea of the existence of a core of thoughts and feelings that are the person's alone. If anyone else could know all that I am thinking or perceive all that I am feeling except in the form I choose to filter and reveal what I am and how I see myself—if anyone could be aware of all this at will—I would cease to have as complete a sense of myself as a distinct and separate person as I have now. A fundamental part of what it is to be an individual is to be an entity that is capable of being exclusively aware of its own thoughts and feelings.

Considerations such as these—and particularly the last one—help us to understand some of the puzzles concerning the privilege against self-incrimination. Because of the significance of exclusive control over our own thoughts and feelings, the privilege against self-incrimination can be seen to rest, ultimately, upon a concern that confessions never be coerced or required by the state. The point of the privilege is not primarily that the state must be induced not to torture individuals in order to extract information from them. Nor is the point even essentially that the topics of confession will necessarily (or even typically) be of the type that we are most unwilling to disclose because of the unfavorable nature of what this would reveal about us. Rather, the fundamental point is that required disclosure of one's thoughts by itself diminishes the concept of individual personhood within the society. For this reason, all immunity statutes that require persons to reveal what they think and believe—provided only that they will not be subsequently prosecuted for what they disclose—are beside the point and properly subject to criticism. For this reason, too, cases that permit the taking of a blood sample (to determine alcohol content) from an unconscious or unwilling person—despite the existence of the privilege—are also defensible. Since a person is not in a privileged position in respect to the alcohol content of his or her own blood, the claim to exclusivity in respect to knowledge of this fact is not particularly persuasive.

In a society in which intrusion into the domain of one's uncommunicated thoughts and feelings was not possible, but in which communications between persons about private things could be intercepted, some of the problems would remain the same. To begin with, because of our social attitudes toward the disclosure of intimate facts and behavior, most of us would be extremely pained were we to learn that these had become known to persons other than those to whom we chose to disclose them. The pain can come about in several different ways. If I do something private with somebody and I believe that we are doing it in private, I may very well be hurt or embarrassed if I learn subsequently that we were observed but did not know it. Thus if I learn after the fact that someone had used a special kind of telescope to observe my wife and me while we were having intercourse, the knowledge that we were observed will cause us distress both because our expectations of privacy were incorrect and because we do not like the idea that we were observed during this kind of intimate act. People have the right to have the world be what it appears to be precisely in those cases in which they regard privacy as essential to the diminution of their own vulnerability.

Reasoning such as this lies behind, I think, a case that arose some years ago in California. A department store had complained to the police that homosexuals were using its men's room as a meeting place. The police responded by drilling a small hole in the ceiling over the enclosed stalls. A policeman then stationed himself on the floor above and peered down through the hole observing the persons using the stall for eliminatory purposes. Eventually the policeman discovered and apprehended two homosexuals who used the stall as a place to engage in forbidden sexual behavior. The California Supreme Court held the observations of the policeman to have been the result of an illegal search and ordered the conviction reversed. What made the search illegal, I believe, was that it occurred in the course of this practice, which deceived all of the persons who used the stall and who believed that they were doing in private something that was socially regarded as a private kind of thing. They were entitled, especially for this kind of activity, both to be free from observation and to have their expectations of privacy honored by the state.

There is an additional reason why the observation of certain sorts of activity is objectionable. That is because the kind of spontaneity and openness that is essential to them disappears with the presence of an observer. To see that this is so, consider a different case. Suppose I know in advance that we will be observed during intercourse. Here there is no problem of defeated reasonable expectations. But there may be injury nonetheless. For one thing, I may be unwilling or unable to communicate an intimate fact or engage in intimate behavior in the presence of an observer. In this sense I will be quite directly prevented from going forward. In addition, even if I do go ahead, the character of the experience may very well be altered. Knowing that someone is watching or listening may render what would have been an enjoyable experience unenjoyable. Or, having someone watch or listen may so alter the character of the relationship that it is simply not the same kind of relationship it was before. The presence of the observer may make spontaneity impossible. Aware of the observer, I am engaged in part in viewing or imagining what is going on from his or her perspective. I thus cannot lose myself as completely in the activity.

Suppose, to take still a third case, I do not know whether I am being observed or overheard, but I reasonably believe that no matter what the appearances, it is possible that I am being observed or overheard. I think it quite likely that the anxiety produced by not knowing whether one is doing an intimate act in private is often more painful and more destructive than the certain knowledge that one is being observed or overheard, despite all precautions. It is possible, for example, that one could adjust more easily and successfully in a world where one could never do things in private than one could in a world where there was always a rational likelihood that one was being deceived about the ostensible privacy in which one was acting. This is so because the worry about whether an observer was present might interfere more with the possibility of spontaneity than would the knowledge that the observer was there. If I am correct, then one of the inevitable consequences of living in a society in which sophisticated spying devices are known to exist and to be used is that it does make more rational the belief that one may be being observed or overheard no matter what the appearances. And this in turn makes engagement more difficult.

There is still an additional reason why control over intimate facts and behavior might be of appreciable importance to individuals: our social universe would be altered in fundamental and deleterious ways were that control to be surrendered or lost. This is so because one way in which we mark off and distinguish certain interpersonal relationships from other ones is in terms of the kind of intimate information and behavior that we are willing to share with other persons. One way in which we make someone a friend rather than an acquaintance is by revealing things about ourselves to that person that we do not reveal to the world at large. On this view some degree of privacy is a logically necessary condition for the existence of many of our most meaningful social relationships.

III

The fourth kind of case that I want to consider is different from the previous three. It is suggested by the example I gave earlier of all of the information that might be made routinely available to me concerning possible appointees to the job of teaching assistant. It concerns the consequences of possessing the technological capability to store an enormous amount of information about each of the individual members of a society in such a way that the information can be retrieved and presented in a rapid, efficient, and relatively inexpensive fashion. This topic—the character, uses, and dangers of data banks—is one that has received a lot of attention in recent years. I think the worries are legitimate and that the reasons for concern have been too narrowly focused.

Consider a society in which the kinds of data collected about an individual are not very different from the kinds of quantity already collected in some fashion or other in our own society. It is surprising what a large number of interactions are deemed sufficiently important to record in some way. Thus, there are, for example, records of the traffic accidents I have been in, the applications I have made for life insurance, the purchases that I have made with my Mastercharge card, the COD packages I have signed for, the schools my children are enrolled in, the telephone numbers that have been called from my telephone, and so on. Now suppose that all of this information, which is presently recorded in some written fashion, were to be stored in some way so that it could be extracted on demand. What would result?

It is apparent that at least two different kinds of pictures of me would emerge. First, some sort of a qualitative picture of the kind of person I am would emerge. A whole lot of nontemporal facts would be made available—what kind of driver I am, how many children I have, what sorts of purchases I have made, how often my telephone is used, how many times I have been arrested and for what offenses, what diseases I have had, how much life insurance I have, and so on.

Second, it would also be possible to reconstruct a rough, temporal picture of how I had been living and what I had been doing with my time. Thus, there might be evidence that I visited two or three stores a day and made purchases, that I cashed a check at the bank (and hence was there between the hours of 10 A.M. and 3 P.M.), that I ate lunch at a particular restaurant (and hence was probably there between noon and 2 P.M.), and so on. There might well be whole days for which there were no entries, and there might be many days for which the entries would give a very sketchy and incomplete picture of how I was spending my time. Still, it would be a picture that is fantastically more detailed, accurate, and complete than the one I could supply from my own memory or from my own memory as it is augmented by that of my friends. I would have to spend a substantial amount of time each day writing in my diary in order to begin to produce as complete and accurate a picture as the one that might be rendered by the storage and retrieval system I am envisaging—and even then I am doubtful that my own diary would be as accurate or as complete, unless I made it one of my major life tasks to keep accurate and detailed records for myself of everything that I did.

If we ask whether there would be anything troublesome about living in such a society, the first thing to recognize is that there are several different things that might be objectionable. First, such a scheme might make communications that were about intimate kinds of things less confidential. In order to receive welfare, life insurance, or psychiatric counseling, I may be required to supply information of a personal or confidential nature. If so, I reasonably expect that the material revealed will be known only to the recipient. If, however, the information is stored in a data bank, it now becomes possible for the information to be disclosed to persons other than those to whom disclosure was intended. Even if access to the data is controlled so as to avoid the risks of improper access, storage of the confidential information in the data bank necessarily makes the information less confidential than it was before it was so stored.

Second, information that does not concern intimate things can get distorted in one way or another through storage. The clearest contemporary case of this kind of information is a person's arrest record. The fact that someone has been arrested is not, I think, the kind of fact that the arrestee can insist ought to be kept secret. But he or she can legitimately make two other demands about it. The person can insist that incorrect inferences not be drawn from the information; that is, the person can legitimately point out that many individuals who are arrested are never prosecuted for the alleged offense nor are they guilty of the offense for which they were arrested. He or she can, therefore, quite appropriately complain about any practice that routinely and without more being known denies employment to persons with arrest records. And if such a practice exists, then a person can legitimately complain about the increased dissemination and availability of arrest records just because of the systematic misuse of that information. The storage of arrest records in a data bank becomes objectionable not because the arrest record is intrinsically private but because the information is so regularly misused that the unavailability of the information is less of an evil than its general availability.

This does not end the matter, although this is where the discussion of data banks usually ends. Let us suppose that the information is appropriately derogatory in respect to the individual. Suppose that it is a record of arrest and conviction in circumstances that in no way suggest that the conviction was unfairly or improperly obtained. Does the individual have any sort of a claim that information of this sort not be put into the data bank? One might, of course, complain on the grounds that there was a practice of putting too much weight on the conviction. Here the argument would be similar to that just discussed. In addition, though, it might also be maintained that there are important gains that come from living in a society in which certain kinds of derogatory information about an individual are permitted to disappear from view after a certain amount of time. What is involved is the creation of a kind of social environment that holds out to the members of the society the possibility of self-renewal and change that is often dependent upon the individual's belief that a fresh start is in fact an option that is still open. A society that is concerned to encourage persons to believe in the possibility of genuine individual redemption and that is concerned not to make the process of redemption unduly onerous or interminable might, therefore, actively discourage the development of institutions that impose permanent marks of disapprobation upon any of the individuals in the society. One of the things that I think was wrong with Hester Prynne's "A" was that it was an unremovable stain impressed upon her body. The storage of information about convictions in a data bank is simply a more contemporary method of affixing the indelible brand.

In addition, and related to some of the points I made earlier, there are independent worries about the storage of vast quantities of ostensibly innocuous material about the individual in the data bank. Suppose nothing intrinsically private is stored in the data bank; suppose nothing potentially or improperly derogatory is included; and suppose what does get stored is an enormous quantity of information about the individual—information about the person and the public, largely commercial, transactions that were entered into. There are many useful, efficient uses to which such a data bank might be put. Can there be any serious objections?

One thing is apparent. With such a data bank it would be possible to reconstruct a person's movements and activities more accurately and completely than the individual—or any group of individuals—could do simply from memory. As I have indicated, there would still be gaps in the picture. No one would be able to tell in detail what the individual had been doing a lot of the time, but the sketch would be a surprisingly rich and comprehensive one that is exceeded in detail in our society only by the keeping of a careful, thorough personal diary or by having someone under the surveillance of a corps of private detectives.

What distinguishes this scheme is the fact that it would make it possible to render an account of the movements and habits of every member of the society and in so doing it might transform the society in several notable respects.

In part what is involved is the fact that every transaction in which one engages would now take on additional significance. In such a society one would be both buying a tank of gas and leaving a part of a systematic record of where one was on that particular date. One would not just be applying for life insurance; one would also be recording in a permanent way one's health on that date and a variety of other facts about oneself. No matter how innocent one's intentions and actions at any given moment, I think that an inevitable consequence of such a practice of data collection would be that persons would think more carefully before they did things that would become part of the record. Life would to this degree become less spontaneous and more measured.

More significant are the consequences of such a practice upon attitudes toward privacy in the society. If it became routine to record and have readily accessible vast quantities of information about every individual, we might come to hold the belief that the detailed inspection of any individual's behavior is a perfectly appropriate societal undertaking. We might tend to take less seriously than we do at present the idea that there are occasions upon which an individual can plausibly claim to be left alone and unobserved. We might in addition become so used to being objects of public scrutiny that we would cease to deem privacy important in any of our social relationships. As observers we might become insensitive to the legitimate claims of an individual to a sphere of life in which the individual is at present autonomous and around which he or she can erect whatever shield is wished. As the subjects of continual observation we might become forgetful of the degree to which many of the most important relationships within which we now enter depend for their existence upon the possibility of privacy.

On the other hand, if we do continue to have a high regard for privacy, both because of what it permits us to be as individuals and because of the kinds of relationships and activities it makes possible and promotes, the maintenance of a scheme of systematic data collection would necessarily get in the way. This is so for the same reason discussed earlier. Much of the value and significance of being able to do intimate things in private is impaired whenever there is a serious lack of confidence about the privacy of the situation. No one could rationally believe that the establishment of data banks—no matter how pure the motives of those who maintain and have access to them—is calculated to enhance the confidentiality of much that is now known about each one of us. And even if only apparently innocuous material is to be stored, we could never be sure that it all was as innocuous as it seemed at the time. It is very likely, therefore, that we would go through life alert to these new, indelible consequences of everyday interactions and transactions. Just as our lives would be different from what they are now if we believed that every telephone conversation was being overheard, so our lives would be similarly affected if we believed that every transaction and application was being stored. In both cases we would go through life encumbered by a wariness and deliberateness that would make it less easy to live what we take to be the life of a free person.

IV

The foregoing constitute, I believe, a connected set of arguments for the distinctive value of privacy. While I find them persuasive, I also believe that some of them are persuasive only within the context of certain fundamental assumptions and presuppositions. And these assumptions and these presuppositions seem to be a good deal more problematic than is often supposed. What remains to be done, therefore, is to try to make them explicit so that they can then be subjected to analysis and assessment. One way to do this is to ask whether there is an alternative perspective through which a number of these issues might be considered. I believe that there is. I call it the perspective of the counterculture because it captures at least some of the significant ingredients of that point of view or way of life. In calling this alternative view the perspective of the counterculture, I do not mean to be explicating a view that was in fact held by any person or group. However, this view does provide a rationale for a number of the practices and ideals of one strain of the counterculture movement in the United States in the 1960s.

I have argued for the importance of reposing control over the disclosure or observation of intimate facts with the actor. One argument for doing so was that intimate facts about oneself—one's fears, fantasies, jealousies, and desires—are often embarrassing if disclosed to others than those to whom we choose to disclose them. Similarly there are acts of various sorts that cause us pain or are rendered unenjoyable unless they are done alone or in the company only of those we choose to have with us.

This is a significant feature of our culture—or at least of the culture in which I grew up. What I am less sure about is the question of whether it is necessarily a desirable feature of a culture. Indeed disagreement about just this issue seems to me to be one of the major sources of tension between the counterculture and the dominant older culture of my country. The disagreement concerns both a general theory of interpersonal relationships and a view about the significance of intimate thoughts and actions. The alternative view goes something like this.

We have made ourselves vulnerable—or at least far more vulnerable than we need be—by accepting the notion that there are thoughts and actions concerning which we ought to feel ashamed or embarrassed. When we realize that everyone has fantasies, desires, worries about all sorts of supposedly terrible, wicked, and shameful things, we ought to see that they really are not things to be ashamed of at all. We regard ourselves as vulnerable because in part we think we are different, if not unique. We have sexual feelings toward our parents, and no one else has ever had such wicked feelings. But if everyone does, then the fact that others know of this fantasy is less threatening. One is less vulnerable to their disapproval and contempt.

We have made ourselves excessively vulnerable, so this alternative point of view continues, because we have accepted the idea that many things are shameful unless done in private. And there is no reason to accept that convention. Of course we are embarrassed if others watch us having sexual intercourse—just as we are embarrassed if others see us unclothed. But that is because the culture has taught us to have these attitudes and not because they are intrinsically fitting. Indeed our culture would be healthier and happier if we diminished substantially the kinds of actions that we now feel comfortable doing only in private, or the kind of thoughts we now feel comfortable disclosing only to those with whom we have special relationships. This is so for at least three reasons. In the first place, there is simply no good reason why privacy is essential to these things. Sexual intercourse could be just as pleasurable in public (if we grew up unashamed) as is eating a good dinner in a good restaurant. Sexual intercourse is better in private only because society has told us so.

In the second place, it is clear that a change in our attitudes will make us more secure and at ease in the world. If we would be as indifferent to whether we are being watched when we have intercourse as we are to when we eat a meal, then we cannot be injured by the fact that we know others are watching us, and we cannot be injured nearly as much by even unknown observations.

In the third place, interpersonal relationships will in fact be better if there is less of a concern for privacy. After all, forthrightness, honesty, and candor are, for the most part, virtues, while hypocrisy and deceit are not. Yet this emphasis upon the maintenance of a private side to life tends to encourage hypocritical and deceitful ways of behavior. Individuals see themselves as leading dual lives—public ones and private ones. They present one view of themselves to the public—to casual friends, acquaintances, and strangers—and a different view of themselves to themselves and a few intimate associates. This way of living is hypocritical because it is, in essence, a life devoted to camouflaging the real, private self from public scrutiny. It is a dualistic, unintegrated life that renders the individuals who live it needlessly vulnerable, shame ridden, and lacking in a clear sense of self. It is to be contrasted with the more open, less guarded life of the person who has so little to fear from disclosures of self because he or she has nothing that requires hiding.

I think that this is an alternative view that deserves to be taken seriously. Any attempt to do so, moreover, should begin by considering more precisely the respects in which it departs from the more conventional view of the role of privacy maintained in the body of this essay, and the respects in which it does not. I have in mind three issues in particular that must be examined in detail before an intelligent decision can be made. The first is the question of the value that the counterculture ideal attaches to those characteristics of spontaneity and individuality that play such an important role in the more traditional view as I have described it. On at least one interpretation both views prize spontaneity and individuality equally highly, with the counterculture seeing openness in interpersonal relationships as a better way of achieving just those ends. On another interpretation, however, autonomy, spontaneity, and individuality are replaced as values by the satisfactions that attend the recognition of the likeness of all human experience and the sameness that characterizes all interpersonal relationships. Which way of living gives one more options concerning the kind of life that one will fashion for oneself is one of the central issues to be settled.

Still another issue that would have to be explored is the question of what would be gained and what would be lost in respect to the character of interpersonal relationships. One of the main arguments for the conventional view put forward earlier is that the sharing of one's intimate thoughts and behavior is one of the primary media through which close, meaningful interpersonal relationships are created, nourished, and confirmed. One thing that goes to define a relationship of close friendship is that the friends are willing to share truths about themselves with each other that they are unprepared to reveal to the world at large. One thing that helps to define and sustain a sexual love relationship is the willingness of the parties to share sexual intimacies with each other that they are unprepared to share with the world at large. If this makes sense, either as a conceptual or as an empirical truth, then perhaps acceptance of the counterculture ideal would mean that these kinds of relationships were either no longer possible or less likely. Or perhaps the conventional view is equally unsatisfactory here, too. Perhaps friendship and love both can and ought to depend upon some less proprietary, commercial conception of the exchange of commodities. Perhaps this view of intimate interpersonal relationships is as badly in need of alteration as is the attendant conception of the self.

Finally, we would want to examine more closely some other features of the counterculture ideal. Even if we no longer thought it important to mark off and distinguish our close friends from strangers (or even if we could still do that, but in some other way), might not the counterculture ideal of openness and honesty in all interpersonal relationships make ordinary social interaction vastly more complex and time-consuming than it now is—so much so, in fact, that these interactions, rather than the other tasks of living, would become the focus of our waking hours?

These are among the central issues that require continued exploration. They are certainly among the issues that the fully developed theory of privacy, its value and its place within the law, must confront and not settle by way of assumption and presupposition.

15

An economic theory of privacy

RICHARD A. POSNER

Much ink has been spilled in trying to clarify the elusive and ill-defined concept of "privacy." I will sidestep the definitional problem by simply noting that one aspect of privacy is the withholding or concealment of information. This aspect is of particular interest to the economist now that the study of information has become an important field of economics. It is also of interest to the regulator, and those affected by him, because both the right to privacy and the "right to know" are becoming more and more the subject of regulation.

Heretofore the economics of information has been limited to topics relating to the dissemination and, to a lesser extent, the concealment of information in explicit (mainly labor and consumer-good) markets—that is, to such topics as advertising, fraud, price dispersion, and job search. But it is possible to use economic analysis to explore the dissemination and withholding of information in personal as well as business contexts, and thus to deal with such matters as prying, eavesdropping, "self-advertising," and gossip. Moreover, the same analysis may illuminate questions of privacy within organizations, both commercial and noncommercial.

I shall first attempt to develop a simple economic theory of privacy. I shall then argue from this theory that, while personal privacy seems today to be valued more highly than organizational privacy (if one may judge by current legislative trends), a reverse ordering would be more consistent with the economics of the problem.

Theory

People invariably possess information, including the contents of communications and facts about themselves, that they will incur costs to conceal. Sometimes such information is of value to other people—

that is, other people will incur costs to discover it. Thus we have two economic goods, "privacy" and "prying." We could regard them as pure consumption goods, the way turnips or beer are normally regarded in economic analysis, and we would then speak of a "taste" for privacy or for prying. But this would bring the economic analysis to a grinding halt because tastes are unanalyzable from an economic standpoint. An alternative is to regard privacy and prying as intermediate rather than final goods—instrumental rather than final values. Under this approach, people are assumed not to desire or value privacy or prying in themselves but to use these goods as inputs into the production of income or some other broad measure of utility or welfare. This is the approach that I take here; the reader will have to decide whether it captures enough of the relevant reality to be enlightening.

Not so idle curiosity

Now the demand for private information (viewed, as it is here, as an intermediate good) is readily understandable where the existence of an actual or potential relationship, business or personal, creates opportunities for gain by the demander. These opportunities obviously exist in the case of information sought by the tax collector, fiancé, partner, creditor, competitor, and so on. Less obviously, much of the casual prying (a term not used here with any pejorative connotation) into the private lives of friends and colleagues that is so common a feature of social life is, I believe, motivated—to a greater extent than we usually think—by rational considerations of self-interest. Prying enables one to form a more accurate picture of a friend or colleague, and the knowledge gained is useful in one's social or professional dealings with that friend or colleague. For example, one wants to know in choosing a friend whether he will be discreet or indiscreet, selfish or generous. These qualities are not necessarily apparent on initial acquaintance. Even a pure altruist needs to know the (approximate) wealth of any prospective beneficiary of his altruism in order to be able to gauge the value of a gift or transfer to him.

The other side of the coin is that social dealings, like business dealings, present opportunities for exploitation through misrepresentation. Psychologists and sociologists have pointed out that even in everyday life people try to manipulate other people's opinion of them, using misrepresentation. The strongest defenders of privacy usually define the individual's right to privacy as the right to control the flow of information about him. A seldom-remarked corollary to a right to misrepresent one's character is that others have a legitimate interest in unmasking the misrepresentation.

Yet some of the demand for private information about other people seems mysteriously disinterested—for example, that of the readers of newspaper gossip columns, whose "idle curiosity" has been deplored, groundlessly in my opinion. Gossip columns recount the personal lives of wealthy and successful people whose tastes and habits offer models— that is, yield information—to the ordinary person in making consumption, career, and other decisions. The models are not always positive. The story of Howard Hughes, for example, is usually told as a morality play, warning of the pitfalls of success. That does not make it any less educational. The fascination with the notorious and the criminal—with John Profumo and with Nathan Leopold—has a similar basis. Gossip columns open people's eyes to opportunities and dangers; they are genuinely informative.

Moreover, the expression "idle curiosity" is misleading. People are not given to random undifferentiated curiosity. Why is there less curiosity about the lives of the poor (as measured, for example, by the infrequency with which poor people figure as central characters in popular novels) than about those of the rich? One reason is that the lives of the poor do not provide as much useful information for the patterning of our own lives. What interest there is in the poor is focused on people who were like us but who became poor, rather than on those who were always poor; again, the cautionary function of such information should be evident.

Samuel Warren and Louis Brandeis once attributed the rise of curiosity about people's lives to the excesses of the press (in an article in the *Harvard Law Review*, 1890). The economist does not believe, however, that supply creates demand. A more persuasive explanation for the rise of the gossip column is the increase in personal income over time. There is apparently very little privacy in poor societies, where, consequently, people can readily observe at first hand the intimate lives of others. Personal surveillance is costlier in wealthier societies, both because people live in conditions that give them greater privacy and because the value (and hence opportunity cost) of time is greater—too great, in fact, to make the expenditure of a lot of it in watching the neighbors a worthwhile pursuit. An alternative method of informing oneself about how others live was sought by the people and provided by the press. A legitimate and important function of the press is to provide specialization in prying in societies where the costs of obtaining information have become too great for the Nosy Parker.

Who owns secrets?

The fact that disclosure of personal information is resisted by (is costly to) the person to whom the information pertains, yet is valuable to others, may seem to argue for giving people property rights in information about themselves and letting them sell those rights freely. The process of voluntary exchange would then ensure that the information was put to its most valuable use. The attractiveness of this solution depends, however, on (1) the nature and source of the information and (2) transaction costs.

The strongest case for property rights in secrets is presented where such rights are necessary in order to encourage investment in the production of socially valuable information. This is the rationale for giving legal protection to the variety of commercial ideas, plans, and information encompassed by the term "trade secret." It also explains why the "shrewd bargainer" is not required to tell the other party to the bargain his true opinion of the values involved. A shrewd bargainer is, in part, one who invests resources in obtaining information about the true values of things. Were he forced to share this information with potential sellers, he would get no return on his investment and the process—basic to a market economy—by which goods are transferred through voluntary exchange into successively more valuable uses would be impaired. This is true even though the lack of candor in the bargaining process deprives it of some of its "voluntary" character.

At some point nondisclosure becomes fraud. One consideration relevant to deciding whether the line has been crossed is whether the information sought to be concealed by one of the transacting parties is a product of significant investment. If not, the social costs of nondisclosure are reduced. This may be decisive, for example, on the question whether the owner of a house should be required to disclose latent (nonobvious) defects to a purchaser. The ownership and maintenance of a house are costly and productive activities. But since knowledge of the house's defects is acquired by the owner costlessly (or nearly so), forcing him to disclose these defects will not reduce his incentive to invest in discovering them.

As examples of cases where transaction-cost considerations argue against assigning a property right to the possessor of a secret, consider (1) whether the Bureau of the Census should be required to *buy* information from the firms or households that it interviews and (2) whether a magazine should be allowed to sell its subscriber list to another magazine without obtaining the subscribers' consent. Requiring the Bureau of the Census to pay (that is, assigning the property right in the information sought to the interviewee) would yield a skewed sample: the poor would be overrepresented, unless the bureau used a differentiated price schedule based on the different costs of disclosure (and hence prices for cooperating) to the people sampled. In the magazine case, the costs of obtaining subscriber approval would be high relative to the value of the list. If, therefore, we are confident that these lists are generally worth more to the purchasers than being shielded from possible unwanted solicitations is worth to the subscribers, we should assign the property right to the magazine, and this is what the law does.

The decision to assign the property right away from the individual is further supported, in both the census and subscription-list cases, by the fact that the costs of disclosure to the individual are low. They are low in the census case because the government takes precautions against disclosure of the information collected to creditors, tax collectors, or others who might have transactions with the individual in which they could use the information to gain an advantage over him. They are low in the subscription-list case because the information about the subscribers that is disclosed to the list purchaser is trivial and cannot be used to impose substantial costs on them.

Even though the type of private information discussed thus far is not in general discreditable to the individual to whom it pertains, we have seen that there may still be strong reasons for assigning the property right away from that individual. Much of the demand for privacy, however, concerns discreditable information—often information concerning past or present criminal activity or moral conduct at variance with a person's professed moral standards—and often the motive for concealment is, as suggested earlier, to mislead others. People also wish to conceal private information that, while not strictly discreditable, would if revealed correct misapprehensions that the individual is trying to exploit—as when a worker conceals a serious health problem from his employer or a prospective husband conceals his sterility from his fiancée. It is not clear why society in these cases should assign the property right in information to the individual to whom it pertains; and under the common law, generally it does not. A separate question, taken up a little later, is whether the decision to assign the property right away from the possessor of guilty secrets implies that any and all methods of uncovering those secrets should be permitted.

An analogy to the world of commerce may clarify why people should not—on economic grounds in any event—have a right to conceal material facts about themselves. We think it wrong (and inefficient) that a seller in hawking his wares should be permitted to make false or incomplete representations as to their quality. But people "sell" themselves as well as their goods. A person professes high standards of behavior in order to induce others to engage in social or business dealings with him from which he derives an advantage, but at the same time conceals some of the facts that the people with whom he deals need in order to form an accurate picture of his character. There are practical reasons for not imposing a general legal duty of full and frank disclosure of one's material personal shortcomings—a duty not to be a hypocrite. But each of us should be allowed to protect ourselves from disadvantageous transactions by ferreting out concealed facts about other individuals that are material to their implicit or explicit self-representations.

It is no answer that, in Brandeis's phrase, people have "the right to be let alone." Few people want to be let alone. They want to manipulate the world around them by selective disclosure of facts about themselves. Why should others be asked to take their self-serving claims at face value and prevented from obtaining the information necessary to verify or disprove these claims?

Some private information that people desire to conceal is not discreditable. In our culture, for example, most people do not like to be seen naked, quite apart from any discreditable fact that such observation might reveal. Since this reticence, unlike concealment of discreditable information, is not a source of social costs and since transaction costs are low, there is an economic case for assigning the property right in this area of private information to the individual; and this is what the common law does. I do not think, however, that many people have a *general* reticence that makes them wish to conceal nondiscrediting personal information. Anyone who has sat next to a stranger on an airplane or a ski lift knows the delight that some people take in talking about themselves to complete strangers. Reticence appears when one is speaking to people—friends, family, acquaintances, business associates—who might use information about him to gain an advantage in business or social transactions with him. Reticence is generally a means rather than an end.

The reluctance of many people to reveal their income is sometimes offered as an example of a desire for privacy that cannot be explained in purely instrumental terms. But I suggest that people conceal an unexpectedly low income because being thought to have a high income has value in credit markets and elsewhere, and they conceal an unexpectedly high income in order to (1) avoid the attention of tax collectors, kidnappers, and thieves, (2) fend off solicitations from charities and family members, and (3) preserve a reputation for generosity that would be shattered if the precise fraction of their income that was being given away were known. Points (1) and (2) may explain anonymous gifts to charity.

Prying, eavesdropping, and formality

To the extent that personal information is concealed in order to mislead, the case for giving it legal protection is, I have argued, weak. Protection would simply increase transaction costs, much as if we permitted fraud in the sale of goods. However, it is also necessary to consider the *means* by which personal information is obtained. Prying by means of casual interrogation of acquaintances of the object of the prying must be distinguished from eavesdropping (electronically or otherwise) on a person's conversations. A in conversation with B disparages C. If C has a right to hear this conversation, A, in choosing the words he uses to B, will have to consider the possible reactions of C. Conversation will be more costly because of the external effects and this will result in less—and less effective—communication. After people adjust to this new world of public conversation, even the Cs of the world will cease to derive much benefit in the way of greater information from conversational publicity: people will be more guarded in their speech. The principal effect of publicity will be to make conversation more formal and communication less effective rather than to increase the knowledge of interested third parties.

Stated differently, the costs of defamatory utterances and hence the cost-justified level of expenditures on avoiding defamation are greater the more publicity given the utterance. If every conversation were public, the time and other resources devoted to ensuring that one's speech was free from false or unintended slanders would rise. The additional costs are avoided by the simple and inexpensive expedient of permitting conversations to be private.

It is relevant to observe that language becomes less formal as society evolves. The languages of primitive peoples are more elaborate, more ceremonious, and more courteous than that of twentieth-century Americans. One reason may be that primitive people have little privacy. There are relatively few private conversations because third parties are normally present and the effects of the conversation on them must be taken into account. Even today, one observes that people speak more formally the greater the number of people present. The rise of privacy has facilitated private conversation and thereby enabled

RICHARD A. POSNER

us to economize on communication—to speak with a brevity and informality apparently rare among primitive peoples. This valuable economy of communication would be undermined by allowing eavesdropping.

In some cases, to be sure, communication is not related to socially productive activity. Communication among criminal conspirators is an example. In these cases—where limited eavesdropping is indeed permitted—the effect of eavesdropping in reducing communication is not an objection to, but an advantage of, the eavesdropping.

The analysis here can readily be extended to efforts to obtain people's notes, letters, and other private papers; communication would be inhibited by such efforts. A more complex question is presented by photographic surveillance—for example, of the interior of a person's home. Privacy enables a person to dress and otherwise disport himself in his home without regard to the effect on third parties. This economizing property would be lost if the interior of the home were in the public domain. People dress not merely because of the effect on others but also because of the reticence, noted earlier, concerning nudity and other sensitive states. This is another reason for giving people a privacy right with regard to the places in which these sensitive states occur.

Ends and means

The two main strands of my argument—relating to personal facts and to communications, respectively—can be joined by remarking the difference in this context between ends and means. With regard to ends, there is a prima facie case for assigning the property right in a secret that is a by-product of socially productive activity to the individual if its compelled disclosure would impair the incentives to engage in that activity; but there is a prima facie case for assigning the property right away from the individual if secrecy would reduce the social product by misleading others. However, the fact that under this analysis most facts about people belong in the public domain does not imply that intrusion on private communications should generally be permitted, given the effects of such intrusions on the costs of legitimate communications.

Admittedly, the suggested dichotomy between facts and communications is too stark. If you are allowed to interrogate my acquaintances about my income, I may take steps to conceal it that are analogous to the increased formality of conversation that would ensue from abolition of the right to conversational privacy, and the costs of these steps are a social loss. The difference is one of degree. Because eavesdropping and related modes of intrusive surveillance are such effective ways of eliciting private information and are at the same time relatively easy to thwart, we can expect that evasive maneuvers, costly in the aggregate, would be undertaken if conversational privacy were compromised. It is more difficult to imagine people taking effective measures against casual prying. An individual is unlikely to alter his income or style of living drastically in order to better conceal his income or private information from casual or journalistic inquiry. (Howard Hughes was a notable exception to this generalization.)

We have now sketched the essential elements of an economically based legal right of privacy: (1) Trade and business secrets by which businessmen exploit their superior knowledge or skills would be protected. (The same principle would be applied to the personal level and would thus, for example, entitle the social host or hostess to conceal the recipe of a successful dinner.) (2) Facts about people would generally not be protected. My ill health, evil temper, even my income would not be facts over which I had property rights, though I might be able to prevent their discovery by methods unduly intrusive under the third category. (3) Eavesdropping and other forms of intrusive surveillance would be limited (so far as possible) to the discovery of illegal activities.

Application

To what extent is the economic theory developed above reflected in public policy? To answer this question, it is necessary to distinguish sharply between common law and statutory responses to the privacy question.

The common law

The term common law refers to the body of legal principles evolved by English and American appellate judges in the decision of private suits over a period of hundreds of years. I believe, and have argued in greater detail elsewhere, that the common law of privacy is strongly stamped by the economic principles (though nowhere explicitly recognized by the judges) developed in this article. That law contains the precise elements that an economically based right of privacy would include. Trade secrets and commercial privacy generally are well protected. It has been said by one court: "almost any knowledge or information used in the conduct of one's business may be held by its possessor secret." In another well-known case, aerial photography of a competitor's plant under construction was held to be unlawful, and the court used the term "commercial privacy" to describe the interest it was protecting.

An analogy in the personal area is the common law principle that a person's name or photograph may not be used in advertising without his consent. The effect is to create a property right which ensures that a person's name or likeness (O. J. Simpson's, for example) will be allocated to the advertising use in which it is most valuable. Yet, consistent with the economics of the problem, individuals have in general no right in common law to conceal discrediting information about themselves. But, again consistent with the economics of the problem, they do have a right to prevent eavesdropping, photographic surveillance of the interior of a home, the ransacking of private records to discover information about an individual, and similarly intrusive methods of penetrating the wall of privacy that people build about themselves. The distinction is illustrated by Ralph Nader's famous suit against General Motors. The court affirmed General Motors' right to have Nader followed about, to question his acquaintances, and, in short, to ferret out personal information about Nader that the company might have used to undermine his public credibility. Yet I would expect a court to enjoin any attempt through such methods to find out what Nader was about to say on some subject in order to be able to plagiarize his ideas.

When, however, we compare the implications of the economic analysis not with the common law relating to privacy but with recent legislation in the privacy area, we are conscious not of broad concordance but of jarring incongruity. As noted, from the economic standpoint, private business information should in general be accorded greater legal protection than personal information. Secrecy is an important method of appropriating social benefits to the entrepreneur who creates them, while in private life it is more likely simply to conceal legitimately discrediting or deceiving facts. Communications within organizations, whether public or private, should receive the same protection as communications among individuals, for in either case the effect of publicity would be to encumber and retard communication.

The trend in legislation

But in fact the legislative trend is toward giving individuals more and more privacy protection with respect to facts and communications, and business firms and other organizations (including government agencies, universities, and hospitals) less and less. The Freedom of Information Act, sunshine laws opening the deliberations of administrative agencies to the public, and the erosion of effective sanctions against breach of government confidences have greatly reduced the privacy of communications within the government. Similar forces are at work in private institutions such as business firms and private universities (note, for example, the Buckley Amendment and the opening of faculty meetings to student observers). Increasingly, moreover, the facts about an individual—arrest record, health, credit-worthiness, marital status, sexual proclivities—are secured from involuntary disclosure, while the facts about business corporations are thrust into public view by the expansive disclosure requirements of the federal securities laws (to the point where some firms are "going private" in order to secure greater confidentiality for their plans and operations), the civil rights laws, "line of business" reporting, and other regulations. A related trend is the erosion of the privacy of government officials through increasingly stringent ethical standards requiring disclosure of income.

The trend toward elevating personal and downgrading organizational privacy is mysterious to the economist (as are other recent trends in public regulation). To repeat, the economic case for privacy of *communications* seems unrelated to the nature of the communicator, whether a private individual or the employee of a university, corporation, or government agency, while so far as *facts* about people or organizations are concerned, the case for protecting business privacy is stronger, in general, than that for protecting individual privacy.

Some of the differences in the protection accorded governmental and personal privacy may, to be sure, simply reflect a desire to reduce the power of government. Viewed in this light, the Freedom of Information Act is perhaps supported by the same sorts of considerations that are believed by some to justify wiretapping in national security or organized crime cases. But only a small part of the recent legislative output in the privacy area can be explained in such terms.

A good example of legislative refusal to respect the economics of the privacy problem is the Buckley Amendment, which gives students (and their parents) access to their school records. The amendment permits students to waive, in writing, their right to see letters of recommendation, and most students do so. They do so because they know that letters of recommendation to which they have access convey no worthwhile information to the recipient. The effect on the candor and value of communication is the same as would be that of a rule that allowed C to hear A and B's conversations about him. Throwing open faculty meetings or congressional conferences to the public has the identical effect of reducing the value of communication without benefitting the public, for the presence of the public deters the very communication they want to hear.

As another example of an economically perverse legislative response to privacy issues, consider the different treatment of disclosures of corporate and of personal crime. The corporation that bribes foreign officials must make public disclosure of the fact, even though the crime may benefit the corporation, its shareholders, the United States as a whole, and even the citizens of the foreign country in question. Yet the convicted rapist, the recidivist con artist, and even the murderer "acquitted" by reason of insanity are not only under no duty to reveal to new acquaintances their criminal activities but are often assisted by law in concealing these activities.

Through the Fair Credit Reporting Act, credit bureaus are forbidden to report to their customers a range of information concerning applicants for credit—for instance, bankruptcies more than fourteen years old and all other adverse information (including criminal convictions and civil judgments) more than seven years old. These restrictions represent an extraordinary intervention in the credit process that could be justified only if credit bureaus systematically collected and reported information that, because of its staleness, had negligible value to its customers in deciding whether credit should be extended. No such assumption of economic irrationality is possible.

These examples could be multiplied, but the main point should be clear enough. Legislatures are increasingly creating rights to conceal information that is material to prospective creditors and employers, and at the same time forcing corporations and other organizations to publicize information whose confidentiality is necessary to their legitimate operation.

A contrary view

I know of only one principled effort to show that individual privacy claims are stronger than those of businesses and other organizations. Professors Kent Greenawalt and Eli Noam of Columbia, in an unpublished paper, offer two distinctions between a business's (or other organization's) interest in privacy and an individual's interest. First, they say that the latter is a matter of rights and that the former is based merely on instrumental, utilitarian considerations. The reasons they offer for recognizing a right of personal privacy are, however, utilitarian—that people need an opportunity to "make a new start" (that is, to conceal embarrassing or discreditable facts about their past), that people cannot preserve their sanity without privacy, and so on. Yet Greenawalt and Noam disregard the utilitarian justification for secrecy as an incentive to investment in productive activity—the strongest justification for secrecy and one mainly relevant, as I have argued, in business contexts.

The second distinction they suggest between the business and personal claims to privacy is a strangely distorted mirror of my argument for entrepreneurial or productive secrecy. They argue that it is difficult to establish property rights in information and even remark that secrecy is one way of doing so. But they do not draw the obvious conclusion that secrecy can promote productive activity by creating property rights in valuable information. Instead they use the existence of imperfections in the market for information as a justification for government regulation designed to extract private information from business firms. They do not explain, however, how the government could, let alone demonstrate that it would, use this information more productively than firms, and they do not consider the impact of this form of public prying on the incentive to produce the information in the first place.

Conclusion

Discussions of the privacy question have contained a high degree of cant, sloganeering, emotion, and loose thinking. A fresh perspective on the question is offered by economic analysis, and by a close examination of the common law principles that have evolved under the influence (perhaps unconsciously) of economic perceptions. In the perspective offered by economics and by the common law, the recent legislative emphasis on favoring individual and denigrating corporate and organizational privacy stands revealed as still another example of perverse government regulation of social and economic life.

16

Privacy and the limits of law

RUTH GAVISON

Anyone who studies the law of privacy today may well feel a sense of uneasiness. On one hand, there are popular demands for increased protection of privacy, discussions of new threats to privacy, and an intensified interest in the relationship between privacy and other values, such as liberty, autonomy, and mental health.[1] These demands have generated a variety of legal responses. Most states recognize a cause of action for invasions of privacy.[2] The Supreme Court has declared a constitutional right to privacy, a right broad enough to protect abortion and the use of contraceptives.[3] Congress enacted the Privacy Act of 1974[4] after long hearings and debate. These activities[5] seem to imply a wide consensus concerning the distinctness and importance of privacy.

On the other hand, much of the scholarly literature on privacy is written in quite a different spirit. Commentators have argued that privacy rhetoric is misleading: when we study the cases in which the law (or our moral intuitions) suggest that a "right to privacy" has been violated, we always find that some other interest has been involved.[6] Consequently, they argue, our understanding of privacy will be improved if we disregard the rhetoric, look behind the decisions, and identify the real interests protected. When we do so, they continue, we can readily see why privacy itself is never protected: to the extent that there is something distinct about claims for privacy, they are either indications of hypersensitivity[7] or an unjustified wish to manipulate and defraud.[8] Although these commentators disagree on many points, they are united in denying the utility of thinking and talking about privacy as a legal right, and suggest some form of reductionism.[9]

This article is an attempt to vindicate the way most of us think and

Reprinted by permission of The Yale Law Journal Company and Fred B. Rothman & Company from *Yale Law Journal* 89:421–71, 1980. © The Yale Law Journal Company, 1980.

talk about privacy issues: unlike the reductionists, most of us consider privacy to be a useful concept. To be useful, however, the concept must denote something that is distinct and coherent. Only then can it help us in thinking about problems. Moreover, privacy must have a coherence in three different contexts. First, we must have a neutral concept of privacy that will enable us to identify when a loss of privacy has occurred so that discussions of privacy and claims of privacy can be intelligible. Second, privacy must have coherence as a value, for claims of legal protection of privacy are compelling only if losses of privacy are sometimes undesirable and if those losses are undesirable for similar reasons. Third, privacy must be a concept useful in legal contexts, a concept that enables us to identify those occasions calling for legal protection, because the law does not interfere to protect against every undesirable event.

Our everyday speech suggests that we believe the concept of privacy is indeed coherent and useful in the three contexts, and that losses of privacy (identified by the first), invasions of privacy (identified by the second), and actionable violations of privacy (identified by the third) are related in that each is a subset of the previous category. Using the same word in all three contexts reinforces the belief that they are linked. Reductionist analyses of privacy—that is, analyses denying the utility of privacy as a separate concept—sever these conceptual and linguistic links. This article is an invitation to maintain those links, because an awareness of the relationships and the larger picture suggested by them may contribute to our understanding both of legal claims for protection, and of the extent to which those claims have been met.[10]

I begin by suggesting that privacy is indeed a distinct and coherent concept in all these contexts. Our interest in privacy, I argue, is related to our concern over our accessibility to others: the extent to which we are known to others, the extent to which others have physical access to us, and the extent to which we are the subject of others' attention. This concept of privacy as a concern for limited accessibility enables us to identify when losses of privacy occur. Furthermore, the reasons for which we claim privacy in different situations are similar. They are related to the functions privacy has in our lives: the promotion of liberty, autonomy, selfhood, and human relations, and furthering the existence of a free society.[11] The coherence of privacy as a concept and the similarity of the reasons for regarding losses of privacy as undesirable support the notion that the legal system should make an explicit commitment to privacy as a value that should be considered in reaching legal results. This analysis does not require that privacy be protected in all cases; that result would require consideration of many factors not discussed here. I argue only that privacy refers to a unique concern that should be given weight in balancing values.

My analysis of privacy yields a better description of the law and a deeper understanding of both the appeal of the reductionist approach and its peril. The appeal lies in the fact that it highlights an important fact about the state of the law—privacy is seldom protected in the absence of some other interest. The danger is that we might conclude from this fact that privacy is not an important value and that losses of it should not feature as considerations for legal protection. In view of the prevalence of the reductionist view, the case for an affirmative and explicit commitment to privacy—vindicating the antireductionist perspective—becomes compelling.

I. The meaning and functions of privacy

"Privacy" is a term used with many meanings. For my purposes, two types of questions about privacy are important. The first relates to the *status* of the term: is privacy a situation, a right, a claim, a form of control, a value? The second relates to the *characteristics* of privacy: is it related to information, to autonomy, to personal identity, to physical access? Support for all of these possible answers, in almost any combination, can be found in the literature.[12]

The two types of questions involve different choices. Before resolving these issues, however, a general distinction must be drawn between the concept and the value of privacy. The concept of privacy identifies losses of privacy. As such, it should be neutral and descriptive only, so as not to preempt questions we might want to ask about such losses. Is the loser aware of the loss? Has he consented to it? Is the loss desirable? Should the law do something to prevent or punish such losses?

This is not to imply that the neutral concept of privacy is the most important, or that it is only legitimate to use "privacy" in this sense. Indeed, in the context of legal protection, privacy should also indicate a value. The coherence and usefulness of privacy as a value is due to a similarity one finds in the reasons advanced for its protection, a similarity that enables us to draw principles of liability for invasions.[13] These reasons identify those aspects of privacy that are considered desirable. When we claim legal protection for privacy, we mean that only those aspects should be protected, and we no longer refer to the "neutral" concept of privacy. In order to see which aspects of privacy are desirable and thus merit protection as a value, however, we must begin our inquiry in a nonpreemptive way by starting with a concept that does not make desirability, or any of the elements that may preempt the question of desirability, part of the notion of privacy. The value of privacy can be determined only at the conclusion of discussion about what privacy is, and when—and why—losses of privacy are undesirable.[14]

In this section I argue that it is possible to advance a neutral concept of privacy, and that it can be shown to serve important functions that entitle it to prima facie legal protection. The coherence of privacy in the third context—as a legal concept—relies on our understanding of the functions and value of privacy; discussion of the way in which the legal system should consider privacy is therefore deferred until later sections.[15]

A. The neutral concept of privacy

1. THE STATUS OF PRIVACY

The desire not to preempt our inquiry about the value of privacy by adopting a value-laden concept at the outset is sufficient to justify viewing privacy as a situation of an individual vis-à-vis others, or as a condition of life. It also requires that we reject attempts to describe privacy as a claim,[16] a psychological state,[17] or an area that should not be invaded.[18] For the same reasons, another description that should be rejected is that of privacy as a form of control.[19]

This last point requires some elaboration, because it may appear that describing privacy as a form of control does not preempt important questions. Were privacy described in terms of control, for example, we could still ask whether X has lost control, and whether such loss is desirable. The appearance of a nonpreemptive concept is misleading, however, and is due to an ambiguity in the notion of control. Hyman Gross, for example, defines privacy as "control over acquaintance with one's personal affairs."[20] According to one sense of this definition, a voluntary, knowing disclosure does not involve loss of privacy because it is an exercise of control, not a loss of it.[21] In another, stronger sense of control, however, voluntary disclosure is a loss of control because the person who discloses loses the power to prevent others from further disseminating the information.

There are two problems here. The weak sense of control is not sufficient as a description of privacy, for X can have control over whether to disclose information about himself, yet others may have information and access to him through other means. The strong sense of control, on the other hand, may indicate loss of privacy when there is only a threat of such loss.[22] More important, "control" suggests that the important aspect of privacy is the ability to choose it and see that the choice is respected. All possible choices are consistent with enjoyment of control, however, so that defining privacy in terms of control relates it to the power to make certain choices rather than to the way in which we choose to exercise this power. But individuals may choose to have privacy or to give it up.[23] To be nonpreemptive, privacy must not depend on choice. We need a framework within which privacy may be the result of a specific exercise of control, as when X decides not to disclose certain information about himself, or the result of something imposed on an individual against his wish, as when the law prohibits the performance of sexual intercourse in a public place. Furthermore, the reasons we value privacy may have nothing to do with whether an individual has in fact chosen it. Sometimes we may be inclined to criticize an individual for not choosing privacy, and other times for choosing it. This criticism cannot be made if privacy is defined as a form of control.

Insisting that we start with a neutral concept of privacy does not mean that wishes, exercises of choice, or claims are not important elements in the determination of the aspects of privacy that are to be deemed desirable or of value. This insistence does mean, however, that we are saying something meaningful, and not merely repeating the implications of our concept, if we conclude that only choices of privacy should be protected by law.

Resolving the status of privacy is easier than resolving questions concerning the characteristics of privacy. Is privacy related to secrecy, freedom of action, sense of self, anonymity, or any specific combination of these elements? The answers here are not constrained by methodological concerns. The crucial test is the utility of the proposed concept in capturing the tenor of most privacy claims, and in presenting coherent reasons for legal protection that will justify grouping these claims together. My conception of privacy as related to secrecy, anonymity, and solitude is defended in these terms.

2. THE CHARACTERISTICS OF PRIVACY

In its most suggestive sense, privacy is a limitation of others' access to an individual. As a methodological starting point, I suggest that an individual enjoys *perfect* privacy when he is completely inaccessible to others.[24] This may be broken into three independent components: in perfect privacy no one has any information about X, no one pays any attention to X, and no one has physical access to X. Perfect privacy is, of course, impossible in any society. The possession or enjoyment of privacy is not an all or nothing concept, however, and the total loss of privacy is as impossible as perfect privacy. A more important concept, then, is *loss* of privacy. A loss of privacy occurs as others obtain information about an individual, pay attention to him, or gain access to him. These three elements of secrecy, anonymity, and solitude are distinct and independent, but interrelated, and the complex concept of privacy is richer than any definition centered around only one of them. The complex concept better explains our intuitions as to when privacy is lost, and captures more of the suggestive meaning of privacy. At the same time, it remains sufficiently distinctive to exclude situations that are sometimes labeled "privacy," but that are more related to notions of accountability and interference than to accessibility.

a. Information known about an individual

It is not novel to claim that privacy is related to the amount of information known about an individual. Indeed, many scholars have defined privacy exclusively in these terms,[25] and the most lively privacy issue now discussed is that related to information-gathering. Nevertheless, at least two scholars have argued that there is no inherent loss of privacy as information about an individual becomes known.[26] I believe these critics are wrong. If secrecy is not treated as an independent element of privacy, then the following are only some of the situations that will not be considered losses of privacy: (a) an estranged wife who publishes her husband's love letters to her, without his consent; (b) a single data-bank containing all census information and government files that is used by all government officials;[27] and (c) an employer who asks every conceivable question of his employees and yet has no obligation to keep the answers confidential. In none of these cases is there any intrusion, trespass, falsification, appropriation, or exposure of the individual to direct observation. Thus, unless the amount of information others have about an individual is considered at least partly determinative of the degree of privacy he has, these cases cannot be described as involving losses of privacy.

To talk of the "amount of information" known about an individual is to imply that it is possible to individuate items or pieces of information, to determine the number of people who know each item of information about X, and thus to quantify the information known about X. In fact, this is impossible, and the notion requires greater theoretical elaboration than it has received until now. It is nevertheless used here because in most cases its application is relatively clear. Only a few of the many problems involved need to be mentioned.

The first problem is whether we should distinguish between different kinds of knowledge about an individual, such as verbal as opposed to sensory knowledge, or among different types of sensory knowledge. For example, assume Y learns that X is bald because he reads a verbal description of X. At a later time, Y sees X and, naturally, observes that X is bald. Has Y acquired any further information about X, and if so, what is it? It might be argued that even a rereading of a verbal description may reveal to Y further information about X, even though Y has no additional source of information.[28]

A related set of problems arises when we attempt to compare different "amounts" of knowledge about the same individual. Who has more information about X, his wife after fifteen years of marriage, his psychiatrist after seven years of analysis, or the biographer who spends four years doing research and unearths details about X that are not known either to the wife or to the analyst?[29]

A third set of problems is suggested by the requirement that for a loss of privacy to occur, the information must be "about" the individual. First, how specific must this relationship be? We know that most people have sexual fantasies and sexual relationships with others. Thus, we almost certainly "know" that our new acquaintances have sexual fantasies, yet they do not thereby suffer a loss of privacy. On the other hand, if we have detailed information about the sexual lives of a small number of people, and we are then introduced to one of them, does the translation of the general information into personal information about this person involve a loss of privacy? Consider the famous anecdote about the priest who was asked, at a party, whether he had heard any exceptional stories during confessionals. "In fact," the priest replied, "my first confessor is a good example, since he confessed to a murder." A few minutes later, an elegant man joined the group, saw the priest, and greeted him warmly. When asked how he knew the priest, the man replied: "Why, I had the honor of being his first confessor."

The priest gave an "anonymous" piece of information, which became information "about" someone through the combination of the anonymous statement with the "innocent" one made by the confessor. Only the later statement was "about" a specific individual, but it turned what was previously an anonymous piece of information into further information "about" the individual. The translation here from anonymous information to information about X is immediate and unmistakable, but the process is similar to the combination of general knowledge about a group of people and the realization that a certain individual is a member of that group.[30]

Problems of the relationship between an individual and pieces of information exist on another level as well. Is information about *X*'s wife, car, house, parents, or dog information about *X*? Clearly, this is information about the other people, animals, or things involved, but can *X* claim that disclosure of such information is a loss of his privacy? Such claims have often been made.[31] Their plausibility in at least some of the cases suggests that people's notions of themselves may extend beyond their physical limits.[32]

A final set of problems concerns the importance of the truth of the information that becomes known about an individual. Does dissemination of false information about *X* mean that he has lost privacy? The usual understanding of "knowledge" presupposes that the information is true, but is this sense of "knowledge" relevant here? In one sense, *X* has indeed lost privacy. People now believe they know more about him. If the information is sufficiently spectacular, *X* may lose his anonymity and become the subject of other people's attention.[33] In another sense, however, *X* is not actually "known" any better. In fact, he may even be known less, because the false information may lead people to disregard some correct information about *X* that they already had.[34] Another difficulty is revealed when we consider statements whose truth is not easily determinable, such as "*X* is beautiful" or "*X* is dumb and irresponsible." Publication of such statements clearly leads to some loss of privacy: listeners now know what the speaker thinks about *X*, and this itself is information about *X* (as well as about the speaker). But does the listener also know that *X* is indeed beautiful? This is hard to tell.[35]

b. Attention paid to an individual

An individual always loses privacy when he becomes the subject of attention. This will be true whether the attention is conscious and purposeful, or inadvertent. Attention is a primary way of acquiring information, and sometimes is essential to such acquisition, but attention alone will cause a loss of privacy even if no new information becomes known. This becomes clear when we consider the effect of calling, "Here is the President," should he attempt to walk the streets incognito. No further information is given, but none is necessary. The President loses whatever privacy his temporary anonymity could give him. He loses it because attention has focused on him.

Here too, however, some elaboration is needed. *X* may be the subject of *Y*'s attention in two typical ways.[36] First, *Y* may follow *X*, stare at him, listen to him, or observe him in any other way. Alternatively, Y may concentrate his thoughts on X. Only the first way of paying attention is directly related to loss of privacy. Discussing, imagining, or thinking about another person is related to privacy in a more indirect way, if at all. Discussions may involve losses of privacy by communicating information about a person or by creating an interest in the person under discussion that may itself lead to more attention. Thinking about a person may also produce an intensified effort to recall or obtain information about him. This mental activity may in turn produce a loss of privacy if new information is obtained. For the most part, however, thinking about another person, even in the most intense way, will involve no loss of privacy to the subject of this mental activity. The favorite subject of one's sexual fantasies may have causes for complaint, but it is unlikely that these will be related to loss of privacy.[37]

c. Physical access to an individual

Individuals lose privacy when others gain physical access to them. Physical access here means physical proximity—that Y is close enough to touch or observe X through normal use of his senses. The ability to watch and listen, however, is not in itself an indication of physical access, because Y can watch X from a distance or wiretap X's telephone. This explains why it is much easier for X to know when Y has physical access to him than when Y observes him.

The following situations involving loss of privacy can best be understood in terms of physical access: (a) a stranger who gains entrance to a woman's home on false pretenses in order to watch her giving birth;[38] (b) Peeping Toms; (c) a stranger who chooses to sit on "our" bench, even though the park is full of empty benches; and (d) a move from a single-person office to a much larger one that must be shared with a colleague. In each of these cases, the essence of the complaint is not that more information about us has been acquired, nor that more attention has been drawn to us, but that our spatial aloneness has been diminished.[39]

d. Relations among the three elements

The concept of privacy suggested here is a complex of these three independent and irreducible elements: secrecy, anonymity, and solitude.[40] Each is independent in the sense that a loss of privacy may occur through a change in any one of the three, without a necessary loss in either of the other two. The concept is nevertheless coherent because the three elements are all part of the same notion of accessibility, and are related in many important ways. The three elements may coexist in the same situation. For example, the psychiatrist who sits next to his patient and listens to him acquires information about the patient,[41] pays attention to him, and has physical access to him. At the same time, none of the three elements is the necessary companion of the other two.

Information about X may of course be acquired by making X the subject of Y's attention. When Y follows, watches, or observes X in any way, he increases the likelihood of acquiring information about X. Similarly, when Y is in physical proximity to X, he has an opportunity to observe and thus obtain information about X. Nevertheless, information about X may be obtained when Y has no physical access to X, and when X is not the subject of Y's attention. It is possible to learn information about an individual by questioning his friends and neighbors, and thus without observing the individual or being in his physical proximity. It is also possible to learn information about an individual entirely by accident, when the individual is not even the subject of attention.[42]

Attention may be paid to X without learning new information about him. The mother who follows her child in order to make sure the child does not harm himself is not interested in gaining new information about the child, nor will she necessarily obtain any new information. Pointing X out in a crowd will increase the attention paid to X, even in the absence of any physical proximity.

Finally, an individual can be in physical proximity to others without their paying attention or learning any new information about him. Two people may sit in the same room without paying any attention to each other, and yet each will experience some loss of privacy.

The interrelations between the three elements may be seen when we consider the different aspects of privacy that may be involved in one situation. For instance, police attempt to learn of plans to commit crimes. Potential criminals may raise a privacy claim concerning this information, but are unlikely to gain much support. The criminal's desire that information about his plans not be known creates a privacy claim, but not a very convincing one. We might be more receptive, however, to another privacy claim that criminals might make concerning attention and observation, or the opportunity to be alone. If constant surveillance were the price of efficient law enforcement, we might feel the need to rethink the criminal law. The fact that these are two independent claims suggests that concern for the opportunity to have solitude and anonymity is related not only to the wish to conceal some kinds of information, but also to needs such as relaxation, concentration, and freedom from inhibition.[43]

Yet another privacy concern emerges when we talk about the right against self-incrimination. Again, the essence of the concern is not simply the information itself; we do not protect the suspect against police learning the information from other sources. Our concern relates to the way the information is acquired: it is an implication of privacy that individuals should not be forced to give evidence against themselves. Similarly, evidentiary privileges that may also be defended' in terms of privacy do not reflect concern about the information itself. The concern here is the existence of relationships in which confidentiality should be protected, so that the parties know that confidences shared in these relationships will not be forced out. In some cases, disclosure will not be sought, and in others the law may even impose a duty against disclosure.

The irreducibility of the three elements may suggest that the complex concept of privacy lacks precision, and that we would do better to isolate each of the different concerns and discuss separately what the law should do to protect secrecy, anonymity, and solitude. Such isolation may indeed be fruitful for some purposes.[44] At present, however, the proposed concept suggests a coherent concern that is generally discussed in extra-legal contexts as "privacy." It therefore seems justified to prefer the complex notion of accessibility to the loss of richness in description that would result from any more particularistic analysis.

e. What privacy is not

The neutral concept of privacy presented here covers such "typical" invasions of privacy as the collection, storage, and computerization of information; the dissemination of information about individuals; peeping, following, watching, and photographing individuals; intruding or entering "private" places; eavesdropping, wiretapping, reading of letters; drawing attention to individuals; required testing of individuals; and forced disclosure of information. At the same time, a number of situations sometimes said to constitute invasions of privacy will be seen not to involve losses of privacy per se under this concept. These include exposure to unpleasant noises, smells, and sights; prohibitions of such conduct as abortions, use of contraceptives, and "unnatural" sexual intercourse; insulting, harassing, or persecuting behavior; presenting individuals in a "false light"; unsolicited mail and unwanted phone calls; regulation of the way familial obligations should be discharged; and commercial exploitation.[45] These situations are all described as "invasions of privacy" in the literature, presumably indicating some felt usefulness in grouping them under the label of "privacy," and thus an explanation of the reasons for excluding these cases from my argument seems appropriate. Such an explanation may also clarify the proposed analysis and its methodological presuppositions.

The initial intuition is that privacy has to do with accessibility to an individual, as expressed by the three elements of information-gathering, attention, and physical access, and that this concept is distinct. It is part of this initial intuition that we want and deem desirable many things, and that we lose more than we gain by treating all of them as the same thing.[46] If the concepts we use give the appearance of differentiating concerns without in fact isolating something distinct, we are likely to fall victims to this false appearance and our chosen language will be a hindrance rather than a help. The reason for excluding the situations mentioned above, as well as those not positively identified by the proposed analysis, is that they present precisely such a danger.[47]

There is one obvious way to include all the so-called invasions of privacy under the term. Privacy can be defined as "being let alone," using the phrase often attributed—incorrectly—to Samuel Warren and Louis Brandeis.[48] The great simplicity of this definition gives it rhetorical force and attractiveness, but also denies it the distinctiveness that is necessary for the phrase to be useful in more than a conclusory sense. This description gives an appearance of differentiation while covering almost any conceivable complaint anyone could ever make.[49] A great many instances of "not letting people alone" cannot readily be described as invasions of privacy. Requiring that people pay their taxes or go into the army, or punishing them for murder, are just a few of the obvious examples.

For similar reasons, we must reject Edward Bloustein's suggestion that the coherence of privacy lies in the fact that all invasions are violations of human dignity.[50] We may well be concerned with invasions of privacy, at least in part, because they are violations of dignity.[51] But there are ways to offend dignity and personality that have nothing to do with privacy. Having to beg or sell one's body in order to survive are serious affronts to dignity, but do not appear to involve loss of privacy.[52]

To speak in privacy terms about claims for noninterference by the state in personal decisions is similar to identifying privacy with "being let alone." There are two problems with this tendency. The first is that the typical privacy claim is not a claim for noninterference by the state at all. It is a claim *for* state interference in the form of legal protection against other individuals, and this is obscured when privacy is discussed in terms of noninterference with personal decisions.[53] The second problem is that this conception excludes from the realm of privacy all claims that have nothing to do with highly personal decisions, such as an individual's unwillingness to have a file in a central data-bank.[54] Moreover, identifying privacy as noninterference with private action, often in order to avoid an explicit return to "substantive due process,"[55] may obscure the nature of the legal decision and draw attention away from important considerations.[56] The limit of state interference with individual action is an important question that has been with us for centuries. The usual terminology for dealing with this question is that of "liberty of action." It may well be that some cases pose a stronger claim for noninterference than others, and that the intimate nature of certain decisions affects these limits. This does not justify naming this set of concerns "privacy," however. A better way to deal with these issues may be to treat them as involving questions of liberty, in which enforcement may raise difficult privacy issues.[57]

Noxious smells and other nuisances are described as problems of privacy because of an analogy with intrusion. Outside forces that enter private zones seem similar to invasions of privacy. There are no good reasons, however, to expect any similarity between intrusive smells or noises and modes of acquiring information about or access to an individual.[58]

Finally, some types of commercial exploitation are grouped under privacy primarily because of legal history: the first cases giving a remedy for unauthorized use of a name or picture, sometimes described as invasions of privacy,[59] usually involved commercial exploitation.[60] The essence of privacy is not freedom from commercial exploitation, however. Privacy can be invaded in ways that have nothing to do with such exploitation, and there are many forms of exploitation that do not involve privacy even under the broadest conception.[61] The use of privacy as a label for protection against some forms of commercial exploitation is another unfortunate illustration of the confusions that will inevitably arise if care is not taken to follow an orderly conceptual scheme.[62]

B. The functions of privacy

In any attempt to define the scope of desirable legal protection of privacy, we move beyond the neutral concept of "loss of privacy," and seek to describe the positive concept that identifies those aspects of privacy that are of value. Identifying the positive functions of privacy is not an easy task. We start from the obvious fact that both perfect privacy and total loss of privacy are undesirable. Individuals must be in some intermediate state—a balance between privacy and interaction—in order to maintain human relations, develop their capacities and sensibilities, create and grow, and even to survive. Privacy thus cannot be said to be a value in the sense that the more people have of it, the better. In fact, the opposite may be true.[63] In any event, my purpose here is not to determine the proper balance between privacy and interaction; I want only to identify the positive functions that privacy has in our lives. From them we can derive the limits of the value of privacy, and then this value can be balanced against others.

The best way in which to understand the value of privacy is to examine its functions. This approach is fraught with difficulties, however. These justifications for privacy are instrumental, in the sense that they point out how privacy relates to other goals. The strength of instrumental justifications depends on the extent to which other goals promoted by privacy are considered important, and on the extent to which the relationship between the two is established. In most cases, the link between the enjoyment of privacy and other goals is at least partly empirical, and thus this approach raises all the familiar problems of social science methodology.

Two possible ways to avoid these difficulties should be discussed before I proceed further. One approach rests the desirability of privacy on a want-satisfaction basis, and the other argues that privacy is an ultimate value. The want-satisfaction argument posits the desirability of satisfying wishes and thus provides a reason to protect all wishes to have privacy.[64] It does not require empirical links between privacy and other goals. Moreover, the notion that choice should be respected is almost universally accepted as a starting point for practical reasoning.[65] The want-satisfaction argument cannot carry us very far, however. It does not explain why we should prefer X's wish to maintain his privacy against Y's wish to pry or acquire information. Without explaining why wishes for privacy are more important than wishes to invade it, the want-satisfaction principle alone cannot support the desirability of privacy. Indeed, some wishes to have privacy do not enjoy even prima facie validity. The criminal needs privacy to complete his offense undetected, the con artist needs it to manipulate his victim; we would not find the mere fact that they wish to have privacy a good reason for protecting it. The want-satisfaction principle needs a supplement that will identify legitimate reasons for which people want and need privacy. This is the task undertaken by an instrumental inquiry. These reasons will identify the cases in which wishes to have privacy should override wishes to invade it. They will also explain why in some cases we say that people need privacy even though they have not chosen it.[66] Thus, these instrumentalist reasons will explain the distinctiveness of privacy.

The attractiveness of the argument that privacy is an ultimate value lies in the intuitive feeling that only ultimate values are truly important, and in the fact that claims that a value is ultimate are not vulnerable to the empirical challenges that can be made to functional analyses.[67] But these claims also obscure the specific functions of privacy. They prevent any discussion with people who do not share the intuitive belief in the importance of privacy. Given the current amount of skeptical commentary, such claims are bound to raise more doubts than convictions about the importance and distinctiveness of privacy.

Thus it appears that we cannot avoid a functional analysis. Such an analysis presents an enormous task, for the values served by privacy are many and diverse. They include a healthy, liberal, democratic, and pluralistic society; individual autonomy; mental health; creativity; and the capacity to form and maintain meaningful relations with others. These goals suffer from the same conceptual ambiguities that we have described for privacy, which makes it difficult to formulate questions for empirical research and very easy to miss the relevant questions. More important, the empirical data is not only scant, it is often double-edged. The evaluation of links between privacy and other values must therefore be extremely tentative. Nevertheless, much can be gained by identifying and examining instrumental arguments for privacy; this is the indispensable starting point for any attempt to make sense of our concern with privacy, and to expose this concern to critical examination and evaluation.

It is helpful to start by seeking to identify those features of human life that would be impossible—or highly unlikely—without some privacy. Total lack of privacy is full and immediate access, full and immediate knowledge, and constant observation of an individual. In such a state, there would be no private thoughts, no private places, no private parts. Everything an individual did and thought would immediately become known to others.

There is something comforting and efficient about total absence of privacy for all.[68] A person could identify his enemies, anticipate dangers stemming from other people, and make sure he was not cheated or manipulated. Criminality would cease, for detection would be certain, frustration probable, and punishment sure. The world would be safer, and as a result, the time and resources now spent on trying to protect ourselves against human dangers and misrepresentations could be directed to other things.

This comfort is fundamentally misleading, however. Some human activities only make sense if there is some privacy. Plots and intrigues may disappear, but with them would go our private diaries, intimate confessions, and surprises. We would probably try hard to suppress our daydreams and fantasies once others had access to them. We would try to erase from our minds everything we would not be willing to publish, and we would try not to do anything that would make us likely to be feared, ridiculed, or harmed. There is a terrible flatness in the person who could succeed in these attempts. We do not choose against total lack of privacy only because we cannot attain it, but because its price seems much too high.[69]

In any event, total lack of privacy is unrealistic. Current levels of privacy are better in some ways, because we all have some privacy that cannot easily be taken from us.[70] The current state is also worse in some ways, because enjoyment of privacy is not equally distributed and some people have more security and power as a result. The need to protect privacy thus stems from two kinds of concern. First, in some areas we all tend to have insufficient amounts of privacy. Second, unequal distribution of privacy may lead to manipulation, deception, and threats to autonomy and democracy.[71]

Two clusters of concerns are relevant here. The first relates to our notion of the individual, and the kinds of actions we think people should be allowed to take in order to become fully realized. To this cluster belong the arguments linking privacy to mental health, autonomy, growth, creativity, and the capacity to form and create meaningful human relations. The second cluster relates to the type of society we want. First, we want a society that will not hinder individual attainment of the goals mentioned above. For this, society has to be liberal and pluralistic. In addition, we link a concern for privacy to our concept of democracy.

Inevitably, the discussion of functions that follows is sketchy and schematic. My purpose is to point out the many contexts in which privacy may operate, not to present full and conclusive arguments.

1. PRIVACY AND THE INDIVIDUAL

Functional arguments depend on a showing that privacy is linked to the promotion of something else that is accepted as desirable. In order to speak about individual goals, we must have a sense of what individuals are, and what they can and should strive to become. We do not have any one such picture, of course, and certainly none that is universally accepted. Nonetheless, privacy may be linked to goals such as creativity, growth, autonomy, and mental health that are accepted as desirable by almost all such theories, yet in ways that are not dictated by any single theory. This may give functional arguments for privacy an eclectic appearance, but it may also indicate the strength of these arguments. It appears that privacy is central to the attainment of individual goals under every theory of the individual that has ever captured man's imagination.[72] It also seems that concern about privacy is evidenced in all societies, even these with few opportunities for physical privacy.[73] Because we have no single theory about the nature of the individual and the way in which individuals relate to others, however, it should be recognized that the way in which we perceive privacy contributing to individual goals will itself depend on the theory of the individual that we select.

In the following discussion, I will note where a difference in perspective may dictate different approaches or conclusions. These different perspectives relate to theories of human growth, development, and personality. It is easy to see that different answers to questions such as the following may yield different arguments for privacy: Is there a "real self" that can be known?[74] If there is, is it coherent and always consistent? If not, can we identify one that is better, and that we should strive to realize? Are human relations something essential, or a mere luxury? Should they ideally be based on full disclosure and total frankness? Or is this a misguided ideal, not only a practical impossibility?[75]

a. Contextual arguments
Some arguments for privacy do not link it empirically with other goals. These arguments contend that privacy, by limiting access, creates the necessary context for other activities that we deem essential. Typical of these contextual arguments is the one advanced by Jeffrey Reiman that privacy is what enables development of individuality by allowing individuals to distinguish between their own thoughts and feelings and those of others.[76] Similarly, Charles Fried advanced a contextual argument that privacy is necessary for the development of trust, love, and friendship.[77] Contextual arguments are instrumental, in that they relate privacy to another goal. They are strengthened by the fact that the link between privacy and the other goal is also conceptual.

A similar argument can be made about the relationship between privacy and intimacy. Here too, it is not simply the case that intimacy is more likely with increasing amounts of privacy. Being intimate in public is almost a contradiction in terms.[78] Such contextual arguments highlight an important goal for privacy, similar to that indicated by examining the possible consequences of a total loss of privacy. We can now move to a detailed examination of more specific functions of privacy.[79]

b. Freedom from physical access

By restricting physical access to an individual, privacy insulates that individual from distraction and from the inhibitive effects that arise from close physical proximity with another individual. Freedom from distraction is essential for all human activities that require concentration, such as learning, writing, and all forms of creativity. Although writing and creativity may be considered luxuries, learning—which includes not only acquiring information and basic skills but also the development of mental capacities and moral judgment—is something that we all must do.[80] Learning, in turn, affects human growth, autonomy, and mental health.

Restricting physical access also permits an individual to relax. Even casual observation has an inhibitive effect on most individuals that makes them more formal and uneasy.[81] Is relaxation important? The answer depends partially upon one's theory of the individual. If we believe in one coherent "core" personality, we may feel that people should reflect that personality at all times. It could be argued that relaxation is unimportant—or undesirable—because it signals a discrepancy between the person in public and in private. The importance that all of us place on relaxation suggests that this theory is wrong, however, or at least overstated. Whatever the theory, people seem to need opportunities to relax, and this may link privacy to the ability of individuals to maintain their mental health. Furthermore, freedom from access contributes to the individual by permitting intimacy. Not all relationships are intimate, but those that are tend to be the most valued. Relaxation and intimacy together are essential for many kinds of human relations, including sexual ones. Privacy in the sense of freedom from physical access is thus not only important for individuals by themselves, but also as a necessary shield for intimate relations.[82]

Because physical access is a major way to acquire information, the power to limit it is also the power to limit such knowledge. Knowledge and access are not necessarily related, however. Knowledge is only one of the possible consequences of access, a subject to which we now turn.

c. Promoting liberty of action

An important cluster of arguments for privacy builds on the way in which it severs the individual's conduct from knowledge of that conduct by others. Privacy thus prevents interference, pressures to conform, ridicule, punishment, unfavorable decisions, and other forms of hostile reaction. To the extent that privacy does this, it functions to promote liberty of action, removing the unpleasant consequences of certain actions and thus increasing the liberty to perform them.

This promotion of liberty of action links privacy to a variety of individual goals. It also raises a number of serious problems, both as to the causal link between privacy and other goals, and as to the desirability of this function.

Freedom from censure and ridicule. In addition to providing freedom from distractions and opportunities to concentrate, privacy also contributes to learning, creativity, and autonomy by insulating the individual against ridicule and censure at early stages of groping and experimentation. No one likes to fail, and learning requires trial and error, some practice of skills, some abortive first attempts before we are sufficiently pleased with our creation to subject it to public scrutiny. In the absence of privacy we would dare less, because all our early failures would be on record. We would only do what we thought we could do well. Public failures make us unlikely to try again.[83]

Promoting mental health. One argument linking privacy and mental health, made by Sidney Jourard,[84] suggests that individuals may become victims of mental illness because of pressures to conform to society's expectations. Strict obedience to all social standards is said inevitably to lead to inhibition, repression, alienation, symptoms of disease, and possible mental breakdown. On the other hand, disobedience may lead to sanctions. Ironically, the sanction for at least some deviations is a social declaration of insanity. By providing a refuge, privacy enables individuals to disobey in private and thus acquire the strength to obey in public.

Mental health is one of the least well-defined concepts in the literature.[85] It appears that Professor Jourard's argument for privacy uses the term in a minimalistic sense: avoiding mental breakdown. Whether mental breakdown is always undesirable is questionable.[86] More serious problems are raised when we examine the link between mental health and privacy. Must chronic obedience always lead to mental breakdown? This is plausible if individuals obey social norms only because of social pressures and fear of sanctions, but this is not the case. Professor Jourard identifies a need for privacy that applies only to those who do not accept the social norms. The strength of his argument thus depends on the likelihood that people reject some norms of their society, and may be adequate only for extremely totalitarian societies. It will probably also depend on the nature of the norms and expectations that are not accepted. Moreover, even if pressures to conform to social norms contribute to mental breakdown, the opposite may also be true. It could be argued that too much permissiveness is at least as dangerous to mental health as too much conformity. One of the important functions of social norms is to give people the sense of belonging to a group defined by shared values. People are likely to lose their sanity in the absence of such norms and the sense of security they provide.[87] Nevertheless, some individuals in institutions do complain that the absence of privacy affects their mental state, and these complaints support Jourard's argument.[88]

Promoting autonomy. Autonomy is another value that is linked to the function of privacy in promoting liberty. Moral autonomy is the reflective and critical acceptance of social norms, with obedience based on an independent moral evaluation of their worth.[89] Autonomy requires the capacity to make an independent moral judgment, the willingness to exercise it, and the courage to act on the results of this exercise even when the judgment is not a popular one.

We do not know what makes individuals autonomous, but it is probably easier to be autonomous in an open society committed to pluralism, toleration, and encouragement of independent judgment rather than blind submissiveness. No matter how open a society may be, however, there is a danger that behavior that deviates from norms will result in harsh sanctions. The prospect of this hostile reaction has an inhibitive effect. Privacy is needed to enable the individual to deliberate and establish his opinions. If public reaction seems likely to be unfavorable, privacy may permit an individual to express his judgments to a group of like-minded people. After a period of germination, such individuals may be more willing to declare their unpopular views in public.

It might be argued that history belies this argument for privacy in terms of autonomy: societies much more totalitarian than ours have always had some autonomous individuals, so that the lack of privacy does not mean the end of autonomy. Even if we grant that privacy may not be a necessary condition for autonomy for all, however, it is enough to justify it as a value that most people may require it. We are not all giants, and societies should enable all, not only the exceptional, to seek moral autonomy.[90]

Promoting human relations. Privacy also functions to promote liberty in ways that enhance the capacity of individuals to create and maintain human relations of different intensities. Privacy enables individuals to establish a plurality of roles and presentations to the world. This control over "editing" one's self is crucial, for it is through the images of others that human relations are created and maintained.

Privacy is also helpful in enabling individuals to continue relationships, especially those highest in one's emotional hierarchy, without denying one's inner thoughts, doubts, or wishes that the other partner cannot accept. This argument for privacy is true irrespective of whether we deem total disclosure to be an ideal in such relations. It is built on the belief that individuals, for reasons that they themselves do not justify, cannot emotionally accept conditions that seem threatening to them. Privacy enables partners to such a relationship to continue it, while feeling free to endorse those feelings in private.[91]

Each of these arguments based on privacy's promotion of liberty shares a common ground: privacy permits individuals to do what they would not do without it for fear of an unpleasant or hostile reaction from others. This reaction may be anything from legal punishment or compulsory commitment to threats to dissolve an important relationship. The question arises, then, whether it is appropriate for privacy to permit individuals to escape responsibility for their actions, wishes, and opinions.

It may be argued that we have rules because we believe that breaches of them are undesirable, and we impose social sanctions to discourage undesirable conduct. People are entitled to a truthful presentation and a reasonable consideration of their expectations by those with whom they interact. Privacy frustrates these mechanisms for regulation and education; to let it do so calls for some justification. In general, privacy will only be desirable when the liberty of action that it promotes is itself desirable, or at least permissible. It is illuminating to see when we seek to promote liberty directly, by changing social norms, and when we are willing to let privacy do the task.

Privacy is derived from liberty in the sense that we tend to allow privacy to the extent that its promotion of liberty is considered desirable. Learning, practicing, and creating require privacy, and this function is not problematic.[92] Similarly, because we usually believe that it is good for individuals to relax and to enjoy intimacy, we have no difficulty allowing the privacy necessary for these goals.

The liberty promoted by privacy also is not problematic in contexts in which we believe we should have few or no norms; privacy will be needed in such cases because some individuals will not share this belief, will lack the strength of their convictions, or be emotionally unable to accept what they would like to do. Good examples of such cases are ones involving freedom of expression, racial tolerance, and the functioning of close and intimate relations. The existence of official rules granting immunity from regulation, or even imposing duties of nondiscrimination, does not guarantee the absence of social forces calling for conformity or prejudice.[93] A spouse may understand and even support a partner's need to fantasize or to have other close relations, but may still find knowing about them difficult to accept. In such situations, respect for privacy is a way to force ourselves to be as tolerant as we know we should be. We accept the need for privacy as an indication of the limits of human nature.

A related but distinct situation in which privacy is permitted is that in which we doubt the desirability of norms or expectations, or in which there is an obvious absence of consensus as to such desirability.[94] Treatment of homosexual conduct between consenting adults in private seems to be a typical case of this sort.[95] Another context in which we sometimes allow privacy to function in this way is when privacy would promote the liberty of individuals not to disclose some parts of their past, in the interest of rehabilitation or as a necessary protection against prejudice and irrationality.[96]

Privacy works in all these cases to ameliorate tensions between personal preferences and social norms by leading to nonenforcement of some standards.[97] But is this function desirable? When the liberty promoted is desirable, why not attack the norms directly? When it is not, why allow individuals to do in private what we would have good reasons for not wanting them to do at all?

Conceptually, this is a strong argument against privacy, especially because privacy perpetuates the very problems it helps to ease. With mental health, autonomy, and human relations, the mitigation of surface tensions may reduce incentives to face the difficulty and deal with it directly. When privacy lets people act privately in ways that would have unpleasant consequences if done in public, this may obscure the urgency of the need to question the public regulation itself. If homosexuals are not prosecuted, there is no need to decide whether such conduct between consenting adults in private can constitutionally be prohibited.[98] If people can keep their independent judgments known only to a group of like-minded individuals, there is no need to deal with the problem of regulating hostile reactions by others. It is easier, at least in the short run and certainly for the person making the decision, to conceal actions and thoughts that may threaten an important relationship. Thus, privacy reduces our incentive to deal with our problems.

The situation is usually much more complex, however, and then the use of privacy is justified. First, there are important limits on our capacity to change positive morality,[99] and thus to affect social pres-

sures to conform. This may even cause an inability to change institutional norms. When this is the case, the absence of privacy may
mean total destruction of the lives of individuals condemned by norms
with only questionable benefit to society. If the chance to achieve
change in a particular case is small, it seems heartless and naive to
argue against the use of privacy.[100] Although legal and social changes
are unlikely until individuals are willing to put themselves on the line,
this course of action should not be forced on any one. If an individual
decides that the only way he can maintain his sanity is to choose private
deviance rather than public disobedience, that should be his decision.
Similarly, if an individual prefers to present a public conformity rather
than unconventional autonomy, that is his choice. The least society
can do in such cases is respect such a choice.

Ultimately, our willingness to allow privacy to operate in this way
must be the outcome of our judgment as to the proper scope of liberty
individuals should have, and our assessment of the need to help ourselves and others against the limited altruism and rationality of individuals. Assume that an individual has a feature he knows others
may find objectionable—that he is a homosexual, for instance, or a
communist, or committed a long-past criminal offense—but that feature is irrelevant in the context of a particular situation.[101] Should we
support his wish to conceal these facts? Richard Posner[102] and Richard
Epstein[103] argue that we should not. This is an understandable argument, but an extremely harsh one. Ideally, it would be preferable
if we could all disregard prejudices and irrelevancies. It is clear, however, that we cannot. Given this fact, it may be best to let one's ignorance mitigate one's prejudice. There is even more to it than this.
Posner and Epstein imply that what is behind the wish to have privacy
in such situations is the wish to manipulate and cheat, and to deprive
another of the opportunity to make an informed decision. But we
always give only partial descriptions of ourselves, and no one expects
anything else. The question is not whether we should edit, but how
and by whom the editing should be done.[104] Here, I assert, there
should be a presumption in favor of the individual concerned.

It is here that we return to contextual arguments and to the specter
of a total lack of privacy. To have different individuals we must have
a commitment to some liberty—the liberty to be different. But differences are known to be threatening, to cause hate and fear and
prejudice.[105] These aspects of social life should not be overlooked,
and oversimplified claims of manipulation should not be allowed to
obscure them.

The only case in which this is less true is that of human relationships, where the equality between the parties is stronger and the essence of the relationship is voluntary and intimate. A unilateral decision by one of the parties not to disclose in order to maintain the relationship is of questionable merit. The individual is likely to choose what is easier for him, rather than for both. His decision denies the other party an understanding of the true relationship and the opportunity to decide whether to forgive, accommodate, or leave. Although we cannot rely on the altruism and willingness to forgive of employers or casual acquaintances, to deny a life partner the opportunity to make informed decisions may undermine the value of the relationship. This is another point at which our theories about human relations become relevant. The extent to which paternalistic protection should be a part of relationships between adults, and the forms such concern may appropriately take, are relevant in deciding this issue.

Limiting exposure. A further and distinct function of privacy is to enhance an individual's dignity, at least to the extent that dignity requires nonexposure. There is something undignified in exposure beyond the fact that the individual's choice of privacy has been frustrated.[106] A choice of privacy is in this sense distinct from a choice to interact. Rejection of the latter frustrates X's wish, but there is no additional necessary loss of dignity and selfhood. In exposure, there is. It is hard to know what kind of exposures are undignified, and the effect such unwanted exposures have on individuals. The answer probably depends on the culture and the individual concerned,[107] but this is nonetheless an important function of privacy.

2. PRIVACY AND SOCIETY

We desire a society in which individuals can grow, maintain their mental health and autonomy, create and maintain human relations, and lead meaningful lives. The analysis above suggests that some privacy is necessary to enable the individual to do these things, and privacy may therefore both indicate the existence of and contribute to a more pluralistic, tolerant society. In the absence of consensus concerning many limitations of liberty, and in view of the limits on our capacity to encourage tolerance and acceptance and to overcome prejudice, privacy must be part of our commitment to individual freedom and to a society that is committed to the protection of such freedom.

Privacy is also essential to democratic government because it fosters and encourages the moral autonomy of the citizen, a central requirement of a democracy. Part of the justification for majority rule and the right to vote is the assumption that individuals should participate in political decisions by forming judgments and expressing preferences. Thus, to the extent that privacy is important for autonomy, it is important for democracy as well.

This is true even though democracies are not necessarily liberal. A country might restrict certain activities, but it must allow some liberty of political action if it is to remain a democracy. This liberty requires privacy, for individuals must have the right to keep private their votes, their political discussions, and their associations if they are to be able to exercise their liberty to the fullest extent. Privacy is crucial to democracy in providing the opportunity for parties to work out their political positions, and to compromise with opposing factions, before subjecting their positions to public scrutiny. Denying the privacy necessary for these interactions would undermine the democratic process.[108]

Finally, it can be argued that respect for privacy will help a society attract talented individuals to public life. Persons interested in government service must consider the loss of virtually all claims and expectations of privacy in calculating the costs of running for public office. Respect for privacy might reduce those costs.[109]

II. The limits of law

One of the advantages of this analysis is that it draws attention to—and explains—the fact that legal protection of privacy has always had, and will always have, serious limitations. In many cases, the law cannot compensate for losses of privacy, and it has strong commitments to other ideals that must sometimes override the concern for privacy. Consequently, one cannot assume that court decisions protecting privacy reflect fully or adequately the perceived need for privacy in our lives.

Part of the reason for this inadequate reflection is that in many cases actions for such invasions are not initiated. The relative rarity of legal actions might be explained by expectations that such injuries are not covered by law, by the fact that many invasions of privacy are not perceived by victims, and by the feeling that legal remedies are inappropriate, in part because the initiation of legal action itself involves the additional loss of privacy. When these factors are forgotten, it is easy to conclude that privacy is not such an important value after all. This conclusion is mistaken, however, as the proposed analysis stresses. Understanding the difficulty of legal protection of privacy will help us resist the tendency to fall victim to this misperception.

It is obvious that privacy will have to give way, at times, to important interests in law enforcement, freedom of expression, research, and verification of data. The result is limits on the scope of legal protection of privacy. I shall concentrate on less obvious reasons why the scope of legal protection is an inadequate reflection of the importance of privacy.

To begin, there are many ways to invade an individual's privacy without his being aware of it. People usually know when they have been physically injured, when their belongings have been stolen, or when a contractual obligation has not been honored. It is more difficult to know when one's communications have been intercepted, when one is being observed or followed, or when others are reading one's dossier.[110] This absence of awareness is a serious problem in a legal system that relies primarily on complaints initiated by victims.[111] In some cases, victims learn of invasions of their privacy when information acquired about them is used in a public trial, as was the case with Daniel Ellsberg.[112] In most situations, however, there is no need to use the information publicly, and the victim will not be able to complain about the invasion simply because of his ignorance. The absence of complaints is thus no indication that invasions of privacy do not exist, or do not have undesirable consequences. Indeed, because deterrence depends at least partly on the probability of detection,[113] these problems of awareness may encourage such invasions.

Ironically, those invasions of privacy that pose no problem of detection, such as invasions through publication, have different features that make legal proceedings unattractive and thus unlikely for the prospective complainant. Legal actions are lengthy, expensive, and involve additional losses of privacy. In the usual case, plaintiffs do not wish to keep the essence of their action private. In a breach of contract suit, for example, the plaintiff may not seek publicity, but usually does not mind it. This is not true, however, for the victim of a loss of privacy. For him, a legal action will further publicize the very information he once sought to keep private, and will thus diminish the point of seeking vindication for the original loss.[114]

Moreover, for the genuine victim of a loss of privacy, damages and even injunctions are remedies of despair.[115] A broken relationship, exposure of a long-forgotten breach of standards, acute feelings of shame and degradation, cannot be undone through money damages. The only benefit may be a sense of vindication, and not all victims of invasions of privacy feel sufficiently strongly to seek such redress.

The limits of law in protecting privacy stem also from the law's commitment to interests that sometimes *require* losses of privacy, such as freedom of expression, interests in research, and the needs of law enforcement. In some of these cases, we would not even feel sympathy for the complainant: the criminal does not need privacy for his autonomy, mental health, or human relations. In other situations, however, the injury is real but legal vindication is considered too costly. Victims realize these facts, and this in turn reduces the tendency to seek vindication through law.

Finally, perhaps the most serious limit of legal protection is suggested by the instrumentalist analysis of privacy above. Privacy is important in those areas in which we want a refuge from pressures to conform, where we seek freedom from inhibition, the freedom to explore, dare, and grope. Invasions of privacy are hurtful because they expose us; they may cause us to lose our self-respect, and thus our capacity to have meaningful relations with others. The law, as one of the most public mechanisms society has developed, is completely out of place in most of the contexts in which privacy is deemed valuable.

These factors indicate that it is neither an accident nor a deliberate denial of its value that the law at present does not protect privacy in many instances. There are simply limits to the law's effectiveness. On the other hand, this does not indicate that there is nothing distinct behind claims for privacy. Emphasis of this point is important, for we must resist the temptation to see privacy as adequately reflected in the law or in reductive accounts. This is also an important reason to seek an explicit commitment to privacy as part of the law.

III. Privacy as a legal concept

My analysis has shown that privacy is a coherent and useful concept in the first two contexts: losses of privacy may be identified by reference to the central notion of accessibility, and the reasons for considering it desirable are sufficiently similar to justify adopting it as a value. Most reductionists do not deny these facts;[116] they assert, however, that privacy is not a useful *legal* concept because analysis of actual legal protection, and claims for protection, suggests that it is not and is not likely to be protected simply for its own sake. I believe this denial of the utility of privacy as a legal concept is misleading and has some unfortunate results. To counteract that view, I therefore argue that the law should make an explicit commitment to privacy.

A. *The poverty of reductionism*

One way to think about "the law of privacy" is to start by asking what privacy is, and proceed to question to what extent the law protects it. This approach raises questions as to why people want privacy, why it is that although they want it they do not make claims for legal protection, and, if they do, why the law is reluctant to respond. Answering these questions gives us a fuller understanding of the scope of actual legal protection and the way the law reflects social needs, the limits of the law in protecting human aspirations, and the need for further legal protection created by changes in social and technological conditions. In contrast, another approach to privacy starts from the legal decisions—or moral intuitions[117] —that define the scope of legal protection for privacy. The practical benefit of this approach is obvious: by reducing decisions to a small number of principles of liability, lawyers and judges are able to rely on legal tradition without having to consult all the cases anew each time a privacy claim is made.

In principle, the starting point should not affect the results of our attempt to find an adequate description of the scope of actual legal protection of privacy. It should not be surprising, however, that these starting from judicial decisions tend to conclude with a reductionist account. First, despite the common use of the term "privacy," the two starting points define different data to be explained. Those scholars who start from decisions, without an external concept of privacy, are led to rely on the concept that may be derived from the decisions themselves. One of the advantages of their enterprise is that their account seeks to explain *all* those cases in which the courts have explicitly invoked the concept of privacy.[118] There is no guarantee that the concepts arising from adjudication will be coherent,[119] however, especially when the theoretical basis for the concept is not settled.[120] An attempt to impose coherence on the use of a single concept in judicial decisions is bound to be misleading when such a coherence does not in fact exist. The reductionists have perceived this lack of coherence in the case of privacy, and have concluded that the best way to describe existing law is with several separate categories of recovery, all designed to protect interests other than privacy and having little else in common.

It is here that the reductionists' starting point has blinded them to other ways to deal with the lack of coherence in judicial decisions. In some cases, the label of privacy has indeed been used to protect interests other than privacy because of the promise and limits of legal categories. In most cases in which a claim of privacy has been made, however, a loss of privacy has been involved. It is for this reason that there are many common features to liability in privacy cases despite the disparate principles that are used as an adequate account of the law. The reductionists cannot explain this unity, and their account obscures it.[121] On the other hand, dealing only with explicit privacy decisions blinds the reductionists to those cases in which the law is in fact used to protect privacy, albeit under a different label.

A second problem with reliance on actual decisions is that the data base is narrow. We deal only with claims that have actually been made, and primarily with cases in which the court has granted recovery. This may be misleading, particularly in areas such as privacy, because there are numerous disincentives for invoking legal protection.[122] Finally seeking to explain the scope of legal protection in order to identify when courts are likely to give a remedy can obscure the reasons why a remedy is not given, which may be crucial for understanding the larger issues.[123]

Starting from the extra-legal concept of privacy enables us to avoid these pitfalls. The account of legal protection resulting from this approach is at least as helpful to practitioners, and also has additional advantages over the reductionist account: it brings to the fore many important observations about privacy and its legal protection, and helps to draw attention to privacy costs.

The primary advantage the approach advocated here exhibits over even the best reductionist account[124] is that it will include within it all legal protection of one coherent value—privacy—in all branches of the law,[125] and under any label. Limited disclosures about individuals, breaches of confidence, the reasons behind testimonial privileges, the right against self-incrimination, and privacy legislation—which have all been discussed in privacy terms but excluded by Prosser's reductionism—will be included.[126] So will be the exclusionary rule and rules of trespass and defamation to the extent they have been used to protect privacy. At the same time, this approach excludes those cases that explicitly refer to privacy in which the concept is invoked misleadingly. Some claims of appropriation,[127] and some claims of immunity from interference,[128] will be excluded. This description thus provides a better picture of current legal protection than does the reductionist account.

The reductionist approach fails even on its strongest claim to adequacy—the exposure of the limits of legal protection of privacy. The primary insight of these accounts is that the law never protects privacy per se, as is indicated by the fact that whenever a remedy for invasion of privacy is given, there is another interest such as property or reputation that is invaded as well. This insight, in general,[129] is quite true, and is certainly important. It reflects the limits of law discussed above. It is nonetheless misleading. It may be true that the law tends to protect privacy only when another interest is also invaded, whereas invasions of other interests may compel protection on their own. It does not follow from this that the presence of privacy in a situation does not serve as an additional reason for protection. Privacy, property, and reputation are all interests worthy of protection. The law grants none of them absolute protection. When two of them are invaded in one situation, recovery may be compelled even though neither alone would suffice. In such cases, the plaintiff would not have recovered had not his privacy been invaded. This operation of privacy is completely obscured by the reductionists.[130]

Besides obscuring the extent of current legal protection, reductionist accounts obscure the continuity of legal protection over time. They give the erroneous impression that the concern with privacy is modern, whereas in fact both the wish to invade privacy and the need to control such wishes have been features of the human condition from antiquity. The common-law maxim that a person's home is his castle; early restrictions on the power of government officials to search, detain, or enter; strict norms of confidence; and prohibition of Peeping Toms or eavesdropping all attest to this early concern.[131] Even when the explicit label of privacy has not been invoked, the law has been used to protect privacy in a variety of ways. Warren and Brandeis, in their famous plea for explicit legal protection of privacy, traced much of this earlier protection by the law of contract, trespass, defamation, and breach of confidence.[132] They offered this tradition of protection as a ground for arguing that the courts could provide remedies for invasion of privacy without legislating a new cause of action in tort.[133] Awareness of this continuity helps us to understand the functions of privacy in our lives, and the changes in circumstances that have led to new claims or protection.

There is nothing in reductionist accounts to suggest insights into why new claims for privacy arise. Nevertheless, understanding what has caused these new claims may be helpful in deciding what to do about them. Despite the tradition of legal protection, it is true that growing concern with losses of privacy is a modern phenomenon. This need not be because of any change in people's awareness, sensitivity, or conception of the essential components of the good life, as Warren and Brandeis implied.[134] Indeed, my analysis of privacy suggests that the functions of privacy are too basic to human life to be so sensitive to changes in perception,[135] and it is in any event doubtful

whether modern man is more sensitive or morally sophisticated than
his predecessors. Moreover, most individuals today have more opportunities for privacy than our ancestors ever did, as well as a greater
ability to regain anonymity after any loss of privacy occurs.

The main reason for this modern concern appears to be a change
in the nature and magnitude of threats to privacy, due at least in part
to technological change. The legal protection of the past is inadequate
not because the level of privacy it once secured is no longer sufficient,
but because that level can no longer be secured. Advances in the
technology of surveillance and the recording, storage, and retrieval
of information[136] have made it either impossible or extremely costly
for individuals to protect the same level of privacy that was once
enjoyed.[137] "Overstepping" by the press, cited by Warren and Brandeis,[138] gives the old invasions of privacy via publication and gossip a
new dimension through the speed and scope of the modern mass
media. We can dramatize this point by noting that the loss of anonymity of public figures is of a new order of magnitude. Many old
stories could not plausibly be written today: Victor Hugo's rehabilitated mayor, Shakespeare's disguised dukes, the benevolent great people who do charity in disguise, are all extremely unlikely in our modern
culture.

The identification of technological developments as a major source
of new concern may be supported by the fact that modern claims
concerning the secrecy and anonymity aspects of privacy have not
been accompanied by new claims concerning physical access: technological advances have affected the acquisition, storage, and dissemination of information, but gaining physical access is a process that
has not changed much.[139] On the other hand, the increase in the
number of people whose profession it is to observe and report, the
intensified activity in search of publishable information, and the changes
in the equipment that enables such enterprises, make it more likely
that events and information will in fact be recorded and published.

Technology is not the whole story, however. The privacy concerns
created by the mass media go beyond the fact that the development
of scandal magazines and investigative journalism lets more people
acquire more information more quickly. An additional problem is
that journalism is crude, and may not do justice to the situation exposed. Partial truths are unsettling because they present a one-
dimensional image of the subject, often without compassion or benevolence. This may be not unlike scandal journalism's old sister,
gossip. The most important difference is that gossip usually concerns
people who are already known in their other facets, and thus partial

truths are less misleading. In contrast, there is no way that most readers of newspapers can correct for the one-dimensional images they receive through print.[140]

The new concern with privacy may also be explained, at least in part, as a tendency to put old claims in new terms.[141] From this perspective, part of the new interest in privacy is not caused by new needs, but rather by new doctrinal moves or hopes for legal change. Privacy has been used to overcome the limitations of defamation;[142] it has been used to avoid such historically loaded legal terms as "substantive due process" and "liberty";[143] and it has been used to avoid basing all entitlements, without differentiation, on the notion of property.[144]

Finally, and perhaps most importantly, reductive accounts reinforce the tendency to overlook the privacy costs that may be involved in a case. Because these accounts suggest that privacy is only a label used to protect other interests, logic would dictate that whenever a privacy question is discussed, the balancing should be among the "real" interests involved. Consequently, privacy is made redundant despite its usage. Although we talk in terms of privacy, the reductionist suggests, what we actually take into consideration are the interests to which privacy is reducible.[145] It is this quality of reductionism that threatens to undermine our belief in the distinctness and importance of privacy, and to have an adverse effect on our policy decisions. The proposed analysis, by clarifying the distinctness and importance of privacy through a functional analysis, enables us to challenge such reductionism.

B. *The case for an explicit commitment to privacy*

There is much to be said for making an explicit legal commitment to privacy. Such a commitment would affirm that privacy is not just a convenient label, but a central value. An explicit commitment would put reductionist accounts in their correct perspective, as attempts to give lawyers and judges a guide to identify cases in which recovery is likely under a given heading. The legal protection of privacy is more than a mere by-product of the protection of other, more "respectable" values. An explicit commitment to privacy would recognize that losses of privacy are undesirable, at least in the circumstances in which such losses frustrate the functions and goals described above. It would recognize that such losses should be taken into account by the legal system, and that we should strive to minimize them.

Clearly, an explicit commitment to privacy does not mean that privacy deserves absolute protection. It does not mean that privacy is the one value we seek to promote, or even the most important among a number of values to which we are committed. This is true for all our values, however. None is protected absolutely, not even those to which a commitment is made in unequivocal terms in the Constitution. Nor would making such a commitment suggest that invasions of privacy would generally be actionable. I have indicated many of the reasons why it is unlikely to expect the law to protect privacy extensively. Making an explicit commitment could not be understood to deny the need for balancing; it would simply identify the factors that should be considered by the legal system.

In positive terms, the case for an explicit commitment to privacy is made by pointing out the distinctive functions of privacy in our lives. Privacy has as much coherence and attractiveness as other values to which we have made a clear commitment, such as liberty. Arguments for liberty, when examined carefully, are vulnerable to objections similar to the arguments we have examined for privacy, yet this vulnerability has never been considered a reason not to acknowledge the importance of liberty, or not to express this importance by an explicit commitment so that any loss will be more likely to be noticed and taken into consideration. Privacy deserves no less.

Further insight about the need for an explicit commitment to privacy comes from study of the arguments made against this approach. First, it may be argued that the American legal system has already made this commitment, and that we should concentrate on answering questions of the scope of legal protection rather than spend time arguing for commitments that have already been made. Questions of scope are no doubt important, and had a commitment to privacy been made and its implications internalized, there would indeed be no further need for an explicit affirmation. But the reductionist literature is at least as influential as that which affirms the distinctness and importance of privacy, and although it is true that some parts of the legal system are informed by an affirmation of privacy, it is equally clear that others are not. For the latter, an explicit commitment to privacy could make an important difference.[146]

A more substantive argument, and one inconsistent with the first, is that we should not make a commitment to privacy because there is no need for further legal protection: we already have all the privacy we could possibly want or need. In those areas in which invasions of privacy are undesirable, the law already provides a remedy. If anything, this argument goes, we need less legal protection today because rising standards of living mean that individuals enjoy more privacy than ever before. Critics emphasize the relatively small number of difficult cases in which we sympathize with the person complaining about invasion of his privacy. In the hundred years of the tort remedy's existence, there as been only one Sidis,[147] one Melvin,[148] one Barber.[149]

It is here that understanding the reasons for the new concern with privacy becomes crucial. It is true that individuals today enjoy more opportunities for privacy in some areas, but this observation, taken alone, is misleading. The rarity of actions is not a good indication of the need for privacy, or of the extent to which invasions are undesirable. We enjoy our privacy not because of new opportunities for seclusion or because of greater control over our interactions, but because of our anonymity, because no one is interested in us. The moment someone becomes sufficiently interested, he may find it quite easy to take all that privacy away. He may follow us all the time, obtain information about us from a host of data systems, record our conversations, and intrude into our bedrooms. What protects privacy is not the difficulty of invading it, but the lack of motive and interest of others to do so. The important point, however, is that if our privacy is invaded, it may be invaded today in more serious and more permanent ways than ever before. Thus, although most of us are unlikely to experience a substantial loss of privacy, we have an obligation to protect those who lose their anonymity. In this sense, privacy is no different from other basic entitlements. We are not primarily concerned with the rights of criminal suspects because we have been exposed to police brutality ourselves. We know that we may be exposed to it in the future, but, more generally, we want to be part of a society that is committed to minimizing violations of due process.

Even if the law had already dealt with all the situations in which privacy should be legally protected, however, an explicit commitment to privacy would still be significant. It is significant in ways that no specific, localized legal protection can be. It would serve to remind us of the importance of privacy, and thus to color our understanding of protection in specific contexts.

The result of this awareness would not necessarily or even primarily be more legal rules to protect privacy. For example, such an explicit commitment to privacy might focus attention on ways to ameliorate the difficulties resulting from the inappropriateness of current legal remedies and legal proceedings. Some thought could go into whether limits on the publicity of judicial proceedings that involve privacy claims could be established without paying too high a price in terms of freedom of expression or fair trials.[150] Moreover, an explicit commitment could increase individual sensitivity to losses of privacy and

thus encourage people to prevent invasions of privacy without reliance
on law at all. It may lead to increased efforts to make it possible to
minimize losses of privacy without invoking the law, through such
efforts as development of technological devices to make leaks from
data systems more difficult. It would also draw the attention of those
whose occupations involve systematic breaches of others' privacy, such
as journalists, doctors, detectives, policemen, and therapists, to the
fact that although some invasions of privacy are inevitable, a loss of
sensitivity about such losses may corrupt the invader as well as harm
the victim.

An explicit commitment to privacy is not vulnerable to the charge
that the law should not protect privacy because its efficacy in doing
so is limited. It might be argued that the contexts within which privacy
has functional value are those in which the law is traditionally reluctant
to interfere. This reluctance stems, at least in part, from an awareness
that some questions cannot and should not be dealt with by the law.
It is unlikely, for example, that the law will ever impose an obligation
on parents to give their children some privacy in order to grow,
develop autonomy, and explore others. We would probably find such
a law an unpalatable interference with liberty. An explicit legal commitment to privacy might make such specific protection of privacy
unnecessary, however. Parents might then realize more fully that privacy is important for their children, and this would lead them to
respect their children's privacy without any direct legal obligation to
do so.

The general commitment would also help in administering the laws.
It could serve as a principle of interpretation, pointing out the need
to balance losses of privacy, perhaps with a presumption in favor of
protecting privacy. It might also supplement existing privacy laws by
identifying improper conduct and invoking the general sense of obligation to obey the laws. A general commitment may thus lead to a
reduction of invasions of privacy even in situations in which the victims
would not have sued had the invasions occurred, either because of
ignorance or for other reasons discussed above.

The functions of a general commitment to the value of privacy as
a part of the law are varied, and cannot be reduced to the amount of
protection actually given to that value in the legal system. Here again,
the commitment to privacy is no different than the commitment to
other values, such as freedom of expression or liberty. As I have
argued before, a commitment to privacy as a legal value may help to
raise awareness of its importance and thus deter reckless invasions.
Most importantly, however, an explicit commitment to privacy will

have an educational impact. This function is of special importance, because most of us enjoy privacy without the need for legal protection. For the most part, what we should learn is how to appreciate our available privacy and use it well. A clear statement in the law that privacy is a central value could make us more aware of the valuable functions privacy can serve. Ultimately, the wish to have privacy must be in our hearts, not only in our laws. But this does not mean that a commitment to the value of privacy should not be in our laws as well.

NOTES

1 The best general treatment of privacy is still A. Westin, Privacy and Freedom (1967). For treatment of a variety of privacy aspects, see Nomos XIII, Privacy (R. Penneck & J. Chapman eds. 1971) (Yearbook of the American Society for Political and Legal Philosophy) [hereinafter cited as Nomos].
2 W. Prosser, The Law of Torts 804 (4th ed. 1971).
3 Roe v. Wade, 410 U.S. 113, 152–55 (1973) (right to privacy cited to strike down abortion statute); Eisenstadt v. Baird, 405 U.S. 438, 453 (1972) (right to privacy includes right of unmarried individual to use contraceptives); Griswold v. Connecticut, 381 U.S. 479, 484–86 (1965) (right to privacy includes right of married couple to use contraceptives). *See generally* Richards, *Unnatural Acts and the Constitutional Right to Privacy: A Moral Theory*, 45 Fordham L. Rev. 1281 (1977); Comment, *A Taxonomy of Privacy: Repose, Sanctuary, and Intimate Decision*, 64 Calif. L. Rev. 1447 (1976) (developing constitutional right to privacy).
4 5 U.S.C. § 552a (1976). For a discussion of the privacy exception to the Freedom of Information Act, 5 U.S.C. § 552(b)(7)(C) (1976), see J. O'Reilly, Federal Information Disclosure: Procedures, Forms and the Law §§ 20.01– 21.10 (1977); Cox, *A Walk Through Section 552 of the Administrative Procedure Act: The Freedom of Information Act; The Privacy Act; and the Government in the Sunshine Act*, 46 U. Cin. L. Rev. 969 (1978).
5 Several constitutional and statutory provisions explicitly recognize the right to privacy. *See, e.g.,* Cal. Const. art. I, §§ 1 (1974 amendment recognizing, *inter alia*, right to privacy); Privacy Protection Study Comm'n, Personal Privacy in an Information Society (1977) (report on various aspects of privacy in U.S. with recommendations for additional protection of privacy).
6 For studies of legal protection in this vein, see, *e.g.,* Davis, *What Do We Mean by "Right to Privacy"?* 4 S.D. L. Rev. 1 (1959); Dickler, *The Right of Privacy*, 70 U.S. L. Rev. 435 (1936); Kalven, *Privacy in Tort Law—Were Warren and Brandeis Wrong?* 31 Law & Contemp. Prob. 326 (1966); Prosser, *Privacy*, 48 Calif. L. Rev. 383 (1960). For a similar study of moral intuitions, see Thomson, *The Right to Privacy*, 4 Philosophy & Pub. Aff: 295 (1975).
7 *See, e.g.,* Kalven, *supra* note 6, at 329 & n.22.

8 This aspect of privacy has been emphasized by Richard Posner. *See, e.g.,* Posner, *Privacy, Secrecy, and Reputation,* 28 Buffalo L. Rev. 1 (1979) [hereinafter cited as *Secrecy*]; Posner, *The Right to Privacy,* 12 Ga. L. Rev. 393 (1978) [hereinafter cited as *Privacy*]. Other commentators have followed his lead. *See, e.g.,* Epstein, *Privacy, Property Rights, and Misrepresentations,* 12 Ga. L. Rev. 455 (1978).

9 All reductionists claim that the concept of privacy does not illuminate thoughts about legal protection. Professor Posner's version is the most extreme: he denies the utility of all "intermediate" values, and advocates assessing acts and rules by the single, ultimate principle of wealth maximization. *E.g., Secrecy, supra* note 8, at 7–9; *Privacy, supra* note 8, at 394.

   The commentators cited in note 6 *supra* accept the utility of some differentiating concepts to denote different interests, such as property, reputation, and freedom from mental distress, but claim that privacy should be reduced to these "same-level" concepts. This form of reductionism is consistent with an acknowledgment that people want privacy, and that satisfaction of this wish does denote an important human aspiration. The essence of this reductionism is the claim that description and evaluation of the law or moral intuitions are clarified by pointing out that we do not have an independent "right to privacy." *See, e.g.,* Davis, *supra* note 6, at 18–24; Kalven, *supra* note 6, at 333–41. This position is frequently found in the literature on privacy. *See, e.g.,* Epstein, *supra* note 8, at 474; Freund, *Privacy; One Concept or Many,* in Nomos, *supra* note 1, at 182, 190–93.

10 This approach may also enhance our understanding and evaluation of the reductionist thesis. *See* pp. 460–67 *infra.*

11 The fact that my analysis demonstrates the value of privacy by showing its contribution to other goals does not make this just another type of reductionism. These instrumental justifications explain why we consider privacy a value but do not mean that we only protect privacy because of these other values. Complex instrumental arguments justify all values save ultimate ones, and perhaps we have no ultimate values in this sense at all. This does not mean that all values are reducible.

12 *See* pp. 425–28 & pp. 437–40 *infra.*

13 Any appearance of circularity here is misleading. To say that the coherence of the descriptive concept of privacy follows from the reasons we have for protecting it does not mean that the privacy we wish to protect is coextensive with the situation identified by the descriptive concept. *See* note 14 *infra.* We must start with a descriptive concept, however, in order to analyze the reasons to value some aspects of privacy.

14 Typical elements that may preempt discussion of desirability are the wishes or choices of the individuals concerned, the nature of the information, or the way in which the information is acquired. One important example is the statement that invasions of privacy are undesirable when the information disseminated is "private." It is clear that the statement must

mean that it is undesirable because the information should be seen as entitled to be kept private, that is, to not become known to the public. For clarity of thought, all of these elements should be excluded from the concept designed to identify the losses themselves. The best discussion of the need for a conceptual scheme that does not preempt questions is Parker, *A Definition of Privacy,* 27 Rutgers L. Rev. 275 (1975). *See generally* R. Gavison, Privacy and Its Legal Protection (1975) (unpublished D. Phil. thesis on file in Oxford, Harvard Law School, and Yale Law School libraries) (discussion of Parker).

15 *See* pp. 456–59 & pp. 467–71 *infra.*

16 Alan Westin has defined privacy as the "claim of individuals, groups, or institutions to determine for themselves when, how, and to what extent information about them is communicated to others." A. Westin, *supra* note 1, at 7. For a discussion of the influence of this definition on the study of privacy, see Lusky, *Invasion of Privacy: A Clarification of Concepts,* 72 Colum. L. Rev. 693, 693–95 (1972). It is interesting to note that Professor Westin also gives a second and quite different description of privacy: "Viewed in terms of the relation of the individual to social participation, privacy is the voluntary and temporary withdrawal of a person from the general society through physical or psychological means. . . ." A. Westin, *supra* note 1, at 7.

17 If we define privacy as a state of mind, we shall not be able to discuss losses of privacy that are unknown to the individual or whether such awareness is relevant to the desirability of such losses.

18 Privacy and the Law, A Report by the British Section of the International Comm'n of Justice ¶ 19 (1970):

> Accordingly, we shall use the word "privacy" in this report in the sense of that area of a man's life which, in any given circumstances, a reasonable man with an understanding of the legitimate needs of the community would think it wrong to invade.

This definition is simply a conclusion, not a tool to analyze whether a certain invasion should be considered wrong in the first place. Gerety, *Redefining Privacy,* 12 Harv. C.R.-C.L. L. Rev. 233 (1977), makes a similar move when he invokes the description proposed in J. Stephen, Liberty, Equality, Fraternity 160 (1967; 1st ed. 1873): "Conduct which can be described as indecent is always in one way or another a violation of privacy." *Id.* at 242. Professor Gerety is quite conscious, however, of the difference between descriptive and normative intuitions. His own definition of privacy invokes descriptive intuitions: "Privacy will be defined here as an autonomy or control over the intimacies of personal identity." *Id.* at 236. He adds, however, that it "carries with it a set of at least preliminary conclusions about rights and wrongs."*Id.*

19 Richard Parker, who is aware of the danger that conclusory definitions may preempt important questions, defines privacy as control over who senses us. Parker, *supra* note 14, at 280–81. Similarly, Professor Fried

defines privacy as control over information. C. Fried, An Anatomy of Values 140 (1970) [hereinafter cited as Values]; Fried, *Privacy*, 77 Yale L.J. 475, 482 (1968) [hereinafter cited as *Privacy*]. Other writers whose definitions of privacy can be understood in these terms are A. Miller, The Assault on Privacy 25 (1971); A. Westin, *supra* note 1, at 7; Beardsley, *Privacy: Autonomy and Selective Disclosure*, in Nomos, *supra* note 1, at 56, 70; Gerety, *supra* note 18, at 236; and Shils, *Privacy: Its Constitution and Vicissitudes*, 31 Law & Contemp. Prob. 281, 282 (1966).

20 Gross, *Privacy and Autonomy*, in Nomos, *supra* note 1, at 169, 169 [hereinafter cited as *Autonomy*]. *But see* Gross, *The Concept of Privacy*, 42 N.Y.U. L. Rev. 34, 35–36 (1967) (defining privacy as "the condition of human life in which acquaintance with a person or with affairs of his life which are personal to him is limited") [hereinafter cited as *Concept*]. Gross does not even refer to his earlier contribution in his 1971 article in Nomos.

21 It will clearly not be a loss in Edward Shils's definition:

> [P]rivacy exists where the persons whose actions engender or become the objects of information retain possession of that information, and any flow outward of that information from the persons to whom it refers (and who share it where more than one person is involved) occurs on the initiative of its possessors.

Shils, *supra* note 19, at 282. The control necessary here is over the outward flow of information, not control over those who receive the information. Hyman Gross has a more complex picture. He suggests whether voluntary disclosure involves loss of privacy depends on whether the recipient is bound by restrictive norms. *Autonomy, supra* note 20, at 171.

22 People may simply be uninterested in an individual, and thus not care to acquire information about him. Such an individual will have "privacy" even if he resents it. To say that an individual controls the flow of information about himself is thus not enough to tell us whether he is known in fact. We also must know whether there are restrictive norms, whether these are obeyed, how the individual has chosen to exercise his control, and whether others have acquired information about him in other ways or at all. The view of privacy presented by Alan Westin is not vulnerable to this difficulty. *See* A. Westin, *supra* note 1.

23 For example, an individual may voluntarily choose to disclose everything about himself to the public. This disclosure obviously leads to a loss of privacy despite the fact that it involved an exercise of control. This much is conceded even by Professor Gross. *Autonomy, supra* note 20, at 171. Moreover, to prohibit the individual from making disclosures is a limitation of his control that would seem to increase his privacy. A similar problem confronts those who seek to promote liberty of action when they are asked whether an individual should be allowed to sell himself into slavery. The sale may be a free exercise of liberty, but the result is a restriction on liberty.

24 I use "enjoys" although individuals would doubtless suffer if exposed to "perfect privacy," and may resent privacy that is imposed on them against

their will. "Perfect" privacy is used here only as a methodological starting point. There is no implication that such situations exist or that they are desirable.

25 *E.g.,* Professor Fried in Values, *supra* note 19, at 140; A. Miller, *supra* note 19, at 25; A. Westin, *supra* note 1, at 7; Beardsley, *supra* note 19, at 56; Professor Gross in *Autonomy, supra* note 20, at 172–74; Shils, *supra* note 19, at 282.

26 Professor Gerety argues that information is part of privacy only if it is "private"—related to intimacy, identity, and autonomy. Gerety, *supra* note 18, at 281–95. Professor Parker suggests that there are times when loss of control over information does not mean loss of privacy, *e.g.,* examinations in which it is revealed the student did not study. Parker, *supra* note 14, at 282.

27 *See* Benn, *Privacy, Freedom, and Respect for Persons,* in Nomos, *supra* note 1, at 1, 11–12 (data banks as paradigmatic privacy issue). Unused data banks do not cause a loss of privacy, of course, because the mere existence of information on file does not make it known to anyone. Access to such data banks does create a threat that losses of privacy may occur. *See generally* Farhi, *Computers, Data Banks and the Individual: Is the Problem Privacy?* 5 Israel L. Rev. 542 (1970).

28 Professor Parker suggests the example of an astronaut whose actions in a spaceship are thoroughly monitored by electrodes that feed data to a control desk. In addition, people at the control desk can observe the astronaut through a television camera. Parker argues that a prohibition against switching off the camera would result in further loss of privacy for the astronaut even though the camera provides no additional information. Parker, *supra* note 14, at 281. Parker seems correct, but not necessarily because loss of control over sensing is involved. The camera may provide people at the control desk with an additional, qualitatively different way to obtain the "same" information, and this may be equivalent to additional information.

29 The "amount" of information may not be as important as the quality and extent of the information. There is a difference between knowing a person, and knowing about him.

30 Another example might be cross-cultural. If we know something about the psychological make-up of a certain class, does a person whom we meet lose further privacy when we learn that he is a member of that class? We certainly may know more "about" him than he might suspect, depending on the probability that he is typical of the class.

31 *See, e.g.,* Cox Broadcasting Corp. v. Cohn, 420 U.S. 469 (1975) (parent alleged that his right to privacy was invaded by identification of daughter as victim of rape-murder); Corliss v. E.W. Walker Co., 57 F. 434 (C.C.D. Mass. 1893), *injunction dissolved,* 64 F. 280 (C.C.D. Mass. 1894) (plaintiffs alleged publication of biography and picture of dead husband and father constituted injury to their feelings).

32 This "extension of self" is a complex phenomenon, and seems highly culture-dependent. In some cases, it may be based on the idea that a person's choices reflect on him; my spouse, my car, and my clothes are part of me in this sense. In cases in which no choice is involved, such as those involving disclosures about parents, children, or siblings, the "extension of self" may be based on a feeling of responsibility for or identification with the other person. *See* Benn, *supra* note 27, at 12.

33 This explains the way in which defamation involves loss of privacy, or at least the threat of such a loss. Even if the defamatory information is false, it attracts attention to the person in ways that may involve loss of privacy.

34 *See* Roberts & Gregor, *Privacy: A Cultural View,* in Nomos, *supra* note 1, at 199, 214 (promotion of privacy through systematic denial of truth).

35 The answer depends on our theories about evaluations. To the extent that some evaluations are susceptible to interpersonal assessment, we may say that such evaluations transmit "objective knowledge." To the extent we consider evaluations subjective only, any informational content is much more complex and limited. The distinction between fact and opinion is important in defamation law's doctrine of "fair comment." Fair comment is privileged, but the facts on which it is based must be accurate. The distinction is notoriously difficult to draw. *See, e.g.,* Titus, *Statement of Fact versus Statement of Opinion—A Spurious Dispute in Fair Comment,* 15 Vand. L. Rev. 1203 (1962).

36 *See generally* The Social Structure of Attention (M. Chance & R. Larsen eds. 1976) (theories of attention).

37 It could be argued that the individual who fantasizes about another person is really thinking about a fictional entity, because the subject of the fantasies has been created by the fantasizer. *But cf.* Van den Haag, *On Privacy,* in Nomos, *supra* note 1, at 149, 152 (arguing that publication of fantasies should be considered invasion of privacy).

38 *See* De May v. Roberts, 46 Mich. 160, 9 N.W. 146 (1881) (finding for plaintiff on these facts). Note that *De May* preceded what is considered the seminal article on privacy, Warren & Brandeis, *The Right to Privacy,* 4 Harv. L. Rev. 193 (1890), by almost a decade.

39 For a comparative study of "spacing" and ways of maintaining physical distances, see E. Hall, The Hidden Dimension (1966).

40 "Secrecy, anonymity, and solitude" are shorthand for "the extent to which an individual is known, the extent to which an individual is the subject of attention, and the extent to which others have physical access to an individual." The fit between these phrases is close but not perfect, and some comments about the different connotations should be noted. "Secrecy" has an unpleasant sense, and "solitude" conjures up an image that may be quite different from the one connoted by "physical access to an individual." For the most part, however, these are small differences. The difference is much greater between "anonymity" and "being the subject of attention." I may stare hard, focusing all my attention on an individual,

without knowing who he is. The subject of my attention is therefore anonymous. On the other hand, even the President has times when he is not the subject of anyone's attention, but we would not call him an anonymous individual. Nevertheless, the aspect of anonymity that relates to attention and privacy is that of being lost in a crowd. If the President could ever be lost in a crowd, he would be anonymous in this context. To draw attention to him in such a case will cost him his anonymity—and his privacy.

41 The psychiatrist acquires information that the patient tells him, and information that the patient furnishes through his gestures, tone of voice, facial expressions, and demeanor. *See* E. Goffman, The Presentation of Self in Everyday Life 2 (1959) (distinguishing between "giving" and "giving off" information). Observation is a key source of information because we always transmit information about ourselves, even in situations in which no verbal communication occurs.

42 This suggests that it may be possible to compare the relative intrusiveness of ways to obtain certain information, *A*, about an individual, *X*. The least intrusive way to acquire the information is to have *X* volunteer it without being asked. A slightly more intrusive way to acquire the information is to ask *X* to provide it. *X* then has control over which questions to answer, and can challenge any that he feels are not necessary or appropriate. Observation of *X* is more likely to generate an amount of information greater than *A*, and thus to create loss of more privacy in this sense. It is also likely to involve physical access, and both observation and physical access may have costs to the individual's concentration, relaxation, and intimacy. *See* p. 447 *infra*. Questioning other individuals about *X* may also elicit an amount of information greater than *A*, and may attract attention to *X* that leads to further loss of privacy. This explains the intrusiveness of "rough shadowing," which is public surveillance that draws attention to the fact that the individual is being followed. *See* Schultz v. Frankfort Marine, Accident & Plate Glass Ins. Co., 151 Wis. 537, 139 N.W. 386 (1913). It is not surprising that courts have found "rough shadowing" actionable as an invasion of privacy. *E.g.,* Pinkerton Nat'l Detective Agency, Inc. v. Stevens, 109 Ga. App. 159, 132 S.E.2d 119 (1963). In contrast, courts have permitted less obvious forms of following and watching for purposes of investigation. *E.g.,* Nader v. General Motors Corp., 25 N.Y.2d 560, 255 N.E.2d 765, 307 N.Y.S.2d 647 (1970); Forster v. Manchester, 410 Pa. 192, 189 A.2d 147 (1963).

43 For a detailed examination of these reasons, see p. 447 *infra*.

44 In a general sense, the similarity of the reasons for protecting all three elements of privacy is sufficient to justify the coherence of the unitary concept. This coherence does not dictate treating all privacy cases the same way, however. It is plausible that legal protection of privacy may emphasize certain aspects more than others. *See* pp. 456–59 *infra* (limits of law) & pp. 465–67 *infra* (rise of new privacy claims). Treatment of the

RUTH GAVISON

privacy issues raised by data systems, for example, may require specific legislation and regulation that is not universally applicable.

45 *See, e.g.,* Committee on Privacy, Report 17–22, 327–28 (1972) (compiling definitions of privacy) [hereinafter cited as Younger Committee].

46 I do not question the value of analyzing legal decisions and rules with a single measure, such as maximizing utility or wealth. *See, e.g., Privacy, supra* note 8, at 394. The price we pay for this illumination is high, however. First, it leads us to assume that we may reach the correct decision by maximizing only one value. Second, it wrongly suggests that we should never create "exclusionary reasons"—concepts, rights, rules, and principles that incorporate some kind of calculus in order to limit the need to consider certain questions in detail. *See, e.g.,* Rawls, *Two Concepts of Rules,* 64 Philosophical Rev. 3 (1955).

47 Adjudicative techniques may cause the coherence of legal concepts to blur. For example, an early case may establish a "right to privacy." This "right" will be invoked in later cases, and as long as the situations are analogous the invocation is proper and illuminating. If a court relies on this right in situations that are significantly different from the early ones, however, it will be for different reasons than those that impelled the original court to grant recovery. The court may be encouraged to do so if it sees this as a way to rationalize a just result that cannot be reached in another way. Even with a just outcome, however, the concept loses its coherence, perhaps irrevocably, because we can no longer know what set of considerations is relevant for invoking it. This loss of coherence has already affected the development of privacy law. *See* pp. 438–40 *infra.*

48 Warren & Brandeis, *supra* note 38, never equated the right to privacy with the right to be let alone; the article implied that the right to privacy is a special case of the latter. *Id.* at 195. The notion of a right "to be let alone" was first advanced in T. Cooley, Law of Torts 29 (2d ed. 1888).

49 *See* W. Prosser, *supra* note 2, at 804 (only characteristic all privacy cases share is right to be let alone). This is not true of only explicit privacy cases, however. Actions for assault, tort recovery, or challenges to business regulation can all be considered assertions of the "right to be let alone." *See* Thomson, *supra* note 6, at 295. Requests for the government to take positive action may be the only claims that cannot be covered under this label; in a contract action, for example, the claim in effect is that the plaintiff should *not* be left alone to his own devices.

50 *See* Bloustein, *Privacy as an Aspect of Human Dignity: An Answer to Dean Prosser,* 39 N.Y.U. L. Rev. 962, 971 (1964).

51 *See* pp. 444–56 *infra* (reasons to protect against losses of privacy).

52 For a similar critique of Bloustein, see *Concept, supra* note 20, at 51–53.

53 *See* MacCormick, *A Note Upon Privacy,* 89 Law Q. Rev. 23, 25–26 (1973).

54 *But cf.* Gerety, *supra* note 18, at 286–88 (effort to explain why files in data banks are related to intimacy, in order to justify seeing them as involving privacy, defined as control over intimate decisions). In fact, this conception of privacy has already created problems in the interpretation of the privacy

exception to the Freedom of Information Act, 5 U.S.C. § 552(b)(7)(C) (1976). *See* Emerson, *The Right of Privacy and Freedom of the Press,* 14 Harv. C.R.-C.L. L. Rev. 329, 351–56 (1979); Kronman, *The Privacy Exemption to the Freedom of Information Act* (forthcoming in J. Legal Stud. (1980)).

55 *See, e.g.,* Emerson, *Nine Justices in Search of a Doctrine,* 64 Mich. L. Rev. 219 (1965) (reasons that led Court to base Griswold v. Connecticut, 381 U.S. 479 (1965), on right to privacy); Ely, *The Wages of Crying Wolf: A Comment on* Roe v. Wade, 82 Yale L.J. 920, 937–43 (1973) (criticizing use of privacy doctrine in abortion cases as misguided effort to avoid discredited "substantive due process" doctrine).

56 *See, e.g., Autonomy, supra* note 20, at 180–81 (danger that corruption of concepts of privacy will have dire consequences); Henkin, *Privacy and Autonomy,* 74 Colum. L. Rev. 1410, 1426–32 (1974). The prediction that privacy would be used to obscure questions of liberty came true in People v. Privitera, 23 Cal. 3d 697, 591 P.2d 919, 153 Cal. Rptr. 431 (1979) (prohibition of laetrile treatments does not violate privacy rights of cancer patients or doctors). The *Privitera* court's conclusion seems correct as far as it goes, but it is arguable that privacy issues were not involved in the case at all. The question was not whether decisions to use laetrile were "personal," but whether the state had a sufficient interest to justify prohibition of a drug that was not proven dangerous. The court's conclusion that privacy was not involved made it oblivious to the liberty and paternalism issues of the case.

57 *See, e.g.,* Griswold v. Connecticut, 381 U.S. 479, 484–85 (1965); P. Devlin, The Enforcement of Morals 1–25 (1968).

58 *See, e.g.,* Van den Haag, *supra* note 37, at 152–53, 166–67 (privacy includes "intrusion" by mail, noise, and smells); Public Utils. Comm'n v. Pollak. 343 U.S. 451, 469 (1952) (Douglas, J., dissenting) (music, news, and propaganda played in transit system buses violated privacy rights of "captive audience"). It seems likely, however, that Justice Douglas's notion of privacy relates more closely to liberty of choice; the Court's opinion held that privacy was not involved because buses are public places. *Id.* at 464–65.

The problem of unsolicited mail also raises few if any privacy issues. The sender has acquired the name and address of the recipient, but this may be done through the telephone directory and thus the loss of privacy appears negligible. The sale of mailing lists is more troublesome. Professor Posner in *Privacy, supra* note 8, at 411, concludes that the economics of the situation justifies such sales without compensation for the recipients, but ignores the possible desire of individuals to be removed from mailing lists. *But see* Privacy Protection Study Comm'n, *supra* note 5, at 125–54.

59 *See, e.g.,* Prosser, *supra* note 6, at 401–07. For the development of the right to privacy and the nature of the first cases, see W. Prosser, *supra* note 2, at 802–04; Dickler, *supra* note 6, at 448–52. Dickler's article was the first scholarly attempt to "redefine" the right to privacy, noting that

the cases could be grouped under three labels (trespass, defamation, unfair trade practices). *Id.* at 435.

60 *See, e.g.,* Pavesich v. New England Life Ins. Co., 122 Ga. 190, 50 S.E. 68 (1905). As Edward Bloustein argues, there is an element of loss of privacy in at least some of these cases. Advertisements may attract attention even when the subjects are anonymous. *See* Bloustein, *supra* note 50, at 985–91.

61 For example, individuals may be commercially exploited if they are compensated for their services at rates below the market price, but this does not seem to involve loss of privacy. Similarly, governmental wiretapping is an obvious example of an invasion of privacy that has not a hint of commercial exploitation.

62 A number of these cases have no relation to privacy whatsoever; the essence of the complaint is not that the plaintiff wants to prevent the use of his identifying features, but simply that he wants to be paid for such use. *See, e.g.,* Zacchini v. Scripps-Howard Broadcasting Co., 433 U.S. 562 (1977); Gautier v. Pro-Football, Inc., 278 A.D. 431, 106 N.Y.S.2d 553 (1951), *aff'd,* 304 N.Y. 354, 107 N.E.2d 485 (1952). In such cases, the doctrine of privacy is completely inappropriate, as noted in Nimmer, *The Right of Publicity,* 19 Law & Contemp. Prob. 203 (1954).

63 Some critics of contemporary society frequently complain that we suffer from too much privacy, that we exalt the "private realm" and neglect the public aspects of life, and that as a result individuals are alienated, lonely, and scared. *See, e.g.,* H. Arendt, The Human Condition 23–73 (1958); Arndt, *The Cult of Privacy,* 21 Austl. Qu., Sept. 1979, at 68, 70–71 (1949). Other social critics emphasize the threat to privacy posed by modern society. *See, e.g.,* V. Packard, The Naked Society (1964). Indeed, much of the privacy literature seems to share the assumption that additional legal protection is needed. Taken together, these two sets of complaints suggest that something is wrong with the contemporary balance between privacy and interaction. Contributions remain to be made to this critical literature.

64 *See, e.g.,* Beardsley, *supra* note 19, at 58 (principle that invasions of privacy are wrong derived from general principle that choice should be respected); Benn, *supra* note 27, at 8–9 (general principle of respect for persons, including principle of respect for their choices, explains our objection to invasions of privacy). To some extent, Benn's discussion goes beyond the want-satisfaction argument when he suggests that there is something especially disrespectful in certain invasions of privacy. *Id.* at 10–12. For a general discussion of want-satisfaction arguments, see Gavison, *supra* note 14.

65 *See, e.g.,* B. Barry, Political Argument 38–43 (1965) (nature of want-regarding justifications and their importance in politics).

66 This is true because we can judge some of the effects of loss of privacy as bad, even if the individual has chosen that loss. An obvious example is the cheapening effect of life in the limelight. Public life, especially in a publication-oriented culture, involves a serious risk that individuals will

receive almost constant publicity. Even though a person is insensitive to his own need for privacy, he may nonetheless need it.

67 *See, e.g.*, Bloustein, *Privacy is Dear at Any Price: A Response to Professor Posner's Economic Theory*, 12 Ga. L. Rev. 429, 442 (1978); Professor Fried in *Privacy, supra* note 19, at 476–78. Both writers stress that the claim of ultimacy strengthens the case for privacy by freeing it from links to other values. At the same time, both conclude by providing justifications that are at least partly instrumental. *Id.* at 478 (trust, love, friendship); Bloustein, *Privacy, Tort Law, and the Constitution: Is Warren and Brandeis' Tort Petty and Unconstitutional as Well?* 46 Tex. L. Rev. 611, 618–19 (1968) (dignity, individuality, inviolate personality). Professor Fried's current position is unclear, however. *See* Fried, *Privacy: Economics and Ethics—A Comment on Posner*, 12 Ga. L. Rev. 423, 426 (1978) ("I am prepared to grant both Posner's and Thomson's attack upon the view which I stated earlier.")

68 The notion of an ever-present, omniscient God exhibits to some extent a willingness to accept, in some context, life with a total lack of privacy. These features of God explain both the comfort and the regulatory force of religious belief.

69 *See, e.g.*, Bloustein, *supra* note 50, at 1003:

> The man who is compelled to live every minute of his life among others and whose every need, thought, desire, fancy or gratification is subject to public scrutiny, has been deprived of his individuality and human dignity. Such an individual merges with the mass. His opinions, being public, tend never to be different; his aspirations, being known, tend always to be conventionally accepted ones; his feelings, being openly exhibited, tend to lose their quality of unique personal warmth and to become the feelings of every man. Such a being, although sentient, is fungible; he is not an individual.

For a similar analysis, see Bazelon, *Probing Privacy*, 12 Gonz. L. Rev. 587, 592 (1977).

70 The contents of our thoughts and consciousness, now relatively immune from observation and forced disclosure, may not always be free from discovery. Lie detectors are only one kind of technological development that could threaten this privacy. *See, e.g.*, Note, People v. Barbara: *The Admissibility of Polygraph Test Results in Support of a Motion for New Trial*, 1978 Det. C. L. Rev. 347; Note, *The Polygraph and Pre-Employment Screening*, 13 Hous. L. Rev. 551 (1976). It is this sense of privacy that George Fletcher uses when he argues that the rule that people cannot be punished for thoughts alone serves to protect privacy. Fletcher, *Legality as Privacy*, in Liberty and the Rule of Law 182–207 (R. Cunningham ed. 1979).

71 It is arguable that only the first concern necessitates legal protection of privacy, whereas the second will be satisfied by any equalization of privacy no matter where the balance is drawn. It is possible, however, that very low levels of privacy are inconsistent with an autonomous and democratic society, even assuming that privacy is equally distributed. *See* pp. 451–56 *infra*. The dangers of unequal distribution of knowledge are dramatically described in G. Orwell, 1984 (1949).

72 There are advantages to working within a single such theory; the conceptual scheme is clear, and may provide a richness of association. On the other hand, because such theories are so different in conceptual scheme and coverage of the human condition, it would require enormous efforts to translate between them. Moreover, adherents of different theories tend to resist other theories as inadequate. It thus seems preferable not to choose a single framework of discussion.

73 *See, e.g.,* Roberts & Gregor, *supra* note 34, at 199–225.

74 Many therapeutic techniques stress the identification of the "real self," explaining deviations from it as inhibitions or repressions. It only makes sense to speak of self-realization and identification if there is a way to separate this self from behavior, which is affected by rationalizations, sublimations, and social controls.

75 The ideal of frankness as the only basis for human relations has been practiced by some participants in the encounter-group movement. *See, e.g.,* W. Schutz, Joy (1969). For a criticism of this ideal of total frankness, see E. Schur, The Awareness Trap (1976); J. Silber, *Masks and Fig Leaves,* in Nomos, *supra* note 1, at 226, 228–31.

76 Reiman, *Privacy, Intimacy, and Personhood,* 6 Philosophy & Pub. Aff. 26, 31–36 (1977).

77 *Privacy, supra* note 19, at 484. Fried suggests that human relations are determined by personal information shared with a partner but no one else. Privacy, which permits individual control over this information, provides the "moral capital" we spend in love and friendship. *Id.* at 484–85. It is not clear from Fried's analysis, however, whether it is useful in assessing the importance of a relationship to examine the amount of personal information shared by the parties. For example, two chess players preparing for a world championship may spend a great deal of time and money in order to acquire a vast amount of information about each other, but we would not say that they had an intimate relationship. Moreover, Fried's argument invokes the weak sense of "control" over information—control over the decision to disclose it, rather than control over the amount of information others actually have. *See* pp. 426–28 *supra* (distinction between two notions of control). Fried's argument at best supports only the right not to disclose personal information, which is usually not threatened anyway. It does not support arguments against gossip, for example. *See id.* at 490. Finally, it may be misleading to suggest that information about ourselves is capital that we spend to create love and friendship, because such information is always being generated and is thus inexhaustible. *See* Reiman, *supra* note 76, at 31–36 (critique of Fried's argument); Rachels, *Why Privacy is Important,* 4 Philosophy & Pub. Aff. 323, 325 (1975).

78 The need for privacy is sufficiently strong, however, that even individuals in "total institutions" develop ways to achieve some intimacy despite near-constant surveillance. *See* E. Goffman, Asylums 173, 223–38 (1961).

79 There are several ways that one can organize functional arguments for

privacy. One obvious approach is to focus on the goals to which privacy
is allegedly linked. Despite the clear attractions of this approach, the
functional analysis I employ is structured around the ways in which privacy
functions to promote goals, rather than on the goals themselves. Thus
the contribution of privacy to autonomy or human relations, which is
achieved in various ways, is mentioned in a number of different places.
This organization is illuminating in identifying the ways in which privacy
operates, which in turn suggests both the possibilities and the limits of
regulation. The repetition in goals is a cost of this approach, but it saves
repetition of functions. Furthermore, this structure points out clearly one
of the important aspects of privacy: the way in which arguments for
privacy are related to its function as a promoter of liberty.

80 The role of privacy in learning is underscored by the fact that one of the
features of underprivileged families considered responsible for their children's failures in school is that most cannot provide the opportunity for
privacy. *See* J. Coleman, Equality of Educational Opportunity 298–302
(1966) (influence of student's background on educational achievement).

81 Relaxed behavior does not necessarily include undesirable conduct; most
kinds of relaxation are not prohibited even though they are unlikely in
public. *See, e.g.,* J. Barth, The End of the Road 57, 58 (1960) (character
who thinks he is alone is observed behaving in ridiculous but not objectionable manner); Rachels, *supra* note 77, at 323–24 (analyzing this scene
in privacy terms).

82 *See, e.g.,* Bloustein, *Group Privacy: The Right to Huddle,* 8 Rut.-Cam. L.J.
219, 224–46 (1977).

83 For example, many pianists refuse to practice in the presence of others,
and not simply to avoid distraction, inhibition, or self-consciousness. They
practice alone so that they are the ones to decide when they are ready
for an audience. It could be argued that privacy thus has its costs in terms
of what the world learns about human achievement; some perfectionists
are never sufficiently pleased with their creations, yet their work may be
superior to much that is made public by others. Even if this were true, it
does not prove that the lost masterpieces would have been created in the
absence of privacy. Perfectionists are just as vulnerable to criticism as
anybody else, perhaps even more so.

84 Jourard, *Some Psychological Aspects of Privacy,* 31 Law & Contemp. Prob.
307, 309–11 (1966). A similar argument is made by Benn, *supra* note 27,
at 24–25.

85 *See* B. Wooton, Social Science and Social Pathology 210–21 (1959) (definitions of "mental health"). It is notable that this concept has been used
in ways that include all the other individual goals mentioned above. For
example, some see autonomy as a sign of mental health; others see the
incapacity to form and maintain human relations as a sign of mental
illness.

86 For privacy's contribution to be desirable, we must value X. Is the avoidance of mental breakdown always desirable? Would we prefer a person

who could adjust to any society, or one who would break down if he had to cope with the requirements of life in a Nazi regime?

87 *See* E. Durkheim, Suicide: A Study in Sociology (1951) (mental breakdown may be affected by absence of social cohesiveness).

88 *See* E. Goffman, *supra* note 78, at 4, 23–25 (individuals are "mortified" and "violated" in mental hospitals).

89 *See* D. Riesman, Faces in the Crowd 736–41 (1952) (relationship between autonomy and nature of society); Benn, *supra* note 27, at 24–26 (argument for privacy in terms of autonomy).

90 Professor Posner suggests an argument of this sort in *Privacy, supra* note 8, at 407. Such an argument could be made about creativity and human relations as well as autonomy. *See* Bloustein, *supra* note 50, at 1006.

91 *See Privacy, supra* note 19, at 485; Sheehy, *Can Couples Survive?* New York Magazine, Feb. 19, 1973, at 35 ("Privacy is disallowed as being disloyal. But if the couple wants intimacy, both partners need to refresh themselves with privacy. That implies also being allowed to withdraw without guilt.")

92 We may, however, question privacy that promotes the learning of skills we consider dangerous, or the development of opinions we consider outrageous, such as opinions favoring bigotry or genocide.

93 *See* G. Allport, The Nature of Prejudice 326–39 (difficulty of making ourselves disregard known prejudices).

94 The distinction between the two types of cases may be illusory, however, if our incapacity to act on our convictions simply indicates doubt in our judgment.

95 Some states still have laws against homosexual relations between consenting adults, *see* Note, *The Constitutionality of Laws Forbidding Private Homosexual Conduct,* 72 Mich. L. Rev. 1613, 1613–14 (1974), and the Supreme Court has refused to declare them unconstitutional, *e.g.,* Doe v. Commonwealth, 403 F. Supp. 1199 (E.D. Va. 1975), *aff'd mem.,* 425 U.S. 901 (1976); *see* Richards, *supra* note 3, at 1319–20. These laws, however, are rarely if ever enforced against consenting adults; the decision not to enforce these laws is thus a decision to let the privacy of the relationship protect the participants from legal sanctions.

96 *See* Melvin v. Reid, 112 Cal. App. 285, P. 91 (1931) (revelation that woman was former prostitute and defendant in murder trial); Briscoe v. Reader's Digest Ass'n, 4 Cal. 3d 529, 483 P.2d 34, 93 Cal. Rptr. 866 (1971) (publication of prior record); *cf. Privacy, supra* note 8, at 415–16 (criticizing *Melvin*); Epstein, *supra* note 8, at 466–74 (deliberate concealment of information as misrepresentation).

97 Alan Westin sees this as one of the major functions of privacy. A. Westin, *supra* note 1, at 23–51. It is important to note that this function would not be as strong in cases in which the level of legal enforcement was high. *See* note 98 *infra.*

98 The fact that such laws are not enforced, *see* note 95 *infra,* may explain why the Supreme Court intervened in the more morally complicated issue of abortion, Roe v. Wade, 410 U.S. 113, 116 (1973), but not in that

of consensual homosexual conduct. A ruling on homosexuality would
have purely symbolic effect, whereas judicial noninterference in abortion
issues would have perpetuated a situation in which safe abortions were
difficult to obtain. *Cf.* Poe v. Ullman, 367 U.S. 497, 508 (1961) (refusing
to strike down statute prohibiting sale of contraceptives because state
did not enforce law).

99   *See* H.L.A. Hart, The Concept of Law 171–73 (1961) (distinction between
law and morality is that law may be deliberately and consciously changed,
whereas morality cannot).

100   To take a famous historical example, Socrates' trial did not make the
case for the principle of academic freedom to the Athenians. Thus, his
public declaration that he would continue teaching was heroic but could
not have been demanded of him.

101   The notion of relevance is crucial, of course. There may be a number
of borderline cases, but some will fall neatly in one of the categories.
The fact that X is sterile is clearly relevant for Y, who wants children
and considers marrying X. The fact that X prefers to have sex with people
of his own gender does not seem relevant, however, to his qualifications
as a clerk or even as a teacher.

102   *Privacy, supra* note 8, at 394–403; *Secrecy, supra* note 8, at 11–17.

103   Epstein, *supra* note 8, at 466–74.

104   For example, we would have less sympathy for an employer who demanded a "yes or no" answer from his employee to the question of
whether the employee had a criminal record or was a member of the
Communist Party. Such an employer may draw unwarranted inferences
if the employee has no opportunity to explain his answer. Professor
Posner has suggested that any such "irrational" conduct by prejudiced
employers will ultimately be corrected by the market, because the vic-
timized employees will command below-average wages, and the unpre-
judiced employers who hire them will obtain a competitive advantage.
Secrecy, supra note 8, at 12 (example of ex-convicts). This is beside the
point, however, because in the interim the employee suffers from high
emotional and economic costs (in the form of irrational stigma and lower
wage rates).

105   *See generally* G. Allport, *supra* note 93 (nature of prejudice).

106   *See, e.g.,* Benn, *supra* note 27, at 6–7; Reiman, *supra* note 76, at 38–39.

107   *See generally* H. Lynd, On Shame and the Search for Identity (1958).

108   *Cf.* NAACP v. Alabama *ex rel.* Patterson, 357 U.S. 449 (1958) (First
Amendment freedom of association includes privacy of political association in order to guarantee effective expression of political views). *See
generally* A. Westin, *supra* note 1, at 23–51 (relation between privacy and
democracy); Bazelon, *supra* note 69, at 591–94 (same).

109   *See, e.g.,* Galella v. Onassis, 353 F. Supp. 196, 207–10 (S.D.N.Y. 1972),
aff'd and modified in part, 487 F.2d 986 (2d Cir. 1973) (plaintiff was
photographed at restaurants, clubs theater, schools, funeral, and while
shopping, walking down street, and riding bicycle); B. Woodward &

S. Armstrong, The Brethren: Inside the Supreme Court (1979) (detailed account of working relationships of Supreme Court Justices). At the same time, it is important to note that restrictions on invasions of public figures' privacy may conflict with the First Amendment. *See, e.g.,* T. Emerson, The system of Freedom of Expression 6–7 (1970); Friedrich, *Secrecy versus Privacy: The Democratic Dilemma,* in Nomos, *supra* note 1, at 105.

The constitutional right to privacy suffers from a split personality. On one hand, the Supreme Court has established a right that covers at least some tort actions. *See* note 3 *supra.* The right may include "the individual interest in avoiding disclosure of personal matters." Whalen v. Roe, 429 U.S. 589, 599 (1977). *But see* Paul v. Davis, 424 U.S. 693, 712–14 (1976) (state circulation of flyer publicizing plaintiff's arrest on shoplifting charges did not violate plaintiff's constitutional right to privacy). On the other hand, it has been suggested that First Amendment developments indicate that those aspects of privacy that conflict with the right to publish true information may be unconstitutional. The issue is far from closed. *See* Emerson, *supra* note 54, at 334–37; Comment, *First Amendment Limitations on Public Disclosure Actions,* 45 U. Chi. L. Rev. 180 (1977). Some have gone so far as to suggest that the conflict between privacy and the First Amendment is illusory, because "privacy" is simply a conclusory word used by the courts. *See* Felcher & Rubin, *Privacy, Publicity, and the Portrayal of Real People by the Media,* 88 Yale L.J. 1577, 1585–88 (1979).

110 An interesting problem of this sort arises in the context of the disclosure exception to the Privacy Act of 1974, 5 U.S.C. § 552a(b) (1976), under which the guarantor of third parties' privacy interests is the government. If people request information about others, the individuals concerned are not notified, and information from files may be disclosed without their permission if the government does not decide to withhold it. *See, e.g.,* Boyer, *Computerized Medical Records and the Right to Privacy: The Emerging Federal Response,* 25 Buffalo L. Rev. 37 (1975) (medical files). The courts are now beginning to examine these problems. *E.g.,* Providence Journal Co. v. FBI, 460 F. Supp. 762, 767 (D.R.I. 1978) (standing under Privacy Act given to individual whose file was sought under Freedom of Information Act); Tax Reform Research Group v. IRS, 419 F. Supp. 415 (D.D.C. 1976) (ordering disclosure of officials involved in White House harassment of "enemies," but keeping targets' identities secret unless they express consent).

111 The problem may be aggravated by the fact that a major invader of privacy is the government, whose interest in exposing its own misconduct is always uncertain. *See, e.g.,* Weidner, *Discovery Techniques and Police Surveillance,* 7 UCLA-Alaska L. Rev. 190 (1978).

112 *See* N.Y. Times, April 28, 1973, at I, col. 4 (reporting break-in to Ellsberg's psychiatrist's office).

113 *See, e.g.,* Andenaes, *The General Preventive Effects of Punishment,* 114 U.

Pa. L. Rev. 949, 960–64 (1966) (risk of detection, apprehension, and conviction is of paramount importance to preventive effects of penal law).

114 A similar problem exists in defamation cases. In such cases, however, the plaintiff seeks a declaration that the publication was not true. Even the successful plaintiff in a privacy action has no guarantee of similar satisfaction. The trend in defamation law has reduced this difference. *See* Gertz v. Robert Welch, Inc., 418 U.S. 323, 377 (1974) (White, J., dissenting) (trend began with N.Y. Times Co. v. Sullivan, 376 U.S. 254 (1964)).

115 *See* Kalven, *supra* note 6, at 338–39 (suggesting that "privacy will recruit claimants inversely to the magnitude of the offense to privacy involved," and thus that law does not need a cause of action that exerts chilling effect on media but does not help worthy plaintiffs). Kalven also draws an analogy between actions for invasion of privacy and actions for breach of promise to marry. *Id.*

116 *See* note 6 *supra*. Richard Posner, however, does not consider privacy a value per se, and this is what makes his version of reductionism extreme. *See* note 8 *supra*. Although some of the points made here apply to Professor Posner's analysis as well, I deal only with moderate reductionists. For a criticism of Posner's approach, see Bloustein, *supra* note 67, at 429–42; Baker, *Posner's Privacy Mystery and the Failure of Economic Analysis of Law,* 12 Ga. L. Rev. 475 (1978).

117 Starting from legal decisions or moral intuitions about the scope of the right to privacy, or the scope of legal protection of privacy, is similar: in both cases what we study is the *conclusion* of a discussion of whether some action is actionable or a violation of a moral right. Thus Thomson's analysis, *see* Thomson, *supra* note 6, shares most of the weaknesses of legal analysis mentioned here. It also shares a similarity of purpose—to give a coherent description of what we have been doing under a single label.

118 Thus, Dean Prosser, the most influential of the reductionists, could offer as a strength of his description that analysis of more than 400 cases of privacy showed that they could all be neatly grouped under four categories of recovery, none of which primarily protects privacy. *See* W. Prosser, *supra* note 2, at 804–14 (setting out four privacy categories of intrusion, disclosure, false light, and appropriation). But in fact, reductionist analyses fail in even their limited attempt to explain precedents. Some cases, frequently discussed in privacy terms, cannot be included under these categories without straining them and weakening their power of description and guidance. For example, Prosser's categories do not encompass claims by individuals under the Privacy Act, 5 U.S.C. § 552a(d)(2)(B) (1976), that some information about them should be deleted or corrected. Moreover, it is unclear whether Prosser could accommodate the "constitutional" right to privacy decisions because he does not have

a category for noninterference in his account. Other accounts do provide such a category, however. *See* Gerety, *supra* note 18, at 261–81; Comment, *supra* note 3, at 1447.

119 The reasons for this are well known by any student of adjudication. Judges tend (and are encouraged) to prefer a just result based on weak doctrine to an admission that current law does not provide a way to justify an otherwise deserved recovery. The price of justice is thus often the coherence of the concepts involved. Privacy is an example of this, as I argue below. Similarly, I suspect that any concept of liberty derived from the constitutional adjudication of the last 100 years will not have much coherence either.

120 Warren & Brandeis, *supra* note 38, is notoriously vague on the conceptual question. For example, the authors never explicitly defined or described what they meant by "privacy." *Compare* Prosser, *supra* note 6, at 392 (Warren and Brandeis meant freedom from publicity) *with* Bloustein, *supra* note 50, at 971 (Warren and Brandeis meant freedom from affronts to human dignity).

121 Dean Prosser himself acknowledges the existence of these "common features," W. Prosser, *supra* note 2, at 814–15, but does not explain why there should be four different torts, dealing with different invasions, and designed to protect interests as distinct as those in reputation, property, and mental tranquility.

122 *See* pp. 456–59 *supra*.

123 One major difficulty is that the cases relied upon by the reductionist in order to derive his concept of privacy will not accurately reflect all the fact situations in which a valid privacy claim could be advanced. This is true because there are many ways to defeat a possibly valid claim based on an alleged invasion of privacy. For instance, conduct may be actionable, but not constitute an invasion of privacy. *See, e.g.,* Peterson v. Idaho First Nat'l Bank, 83 Idaho 578, 367 P.2d 284 (1961). A loss of privacy may have occurred, but not as the result of conduct considered undesirable, as in the case of a loss of privacy resulting from certain research activity and from investigations to verify plaintiff's statements or damage claims. *See, e.g.,* Fed. R. Civ. P. 35 (court may order parties to submit to mental or physical examination by physician). Even when the conduct is undesirable, it may not be actionable because it has not passed a certain threshold. *See, e.g.,* Virgil v. Sports Illustrated, Inc. 424 F. Supp. 1286, 1289 (S.D. Cal. 1976) (publication of fact plaintiff extinguished cigarettes in his mouth, dove off stairs to impress women, hurt himself in order to collect unemployment benefits, spent his time body-surfing, ate insects, and participated in gang fights as youngster, was "not sufficiently offensive" even to create jury question). Finally, courts may deny recovery even when the conduct is prima facie actionable because the defendant can establish a defense, which usually means that some competing interest is judged to be more important in the circumstances. The most important such defense raises the First Amendment, claiming that publication is

of sufficient public interest to override individual privacy. *See, e.g.,* Time, Inc. v. Hill, 385 U.S. 374, 388–91 (1967) (First Amendment bar to invasion of privacy claim).

124 Dean Prosser's account has been incorporated into the Restatement (Second) of Torts § 652A (1976), but it is not the best of the reductionist works. For example, there are explicit privacy cases that do not fit neatly into any of his categories, and Prosser's attempt to accommodate them strains the categories and deprives them of much force. One such group of privacy cases is that in which the plaintiff has attention attracted to him against his will. Prosser does not have such a category and must squeeze these cases into "intrusion." W. Prosser, *supra* note 2, at 808–09. Another group of cases is that in which the plaintiff must answer certain questions as a condition of employment. Prosser groups one such case, Reed v. Orleans Parish School Bd., 21 So.2d 895 (La. App. 1945), under "public disclosure of private facts," W. Prosser, *supra* note 2, at 810 n.89, although no public disclosure was involved. Similarly, he groups Fifth Amendment cases of impelled self-incrimination under "intrusion." *Id.* at 807. For a detailed exposition of his account and its shortcomings, see R. Gavison, *supra* note 14.

125 One of Prosser's problems is that he deals only with the law of torts, and cannot adequately discuss protection of privacy in other contexts. There is nothing illegitimate about dealing with one branch of the law for practical purposes, of course. For an example of the broader perspective gained through a synoptic view, however, see Bloustein, *supra* note 50.

There is no doubt that the only way to defeat the dangerous hegemony of Dean Prosser's account of legal thinking is by actually working out the description of the law of privacy that would follow from the proposed analysis, including sufficient detail so that practitioners and judges could rely on this description. I have tried to outline such a description in R. Gavison, *supra* note 14. For the gains of this analysis in the much simpler context of Israeli law, see R. Gavison, *The Minimum Area of Privacy— Israel,* in Israeli Reports to the Tenth International Congress of Comparative Law 176 (1978).

126 *See, e.g.,* Note, *Formalism, Legal Realism, and Constitutionally Protected Privacy Under the Fourth and Fifth Amendments,* 90 Harv. L. Rev. 945 (1977); Note, *Medical Practice and the Right to Privacy,* 43 Minn. L. Rev. 943 (1959). Dean Prosser excludes cases of limited disclosure because he insists that one element of the "genuine" privacy tort is publicity, and that limited disclosure is not enough. W. Prosser, *supra* note 2, at 909–12.

127 *See* p. 440 *supra.*

128 *See* p. 439 *supra.*

129 There are at least some cases in which recovery for invasion of privacy has been given in which no other interest was involved (unless we take "freedom from mental distress" to be a distinct interest, which would engulf all privacy claims and many others as well). *See, e.g.,* Melvin v. Reid, 112 Cal. App. 285, 297 P. 91 (1931) (motion picture disclosed

current identity of former prostitute who had been acquitted in murder
trial seven years earlier).
130 De May v. Roberts, 46 Mich. 160, 9 N.W. 146 (1881), is probably best
explained in such terms. Such a combination of motives appears in many
of the appropriation cases. *See, e.g.*, Pavesich v. New England Life Ins.
Co., 122 Ga. 190, 50 S.E. 68 (1905). For the relevance of privacy rhetoric
in explaining decisions, and as an argument against Posner's reductionism, see Epstein, *supra* note 8, at 461–65.
131 A certain sphere of privacy has been protected from the earliest times.
Anglo-Saxon law and German tribal law protected the peace that attached to every freeman's dwelling, and offered compensation for damage to property, insulting words, and the mere act of intrusion. 1 Die
Gesetze der Angelsachsen Abt. 8, 15, 17, Hl. 11, Af. 40, Ine 6–6.3
(F. Liebermann ed. 1903); 1 F. Pollock & F. Maitland, The History of
English Law 45 (2d ed. 1968).
   The notion that one's home is protected from arbitrary intrusions by
government officials finds little support in the polemics of reformers
until the late 16th century and no support in case law until the 18th
century. Medieval kings did not make available writs *de cursu* against
lawless royal officials, though periodically they did permit inquiry into
such official misconduct. *See* H. Cam, The Hundred and the Hundred
Rolls, an Outline of Local Government in Medieval England (1930).
Manorial bailiffs, subject to local custom, the sheriff, tax collector, and
creditors, subject to the limits on distraint proceedings, could enter a
freeman's home restrained more by trespass liability than by any requirement of a warrant. 2 F. Pollock & F. Maitland, *supra*, at 575–78.
   We know less about entry into the home to gather evidence for criminal
law enforcement. The procedure for neighbors, jurors, and later mag-
istrates to conduct such investigations is hidden by the use of the general
issue, the rudimentary law of evidence, and the informality and local
context of the criminal law. *See* S. Milsom, Historical Foundations of the
Common Law 357, 360 (1969); Baker, *Criminal Courts and Procedure at
Common Law 1550–1800*, in Crime in England 1550–1800 at 15, 16–17,
38–39 (J. Cockburn ed. 1977). It is unlikely that there were any real
checks on evidence-gathering other than general tort liability. *But see*
Samaha, *Hanging for Felony: the Rule of Law in Elizabethan Colchester*, 21
Hist. J. 763, 768–71, 774–75 (1978) (claiming early notions of rule of
law and evidence procedure).
132 Warren & Brandeis, *supra* note 38, at 197–214.
133 This reliance on the history of legal protection makes Warren and Brandeis's article one that "does model better than anything in the literature
the emergence of a common law principle." Wellington, *Common Law
Rules and Constitutional Double Standards: Some Notes on Adjudication*, 83
Yale L.J. 221, 252 (1973).
134 Warren & Brandeis, *supra* note 38, at 193 ("Thus, in very early times,
the law gave a remedy only for physical interference with life and prop-

erty . . . . Later, there came a recognition of man's spiritual nature, of his feelings and his intellect.")

135 In this sense, privacy may indeed be related to defamation, which is one of the oldest concerns of law. *See* S. Milsom, *supra* note 131, at 332–43; N. Rakover, Defamation in Jewish Law (1964).

136 *See, e.g.,* P. Hewitt, Privacy: The Information Gatherers (1977); A. Miller, *supra* note 19; J. Rule, Private Lives and Public Surveillance (1973); A. Westin, *supra* note 1, at 158–68.

137 *See, e.g.,* Younger Committee, *supra* note 45, at 153–76.

138 Warren & Brandeis, *supra* note 38, at 196.

139 Not only has this process remained the same, but this is the area in which rising standards of living and safety have brought the most dramatic increases in privacy. *See Privacy, supra* note 8, at 396–97 (privacy increases with wealth of society).

140 A powerful literary illustration is provided by H. Böll, The Lost Honor of Katharina Blum (1975).

141 *See* notes 47, 119 *supra.*

142 Once it became established that truth was an absolute defense to a defamation claim, *see* Harnett & Thornton, *The Truth Hurts: A Critique of a Defense to Defamation,* 35 Va. L. Rev. 425 (1949), the only way to make truthful publications actionable was to develop new privacy doctrine. *See* Wade, *Defamation and the Right to Privacy,* 15 Vand. L. Rev. 1093, 1109, 1120 (1962) (approving use of privacy to overcome limitations of defamation).

143 *Compare* Lochner v. New York, 198 U.S. 45 (1905) (liberty of contract) *and* Griswold v. Connecticut, 381 U.S. 479, 481–82 (1965) (refusing to apply substantive due process) *with id.* at 485–86 (right to privacy). For a critical discussion of this move, see Ely, *supra* note 55, at 937–43.

144 Warren & Brandeis *supra* note 38, had this in mind when they insisted that privacy be protected as "personality," not as a property interest. *Id.* at 205–08. Privacy has been used to protect property, however. *See* pp. 439–40 *supra.* Professor Posner in *Privacy, supra* note 8, at 393–404, argues for an undifferentiated conception of privacy as a kind of property, and Thomson, *supra* note 6, at 303–06, notes that much of the privacy rhetoric is based on "ownership" grounds.

145 The most extreme example of such an analysis is Posner's. *See Privacy, supra* note 8; *Secrecy, supra* note 8. But the price that may be exacted by such an approach if it is used to make policy decisions about the scope of desirable legal protection becomes clear in works such as Kronman, *supra* note 54, and Felcher & Rubin, *supra* note 109, because these commentators actually conclude that privacy should not be considered an independent and distinct value.

146 *See* note 109 *supra* (conflict between privacy and freedom of expression).

147 Sidis v. F-R Publishing Corp., 34 F. Supp. 19 (S.D.N.Y. 1938), *aff'd,* 113 F.2d 806 (2d Cir.), *cert. denied,* 311 U.S. 711 (1940) (magazine story about former child prodigy describing his current activities).

402   RUTH GAVISON

148 Melvin v. Reid, 112 Cal. App. 285, 297 P. 91 (1931) (movie about former prostitute acquitted of murder seven years earlier).
149 Barber v. Time, Inc., 348 Mo. 1199, 159 S.W.2d 291 (1942) (picture taken of "insatiable eater" in hospital bed).
150 Limits on the publicity of judicial proceedings, for various reasons, are not unknown. *See, e.g.,* Gannett Co., Inc. v. DePasquae, 99 S. Ct. 2898 (1979) (pretrial criminal hearings may be closed to press). In most situations, the imposition of criminal sanctions for truthful disclosures would probably not be upheld. *See* Landmark Communications, Inc. v. Virginia. 435 U.S. 829 (1978) (First Amendment does not permit criminal sanctions of third persons who publish truthful information about confidential proceedings before state judicial review commission). Other measures limiting the possibility of publication may be constitutional, however. *See, e.g.,* Cox Broadcasting Corp. v. Cohn, 420 U.S. 469, 491 (1975) (although First Amendment does not permit sanctions for accurate publication of rape victim's name obtained from public records, Court reserves "broader question" whether state may "protect an area of privacy free from unwanted publicity"); N.Y. Civ. Rights Law §§ 50, 51 (McKinney Supp. 1976) (recent amendment to privacy statute in response to *Cox Broadcasting*).

17

Privacy and intimate information

FERDINAND SCHOEMAN

I knew the mass of men conceal'd
Their thought, for fear that if reveal'd
They would by other men be met
With blank indifference, or with blame reproved;
                  from Matthew Arnold's "The Buried Life"

Privacy itself is suspect as a value. It makes deception possible and provides the context for concealing things about which we may feel ashamed or guilty. Embarrassed by this feature, defenders of privacy often argue that privacy is a necessary response to a social and political world that is insufficiently understanding, benevolent, respecting, trustworthy, or caring. I shall call this rationale for privacy "reactive." This response assumes that we would no longer care who knows the most intimate facts about ourselves were the world morally improved. Some have even suggested that, divorced from its prudential motivation, a proclivity for privacy should be seen as an attitude that impedes the realization of a sense of community and at the same time makes the individual more vulnerable to selective disclosures on the part of others. [If everything about a person is already known by others, that person need not fear revelations. If he (or she) discovers that others are more like him than he first suspected, he is less subject to the intimidations engendered by a sense of comparative inferiority.]

Philosophers and legal theorists have discussed privacy as valuable independent of its effectiveness in protecting persons from a morally harsh world. Charles Fried,[1] Robert Gerstein,[2] James Rachels,[3] and Richard Wasserstrom,[4] have elaborated the ways in which the intimate qualities of some interpersonal relationships would not be possible outside the context of privacy. Ruth Gavison,[5] Jeffrey Reiman,[6] Richard Wasserstrom,[7] Robert Gerstein,[8] and Stanley Benn[9] have pointed out how certain intimate dimensions of the self (having to do with the creation or discovery of moral character) would be truncated or debased without respect accorded to the individual's claim to control personal information. In the vein of these theorists, I would like to add to the discussion of the place of privacy as a value independent of its feature of protecting people from an imperfect social world. In this chapter I will elaborate themes others have introduced as well as suggest some new ones. Essentially I hope to show that on balance, outside of special contexts, revelation of self is not to be thought of as desirable in itself and may be detrimental. I hope to persuade readers that respect for privacy marks out something morally significant about what it is to be a person and about what it is to have a close relationship with another. Put abstractly, I shall argue that respect for privacy reflects a realization that not all dimensions of self and relationships gain their moral worth through their promotion of independently worthy ends.

I

I shall begin by discussing the question of whether revelation of self is good, except in those special contexts when it enables others to injure one's interests. Let me begin with the presumption that, prudent mistrust aside, more knowledge about a person is better. One implication of this view, a view entertained by Richard Wasserstrom[10] and endorsed by Richard Posner,[11] is that it is a better state of the world, other things being equal, if when I go to the dry cleaners to pick up my pants the attendant and I also share our innermost feelings and attitudes, despite the fact that we have no close relationship. The claim is that even outside the context of an especially close relationship, it is somewhat better for people to know more about one another than it is for them to know less. This attitude strikes me as most implausible but enlightening. It can be used to illustrate how much of what is good about people sharing and knowing one another intimately is contextually dependent.

As things now stand, people generally reveal intimate parts of their lives only to persons in contexts in which some special involvement is anticipated. It is, accordingly, very awkward to be going about one's business and be confronted with a plea or expectation for personal involvement which, by hypothesis, is unoccasioned by the relationship. Although sometimes welcome, generally such pleas are disturbing for they seem to give us less control over where we will expend our emotional resources. The reason for being reserved in these situations is not fear of being harmed by the content of one's revelations, but rather a realization that such situations call for something personally important to be given without first assuring that it is given freely. It does not seem plausible to suggest that it would be better if people generally revealed intimacies without really caring about the emotional attachments normally associated with such revelations; the very intimacies such revelations characteristically promote would have a harder time surfacing if they were deprived of their social and personal significance.

Three exceptions to this position should be noted and explained. First, there are times when a person so desperately needs the concern of others that something like an insistence on intimacy is legitimized. (Crisis may occasion temporary intimacy.) This concession in no way goes to showing that in normal situations such revelations are appropriate. Second, the publication of personal diaries, autobiographies, poems, confessions, and the like, though revealing of personal intimacies, hardly seems to warrant moral disapproval, as the position here advocated about reserve would seem to suggest. In response, we can observe that unlike personal disclosure, the publication of personal information leaves others completely free emotionally to take whatever attitude they want toward the writer. Even though the point of the writing may be to affect others in a personal way, there is still the distance that publication imposes that differentiates this communication from person-to-person revelations. Third, it may be pointed out that we often talk to complete strangers about intimate matters and that the frequency with which this occurs suggests that something important is being missed in the analysis presented. In considering this argument, it is important to notice that a stranger is someone uninvolved in the web of one's ordinary social relationships and someone one expects to stay uninvolved. Thus to a certain extent, revelations to a complete stranger are largely equivalent to publication because the expectation of involvement is so remote. The stranger provides an objective perspective—a perspective people admittedly find very useful to confront. The fact that one is in a position to tell a stranger things of an intimate nature does not suggest that it would be good to tell the same things to someone with whom one has an ongoing relationship. Our relationship with these people would become very different if intimate sharing were made a part of it. (Below I take up the question of the desirability of redefining relationships so as to include such intimacy.)

The emphasis in discussion of these exceptions has been on the demands revelations place upon the listener. Now, I shall discuss in detail difficulties for the person who is doing the revealing. Essentially, I shall argue that what is revealed in abstract contexts may not be at all what the revealer intends to convey.

What makes information private or intimate for a person is not just a function of the content of the information; it is also a function of the role the information plays for the person. One facet of this role is that the information is to be regarded as special and thus only revealed in certain contexts—contexts in which the very giving of the information is valued as a special act, and where the information so given will be received sympathetically. We tend to think of private information as pertaining to primarily embarrassing or wrongful conduct or thoughts. I think that what makes things private is in large part their importance to our conceptions of ourselves and to our relationships with others. To entrust another with intimate information is not primarily to provide the other with an arsenal that could prove detrimental to ourselves if revealed to the world. Perhaps the most significant aspect of what the revealer of intimate information has to convey is that *the information matters deeply to himself*. Typically, this involves a trust that the other will not regard the revelation as inconsequential, as it would be to the world at large. What is conveyed to someone uninvolved is different in an essential way from what is intimately conveyed. Selective self-disclosure provides the means through which people envalue personal experiences which are intrinsically or objectively valueless.

Perhaps the closest analogy to what I am trying to express about intimate information is our attitude toward a holy object—something that is appropriately revealed only in special circumstances. To use such an object, even though it is a humble object when seen out of context, without the idea of its character in mind is to deprive the object of its sacredness, its specialness. Such an abuse is regarded as an affront, often requiring ritual procedures to restore the object's sacred character. (Note that there are certain uses which are permitted even though not devotional in nature: use for educational purposes, for example.)

Supportive of this analogy between the private and the sacred are some literary treatments of privacy invasions. Incursions into one's privacy, one finds, are described as *pollutions* or *defilements*. In Henry James's novel *The Reverberator* we find Gaston Probert trying to explain to his fiancée, Francie Dosson, just what her revelations of family matters to, and the subsequent publication in, a society newspaper has meant to his family. Gaston puts it this way: "They were the last, the last people in France, to do it to. The sense of excruciation—or pollution."[12] We also find the theme of privacy invasion as defilement explored in Athol Fugard's play, *A Lesson from Aloes*. The South African secret police have ransacked Piet and Gladys Bezuidenhout's house. They discover Gladys's diary and read it, despite the fact that there is nothing significant in it to anybody but Gladys. Gladys, trying to explain to her husband just how defiling the experience was, speaks as follows:[13]

There, I've cancelled those years, I'm going to forget I ever lived them. They weren't just laundry lists, you know. There were very intimate and personal things in those diaries, things a woman only talks about to herself. Even then it took me a lot of trust and courage to do that. I know I never had much of either, but I was learning. (*Her hysteria begins to surface again*) You were such a persuasive teacher, Peter! "Trust, Gladys. Trust yourself. Trust Life." There's nothing left of that. (*She brandishes her diary*) Must I tell you what I've been trying to do with this all day? Hide it. It's been behind the dressing table . . . under the mattress.

Can you think of somewhere really safe? Where nobody would find it, including yourself? There isn't is there? Do you know what I would really like to do with this? Make you eat it and turn it into shit . . . then maybe everybody would leave it alone. Yes, you heard me correctly. Shit! I've learned how to use my dirty words. And just as well, because there's no other adequate vocabulary for this country. Maybe I should do that in case they come again. A page full of filthy language. Because that is what they were really hoping for when they sat down with my diaries. Filth! . . .

If you were to tell me once more that they won't come again . . . ! To start with, I don't believe you, but even if I did, that once was enough. You seem to have a lot of difficulty understanding that, Peter. It only needs to happen to a woman once, for her to lose all trust she ever had in anything or anybody. They violated me, Peter. I might just as well have stayed in that bed, lifted up my nightdress and given them each a turn. I've shocked you. Good! Then maybe now you understand.

Not only is it a violation of an individual if intimate information is forced or tricked out of the person, or if a confidence is betrayed, as the literary examples here illustrate, but even the person himself who feels something special about this information may be insufficiently sensitive to the role of this information in his own mind. (Perhaps we should say that a person can violate his own privacy.) Probably every person has had the experience of telling another something very important, something that is unappreciated as special by the listener. This information, we learn, is really only meant for those who will treat it as something that matters *because it matters to the speaker*. Otherwise the most we have is a good or interesting story; often not even that. By being shared with others who cannot really appreciate the personal significance of certain information, such information loses some of its special character for the revealers. The kind of connectedness that is a prerequisite for intimate sharing must be present for this kind of appreciation to emerge. Otherwise the effort at communicating will misfire.

I have been arguing that the revelation of intimate information should be regarded as appropriate only in certain contexts, and that indeed, in a sense this kind of revelation *cannot* take place outside such a context. When it does take place outside the proper setting, a sense of violation is occasioned, whether the revelation was voluntary or not. Let me now address the question: Would the world be a better place if everyone shared the kind of relationship in which it was appropriate to make private disclosures? In response, let me begin by noting that different kinds of relationships require different qualities of persons. For instance, qualities which make persons good friends may make them unsuitable for a supervisor–supervisee relationship. There need not be any defect in the persons either as friends or as workers; qualities required in each relationship may be mutually exclusive. For a host of reasons, personal characteristics may determine that a person feels more comfortable in, and gains more out of, certain personal settings than others. Such concerns cannot be irrelevant to the capacity and desirability for intimacy. It is worth noting that in many of our important relationships emotional distance between the parties is crucial. For instance in a lawyer–client relationship, a psychotherapist–patient relationship, or even a student–teacher relationship it is not ideal that there be unbounded emotional involvement between the parties. These relationships require an objectivity of judgment that would be counterproductive to eliminate. Conversely, such professional detachment would be inappropriate in relationships in which identification with the other is a central feature of the relationship, as in parent–child relationships, friendships, and marriages.

People have, and it is important that they maintain, different relationships with different people. Information appropriate in the context of one relationship may not be appropriate in another. Such observations have been captured by sociological notions such as "audience segregation," "role," and "role credibility."[14] Such notions have been introduced to help describe or explain how the effectiveness of our relationships to various people in diverse contexts depends on limited access to persons or, more precisely, on access to limited dimensions of persons. Though some of our important relationships and aspirations involve intimacy with others, some are focused on really quite limited and objective interactions. As Ruth Gavison has argued,[15] part of our capacity to work with others in professional contexts may depend on remaining uninvolved in personal, political, moral, and religious aspects of the other. Accordingly, if a person finds the discussion of his own or anyone else's intimate life inappropriate in many contexts, it is not necessarily because he has anything to be ashamed about or anything for which he should feel guilty. It is that there are various dimensions of a person which it is important to develop, only some of which may involve intimate sharing. The integrity of different spheres of a person, and the ultimate integrity of the person, depends on that person's capacity to focus on one dimension at a time. This defense of privacy has nothing to do with lack of trust or good will generally, or with any fact about the moral imperfections of the world.

Some writers have equated nondisclosure of self to others as tantamount to fraud, hypocrisy, deceit.[16] Keeping people ignorant about what one is like in spheres they are not part of, or have no reasonable claim to knowledge about, is in no way morally tainted behavior. Generally, so long as a person does not misrepresent himself to those who, within the relevant domain, reasonably rely on his projected image, that person is not acting deceptively.

Related to the concern that role segregation is deceptive or hypocritical is the claim that it would be better if people exhibited coherence across the different roles they maintain. For instance, what one is like as a professional would in relevant ways be indicative of what one is like as a family member, as a citizen, as a friend, as an athlete, and so on. Though what I shall have to say here is admittedly sketchy and speculative, there does seem to be evidence of a psychological nature that relates to this issue. Different conceptions of what it is to be a person do bear on the issue of an individual's personality coherence and the role of privacy. According to the commonsense view, there is a core personality that is integrated but puts on various guises (for various purposes) in particular contexts. The picture is of a character standing behind various masks, none of which is really the actor, with the ability of discarding all the personae and revealing the true core. From this view, we can distinguish authentic responses of an individual from those that are role-governed, context-dependent, and inauthentic. On this account, privacy serves to protect a person's intimate self through concealment. Privacy permits pretense.

There is another view according to which there may be no unified core personality that exhibits authentic or inauthentic responses to circumstances. Instead there are diverse facets of personality that are brought into play in various contexts. These facets of self are not personae that some central self dons in its inauthentic mode. Rather these selves actually constitute the person. A person is something like a corporation of context-dependent characters. Any coherence between dimensions is something achieved and not something naturally implicit in the person.

On this second view it is still possible for people to be deceptive or inauthentic. The reference self is simply not the central core; it is the particular dimension of self that is specific to the prevailing context. Roles are not the masks of personality but the very medium within which personality is attributable to people. Privacy from this perspective supplies the condition for the expression and fulfillment of different dimensions of self, all of which may be equally real. It is important to emphasize that the attribution of dimensionality to individuals does not mean that people are multiple personalities in a clinical sense. Rather this view states that one may operate with different values and sensitivities in these different modes without being either schizophrenic or deceptive.

Psychologists who have advanced this second view of the self have done so on the basis of clinical and experimental findings.[17] Their most dramatic evidence is that certain consequences that would be anticipated on the basis of the commonsense view of self are frequently not what is found. On the commonsense view an individual's behavior in one setting should be quite predictable on the basis of his behavior in other settings. This is not the case. What is found is that knowledge about a person in one context is of little predictive value when anticipating behavior in dissimilar contexts. Instead, what proves to be a better predictor of behavior is knowledge of how others, however varied in personality, have behaved in the particular context at issue. Knowing the context of behavior and knowing how others have responded to this context prove to be more reliable indicators of behavior than does knowing how an individual has behaved in other contexts. There is more uniformity in behavior among different individuals in the same context than there is in the same person over a range of different contexts.

This evidence may suggest that there is no core self; one of the key functions that the core self is supposed to serve is to account for the consistency of behavior through diverse contexts and times. If the effect is not present, there is less reason to posit the cause. The results of the experiments cited above suggest there is some basis for thinking that privacy may play a central role in personality development. Privacy may provide the contexts in which various facets of personality can develop.

There are situations which require unusually high coherence between roles or even require that there be only one role in the agent's life. Someone who joins a monastic order has apparently committed himself to leading only a monastic life, or at least to doing only things consistent with that life. People who present themselves in such roles indicate to others that all their dimensions can be expected to conform to the ideals of their self-proclaimed ideal self. Such roles may preclude much of what would normally count as private domains. Although there are obviously things to admire about such choices, it is also apparent that there are costs in terms of aspects of the self that must be foregone.

II

Are there domains of life which are inherently private? Several positions have been developed in the literature in answer to this question. According to some, what it is that is regarded as private is culturally determined and respect for a person's privacy is primarily symbolic in significance.[18] According to a related position, what is private is determined by each particular relationship.[19] Relationships define which parts of another's life one can legitimately inquire into and which are beyond one's legitimate ken. According to still others, what is private is determined by what area of one's life does not, or tends not to, affect the significant interests of others.[20]

The last criterion is subject to the following difficulty. Whatever one might claim as private can cease being such if others manage to generate a stake in that state of affairs. With such a criterion one no longer maintains control over what would otherwise seem a private part of one's life. For instance, so long as one is in a position to make a large bet on any matter relating to another's life, that matter ceases to be private because of the interest one acquires in uncovering this facet of another's life. Additionally, if we think of the large investments certain institutions have in tracking down intimate details of various people's lives, we should have to concede that these details are not really private after all. While we may want to be somewhat utilitarian in considering how much weight to give to individual privacy claims, I think that there is little persuasive about the position that the "self-regarding" aspects of life are at the same time the private aspects.

A related criterion of the private, it could be suggested, is that it be the domain of a person's life which the individual is generally in the best position to manage well. Assigning rights over this area to anyone else, the suggestion continues, would result in lower overall benefits. One may concede the point that individuals should control those parts of their lives which they can best manage without thinking that this constitutes a criterion of the private. Although a physician might be in the best position to regulate how we should care for our bodies, this remains a private matter.

Although there are many things that we regard as private, some of these things seem essentially private because they are central to us— because they define what we are emotionally, physically, cognitively, and relationally. We might say about these categories that we consider information relating to them presumptively private. Other values may offset our interest in protecting an individual's privacy in any particular context, nonetheless, roughly speaking, one's private sphere in some sense can be equated with those areas of a person's life which are considered intimate or innermost. Though categories like parent, poet, and patriot have the meaning they do in a social context, it is their centrality to identity which makes these roles part of a person's private dimension.

This view is my basis for rejecting the second criterion of the private mentioned above: the view that each relationship defines what is private to it. It may be true that depending on our relationship we will regard some pieces of information appropriate for some to inquire into and others not. This fact does not settle what it is that is private. Even if we think that it is appropriate for a psychiatrist or a spouse to ask us about various things, this does not mean that such topics are not private matters. It is just that the norms permit some people access to our private domains.

The position advocated here might be challenged by observing that qualities such as age, race, family status, profession, and general appearance are central to us even though we do not generally regard these as private. And other characteristics are taken as private even though they do not have much to do with what is central to our lives or with the integrity of our intimate selves, for example, annual income. The qualities that I mention as central but which are not regarded generally as private are those that would be either very difficult to conceal if one were to have any social existence at all, or else central to one's public role and thus counterproductive to keep private for that reason. With respect to those things that are not central to people but about which people feel a sense of privacy, these might generally be regarded as sensitive topics because of the reactive concerns we all share or because of socially conditioned norms. In any event, in saying that the realm of the intimate is essentially private or marks off what is the private realm, I am not saying that there are not other bases for people feeling private about certain matters. Everyone would concede that much of what people regard as private is a culturally conditioned sensitivity. The issue is whether culturally distinctive norms determine all of what is regarded as private, and I am arguing that the answer to this is no.

Numerous lawyers and philosophers have accused those who introduce privacy terminology when discussing state regulation of birth control and abortion as confused.[21] Still, if one thinks that whether a married couple uses birth control is a *private matter* and for that reason not within the proper domain of state regulation, the sense of privacy I am advocating is vindicated. Even if some pressing need legitimized state involvement with such decisions, they would remain private decisions in the sense that they related to intimate elements of life. (They would cease to be private in the sense of answering who had final legal authority to make decisions here.)[22] The centrality of decisions concerning birth control and abortion to intimate relationships and intimate aspects of oneself *makes* such issues privacy issues.

One might ask how am I differentiating the notion of the private from the notion of the intimate. Although I have regarded the intimate as a criterion of the private, labeling something as part of one's private realm indicates that there are norms of nonintrusion which apply to that area of a person's life. Labeling an area one of intimacy does not carry the same normative associations. The relationship between the two is, however, internal.

III

I have argued that respect for privacy enriches social and personal interaction by providing contexts for the development of varied kinds of relationships and multiple dimensions of personality. I have also suggested that while one can usually share informational aspects of oneself without apparent limit, sharing what is significant to one about this information is effectively limited to special kinds of relationships, and that we have independent reasons for not taking as an ideal the generalization of such special relationships to encompass all our interactions with others. Let me now move on.

The general point I wish to advance in this section is that respect for privacy signifies our recognition that not all dimensions of persons or relationships need to serve some independently validated social purpose. A private sphere of valuation must be morally recognized. My position involves two arguments. First, part of what is meant by respecting persons as persons is the acknowledgment that what has meaning for one individual thereby gains presumptive moral value independent of its promotion of socially valuable ends. Second, the personal basis of value is best kept located in the private realm generally; otherwise it will atrophy and be subsumed by public standards of value.

I start with the thesis that the individual is a source of value. A number of considerations are important to keep in mind. First, if the only morally recognizable point of a person's activities were to consist in the degree to which his activities assisted other people's projects, we would have a self-defeating and groundless situation. Some things must be good for persons, independent of their effects on others, or else there would be no point to helping others in the first place. Second, what is important to a person about pursuing goals is not only the objective relevance of the goals themselves but also their personal relevance—the fact that they are his goals.[23] It would be wrong to say of a person that his attachment to his objective should not count in assessing whether it is worth his while to pursue that end. And it would be wrong to say that his attachment should have no independent bearing on others' evaluations and pursuits. Without an individual's capacity to create value in something by valuing it, what we are left with is respect for values but no respect for persons as such. The respect for persons would be derivative only to the extent to which persons happened to value what was really and independently valuable. On such a view persons would have only instrumental or incidental value insofar as they promoted the right objectives. This is not to say that the fact that a person forms an objective is to be taken by others as a decisive reason for valuing and facilitating that objective. It is only to say that this valuation by the individual must be accorded moral weight independent, to a certain degree, of its overall consequences for society.

One could object to this position on the ground that what is valuable in an individual's idiosyncratic objectives is not the object of his or her loyalties as such, which may be neutral or detestable, but rather the *process through which the individual exercises autonomy*. Focusing on the desirability of autonomous choice provides sufficient basis for respect for individuals without having to further suppose that individuals add value to the objectives themselves by valuing them.[24] In response, one can observe that the values or loyalties one adheres to may not reflect autonomous choice in a direct sense and insofar as the agent sees it. For instance, a person may think that it is only through subjection to something over which he has no legitimate choice that he satisfies important objectives, for example, subjection to moral principles and rules or to divine commands. (One could then respond that even such first-order subjection reflects autonomy but at a higher level; the problem can be reiterated at each level.) Why should we judge that it is because a value reflects autonomous choice, and not inner meaning, that a person's objectives gain presumptive value? It seems much more plausible to suggest that whatever value autonomy has derives from its provision of prospects for meaningful existence than to say that the value of inner meaning derives from its reflection of autonomy.

It is no accident that some of our institutions that protect people's loyalties to ends which are potentially antagonistic to social well-being (such as testmonial privileges generally and the protection against self-incrimination specifically) generally were secured in a context of freedom of conscience,[25] which is an aspect of protection of intimacy. The essence of such struggles is the argument that there is within each individual some part that is not to be exploited even for socially or politically worthy ends. The medieval notion of *subsidiarity* can be usefully applied here. Subsidiarity involves regarding the political state as limited in its scope to certain domains of a person's life. This view specifically regards the state as not being competent to involve itself with determinations in matters of conscience or inner meanings generally. This position need not imply that the state does not have the ability or capacity to be effective in such areas. More pertinent to our concern is the theory's insistence that whatever the state's ability or capacity to mold consciences, it is violative of a person to do so.

Privacy, I wish to suggest, insulates individual objectives from social scrutiny. Social scrutiny can generally be expected to move individuals in the direction of the socially useful. Privacy insulates people from this kind of accountability and thereby protects the realm of the personal. When in conflict with social aims, private objectives tend to be devalued. For example, discussing parent–child relationships, nearly all the vast literature cites the best interest of the child as the sole basis for legitimizing parental control over the child. These discussions leave out entirely the interest parents and children alike have in maintaining intimate involvement (except as it promotes the child's well-being). This interest in intimacy must be taken into account when characterizing the moral basis for family autonomy. It is in such contexts that important aspects of personality develop. Something important is obscured when the family is seen as having primarily social, rather than personal, objectives.[26]

I believe it is important in a society for there to be institutions in which people can experience some of what they are without excessive scrutiny. Privacy is such an institution. Privacy involves norms that allow the pursuit and development of aims and relationships that count simply because the people involved find meaning in them. Privacy, I want to argue, provides the context for personal objectives being respected. I have suggested there is nothing wrong with people pursuing personally validated objectives, even though these do not serve the interest of everyone or enhance the autonomous status of others.

I have argued in this chapter that from a number of perspectives privacy is important independent of its *reactive* function of protecting people from the morally unscrupulous, or merely suboptimal, qualities of others. Privacy is important with respect to the multidimensionality of persons and with respect for the personal or inner lives of people. Dimensionality and inner meaning together provide the primary bases for defending the nonreactive importance of privacy.

NOTES

For helpful comments and discussions I am indebted to Herbert Fingarette, Kent Greenawalt, Teri Bell, Michael Gardner, Sara Schechter-Schoeman, Evelyn B. Pluhar, and Linda Weingarten.

1 Charles Fried, "Privacy," 77 *Yale Law Journal* (1968) 475–93.
2 Robert Gerstein, "Intimacy and privacy," 89 *Ethics* (1978) 76–81.
3 James Rachels, "Why privacy is important," 4 *Philosophy and Public Affairs* (1975) 323–33.
4 Richard Wasserstrom, "Privacy: some arguments and assumptions," in Richard Bronaugh, ed., *Philosophical Law*, Westport, Conn.: Greenwood Press, 1978.
5 Ruth Gavison, "Privacy and the limits of law," 89 *Yale Law Journal* (1980) 421–71.
6 Jeffrey Reiman, "Privacy, intimacy, and personhood," 6 *Philosophy and Public Affairs* (1976) 26–44.
7 Richard Wasserstrom, "Privacy: some arguments and assumptions," in Richard Bronaugh, ed., *Philosophical Law*, Westport, Conn.: Greenwood Press, 1978.
8 Robert Gerstein, "Privacy and self-incrimination," 80 *Ethics* (1970) 87–101.
9 Stanley Benn, "Privacy, freedom and respect for persons," in J. R. Pennock and W. Chapman, eds., *Nomos XIII: Privacy*, New York, Atherton Press, 1971.
10 Richard Wasserstrom, "Privacy: some arguments and assumptions," in Richard Bronaugh, ed., *Philosophical Law*, Westport, Conn.: Greenwood Press, 1978.

11 Richard Posner, "The right to privacy," 12 *Georgia Law Review* (1978) 393–422.

12 Henry James, *The Reverberator,* New York: Grove Press, 1979, p. 190. See also Helen Lynd, *On Shame and the Search for Identity.* New York: Harcourt, Brace & Co., 1958.

13 Athol Fugard, *A Lesson from Aloes,* New York: Random House, 1981, pp. 27–28.

14 Erving Goffman, *The Presentation of Self in Everyday Life,* Garden City: Doubleday, 1959.

15 Ruth Gavison, "Privacy and the limits of law," 89 *Yale Law Journal* (1980) 87–101.

16 See the works of Posner, Wasserstrom, and Goffman already cited for expressions to this effect.

17 Walter Mischel, *Personality and Assessment,* New York: John Wiley, 1968, chapter 5.

18 Charles Fried, "Privacy," 77 *Yale Law Journal* (1968) 475–93.

19 James Rachels, "Why privacy is important," 4 *Philosophy and Public Affairs* (1975) 323–33.

20 H. J. McCloskey, "The political ideal of privacy," 21 *Philosophical Quarterly* (1971) 303–14, and "Privacy and the right to privacy," 55 *Philosophy* (1980) 17–38.

21 Louis Henkin, "Privacy and autonomy," 74 *Columbia Law Review* (1974) 1410–33; Ruth Gavison, "Privacy and the limits of law" 89 *Yale Law Journal* (1980) 421–71, esp. 438ff.; Hyman Gross, "Privacy and autonomy," in J. R. Pennock and J. W. Chapman, eds., *Nomos XIII: Privacy,* New York: Atherton Press, 1971; and Hyman Gross, "The concept of privacy," 42 *New York University Law Review* (1967) 35–54.

22 Stanley I. Benn and Gerald Gaus, "The Public and the private: concepts and action," in Stanley I. Benn and Gerald Gaus, eds., *The Public and the Private in Social Policy,* London: Croon Helm and St. Martin's Press, 1983, pp. 3–27.

23 See Thomas Nagel, "The Limits of Objectivity," in Sterling McMurren, ed., *The Tanner Lectures on Human Values,* Salt Lake City: University of Utah Press, 1980, 75–140; Bernard Williams, "Persons, character and morality," in Amelie Rorty, ed., *Identity of Persons,* Berkeley: University of California Press, 1976, 197–216; and Samuel Scheffler, *The Rejection of Consequentialism,* Oxford: Oxford University Press, 1982, especially chapter 2.

24 Evelyn Pluhar suggested this problem in her "Commentary on 'privacy and intimate information,'" presented at the 1983 American Philosophical Association, Western Division, meetings.

25 See Leonard Levy, *Origins of the Fifth Amendment,* Oxford: Oxford University Press, 1968. Interestingly, even Jeremy Bentham, who was hostile to testimonial privileges generally, acknowledged the priest-penitent privilege since it recognized a Catholic's institutionally defined duty to confess transgressions, and thus was a requirement of religious freedom.

26 For an extensive defense of this claim see two works by Ferdinand Schoeman: "Rights of children, rights of parents, and the moral basis of the family," 91 *Ethics* (1980) 6–19, and "Childhood competence and autonomy," 12 *The Journal of Legal Studies* (1983) 267–87.

Selected bibliography

This bibliography is far from complete. For a much fuller and richer guide to the privacy literature, one is advised to look at the bibliography prepared by David O'Brien, referenced below.

Altman, Irwin. 1975. *The Environment and Social Behavior: Privacy, Personal Space, Territory, Crowding.* Monterey: Brooks/Cole Publishing Co.
   1977. Privacy regulation: culturally universally or culturally specific? *Journal of Social Issues* 33: 66–84.
Arendt, Hannah. 1958. *The Human Condition.* Chicago: University of Chicago Press.
Beardsley, Elizabeth. 1971. Privacy: autonomy and selective disclosure. In *Nomos XIII: Privacy,* J. R. Pennock and J. W. Chapman, eds. New York: Atherton Press, pp. 56–70.
Benn, Stanley I. 1971. Privacy, freedom and respect for persons. In *Nomos XIII: Privacy,* J. R. Pennock and J. W. Chapman, eds. New York: Atherton Press, pp. 1–26.
Benn, Stanley I. 1978. Protection and limitation of privacy. *Australian Law Journal* 52: 601–612, 686–92.
   1980. Privacy and respect for persons: a reply. *Australian Journal of Philosophy* 58: 54–61.
Benn, Stanley I., and Gaus, Gerald. 1983. *The Private and Public in Social Policy.* London: Croon Helm and St. Martin's Press.
Bloustein, Edward. 1964. Privacy as an aspect of human dignity: an answer to Dean Prosser. *New York University Law Review* 39: 962–1007.
   1978. *Individual and Group Privacy.* New Brunswick, N.J.; Transaction Books.
Bok, Sissela. 1982. *Secrets: On the Ethics of Concealment and Revelation.* New York: Pantheon.
Böll, Heinrich. 1975. *The Lost Honor of Katharina Blum.* New York: McGraw-Hill.
Boyd v. United States, 116 U.S. 616 (1886).
Bulmer, Martin. 1979. *Censuses, Surveys and Privacy.* New York: Holmes and Meier.
   1982. *Social Research Ethics: An Examination of the Merits of Covert Participant Observation.* New York: Holmes and Meier.

1982. The research ethics of pseudo-patient studies: a new look at the merits of covert ethnographic methods. *The Sociological Review* 30: 627–46.

Cavell, Stanley. 1979. *The Claims of Reason*. Part IV. Oxford: Oxford University Press.

Conrad, Joseph. 1910. *Under Western Eyes*. New York: Doubleday.

Davis, Frederick. 1959. What do we mean by "right to privacy?" *South Dakota Law Review* 4: 1–24.

Ely, John. 1973. The Wages of crying wolf: a comment on *Roe v. Wade*. *Yale Law Journal* 82: 920–50.

Emerson, Thomas. 1979. The right of privacy and freedom of the press. *Harvard Civil Rights—Civil Liberties Law Review* 14: 329–60.

Epstein, Richard. 1978. Privacy, property rights and misrepresentations. *Georgia Law Review* 12: 455–74.

1980. A taste for privacy? Evolution and the emergence of a naturalistic ethics. *The Journal of Legal Studies* 9: 665–81.

Felcher, Peter, and Rubin, Edward. 1979. Privacy, publicity, and the portrayal of real people by the media. *Yale Law Journal* 88: 1577–1622.

Flaherty, David. 1972. *Privacy in colonial New England*. Charlottesville: University of Virginia Press.

Flaherty, David, Hanir, Edward, and Mitchell, S. Paula. 1979. *Privacy and Access to Government Data for Research: An International Bibliography*. London: Manrell Publishing.

Fontane, Theodor. 1976. *Effi Briest*. New York: Penguin.

Fried, Charles. 1968. Privacy. *Yale Law Journal* 77: 475–93.

1978. Privacy: economics and ethics, a comment on Posner. *Georgia Law Review* 12: 423–28.

Gavison, Ruth. 1980. Privacy and the limits of law. *Yale Law Journal* 89: 421–71.

Gerety, Tom. 1977. Redefining privacy. *Harvard Civil Rights–Civil Liberties Law Review* 12: 233–96.

Gerstein, Robert. 1970. Privacy and self-incrimination. *Ethics* 80: 87–101.

1978. Intimacy and privacy. *Ethics* 89: 76–81.

1979. Demise of Boyd: self-incrimination and private papers in the Burger court. *UCLA Law Review* 27: 343–97.

1982. California's constitutional right to privacy: the development of the protection of private life. *Hastings Constitutional Law Quarterly* 9: 385–427.

Glancy, Dorothy. 1979. The invention of the right to privacy. *University of Arizona Law Review* 21: 1–39.

Godkin, E. L. 1890. Rights of the citizen, part IV–to his own reputation. *Scribner's Magazine* 8: 58–67.

Goffman, Erving. 1959. *The Presentation of Self in Everyday Life*. Garden City: Doubleday.

1961. *Asylums*. Garden City: Doubleday.

1963. *Behavior in Public Places*. New York: Free Press.

Goldman v. United States, 316 U.S. 129 (1942).

Gouled v. United States, 255 U.S. 298 (1921).

Greenawalt, Kent. 1967. Wiretapping and bugging: striking a balance between privacy and law enforcement. *American Judicature Society Journal* 50: 303–9.

1968. The consent problem in wiretapping and eavesdropping: surreptitious monitoring with the consent of a participant in a conversation. *Columbia Law Review* 68: 189–240.

1974. Privacy and its legal protections. *Hastings Center Studies* 2: 45–68.

1981. Silence as a moral and constitutional right. *William and Mary Law Review* 23: 15–71.

Gregor, T. A. 1970. Exposure and seclusion: a study of institutionalized isolation among the Mehinachu Indians of Brazil. *Ethnology* 9: 234–50.

1974. Publicity, privacy and Mehinachu marriages. *Ethnology* 13: 333–49.

Griswold v. Connecticut, 381 U.S. 479 (1965).

Gross, Hyman. 1964. *Privacy – Its Legal Protection*. New York: Oceana Publications.

1967. The concept of privacy. *New York University Law Review* 42: 34–54.

1971. Privacy and autonomy. In *Nomos XIII: Privacy*, J. R. Pennock and J. W. Chapman, eds. New York: Atherton Press, pp. 169–181.

Hall, Edward T. 1966. *The Hidden Dimension*. Garden City: Doubleday.

Halmos, Paul, 1952. *Solitude and Privacy*. London: Routledge & Kegan Paul.

Henkin, Louis. 1974. Privacy and autonomy. *Columbia Law Review* 74: 1410–33.

Hill, Alfred. 1976. Defamation and privacy under the First Amendment. *Columbia Law Review* 76: 1205–1313.

Hoffa v. United States, 385 U.S. 293 (1966).

Hudson, Stephen, and Husak, Douglas. 1979. Benn on 'Privacy and respect for persons.' *Australian Journal of Philosophy* 57: 324–29.

James, Henry. 1886. *The Bostonians*. New York: Macmillan.

1888. *The Reverberator*. New York: Macmillan.

1888. *The Aspern Papers*. Reprinted (1962) in *The Turn of the Screw and Other Short Novels*. New York: Signet.

1944. The death of the lion. In *Stories of Writers and Artists*, F. O. Matthiessen, ed. New York: New Directions.

1946. The private life. In *Fourteen Stories by Henry James*, David Garnett, ed. London: Rupert Hart-Davis.

Kalven, Harry, Jr. 1966. Privacy in tort law – were Warren and Brandeis wrong? *Law and Contemporary Problems* 31: 326–41.

Karst, Kenneth. 1966. "The files": legal controls over the accuracy and accessibility of stored personal data. *Law and Contemporary Problems* 31: 341–76.

1980. Freedom of intimate association. *Yale Law Journal* 89: 624–92.

Katz v. United States, 389 U.S. 347 (1967).

Kelman, Herbert. 1977. Privacy and research with human beings. *Journal of Social Issues* 33: 169–95.

Kronman, Anthony. 1980. The privacy exemption to the freedom of information act. *The Journal of Legal Studies* 9: 727–74.

Landynski, Jacob. 1966. *Search and Seizure and the Supreme Court: A Study in Constitutional Interpretation*. Baltimore: Johns Hopkins University Press.

Lasson, Nelson. 1937. *The History and Development of the Fourth Amendment to the United States Constitution*. Baltimore: Johns Hopkins University Press.

Laufer, Robert, and Wolfe, Maxine. 1977. Privacy as a concept and a social issue: a multidimensional theory. *Journal of Social Issues* 33: 22–42.

Levy, Leonard. 1968. *Origins of the Fifth Amendment*. Oxford: Oxford University Press.

Lewis v. United States, 385 U.S. 206 (1966).

Lynd, Helen Merrell. 1958. *On Shame and the Search for Identity*. New York: Harcourt Brace & Co.

Manley, Jared. 1937. April Fool! *The New Yorker*. Aug. 14, 1937, 22–26.

McCloskey, H. J. 1971. The political ideal of privacy. *Philosophical Quarterly* 21: 303–14.

1980. Privacy and the right to privacy. *Philosophy* 55: 17–38.

Merton, Robert. 1964. *Social Theory and Structure*. New York: Free Press.

Miller, Arthur. 1971. *The Assault on Privacy*. Ann Arbor: The University of Michigan Press.

Murphy, Robert. 1964. Social distance and the veil. *American Anthropologist* 66: 1257–74.

New York Times v. Sullivan, 376 U.S. 254 (1964).

O'Brien, David. 1979. *Privacy, Law and Public Policy*. New York: Praeger Special Studies.

1980. *The Right to Privacy: Its Constitutional and Social Dimensions: A Comprehensive Bibliography*. Austin: Tarlton Law Library, University of Texas Law School.

Olmstead v. United States, 277 U.S. 438 (1928).

On Lee v. United States, 343 U.S. 747 (1952).

Parent, W. A. 1983. Privacy, morality and the law. *Philosophy and Public Affairs* 12: 269–88.

Parent, W. A. 1983. Recent work on the concept of privacy. *American Philosophical Quarterly* 20: 341–356.

Parker, Richard. 1974. A definition of privacy. *Rutgers Law Review* 27: 275–96.

Pennock, J. R. and Chapman, J. W., eds. 1971. *Nomos XIII: Privacy*. New York: Atherton Press.

Plamenatz, John. 1974. Privacy and laws against discrimination. *Rivista Internazionale di Folosopfia del Diritto*. 4: 443–55.

Polyviou, Polyvios. 1982. *Search and Seizure: Constitutional and Common Law*. London: Duckworth & Co.

Posner, Richard. 1978. An economic theory of privacy. *Regulation* (May/June): 19–26.

1978. The right of privacy. *Georgia Law Review* 12: 393–422.

1979. Privacy, secrecy and reputation. *Buffalo Law Review* 28: 1–55.

Prosser, William. 1960. Privacy. *California Law Review* 48: 383–423.

Rachels, James. 1975. Why privacy is important. *Philosophy and Public Affairs* 4: 323–33.

Reiman, Jeffrey. 1976. Privacy, intimacy and personhood. *Philosophy and Public Affairs* 6: 26–44.

Report of the Commission on Personal Privacy. 1982. State of California.

Richards, David. 1982. *Sex, Drugs, Death and the Law: An Essay on Human Rights and Overcriminalization*. Totowa, N.J.: Rowman and Littlefield.

Roberts, John, and Gregor, Thomas. 1971. Privacy: a cultural perspective. In *Nomos XIII: Privacy*, Pennock, J. R. and Chapman, J. W., eds. New York: Atherton Press.

Roe v. Wade, 410 U.S. 367 (1973).

Scanlon, Thomas. 1975. Thomson on privacy. *Philosophy and Public Affairs*. 4: 315–23.

Schoeman, Ferdinand. 1982. Friendship and testimonial privilege. In *Ethics, Public Policy, and Criminal Justice*, Frederick Elliston and Norman Bowie, eds. Cambridge: Oelgeschlager, Gunn and Hain.

1984. Privacy and intimate information. In *The Philosophical Dimensions of Privacy: An Anthology*, Ferdinand Schoeman, ed. Cambridge: Cambridge University Press.

1984. Privacy and police undercover work. In *Police Ethics: Hard Choices in Law Enforcement*, William Heffernan and Timothy Stroup, eds. New York: John Jay Press.

Schwartz, Barry. 1968. The social psychology of privacy. *American Journal of Sociology* 73: 741–52.

Shils, Edward. 1966. Privacy: its constitutional vicissitudes. *Law and Contemporary Problems* 31: 281–306.

Sidis v. F-R Publishing Company, 113 F.2d 806 (2d Cir. 1940).

Silverman v. United States, 365 U.S. 505 (1961).

Simmel, Georg. 1950. The secret and the secret society. In *The Sociology of Georg Simmel*, Kurt Wolff, ed. Glencoe: Free Press.

Stephen, James Fitzjames. 1873. *Liberty, Equality and Fraternity*. New York: Henry Holt and Co.

Symposium: Privacy. 1966. *Law and Contemporary Problems* 31.

Symposium: Privacy as a behavioral phenomenon. 1977. *Journal of Social Issues*. 33.

Symposium: Privacy and economics. 1978. *Georgia Law Review* 12.

Taylor, Telford. 1964. *Two Studies in Constitutional Interpretation*. Columbus: The Ohio State University Press.

Thomson, Judith Jarvis. 1975. The right to privacy. *Philosophy and Public Affairs* 4: 295–314.

Wacks, Raymond. 1980. The poverty of "privacy." *Law Quarterly Review* 96: 73–89.

Ware, W. H., and Parsons, C. 1976. Perspectives on privacy: a progress report. *The Bureaucrat* 5: 141–56.

Warren, Samuel, and Brandeis, Louis. 1890. The right to privacy. *Harvard Law Review* 4: 193–220.

Wasserstrom, Richard. 1978. Privacy: some arguments and assumptions. In *Philosophical Law*, Richard Bronaugh, ed. Westport: Greenwood Press.

Weiss, Paul. 1983. *Privacy*. Carbondale: Southern Illinois University Press.

Westin, Alan. 1967. *Privacy and Freedom*. New York: Atheneum press.

Westin, Alan, and Baker, Michael. 1972. *Data Banks in a Free Society*. New York: Quadrangle/New York Times Book Co.

Winfield, Percy. 1931. Privacy. *Law Quarterly Review* 47: 23–42.

Winston, Kenneth. 1975. Self-incrimination in context: establishing procedural protections in juvenile and college disciplinary proceedings. *Southern California Law Review* 48: 813–51.

Wolfe, Maxine, and Laufer, Robert. 1974. The concept of privacy in childhood and adolescence. In *Man–Environment Interaction: Evaluations and Applications*, D. H. Carson, ed. Washington, D.C.: Environment Design Research Association.

Index of names